WALT WHITMAN

WALT WHITMAN

A GAY LIFE

GARY SCHMIDGALL

A WILLIAM ABRAHAMS BOOK

DUTTON

DUTTON
Published by the Penguin Group
Penguin Putnam Inc., 375 Hudson Street,
New York, New York 10014, U.S.A.
Penguin Books Ltd, 27 Wrights Lane,
London W8 5TZ, England
Penguin Books Australia Ltd, Ringwood,
Victoria, Australia
Penguin Books Canada Ltd, 10 Alcorn Avenue,
Toronto, Ontario, Canada M4V 3B2
Penguin Books (N.Z.) Ltd, 182–190 Wairau Road,
Auckland 10, New Zealand

Penguin Books Ltd, Registered Offices:
Harmondsworth, Middlesex, England

First published by Dutton, an imprint of Dutton Signet,
a member of Penguin Putnam Inc.

First Printing, September, 1997
10 9 8 7 6 5 4 3 2 1

 REGISTERED TRADEMARK—MARCA REGISTRADA

Library of Congress Cataloging-in-Publication Data:

Schmidgall, Gary.
    Walt Whitman : a gay life / by Gary Schmidgall.
        p.   cm.
    "A William Abrahams book."
    Includes bibliographical references and index.
    ISBN 0-525-94373-0 (acid-free paper)
    1. Whitman, Walt, 1819–1892—Relations with men.   2. Homosexuality and literature—
United States—History—19th century.   3. Poets, American—19th century—Biography.
4. Gay Men—United States—Biography.   I. Title.
PS3232.S36   1997
811'.3—dc21
[B]   97-14311
                                                                                                 CIP

Printed in the United States of America
Set in Goudy
Designed by Leonard Telesca

This book is printed on acid-free paper.

Contents

3

WALT & HIS BOYS: "TO SEEK MY LIFE-LONG LOVER" 153

4

WALT & HORACE: "MIRACLES FOR MYSELF" 225

LIST OF ILLUSTRATIONS

Fatigued by their journey they sat down on Nature's divan whence they regarded the sky. Pressing one another's hands, shoulder to shoulder, neither knowing why, both became oppressed, their mouths opened, without uttering a word they kissed one another. Near them the hyacinth and the violet marrying their perfume, on raising their heads they both saw God who smiled at them from his azure balcony: Love one another, said he, it is for that I have clothed your path in velvet; kiss one another, I am not looking. Love one another, love one another and if you are happy, instead of a prayer to thank me kiss again.

—from a Walt Whitman notebook

WALT & US:
A FOREWORD

After a man disappears, the mists begin to gather,
then fallacy of one degree or another, then utter myth,
irresistibly mystifying everything. It is a lamentable twist
in history.

—Walt Whitman

O N A PLEASANT Sunday afternoon in the spring of 1889, Walt Whitman's brawny young nurse Ed Wilkins rolled his seventy-year-old charge out of the little Mickle Street house in Camden, New Jersey, in a new wheelchair purchased from Wanamaker's a month before. Their destination was the nearby dinner table of an old and dear friend, Tom Harned, and his family. Whitman's faithful Boswell, Horace Traubel, was on hand and recorded that Walt "rejoiced exceedingly" to hold Tom's baby on his lap. When the baby tugged on his beard, he chuckled. "Never mind—he is only trying to discover what kind of a critter I am—let him pull whatever he chooses." And he enthused further, perhaps ill-advisedly: "The dear babies! It is the Whitman trait to love women, babies, and cattle: that is a demonstrated feature."

Would that biographers were as fortunate as the Harned baby in their efforts to discover what kind of a critter the author of *Leaves of Grass* was. Out in company, especially such mixed company as the Harned hearth afforded, Whitman was his unfailingly jovial, open-hearted, unflappable self. But in private, when more adult parties came prying, it was an oft-demonstrated Whitman feature to very quickly lose his charm and "good gray" aura of benignity. He most decidedly disliked *them* pulling him wherever they chose. John Burroughs, the most trenchant of all the writers on Whitman who knew him personally or observed him while he lived, expressed perhaps the earliest and best summary of the poet's biographical "difficulty." Just two months before Walt's death in March 1892, Burroughs wrote to Traubel with a critique of Traubel's essay comparing Whitman to

Lowell: "W. is so hard to grasp, to put into a statement. One cannot get to the bottom of him; he has so many bottoms, he is bottomed in nature, in democracy, in science, in personality—you did well in getting your lever under him as far as you did."

Whitman, as Burroughs implied, was a man of spectacular inconsistencies and paradoxes. One month he could declare that his "own tendencies—inherent belongings" leaned in favor of "buoyancy, joy, confidence." A few months later, however, he could morosely conclude that the "average human critter is bad. . . . Certainly, in our social life all is villainy and dollars and cents—is rotten to the core—men grasping, grasping, toiling, fighting, full of venom and bitterness." "The state of society," he added, "is deplorable—deplorable beyond words." This dandy-in-woolens could also declare that "style is to have no style," yet his style is as distinctive and immediately identifiable as any in American literature, except perhaps for Emily Dickinson's.

But it is surely the paradox of Whitman the Autobiographer that most concerns and provokes those who choose to write about him. This paradox consists, first, in the blatancy of the self-revelation in Whitman's published work. With much justice, he summed up for Traubel in 1890, "I should say that anyone, to get hold of me,—the bottom of the big book—all I have written—would see that all my work is autobiographical—yes, and that this autobiography finds its center and explication in the poems—in *Leaves of Grass*."* A short time later Traubel responded to a friend's idea that Whitman should pass his time writing "autobiographical notes" by saying it would be "almost farcical to write any autobiography deliberately, when all *Leaves of Grass* and the prose was autobiography if anything." At which Whitman laughed and said, "You are right about it—right." Added to this, of course, was his scrupulously crafted pose as an eager, exultant, no-holds-barred self-singer and his casting of the lucky reader as a trusted intimate. "This hour I tell things in confidence, / I might not tell everybody but I will tell you," he promised in "Song of Myself." In the more sex-charged *Calamus* poems written a few years later, he beckoned: "Come, I will take you down underneath this impassive exterior."

But Whitman's most salient character trait was a desire to have his cake and eat it: to be "Both in and out of the game," "One of that centripetal and centrifugal gang," and also "Open but still a secret." And so, he wanted to tell *all* about "Walt Whitman, an American" (another prior title of "Song of Myself") and—at least about certain sensitive parts of

---

*Asterisks in the text refer to endnotes (pp. 347ff.) that contain further elaboration or additional relevant material.

his life—to tell *nothing*. The paradox of Whitman the Autobiographer, then, is that when concerned with the profoundest realities of his life—most obviously the reality of his homosexuality, which is the main subject of this book—the poet became much more wary, devious, and, as several friends said he was expert at being, suddenly granite-faced and forbidding. Every now and then, he slips into *Leaves of Grass* a frozen glare at the probing life-writer. "Do you suppose yourself advancing on real ground toward a real heroic man?" he challenges in *Calamus* #12; "Have you no thought, O dreamer, that it may be all maya, illusion?" To the future historian of his life he says bluntly: "I do not tell the usual facts, proved by records and documents." And he warns his biographer Rosencrantzes and Guildensterns in "To a Certain Civilian" that "you will never understand me."

Traubel, a bank clerk in his thirties who visited Whitman nearly every day during the poet's last four years, very quickly became sensitive to his tetchiness over delicate questions. "He hates to have anyone fire a fast question at him," Traubel noticed, and on another occasion he observed, "W. is a slow answerer but he always answers to the point. That is, if he wants to answer at all. Sometimes he don't." With nosey civilians, it was usually "don't." Early in Traubel's visits, Whitman summarized, "I am always uneasy about the inquirers when they come buzzing about: they get on my skin and irritate me." Several months later he exploded, "God Almighty how I hate to be catechized!" William Ingram, an old Quaker tea merchant and friend of Walt's, proved an especially bold catechizer, and Whitman repined about him: "He is a questioner—a fierce interrogator: I am disturbed by his boisterous questions: rattled by them, as the boys say: I am not fond of being catechized—indeed, rather run from it." Then he adds a candid remark about his clam-shell instincts: "I am not fond of questions—any questions, in short, that require answers." Even the Englishwoman Anne Gilchrist, who fell in love with him from afar and came with amorous intentions to Philadelphia for a three-year siege, had to admit in the end: "Walt Whitman and I have been the profoundest of friends, but even between us my inevitable questions have badly cracked the rope." One can well imagine why.

The ease and suddenness with which Whitman could hoist his drawbridge was, in fact, a regular and occasionally hilarious topic in the cluttered Mickle Street study. In 1889 John Addington Symonds—an Englishman who for years had eagerly hoped to cajole Whitman into acknowledging the homosexual themes of *Leaves of Grass*—wrote to ask about poems that had been deleted from the early editions. Especially in the case of two eloquent gay lyrics, *Calamus* #8 ("Long I thought that knowledge alone would suffice me") and *Calamus* #9 ("Hours continuing long"), Symonds was venturing into a sensitive matter. Whitman of course temporized and said nothing. John Clifford, that rara avis of the day, a liberal preacher willing to read Whitman from his pulpit, heard about this and joked that "it is good he is 3,000 miles off: it saves him the disappointment of putting his questions to Walt and having them avoided." When Traubel reported this remark to Whitman, he replied: "So Clifford has heard I dislike to be asked questions?" "Not *heard* of," Traubel retorted, "but has observed it himself."

One December day in 1890 the familiar Whitman silence was unintentionally on display. Traubel brought a somewhat understated friend by to talk with Walt. The friend said afterward, "Curiously, W. never answered one of my questions." Next day, Walt remarked, "What a quiet young man that was you brought yesterday!" He was by then hard of hearing and had not caught any of the questions! As Traubel explained: "I am often asked when I take strangers there, why it is I cast my voice to such a pitch."

Whitman is an intimidating subject for biography because his instinct was to treat inquirers not like the whispery-voiced young man but like Symonds: to *pretend* not to hear. And when that did not work, he was not above lying. When Symonds wrote him in 1890 with a more confrontational catechism about the homosexuality of the *Calamus* poems, the exasperated and flustered Whitman recoiled from the threatening implication with his famous red herring about fathering six children in a darkly veiled past. On a more mundane level, he admonished Traubel one day not to convey bad news about his health to a dear Canadian friend: "I don't want Bucke to know the worst. . . . he worries over bad news: write him in a cheerful vein—lie to him, buoy him up."

Whitman learned from the bitter experience of hostility to his first three *Leaves of Grass* editions that "the worst" about his sexuality and sexual life could also not be spoken about candidly. His most succinct statement about these early attacks—"I expected hell: I got it"—goes far in explaining why, after the first three editions, Whitman began to exercise that faculty which the phrenologists said he had in such abundance: caution. "Thirty years ago or more a circle of *célèbres* in phrenology gave my head a public dissection," he told Traubel, and they "marked my caution very high—seven and over. Their seven [the phrenologists' highest rating] was backed by my experience with myself." In four short years he had learned his lesson: the opening line of the 1860 poem "Debris" asserts, "He is wisest who has the most caution." Caution was also the trait Whitman famously chose to emphasize in 1884 to Edward Carpenter, a visiting Englishman who would later become an important advocate for tolerance of homosexuality. He likened himself to a furtive hen stealthily hiding her eggs in a hedgerow, and he also told Carpenter, "I think there are truths which it is necessary to envelop or wrap up." To this furtive hen we shall return.

Whitman surely considered the "truths" of sexuality and one's private sexual life to be among the subjects ripe for mystification or concealment. His efforts to cheer and "buoy up" his mainstream American readership by enveloping and wrapping these truths were various and often ingenious. One way to keep the sexual catechizers at bay, however, was more drastic: simply destroy that part of the historical record in his own possession. Some believe that on two occasions, in 1873 and 1888, Whitman destroyed letters he had received from Peter Doyle, one of the most important of his loving "comrades," and the Traubel conversations make it clear Whitman was not shy about burning potentially compromising material. Letters—some of them anonymous, full of venom, and probably homophobic—went straight into the stove before Traubel could get a look at them. (Thomas Mann behaved similarly. He is known to have destroyed diaries at least three times: first in 1895 when he was twenty—probably in response to the trial of Oscar Wilde—then in the thirties, when he feared Nazi discoveries, and finally in the summer of 1945, when some early diaries were incinerated. At the age of seventy-five, in 1950, after describing his latest infatuation with a young man, Mann wondered if another bonfire was necessary . . . but then decided at long last to fling caution to the winds.)

Within months of beginning his daily visits, Traubel became an archival packrat, carting off anything and everything Whitman was of a mind to discard. One day he arrived to find Whitman throwing things away, and this revealing set-to resulted:

> I broke in: "What the devil do you do that for?" He laughed outright: "Now you're fierce again. . . . What the hell's all that stuff good for now except to lumber up the house?" I was serious about it: "Anyway—let me judge of that for myself. I've got plenty of room home for anything you want to throw away." He looked at me fixedly: "You seem to be very earnest about it. I don't know but that I've got any prejudice against saving it. But, Horace—most of that stuff is best destroyed—for many reasons best." Still I insisted. Then he smiled and concluded: "I promise to throw some of it your way— some of it—though there is a bit here and there too sacred—too surely and only mine—to be perpetuated."*

Some weeks later the scene was replayed with new dialogue:

As I was leaving W. remarked: "I was destroying some papers today but saved a few for you." I kicked at once. "I knew you would growl—but no matter—you growl but you do not bite. I am, in fact, Horace, saving you all the essential things—things that make history: what I chuck away or burn up is not worth keeping either for your purposes or mine."

Traubel's purposes were clear, and he stated them in the preface to his first volume: "To set down the record. Then to get out of the way myself." What *Whitman*'s purposes were cannot be so simply stated, but it is surely plausible to assume that many of those manuscript papers and much correspondence "too sacred—too surely and only mine" to be vouchsafed to the eyes of posterity had to do with sexual encounters and affairs of the heart.

All his sensitive personal papers Whitman treated rather like the "great secret" of his past life that he got into the habit of tantalizing Traubel with. After some months of coy hints, Horace was still probing playfully. "I reminded W. that I was losing sleep and meals in my anxiety over the 'surprise' that he still held back." Silence. Three days later, Whitman brings up the subject again. "I pricked up my ears. Was the revelation about to come? He saw my interested face. 'Are you ready for it?' I laughingly replied: 'I'm leanin' up against myself strong!' " Whitman then tried to palm off a few idolatrous letters from a budding young (and gay) writer named Bayard Taylor, but Traubel was not fooled and persisted for several more months. How Traubel was further teased about this secret we shall see later; the point to make here is that, as far as we know, Whitman, who professed to prefer the "let-it-go" rather than the "judicial" man, finally never let go with his surely amorous secret. Perhaps it was part of Traubel's revenge to needle Walt about being a bachelor. One day the poet said it was good for a boy to "have a girl," and Traubel exclaimed, "And that from a bachelor!" Whitman's reaction was perhaps revealing. "He snapped back half in fun and much in earnest: 'Not too much of a bachelor, either, if you knew it all!' This fling was so dead-set with its teeth shut that I thought he might go on some on the subject. But he was silent and I went home."

In addition to the suppressions and secrecies of his private life, Whitman also worked hard to enwrap the truths of his sexuality in his published writings. Where his poetry is "difficult," it is often because of the methods of furtiveness, calculated ambiguity, and closeted concealment with which Whitman cushioned, so to speak, many of his most strikingly bold assertions about sex and sexuality in *Leaves of Grass*. The eminent gay poet James Merrill described in his memoir almost exactly the same *modus operandi*, which he employed in his early poetry: "I never doubted that almost any poem I wrote owed some of its difficulty to the need to conceal my feelings, and their objects. Genderless as a figleaf, the pronoun 'you' served to protect the latter, but one couldn't be too careful. Whatever helped to complicate the texture—double meanings, syntax that William Empson [author of *Seven Types of Ambiguity*] would have approved—was all to the good." The early *Leaves of Grass* editions are filled with such "difficulty" generated by an author with a sexual disguise to maintain. Merrill, incidentally, also described himself at the outset of his career as a poet who felt "stifled, unable to express a thought, my thoughts being primarily erotic"—a perfect précis of Whitman in the early 1850s, just before the volcanic eruption of his own erotic thoughts in the first *Leaves*.

Nearing the age of fifty, the Greek poet Constantine Cavafy looked back upon his life and described a necessary "difficulty" for his biographers that is very similar to what we encounter in Whitman and Merrill. In a poem appropriately titled "Hidden Things" (and which he never allowed to be printed in his lifetime), Cavafy ascribed this difficulty to the "obstacle" of his homosexuality and the need to be furtive about it. The poem, composed in 1911, deserves quotation in full, for it not only alludes to the "concealed but substantial life" in the great poems of the early *Leaves* editions, it also encourages us, at its end, to reach for a keener awareness of how the "obstacle" functions in Whitman's work:

> From all I did and all I said
> let no one try to find out who I was.
> An obstacle was there that changed the pattern
> of my actions and the manner of my life.
> An obstacle was often there
> to stop me when I'd begin to speak.
> From my most unnoticed actions,
> my most veiled writing—
> from these alone will I be understood.
> But maybe it isn't worth so much concern,
> so much effort to discover who I really am.
> Later, in a more perfect society,
> someone else made just like me
> is certain to appear and act freely.

In his last year—a year that still found Harvard banning his poems from its library—Whitman said to Traubel with ironic whimsy, "It is one of my dreads that there may come a time, and people, to *exposit, explicate Leaves of*

Grass." One would like to think that, society having become more nearly perfect in respect of homosexual rights since 1911, we should be able, in Cavafy's phrase, to act—and read—more freely in the presence of *Leaves of Grass.* At the end of his writing career, Whitman felt exactly as Nietzsche did: "The time for me hasn't come yet: some are born posthumously." I hope *Walt Whitman: A Gay Life* will be able to assist at this birth.

❧ ❧ ❧

The "good gray" poet was not only an expert in the "veiled writing" of which Cavafy wrote but also an expert at intimidation. One day he rather forlornly admitted to Traubel that he had lost in his old age the ability to say "something very snubbing to a fellow I thought impudent." Modern writers on Whitman, especially those with collegiate affiliations, have special reason to feel intimidated by him, since he left countless snubbing and often agreeably eloquent squelches of biographers, literary critics, and university professors who "esteem themselves great punkins."

As one might guess of a poet who did not scruple to publish unsigned and profoundly flattering reviews of his own work, Whitman became a very careful and sometimes harsh-judging critic of biography in general and Whitman biography in particular. When a life of Jesus appeared, he ejaculated, "Poor Jesus!—to have come down these eighteen hundred years, to be biographized by us moderns! He hardly deserved it!" As to his own life story, there is more than a grain of truth in some of his assessments. Take, for instance, Edmund Clarence Stedman, a fairly close acquaintance whom Whitman rather liked for company and grudgingly admired. Yet when Stedman published a study of him, Walt brusquely concluded: "Stedman is cute [i.e. acute] but hardly more than cute—not a first hander—a fine scholar, with great charms of style, fond of congregating historic names, processional, highly organized, but not in the windup proving that he is aware of what all his erudition, even all his good will (he has plenty of that, God bless him!), leads up to. I should not say such things, should I? I am a hell of a critic."* And so he was. This view happens to apply to many of the books on this most written-about of all American authors that have been published in the last century. About them I have mostly found myself feeling rather the way Whitman felt about all the paintings he had sat for over the years: "I am persuaded that my painter has not yet arrived. I know I have been very successfully taken—taken in all sorts of habits and hours—but somehow there is an elusive quality which so far no one has caught."*

What biographer sets forth without thinking that he will finally capture the "elusive quality" of his subject? I am no exception, and my temerity is born of confidence that sexuality was the elusive quality to which Whitman was referring. He was, I think, also subtly alluding to sex when, several months later, he praised Heinrich Heine and "all the big fellows" of poetry with words extremely significant for anyone approaching *Leaves of Grass*. "In all imaginative work, all pure poetic work," Whitman said, "there must especially come in a primal quality, not to be mentioned, named, described, but always felt when present: the direct off-throwing of nature, parting the ways between formal, conventional, borrowed expression and the fervor of genuine spirit." As we shall see, the primal quality for Whitman was sex, and this was of course "not to be mentioned"—could not possibly be "named"—in mid-nineteenth-century America. Yet the glory of *Leaves* is that sex is, as he put it, "always felt when present" in his poems, and it is present remarkably often, much to the sometimes amusing consternation of Whitman's many academic critics.

Anyone connected with academe is bound to feel a little squeamish in Whitman's presence, since he so heartily despised the ivory tower and its inhabitants. "I consider it the bane of the universities, colleges," he once complained, "that they withhold, withdraw, men from direct, drastic contact with life."* To such "formal-cut men in literature" the "drastic" life, particularly the drastic sexuality, of *Leaves of Grass* was bound to be impossible to accept, let alone understand. "They like portions, beauties, what they would call 'gems'—do not see more. But it took more than *that* to compass *Leaves of Grass*. The thread connecting all was never penetrated by such men." One university man wrote him cordially, but Whitman still rankled, and reiterated his main objection: "His letter is friendly but he has the excessive caution of the university man. The scholar swells rarely—I may say never—let themselves go." Scholar "swells" of this ilk have dogged Whitman up to the present day, and they are most conspicuously revealed when they approach the most "drastic" of the poems in *Leaves of Grass*, the *Calamus* sequence. Paul Fussell, in reviewing the *Comprehensive Reader's Edition* in 1967, for instance, built up a fine head of steam over the "euphemisms and awkward genteelisms" that "conspicuously mar" the notes on the *Calamus* poems: "It would be hard indeed for a reader of [Blodgett and Bradley's] edition to gather that Whitman was a homosexual whose program for national reform . . . was an infinitely careful and delicate extension of his most passionate internal longings for affection."* The sometimes downright hilarious genteelisms of even more recent studies of Whitman brighten several pages in Chapter 2.

Shaw called every profession a conspiracy against the laity, and it was in this vein that Whitman all his authorial life hewed to the layman's viewpoint. "I do not value literature as a profession," he told Traubel, "I feel about literature what Grant did about war. He hated war. I hate literature. I am not a literary West Pointer." Doubtless part of his antipathy to Shakespeare (and his frequently expressed temptation to believe the plays were written by somebody else) was the mere fact that the Bard was hostage to the professors. "Do you suppose," he asked Traubel, "I accept the almost loony worship of Shakespeare—the cult worship, the college-chair worship? Not a bit of it." No wonder Harvard's "great punkins" never chose to invite Whitman to campus, though many Harvard students were eager for him to come. And as for all the bluenosed New York literati—mostly college graduates, of course—he witheringly concluded: "They are mainly a sad crowd—take the whole raft of them." Part of his deep admiration for the Cambridge University–educated Carpenter was the fact that he survived with his humanity intact; "he was a university man, yet managed to save himself in time: plucked himself from the burning."

Whitman was surely not surprised that preachers, prigs, and stuffy university professors of the eastern seaboard did not grasp "the thread connecting all" in *Leaves of Grass*. As he said, he expected hell and got it. When Traubel let it be known to an old man that he knew Whitman, the stranger asked, "He's the fellow who wrote a smutty book?" To which Traubel curtly replied, "Smutty people consider it smutty." "Smutty" was a common view of *Leaves of Grass*, certainly of the three early editions. It was a view probably more often than not held by those who never actually read it or any poetry at all. The "smutty" party heartily damned the author to the end of his days. In August of 1890 Whitman handed Traubel a letter from Canada, with the words "here is a woman who is afraid I am to be damned—bless her! . . . it's of the same parcel with others I get from day to day." But, though there were plenty of them, the damns were not unanimous, as Whitman explained to Horace: "For a long time all I got out of my work was the work itself and a few amens. . . . I was not only not popular (am not popular yet—never will be) but I was *non grata*—I was not welcome in the world." Splendidly and happily wrong though he was on the question of his future fame, Whitman's remark about the "few amens" was accurate.

The present study, in a sense, is largely about those particular "amens" that were uttered by the select few readers of *Leaves of Grass* who did not see smut in its pages but rather a thrilling invitation to self-recognition, fraternity, and empowerment. Doubtless amens were uttered in 1855, 1856, and 1860 for many reasons, but the main interest here will be in the "amens" of readers who responded to the "secret and divine signs" of its gay subtext. These are the readers whom, I believe, Whitman was quite consciously addressing, though often with extremely careful disguise and artifice. Only readers with an awareness of the unspoken or barely hinted bases of sexual kinship and capable of a certain diplomacy of reticence were to be admitted from the vast pool of "civilians" into this special intimacy. Such readers, it might be said, had to behave rather as Horace Traubel did in gaining the complete—well, *almost* complete—confidence of Whitman. (Traubel, incidentally, eventually married and fathered two children, but marriage then, as now, was no guarantee of certain knowledge about a husband's sexuality. Symonds himself fathered three daughters. In fact, a recent biography of Whitman's boyfriend Peter Doyle includes the mention of one Gustave Wiksell as Traubel's "lover."* The nine volumes of conversations between Whitman and Traubel often betray a deeply affectionate, emotional, loving relationship, which is described in the last chapter.)

Anyone desiring intimacy with Whitman and his sexual life would be well advised to mimic Traubel's brilliantly disarming diplomacy. Whitman had to be ingratiated and relaxed into a communicative mood, and Traubel sensed early on how this could be done: "My method all along has been to not trespass and not ply him too closely with questions necessary or unnecessary. When a lull occurs I sometimes get him going again by making a remark that is not a question. Other times we sit together for long seances of silence, neither saying anything. One evening during which we had not done much more than sit together, he on his chair, I on his bed, he said: 'We have had a beautiful talk—a beautiful talk.' " Three weeks later, Traubel must have been thrilled to learn from Whitman himself how well this strategy was working. Indeed, the scene turned into a kind of male-bonding epiphany:

"Horace, you are the only person in the world whose questions I tolerate: questions are my bête noire: even you at times, damn you, try me: but I answer your questions because you seem to me to have a superior right to ask them. . . ." He laughed. "Now, Horace, you see how much I love you: you have extorted my last secret. You have made me tell you why you are an exceptional person—you have forced from me an avowal of affection." He was quite lively for an instant while making this sally. Then he relapsed—looked miserable, as if to go to pieces. I went to him. "Help me to the bed," he said. This I did. He sank on the pillow. Closed his eyes. I reached down and kissed him. He said "Good night" without opening his eyes. I said "Good night" and left.*

The powerful moment here, when Whitman suffered a miserable reflex at having revealed his loving feelings, may hint why he never divulged his "great secret."

In any event, Traubel's skillful and genuine congeniality gave him, and us, extraordinary and revealing entré to Whitman-behind-the-scenes that civilian writers could not hope for. He got to know his man very well . . . where his emotional solar plexus lay. One day, for example, Whitman gave him an old Civil War letter in which he was informed about a soldier he had known who was then convalescing in Boston. After reading it aloud, Traubel said he could guess which sentence in the letter pleased Whitman. He chose correctly ("He is very lonesome lying here with no Walt Whitman to cheer him up"), and Walt responded, "You are a first-rate guesser: you keep a little ahead of me every time." Traubel took this chance to say, "I am still waiting for that surprise," but all he got was: "A day or two more and you may come to your own."

Though Whitman never came clean, he did become greatly attached to Traubel. In fact, he began to think of Traubel as a kind of heaven-sent soulmate. Fairly early in their conversations, on an evening when Whitman seemed "very affectionate in his manner," the poet asked him to come over to him.

> I went over. He took my hand. "I feel somehow as if you had conse-
> crated yourself to me. That entails something on my part: I feel
> somehow as if I was consecrated to you. Well—we will work out the
> rest of my life-job together: it won't be for long: anyway, we'll work it
> out together, for short or long, eh?" He took my face between his hands
> and drew me to him and kissed me. Nothing more was then said. I went
> back to my chair and we sat in silence for some time.

After a month passed, in fact on the day Whitman signed his last will, Horace advanced to the status of an authorized biographer. "Some day you will be writing about me: be sure to write about me honest: whatever you do do not prettify me: include all the hells and damns."* Traubel eventually quoted this admonition in his preface to his first volume of *With Walt Whitman in Camden*.

While the effect of the whole is one of honesty and credible capture of Whitman's personality, it has to be said there is not a single shocking or daring revelation, piece of news, or gossip in all nine volumes. Traubel's project was an eminently polite and well-mannered one. Still, there are for the attentive reader many revealing glimpses into Whitman's gay emotional and artistic economy, glimpses behind the walls of reserve (and of the Closet) that he erected to protect his privacy. That Whitman was quite intentionally allowing Traubel to peer behind the "real Me" of his poetic persona he made clear, I believe, when he favorably compared Traubel's project with the work of a "formal" contemporary Whitman biographer like William Sloane Kennedy: "I see more value in the matter you are piling together . . . personal memorabilia, traits of character, incidents, habits—the pulse and throb of the critter himself." Whitman also appears to have been conscious that—if not by revelation of astounding secrets in actual words, then by a kind of relentless osmosis—he was revealing something substantial about the gay affiliations of his prime of life. This is shown, I believe, in a remarkable ebullition that took place on a December evening in 1890.

Traubel's entry begins: "Happy this night's 20 minutes with W.! He sat in his own room—warmed by his own rosy fire—though the cold out-of-doors was crisp and severe. He kept my cold hand—said: 'Its cold is no offense—refreshing, rather.' " At the end of the twenty minutes Whitman, still fervent after delivering a short encomium to American democracy, told Traubel as he was about to depart that "the public has no notion of me as a spiritualistic being. Apart from a few—a very few—of you fellows—my *entourage*, household—you, Doctor [i.e. Bucke], perhaps several others—no one understands that I have my connections—that they are deep-rooted—that they penetrate shows, phenomena." Here Whitman was, in effect, telling Traubel that he truly had been taking him, as he had said in *Calamus*, down underneath an impassive "public" exterior to reveal personal truths. His diction is, as always, very careful, yet surely "spiritualistic" can be read as "sexual" too. Indeed, his reference to "connections" that are "deep-rooted" might well remind one of probably the most famous obiter dictum Whitman ever uttered to Traubel: "sex, sex: always immanent . . . sex, sex: the root of roots: the life below the life!"*

Scarcely any other autobiographical matter is more tantalizing and significant than how Whitman's homosexual "connections" penetrated the "shows" and "phenomena" of his public life and published works. Hints of the existence of his gay fraternity—those, as he once put it, who "belonged to our circus"—are not infrequent in Traubel's 4,800 pages (the last two volumes, covering the final year of conversations, were only recently published). A few can be usefully mentioned here at the outset. Some, naturally, concern the reception of *Leaves of Grass*. It is easy, for instance, to consider that Whitman was speaking of the gay artist operating from within the Closet when, in mid-bite at table, he made an extraordinary remark. "At one point in the dinner, he sat with a piece of chicken suspended on his fork and entered into quite a talk about the 'meaning' of *Leaves of Grass*, that it 'can never be understood but by an indirection,' adding, 'It stands first of all for that something back of phenomena, in phenomena, which give[s] it all its significance, yet cannot be described—which eludes definition, yet is the most real thing of all.' Then finishing his bite . . ." The most real thing of all in the early editions of *Leaves*, I believe, is sex, and the "something" behind its superficial phenomena is Whitman's self-consciousness of his sexuality. It of course had to "elude definition."

A code word for this aberrant and unrevealable sexuality in Whitman's day was "Greek," and several times in the conversations the Greek partisanship of Whitman and *Leaves* is acknowledged. He recalled, for instance, about Samuel Longfellow, one of his early defenders, "away back he was a student of *Leaves of Grass*, I was told—liked it, called it Greek—said I was the most Greek of the moderns." Whitman seemed not displeased to add that Longfellow was alluding not so much "to the form as to the spirit of the book—the underlying recognition of facts which were the peculiar property of the Grecian." One year later, Whitman quite happily associated *Leaves* with things Greek and even added "gay" to the mix. This was when he spoke admiringly of his Whitman-quoting preacher friend: "Clifford is quite Greek, isn't he? Even decidedly, markedly, Greek?—what I call gay-hearted, buoyant—especially gay-hearted—I am fond of calling *Leaves of Grass* gay-hearted."

Several times, incidentally, Whitman used the word "gay" in a way that makes one suspect it was already capable of carrying a "homosexual" connotation at mid-century. Perhaps the most evocative instance of "gay" appearing in a same-sex context is this buoyant passage that Whitman probably jotted down early in 1855 or before—that is, exactly when he was preparing his first *Leaves of Grass* edition for publication:

> How gladly we leave the best of what is called learned and refined society, or the company of men from stores and offices, to sail all day on the river amid a party of fresh and jovial boatmen, with no coats or suspenders, and their trowsers tucked in their boots.—Then the quick blood within joins their gay blood and the twain dances polkas from the bottom to the top of the house, long constraint in the respectable and money-making dens of existence, a man emerges for a few hours and comes up like a whale to spout and breathe.

Behind this harmless allusion to the nineteenth-century commonplace of men dancing with each other ("ram reels" or "bull dances" they were called), the early *Leaves* editions would soon show, an aggressive urge toward homosexual liberation was at play. The powerful image of a breaching whale is thus extraordinarily apt to both the gaiety and the emergent gayness in Whitman's verse.

Apt, too, is the positively Nietzschean image of those jovial boatmen polkaing with each other through the house. Nietzsche, who shared

Whitman's admiration for the homoerotics of classical Greek pedagogy, asserted that any higher culture resembled a "daring dance" requiring "strength and flexibility," and he valued most those books that "teach us to dance."* Of such books Nietzsche explained, "There are writers who, by portraying the impossible as possible ... elicit a feeling of high-spirited freedom, as if man were rising up on tiptoe and simply had to dance out of inner pleasure." Walt Whitman was such a writer. Though his imagery was largely that of heroic vocalism rather than dance, his aim was Nietzsche's: to encourage his readers to free themselves from respectable and refined society and revel in the "inner pleasure" of their own unique personality—and sexuality. Pure Nietzsche, therefore—and one might also say pure Stonewall—is Whitman's credo of radical self-assertion in "Song of Myself": "The boy I love, the same becomes a man not through derived power, but in his own right, / Wicked rather than virtuous out of conformity or fear."

On the festive occasion of his seventy-second (and last) birthday dinner, having been plied with champagne by Mrs. Harned, Whitman, with a delightful unintended double entendre, called Symonds "essentially the most splendid person England has produced . . . very cute; very penetrative; very Greek—thoroughly Greek." That "Greek" was synonymous with laissez-faire attitudes toward sexual behavior is strongly suggested by Whitman's delight whenever *Leaves of Grass* was praised for its Greek spirit. This happened, for example, just a month before he died. An Englishman named T. W. Rolleston, in a letter from Wimbledon, expressed fear that there was "not enough genuine culture" in 1892 America to allow a full embrace of Whitman, and he explains: "I mean the culture gained from absorbing the spirit of the great Greek poets & thinkers—the men who faced the problems of the world & its phenomena in the freest and sincerest spirit ever known." Walt relished this (he himself often used "phenomena" as a polite euphemism for sex and sexuality) and asked Traubel to reread the passage: "On *Greek* culture? Read that again—read it slow." Horace did so, and Whitman remarked: "Altogether, Horace, that is one of the best of our recent letters. It goes near bottom." As so often, sexuality hovers behind one of the "bottom meanings" of *Leaves of Grass*.

In 1920s Germany, by the way, when Thomas Mann sought to counter the blood brotherhood of right-wing militarism, one of his strategies was to make much of Whitman's trumpeting of an erotic democracy. In the stunningly bold speech "On the German Republic" in which he declared "Eros as statesman," Mann, too, emphasized the Greek spirit of the "raging and reverent" *Calamus* poems, calling Whitman's worship of the "electric" body "Hellenism born anew as the spirit of American democracy." A few years later, in 1923, Mann contributed an article to a New York periodical in which he associated Whitman not only with Greece but with his great philosophical idol: "Nietzsche's place is where the spirit of Greece is fused with the lyrical spirit of American democracy, the universal spirit of Walt Whitman."

Of course, "Greek" could also be a term of opprobrium, as Walt hinted when, after a friend remarked that "the Greeks still make excellent wines," he retorted, "then you see they are not altogether degenerate!" In March 1890 a public discussion of *Leaves* took place in Philadelphia, and a fellow named Sulzberger questioned whether the "comradeship" announced in *Calamus* was not "verging upon the licentiousness of the Greek." Traubel noted how Whitman took the query "seriously" and commented, "he meant the handsome Greek youth—one for the other?—Yes I see! and indeed I can see how it might be opened to such an interpretation." And then Whitman launched into a long defense of the word "calamus," which he had taken from the *Calamus aromaticus* plant, whose phallus-shaped spadix was so apt for his most homoerotic poem cluster: "I like it much—it is to me, for my intentions, indispensable—the sun revolves about it, it is a timber of the ship—not there alone in that one series of poems, but in all, belonging to all." This is yet another bold allusion to that sexual "most real thing of all" behind the "phenomena" of *Leaves of Grass*. In this same tirade, which Traubel reports was uttered "with a great vehemence," Whitman also praised "comradeship," one of his self-chosen code words for male-male bonding, and bemoaned the undemonstrativeness of American men (though he had "seen the boys down in the war, in the hospitals, embrace each other, cry, weep").

Months earlier, in the fall of 1888, Traubel asked Whitman, "What comes before comradeship?" and the reply was "Nothing." This was apropos an old draft letter Walt had found while rummaging among his memorabilia. It was dated 1870 and addressed to his "Dear loving comrade" Benton Wilson, one of his Civil War boys. Whitman gave the letter to Traubel and, rather unusually, told him not to read it aloud. Among its moving protestations are these: "Sometimes, after an interval, the thought of one I much love comes upon me strong and full all of a sudden. . . . I have been and am now thinking so of you, dear young man, and of your love, or more rightly speaking, our love for each other—so curious, so sweet, I say so *religious*—We met there in the Hospital—how little we have been together—seems to me we ought to be some together every day of our lives—I don't care about talking, or amusement—but just to be together, and work together, or go off in the open air together. . . ." After reading the letter in silence, Traubel looked up to find Whitman teary-eyed. Still, Walt pulled himself together for another spirited outburst about gay fraternity (indeed, gay liberation) when Horace said to Walt that letters like this one were "the best gospel of comradeship in the language—better than the *Leaves* itself." "Comradeship—yes, that's the thing," Whitman agreed, "getting one and one together to make two—getting the twos together everywhere to make all: that's the only bond we should accept and that's the only freedom we should desire: comradeship, comradeship."

Many of Whitman's countless more general pontifications on the subject of tolerance, of course, can and should be read as conforming with his more explicit apologies for comradeship and "adhesiveness," another of his code words for same-sex relationships. One thinks for example of his resentment of "all the puritan criticism" of Heinrich Heine, whom Whitman viewed (rather as he liked to view *himself*) as "a genuinely great soul—not yet justly measured: hot, turbulent . . ." Or his view that "America means above all toleration, catholicity, welcome, freedom—a concern for Europe, for Asia, for Africa, along with its concern for America. It is . . . a fact everywhere preciously present." On another occasion, Walt eulogized a just-deceased member of the Whitman inner circle and emphasized again the theme of toleration: "Dick was a Walt-Whitmaniac in the common ways of life . . . hospitable to all sorts of men, all forms of thought, all contrasts of life." All sorts of men, indeed.

Not surprisingly, *Leaves of Grass* generated many eloquent colloquies that, in their context, insist upon the free embrace of the body and its sexuality. None, I think, is more poignant than the one evoked on a summer evening in 1888, when Whitman launched into a monologue about the critics of *Leaves* who "condemn it without reading it," about others who with "dismal growl" are always asking, "here, Walt Whitman, what do you mean?" and, finally, about all the pressure he had felt "to concede a point here and there to conciliate the howlers." Then he paused. Traubel, with cool nerve, played his conversational cards just right: "I was wholly silent. He then went on with the same line of thought." Whitman liked to point out the influence of his mother's Quakerism upon him, and he did so now, movingly. Indeed, the words he uttered constitute the best expression of the Whitman credo we have. They are especially pertinent here because they in effect address the ineluctable fact of one's sexuality and the wisdom of accepting it. Of his refusal to bow to all the "brilliant assaults" of which he had "been a victim," Whitman continued:

> I have a deeper reason than all that . . . a reason that always
> seems conclusive, to say the last word—the conviction that the

thing is because it is, being what it is because it must be just that—as a tree is a tree, a river a river, the sky the sky. A curious affinity exists right there between me and the Quakers, who always say, this is so or so because of some inner justifying fact—because it could not be otherwise. I remember a beautiful old Quakeress saying to me once: "Walt—I feel thee is right—I could not tell why but I feel thee is right!"—and that seemed to me to be more significant than much that passes for reason in the world.

🌿   🌿   🌿

A tree must be a tree—here one thinks immediately of the autobiographical solitary live-oak that figures so movingly in *Calamus #20*—and a gay man must be a gay man.

The present biography is largely devoted to this aspect of Walt Whitman's life and writings. Yet I am not unmindful that Whitman himself once complained, sharply and sensibly, about those who emphasize one aspect of a life at the expense of all others. "You remember what I said the other night about Bret Harte—men of that stamp," he said to Horace one day, "how they take up a single phase of our life—lay such stress on it that it would be supposed all was concentrated there—there was no other life—when in reality this is but a drop in the sea." The result of such "concentrated" biography, of course, is a multiplicity of Whitmans, as the subject himself observed: "I meet new Walt Whitmans every day. There are a dozen of me afloat."

My justification—my defense, if you will—for preferring to concentrate on the gay Whitman is simply that it is about time. About time, that is, for a poet who believed sex was the "most sensitive spot" in *Leaves of Grass*—and who so long ago expressed amazement at "how people reel when I say father-stuff and mother-stuff and onanist and bare legs and belly! O God! you might suppose I was citing some diabolical obscenity. Will the world ever get over its own indecencies . . . ?" Hitherto, scholarship has given us Whitman the *Thinker*, Whitman the *Poet and Person*, Whitman the *Magnificent Idler*, Whitman *An American*, Whitman the *Poet of Democracy*, Whitman the *Prophet of the New Era*, Whitman the *American Giant* and *Builder for America*, Whitman the *Yankee Redeemer*, Whitman the *Friend*, Whitman the *Legend*, and (more than once) plain old Whitman the *Man*. Why should we not, by way of ameliorating the imbalance of emphasis at this late date, have something like Whitman the *Gay Lover*, or *Pre-Stonewall Prophet*, or *Bather in Sex*?

Several who have written on Whitman since the Stonewall uprising of 1969 have begun to show the way, and the time now seems ripe for a systematic attempt to turn the tables on the mythic, mist-engulfed Whitman and to set in his stead the flesh-and-blood—which is to say the sexual—Whitman.* There is, I like to think, warrant for what some may feel is a drastic reappraisal in an observation Walt uttered, "as if stirred by great feeling," to Horace one day: "It does a man good to turn himself inside out once in a while: to sort of turn the tables on himself. . . . It takes a good deal of resolution to do it: yet it should be done—no one is safe until he can give himself such a drubbing: until he can shock himself out of his complacency. . . . if we don't look out we develop a bumptious bigotry—a colossal self-satisfaction, which is worse for a man than being a damned scoundrel."

There are other reasons for the tight biographical focus of this study. One, I hasten to repeat, is the conviction that Whitman's sexuality was the paramount influence upon his oeuvre. In other words, I am operating, as I did in *The Stranger Wilde,* on the assumption that Friedrich Nietzsche was correct in asserting that "the degree and kind of a person's sexuality reach up into the ultimate pinnacle of his spirit." Countless are Whitman's assertions—especially those made in letters or private conversation, where he was more free to express himself—of the primacy of sex in his poetry. Even from his deathbed he could insist spiritedly upon the "heroic animality of the *Leaves*" and rise in fury at "how these damned saints affect a carriage of anti-animality." A few days later he warned well and truly that critics "can hardly realize the *Leaves*" if they "do not reach the tapstone—face its physiological, concrete—might almost call it, its brutal, bloody—background, base." And then he expresses pity mingled with disgust at those critics who, averting their gaze from the "physiological," miss the forest for the trees: "There are parts, features, faculties, detached bits, beauties, perhaps—these the fellows got—but the unitariness, the uncompromising physiology, backing, upholding all—that they do not see, do not catch the first glimpse of." Strong words . . . and words unpublished until 1996. Yet they apply to much "processional" Whitman commentary of the last century.

Another reason is rather more selfish, though certainly Whitmanesque: I would like to think I am *con amore* with my subject. Horace Traubel's father was a lithographer and artist who seemed to love his work, and Whitman said one day, thinking of him, "to be *con amore* with your work . . . signifies a world of advantage to start with." Many of the scholarly and belletristic books on the groaning Whitman shelf that I have read seem to lack this advantage, and I am sanguine enough to imagine that my own experience as a gay man may confer some advantage on me, at least as an explorer of the Whitman who most interests me. And let there be no doubt that this interest is shamelessly and elaborately autobiographical. Thinking about Whitman's life and work has, on eerily numerous occasions, proved an invitation to think about my own life. Such self-indulgence must play a part in any responsive biography, but in Whitman's case it is particularly apropos. One day Traubel interrupted his reading of an idolatrous letter written to Walt by the author of *Dracula* to observe that "autobiography is the only real biography."* To which, I was immensely relieved to learn, Walt added his "amen" and said, "It's absorbingly interesting." The reason for his agreement on this point is perhaps to be found in this observation from an early Whitman notebook: "A man only is interested in any thing when he identifies himself with it."

What follows is thus by no means a full life. I will be ignoring many interesting or significant aspects of Whitman's biography—Whitman's broader cultural milieux, his political affiliations, his education, his European reception—happy in the knowledge that others have already been there and done that. Being devoted principally to sexual identity, sex, and love, the following pages will necessarily be mainly focused on the most pertinent time of Whitman's life: his prime. He had occasion to define this prime himself when he remarked on how the twenty-nine-year-old Traubel invariably answered "well" whenever the poet asked about his health: "It is so great—so superb—to be always well. However, these are your years to expect it—from eighteen to forty-five—halcyon days, sure enough." And Whitman then added a remark that, of course, applied spectacularly to himself: that "if there's anything in a man, physically or mentally, it's sure to come out, to give an account of itself, along through that stretch of life."

This stretch of Whitman's life would be 1837 to 1864, but the "halcyon" years when he came into both a physical (let us say sexual) and mental (let us say artistic) prime can be more narrowly located in the decade of the 1850s. Whitman's "youth" and his coming-out as a poet and homosexual were somewhat delayed, as sometimes happens in gay lives (Oscar Wilde also achieved true flamboyance only in his midthirties). In fact, Whitman, perhaps thinking of himself, suggested one day with a fine unintended pun that "slow fruit" is the best. Traubel read aloud an idolizing letter from a young Englishman—who, incidentally, later became a member of Wilde's gay coterie—and Walt observed, "That sounds very ripe for a boy of eighteen. . . . It is singular how soon some natures come to a head and how long it takes others to ripen, though I believe, as a rule, the slow fruit is the best," *Leaves of Grass* was slow fruit indeed, but it was written by a still essentially youthful Whitman albeit not to the eye (he had gone quite gray by thirty). This, by the way, is perhaps the place to note that each of the first three truly epochal fictions of homosexual liberation was written by a slow fruit who was thirty-five years old at the time: *Leaves of Grass*, *The Picture of Dorian Gray*, and Thomas Mann's *Death in Venice*.*

Another tightening of focus follows unavoidably: only the first three of Whitman's ten editions of *Leaves of Grass*—the editions of his "halcyon days"—will matter much in this study. Fortunately, and not coincidentally, all but a very small handful of his greatest poems appeared in these three editions of 1855, 1856, and 1860. In his youth Whitman had greatly admired the rather masculine-looking actress Charlotte Cushman, who had in fact played the roles of Romeo and Hamlet and whom Whitman had called "a noble fellow." Many years later Whitman recalled, "Charlotte Cushman's great acting was done in her earlier days before she was famous." That view perfectly, if unwittingly, describes Whitman's own transformation from an unknown singer of the sexually electric body to a famously good gray bard.

The great early poems were also poems of a youthful sexual prime. This surely explains one aspect of the reception of *Leaves* that Whitman himself began to notice with bemusement. Thinking of many readers like Edmund Gosse and Bayard Taylor, who idolized him in their youth and then fell away, Whitman observed: "The young fellows seem rather bowled over by me: [then] they get respectable or something and I will no longer do. . . . I suppose I don't wear well—that's what's the matter: I fool 'em for a time, when they're in their teens, but when they grow up they can no longer be deceived." Here is yet another unwitting comment on the progress of Whitman's career. For he himself became more respectable, became more "mature" and "adult" and aware (as only the aged or cynical can be) that love and sexual joy are merely deceits. But it is the youthful poet—who was bowled over by sex, and whose sexual poetry can still bowl over a reader— who will preside over the following chapters.

Not all of Walt's remarks about the difference between the early and the late Whitman—and the vastly greater stature of the former—were inadvertent. The most poignant and witty one I have come across was made about a month after his musing on turncoats like Gosse and Taylor. Naturally, sex was at issue. Whitman had dug up a gushing letter of Taylor's written more than twenty years before. Amid its purple prose: "There is not one word of your large and beautiful sympathy for men which I cannot take into my own heart, nor one of those subtle and wonderful physical affinities you describe which I cannot comprehend *etc*." After Traubel read it aloud, Whitman remarked that Taylor, who for years had been writing very genteel lavender-tinged poetry and fiction, had lately been "quoted against me—especially against the sex poems." This set Whitman off on the whimsical thought of how he would feel if the vigorous sexuality of his early poems were finally embraced: "I wouldn't know what to do, how to comport myself, if I lived long enough to become accepted, to get in demand, to ride on the crest of the wave. I would have to go scratching, questioning, hitching about, to see if this was the real critter, the old Walt Whitman—to see if Walt Whitman had not suffered a destructive transformation—become apostate, formal, reconciled to the conventions, subdued from the old independence."

A more accurate description of the transformation of *Leaves of Grass* after 1860 (and a better sanction for riveting attention on the first three editions) could not be wished. As Whitman's post–Civil War years rolled on, he did become reconciled to the conventions—the social, political, poetic, and sexual conventions. At least as a public figure, he moved relentlessly in a direction away from heterodoxy and toward orthodoxy; became, in other words, more and more of a democrat and majoritarian. In the privacy of Mickle Street, though, he felt more free to flare up in the style of the early, preapostate Walt Whitman. He did so when Dr. Bucke carped, "Walt, you seem determined to be in the minority," and he answered, "Yes, I do: that's the only safe place for me."

The following chapters focus on Walt Whitman as a gay man finding his voice, finding sex, finding love, finding friendship. Though the chapters are thematic, they are ordered more or less chronologically. For it appears that Whitman discovered opera and his own heroic throat just before he made his great "phallic choice" for himself and America. And it was in his subsequent decades that he not only searched for another man with whom to wander hand in hand "apart from other men" but also continued to pursue the political "institution of the dear love of comrades," as he phrased it in *Calamus #24*.

"Walt & Marietta," the first chapter, is thus about Whitman as an opera queen, with all the ramifications this experience had for his sexual and poetic coming-out. Much discussion of the nexus between opera and homosexuality has appeared of late, and I was, in fact, nearly tempted to title this chapter "The Real Queen's Throat," in allusion to a recent screwball comedy of a book on the subject.* For Whitman, it was most emphatically *not* over when the fat lady Marietta Alboni sang to him for the first time; indeed, his ascent to true artistic mastery began at almost exactly that ecstatic moment in his life.

In the second chapter, "Walt & Boss-Tooth," I evoke a plausible sexual life for Whitman by drawing from his published poetry, fiction, and prose, his correspondence, notebooks, daybooks, miscellaneous manuscripts, and private conversations. Along the way I look into the droll history of the sexual encounters of critics and biographers with Whitman, as well as some of the ways Whitman himself censored and expurgated *Leaves* in the course of writing and revision.

In "Walt & His Boys" I attempt to reconstruct Whitman's lifelong search for a "Lover divine and perfect Comrade," looking first at his attitudes toward women, then at the characteristic emotional dynamics of the male relationships he favored, the ideals he pursued. The chapter then moves into a discussion of several young men who were important in what he called his "passional" life.

Finally, Chapter 4 focuses on the extraordinary relationship that developed between Whitman and the last dear young friend and phenomenally assiduous Boswell of his final four years, Horace Traubel.

The afterword that follows is a biographer's *jeu d'esprit*. Whitman saw himself "as connecter, as chansonnier of a great future," and he certainly "connected" with me in several curious, sometimes startling ways in the course of my work on this project. I describe in these pages the very Whitmanesque conjunctions of biography and autobiography that now and then occur between the lines of the preceding chapters.

Whitman added two substantial annexes to his last *Leaves of Grass* editions. My annex, too, is a long one but, I contend, crucial to understanding not only Whitman's posthumous reception but also the significant part he played (along with André Gide, Thomas Mann, and—most especially—Oscar Wilde, in their respective countries) in the movement now referred to as "gay liberation." Whitman believed only "future ages" would truly understand his work. In respect of his superbly mischievous, subversive, but very cleverly masked philosophy of sexuality, he was certainly correct. His boldness and acuity are only now becoming thoroughly apparent. And now that they are, the extraordinary similarities with Wilde, the English-speaking world's other great nineteenth-century gay celebrity and liberator from the constraints of moralists, are emerging as well.

In the annex, then, I consider how Whitman and Wilde pursued in similar way their demands for spiritual, intellectual, and artistic freedom. In effect, they laid the rhetorical bases for a philosophy of gay liberation. My context is the famous 1882 meeting of the two men in Camden, and I focus on several of their important shared modes of achieving, even within the confines of the Closet, room for the expression of their ebullient personalities, their sexuality, and their subversive cultural agendas. I conclude with a reading of Wilde's finest children's tale, "The Fisherman and His Soul," as a brilliant if small-scale reiteration of the liberating themes in *Leaves of Grass*.

I was delighted to indulge in a pun when I chose the title for *The Stranger*

Wilde, knowing that the author of *The Importance of Being Earnest* would not have objected. About the play on "gay" in the title of this book I am more fretful, not least because Whitman never punned. One day he showed Traubel an old Civil War safe-conduct pass and, referring to its being a worthless curio, said "it won't pass for money." Traubel expressed his surprise at the pun, but Whitman swore it was unintended. "Did you ever know me to pun? It's not in my line at all. I am guilty of most [of] the real bad sins but that bad sin I never acquired."

Nevertheless, I would like to have the word "gay" read both in the primary nineteenth-century sense of cheerful exuberance and in the sense of male homosexual. The older meaning still goes far in capturing the essential Whitman spirit, but so, too, does the newer one that now seems to have banished all rivals. I want to emphasize this late-coming meaning not only because, as mentioned before, I have a sneaking suspicion that the word, spoken in the right company, may long have had something of its familiar post-Stonewall ring, but also because the pun is in the spirit of Whitman's coopting of words like "adhesive" and "comrade" to expand the vocabulary for the demonstration of male-male affection, which he believed was very inadequate in America. And of course the modern meaning of the word is sometimes superbly true to Whitman's thrust when it appears in his verse—perhaps most wonderfully in these lines from 1856 that anticipate the ideals of post-Stonewall gay and lesbian advocacy:

> In the best poems re-appears the body, man's or woman's,
>   well-shaped, natural, gay,
> Every part able, active, receptive, without shame or the need of
>   shame.*

In addition to the pun in the title, there is another distinctly un-Whitmanlike aspect to this book: it carries a dedication. There are no Whitman dedicatees, and it is fascinating to ponder why. The poet's own explanation is hardly convincing but may have to do: "I do not know why—probably there is no why. Dedications have gone out of vogue—are no longer regarded as necessary." Nor might Whitman have liked my choice of two dedicatees who have been university men for the thirty years they have been companions—and for all the time I have been fortunate enough to know them. Happily, though, these are uncommon "scholar swells." Like Whitman's deeply admired Edward Carpenter, they have managed to pluck themselves from the burning.

For their assistance or advice I am delighted to acknowledge and thank Girvice Archer Jr., Jeanne Chapman, the late Vera Brodsky

Lawrence, Ann Marlowe, Marybeth McMahon, Vincent Newton, Paul Robinson, G. Thomas Tanselle, and Marvin Tartak.

Finally, I would like to note that Allen Ginsberg died a few days before this book left my hands for the last time. He was not so much Whitman's unparalleled twentieth-century heir as he was his reincarnation. Attempting to explain himself to his father in the late 1950s, Ginsberg wrote, "Whitman long ago complained that unless the material power of America were leavened by some kind of spiritual infusion, we would wind up among the 'fabled damned,' " and he added that the "only way out is individuals taking responsibility and saying what they actually feel." My readers will quickly understand why I am deeply disappointed that this study came too late for the author of "Howl!" to cast his eyes upon it.

1

WALT & MARIETTA:
ENTER THE DIVO

If you have the voice, sing.
—Ovid, *The Art of Love*

She roused whirlwinds of feeling within me.
—Walt Whitman

AN OLD MAN, Walt Whitman took it in mind one day to jot down on a scrap of paper the names of all the celebrities he had personally seen during his life. He was able to include seven presidents on this list, as well as literary giants like Bryant, Cooper, Emerson, Longfellow, and Poe. And he added such luminaries as the Marquis de Lafayette, Aaron Burr, John Jacob Astor, the tragedians Edwin Forrest and Junius Brutus Booth, and the Quaker stem-winder Elias Hicks. Of the twenty-one names on Whitman's list, only one is a woman's: Marietta Alboni. Who was she? And what caused the elaborately misogynistic poet to choose her for this singular honor to her sex?

These are momentous questions, I believe, for anyone interested in probing the strangest miracle in the history of American letters—the appearance in the summer of '55 of *Leaves of Grass*, that great original sheaf of poems from the pen of a man who had formerly been an itinerant (and possibly disgraced) schoolteacher, blowhard journalist, doggerel poet, hack story writer, Broadway loafer, and sometime carpenter and homebuilder. But before we make our acquaintance with the stupendous Italian opera singer Marietta Alboni or consider the ecstatic joys she gave the poet, we must pause and reflect a little on a very peculiar thirty-three-year-old who, from boyhood called Walt by his family and friends, was known to the world, mainly through his journalistic editing and writing, as "Walter" or "W." Whitman. I speak, to be more specific, of the Walter Whitman who, on an early summer evening in 1852, sat expectantly in Metropolitan Hall along with a few thousand other New

Yorkers awaiting Alboni's appearance at her first American concert. Thirty years later Whitman reminisced, "I heard Alboni every time she sang in New York and vicinity." He had earlier boasted of his delight in taking his usual seat in New York's theaters "by night among the sudorous or sweaty classes," and I am taking him at his word that he was indeed present for Alboni's debut in Metropolitan Hall on that long-ago evening.

I call this Walter Whitman very peculiar, though not because one could spot him in the audience at the large hall on Broadway above Bleecker Street, thirsty for an evening of stupendous bel canto fireworks. Opera was the grandest entertainment in town, and this was a golden age in New York City for opera, especially Italian opera. The northeastern seaboard of America had in recent years been discovered by major European singers and their managers to be ripe for vocal exploitation. Indeed, Alboni had arrived in the city—with no little bravado, some aficionados thought—just a week after the "Swedish Nightingale" Jenny Lind departed America following a sensational tour managed by P. T. Barnum. And opera had also begun to catch the imagination of Whitman himself. In his editorials he regularly protested vociferously against the foisting of effete European culture upon robust, sinewy Americans. "What perfect cataracts of trash come to us at the present day from abroad," he opined in the Brooklyn *Daily Eagle*. For opera, however, he appears to have made a striking exception, and his experience of professional singers was by no means scanty. In 1851 he boasted in the *Evening Post* of "traveling through the fifteen years display in this city of musical celebrities, from Mrs. Austin up to Jenny Lind," which would mean that he began attending vocal performances as a teenager sometime in the late 1830s.

Whitman's presence at Alboni's debut was far from peculiar, too, because news from Europe about her stupendous contralto voice had been extremely favorable, notwithstanding ribald rumors about an enormous physique. This high praise must have made Whitman's attendance almost mandatory, in spite of weather so warm that, according to the *Post*, it drove "many of our regular concert-goers out of town" and left a thousand empty seats. At least one reviewer grimaced at the notion of being present in such heated weather: "In the present limp state of linen, a cooler prospect than a two hours' seething with four thousand mortal men and women in a huge cauldron of brick and mortar would be welcome; but if we must choose between boiling with Alboni and not boiling without Alboni, by all means, let us boil."* Perhaps, too, her advance publicity, which the *Musical Times* said left "an impression of something masculine and *brusque*," was just what might have goaded Whitman into buying a ticket. His tastes, after all, were for the "manly" in all things, and he had made his disgust at the porcelain-skinned, piccolo-voiced soubrette species of female vocalist quite clear hitherto in his occasional published opera reviews. Jenny Lind, for example, had left him quite cold.

No, I am inclined to call this Whitman of the summer of 1852 peculiar not on account of his operatic devotions but rather because this Whitman was so spectacularly commonplace and matter-of-fact a young man. He was, well, so *un*operatic. At the no longer young age of thirty-three, what had he to show for himself?

HERE AT LAST IN BABYLON: THE EARLY YEARS

Not yet a teenager, Whitman began his working life in 1830 as an office boy for a lawyer, then for a doctor, while living with his family in Brooklyn. By his early teens he had moved on to the positions of printer's devil and compositor at several newspapers, including the Long Island *Patriot* and *Star*. But when his family moved back to the country near his North Shore birthplace, he put his foot down and, in common-enough rebellion, refused to do farm work. So, at the incredible age of seventeen, Whitman, whose own formal education petered out by the age of eleven, turned to teaching. The young pedant grazed in several rural Long Island towns, never, apparently, persuading the citizenry in any of them (or himself) that a permanent position was desirable. He was clearly unable to quite picture himself becoming one of those "eccentric specimens of the masculine race" called country schoolteachers. Sexual scandal, as we shall see in the next chapter, may also have helped to cut his classroom career short a few years later.

Herman Melville ended his feckless early stab at a teaching career by adventurously shipping out to the Pacific on a whaler. Whitman staidly remained closer to home. In June 1838 he somehow induced backers to set him up as the founding editor of the Long *Islander* at Huntington, near his birthplace; the first issue appeared just after his nineteenth birthday. This weekly became rather less weekly as Whitman's interest waned and his horseback paper-route trips became more leisurely and meandering, and in a year's time his investors got fed up and sold the Long *Islander* out from under him. Several more stints as an itinerant Long Island school-teacher followed, after which Whitman found his way back to Brooklyn and New York. He had lived there with his family from the age of four to fourteen, and quite obviously those formative years had convinced him that in the "brick-and-pine Babel" to the west his pleasure lay.

For most of the 1840s—Whitman's twenties—he worked in the newspaper trade, at first as a printer in the pressroom of the *New World*, later writing for or editing several weeklies and dailies like the *Aurora*, the Brooklyn *Daily Eagle*, the *Sun*, the *Tattler*, the *Democrat*, and the *Sunday Times*. Finally, in 1848, having quit or been fired from the *Eagle*, he set out for New Orleans to take up the position of editor at a new paper called the *Crescent*. He lasted two months there, resigning in late May, and by early September he was back in New York editing another start-up paper, the Brooklyn *Freeman*. The next year, 1849, he opened his own small printing office and bookshop on Myrtle Avenue in Brooklyn.

Within a year or two Whitman's short attention span as an employee or proprietor appears to have prevailed once again, and he abandoned the publishing world entirely. Though details of Whitman's activities and whereabouts are extremely scanty for this period, it appears that for the next several years, the early 1850s, he became an entrepreneurial carpenter and house builder. He seems to have fared about as poorly as his father, who had pursued these same trades for many years. Whitman thus had little material wealth to show for more than a decade of busyness spent making his way in America's great commercial and sexual Babylon on that evening Marietta Alboni first opened her throat in the New World. Indeed, the first words she sang were splendidly apropos: *Eccomi alfine in Babilonia*—"here I am at last in Babylon." Unless he still had access to a press pass from his journalistic days, Whitman probably chose to buy for Alboni's debut a cheap place in the upper tier of Metropolitan Hall, where the vestless "roughs" and shirtsleeved "b'hoys," whose company he preferred in any case, sweated and had a rowdy good time.

Nor did Walter have the fame he had hankered after. Whatever the quality of his mortises and tenons, he could claim no distinction as a poet—or as a fiction writer, belletrist, or journalist-editor, for that matter. All through the 1840s and early 1850s, Whitman was a steady but very minor and sporadic presence in New York papers and magazines. Biographers and critics have unanimously accounted his early poetry, which he began in 1840 to publish every once in a while, very bland stuff, indistinguishable from the countless chunks of poetasting produced to satisfy the appetite of the city's numerous weeklies and dailies. Mostly it was rhymed, and Whitman favored clipped, plodding tetrameter lines arranged in lock-step ballad stanzas. These poems never rise above the arch or maudlin and carry such titles as "Fame's Vanity" and "The Punishment of Pride." Their only occasional interest lies in the autobiographical themes that now and then shine through the doggerel, as for example in "The Play-Ground"—

O, lovely, happy children!
I am with you in my soul;
I shout—I strike the ball with you—
With you I race and roll.

—or in what, I will later argue, can be thought of as Whitman's first gay poem, "The Love That is Hereafter." Its concluding stanza:

For vainly through this world below
We seek affection. Nought but wo
Is with our earthly journey wove;
And so the heart must look above,
Or die in dull despair.

Only one poem written in the period Before Alboni, "Resurgemus," dispenses with rhyme and stanza form and has the rhythmic flexibility and freedom that we associate with the *Leaves of Grass* Whitman. This poem about the European revolutionary movements of 1848 (Latin *resurgere* = to rise up again) is more than sixty lines long and begins:

Suddenly, out of its stale and drowsy air, the air of slaves,
Like lightning Europe le'pt forth,
Sombre, superb and terrible,
As Ahimoth, brother of Death.

Not surprisingly, this poem, which appeared in the New York *Tribune* in June 1850, is the only one of the dozen or so he had written up to then that Whitman allowed into the 1855 *Leaves*.* "Resurgemus," a brief breath of fresh poetic air from Whitman's quill, was a decidedly exceptional performance. For the rest, there was in his stale and drowsy verse no hint of the poet who would leap forth on the literary scene something like lightning— superbly but far from sombrely—a few years later with *Leaves of Grass*.

Whitman's prose fiction of the decade of the 1840s bulked much larger than his poetry. Unlike the tiny, exquisite juvenile novels of Jane Austen, which so amusingly foretell the mature author, there is nothing in the art of Whitman's short stories (though much in their autobiographical subtexts) to prepare us for epoch-shattering work to come. These two dozen short pieces are miniature potboilers, in which Whitman often unappetizingly blends callow archness, sentimentality, and blatant melodrama. Among their titles are "The Child and the Profligate," "The Tomb Blossoms," "The Half-Breed: A Tale of the Western

Frontier," "Dumb Kate.—An Early Death," "One Wicked Impulse!" and, prophetically, "The Boy Lover." His first published story, "Death in the School-Room (A FACT)," appeared in 1841 and featured a pedant-villain named Lugare: "Hasty to decide, and inflexibly severe, he was the terror of the little world he ruled so despotically." We leave Lugare at the moment of discovering that a sickly boy he has been flogging for inattention is in fact dead: "His countenance turn'd to a leaden whiteness; the ratan dropp'd from his grasp; and his eyes, stretch'd wide open, glared as at some monstrous spectacle of horror and death. The sweat started in great globules seemingly from every pore in his face; his skinny lips contracted, and show'd his teeth. . . ." In his succeeding stories Whitman managed to tame such breathtaking garishness a little, but he was never able to eradicate it entirely from his narrative style.

His longest fiction of this period was *Franklin Evans, or The Inebriate,* a lurid temperance novel that appeared in the *New World* in 1842 and again, in revised form, in 1846 in the Brooklyn *Daily Eagle.* Though the autobiographical interest of the story is enormous and will claim our attention in Chapter 2, its artistic interest is minuscule indeed. Obviously, Whitman the self-proclaimed poet of America soon came to look upon it as a skeleton in his closet, and he quite successfully managed to keep it hidden there for decades. Already with the 1846 reprinting, in fact, he got some distance away from it by making its author one "J.R.S." His first recorded mention of *Franklin Evans* was in a conversation with Horace Traubel in 1888, when he confessed it had been written because the offer of a "cash payment" from the *New World* was too tempting. "I was so hard up at the time . . . I set to work at once ardently on it (with the help of a bottle of port or what not)." Nearly a half century later, Whitman could afford to be blunt about the god-awful product: "In three days of constant work I finished the book. Finished the book? Finished myself. It was damned rot—rot of the worst sort— not insincere, perhaps, but rot, nevertheless: it was not the business for me to be up to. I stopped right there: I never cut a chip off that kind of timber again."

Another writerly business Whitman sought for several years to be "up to" was the producing of countless, sometimes anonymous, editorials, feuilletons, and filler paragraphs for various New York newspapers. Much of this ephemera has been collected, and it all now makes reading that is at best unintentionally droll, at worst merely tedious. Eloquent turns of phrase are nonexistent, and Whitman displays himself as far from a deep thinker or feeler. Even when his heart seems in the right place, as when he lambastes legislators in Albany for entertaining a law for "making all practices of licentiousness penal," his editorial style often veers toward the inflated and pontifical: "We are no friends to the fearful caprice of mobs. But the iron arm of the thousand fingered law is as tyrannical—interferes as unjustly and oppresses as cruelly—as ever did the sans culottes of Robespierre's day, or the Protestant rabble of the imbecile Lord George Gordon." In 1846 he took on the Post Office in his usual table-thumping style: "There is not a fact which can bring more irrefragable evidence to prove itself, than that the Post Office Department of the United States is the most mismanaged 'concern' of any general institution in the world! It is a living oration and argument against the power of the government to compete with individual enterprise. . . . We want an active Yankee—a fellow who is 'up to the age'—in that Department."

He was not out after subtlety, and a bubbly effrontery often animated his journalese, as when he took his *Aurora* readers on a tour of lower Manhattan in March 1842: "A door or two further is Tammany Hall, the Mecca of democracy—the time-honored, soul-endeared holy of holies, to all who go for anti-monopoly. . . . Now you come into the region of Jews, jewelry, and second-hand clothing. Here and there, the magic 'three balls' hold out hope to those whose ill luck makes them grasp at even the smallest favors. . . . If you turn right, you will come into some of the dirtiest-looking places in New York . . . quite thickly settled with German emigrants." On the subject of elected officials he was regularly rambunctious: "Few evils are greater in these blessed United States, than the officiousness of the law-making powers. They meddle with every thing, and derange every thing," Whitman opined, adding, "If the legislative ninnies were allowed to meet together only once in a great while, we would be much the better off."

Sometimes he would deploy his hectoring style on minicrusades distinctly pertinent to his subsequent homoerotica. A July 1846 *Eagle* editorial with the headline BROOKLYN YOUNG MEN.—ATHLETIC EXERCISES begins, "In our sun-down perambulations, of late, through the outer parts of Brooklyn, we have observed several parties of youngsters playing 'base,' a certain ball game." Whitman, who as a wheelchair-bound old man would delight in watching baseball players on the Camden town common, adds, "We wish such sights were more common among us." Then he goes on to complain that "the practice of athletic and manly sports" by "the young men of nearly all our American cities are very deficient." And the creator of the thrilled gazer upon twenty-eight young male bathers in "Song of Myself" also authored a long editorial urging free baths for Brooklyn under the headline BATHING—CLEANLINESS—PERSONAL BEAUTY. With the verve of today's promoters of fitness centers, Whitman wrote, "As a matter of personal beauty, too, the bath is important. It gives the complexion a clear and wholesome tint, blending the red and white together upon the cheeks, and freeing the system from a hundred gross humors, all poisonous to personal good looks."

Nor was Whitman above some very cheeky silliness in his eagerness to fill up the little blank spaces in his layout. One day he jauntily contrived to review a book (Dumas's *Count of Monte Cristo*) without having read it: "Sparkling in quality and plentiful in quantity appears to be this work—*appears*, for we confess to not having read it. There are certainly, however, a pleasant gracefulness and vivacity in Dumas' writings—that we can say from our knowledge of his former works." On 6 June 1847, *Eagle* readers were stunned to learn there was a

PAUCITY OF NEWS

Never were matters in the news line duller than
they are today.

One is bound to wonder how the future greatest of American poets could have been gestating at the same time he was scrambling about to inform his *Eagle* readers that

Carelessly knocking a man's eye out with a
broken axe, may be termed a *bad axe-i-dent*.

Or concocting such blithe fillers as "J.J. Astor has given $500 to the Fund for Firemen's widows and orphans? How on earth could he spare it?" and "What do you think, Sir Reader, when we tell you that three ladies' slippers were 'pulled off' and bestowed on us this morning. We have 'em now—in a glass of water!" Or browbeating impresarios with an IMPORTANT ANNOUNCEMENT demanding the "polite means of a special invitation" and "gratuitous tickets" if they expected the *Eagle* to appear at their theatrical events. Or giving a rival editorialist a Bronx cheer: "If the *Boston Post* is green enough to doubt any thing positively affirmed in the Brooklyn *Eagle*, we quite despair of the Republic—at least the eastern section." Or cheekily transacting his own business, as in this larky personal:

RECEIVED WITH THANKS

A pretty bouquet from Bob.

And who, we are tantalized, might Bob have been? One of his very early boyfriends? In April 1846 Whitman published six pithy rules for "How to Write for a Newspaper." The first rule was "Have something to write about," and it must be said that he did not always follow this rule himself.

Walter Whitman's parents, family, and friends, not to mention a large wake of aggravated former employers, might well have been forgiven for wondering, in the summer of 1852, if the feckless fellow would ever come to anything. Whitman himself obviously began to wonder about this, too. There is a poignant passage in "Crossing Brooklyn Ferry," perhaps the finest of the new poems in the 1856 *Leaves of Grass*, in which he looks back on a harrowing time of erosion in self-confidence as he reached his thirties with so little accomplished:

> It is not upon you alone the dark patches fall,
> The dark threw its patches down upon me also,
> The best I had done seem'd to me blank and suspicious,
> My great thoughts as I supposed them, were they not in
> reality meagre?

As it happens, there is some even earlier evidence of Whitman's miserable and accurate self-awareness (for what he had produced *was* blank and meagre) before he ferried across his poetical Rubicon in 1855. The transparent autobiography in his early writing has already been remarked upon, and it is on fascinating display in a story titled "The Shadow and the Light of a Young Man's Soul," which he published in the *Union Magazine* in June 1848.

This little story—just three thousand words long yet still seeming a bit overstuffed—offers an uncannily prophetic glimpse of the blank, suspicious "Walter" before he transformed himself into the magnificently ego-effusing "Walt." His alter ego here is named Archibald Dean, and he, too, loves the city, "living out of which he had so often said was no living at all." Alas, he is forced by poverty to emigrate to a country school district to teach for "poor pay and coarse fare." Archibald's waywardness frets his widowed mother, just as Walt probably felt his own laziness concerned his mother, Louisa Whitman: "What troubled her much, perhaps most, was the way of her son Archibald. 'Unstable as water,' even his youth was not a sufficient excuse for his want of energy and resolution; and she experienced many sad moments, in her maternal reflections, ending with the fear that he would 'not excel.' " And Archie, apparently like Walt himself, lets "his heart sink within him" whenever he has to show signs "of the necessity for labor, or of the absence of funds."

Archie, like the speaker in "Crossing Brooklyn Ferry," is pretty hard on himself. Though unsullied by any of "the darker vices which are so common among the young fellows of our great cities," the basically "benevolent, candid soul" still tends to contemplate "the dark side of his life entirely too often," pining especially "over his deficiencies, as he called them, by which he meant mental as well as pecuniary wants."

Trapped in rural tedium, Archie emits a *cri de coeur* to his mother in a letter that sounds written from Whitman's own experience. He had, after all, actually resided with his family for a time in Babylon, Long Island, but it was clearly the greater Babylon to the west that always beckoned him. "Mother, my throat chokes, and my blood almost stops," says Archie, "when I see around me so many people who appear to be born into the world merely to eat and sleep, and run the same dull monotonous round—and think that I too must fall in this current, and live and die in vain!" (Whitman's extreme closeness to his mother is reflected in an autobiographical parenthesis in the story: "strange as it may seem to most men, she was also his confidential friend." Other Whitman hallmarks: Archie's delight in the "refreshing influence" of "open-air nature" and his penchant for "morning rambles" and "evening saunters.") Surely, such a passage alludes to the "dark patches" of depression Whitman himself must have experienced now and again between 1840 and 1855. It also alludes to the dull, monotonous round of his attempts at versifying, the mediocre stories of which this was one, and the unproductive grind of newspaper work that had carried him into early middle age.

In the first half of his story, then, Whitman, with Bunyanesque allegorical blatancy, precipitates Archie into a Slough of Despond. In the last half, with almost hilariously orotund, preachy clichés, he undertakes to buck his hero up from his summer of rustic discontent: "To the young man, with health and a vigilant spirit, there is shame in despondency. Here we have a world, a thousand avenues to usefulness and to profit stretching in far distances around us. Is *this* the place for a failing soul? Is *youth* the time to yield, when the race is just begun?"

The author achieves a miraculously "changed spirit" in his hero by the sole device of having Archie hear the "history" of an "ancient, bony, yellow-faced" local spinster. It appears that she devoted her entire adult life to amassing the money to repossess her family's farm, which had been lost because of the "extravagance and dissipation" of her father. "Long—long—long years passed; youth fled (and it was said she had been quite handsome)" as she pursued her goal. Finally, she "conquered her object! She not only cleared the farm, but was happy in furnishing her old father with a home there for years before his death." Archie takes the story to heart, feels it "as a rebuke—a sharp-pointed moral to himself and his infirmity of purpose," and commences very methodically to work out a "revolution in his whole make." "The change was not a sudden one," our author tells us. "But his heart was awakened to his weakness; the seed was sown; Archie Dean felt that he *could* expand his nature by means of that very nature itself." The story ends with an outburst of benevolence, and we bid farewell to a stunningly transformed Archie: "With an iron will he substituted action and cheerfulness for despondency and a fretful tongue." He now succeeds in finding employment in the city and lives (with his mother) happily ever after. Whitman, in the story, emphasizes with italics that the story within the story (an awkward device he favored) was a true one: *"the foregoing incident is a fact."* The stagy device of the maiden farmer was apparently purloined from real life.

I have paused so long over this artless story and its not sharp- but blunt-pointed moral because, in a very curious, revealing way, it is "a fact" that Walt Whitman was Archibald Dean. "The Shadow and the Light of a Young Man's Soul," obviously written as a wish-fulfillment fantasy to solace Whitman's own existence, happens to contain a brilliant prophecy of his future. It is inaccurate, really, only when we are told that Archie's "great change" of spirit and worldview was not a sudden one. Whitman's own transformation was most certainly a sudden one. For during the years 1853–55, while sawing, hammering, and hibernating more or less from the writing game in the periodical press, he experienced a "revolution in his whole make" that suddenly made it impossible for him to write poems with titles like "Each Has His Grief," stories like "The Shadow" itself, or high-pitched editorial blasts and counterblasts. Somehow, he summoned up the courage to act as his hero Archibald Dean had several years before: "He met his fortunes as they came, face to face, and shirked no conflict. Indeed, he felt it glorious to vanquish obstacles." He became able, quite precisely as Archie did, to "expand his nature by means of that very nature itself."

In other words, Whitman was enabled to write *Leaves of Grass*, a poetic tour de force that, to put it mildly, shirked no conflict and sought to vanquish cultural obstacles of Himalayan immensity. With an iron will and breathtaking self-composure, he forced mid-nineteenth-century America to submit to a new dispensation, a new personality, a new poetic—and a new sexuality. With the first three editions of *Leaves of Grass*, Whitman emerged from the Closet, leaving in it not only a meretricious sexual identity but a meretricious and mediocre artistry as well. He gained access, as he would later phrase it, to

The body permanent,
The body lurking there within thy body,
The only purport of the form thou art, the real I myself . . .

And his clarion call for such access as every human being's birthright awakened America just as much as the Romantic horn of Victor Hugo's (and Verdi's) Hernani had shattered the Neoclassical verities and complacencies in Europe a generation before.

How can this astonishing *resurgemus* possibly be explained? The all-too-visible prestidigitation of the author in "The Shadow" ensures that the revolution in Archibald Dean's "whole make" holds small interest. Not so the spiritual revolution that gave us a volume of poetry in 1855 that appeared, startlingly, with no name on the title page. All the reader saw was a facing-page engraving of a handsome bearded man in a wide-brimmed hat and open-collared shirt standing in a relaxed contrapposto, head slightly cocked and one hand on his hip, the other in his pants pocket. Because this volume is now universally considered the single most important title in American poetry (the obvious counterpart to the 1609 first edition of Shakespeare's *Sonnets*), the revolution that produced it has evoked enormous fascination. But because Whitman left almost no record of his Manhattan and Brooklyn activities, whereabouts, friendships, and love life in the few years before 1855, explaining the great revolution has necessarily entailed speculation and the sifting of circumstantial evidence. Whitman's tantalizingly "lost" years of 1851–55 or so, in fact, are precisely like the period in Shakespeare's life, circa 1582–90, that immediately preceded his stunning debut on the London stage. Virtually nothing is known about them, either.*

What, then, caused the chrysalis-poet of

So, welcome death! Whene'er the time
    That the dread summons must be met,
I'll yield without one pang of fear,
    Or sigh, or vain regret.

to emerge from his cocoon with such colorful flamboyance and greet his readers in the summer of 1855 with this memorable opening recitative:

I CELEBRATE myself,
And what I assume you shall assume,
For every atom belonging to me as good belongs to you.

I loafe and invite my soul,
I lean and loafe at my ease . . . . observing a spear of summer grass.

What, to phrase the question more tendentiously, suddenly released the enormous creative energies of the poet's mouth and throat, which for so many years had lain closed or obstructed within his "body permanent"? And, because the mouth and throat are the primary erogenous zone after the genitals themselves (and are particularly active in the forms of homosexual intercourse), we are led inevitably to the corollary question: what released Whitman's exuberant celebration of sexuality—more particularly homosexuality—and caused him to associate it so intimately with heroic vocalism in *Leaves of Grass*, where "sing" and "song" occur well over 250 times, along with more than two hundred other terms of musical art?*

If any person from Whitman's "lost years" can help us resolve this supreme puzzlement about his achievement as a poet, it is Maria Anna Marzia Alboni. It is peculiarly in the power of this fabulous Italian contralto, born at Città di Castello in 1823, to aid us in solving our mystery. This woman, I will argue, can tell us more about the admirer of the "beautiful masculine Hudson," the celebrator of "turbulent manly cities," the author of "lusty lurking masculine poems," the rapt listener to the "voices of young men [who] loudly and musically call me by my nighest name" than any of those twenty famous men on his list.

Marietta Alboni, moreover, can help us not only with the mystery of how *Leaves of Grass* came to be but with the mystery of what the poems mean. Whitman was proud of his secrecies and trickiness. In an unsigned review of the first edition, he bragged that his "distinct purposes" were "curiously veiled" and added that it was the author's "pleasure to elude you and provoke you for deliberate purposes of his own." The reader who wants "to

Steel engraving by Samuel Hollyer of an 1854 daguerreotype of Walt Whitman, which appeared as a frontispiece for the first edition of Leaves of Grass *in 1855.*

prove and define" *Leaves of Grass*, he warns in an introductory poem, must provide "the main things" himself. A few years before he died, Whitman explained with a musical image just what those "main things" in the knotty business of interpretation are:

> To get the final lilt of songs,
> To penetrate the inmost lore of poets . . .
> To diagnose the shifting-delicate tints of love and pride
>   and doubt—to truly understand . . .

Who better than Alboni, one of the supreme executants of nineteenth-century bel canto opera, to help us penetrate a little into Whitman's "inmost lore" and find the right tempo for the "final lilt" of his poems?

For she is the solitary singer on Whitman's list. She is, in fact, a potent-voiced progenitor of that overwhelmingly affecting and liberating vocalist, the mocking-bird in the greatest of the new poems in the 1860 *Leaves of Grass*:

> O you singer solitary, singing by yourself, projecting me,
> O solitary me listening, never more shall I cease perpetuating you . . .

Alboni "projected" Whitman in various powerful ways, and the memory of her performances proved indelible. And, to vary his own phrase, she also penetrated Whitman's inmost sexual lore. For operatic singing and sexual performance have more in common than the athleticism they both obviously require. The voice theorist Marie-France Castarède has argued in her study *La Voix et ses sortilèges* that the sound of an operatic voice is decidedly phallic, penetrating the body and feminizing it, and Paul Robinson, pursuing her view further, observes that there is "an isomorphism between operatic singing and sexual performance": "it is no accident that we speak of a voice 'climaxing' on a high note, or compare the ascending and declining vocal trajectory of the typical operatic phrase to the tumescence and detumescence of sexual arousal."* Small wonder, then, that Whitman in his manuscript jottings would write of desiring to hear a soprano who "lithely overleaps the stars, and convulses me like the love-grip of her in whose arms I lay last night."

The rapture, both musical and erotic, of America's future virtuoso "Chanter of Personality" at hearing Alboni for the first time can be fairly easily imagined, for the reviews, as we shall see below, were unanimously ecstatic. But before we join La Alboni and Walt and sample the pleasures she supplied, we must do our operatic homework and explore the experience of opera that Whitman brought with him to Metropolitan Hall on 23 June 1852. Many, aside from Whitman himself on several occasions, have asserted the importance of opera for *Leaves of Grass*, beginning a century ago with his close acquaintance John Burroughs. He wrote in 1896 that Whitman's work was "doubtless greatly influenced by the opera and the great singers."* Robert Faner, a half century later, concluded that the "implication is inescapable that during his most important creative years Whitman was absorbed in opera to a degree almost incredible." And more recently John Dizikes, in his 1993 cultural history of opera in the United States, stated boldly and, I think, justly: "Opera's greatest contribution to American culture in the 19th century was the poetry of Walt Whitman." But no one has yet fully or satisfyingly grasped the importance of Marietta Alboni or explained why opera, of all art forms, should have played so crucial a role in his emergence from the closet of mediocrity—and the Closet of sexuality.

WALTER GOES TO THE OPERA

Whitman's first known scribal brushes with opera were not auspicious. He fell quickly into the time-honored tradition of taking cheap shots at "the agonized squalls, the lackadaisical drawlings, the ear-piercing shrieks, the gurgling death-rattles" to be heard in the Italian opera at Palmo's Theater in the spring of 1846. This was the satiric spirit of Josh Billings, who observed, "I hav seen wimmen in opera, and also hav seen them in fits, and I prefer the fits, for then I know what tew do for them." The following winter, the prematurely jaded cub reporter for the *Daily Eagle* pronounced himself disgusted with the "dancing school bows and curtsies and inane smiles, and kissing of the tips of a kid glove" of the typical soubrette soprano and "absolutely sick to nausea of the patent-leather, curled-hair, 'japonicadom' style" of the lyric stage. And it was in this same review that Whitman famously compared European/operatic "art music" unflatteringly with the homely "heart music" of the popular Hutchinson family singers.

The next summer, of 1847, he reported more favorably on Anna Bishop, "an Englishwoman, considerably Italianized," in Donizetti's *Linda di Chamounix*. The exertions of her "purest soprano" put him pleasantly "in mind of the gyrations of a bird in the air," but the faint-hearted critic adds, "the heat and the crowd prevented our staying to see more than the first act." Later, he would brainstorm a few ideas for creating a native "American opera," among them the perky notion of putting "three banjos (or more?) in the orchestra" and letting them "accompany (at times exclusively) the songs of the baritone or tenor."

Whitman became, in these early years, a practical, vigorous, unpretentious visitor to the opera—a devotee, it seems, in no danger of turning into a tsk-tsk-ing aficionado like, say, the snobbish diarist George Templeton Strong. He did not bother the fine points too much. Four decades later, he recalled that his "enjoyment was altogether untechnical: I knew nothing about music: I simply took it in, enjoyed it, from the human side: had a good ear—did not trouble myself to explain or analyze." But he did prepare himself conscientiously for performances. In notes he made around 1855 for an essay on operagoing, he worried about those who might attend an Italian opera unprepared and then not like it. "If the piece is unknown to you, it were better to procure the English translation of it beforehand and read it over once or twice," Whitman advises, "for it destroys all the enjoyment of music to follow it, page by page during the performance." In "my opera days," Whitman later told Traubel, "I always took care to get a libretto the day before, then took care to leave it at home on the day itself!"

He also liked the relatively relaxed all-male atmosphere (and cheaper seats) of the upper tiers, "among men in their shirt sleeves—the sunburnt, the unshaven, the huge paws." His favorite kind of audience, for operas or plays, was one where "slang, wit, occasional shirt sleeves, and a picturesque freedom of looks and manners, with a rude good-nature and restless movement, were generally noticeable." In 1846, in fact, Whitman wrote a short piece under the leader "Don't be so 'Mortal Genteel!'" in which he urged, "During the intervals of the performance be not afraid of talking, laughing and moving.—You are not having daguerreotypes taken. . . . it comes over one like a chill to see so many persons perched, as it were, on their propriety."

Whitman liked it when the rambunctious atmosphere inside New York's midcentury theaters mimicked that of the Broadway pageant. The years of his first gusts of operatic pleasure were exactly those during which he began cultivating his wide circle of young male friends (a circle that was probably becoming more and more homosexual, too). He even made explicit the connection between the two kinds of voices he loved best in a collection of notes on vocabulary and elocution that he compiled in the 1850s: "The great Italian singers are above all others in the world from causes quite the same as those that make the voices of the native healthy substrata of Mannahatta young men, especially the drivers of horses, and all whose work leads to free loud calling and commanding, have such a ring of freshness." From this bizarrely mixed chorus of sopranos and streetcar drivers, tenors and foretopmen, would come the ring of freshness in "Song of Myself" and many another early Whitman aria.

Whitman's Jacksonian instincts, of course, made him happier when he was in an opera house that was "democratic." That is, an opera theater with no private boxes. One such was Palmo's, a 1,200-seat venue where all tickets were $1. (Whitman may also have appreciated the restaurant-cum-bathhouse and the saloon Palmo ran on the same premises.) Indeed, it was a fortunate coincidence that Alboni's first Manhattan performances were under the aegis of an impresario, E. A. Marshall, who refused to employ the aristocratic subscription-ticket system. On the front page of *The Musical World and New York Musical Times* of 15 January 1853, adjoining the review of Alboni's debut in a fully staged opera, is an exultant editorial that begins: "We have it, at last. Italian Opera is established in New York on a *democratic*, and, consequently, on a paying basis. Those contemptible 'subscription' times . . . have now passed away, never, we trust, to return." The editorialist estimates there are "this day forty thousand persons in New York (including strangers) who can afford, and doubtless intend, to hear Alboni and [the German soprano Henriette] Sontag in opera. As long as these persons are conscious that . . . no favored few have monopolized all the best seats for the season—that they are at perfect liberty to dress as they please—that, in short, there is no 'exclusiveness,' or 'style,' or clannishness of any kind recognized, they will be candidates for tickets."

The result was as *The Musical World* predicted, and must have made Whitman feel quite comfortable. "The audience" for Alboni's debut as Rossini's Cinderella, reported the *Courier and Enquirer*, was "much more heterogenous than operatic audiences usually are. The learned and the unlearned, the cultured and the un- in the gentle art."

That Whitman perfected his knowing operagoer's pose at precisely the same time he perfected his poetic voice is charmingly evidenced by a piece he published in *Life Illustrated* a few months after *Leaves of Grass* appeared. In it he promises to "bring the opera to you—even the Italian Opera—in full bloom." For this excursion, the self-appointed docent chose a performance of Verdi's "noble opera" *Ernani* at the brand-new Academy of Music on Broadway at Fourteenth Street, "the largest amusement-building in New York," we are told, "and one of the largest in the world." Whitman devotes most of his space to a wry description of the premises and the audience that is worthy, almost, of Edith Wharton or Willa Cather. We see "proud, fat, pampered horses" and liveried footmen deliver members of the City's chic "upper ten[-thousand]" from their carriages. Later, from the middle of the parquet, Whitman casts a look around the boxes: "What an air of polished, high-bred, deliberate, heartless, bland, superb, chilling, smiling, repelling fashion!" A hasty synopsis of the plot makes the reporter a bit self-conscious, and he warns: "It is novel, of course, being far, very far from what you were used to—the church choir, or the songs and playing on the piano, or the nigger songs, or any performance of the Ethiopian minstrels, or the concerts of the different 'families.' "

The starring tenor of the evening, Marini, is pronounced "a magnificent artist," but Whitman falls, as aficionados so often do, into nostalgic lament for more glorious voices of earlier days. "The young and manly Ernani used to be well played by [Geremia] Bettini, now at the Grand Opera in Paris. Bettini was a beautiful, large, robust, friendly, young man—a fine tenor." Though the entire Academy of Music cast is pronounced good, "we shall never lose the recollection of the pleasure of those other singers."

Whitman's feuilleton was mainly cheeky and inevitably patronizing. After all, it was intended, he said, for "a country reader, or young person, who has no experience at all in theater-going." (It could have been worse: in a manuscript version he begins his definition of opera, "For the information of you, our unsophisticated companion . . .") And he does dwell on the very basics, explaining that "in the grand opera every thing is done by music" and "the book of the opera" sold in the lobby is "the original Italian words of the piece on one page, and an English translation off against them." One could be forgiven for assuming the author was among that legion who are thankful for opera only because it offers such a fat target for satire.

Except, that is, for one short but curiously purple passage in the essay. It is the only passage, in fact, that gibes with what we learn from hints in the manuscripts and notebooks, certain passages in Leaves of Grass, and later reminiscences, namely, that Whitman was deeply, shatteringly affected by the Italian opera performances he heard in New York City in the early 1850s. In this paragraph Whitman asserts that opera, ably performed, can deliver to the receptive listener a new personal identity: "A new world—a liquid world—rushes like a torrent through you. If you have the true musical feeling in you, from this night you date a new era in your development." And opera, dear reader, can also reveal to you your own voice: "If you are a vocalist, you see you did not previously know how to even open your mouth. You did not know how to express the simplest sounds properly. These singers do it all so much easier, and incomparably better. This is science! This is art! You envy Italy, and almost become an enthusiast."

The strange coexistence of satire and epiphany in Whitman's *Ernani* jaunt calls to mind a remarkable entry in the diary of Whitman's idol, Ralph Waldo Emerson, describing an operatic performance Emerson had attended in Naples in 1833. The entry begins, as Whitman's essay does, with blasé indifference: "I could not help pitying the performers in their fillets & togas, & saw their strained & unsuccessful exertions & thought on their long toilette & personal mortification at making such a figure. There they are—the same poor Johns & Antonios they were this morning, for all their gilt & pasteboard." But then a curious thing happened to Emerson as he sat bemusedly detached from the exaggerated antics on stage.

A natural, passionate, and potent-voiced singer appeared and transformed the theatrical event, leaving Emerson elated and awed: "the moment the prima donna utters one tone or makes a gesture of natural passion, it puts life into the dead scene. I pity them no more. It is not a ghost of departed things, not an old Greece & Rome but a Greece & Rome of this moment. It is living merit which takes ground with all other merit of whatever kind—with beauty, nobility, genius, & power." The lesson Emerson drew from this aesthetic catharsis, and which he confided to his diary, is a peculiarly—and prophetically—Whitmanesque one: "O trust to Nature, whosoever thou art. . . . Trust your simple self & you shall stand before genuine princes."

Manifestly, Whitman also became spectacularly captivated by opera, and this appears to have happened in the early 1850s. That his upward operatic trajectory was well on its way even by 1851 is eloquently suggested by one of his "Letters from Paumanok" published on 14 August of that year. In it he favors his readers with an exultant recreation of a visit to a performance on 8 August of Donizetti's *La Favorita* at the Castle Garden theater situated in the Hudson River just off the Battery. Emerson's Neapolitan thrill pales by comparison with Whitman's ecstatic encomium, which is but one of several precursors to the "enthusiast" passage that later appeared in *Life Illustrated*.

Here is an author obsessed, ravished by the human voice—especially that of the tenor Bettini, whose "clear, firm, wonderfully exalting notes, filling and expanding away, dwelling like a poised lark up in heaven, have made my very soul tremble." Emerson is again echoed in Whitman's assertion that Bettini's singing has "breathing blood within it . . . none have so thoroughly satisfied, overwhelmed me, but this man. Never before did I realize what an indescribable volume of delight the recesses of the soul can bear from the sound of the honied perfection of the human voice." Whitman adds, "The *manly* voice it must be, too. The female organ, however curious and high, is but as the pleasant moon-light"—another insult to the daintily chirping type of soprano.

A dozen years later, Whitman's brother Jeff heard a tenor who reminded him of Bettini and hastened to tell Walt: "He is in looks and acting almost a likeness of Bettini (the tenor whom we used to admire so much). . . . He certainly would carry you back to the old Castle Garden and Bettini singing 'Spirit O' Gentil [sic].' " It is no wonder Jeff remembered Bettini so fondly, for Walt's "Letter from Paumanok" contains a grand rhetorical question in praise of Bettini that ranks as one of the most memorable expressions of the soul-smiting power of the human voice:

> Have you not . . . while listening to the well-played music of some band like [Castle Garden impresario] Maretzek's, felt an over-whelming desire for measureless sound—a sublime orchestra of myriad orchestras—a colossal volume of harmony, in which the thunder might roll in its proper place; and above it, the vast, pure Tenor,—identity of the Creative Power itself—rising through the universe, until the boundless and unspeakable capacities of that mystery, the human soul, should be filled to the uttermost, and the problem of human cravingness be satisfied and destroyed?

But then, what excitement still awaited Whitman! He had not yet heard the voice of Marietta Alboni.

The ecstasy over Bettini can, I think, be considered a seminal moment in Whitman's midlife and the crisis that was shortly to occur in it. The "Letter" ends with an epiphany on Bettini's rendition of the "sweet music of Donizetti": "Pure and vast, that voice now rises, as on clouds, to the heaven where it claims audience. Now, firm and unbroken, it spreads like an ocean around us. . . . Thanks, limner of the spirit of life, and hope and peace; of the red fire of passion, the cavernous vacancy of despair, and the black pall of the grave." And Whitman adds a last short paragraph that stares into the future and toward his own buoyant yea-saying poems to come: "I write as I feel; and I feel that there are not a few who will pronounce a Yes to my own confession."

By his own account, Whitman was notably prepared for this operatic liberation from his mundane voice by reading George Sand's sprawling novel *Consuelo*, which appeared in America in translation in the 1840s. Its heroine is a simple country girl who becomes an opera singer of great fame. A half century later, Whitman found the tattered novel amid the clutter of his house in Mickle Street and reminisced to Traubel, "I have always treasured it: read, read, read, never tiring. The book is a masterpiece: truly a masterpiece: the noblest work by George Sand—the noblest in many respects, on its own field, in all literature."*

Sand based *Consuelo* on the soprano Pauline Garcia Viardot (1821–1910) and particularly emphasized the heroine's achievement of complete mastery over her public, notwithstanding being "decidedly ugly" and a foreigner in Italy (a Spaniard, she is nicknamed La Zinga-rella, or the gypsy). Sand's description of Consuelo's stunning debut in a small rural church remained with Whitman for many years, for in an 1860s notebook we have this jotting on the subject of effective oratori-cal style:

> The broad and sweeping method of the Italian masters of music.
> Style.
> Free, rich, *broad* and full of *strength* and suppleness (as Consuelo's Italian method in the village church with Hadyn [sic]—which first confounded, then carried away and made enthusiastic the congregation . . .)

Consuelo's subsequent conquest of Venice is in the beloved tradition of sudden stardom. She enters the stage "self-possessed and serious . . . with a propriety of manner equally devoid of humility and coquetry." She then delivers a recitative "with so firm a voice, with accents so lofty, and a self-possession so victorious, that cries of admiration from the very first resounded from every part of the theater" (a triumph Alboni would exactly reenact in Metropolitan Hall). Her bravura aria is interrupted ten times; she is recalled to the stage seven times amid "thunders of applause"; and "all the furor of Venetian dilettantism displayed itself in all its ridiculous and absurd excess."

Sand's heroine, we shall soon see, perfectly prepared Whitman for the real-life revelation that Marietta Alboni was to prove. Consuelo, we learn, sings "with as little effort and labor as others might have in merely breath-ing." She is "absolutely devoid of coquetry" and exhibits an utterly ingrati-ating "cheerful frankness and confiding good nature which inspired a sympathy equally rapid and irresistible." "Ignorant of finesse," Consuelo is a perfectly Whitmanesque figure who knows that the impressions of "open-ness and candor . . . are far more powerful weapons." And finally, Consuelo exhibits that deep sense of self-worth without which it is hard to imagine success before an opera-house public: "She felt the necessity of belonging to herself—that sovereign and legitimate want, the necessary condition of progress and development of the true artist."

The climax of the novel consists of Consuelo's grand entry, in an opera called *Zenobia*, into her full personal artistic identity. It is no effort to imagine the author whose great poem opens with the line "I celebrate myself" being powerfully struck by this passage: "It was the first time that Consuelo filled a part in which she could be herself—in which she could manifest, in their full force, all her purity, strength, and tenderness, without, by an artificial effort, identifying herself with an uncongenial character. She was able to forget her painful task, abandon herself up to the inspiration of the moment, and drink in the deep and pathetic emotions . . . which were revealed to her, as it were, by the magnetic influence of a sympathetic audience. . . . Hitherto she had ever asked herself whether she could not have done better, but now she felt that she had revealed all her power and, almost heedless of the thunders of acclamation, she applauded herself in her secret soul." Picture Walt Whitman just before the Fourth of July 1855, on the eve of the appearance of *Leaves of Grass*, in approximately this same frame of mind: applauding himself in his secret soul.

All successful artists, but especially stage performers, must learn how to applaud their own "secret soul" and captivate their audience by sheer force of personality. The exhilarating thrill of grasping command of the stage for the first time figures at some point in most singers' life stories, as it does, for instance, in Willa Cather's variation on the *Consuelo* tale, *The Song of the Lark*, which Cather based on the life of the soprano Olive Fremstad. The same thrill also figures poignantly in the memoirs of Clara Louise Kellogg, the first American-born singer to enjoy a stellar European career. Kellogg is charmingly candid about her rawness as a human being before coming into her artistic majority: "I knew nothing of life, for my puritanical surroundings and the way in which I had been brought up were developing my personality very slowly." She recalls a critic of her debut performance in *Rigoletto* complaining about her too-intellectual, unpassionate heroine and adds, "The man who wrote that was quite correct. He had discovered the Puritan maid behind the stage trappings of Gilda."

Kellogg speaks fascinatingly, too, of "that 'incubating period' before my first appearance in opera" when she became conscious of what distinguishes the sublime from the ridiculous on the stage: "I was studying gesture then—the free simple, *inevitable* gesture that is so necessary to a natural effect in dramatic singing; and during the beautiful melody, *A te, o cara* [in Bellini's *I Puritani*], which he sang in the first act, [the tenor Pasquale] Brignoli stood still in one spot and thrust first one arm out, and then the other, at right angles from his body, twenty-three times. I counted them, and I don't know how many times he had done it before I

began to count! 'Heavens!' I said, 'that's one thing not to do, anyway!' "
Later, by the way, she found herself on stage with Brignoli, who forbade
physical contact from his colleagues during a performance: "Imagine
playing love scenes," Kellogg wrote, "with a tenor who did not want to be
touched."

Kellogg's "incubating period" came to an end with a real-life moment
of truth like Consuelo's: her Boston debut as Donizetti's Linda di
Chamounix before a dishearteningly small audience. She writes perceptively about this—and in a way very pertinent to Whitman. "As Linda I
do not think that I showed any great intellectual improvement over
Gilda, but I certainly acquired a certain confidence and authority. I sang
and acted with more ease; and for the first time I had gained a sense of
personal responsibility toward, and for, the audience. When I beheld only
three hundred people and determined to win them, and win them I did, I
came into possession of new and important factors in my work. This consciousness and earnest will-power to move one's public by force of one's
art is one of the first steps toward being a true *prima donna*."

By the time, a few months earlier, when Whitman heard Kellogg in
the role of Linda, his own "incubating period" was several years behind
him. And for even longer (at least since his "Letter" about Bettini in
1851) he had been displaying an extraordinary fascination with the
nature of artistic power and the determination of the vocalist—be he or
she an actor, an orator, or a singer—to "win" the audience. The lessons
she had learned about the "simple, *inevitable*" gesture and about "*personal
responsibility*" to the audience are the foundation of the first three editions of *Leaves of Grass*.

OPERA'S SUPERB SUGGESTIONS

When the tenor Brignoli died in 1884, Whitman, not holding his primitive acting against him, wrote "The Dead Tenor" in his honor. It includes
these moving lines:

> (So firm—so liquid-soft—again that tremulous, manly timbre!
> The perfect singing voice—deepest of all to me the lesson—trial
>   and test of all:)
> How through those strains distill'd—how the rapt ears, the soul of
>   me, absorbing
> *Fernando's* heart, *Manrico's* passionate call, *Ernani's*, sweet
>   *Gennaro's*,

I fold thenceforth, or seek to fold, within my chants transmuting,
Freedom's and Love's and Faith's unloos'd cantabile.

The poem focuses eloquently on the two central questions of this chapter: What *was* for Whitman the "deepest" lesson of opera? And what, by
extension, is the deepest lesson of Whitman's poetry? The answers may
be the same; they may both have to do, simply, with *receiving the voice.*
Receiving, that is, in the sense of allowing the invading power of another's voice to confer the courage to use one's own voice . . . to utter
one's own "unloos'd cantabile."

That opera was responsible for Whitman's recognition of this primal
lesson is suggested in many small though poignant ways. On a scrap of
paper, for instance, he one day made a list of all the words that might
describe the poems he was writing in the mid-1850s. "Leaf" and "Song"
are among them, but it also occurred to Whitman that several other
musicianly epithets might be suitable too: chant, psalm, hymn, carol,
cavatina, caprice, fantasia, canticles, songlet. Imagine the pleasure of
opera lovers today if he had chosen instead to title his great poem
"Cavatina of Myself."

The intimate connection of "Song of Myself" with opera is perhaps
even more evocatively suggested by a leaf of paper now in the collection
of Duke University. On one side are the lines "I am your voice . . . / I
celebrate myself to celebrate every man and woman"—lines that would
become the more succinct "I celebrate myself." On the other side is an
explicitly operatic "translation" of this notion of self-voicing being inextricable from self-development:

> To sing well your part of an opera is excellent; but it is not
> enough.—You should be master of the composers of all operas—and
> of all tenors—and of all violins and first violins,—for they were all
> men like yourself, and perhaps less developed than yourself.

Precisely the same yoking of self-culture and vocalism in the contempla-
tion of the poet's vocation occurs in one of the most important and
exciting of Whitman's extant manuscripts, which appears to predate the
first edition of *Leaves of Grass.* It begins with an expression of the primacy
of the self: "The one duty under which a man or woman is bound to himself or herself is the enfolder of every bit that follows.—That is the only
independent, living entire obligation." The individual, Whitman continues, must always be balancing the "boundless account" of the world
"with his own soul." He then records his view "Of the Poet," who must

finally be the bringer of "entire health, both of spirit and flesh, the life of grace and strength and action, from which all else flows." In what form shall such a savior appear? we are naturally eager to learn.

On the next sheet of this manuscript, we discover that it will be as an operatic tenor or soprano. Whitman's manuscript shows that he struggled through several versions of his answer to this deep question. What one must piece together from these versions ranks, nevertheless, as an operatic epiphany just as memorable as James Joyce's wonderful description in *Ulysses* of the climactic high B-flat in the aria *M'appari*.* Whitman fantasizes:

> I want that tenor, large and fresh as the creation, the orbed parting of whose mouth shall lift over my head the sluices of all delight yet discovered for our race.—
> I want the soprano that lithely overleaps the stars, and convulses me like the love-grip of her in whose arms I lay last night.—I want an infinite chorus and orchestrium, wide as the orbit of Uranus true as the hours of the day, and filling my capacities to receive, as thoroughly as the sea fills its scooped out sands.—I want the chanted Hymn whose tremendous sentiment . . . shall uncage in my breast a thousand wide-winged strengths and unknown ardors and terrible extasies—putting me through the flights of all the passions—dilating me beyond time and air—startling me with overtures of some unnamable horror—calmly sailing me all day on a bright river with lazy slapping waves—stabbing my heart with myriads of forked distractions more furious than hail or lightning—lulling me drowsily with honeyed morphine—tight'ning the fakes of death about my throat, and awakening me again to know by that comparison, the most positive wonder in the world, and that's what we call life.

This would in time become (though much toned down, bowdlerized, and truncated) the passage in Section 26 of "Song of Myself" that begins, "I hear the chorus, it is a grand opera, / Ah this indeed is music—this suits me."

Sometime after jotting these feverish lines, Whitman uncaged his breast and produced the first edition of *Leaves of Grass*, which made very clear that the music of grand opera suited him. In a "Ramble" on the subject of "English in America," Whitman looked about the "poor, indigent, watery affair" of American letters and found "no full, free utterance . . . no abandonment." Where, he asked rhetorically, "is the theory of literary expression that . . . absorbs the superb suggestions of the Grand Opera?"

There was no such theory on the American scene, of course. Walt Whitman himself would produce it. He would costume his poetry in it.

The threshold suggestion of opera is that the voice must be carefully cultivated. Training, exercise, hygiene must be observed. The critic Richard Grant White, in summing up Kellogg's career, remarked that she was "somewhat lacking" in strength of voice, body, and emotional expression. But then he adds, "on two other points she was amply furnished: she had strength of character and strength of will. She persevered. Her voice grew stronger by exercise, as also did her body."

Clearly, Whitman had many years before taken to heart Kellogg's conviction that the voice required gymnastic cultivation. Images of the vocalist's strength of character abound in his poems. "I exultant," he announces in the first poem of the 1860 edition, "will now shake out carols stronger and haughtier than have ever yet been heard upon the earth" ("shake" being then the usual term for a trill). His boast in the 1855 version of "Song of Myself"—"I fling through my embouchures the loudest and gayest music"—perhaps explains why Thoreau chose to describe *Leaves of Grass* as "an alarum or trumpet-note ringing through the American camp." Visits to the opera house made clear to Whitman that the power to utter haughty carols and stentorian high notes is not casually won. Among his notes for "A Visit to the Opera" is a section entitled "long study and practice needed to make a singer." On another scrap he notes that an operatic singer must "practice two, three, or four hours, every day—perhaps continuing patiently for six or eight years."

Whitman, always obsessively health-conscious, now became highly conscious of the need for vocal hygiene. In notes on "Italian Singers in America," he observed, "The voice is a curious organ, and follows the general health for good or evil.—The body must be vigorous and sound, before the voice can be so." He then offers this regimen: "Excess, habitual intoxication, voluptuousness, bad blood, starvation, dyspepsia, a sunken chest, &c, &c, are all obstacles in the way of fine vocal utterance." In another manuscript is this draconian advice on "the rigid pre-requisites of a great voice": "Fat, gluttony, swilling beer, gin, 'soda,' coffee, or tea— these ... make the voice thick, put flem in the throat.... *Drink water only.*" In rather more explicit notes for a lecture he never delivered, Whitman warned: "Drinking brandy, gin, beer, is generally fatal to the perfection of voice;—meanness of mind the same ... masturbation, inordinate going with women, rot the voice." He then alludes, in a passage already quoted, to the two classes of city denizens whose vocalism delighted him most in the 1850s: "the great Italian singers" and "the native healthy substrata of Mannahatta young men, especially the drivers

Detail of a Whitman manuscript in which he reiterates the influence of vocal music on Leaves of Grass. The first biography of Whitman, Richard Maurice Bucke's Walt Whitman of 1883, contained large passages that were in fact authored by the poet himself. Pictured here is one such insertion, in which the poet attributes the "rich, broad, rugged rhythm and inimitable interior music" of his poems to their gestation during years when he was "saturated . . . with the rendering, by the best vocalists and performers, of the best operas and oratorios." Immediately following this passage, Whitman saw to it that Bucke inserted an article by Fanny Ritter recording his adoration for Alboni; this praise is quoted on page forty-five. Courtesy of the New York Public Library.

of horses." And Whitman certainly took his own advice, studying scrupulously the vocalism of healthy Mannahatta young men and avoiding, if not masturbation, certainly any "inordinate going with women."

Whitman's growing preoccupation with—and rapture in the presence of—the trained and athletic voice produced several magnificent poems about heroic utterance in the 1860 edition: "Vocalism," "That Music Always Round Me," "A Word Out of the Sea" (later "Out of the Cradle . . ."), and "To a Certain Cantatrice." Though first conceived as an homage to orators, "Vocalism" brilliantly evokes the complex, arduous regimen that brings us "the practis'd and perfect organ." "Are you full-lung'd and limber-lipp'd from long trial? from vigorous practice? from physique?" he challenges. The "right voice"—that rare voice that makes us tremble—comes only

> After a loosen'd throat, after absorbing eras, temperaments, races,
>   after knowledge, freedom, crimes,
> After complete faith, after clarifyings, elevations, and removing
>   obstructions . . .

Toward such a voice "swiftly hasten all—none refuse, all attend." Nowhere in Manhattan was this charisma more apparent than in the enormous audiences that convened in the Academy of Music, Metropolitan Hall, Niblo's, the Astor Place Opera, Palmo's, and Castle Garden to hear the finest stars of the Italian opera.

Manifestly, Whitman absorbed in these venues the second superb suggestion of the grand opera, which is captured in these lines (note the allusion to his own callow earlier views about opera):

> That music always round me, unceasing, unbeginning, yet long
>   untaught I did not hear,
> But now the chorus I hear and am elated,
> A tenor, strong, ascending with power and health . . .
> A soprano at intervals sailing buoyantly over the tops of
>   immense waves . . .

The suggestion is that the voice must be a *soloist's*, a voice that can ride above the "triumphant tutti" and boast the stamina for "striving, contending with fiery vehemence to excel" one's colleagues. Only possessed of such a voice can one hope to be, as he wrote in another poem, the "chief histrion" who "Down to the footlights walks in some great scena, / Dominating the rest."

Here we are firmly in the world of the diva and the divo. This was the calculated, self-vaunting style of the opera star, which he could have been alluding to when he mulled over the ideal style for lecturing: "An animated *ego-style* . . . involving self-esteem decision, authority." In a similar note about lectures—"Broad, free"—Whitman refers specifically to the "broad and sweeping method of the Italian masters in music." He then admonishes himself to apply the audience-conquering lesson of *Consuelo*: "Free, rich, *broad* and full of *strength* and suppleness . . . as Consuelo's Italian method in the village church . . . which . . . carried away and made enthusiastic the congregation." This is no style for the mere comprimario. "Play the old role," Whitman admonishes from his Brooklyn Ferry, "the role that is great or small according as one makes it!" But we can see that the role the poet intended for himself on the Manhattan stage was strictly of the "great" variety. The playwright Terrence McNally, in his recent *Master Class*, has the character of Maria Callas explain, "Art is domination. It's making people think that for that precise moment in time there is only one way, one voice. Yours." Clearly, that was the effect Whitman was after in his first edition of *Leaves of Grass*.

The ego-style of opera was just as clearly required. "When a grand and melodious thought is told to men for the first time," he observed (probably as he wrote *Leaves of Grass*), "down and within their hearts each one says, That music! those large and exquisite passages! where have I heard them before?" In order to deliver the large and exquisite passages in his cavatinas of himself, Whitman demanded the stage to himself. The "greatest poet," he wrote in the 1855 preface, "is complete in himself. . . . He is not one of the chorus." And, true to his word, he could announce in 1860, "Solitary, singing in the West, I strike up for a New World." Not many Americans sensed at the time that Whitman was alone at center stage of American poetry, but it is now clear that he was. D. H. Lawrence called Whitman "a very great poet . . . of the transformations of the soul as it loses its integrity," a poet "of the soul's last shout and shriek, on the confines of death." Which is to say, of course, that Whitman was the most operatic of all American poets.

To succeed in this virtuoso performance appears to have required of Whitman the same elaborate, sometimes fretful nerving-up and marshaling of wits, resources, powers that the opera singer must indulge. Here, in some very shrewd notes on the ideal style to assume before an audience (they echo Kellogg on the "inevitable" gesture), Whitman rehearses the best way to command the stage:

Restrain and curb gesture. Not too much gesture. Animation and life may be shown in a speech by great feeling in voice and look. Interior gesture, which is perhaps better than exterior gesture. . . . all this about 'interior gesture' and a flowing forth of power, simply is: that so much must have been generated, such an exhaustless flood of vitality, tone, sympathy, command and the undeniable clinch (all the product of long previous perfect physique through food, air, and exercise, &c &c) that a subtle something equivalent to gesture and life, plays continuously out of every feature of the face and every limb.

The same delicate combination of charm, self-consciousness, concentration, and force that can lead to sexual conquest is at work here, as the executant achieves his consummating "undeniable clinch" with the audience—an analogue, surely, to the orgasmic "love-grip" evoked by the trained soprano in "Song of Myself."

The complexity of this task is daunting and requires, Whitman makes clear, infinite attention to detail, relentless calculation. This is the only way, finally, to freedom and power on the stage, as Clara Louise Kellogg makes vividly clear in her memoirs:

My freedom of gesture and action came from nothing but the most complete familiarity with the part and the detail of everything I had to do. In opera . . . everything has to be timed to a second and a fraction of a second. One cannot wait for unusual effects. The orchestra does not consider one's temperament, and this fact cannot be lost sight of for a moment. . . . For it is only in the most rigidly studied accuracy of action that any freedom can be attained. When one becomes so trained that one cannot conceivably retard a bar, and cannot under-time a stage cross nor fail to come in promptly in an *ensemble*, then, and only then, can one reach some emotional liberty and inspiration.

Whitman wrote his poetry with the same scrupulous detachment, as he had occasion to explain when Swinburne ventured to compare him with William Blake. "Both are mystics, extatics," Whitman granted, but there was "a vast difference" between himself and Blake: "Whitman, though he occasionally prances off or takes flight with an abandon & capriciousness of step or wing, and a rapidity & whirling power, which quite dizzy the reader in his first attempts to follow, always holds the mastery over himself, &, even in his most intoxicated lunges or pirouettes, never once loses control, or even equilibrium."

This, pure and simple, must be the method of any successful interpreter of the Italian bel canto repertory. Whitman urged upon himself the personal slogan of "Boldness. Nonchalant ease and indifference," and that is precisely the pleasant fiction that spectacular singers are always attempting to foist upon their public. But few listeners are ever truly fooled. We come away from any fine bel canto performance—which inevitably involves stunning breath control, gorgeous phrase sculpting, suave acrobatics, and risk-taking nerve—thinking of the executant exactly as Paul Zweig thought of the author of *Leaves of Grass*: "Whitman's bag of tricks is deep."

And we can be certain, too, that the singer has much fear to hide in this risky vocation. The fear, for instance, that Whitman expressed—prophetically for himself—in these lines published near the end of his dozen or so years of avid operagoing: "Perhaps soon some day or night while I am singing my voice will suddenly cease." Or the eternal fear of the opera singer that so much utterance "with electric voice," so much defiance of physiology, will in the end prove self-destructive:

> Nature . . . is taking advantage of me, to dart upon me,
>   and sting me,
> Because I was assuming so much,
> And because I have dared to open my mouth to sing at all.

The early editions of *Leaves of Grass* are steeped in this consciousness of a singer always mindful of his "equilibrium" in treacherous waters. He wrote truly of this "ego-style" in the 1856 edition—"The song is to the singer, and comes back most to him"—and a few years later heard every American "singing what belongs to him or her and to none else."

Zweig has archly observed that "if there is one thing Whitman surely never was, it is unself-conscious" and that Whitman had a remarkable ability to "orchestrate his presence." This is because the poet, having concluded that he would be America's great literary vocalist, knew that the method of the great singers he heard in the opera theaters of Manhattan was the only method for him. Hence so many self-admonishments among his manuscripts, like the following, which even today still constitute splendid advice for the would-be primo tenore or prima donna:

A rule in Elocution.

Not to wobble or quiver or duck the head, but keep it easily and equably erect with steady grace,
  measured and slow—measured—measured—measured

One part or spot, however small, there should be in every address where the speaker is *all out.*

Hasting, urging, resistless,—no flagging . . . florid—spiritual—good, not from their direct but indirect meanings—to be perceived with the same perception that enjoys music . . .

Fiercely and with screaming energy [he writes, after making some notes for an "American opera"]

a good word—*use it*
VERVE—(pron. just like *verse*)
Fr. excitement of imagination such as animates a poet, artist or musician, in composing or performing—rapture, enthusiasm spirit, energy

"Verve," in fact, is perhaps the best word there is for expressing the essence of Whitman's first three *Leaves of Grass* editions. Not coincidentally, "verve" also ideally translates that favorite phrase of Italian composers, Verdi especially, for passages that demanded robust bravura: *con slancio.*

The payoff for all this concentrated calculation, of course, is the utterly unexpected, captivating debut in which the vocalist suddenly assumes what Kellogg so aptly called personal responsibility. A performance, in other words, in which the stunning, never-before-heard voice of a "real Me" takes an audience by storm. *Leaves of Grass* is, in fact, Whitman's debut opera, its first poem a gigantic virtuoso entrance aria establishing with a diva's hauteur, as he phrased it, "My own voice, orotund sweeping and final."

The 1855 edition is rich in passages that underscore the momentous operatic nature of the occasion. The audience assembles; the moment of truth approaches: "Come my boys and girls, and my women and household and intimates, / Now the performer launches his nerve. . . . He has passed his prelude on the reeds within." The houselights dim: "The preparations have every one been justified; / The orchestra have tuned their instruments sufficiently . . . . the baton has given the signal." Appropriately arresting entrance music sounds: "the trill of a thousand clear cornets and scream of the octave flute and strike of triangles."

Finally, the imperious entrance: "Do you take it I would astonish?" (And the aural invitation "come listen all!"—which echoes the *Uditemi!* preceding so many Italian opera arias—would be added in 1867.)

Magically, the "dumb voices" in the audience are vicariously given utterance by the soloist: "Through me forbidden voices, / Voices of sexes and lusts . . . . voices veiled, and I remove the veil, / Voices indecent by me clarified and transfigured." The audience levitates—"I dilate you with tremendous breath . . . . I buoy you up"—and the divo finally conquers everyone in the darkened theater: "My voice goes after what my eyes cannot reach, / With the twirl of my tongue I encompass worlds and volumes of worlds." And yet again, the erotic love-grip, the undeniable clinch with the audience: "I have embraced you, and henceforth possess you to myself."

"I hear the sound of the human voice . . . . a sound I love," Whitman wrote in that first version of "Song of Myself." But what truly resonates in the poem—in the 1855 *Leaves of Grass* as a whole—is the sound of Personality. The most fundamental, and superb, of all grand opera's suggestions is simply that Personality, the "real Me," demands bold vocalism, bold histrionics, bold launching of oneself *"all out"* at just the right moment. Above all, voice.

Many years later, Whitman cast some telling backward glances upon the time that preceded his spectacular debut. Two of these, I think, illuminate the intersection he made between Personality and Voice and are especially interesting. In the first, from the preface to *November Boughs* (1888), a debutant gathering his forces is recalled. Whitman's chronology is specific and most significant:

After continued personal ambition and effort . . . I found myself remaining possess'd, at the age of thirty-one to thirty-three [i.e. 1850–52], with a special desire and conviction. Or rather, to be quite exact, a desire that had been flitting through my previous life, or hovering on the flanks, mostly indefinite hitherto, had steadily advanced to the front, defined itself, and finally dominated everything else. This was a feeling or ambition to articulate . . . my own physical, emotional, moral, intellectual, and aesthetic Personality [and then] to exploit that Personality, identified with place and date, in a far more candid and comprehensive sense than any hitherto poem or book.

In other words, Whitman's tenor required a vehicle at this juncture. He knew what he wanted to exploit but not yet how to do so. This he was to learn largely from his visits to the legitimate and lyric theaters of Manhattan, as he explains in the second passage. It is another of Whitman's brief meditations on the physiology and philosophy of the voice:

> [T]he human voice is a cultivation or form'd growth on a fair native foundation. This foundation probably exists in nine cases out of ten. Sometimes nature affords the vocal organ in perfection, or rather I would say near enough to whet one's appreciation and appetite for a voice that might be truly call'd perfection. To me the grand voice is mainly physiological—(by which I by no means ignore the mental help, but wish to keep the emphasis where it belongs). Emerson says *manners* form the representative apex and final charm and captivation of humanity: but he might as well have changed the typicality to voice. . . . it finally settles down to *best* human vocalization. Beyond all other power and beauty, there is something in the quality and power of the right voice (*timbre* the schools call it) that touches the soul, the abysms.

Whitman then lists some of the "celebrated people possessing this wonderful vocal power, patent to me, in former days." Among them is the actress Fanny Kemble, the tenor Bettini, and "the old actor Booth," whom Whitman admired for his "magnetism" and "electric personal idiosyncrasy." But the memorable vocal celebrity Whitman chooses to mention first is Alboni, whom he also singled out with imagery from the flow of electrons, referring in a chat with Traubel to the "magnetism" of her voice. "What a joy, a grandeur, an illimitable inspiration!"

A few days later, mention was made of a favorite Delaware ferryboat captain and musician, Ed Lindell, who denigrated "the importance of the human voice." To which Whitman responded, "I doubt if he has ever heard a voice that justifies what we call vocal powers: the great, overwhelming, touching, human voice—its throbbing, flowing, pulsing qualities. Alboni—or that strange, awkward, obesely ridiculous figure, the Italian who recently died—oh yes! Brignoli. Such voices—do they not justify all—explain all?" Another substantial comment on Alboni recorded by Traubel was uttered on 19 February 1890: "I never think of Alboni but I think of the finest voice, organ, that ever was. Her contralto—what a purity! what a range! And whatever her change of pitch, there was no loss of power, of integrity."

THE ELEPHANT WHO SWALLOWED A NIGHTINGALE

In 1842, at the age of nineteen and after having been favored by the eminent Gioachino Rossini with free vocal lessons for three years, Marietta Alboni made her operatic debut in Bologna. She moved quickly on to European fame with successes at St. Petersburg, London (where she bested rival divas Giulia Grisi and Jenny Lind), and finally Paris. There, at the Théâtre Italien on 2 December 1847, her debut as Arsace in *Semiramide* caused unexpected and total delight. The *Gazette musicale* reported: "Not a single bravo saluted her entrance. There was complete silence right up until one heard the admirable sounds of that voice so powerful and yet so moderate in its power. The silence did not last long, and the singer was soon hearing the applause, the acclamation, to which we have now accustomed her ear." A few years later, on 10 May 1850, she made her stunning debut at the Opéra in Meyerbeer's *Le Prophète* in the role of Fidès, succeeding Pauline Viardot (Sand's inspiration, it will be recalled, for *Consuelo*). Théophile Gautier's ecstatic review began, "La Alboni has been heard at the Opéra before only as a recitalist, and we all know what success that has brought her. A voice more fresh, more silvery, more sympathetic, more flexible or better managed has never been heard before an orchestra or a charmed public. So much grace and so much force, so much power and lightness! One voice so feminine and at the same time so masculine! Juliet and Romeo in the same throat!"

After further touring in Europe, Alboni crossed the Atlantic. She arrived in New York in early June of 1852 and stayed for exactly one year. Her metropolitan performances (she also sang in Boston, Philadelphia, and Saratoga Springs) consisted of about a dozen recitals in June, September, and October, then winter and spring 1853 appearances in nearly a dozen fully staged operas. It was, by unanimous journalistic account, a glorious year for Alboni, and it began with the late-June recital at Metropolitan Hall.

The circumstances were far from auspicious. Refusing to be be-Barnumed as Lind had been, she enjoyed little fanfare on her arrival, and not all of her advance publicity had been flattering. Prima donnas of ample physique are peculiarly susceptible to vulgar quips: Monstrous Cabaret or Monsterfat for Montserrat Caballé or Jus' Enormous for Jessye Norman, to mention a few recent cruel examples. Alboni was no exception, thanks notably to Rossini's heartless but eminently repeatable remark about her swallowing a nightingale. Richard Grant White recalled thirty years later, "All that was known of her was that she was much thought of in Europe, and that she was very stout; so that there was a poor joke current at the time that 'she was not all bony, but all fatty.' "

The weather, as already noted, was also unusually warm, leaving many seats empty, though the *Post* reported the remainder were filled by a "brilliant and enthusiastic audience."

Alboni chose for her Manhattan entrance aria a scene from an opera by her former mentor. Arsace's spectacular recitative and cavatina from *Semiramide* had become her calling card. In choosing it she doubtless recalled how, five years earlier, this bravura aria had instantly defrosted the audience at her London debut. "At my first entrance the public received me with a glacial coolness that would have abashed any other artist." Instead, she chose to behave like the fearless "new" Archie Dean of Whitman's story. "Upon me this had the opposite effect. I said to myself: nothing is expected of me; therefore what I do will be the more appreciated. As if by magic, I put my fear to one side and attacked with confidence the aria *Eccomi alfine in Babilonia!* By the words *è questo di Belo il tempio* [the second line of the recitative] my public was conquered, and I surpassed myself in everything that followed. It was really splendid."

Alboni's obvious desire to repeat this happy history was brilliantly fulfilled. George William Curtis described the great moment in the *Tribune*: "When she was about to commence, the audience were breathless with attention. A pin might be heard fall. She had not got through the first line when the quality of her voice was revealed to the evident delight of the whole audience, who, at the end of the second line, could no longer retain their impulse to give expression to their feelings and shouted 'bravo, bravo' in the most impassioned manner. Two or three shakes in this gem were exceedingly beautiful and the cadence [i.e. cadenza] was performed in a style of finish that proved the accomplished *artiste*. The applause was most tumultuous, and she was called out amidst renewed and prolonged expressions of the greatest enthusiasm." White, for the *Courier*, reported the recitative done in "large, simple, and grand" style and the aria itself "admirable." The *Evening Post*, describing her voice as "rich, mellow, copious, well-modulated and luscious," reported that "the *debutante* had achieved an unquestionable success," inundating the audience with a "full flood of sound, yet clear and sparkling, and capable of the easiest management." She was rewarded by a "tempest of applause."

To apparently unanimous stupefaction, Alboni continued to surpass herself as her program unfolded, notably by offering in the drinking song from *Lucrezia Borgia* "the most beautiful shake, and at the same time of the longest duration, we ever heard" (this trill "produced a *furore* of excitement," said Curtis). Then she sang a duet from Donizetti's *Don Pasquale* with the tenor Sangiovanni so sweetly that it had to be encored;

Three cartes de visite of Marietta Alboni. The earliest, published by Gurney & Son, shows her seated in elaborate dress and is probably from a daguerreotype made during her year in America in 1852–53. The image of her in costume holding a staff dates from the 1860s; it may show her as the Queen in Donizetti's Anna Bolena, one of several soprano roles she sang. Also from the 1860s is the portrait of her seated with a fan. Courtesy of Girvice Archer, Jr.

it was "moonlight made audible," said White. Finally, "she electrified the audience" with the climactic rondo *Non più mesta* from Rossini's Cinderella opera. Curtis pronounced this a "crowning triumph of the night" and reported that "the whole audience rose and waved their hats and handkerchiefs in the most excited manner, while she laughed all the time as if she was enjoying a very good joke." That this choice, too, was a shrewd one is suggested by what the French critic de Rovray said many years later about Alboni's *Non più mesta*: "If anyone were to ask me what piece of vocal music I had heard most perfectly executed in all the years I have been going to the theatre, I would answer without hesitation: the rondo from *La Cenerentola* as sung by Alboni. Art can go no further. It is perfection carried to the outermost limits!"

At her next appearance two days later, the *Musical Times* reported, Alboni's thrilling vocalism and the heat were unabated: "Men dissolved in rapture and perspiration simultaneously."

As with any sudden operatic revelation, there was much competition in the first Alboni reviews to describe and praise the new vocal wonder. Curtis kept reasonably calm in his delight: "The characteristics of her voice are great power, strength, and volume, not only without coarseness, but of the finest, softest and richest texture, depth and great purity, with a most remarkable sympathetic touching quality." White let fly more deliriously. Alboni's voice, he gushed, "comes bubbling, gurgling, gushing from that full throat and those gently parted lips, and reminds us of draughts of which poets have sung, but of which bacchantes have only dreamed. A child, on hearing it, must needs have visions of seas of amber jelly floating before his enamored mental vision, so materially rich, honeyed and pellucid it is." The *Post* oozed similar bedazzlement: "a spontaneous gush, or bubble, of sounds . . . a fountain of rich, ambrosial wine . . . perfect pyrotechnic display . . . varied, brilliant, deep, swelling, ecstatic." No one present, it seems, would have objected to Curtis's summary judgment: "There is no living contralto voice equal to it. There never, perhaps, was such a contralto voice before. It is the very soul and essence of melody."

The ravishing debut vindicated Ovid's wry suggestion in *The Art of Love*: "Let women learn to sing; with many of them voice instead of face has been the procuress."* Her singing had a deliciously cosmetic power. There was much gentlemanly effort to avoid the temptation to carp about what the *Home Journal* bluntly called her "avoirdupois weight." The *Post* reported, apparently with relief, "She is not enormously large, while her features are fine, and have made a narrow escape from beauty." White was equally diplomatic: "Although her amplitude exceeds even the most accommodating standard of symmetry, her features are unquestionably fine, and her face needs only a little attenuation to be decidedly handsome." Thirty years later, he added to this assessment, obviously with a generosity conferred by nostalgia: "In fact, Alboni's face was a noble one of the pure Italian type, and very charming in its expression. . . . Her smile was charming, and not only because it revealed the whitest of coral-set teeth; and her laugh infected the air around her with hilarity. It was impossible not to laugh with her." Clearly, the occasional allusions to Alboni's physique—"a young Falstaff in short petticoats" or "the blithe Bacchus in ample skirts"—had been intended affectionately.

That Whitman himself, following Ovid, was among those utterly disarmed by the contralto's artistry he made clear in his one description of her physique: "Alboni is a fully developed woman, with perfect-shaped feet, arms, and hands.—Some thought her fat—*we* always thought her beautiful.—Her face is regular and pleasant—her forehead low—plentiful black hair, cut short, like a boy's—a slow and graceful style of walk—attitudes of inimitable beauty, and large black eyes." That emphatic *we* is superb. It is the male-bonded *we* of the camerados of the upper tier.

Alboni succeeded in surpassing the triumph of her debut in several recitals in September and early October. The first, before more than five thousand spectators at Metropolitan Hall, left "the house in ecstasy with her rich, full, round notes," said the *Tribune*. At the recital on 18 September, reported the *Home Journal*, she was showered with more than a hundred bouquets. Toward the end of the month, critics were beginning to feel the strain of constant praise. "The fame of this great artist is so thoroughly established in this City, and her performances so equal in their perfection," wrote Curtis in the *Tribune*, "that criticism has become almost a work of supererogation."

In October, though, Alboni obliged the pleasure-weary critics to soldier on when her repertory expanded beyond Rossini and Donizetti. "In those grand inspirations of Bellini, which seem such simple outpourings of intense passion, her incomparable voice, her majestic phrasing and calm strength find fit subjects," said the *Tribune*. The recital on 13 October left the same reviewer feeling that "the heart-throbs of tragedy mark every cadence of her voice." In the final recital, on the fifteenth, Alboni displayed her usual "superb awareness of conscious power and superiority," especially in the *Casta diva*: "We have heard that aria sung by the most famous singers, but never by any that gave it so *internal* a meaning, or poured it forth with such a majesty of power as Alboni."

Assessing this series of tours de force, the *Albion* (23 October) was even willing to rank Alboni above all the prima donnas who had hitherto come to America, even above Jenny Lind. They "must all succumb we think to that rare development of the 'beautiful Italian instinct' which we have seen in Alboni. . . . Her singing is not only the most perfect of its kind, but by far the most intrinsically gratifying."

Six weeks later, Alboni ignited another concentrated furor with a series of operas at the Broadway Theater, first *Cenerentola* (27 and 30 December), then Donizetti's *Daughter of the Regiment*, and Bellini's *Sonnambula* and *Norma*. When she had offered her fairy-tale heroine in Paris, Gautier wittily granted that Alboni "is certainly not physically the Cinderella one dreams of . . . a pained sadness within that athletic and triumphant body is scarcely imaginable. If she wished, this robust Cinderella could crush her lean, wicked sisters with one finger." But Gautier was won over by the "unimaginable perfection" of Alboni's singing. White had the same reservations: "The stage did not increase her attractions. She was not an actress; she was not a great operatic prima donna; she was a singer simply and absolutely—the greatest singer of her half-century; nothing more. . . . Nor was her figure at all suited to Cinderella, to Amina, or to the Daughter."

And yet, Alboni triumphed. The *Courier* reported, "Three or four times during the evening she electrified her hearers," especially with the rondo ("what we all came to hear"). In *Daughter*, said the *Tribune*, "the amiable cantatrice was replete with good humor which made all human nature in the house kin," and the *Post* found that her "careless, good-natured, jolly manner is much better suited to a *Vivandière* than the coquettish graces of the French ladies who take the *rôle*." The *Home Journal* was bowled over by Alboni in the music lesson scene, which filled "the vast and crowded theatre with the most magnificent and stirring music that ever flowed from the throat of woman." The *Courier* urged readers to hurry for tickets to the second performance that evening: "Sometimes there are sham successes but Madame Alboni's is not among them."

Alboni followed these two comic romps with the grand pathos of Bellini. Her performance as Bellini's sleepwalker the *Albion* declared "positively one of the greatest we ever witnessed upon the lyric stage," and the *Courier* declared the memory of all previous Aminas banished by Alboni, even though she appeared on stage "a portly person, with a short neck and hair cut close above it like that of a boy." "Amina's grief, when Alboni is Amina, is grand," its critic enthused. "She is no whining, puling girl. With Alboni both grief and joy are heroic."

No wonder that, two weeks later when Alboni brought out her *Norma*, the excitement was unparalleled. "Last evening, Alboni appeared at the Broadway Theater in *Norma*," reported the *Herald*, "and drew such a crowd as never before was congregated within its walls. From an early hour on Wednesday, every seat in the boxes was bought up, and yesterday five dollars were offered for secured seats. . . . Hundreds upon hundreds had their money returned to them at the door, after every passage was filled to overflowing with persons standing and wedged so close together that there was no possibility of passing to or fro. . . . So much money never was received before, on any single night, in Broadway theatre." We know that Whitman attended this performance or the one that took place the next evening. Indeed, given the boast already quoted, he may have attended both. How the audacious contralto succeeded in this most challenging and extremely popular soprano role—and how Whitman responded to her Norma—we must delay considering for a moment. Suffice it to say that, though she appears never again to have sung the role, she did not disappoint her eager-to-be-delirious fans on this occasion.

Alboni's third and final vocal extravaganza in Manhattan took place at Niblo's Theater, with appearances in six new roles and encores of *Sonnambula* and *Daughter*. This season opened with *Don Pasquale* on 23 March 1853. The *Tribune* found her "in excellent voice" and was "pleased to observe that she never condescended to use the yow-yow passages of the lower register to secure applause." Her Rosina in *Il Barbiere di Siviglia* on 4 April was found "entirely delicious" by the *Home Journal*: "Some singers surprise and astonish: she thoroughly satisfies." Her revival of the sleepwalker Amina left the *Courier* wondering, "What need to reiterate a monotone of unqualified praise." The *Herald* was on hand, too, and—clearly enjoying, like Whitman, not technically but "from the human side"—refused to be bothered by Alboni's downward transposition of the soprano part: "Amina will henceforth rank as one of the greatest, if not the greatest, of Mad. Alboni's roles. . . . Jenny [Lind], great as she was, never took a house by storm in the *Ah! non giunge* as Alboni does. Learned critics object, we believe, to the introduction of her lower notes, but they impart a real sense of pleasure; and we, who love music as an enjoyment, and not as a study, are profoundly grateful to Providence for having bestowed them on our prima donna."

The *Musical World* offered a lovely turn of phrase for her appearance as Leonora in Donizetti's *La Favorita* on 8 April: "She melted upon the susceptibilities of the audience like a snow-flake." The *Albion* reviewer was also present and, throwing caution to the wind, nominated it "the greatest operatic representation we have ever witnessed in New York." But this triumph was soon upstaged by the *Lucrezia Borgia* on 22 April. Its cast, led by "the peerless Alboni," said the *Albion*, produced "certainly the greatest operatic performance ever witnessed in this hemisphere." The *Courier* said of her in the pants role of Orsini, "the true bacchanalian spirit beamed in her face." The *Post* declared her "particularly triumphant" in the drinking song. A few days later she charmed the *Evening Post* in Rossini's *La Gazza ladra*: "Alboni, who looked very sweetly in the simple rustic part of Ninetta, was never more sparkling and delicious." And her last operatic performance was as Zerlina in *Don Giovanni*. "With what naive and rustic coquetry she went through the part," said the *Courier* reviewer.

The now-beloved contralto's farewell to America, a benefit recital for the conductor Arditi late in May, proved a characteristic triumph. "All, from first to last, was equally glorious, equally rich, equally perfect throughout," said the *Albion*. Among several bravuras included this evening were the third-act finale from *Ernani*, in which Alboni sang the baritone role of Carlo Quinto, a last outing for Norma's *Casta diva*, Amina's *Ah! non giunge*, and Rossini's florid *Di tanti palpiti* from *Tancredi*.

Sensing the end of a brief but gorgeous era, reviewers caught their breath and paused to assess her. "We have heard the last delicious strains," said the *Daily Times*, "of the best and most fascinating singer of the age. The chain of enchantment is broken, and we may go home to our pianos and play dismal requiems." The *Albion* concluded, "Alboni has left her mark upon the musical taste of this city, which time cannot efface." Especially remarkable was her grand simplicity, which compared so favorably with Henriette Sontag's "superfluous *arpeggios*" and Jenny Lind's "cold and feelingless *cadenzas*." Indeed, it was held up as a great mark of honor that Alboni was "never guilty of introducing a superfluous *trill*, no matter what the temptation." "And so farewell," ends the review, "to the perfect, incomparable Alboni! We shall not soon look upon thy like again!" *Di tanti palpiti*, indeed.

And then the vocal palpitations ended. Alboni sailed for France on the first of June, soon married an Italian count, and by 1863 had abandoned her career. Widowed shortly afterward, she settled into a long Parisian retirement, emerging to sing rarely (at Rossini's funeral in 1868, for example), and died at the age of sixty-eight in June 1894, an august but melancholy reminder of a golden era of vocalism. An obituary in *Le Menestrel* praised her as "one of the last glories—and the most sparkling—of the beautiful art of Italian singing, whose traditions she learned from Rossini himself and which is not heard at all today, when song and expression have been replaced by endless declamation and reckless vociferation." Her grave is in Père-Lachaise, near that of another dear Whitman acquaintance with a low, musical voice, Oscar Wilde.

Three decades after her American *annus mirabilis*, the veteran reviewer White remembered Alboni in the most impressive terms, calling her "probably the greatest singer the world has seen since Malibran." Hers was a voice "to which no other that has been heard for fifty years can be compared either in volume or in quality,—and the method absolutely perfect, and a style the charm of which can hardly be expressed in words. . . . Excepting Malibran, no singer, not even Jenny Lind, did so much as Alboni did to elevate and purify the taste of the higher class of music lovers. She became the model, the standard by which others were to be tried." White emphasized the nature of Alboni's magic by recalling a particular phrase in Amina's aria *Ah! non credea* as she sang it: "Now, after almost thirty years, I can hear with my mind's ear the marvelously, almost miraculously, beautiful way in which she uttered the few notes of this simple phrase . . . and which, passing in an instant, almost in the twinkling of an eye, yet had in every note . . . and in its conception as a whole, and in its execution, an enchanting, subduing charm which produced a feeling of mingled transport and humiliation. One was almost tempted to go and kneel down before her and do something abject in grateful acknowledgment of this manifestation of supreme musical divinity."

VENUS CONTRALTO

Walt Whitman was transported in precisely this fashion by Alboni's singing. By curious and telling coincidence, in fact, it is also the role of Amina that evoked Whitman's famous expression of the contralto's supreme musical divinity. In the last of his memorable opera-inspired poems, "Proud Music of the Storm" (1869), the poet recalls to mind some of "Italia's peerless compositions" that had thrilled him years before: "poor crazed Lucia's eyes' unnatural gleam"; Ernani hearing "the infernal call, the death-pledge of the horn"; the "trombone duo, Libertad forever!" of *I Puritani*; and Fernando's "Song of lost love" in *La Favorita*. Then, climactically:

> Awaking from her woes at last retriev'd Amina sings,
> Copious as stars and glad as morning light the torrents of her joy.
>
> (The teeming lady comes,
> The lustrious orb, Venus contralto, blooming mother,
> Sister of loftiest gods, Alboni's self I hear.)

Those lines and "To a Cantatrice" (this is the 1860 version)—

Here, take this gift!
I was reserving it for some hero, orator, or general,
One who should serve the good old case, the progress
    and freedom of the race, the cause of my Soul;
But I see that what I was reserving belongs to you just
    as much as any.

—constitute Whitman's poetic acknowledgment of Alboni's artistry. But he left several other reminiscences about her, and these, I believe, are worth surveying before we consider the precise reasons why she so profoundly served the "cause" of this poet's soul.

The earliest of these comes among the remarks on Italian singers in America that he compiled in 1858: "The best songstress ever in America was Alboni.—Her voice is a contralto of large compass, high and low—and probably sweeter tones never issued from human lips. The mere sound of that voice was pleasure enough." In his 1882 memoirs, *Specimen Days*, he recalled "certain actors and singers" who had "a good deal to do with the business" of gestating *Leaves of Grass*: "I heard, these years, well render'd, all the Italian and other operas in vogue." Whitman then mentions seventeen operas, among them several in which Alboni scored triumphs; as usual he gives her pride of place: "I heard Alboni every time she sang in New York and vicinity—also Grisi, the tenor Mario, and the baritone Badiali, the finest in the world." In a later, more elaborate sketch of "the best dramatic and lyric artists I have seen in bygone days," Whitman wrote, "Perhaps my dearest amusement reminiscences are those musical ones. I doubt if ever the senses and emotions of the future will be thrill'd as were the auditors of a generation ago by the deep passion of Alboni's contralto (at the Broadway Theatre, south side, near Pearl street)—or by the trumpet notes of Badiali's baritone, or Bettini's pensive and incomparable tenor in Fernando in *Favorita*."

Memories of Alboni haunted the poet for a very long time. Pasted in one of his notebooks is this brief newspaper clipping from 1890: "Mme. Alboni celebrated the completion of her seventy-fourth [in fact sixty-seventh] year last week at her house in the Cours la Reine, Paris. Notwithstanding her years, Mme. Alboni, it is said, sang the air from 'The Prophet' with a powerful dramatic sentiment and a superb voice that recalled the brilliant triumphs of this incomparable Fides." This is surely the basis for Whitman's last published reference to Alboni, which puts her in the most estimable company: "Seems to me now when I look back, the Italian contralto Alboni (she is living yet, in Paris, 1891, in good condition, good voice yet, considering) with the then prominent histrions

Booth, Edwin Forrest, and Fanny Kemble and the Italian singer Bettini, have had the deepest and most lasting effect upon me. I should like very well if Madame Alboni and the old composer Verdi (and Bettini the tenor, if he is living) could know how much noble pleasure and happiness they gave me then, and how deeply I always remember them and thank them to this day."

Several other remarks about Alboni that Whitman made in conversation have come down to us and are in the same exalting vein. In August 1888, he happened to recall that Traubel's father was "a considerable something of a singer once upon a time." Thus commences this train of thought: "A baritone was he? It is a noble voice. Ask him for me if he ever heard Badiali: Badiali was the superbest of all superb baritones in my time—in my singing years. Oh! those great days! great, great days! Alboni, Badiali, in particular: no one can tell, know, even suspect, how much they had to do with the making of *Leaves of Grass.*" And Whitman added, "My younger life was so saturated with the emotions, raptures, uplifts, of such musical experiences that it would be surprising indeed if all my future work had not been colored by them."

Whitman expressed similar sentiments about Alboni to Fanny Ritter, who reported him as saying, "Her mellow, powerful, delicate tones, so heartfelt in their expression, so spontaneous in their utterance, had deeply penetrated his spirit, and never, as when subsequently writing of the mocking-bird or any other bird-song, on a fragrant, moonlit summer night, had he been able to free himself from the recollection of the deep emotion that had inspired and affected him while he listened to the singing of Marietta Alboni."* In a conversation with Traubel in March 1889, Venus contralto stood all alone on her pedestal: "For me, out of the whole list of stage deities of that period, no one meant so much to me as Alboni, as Booth: narrowing it further, I should say, as Alboni alone." And again, a few months later, enormous praise for Alboni alone came when Whitman spoke of "the consciousness of abounding presence in a fine organ—a superb voice—I have known some—Alboni's 40 years ago—the magnificent contralto."*

More than two years later and not long before Whitman's lungs finally gave out, Alboni still occupied unchallenged her place of eminence in his memory. On one of the increasingly rare occasions when Horace found him "in great good trim" and talkative, the conversation reached a climax with a last glowing expression of how completely Marietta had transfixed him. No being more than Alboni had moved and possessed him, Traubel reported Whitman as saying. "She roused whirlwinds of feeling within me." He also reasserted his conviction of her physical beauty, even though "none about me or people generally" agreed with him. And, while Italian opera may have sunk in popularity by the 1890s under Wagner's ascending star, it reigned supreme when *she* sang it. If greatness "was not in the opera then it was in her," Walt insisted. "She shed tears, real tears. I have been near—often within a seat or two—and seen her." This final bravo, Traubel records, created at the bedside "an atmosphere . . . crimsoned with good blood and sympathy."

We come now to the obvious and momentous question, which can be asked in several ways. What caused Marietta Alboni in particular to appeal so strongly to Whitman? What caused *this* singer to produce in him such rapturous uplift? He once remarked to Traubel that he was "particularly susceptible to . . . voices of range, magnetism: mellow, persuading voices." The first three desiderata are no trouble. Alboni's astonishing range was always her most salient feature. Asked to sign a guestbook once, she simply wrote:

La mia estenzione.
   —Marietta Alboni

The magnetism of her vocal presence and the mellowness of her luscious voice we have seen consistently praised in her American reviews. But what made hers a *persuading* voice for Whitman?

The answer to these questions lies in the editions of *Leaves of Grass* produced during what he called his "singing years." For as one becomes more familiar with the reception of Alboni by New Yorkers and our poetic "son of the brawny and tall-topt city," the more clearly one sees behind Whitman's amorous "real Me" the shadow of his Venus contralto. To repeat the supreme insight in Whitman, "We convince by our presence," and it will not be difficult to discern the extraordinarily convincing presence of Alboni in *Leaves of Grass*. Many of her most salient characteristics as an artist must have helped to *persuade* Whitman that creating his "real Me" was not merely possible but imperative.

AURAL BEAUTY: "Things base and vile," wrote Shakespeare, love can transform to "form and dignity." The voice has a similar power. No form of vocalism teaches this lesson more convincingly than opera, where powerful projection requires a physique incompatible with conventional notions of beauty. The lesson figured, for example, in the composition of *Aida*. When Verdi worried the audience might laugh if an ugly soprano were referred to in the dialogue as "beautiful," his librettist Ghislanzoni rightly pooh-poohed him: "In the opera house all women are beautiful or at least are made beautiful by the idealism of music. . . . Even if we have a monster from Lapland on stage, the public will go into ecstasies."

Whitman learned the same lesson from Alboni. When this fat lady sang, as he put it himself, "*we* thought her beautiful." By the time Whitman was prepared to launch his amorous cavatina

Walt Whitman, circa 1854, just after the departure of Alboni for Europe and before the appearance of the first edition of Leaves of Grass. *Courtesy of the Trent Collection, Duke University Library.*

of sex and youth, he was well into middle age, gray-bearded and certainly not conventionally handsome. An acquaintance who knew him in the early 1850s said, "He was quite gray at thirty. He had a look of age in his youth, as he now has a look of youth in his age." But everywhere in *Leaves of Grass* is manifest the vocal idealism that gives the poet confidence to become "undisguised and naked" in spite of "this swarthy and unrefined face—these gray eyes, / This beard—the white wool, unclipt upon my neck," as he describes himself in *Calamus* #19.

ONE OF THE BOYS: Whitman dreamed in the late 1850s of an ideal "city of robust friends—Nothing was greater there than manly love." And he loved, in real life, to feel the "electric force and muscle from perhaps 2000 full-sinew'd men" as he sat in the upper tier of a Manhattan theater. Alboni, with her hair "cut short, like a boy's" and that voice with a manly dose of Romeo in it, must have gratified his predilections enormously. (His own voice, it seems, had an androgynous tang to it: Richard Bucke, in his 1883 biography, called him a "sort of male castrato; a false soprano." This did not please Whitman at all, and he saw to it that the remark was deleted.)

Alboni appears to have been the ideal antidote to the frilly, kid-gloved soubrette who so riled Whitman in his early operagoing days. She wore her hair "without comb, ribbon, or ornament." An 1848 Parisian pamphlet on Alboni explained that she wore her hair "à la Titus" as "one of the exigencies of her employment: for, being a contralto, Alboni almost always plays the roles of men." In fact, her repertory of over forty roles included only a dozen male characters, and she sang only one of these pants roles—the much-praised Orsini in *Lucrezia Borgia*—in America. Yet her hairstyle may indeed have been a matter of personal, happily Whitmanesque fashion-be-damned taste.

In any event, the tomboyish bent of Alboni's nature flourished when she dueled the extremely elegant, ladylike Sontag in simultaneous productions of *The Daughter of the Regiment* in January 1853. She won handily, utterly charming the audience by playing the drum "in a style that would pass muster in a French barracks" (*Home Journal*), skillfully banishing all "fine ladyism" from the role (*Courier*), and exuding enormous pleasure in "the frank and gay life of the camp" (*Tribune*). Poor Sontag never had a chance. "It is better to hear Alboni sing one good song, than Sontag through an opera," was the harsh judgment of *Putnam's Monthly*. Given his tastes, Whitman would doubtless have agreed.

When Alboni essayed the quintessentially pert role of Rosina in *Barbiere*, the *Tribune* reviewer had to admit, "She is not so admirable in the delicate, arch humor of this character, as in the broad, rollicking fun she imparts to the Daughter of the Regiment." Some divas seek to dominate the audience with imperious poise, and to these Whitman was obviously allergic: "why should I venerate and be ceremonious?" he asks in "Song of Myself." The reviews for Alboni show that she was a diva of a different cut—a blithe, broad-shouldered, come-hither diva around whose shoulder one might put a companionable arm, a form of physical contact Whitman especially liked. The first acquaintance of the *Herald* reviewer with her left him feeling exceedingly cozy: "She has a most good-humored, good-looking, good-natured face, almost a jolly expression of countenance, which suggests the homely proverb of 'laugh and be fat.' "

This unladylike, almost fraternal buoyancy doubtless explains Alboni's huge success with the moment, in *The Daughter of the Regiment*, when the tomboy heroine must tearfully part from her comrades. "With her handkerchief pressed upon her streaming eyes," reported the *Home Journal*, "she poured forth a flood of melting lamentation that can never be forgotten by any that heard it." The text for this moment could practically be these words from the last of the *Calamus* poems: "how happy you were if I could be with you and become your comrade."

And positively eerie is the foreshadowed future for Whitman in the

Marietta Alboni in the title role of the "heroic opera" Tancredi, *the first stupendously successful opera by her early mentor, Gioachino Rossini.* Tancredi *was one of more than a dozen male characters Alboni assumed in her career, though she sang only one, Orsini in Donizetti's* Lucrezia Borgia, *in New York. Whitman was surely familiar with* Tancredi's *music. It was part of the first season of Italian opera in New York, at the Park Theater in 1825, and its most famous aria, "Di tanti palpiti," became extremely popular as a coloratura display piece. The impossibly cinched waist here must be taken with salt, but the head accords with Whitman's description: "Her face is regular and pleasant—her forehead low—plentiful black hair, cut short, like a boy's." Courtesy of Girvice Archer, Jr.*

way the *Musical World* chose to cast its vote for Alboni's military lass: "We prefer Alboni's Maria to Sontag's; simply, we suppose, because it accords best with our nature. Were we a soldier, lying on the damp, cold ground, with a saber cut across our cranium and our countenance, ploughed up by a musket ball, we should hail the appearance of Alboni's Maria with delight—with inexpressible joy. We know she would bind up our wounds, and nurse us back to health in the most kind, loving and womanly manner imaginable. But we should not be so glad to see Sontag's. . . . She would be apt to leave our couch of suffering to attend a ball." The sunny air of comradely intimacy that Alboni cultivated is, of course, a main element of *Leaves of Grass*. Whitman boasts in "Song of Myself," "I dilate you with tremendous breath, I buoy you up," and Alboni, with her spectacular breath control and exuberant good nature, obviously performed the same feat for her audiences.

Before we turn from the "manly" charms of Alboni's voice and stage personality, it is worth noticing another way in which her transgression of orthodox concepts of gender may have appealed strongly to Whitman. This is a transgression performed by all operatic divas as soon as they open their mouths: emitting sounds just as stentorian and authoritative as their male colleagues, they utterly annihilate the notion that one gender is "superior," the other "inferior." In his attempt to explain the nexus between opera and gay men, Paul Robinson pursues the ramification of this perceptively. Speaking of heroic-scale opera stars (like Alboni), he observes, "We ought not to be surprised that this particular creature—the transgressive female opera singer—should have become an object of identification with homosexuals. The opera diva, after all, gives the lie to prevailing asssumptions about sex and gender. She explodes the system. Small wonder that men whose sexual desires are also stigmatized by the same system of assumptions should find in the diva a kind of spokesperson."*

Surely, something like this identification was at work in Whitman's psyche when he capitulated so wholeheartedly to Alboni. Indeed, this was probably also what caused him to respond so emphatically to the diva in *Consuelo*, created by George Sand (herself a notable rebuke to the patriarchy) to explode patriarchal orthodoxy. And the subversive Willa Cather later did the same thing with her diva-heroine Thea Kronberg in *The Song of the Lark*. There may also be, here, a hint of the reason why *Leaves of Grass* was so warmly received by the more freethinking of Whitman's contemporary female readers. In his vigorous embrace of the democracy of gender on the operatic stage and his constant metaphorical use of opera's terms in his verse, these female readers must have sensed Whitman's fundamental urge, in Robinson's phrase, to explode the patriarchal system.

A GIFT TO BE SIMPLE: In his last months, Whitman offered his two cents on plans for a dinner party that he himself was too ill to attend: "I think a quiet affair, a dozen or so of you, would not hurt." Then he added, characteristically, "Do not be afraid to grapple with simplicity. Our fel-

lows are too much bent upon display—big setouts, dishes, waiters, cur-
tains, luxurious surroundings. But with us that ought all to be taboo."
Simplicity, said Whitman, is the sunshine of life. That was why Shakespeare, especially the clotted, aristocratic comedies, stuck in his craw.
"What play of Shakespeare, represented in America," he asked in one of
his early anonymous reviews of Leaves of Grass, "is not an insult to
America, to the marrow in its bones?" But why, if he derided one over-
wrought bequest of the Old World, namely the oeuvre of "tangled and
florid Shakespeare," would he be so taken with deeply Old World grand
opera? Why did the most virtuosic vocal writing in operatic history, that
of the Italian bel canto repertory, so inspire him? Again, Alboni may
help us to understand.

This is because the great gift in art is to achieve simplicity in the midst
of complexity, to *focus* complex thoughts, desires, and fears, to deploy
enormous expressive powers dexterously, intensely. All superior operatic
executants share this power, and Alboni appears to have done so. Pougin
wrote of her having "the same beautiful simplicity of style, the same
warmth of sentiment" as the sublime Giuditta Pasta, and this note is often
struck in the American reviews. She grappled brilliantly with simplicity.

Alboni made such a memorable effect as Donizetti's Daughter, said
the Herald, because she "acted so naturally and with such a graceful simplicity." When she unveiled her Bellini style in recital with arias from
Norma and Sonnambula, the Tribune observed that "no bustling energy of
action, no external demonstration of feeling could so touch the soul, and
so affect it with the very essence of dramatic interest, as the simple
singing of these pieces." Reviewers expressed particular delight in her
lack of affectation. The Herald noticed this immediately in her debut
recital: "She has not the slightest affectation about her." "She touches
the soul by the pure and hearty sentiment with which she renders the
music of the Italian masters," said the same reviewer of a subsequent
recital. Later, the Tribune praised the "naif, unconstrained" quality of her
"excellent acting" and her gratifying "absence of artificiality."

Critics also gratefully acknowledged that, just as Alboni eschewed the
off-putting tics of prima donnaism, she also refused merely to flaunt her
virtuosity. The Herald noticed at her debut, "She uses very little embel-
lishment—which in her case would be like gilding refined gold," and at
her first fall recital the Tribune was pleased that she "rendered the music
. . . as brilliantly, more *purely*, and with less extraneous ornament, than
any whom we can call to mind." The reviewer later delighted to report
that her outing as the heroine in Don Pasquale was blessedly free "of
extra-super cadenza-making."

Just a week before, the *Musical World* published on its front page a translation of Franz Liszt's attack upon Alboni's archrival Sontag and all "throat-virtuosos" and "luxury-artistes" of her ilk. "To hear her sing," Liszt wrote, "is a purely aristocratic, luxurious enjoyment; and for the very reason that it pre-supposes, on the part of those participating, the most absolute *passiveness*." This "*artificial* and *luxurious* Art," this art of "*self-seeking virtuose-dom*," Liszt asserts, is the "insidious enemy of all genuine, and—as Richard Wagner truthfully says—*necessity-born Art*." Only this latter art can summon the listener "into a kind of *individual activity*." Artificial and luxurious art was likewise anathema to Whitman.

Whitman all his life despised the "boudoir amours and parlor fripperies" of the Manhattan aristocracy, especially (we have seen) when this luxurious lifestyle was on display in the city's opera houses. Not surprisingly, he never even mentions Sontag, the darling of the corseted and fur-lined classes, in his operatic reminiscences. Obviously, Whitman was of Liszt's and Wagner's mind. Alboni's simple, passionate, and emotionally penetrating art put her clearly in the Liszt-Wagner party, the Whitman party, in this controversy, as the poet made clear in his wry criticism of that supreme example of the "luxury-artiste," Jenny Lind: "The Swedish Swan, with all her blandishments, never touched my heart in the least. I wondered at so much vocal dexterity; and indeed they were all very pretty, those leaps and double somersets. But . . . there was a vacuum in the head of the performance. Beauty pervaded it no doubt, and that of a high order. It was the beauty of Adam before God breathed into his nostrils." No wonder that Whitman, in editing Richard Bucke's *Walt Whitman* for publication in 1883, insisted on deleting the sentence, "Jenny Lind's singing, too, had greatly influenced him," thus leaving a passage devoted entirely to praise of Alboni.

Just one year after Whitman published his pan of Jenny Lind, Venus contralto would enter his life to assist in filling the "vacuum in the head" of his own performance as a poet and breathing life into the nostrils of the "real Me." His often-expressed gratitude to Alboni urges us, I think, to conclude that she played an important part in drawing him into the "individual activity" of *Leaves of Grass*, as stunning an example of "necessity-born art" as the annals of American literature afford.

NONCHALANCE: One acquaintance of Whitman's in the early 1850s observed that his "singular coolness was an especial feature. I have never seen him excited in the least degree: never heard him swear but once." In the remainder of the decade, the poet worked hard and successfully to perfect the art of seeming (if not necessarily being) laid-back. "Boldness.

Nonchalant ease and indifference," we have noticed, was to be—truly
became—his "personal slogan." By the 1860 edition, the poet could
justly claim complete success in his efforts to "find a new unthought-of
nonchalance with the best of Nature! / To have the gag remov'd from
one's mouth!"*

Many superbly nonchalant Italian singers inspired Whitman to
remove that gag, notably the "broad-chested feller" Cesare Badiali, whose
"absolute ease of demeanor" so impressed him. But Alboni was surely his
greatest teacher of nonchalance. Deploying a similar image of suddenly
found heroic voice, Whitman admonishes in "Song of Myself," "Loafe
with me on the grass, loose the stop from your throat." A few years before
loosing the stop on his own throat, he had often loafed in sybaritic ease
with Marietta on the Manhattan stage.

When Alboni debuted in Paris, the *Gazette musicale* professed astonishment that she could sing difficult music with such ease: "Alboni sings
. . . without effort, without fatigue, without the slightest movement of
the body, yet not without physical expression. She smiles with her lips
and with her face. She excels in song that is graceful, audacious, triumphant. She was born for the bravura aria."* This theme of audacious
ease became the leading theme of Alboni's American reviews. Self-ease
is immediately apparent and charismatic, and Alboni practically won her
audience before singing a note. "Her large laughing eye expresses an
infinity of good nature," reported the *Mirror* just after her arrival. R. Storrs
Willis met her just before the debut and wrote in the *Musical Times*
of "one of those comfortable, nonchalant, delightful creatures, whom it
puts one in perfect good humor with himself and the world occasionally
to see."

Her recitals confirmed this advance publicity. The *Herald's* report on
her debut, in fact, virtually translates the praise of the *Gazette musicale*:
"And what is so peculiar to Alboni, those luscious notes gush from her
without an effort. What has been said by some of the Swedish nightingale, but is not true of her, is true of Alboni—that she sings like a bird—
with such ease does she glide through the mazes of the melody. She does
not appear to have much dramatic power. She scarcely moves a muscle."
The *Courier* agreed: "She seems to give no thought to what she does, but
merely to let the flood of her song pour itself forth."

At her fall recitals Alboni carried unprepossessing heroism to new
heights. At the opening one, reported the *Tribune*, she appeared before
the enormous crowd in Metropolitan Hall "with hair dishevelled, and
calm indifferent manner." Of her *Una voce poco fa* the reviewer wrote
that "she sang through the delicious *allegro* with as much *sangfroid* as

though the public was a matter of total indifference." The *Courier* like-wise noted that she sang "with seeming pleased and unconscious careless-ness." Of course, she still succeeded in leaving the audience "in ecstasy." Later, she presented to the *Home Journal* "a picture *in large* of placid, smiling and gracious content. Her welcome was cordial, not vehement, and her responsive smiles showed resplendent teeth." At an October recital she romped through an obstacle course titled "Musical Difficulties Solved," said the *Herald*, "with a nonchalance that showed that nothing in the shape of difficult passages (with which the music abounded) came amiss to her."

In opera, Alboni's triumphant ease did vitiate somewhat the dramatic force of her impersonations, but the critics did not seem unhappy with such compromises. Her Cinderella, said the *Albion*, was "distinguished by the superbest indolence," and in her Leonora in *La Favorita* "there was no straining for effect: all was easy, natural and beautiful." *Putnam's Monthly* caught the drollery of her laid-back Maria with a wry turn of phrase: "The brisk, pert little daughter of the regiment could not fail to be amusingly personated by the tropical amplitude of our languid contralto."

Putnam's, in January of 1853, summed up Alboni's initial opera season in terms that bring us back again, emphatically, to Whitman and his *Leaves of Grass*. She is said to have a "voice that is always captivating, smooth, luscious and sympathetic" and which is deployed "with a languid heroism . . . a frank and unaffected demeanor." Languid heroism: perfect phrase for a poem (and a life's work) that begins, "I loafe and invite my soul, / I lean and loafe at my ease." Perfect phrase, too, for the poet who would in a few years boast that he and his "Manhattanese" comrade/lover are "two natural and nonchalant persons." The title of the quintessential Whitman poem "Me Imperturbe," new in 1860, could have been Alboni's motto, for even in so vivacious a character as Rosina the *Albion* critic could record that she displayed an "imperturbable repose of manner."

Attempting to explain, in 1889, why he had made such successful love with the photographer's camera during his life, Whitman said to Traubel, "I think the greatest aid is in my *insouciance*—my utter indiffer-ence: my going as if it meant nothing unusual."* Yet another lesson that the languid heroine taught Whitman so well.

THE GREAT MS. NORMA

Marietta Alboni displayed, in spectacular fashion, a casual, self-delighting pride. Her Amina, said the *Tribune*, "revels in its own perfection." The

Albion's critic, responding to the very same performance, noticed this too and offered perhaps the most important—certainly the most Whitmanesque—critical insight evoked by the entire American tour: "It has been remarked that Alboni's singing seems to give herself a pleasure almost equal to that of her hearers. Therein lies the secret. Without this, the most consummate art, the most exquisite voice imaginable, would be comparatively powerless. The songstress *believes* in her singing herself." The twelve poems of the first *Leaves of Grass* could not have been written without a similar self-confidence. Whitman, in fact, alluded to the quasi-operatic flaunting of his new book when he asked these impertinent rhetorical questions in one of his anonymous self-reviews: "Do you think the best honors of the earth are won so easily, Walt Whitman? Do you think city and country are to fall before the vehement egotism of your recitative of yourself?" Though in fact they did not, the sanguine author clearly hoped city and country would fall prostrate before his vocalism, just as he and his camerados of the upper tier did for Marietta.

The very words that begin the stupendous entrance aria of "Song of Myself" express precisely the self-conscious pride that must inspire every great opera singer just before the curtain rises: "I celebrate myself . . ." Reveling in one's own perfect self while at the same time "assuming" a role, "every atom" of it, and then making it "belong" to the audience: this is the ultimate performative triumph for both the singer and the poet. The only difference, Whitman truly observed a few years after Alboni's departure, is that "singers do not live long—only the poet lives long." This melancholy remark is especially poignant in Alboni's case. So much, and such unanimous, praise naturally awakens the desire, in Shakespeare's phrase, to "call back yesterday, bid time return." How one would love to hear what she sounded like. To be vouchsafed just one performance and be able to share the pleasure of Whitman and his contemporaries!

If such were possible, who would not choose the *Norma* at Metropolitan Hall on 27 January 1853? The experience sojourned long in Whitman's memory. Surely it is Alboni's infanticidal priestess who is recalled in "Proud Music of the Storm" (1869): "Across the stage with pallor on her face, yet lurid passion, / Stalks Norma brandishing the dagger in her hand." Much later, Whitman wrote of being deeply moved at the sight of the "superb severity" of Niagara Falls on a June afternoon in 1880: "Brief, and as quiet as brief, that picture—a remembrance always afterwards." And then he adds, "Such are the things, indeed, I lay away with my life's rare and blessed bits of hours, reminiscent, past—the wild sea-storm I once saw one winter day, off Fire island—the elder Booth in

Richard, that famous night forty years ago in the old Bowery—or Alboni in the children's scene in *Norma*. . . ."

The desire to hear Alboni as Norma is, in one respect, predictable enough. As the *Herald* explained in its review the day after she first sang the role, it is "regarded by the critics as the great test of a *prima donna* in lyric tragedy." Whitman himself implies in "The Dead Tenor" that the "perfect singing voice" can only live when it submits to "the trial and test of all," and *Norma* was thus a very familiar opera in Whitman's day because (as with *Hamlet* for classical actors) its title role offered the supreme challenge to artistic accomplishment. Familiarity breeding humor, if not contempt, *Norma* soon fell prey to the busy devisers of opera travesties. In addition to Mrs. *Normer* were such punny send-ups as *Herr Nanny* (*Ernani*), *The Roof Scrambler* (*Sonnambula*), *Fried Shots* (*Der Freischütz*), and *The Cat's in the Larder* (*La Gazza ladra*). *Norma* remains the supreme test today, though sopranos very rarely risk taking up "this terrifying score," as it was called by the eminent early twentieth-century Norma, Ester Mazzoleni, whose uncle, the tenor Francesco Mazzoleni, had been admired by Whitman.

But the poet would have had a special reason to be fascinated by this *Norma*. The profound interest of Alboni's priestess lies in the fact that the role was, in essence, her own personal, self-delighting, and risk-laden *Leaves of Grass*. Conversely, Whitman's 1855 edition was his Norma: a courageous, startling, unrepeatable quantum leap into a new vocal world.

Why was Alboni's Norma such a Whitmanesque adventure? Obviously, because it constituted a "trial and test of all," a tremendous risk of her powers of execution. Also because it embodies the will to astonish; "Do you take it I would astonish?" asks the self-singer in his grand equivalent to *Casta diva*. Also because—just as Whitman challenged the boundaries of sexuality and sex talk—Alboni wished to challenge the arbitrary boundary that separates sopranos from contraltos. "Yes, this queen of contraltos," wrote Richard Grant White, "not content with all the triumphs she had achieved, hankered after *Norma*, the part of all parts for which she was most unfitted both in voice and in person, and to which her style was not less suited." Alboni, in short, wanted *more*.

And—here is the ultimate Whitman touch—she wanted more in order to *pleasure herself*. We know this because White one day paid the contralto a visit in her Manhattan apartment and recorded this charming conversation:

Presently, nodding her handsome head to me, she said, *"Un segreto!"* and then drew back, and looked at me with an arch smile, like a child.

"*Per esser felice!*" I rejoined, luckily thinking of the Brindisi [aria in Donizetti's *Lucrezia Borgia*] which she sang so splendidly.*

"*Si, si!*" she merrily cried, clapping her fat hands. . . . Then, with mock gravity, she said: "*Quando io saro stata buon' ragazza per lungo tempo, voglio mi fare una presenta* [When I have been a good little girl for a long time I mean to make myself a present]," adding, in reply to my look of inquiry, "*La Norma. Lo cantero per piacere solo.* [Norma. I shall sing it only for pleasure.]"

"Why not sing it now?" I asked.

"Ah," she replied, "one must scream a little to sing Norma, and I do not yet know how to scream."

That last bit of wonderful vocal wisdom should remind us of Whitman's stage direction to himself: "Fiercely and with screaming energy." Coincidentally, White attended the second *Norma* and was particularly struck by how "fiercely impetuous" Alboni was in her scene with the children.

Alboni, obviously, did not delay this present to herself for very long. The fact that she had given her Manhattan public a taste of *Casta diva* in her fall recitals to spectacular praise may have encouraged her to think she had consummated her ability to scream. The *Tribune* could scarcely believe its ears: "The heart-throbs of tragedy mark every cadence of her voice, and her tones and modulations convey the idea of a deeper emotion, a more inward and real sentiment." "It is difficult to describe the flow of that exhilarating strain from her lips," chimed in the *Courier*, "seeming as it did to unite brilliance, majesty, and tenderness." The audience was left "in a tumult of delight and wonder." The scena was encored at the next recital before three thousand people, and the *Herald* opined that it sounded "as good as new, notwithstanding it has become almost as old as Old Hundred." Alboni's congregation was clearly primed for the entire role.

Nearly three months later, the gift to herself and Manhattan finally arrived. The *Albion* said that it was "the most overcrowded house we ever saw at the Broadway," with the audience, according to the *Herald*, "on the tip-toe of expectation," especially for the *Casta diva*. And it was able to report that Alboni "fully justified the expectation formed of her in the great *role* of the Druidess. Thunders of applause, and shouts of 'brava' resounded through the house in rapid succession, and the most intense enthusiasm prevailed. Her triumph was one of the greatest ever achieved by a vocalist in this city." The *Casta diva* she poured forth in "a voice fresh as a gushing spring, and sweet as the softest warbling of the lark when it soars to heaven's gate. There was a depth of feeling in her tone that touched every heart, and the fervor of her devotion which she expressed in the *andante* beautifully contrasted with the hope and joyous exuberance of the *allegro*." But the pièce de résistance proved to be (as it did in Whitman's cherished memory) the scene with the children, in which she evinced "all of the tenderness of the mother's heart." The *Herald* summarized, "The great characteristics of Alboni's Norma are majesty in the acting—tenderness, sweetness and tremendous power in the recitative and in the songs."

To White's amazement, he was also totally won over, though thirty years later he could more coolly grant that the triumph was achieved at some expense to Bellini: "To my surprise, she not only sang the music with passion and with fervor, but in her action showed intuitions of dramatic power which I had never before remarked in her. . . . It was a very great performance, regarded from a certain point of view; but Norma-ly it was open to objection. Much of the music was transposed; and, on the other hand, her figure was composed of such a connected system of globes and ellipses [gallant euphemism!] that it was impossible to accept her as the Grand Priestess of the Druids." But most in the audience, it appears, were of the *Albion*'s more generous view: "who could ever have imagined that Bellini's Norma, sung half a note lower than written, could produce a deeper and more heartfelt impression than it ever did in the original key?"

Pity the poor assisting artists, however, especially the hapless Adalgisa, a Madame Seidenburg. The *Albion* noticed Alboni's downward transpositions "brought the role rather too low for that lady's compass." And the *Herald* critic, having exhausted himself with superlatives, ended lamely: "We have said so much of the prima donna, that we have no room left to say anything of those who supported her; nor is it necessary, for Alboni 'is a host in herself.' "

Whitman desired precisely the same kind of triumph for the heroically idiosyncratic persona of *Leaves of Grass*, and nothing makes this more clear than the numerous images of the stage-dominating divo that he scattered through the "rave" reviews he wrote anonymously for the first edition:

> One of the roughs, large, proud, affectionate . . . his posture
> strong and erect, his voice bringing hope and prophecy.

> Self-reliant, with haughty eyes . . . steps Walt Whitman into
> literature.

He makes audacious and native use of his own body and soul.

The first glance out of his eyes electrifies him with love and
    delight.

Whitman put himself even more explicitly and emphatically in Alboni's
company when he wrote to Emerson in 1856, "Strangle the singers who
will not sing you loud and strong."

THE DIVO RETIRES

In the New York *Saturday Press* of 7 January 1860 appeared an unsigned
article, almost certainly by Whitman, titled "All About a Mocking-Bird."
In it we learn that "Walt Whitman's method in the construction of
his songs is strictly the method of the Italian Opera," and the "bold
American" reader is admonished, "in the ardor of youth, commit not
yourself, too irretrievably, that there is nothing in the Italian composers,
and nothing in the Mocking-Bird's chants. Pursue them awhile—
listen—yield yourself."

Two months later, Whitman left for his Boston printer with the
manuscript of the third edition of *Leaves of Grass* under his arm. Less
than a year after it appeared, the author attended a Friday evening performance of "positively the last night of the season" at the Academy of
Music. "By universal request," said the *Tribune* notice, Clara Louise Kellogg, the amazing debutante of the season, would "renew her triumph" in
the title role of *Linda di Chamounix*. It was to prove the most portentous
evening of Whitman's life.

The Secession War had begun that Friday morning. Next day the *Tribune* reported, "The Jeff Davis rebellion . . . commenced formal war upon
the United States by opening fire on Fort Sumter at 4 o'clock yesterday
morning." Whitman recalled, "News of the attack on fort Sumter and *the
flag* at Charleston harbor, S.C., was receiv'd in New York city late at
night (13th April, 1861) and was immediately sent out in extras of the
newspapers. I had been to the opera in Fourteenth street that night, and
after the performance was walking down Broadway toward twelve
o'clock, on my way to Brooklyn, when I heard in the distance the loud
cries of the newsboys."

The moment when—after the bravura and bravos inside the Academy
of Music—Whitman suddenly found himself among a crowd that "listen'd silently and attentively" to a telegram with the fearful news marks

the great Continental Divide in the poet's life. Opera was suddenly eclipsed for Whitman, just as it was for audiences and artists of the day. As Kellogg, the just-fledged star, observed, "The American people found the actual dramas of Bull Run, Big Bethel, and Harper's Ferry more absorbing . . . and the airs of *Yankee Doodle* and *The Girl I Left Behind Me* more inspiring than the finest operatic *arias* in the world." The effect on the city's operatic life Whitman captured in a poem written at the war's end: "O superb! O Manhattan, my own, my peerless! . . . How your soft opera-music changed, and the drum and fife were heard in their stead."

But the Civil War did not completely curtail Whitman's operagoing. In 1863 he wrote a long, charming letter to a young soldier in Washington describing a performance of *La Favorita* he had attended at the Academy of Music. He concludes, with approximate chronological accuracy: "Such singing and strong rich music always give me the greatest pleasure—and so the opera is the only amusement I have gone to, for my own satisfaction, for last ten years." And around 1870 Whitman took his boyfriend Peter Doyle to a performance of "Polyato" (i.e. Donizetti's *Poliuto*) during a week's visit to New York. We also have an 1872 letter sent from Brooklyn to Peter Doyle in Washington in which Whitman reports, "I have been to the Italian Opera twice, heard [Christine] Nilsson both times—she is *very fine*—One night *Trovatore* & one, *Robert* [*le Diable* by Meyerbeer], with Brignoli—both good." One hopes Brignoli's thespian skills had improved by then. Four years later, Whitman took his sixteen-year-old niece Mannahatta for the treat of hearing Brignoli sing his "superb" *Spirto gentil* in a *Favorita* at the Philadelphia Academy of Music.

Still, Whitman's earnest "singing years" were cut short, first by the Civil War and then by the paralytic stroke and move to New Jersey that occurred in 1873. Opera receded from his life to a drastic and melancholy degree. Though it became almost a critical cliché that his poetry was Wagnerian, Whitman seems never to have attended a Wagner performance. And his reaction to the analogy was mainly puzzlement: "So many of my friends say Wagner is *Leaves of Grass* done into music that I begin to suspect there must be something in it. . . . I was never wholly convinced—there was always a remaining question. I have got rather off the field.—the Wagner opera has had its vogue only in these later years since I got out of the way of going to the theater."*

This was to be Whitman's typical pose for his last decades—the elderly devotee whose eyes are focused in permanent retrospect. In an 1881 essay on contemporary American poetry, he made it clear his heart lay with the old-fashioned Alboni repertory: "The music of the present,

Wagner's, Gounod's, even the later Verdi's, all tends toward this free expression of poetic emotion, and demands a vocalism totally unlike that required for Rossini's splendid roulades, or Bellini's suave melodies." When Traubel attended a performance of Verdi's *Otello* in 1888, Whitman asked, "Is it our opera—the vocalism of the new sort? or is it still the old business lingering on?" Traubel wisely answered that it was both and said he had always thought Whitman liked "the old operas." "I do like them—at least I did," Whitman poignantly replied, "but their age is gone."

The trajectory of Whitman's opera experience follows very precisely the trajectory of any spectacular diva's career, just as it mimics his own career as a poet. First, there is the period when one takes in the world, when one *listens* and learns. "Alboni fills up the ear's craving," said the *Tribune* of her operatic debut, and there could have been no more craving an ear in her audience than Whitman's. Here, in these lines from the "grand opera" scene of "Song of Myself," we perhaps have the future poet sitting raptly in the third tier of the Broadway Theater as the imperturbable Alboni sings:

> Now I will do nothing but listen,
> To accrue what I hear into this song, to let sounds
>   contribute toward it.

Second comes the debut and a glorious prime, when one enters upon the stage "with strong music" and is able to sing it "loud and strong." Then, after a time, the first awareness of erosion and shaken self-confidence. "As I Ebb'd with the Ocean of Life," written at the end of Whitman's poetic prime, captures uncannily the effect of a diva losing her nerve: "baffled, balk'd," he becomes aware of the gossipy "blab whose echoes recoil upon me," of the "distant ironical laughter" in his audience at his expense, and of the world stinging him because he has "dared to open my mouth to sing at all." And finally comes the inevitable downward slope: the aging and growing recalcitrance of the voice, the increasing tendency to *imitate* rather that *be* one's artistic self, the (sometimes amusingly extended) farewell performances, and finally retirement.

Whitman beautifully caught the pathos of his own vocalist's ending in just two lines: "So I pass, a little time vocal, visible, contrary, / Afterward a melodious echo, passionately bent for . . ." It is always especially sad when a tremendously gifted singer proves cometlike and is vocal for only "a little time." (One thinks of the sadly brief primes of the sopranos Ljuba Welitsch, Anita Cerquetti, and Elena Suliotis, for example.*) Alboni's career, though it lasted a goodly fifteen years, still was accounted a career cut short when she married Count Pepoli and retired in 1863. The poet's prime was much shorter, more in the vein of Welitsch, who flourished (from about 1947 to 1952) at precisely the same time of life—mid to late thirties—as Whitman.

This prime lasted a mere five years. Whitman appears to have sensed, as he completed his poems for the third edition, that his vocalism was in jeopardy. The lines just quoted are from "So long!"—the perfectly apt poem he chose to conclude the 1860 edition. "I sing the endless finalés of things," he boasted, and over the last thirty years of his life he certainly became an expert in the performance of operatically extended farewells. Like the fat lady milking her fatal *aria di sortita*, he was "loth, O so loth to depart! / Garrulous to the very last."

Paul Zweig writes brilliantly of the supreme bravura aria of Whitman's vocal prime, "Song of Myself," as being no poem at all but "a reckless present tense; this is a voice becoming naked . . . a voice discovering itself to you and to itself."* "Reckless present tense" is an ideal phrase for capturing the power, pathos, and momentariness of heroic vocal utterance. It is "real" only at the moment when the mouth is orbically flexed and "pouring and filling" full the listener's craving ear. All that follows can be at best but a shadow of the dizzying, ecstatic present moment. As Whitman so finely phrased the notion in "Song," "It throbs me . . . I am exposed . . . my windpipe squeezed in the fakes of death."

Alboni lived long in such a shadow. Kellogg recounted the drollery of sharing the Albert Hall stage with the contralto, then past her prime, and telling her how honored she was to do so. "She bowed and smiled. She was a very, very large woman, heavily built, but she carried her size with remarkable dignity. I was considerably amused when she replied: 'Ah, Mademoiselle, I am only a shadow of what I have been!' " In his later years, Whitman often expressed this sentiment, and he often did so in terms of musical vocalism. In a splendid poem on aging, "A Hand-Mirror"—also new in the 1860 edition—he observes, "No more a flashing eye, no more a sonorous voice or springy step." "You, old throat! one cadenza for me—what I have been" and "O old throat! what have you been?" are manuscript lines that Whitman deleted from "So long!"

The hitherto electric voice is given to uttering a "muffled sonorous sound" in "Yonnondio" (1884). Several poems in *The First Annex: Sands at Seventy* (1888) almost caricature a retired divo. In "A Carol Closing Sixty-Nine" the caroler feels a "strange inertia," and in "Queries to My Seventieth Year" he is "Dull, parrot-like and old, with crack'd voice harping." In "My

Canary Bird," the devotee of the great Alboni solaces himself with the warble of his "caged bird ... Filling the air, the lonesome room, the long forenoon." In a poem published a year before his death, he seeks to "chant old age" but can do so only "in careless trill," producing not arias but mere "recitatives."

In fact, there are many "aural" and "operatic" ways to describe Whitman's long vocal decline. One can see it, for example, in the way Whitman transformed himself after 1860 from a soloistic partisan of the "sovereign person" (Democratic Individual) into a kind of one-man chorus offering fanfares for "representative man" (Democratic Nationality). His metier changed from that of opera's "chief histrion," the tutti-surfing tenor or soprano, to that of the stage basso, whose voice, Whitman wrote, typically shudders "lusciously under and through the universe." Assuming a prophet's and chorus-leader's mien, he became more the Zaccaria of Verdi's *Nabucco*, the booming hero of Rossini's *Mosè in Egitto* (a work performed at the Brooklyn Academy of Music the day after the war began), or the priestly comprimario Oroveso rather than the heroic priestess in *Norma*. He ceased to be the outrageous boundary-trespassing divo and modulated into the obligatory paterfamilias bass of many an opera's dramatis personae.

Whitman, in short, made good on his 1860 promise to "make poems, songs, thoughts, with reference to ensemble." In one of his typically bombastic later poems, in fact, he quite explicitly states that he has no suave solo melodies à la Bellini to sing, but merely some astral choral "whole" to celebrate:

> No special strains to sing, none for itself,
> But from the whole resulting, rising at last and floating,
>   A round full-orb'd eidólon.

This is a far cry from Whitman's exultant "The song is to the singer, and comes back most to him" of 1856.

Whitman also began to moderate himself in ways utterly unoperatic. He began, it would seem, to act upon the admonishment we find in one of his notebooks: "Avoid ... the whole of the *lurid* and *artistical* and *melodramatic* effects.—Preserve perfect calmness and sanity." A fine instance of Whitman's transit from his operatic emotions of the 1850s to the nostalgia-laced "sanity" of his last decades comes early, in an 1870 letter to Doyle describing a "beautiful quiet Sunday forenoon." He tells of listening for three hours to a young widow neighbor of his mother singing in her parlor: "she has a voice not powerful & ornamental as the opera

*Portrait by Alexis Pérignon of Marietta
Alboni in 1870, after her career ended,
holding a score of her former mentor Rossini
(one of her last public performances was at
his funeral in 1868). Courtesy of the Musée
Carnavalet, Paris.*

ladies, but with that something, pleasing & tender, that goes to the right spot—sings good old hymns & songs—I have enjoyed it greatly."

To achieve such calm sanity, Whitman, in the course of revising his poems, systematically toned down his use of three thoroughly operatic rhetorical devices that he had lavishly deployed to melodramatic effect. Many arias from the Whitman-Alboni repertory begin with an "O" and "Ah" (the rhetorical term for this is *ecphonesis*, from the Greek "to cry out"); the Whitman corpus is rich in them. But they were often pruned for later editions of *Leaves of Grass*. The same is true of that more obvious invitation to melodrama, the exclamation point. With the 1860 edition, Whitman also began to suppress the silence-demanding, musically effective ellipses in his poems.

The result of all these changes, of course, was to make his poems look on the page less and less like the opera librettos he had so carefully read in his "singing years." And paradoxically, his poetry became more and more susceptible to criticism in the same terms commonly deployed to satirize opera. Robert Louis Stevenson's thumbnail sketch of Whitman's poetic style, for instance—"a most surprising compound of plain grandeur, sentimental affectation, and downright nonsense"—could also describe *Il Trovatore* or *La Favorita*.

In Whitman's very rhythm, too, one can sense a distancing from the opera world in the later years. It becomes harder to get his "final lilt" because the lively waltzes, boleros, and dotted rhythms of the bel canto repertory seem to have been swamped either by the "sobbing dirge of Nature" or the Civil War's "dirge, the voices of men and women wreck'd." "I love well the martial dirge," Whitman wrote in 1865, and perhaps his finest Civil War poem is the "Dirge for Two Veterans" (set

finely to music by Kurt Weill). Indeed, in notes for an opera scribbled in
the late 1860s, war is the theme and the dirge predominant:

> in Hospital.—
> —? some typical appropriate
> ?*tune*, or ?hymn or ?something
>> played by the band (?some dirge or ?opera passage or ?march)
>>> *Calling up the whole*
>>> *dead of the war*
>> The march in last act of *La Gazza Ladra*

Whitman ends his jotting with the call for "a strong *triumphal* instrumental & vocal *chorus*." We are obviously no longer in the opera house
but in the concert hall, listening to something like the end of Beetho-
ven's Ninth. Indeed, the most characteristic music-poem of Whitman's last thirty years, "The Mystic Trumpeter" (1872), is but another,
and decidedly more bathetic, version of Schiller's "Ode to Joy." Its
ending:

> The ocean fill'd with joy—the atmosphere all joy!
> Joy! joy! in freedom, worship, love! joy in the ecstasy of life!
> Enough to merely be! enough to breathe!
> Joy! joy! all over joy!

But it was not, apparently, enough to *sing*. His current "halcyon days," as
he wrote in the 1888 poem of that name, were the "quietest" of all.

Put another way, Whitman's rhythmic sense became increasingly
minimalist with the passing years. The taste for Rossini, Bellini, and
Donizetti slowly transformed, one might say, into a taste for the hyp-
notic, repetitive music of the New Age (Philip Glass, say) and of Nature.
This is strikingly apparent in the recollection of a summer night in 1876
in which the "reedy monotones" of katydids are apostrophized:

> . . . a long, chromatic, tremulous crescendo, like a brass disk whirl-
> ing round and round, emitting wave after wave of notes, beginning
> with a certain moderate beat or measure, rapidly increasing in
> speed and emphasis, reaching a point of great energy and signifi-
> cance, and then quickly and gracefully dropping down and out. Not
> the melody of the singing-bird—far from it; the common musician
> might think without melody, but surely having to the finer ear a
> harmony of its own; monotonous—but what a swing there is in the

brassy drone, round and round, cymballine—or like the whirling of brass quoits.

A more eloquent evocation of New Age music could hardly be wished, and Whitman clearly contrasts the insects' "piquant utterances" with Italian opera's melodious, mocking-bird song. This was the musical style for a poet becoming attuned to "Labial gossip of night, sibilant chorals," to "Whispers of heavenly death," and to the "deep musical drone of . . . some bumble-bee symphony."

Whitman also became, in his later years, a poet far more attuned to, and eager to express, the visual at the expense of the aural. In "A Broadway Pageant" (1860), a watershed poem in which Whitman turns away from his former marauding, roughneck life to entertain his vocation as America's Bard, occurs the telling phrase, "See my cantabile!" Whitman became like the "superior landscape painter, some fine colorist" he mentions in *Specimen Days*, fussily attending to "strange effects in light and shade" and "delicate color-effects." The connoisseur of opera pretty much vanished, except as a listener after "the flageolet-note of a quail" or the wood-thrush's "sweet, artless, voluntary, simple anthem," or the meadowlark's "liquid-simple notes, repeated at intervals, full of careless happiness and hope."

On a serene spring night in 1880, after dinner with friends, Whitman heard a voice from the church across the street singing a Lutheran hymn, a contralto voice. His description of the effect is lovely, but it is the description of a painter, not the opera lover who once had heard the great Alboni. "The air was borne by a rich contralto. For nearly half an hour there in the dark . . . came the music, firm and unhurried, with long pauses. The full silver star-beams of Lyra rose silently over the church's dim roof-ridge. Vari-color'd lights from the stain'd glass windows broke through the tree-shadows. And under all—under the Northern Crown up there, and in the fresh breeze below, and the *chiaroscuro* of the night, that liquid-full contralto."

FINALE OF THINGS

Some reminders of how opera relaxed its love-grip on Whitman are startling. Consider, for example, the "recitative" he published in 1876 in praise of a "Fierce-throated beauty" who rejects, as he himself did, all the "sweetness debonair of tearful harp or glib piano" of paltry parlor music (he made fun of those who called a "pianner player" a "pee-a-nist").

Another stalwart "trained soprano" such as Whitman exalted in "Song of Myself," one might guess. But no: the poem is a paean "To a Locomotive in Winter."

Or there is the experience of reading "Thou Mother with Thy Equal Brood" (1872), a very good example of bad late Whitman, at once earth-treading and bombastic. It's also another damned "recitative." One plows through its feast of abstraction about Democracy, the Modern, Time, and Union and then comes to the lines:

> Emblem of general maternity lifted above all,
> Sacred shape of the bearer of daughters and sons,
> Out of thy teeming womb thy giant babes in ceaseless
>   procession issuing . . .

The memory of the poet's "singing years" here is jolting. How much more exciting than this "federal mother," one cannot help feeling, is that operatic mother Norma in "Proud Music of the Storm," with lurid passion in her face and a dagger in her hand. And how much more thrilling and evocative of Whitman's finest poetry the "teeming lady" he once saw on the stage of the Broadway Theater. In 1870 Bret Harte, then editing the *Overland Monthly* in San Francisco, rejected Whitman's garrulous "Passage to India" with a similar complaint. "I fear," he said, the poem "is too long and too abstract for the hasty and the material minded readers of O.M." In the summer of 1888, Whitman told Traubel, "I am no longer a theatre-goer—perhaps I have lost the theatrical perspective—I have not seen plays for a long time." That remark applies to both the legitimate and the lyric theater, and it seems obvious that the loss of the poet's "theatrical perspective" contributed to the declining quality of his later poems.

The disconcerting irruptions of theater memories in the later poetry are salutary. For they serve to remind us that—notwithstanding the very title and out-of-doors ambiance of *Leaves of Grass* (we first glimpse the poet at his ease "observing a spear of summer grass")—the work is a *theater* piece. The "site" of its earliest editions is as much that of the parquet, proscenium, and gaslit theater lobbies of Broadway and the Bowery as it is of the beaches of "fish-shape Paumanok" or Mannahatta's "populous pavements."

Whitman, we have seen, several times acknowledged in print and conversation the influence of opera, but the most touching and private acknowledgment he left behind occurs in a short note he probably jotted between 1853 and 1855, that is, during the short time that passed after

Marietta Alboni sailed away and *Leaves of Grass* appeared. This jotting divulges the book's raison d'être, which is to celebrate the gust of pleasure one feels at escaping from the parlor, from indoors and propriety, and respiring freely in the open air. ("Outdoors is the best antiseptic ever" is among his *Leaves of Grass* notes.) But breathing deeply, these lines suggest, Whitman learned not only on the beaches and in the salt-marshes of Long Island but also indoors, at the opera house:

> Poem—illustrating (*Good moments*)
> soul in high glee all out (exquisite state of feeling of happiness—
> some moments at the opera—in the woods)*

2

WALT & BOSS-TOOTH:
"SINGING THE PHALLUS"

Yet still sex, sex: the root of roots: the life below the life!
—Walt Whitman

He was compelled to act,—to do the thing instead of saying it.

—John Burroughs

ALT WHITMAN IS, in the literal sense of the word, the most touching of all American poets. He is the supreme celebrator of close physical proximity and the thrill of sexual arousal that may attend it: the "touch of face to face," the "long sustained kiss upon the mouth or bosom," the "shuddering longing ache of contact," and the embrace so ardent and muscular that "you cannot unloose me." He was the poet of "bellies press'd and glued together" with sweat or semen and of the convulsive "love-grip" of the "Thruster holding me tight and that I hold tight!" "Push close my lovers" was his motto.

Often, but most strikingly in "Song of Myself," Whitman made thrilling and momentous the simple extension of the hand and fingers to touch the body of another, as Michelangelo did with God's hand extended to Adam's in the Sistine Chapel:

> I merely stir, press, feel with my fingers, and am happy,
> To touch my person to some one else's is about as much as I can
>   stand.
>
> Is this then a touch? quivering me to a new identity,
> Flames and ether making a rush for my veins . . .

Many of Whitman's most splendid poems describe such tremulous attainment of new spiritual and sexual identity, through the simple but tan-

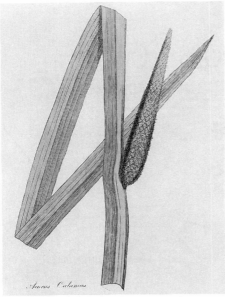

Acorus Calamus

A leaf and spadix of the calamus plant, from William Woodville's Medical Botany *of 1832. Woodville observed that this species "usually grows in stagnant waters, and the sides of rivers, producing its flowers in May and June" and is "the only true aromatic plant indigenous to northern climates." It was also called* Calamus aromaticus *or* odoratus, *sea-sedge, myrtle sedge, and sweet sedge. Thoreau knew it as sweet flag or critchicrotches and noted its aroma: "How agreeable and surprising the peculiar fragrance of the sweet flag when it is bruised." William Salmon, in his* Botanologia *of 1710, reported that the spirit derived from Calamus made "a Noble and Generous Cordial, chears the Heart, revives the Spirits, and strengthens Universal Nature." He also recommended it as a cataplasm—applied "to the Testicles, it wonderfully abates their Swelling." Whitman saw a stand of the plant on a Delaware River excursion late in life and rhapsodized, "Leaves of Grass! The largest leaves of grass known! Calamus! Yes, that is calamus! Profuse, rich, noble, upright, emotional!"*

talizing act of touching. Indeed, the poet intended his poetry to be ratified by the tactile handling of that most physically intimate edition (the third) of *Leaves of Grass*, his surrogate body: "this is no book, / Who touches this touches a man." In the most elaborate self-sketch Whitman ever produced of himself in his prime, the "Broad-Axe Poem" of 1856, he calls himself a "Persuader always of people to give him their sweetest touch."

The most common gesture of public physical intimacy in Whitman involves a "reaching around of arms." In "Song of Myself," the poet offers to show his readers the sights, for instance, with "My left hand hooking you round the waist" and envisions a rural jaunt with his "right and left arms round the sides of two friends, and I in the middle." Several instances of such casual embrace occur in the second edition of *Leaves of Grass*. Whitman boasts in "Crossing Brooklyn Ferry" of the young men who call him by his "nighest name" and of the pleasure he feels at the touch of "their arms on my neck." He calls himself, in the "Broad-Axe Poem," a "Passer of his right arm round the shoulders of his friends." He is happy to observe, in "Salut au Monde," groups of "old men going slowly with their arms about each other's necks." In the city, too, this casual physicality is apropos, as he asserted in the 1860 edition. In *Calamus #10*, the poet asks future biographers to remember him as one who often "saunter'd the streets, curv'd with his arm the shoulder of his friend, while the arm of his friend rested upon him also." And all his experiences as a male nurse are finely captured in the two lines that end one of his most powerful Civil War poems, "The Wound-Dresser": "Many a soldier's loving arms about this neck have cross'd and rested, / Many a soldier's kiss dwells on these bearded lips."

But many embraces in *Leaves of Grass* are more fraught with sexual and political insinuation. Among the "beautiful" sleepers lying together unclothed in the dream vision of "The Sleepers" is the friend who is "inarmed by friend." Following attentively the embraces in Whitman, we soon and almost imperceptibly glide into forbidden territory. The erotic temperature rises, as mundane physical gestures become sexually italicized. In *Calamus #32*, for example, the poet offers a vivid snapshot of "two simple men" performing the "parting of dear friends" on a pier: "The one to remain hung on the other's neck and passionately kiss'd him, / While the one to depart tightly pressed the one to remain in his arms." At the poem's beginning, Whitman challenges the reader to wonder why he would record this moment amid all "the vaunted glory and growth of the great city spread around me." Given the context of the *Calamus* sequence in which the poem appears, the answer, though not vouchsafed by the author, is clear: Unlike the other casual bystanders on the pier who witness this (seemingly) innocuous moment of sweet sorrow, his own sexual instincts are thrilled at observing "passional relations" publicly and licitly displayed.

Whitman's implication in "What Think You"—that men should be able to embrace unabashedly in this way on less momentous occasions—becomes a plank in his urban political platform elsewhere in *Calamus*. Perhaps only those who have spent time in the few neighborhoods in America where men can walk casually down the street arm in arm without fear—Chelsea in New York, West Hollywood in Los Angeles, the Castro in San Francisco—would now be likely to read as Whitman intended it the phrase "Arm'd and fearless" that describes the "two boys together clinging" in *Calamus #26*. The image has less to do with guns (Whitman's brother said he "would have nothing to do with" guns), than with the fearlessness one feels inarmed by a true friend and lover. *Calamus #26* is a poem of empowerment, and the embrace is crucial to its effect. The "two boys" find themselves

> Power enjoying, elbows stretching, fingers clutching,
> Arm'd and fearless, eating, drinking, sleeping, loving,
> No laws less than ourselves owning . . .*

Calamus #5, which Whitman broke asunder and scattered to muted effect in later editions of *Leaves of Grass*, is another of his empowerment poems. It boldly announced that "Those who love each other shall be invincible" and reached its climax with the image of arms about the neck:

> I will plant companionship thick as trees along all the rivers of
>   America, and along the shores of the great lakes, and all over
>   the prairies,
> I will make inseparable cities, with their arms about each other's
>   necks.

One can see why these lines would so appeal to the later, more asexual and stentorianly "Democratic" Whitman, who cannibalized them for a poem blandly called "For You O Democracy." But when he first wrote them he had something more personal, potent, and sex-charged in mind. One can see this in *Calamus* #4, where the image of arms about the neck occurs in an explicitly erotic context. The poet finds himself alone and wandering by a luxuriant pondside in spring and is visited by the memory of a "troop" of former lovers:

> Some walk by my side, and some behind, and some embrace my
>   arms or neck,
> They, the spirits of friends, [here in his ms. Whitman included
>   "lovers, comrades"] dead or alive—thicker they come, a great
>   crowd, and I in the middle . . .

Whitman's self-censorship, as always, is fascinating. For it reveals him stepping back from the erotic implications of his image, in this case the image of arms hanging around the neck of another.

The image, like all body language, is subject to interpretation. It can be "read" innocently as an un-electric gesture of homosocial bonhomie, just as one reads the familiar pictures of exultant athletes hugging each other in victorious deshabille in the sports sections of newspapers. Or it can be read with more sexual point. Whitman asserted as much when he boasted of himself in "Spontaneous Me" (1856) as the author of "lusty, lurking, masculine poems" and of this poem as a projection of the "hankering" phallic real Me between his legs: "This poem drooping shy and unseen that I always carry, and that all men carry." And his poetry, like his own "phallic thumb of love," is certainly subject to "spontaneous" arousal when the right "Love-thoughts" are evoked, when a tantalizing "love-odor" caresses his nostrils, or when he encounters in the darkness a sought-after "love-yielding." When this occurs, the "arm'd and fearless" sidewalk saunter of two men becomes a hint of what can happen, as he says in "Spontaneous Me," in "the privacy of the night," when arms hang upon the neck to more earnest purpose.

Whitman preceded his boast about lusty masculine poems with perhaps the most daringly erotic metaphor of his entire career, a metaphor that implicates all the arms-around-the-neck imagery in his poems. In his flamboyant preface for the first edition, he asserted that the "greatest poet" (like himself) will attract his country "body and soul" to him and will "hang on its neck with incomparable love and plunge his semitic muscle into its merits and demerits." In the 1856 edition, in his "Poem of Many in One," he repeated these words almost verbatim (only in the 1871 edition did Whitman correct "semitic" to "seminal"). This is pure Whitman of the sex-drenched first three editions of Leaves of Grass: graphic, rough, over-the-top, but also—in the phrases of that other garrulous and cunning mystifier, Hamlet—full of "antic disposition" and "ambiguous giving out." The effrontery of likening cultural interrogation to phallic penetration is captivating but does not entirely obscure the really important, if lubricious, question: where is that metaphorical muscle plunging?

Is it plunging, missionary-style, into the vagina of a woman lying absolutely still, as Sylvester Graham exhorted nineteenth-century women to do in order to conserve the man's "vital fluid"? (He also invented the Graham cracker.) Is it plunging intercrurally with a man, or merely moving rhythmically up and down with convulsive throb on his belly? The seminal muscle plunges into "merits and demerits." Are these merely the two buttocks (of woman or man), or could versatility be the point—and a reference, therefore, to different orifices? Is the poet thus referring to the plunge of oral and vaginal, or even anal, intercourse with a woman—or to the plunge of the phallus into the anus and the sucking mouth of another man, as seems to happen when the "truant" lover "laps" the phallic "ear of rose-corn, milky and just ripened" in the dream-time of Whitman's erotic nocturne "The Sleepers" in its 1855 version: "The white teeth stay, and the boss-tooth advances in darkness, / And liquor is spilled on lips and bosoms"? In any event, arms hanging upon the neck of one's partner would facilitate many of these forms of sexual intercourse.

Whitman, of course, does not answer our question. As so often, he hits with his sexual image and runs, leaving the predilections of the reader to guide speculation about the sexuality and Kamasutra involved. He treats us rather as Iago, another cunning mystifier and one with Whitman's taste for sexual explicitness, treats Othello: he gives us just enough sexual hints to be "probal to thinking," then allows us to draw our own conclusions. Like Iago, he is full of erotic "imputations and strong circumstances" that lead "directly to the door of truth," but he deftly leaves us to open the door ourselves. And nothing seems to have given the self-described "furtive old hen" more pleasure than to cluck derisively through his beard at his critics and would-be explainers, "Wrong door!" He was also manifestly capable of harrumphing "Wrong door!" even when a particularly attentive reader—John Addington Symonds, for example—opened the right door and made bold to confront him.

For nearly twenty years Symonds, in his letters from England, egged Whitman on to say the obvious about *Calamus*, namely, that it was about (as Whitman himself put it) "the passional relations of men with men." It is amusing to watch the poet rankle under the interrogation. In 1888, for instance, he says of a letter written sixteen years before, "it drives me hard—almost compels me—it is urgent, persistent: he sort of stands in the road and says: 'I won't move till you answer my question.' " A month later another Symonds letter, this one from thirteen years before, is read out loud by Traubel, and Whitman fusses yet again: "he harps on the *Calamus* poems again. . . . I don't see why it should but his recurrence to that subject irritates me a little. . . . I suppose you might say—why don't you shut him up by answering him? There is no logical answer to that. . . . I suppose the whole thing will end in an answer some day. It always makes me a little testy to be catechized about the *Leaves*—I prefer to have the book answer for itself." And Whitman adds, "for thirty years my enemies and friends have been asking me questions about the *Leaves:* I'm tired of not answering questions. . . . Anyway, I love Symonds. Who could fail to love a man who could write such a letter? I suppose he will yet have to be answered, damn 'im!" Symonds's third degree, of course, would climax two years later, in 1890, with the most hilarious lie of Whitman's career, the one about fathering six children.

And so it is, too, with the question about the plunging seminal muscle. Whitman leaves us on our own. Pondering what he, in his libidinous heart of hearts, had in view when he ventured his carnal metaphor in 1855 is intriguing enough, but the far more provocative and entrancing question this image invites us to ask—the question the following pages will entertain—is the quite simple, shameless question: where was Whitman inclined to plunge his own seminal muscle?

THUMB OF LOVE—UPRIGHT, EMOTIONAL

His sheer sex-happiness—his utterly unmystic erotic deliria—invites the question. Ridiculing all the polite drawing-room "blurt . . . about virtue and about vice," Whitman insisted not merely on the deliciousness of sex but the deliciousness of talking about it. As John Burroughs observed early on, he "applied to the morbid sex-consciousness" of his day "the heroic treatment; he has fairly turned it naked into the street." How Whitman would have enjoyed the pose of heroic nudity of Rodin's *Balzac,* which infuriated the army of Philistia in turn-of-the-century France in just the way *Leaves* did midcentury America. He often strikes that defiant, shameless, sturdy pose in his early editions.

The heroic treatment, as Burroughs adds, meant not mere airy euphemism, either, but riveted attention to sexual *acts*: "being an artist, a creator, and not a mere thinker or preacher, he was compelled to act,—to do the thing instead of saying it." When Whitman announces that he will "effuse egotism and show it underlying all," his very first order of business is naturally to attend to "sexual organs and acts!" And when he demands freedom for the "most copious and close companionship of men" in *Calamus #25,* he insists that the "blades" of this companionship must grow in the form of "words, acts, beings." The poem leaves no doubt that the "acts" he has in mind are sexual. That "copious," of course, is typically sly diction that carries a hint of seminal discharge, and the men he lauds are possessed of "sweet and lusty flesh" and are "choice and chary of its love-power." (Whitman, ever more chary of his reputation after the Civil War, deleted this last phrase from all post-1860 editions.) A nineteen-year-old Thomas Mann wrote to his closest confidant, referring to the genitalia: "you don't need to despise your lower regions so entirely . . . the lower regions contain a huge amount of poetry—one only has to develop it beautifully into feelings and mood." This, in few words, is the fundamental view of the author of the first editions of *Leaves of Grass.*

Whitman's impatience with mere verbal foreplay is amusingly apparent in the notes he made on reading the *Phaedrus.* He clearly wanted to identify himself with Plato, recording several obvious parallels: Plato got his name "from his broad breast & shoulders—Plato = platitude, broad"; "was a poet & traveler"; "had a school, in Athens, & was a teacher"; "never married." But he had little patience with the close reasoning of the dialogue style. The passages in which Socrates takes his defense of platonic love "into higher and purer regions" annoyed him: "There is . . . too much of mere verbal point & distinction—it is often quite a nuisance, being carried on tediously and interminably." However, his interest perked up considerably at the passages where the "youth of exceeding beauty" who "had very many lovers" and the manner in which he disposed of his "favors" were discussed. Indeed, Whitman remarks that these passages are "quite rhythmic, even in translation."

He especially liked it when the rhythm became sexual: the close-contact-in-the-gymnasium, lying-down-together, and kissing-and-fondling parts. Whitman marked out "as very significant" the sections of the Henry Cary translation he was reading in which two male lovers "are laid down together" and one is "unable to refuse, as far as in his power, to gratify his lover in whatever he requires." Apparently, this couple does not go all the way. Another, more daring couple adopts "a coarser and less philosophic mode of living"; they meet and are soon found to have "made and consummated that choice which most men deem blissful." Of such an image of *al fresco* intercourse Whitman would make much in *Leaves of Grass*.

Lysis, another Platonic dialogue, also caught Whitman's fancy. Here, he summarized, "Lysis is a beautiful youth whom [Hippothales] loves & pines for." Perhaps he identified with Hippothales, who is given to composing extravagant poems and songs on his darling. The *Calamus* sequence was written in the young man's ebullient, demonstrative spirit. Certainly Whitman identified with Socrates, who boasts that he has received from heaven the gift for detecting "at a glance both a lover and a beloved." Whitman also transcribed in his notes a paragraph in which Socrates confesses that he has "a fond desire for the possession of friends . . . so fond am I of intimate friends." The subject of *Lysis* is "the course of conduct or conversation that a lover ought to adopt in order to render himself agreeable to the object of his affection." The purpose of this courtship is thus by no means idle; it is to *possess* the intimate friend—to charm one's beloved into bed and achieve sexual possession. With Whitman, there was no possession of genuine consequence without sex: "sex, sex: always immanent," he admonished Horace Traubel, "here with us discredited—not suffered: rejected from our art: yet still sex, sex: the roots of roots."

Whitman's signature poem shows this time and again. Notwithstanding its title, "Song of Myself" is most emphatically a poem of two bodies—"Long I was hugg'd close—long and long"—and of sexual possession. Like the two lovers in the *Phaedrus*, whose consummation is achieved without an actual description, one suddenly finds oneself, when reading Section 40, to have been in bed at night with Whitman . . . and possessed. Again, arms and neck come into play: "here is my neck . . . hang ["press," more daringly, in an earlier ms.] your whole weight upon me." And suddenly the *fait* is *accompli:*

> I have embraced you, and henceforth possess you to myself,
> And when you rise in the morning you will find what I tell you is so.

No wonder a reading of "Song of Myself" can leave one with an ener-vated "morning after" feeling—not necessarily disagreeable—of having been subjected to a long bout of athletic lovemaking with a "top" man. A thruster has held one tight. No wonder, either, that when Bronson Alcott visited Whitman in 1856 he noticed three pictures pasted on the rude walls of his bedroom: a Hercules, a Bacchus, and a satyr.

Sexual possession is achieved by the phallus, so the iconography on Whitman's bedroom wall was absolutely perfect and thoroughly re-vealing. He is, after all, probably the most gaily, muscularly, and relent-lessly phallic writer in the annals of literature and was eager to present himself as a "manly" and "robust" explosion of virility (now we might say "butch" or "macho"). Indeed, Alcott had met Whitman a month before glimpsing his bedroom wall and recorded a quite prescient thumbnail sketch of the poet: "Broad-shouldered, rouge-fleshed, Bacchus-browed, bearded like a satyr, and rank."

When one begins to dwell on the phallic presence in the early edi-tions of *Leaves of Grass*, "rank" seems truly the *mot juste*. The urge toward tumescence, the imagery of arousal, the thrilling sensation of vessels dilating with blood are ubiquitous in his poems. As Whitman explained to a Dutch admirer with very well chosen verbs, "My verse strains its every nerve to arouse, brace, dilate, excite." Whitman's well-known vaunt that he would "chant the chant of dilation or pride," in fact, carries a delectably apropos (if perhaps unintended) sexual pun, for not only can "dilation" refer to the expansion of a bodily organ, but among the mean-ings of "pride" is lust and the heat of animals receptive to sexual activity ("as salt as wolves in pride," says Iago, to imply lecherousness).

"Something I cannot see," says Whitman in "Song of Myself," "puts upward libidinous prongs." That invisible something, of course, can be intensely *felt*: it is the pent-up aching pressure of sexual energy eager for release. Many of the most exciting moments in Whitman's poetry are attended by the rising of such libidinous prongs, as when the "limpid liquid" within the young man of "Spontaneous Me" strains toward ejaculation: "The vex'd corrosion so pensive and so painful, / The torment, the irritable tide that will not be at rest."

One becomes accustomed to reading Whitman's early poems just as the poet "reads" the "ample and spheric earth" in *Calamus #36*:

> I now suspect there is something fierce in you, eligible to burst
> forth;
> For an athlete is enamoured of me—and I of him,
> But toward him there is something fierce and terrible in me,
> eligible to burst forth,
> I dare not tell it in words—not even in these songs.

But Whitman *is* telling us in words (though words he was confident only sexual cognoscenti would fully grasp) what is eligible to burst forth and always threatening to do so: the phallus. And it does burst forth in a variety of colorful phrases in his poems: thumb of love, man-root, love-root, *Calamus* root, slow rude muscle, firm masculine colter ("colter" being the sharp blade attached to the beam of a plow), sharp-toothed touch, tooth-prong, manly maple tooth. The violence and sheer over-mastering strength of sex are not easy to ignore in Whitman's phrasing. This generates much of the excitement of Whitman's early erotic poems, especially at the characteristic moments when these "lurking" poems cease their shy, flaccid "drooping." Louis Simpson has ventured that Whitman's "most ecstatic passages are descriptions of sexual intercourse or frottation," but Whitman long ago anticipated this aperçu in his remark to Traubel that there was "a close connection—a very close con-nection—between the state we call religious ecstasy and the desire to copulate."

In *Calamus #25* Whitman praised the "never-quelled audacity" of men who go with "their own gait, erect," and it is tempting to free-associate just a little and think of how the erect phallus presides over *Leaves of Grass*. His research for the volume encourages one to do so, for in his daybook he recorded this about "Phallic festivals": "Wild mirthful processions in honor of the god Dionysus (Bacchus) in Athens, and in other parts of Greece—unbounded licenses—mocking jibes and irony." This note becomes his reference, in "Song of Myself," to "Dancing yet through the streets in a phallic procession." Also among his manuscript jottings is this strange unisex vaunting of the phallus: "see here the phallic choice of America, a full-sized man or woman—a natural, well-trained man or woman / (The phallic choice of America leaves the finesse of cities . . .)." This notion Whitman would eventually transform into his "singing the phallus" and "the muscular urge" in *Enfans d'Adam #2* of 1860.

Those lines about the phallic choice of America did not get into *Leaves of Grass*, but then they were scarcely needed, so obvious is it that Whitman was making the phallic choice on America's behalf. Everywhere, there is arousal and dilation as he pursues his agenda of encouraging "the genital impulse of These States." In *Enfans d'Adam #12* (1860) the satyric vagabond ("Lusty, phallic, with the potent original loins") boasts of bathing his Adamic songs in sex. In *Chants Democratic #4* (1860) he gives the American Soul two "equal hemispheres"; one (Love) is spiritual, the other (Dilation or Pride) physical. In "Song of the Banner at Daybreak" of 1865, just before Whitman began systematically to neuter his utterances, tumescence on the subject was still possible: "My limbs, my veins dilate, my theme is clear." But one must now look harder, and more fancifully, for the hints of arousal. By the time of "Gods" (1871), Whitman was well on his way to withdrawing from the phallus and the sexual arena to the "higher and purer regions" of Platonic forms. He began to delete his genital impulses—even cut the line about the "genital impulse of These States" from all post-1860 editions. There is no new talk about "love-flesh tremulous aching" or "mad-sweet drops" of semen or the arched, thrusting torso with its "pendant" phallus or the "sensitive, orbic, underlapp'd brothers" that hang below it. The "perfect Comrade" becomes bodiless and "divine." Whitman's "dilation" is bloodless now. The lover is "Complete in body and dilate in spirit," but we are obliged to take it on faith that a dilated phallus completes this body.

Whitman's phallic thrill never vanished entirely, though to observe it in action it becomes increasingly necessary to accost him in private and listen with well-cocked ear. One late afternoon during his last summer, for example, he made a three-mile excursion with the newly married Traubels and his nurse Warrie Fritzinger to Pea Shore on the Delaware River. Along the way, Whitman caught sight of a stand of that marsh grass with the phallus-shaped flower that, more than thirty years before, he had made the focal device on his poetical coat of arms. In a wonderful outburst, recorded by Horace Traubel, Walt's thrusting "spirit of 1860" revived momentarily: "Leaves of Grass! The largest leaves of grass known! Calamus! Yes, that is calamus! Profuse, rich, noble, upright, emotional!"*

It is very tempting, too, to revel in the further delightful unintended (or were they intended?) sexual double entendres of Walt's advice, offered virtually from his deathbed several months later, to an idolatrous visiting Englishman who wished to gather some *Calamus aromaticus* as a souvenir. Here is Walt's advice on cruising for calamus: "you must be careful how you look it up. There's a counterfeit calamus, which is only a rush—has no root. But calamus itself, the real thing, has a thick bulby root—stretches out—this way—like the fingers spread . . . You can easily get it—pulls up. Oh! yes! You will know it by the root, which is really the *only* way to know it." Dare one venture that it is only by pulling with fingers spread for the thick man-root that we can encounter the "real thing"—the poet who wrote *Leaves of Grass*?

Whitman had great fun, earlier in life, while his phallic choice lasted, while "hot wishes" were still eligible to burst forth . . . and while he still felt the urge to describe them in his poetry. Whitman had a reputation for laziness and loafing, which he did much to encourage: "I loafe and invite my soul" is his memorable opening for "Song of Myself." But omphaloskepsis was not his quintessential pose. His gaze was drawn further down; phalloskepsis was his most earnest pastime:

> To speak! to walk! to seize something by the hand!
> To prepare for sleep, for bed—to look on my rose-colored flesh,
> To be conscious of my body, so amorous, so large . . .

How delighted, in his sexual heyday at least, Whitman would have been with Allen Ginsberg's admiring phallicism: "his mind was so expansive that it was completely penetrant." Who touches *Leaves of Grass*, that is, touches a very large, upright, and emotional tool—a witty notion that gives an apt, if whimsical, spin to some of Whitman's most famous lines: "I am large, I contain multitudes" is worthy of a heroic seminal muscle; "It is time to explain myself—let us stand up" allows the poet to advance, like the bull, "to do his masculine work." And "Dash me with amorous wet, I can repay you" is yet another reminder that "Song of Myself" is finally a poem of two bodies.

Like so much of the sexual imagery in Whitman, this picture of two bodies with potent original loins and phalluses reared for ejaculation brings us back to the question: where did Whitman himself plunge his seminal muscle?

READING WHITMAN'S SEX

Shortly before publishing the 1860 edition, Whitman confided to a notebook, "I write with reference to being far better understood then [in "future ages"] than I can possibly be now." His principal reason for thinking this depressing thought, no doubt, was the radically heterodox sexuality in which his forthcoming *Leaves of Grass* was bathed. If buoyant naiveté or reckless optimism had encouraged him to fantasize that the many-pronged libidinousness of his earlier editions would wash in mid-century America, he was obviously disabused of this illusion in short order. Thirty years later Whitman recalled for Traubel the rancorous reception and its chief cause: the sex. Or, as a critic in the New York *Herald* would put it, Whitman's "disgusting Priapism." Sex, the poet said, "was the thing in my work which has been most misunderstood—that has excited the roundest opposition, the sharpest venom, the unintermitted slander, of the people who regard themselves as the custodians of the morals of the world. Horace, you are too young to know the fierceness, the bitterness, the vile quality, of this antagonism. . . . You have only heard the echoes of that uproar."

The "uproar" has been continuous since 1855, though decibel levels have varied to some extent from generation to generation. And what is astonishing about the uproar is the extraordinary spectrum of responses the sex in Whitman has evoked from the very beginning. Some readers, like Emerson, take the high road ("I give you joy of your free and brave thoughts"); others, like Thoreau, the low one ("It is as if the beasts spoke"). Willa Cather was perhaps the first to actually call him "that dirty old man," but Jorge Luis Borges, on the other hand, professed that he found "a great chastity, a great purity" in him. And the spectrum has been just as wildly various when the autobiographical implications of Whitman's sexual matter are addressed, as he urged us to do in *Leaves of Grass* and in all his talk about the proud primacy of sex in life (his own and his reader's). "I cannot too often reiterate," he wrote in 1888, that his magnum opus "has mainly been the outcropping of my own emotional and other personal nature." "Other personal" is, of course, a typical late-Whitman finesse for "sexual."

But there are many ways to think about the "outcroppings" of personal emotions in Whitman's poetry. As it happens, the full spectrum of response to them was neatly expressed by W. H. Trimble in one of the earliest Whitman studies, his *Walt Whitman and* Leaves of Grass: *An Introduction* of 1905. Trimble came to what he called Whitman's "Songs of Sex" and offered us a view of the great fork in the critical road for anyone who is curious about the plunge of Whitman's seminal muscle:

Whitman inserted, in many of his poems, lines and sentiments which—to the ordinary reader—are not only shocking and offensive, but are liable to produce the impression that they were written by a man who lived a licentious life, and who allowed his fine intellect to wallow in impure and abominable ideas. Whereas in reality Whitman's life appears to have been remarkable for its manliness and cleanliness; and his greatest aim was to give his fellow-men a helping hand in the direction of purity.

Here, with pristine clarity (Whitman might have enjoyed the phallic "inserted"), the dilemma presented to the custodians of the world's morals by *Leaves of Grass* is shamelessly articulated, namely, how to deal with all the rank sexual content in "polite" and "respectable" terms. The crucial feat for these custodians who wished to give Whitman the benefit of the doubt—and here Trimble proved brilliant—was to become an "extraordinary" reader, a reader who exists above and beyond sex, in the "higher and purer regions" that made Whitman so impatient when he read Plato's dialogues. His technique, which would prove very common in the first century of Whitman criticism, was to be (or pretend to be) blind to the sex in Whitman. Thus in Trimble's little book there are sections on Religion, on Prudence, Charity, and Personal Force, and on Death and Immortality. But his discussion of sex is devoted entirely to the *Children of Adam* poems; the *Calamus* sequence is not even mentioned! And Trimble never sings the phallus; instead of that appendage he refers abstractly to "the reproductive organs."

Twenty years earlier Edmund Clarence Stedman, in his essay on Whitman in *Poets in America* (1885), had performed a similarly elaborate feat of averting his eyes from the seminal muscle. First he expressed concern that the poet's "physical excursions" were "too anatomical and malodorous," but in the end he proved himself yet another "extraordinary" reader, focusing entirely on heterosexual "acts of procreation and reproduction" and urging that we "presuppose" Whitman's "honesty of purpose." Otherwise, he says, "his objectional phrases and imagery would be outlawed, not only of art but of criticism."

Leaves of Grass has borne much over the last century and a half from such high-minded fools as Trimble and Stedman with their rose-colored glasses. *Leaves of Grass* has had its share of hostile "ordinary" readers in Trimble's sense, too, the ones who know "impure and abominable ideas" when they see them and are willing to say so. One of its first reviewers, Rufus Griswold, saw them and exploded with vituperation over this "mass of stupid filth" and "gathering of muck" in Whitman's verse. But out of regard for "ears polite" he refused to be more explicit than quoting at the end of his review the legal Latin boilerplate for sodomy: *Peccatum*

illud horribile, inter Christianos non nominandum. This was the sort of con-
demnation Whitman complained about so heatedly in his reminiscences
to Traubel. And no wonder: such priggish bullying doubtless lost *Leaves
of Grass* many a reader. Emily Dickinson was apparently one. In April
1862 she wrote to Thomas Higginson, "You speak of Mr Whitman—I
never read his Book—but was told he was disgraceful."

Still, it is a nice question whether *Leaves* has suffered more from the
ameliorative instincts of high-minded, asexual critics unaware of or
unwilling to acknowledge its erotic transactions—or from the Argus-eyed
Griswolds who recognize the potently subversive sexual agenda and
react with understandable, and not entirely inappropriate, hysterics.
Thoreau shrewdly hoped the former would predominate; he thought it
would be best if Whitman's poems were to find readers "so pure, that they
could read them without harm, that is, without understanding them."
Leaves has found many such readers, still finds them today. Whitman,
of course, must have expected that his poems would be read by both idiots
and savants of sex and those of every level of sophistication in between,
and that their interpretations would differ enormously, though the sheer
depth of the passions his poetry evoked in his lifetime (both cordial and
hostile) may have taken him aback. Indeed, he developed a thick hide, not
to mention sarcastic humor, in dealing with the genitally phobic. In 1888,
for instance, he reported to Traubel, "A man was here the other day who
asked me: 'Don't you feel rather sorry on the whole that you wrote the sex
poems?' I answered him by asking another question: 'Don't you feel rather
sorry on the whole that I am Walt Whitman?' "

After tasting for those first few years the variety of responses to the
athletic sexuality in *Leaves*, Whitman paused in the midst of writing his
most adventurously erotic poem cluster to wonder out loud about the
demography of his audience:

Who is now reading this?

May-be one is now reading this who knows some wrong-doing of
    my past life,
Or may-be a stranger is reading this who has secretly loved me,
Or may-be one who meets all my grand assumptions and egotisms
    with derision,
Or may-be one who is puzzled at me.

This fascinating analysis in *Calamus* #16 lays out the four main sectors of
Whitman readers. In the first cohort are those denizens of Broadway, the

Bowery, and Brooklyn who might have known him personally and heard the gossip about (or seen with their own eyes) his commission of a wrongdoing—perhaps a lover's infidelity or the contravention of a sodomy or prostitution statute. Then there are those "strangers" who would read the steamy *Calamus* poems and happily recognize a kindred sexual spirit. We will see later that Bram Stoker, the author of that homoerotic extravaganza *Dracula*, was such a reader. In 1872, at the age of twenty-four, he wrote Whitman a wonderfully effusive letter thanking him for "many happy hours" spent reading his poems "with my door locked late at night." (By strange coincidence, Stoker went on to marry the woman to whom Oscar Wilde had first offered his hand, Florence Balcombe.)

The third category embraced all of Whitman's despised fancy, parlor-bound literary critics and custodians of morals—the prudes and puritans, as he wrote in his open letter to Emerson in 1856, who were wedded to "the fashionable delusion of the inherent nastiness of sex, and of the feeble and querulous modesty of deprivation"—the Griswolds, Anthony Comstocks, and *Boston Posts* (whose reviewer opined in 1860 that "both Whitman's *Leaves* and Emerson's laudation had a common origin in temporary insanity"). And finally, in the fourth category, the puzzled fence-sitters, like Stedman, who could admit that Whitman was "too anatomical and malodorous withal" and yet be eager to assume that his "loyal reliance upon the excellence, the truth, of nature" was genuine.

Even deeply sympathetic readers could end up in such a rhetorical quandary, as Symonds did in the candid appreciation he published the year after Whitman died (and on the day of his own death). Symonds found "a distinctly sensuous side to his conception of adhesiveness," but elaborately avoided the *acts* that might result from this sensuality with the usual verbiage of noble asexuality: "Whitman possessed a specially keen sense of the fine restraint and continence, the cleanliness and chastity, that are inseparable from the perfectly virile and physically complete nature of healthy manhood." One has to admire the ingenuity of deploying so many epithets—*restraint, continence, cleanliness, chastity, healthy*—designed to make moral custodians feel good in the course of a chapter that, in fact, urges a more generous "new chivalry" toward "those unenviable mortals who are the inheritors of sexual anomalies." That is, homosexuals.

Long gone are those very first readers who had known Whitman personally or as a conspicuous celebrity loafer in his "wrong-doing" heyday of 1845–1860. As for the second cohort, over the first century many homosexual readers must have loved *Leaves* secretly, but few divulged their response in correspondence. Even fewer ventured publication, and then usually with the seven-veiled diffidence of a Symonds. For the most part, therefore, the subject of Walt's seminal muscle has been left to members of the last two groups of readers: the derisive moralists and the puzzled high-minders. The views of these Keystone sexologists—who could not even address their subject in print until early in this century— now make droll, occasionally hilarious reading.

In 1913, for example, a Dr. W. C. Rivers published a pamphlet called *Walt Whitman's Anomaly*—its sale, said the title page, being restricted to "Members of the Legal and Medical Professions." Rivers boldly (for his day) concludes that Whitman was a homosexual. Among the dead give-aways: his delight in "cooking, not as a sportsman sometimes will, but for its own sake"; his ability to "talk about clothes with a woman's knowledge"; his "feminine pity for military suffering"; and the "rows of kisses marked upon the paper with crosses" in his "love letters" to Peter Doyle. When Rivers comes to ask "the question as to whether Whitman confined his feelings of affection for his own sex to the emotional sphere only, or whether they found physical vent," he is able to save the poet from *pec-catum horrible* by emphasizing his "invariable" passivity. "Partly on account of the passivity noticed, there is no need to charge the poet with the grossest unnatural indulgence of an active kind, but that he experienced orgasm seems certain ... probably masturbation." Rivers adds, with cheerful, mind-boggling effrontery, "For Whitman mere contact would suf-fice," and ends with the boast that his analysis is "as sound as an anvil."

Even such a patronizing step "forward" as *Walt Whitman's Anomaly* was bound to aggravate the high-minders and excite the instincts of homophobic denial. Thus, Bliss Perry, the Harvard professor and distin-guished literary critic who had written one of the first Whitman studies, wrote an aghast letter to Rivers saying that "there has never been the slightest evidence that Whitman practised homo-sexuality." He said he had talked "very frankly" with most of Whitman's "surviving friends" and "never heard, in talk or in print until last year, any rumor of the charge of homo-sexuality." He even adduced personal acquaintance with the aging Peter Doyle—"a big Irishman, with a sense of humor."

With the 1920s, however, denial required more arduous effort, as typi-fied by the prominent and indefatigable Whitman scholar Emory Hol-loway. His 1926 biography won the Pulitzer Prize (in it he says the *Calamus* poems were born of "an unhealthy mood"), but several years ear-lier he published a short article in *The Dial* on "Walt Whitman's Love Affairs." Here he began his decades-long pursuit of the woman or women who might have fathered the children of which Whitman boasted to Symonds, but he also rather touchingly expressed the beginnings of tortured doubt about the poet's sexuality. For Holloway had discovered in Whitman's manuscripts that the woman loved by the poet in "Once I Pass'd through a Populous City" was originally *a man*. He also discovered in the notebooks emotional "perturbation" that Whitman felt over a "her" identified in cipher as "16" or "164" (he was never able to divine that the sixteenth and fourth letters of the alphabet were P and D, that is, Peter Doyle, about whom much more in the next chapter).

Thinking such evidence "abundantly unclear," Holloway in the end included himself among Whitman's "puzzled" cohort. His conceding that the manuscript history of "Populous City" "goes far . . . toward showing that Whitman retained in his maturity some of the sexually indiscriminate affection of childhood" was a high-minder's compromise. Yet in his biography he finally cast his vote for denial and asserted, without any credible evidence, that the famous red herring about a heterosexual New Orleans liaison was "substantially true." And in 1932 he would assert even more aggressively, but quite without citations to support his view: "That Whitman had known the love of woman, and given physical expression to it though not married, is obvious to students of his poetry."

Holloway's fairly honest fretting nearly passes as the essence of probity, however, compared to most of the "grand assumptions" that have been made about Whitman's sexual intercourse. Two typical mid-twentieth-century examples of the baseless generalization, homophobia, and plain flatulence that tend to be combined in these utterances are Henry Seidel Canby's *Walt Whitman: An American* (1943) and Van Wyck Brooks's *The Time of Melville and Whitman* (1947). Canby's not uncommon ploy was to consider "love" to be given "sexual" expression in the *Enfans d'Adam* cluster and "spiritual" expression in *Calamus*. Though disinclined to credit Whitman's fathering of children, he prefers to finesse Whitman's never marrying by attributing it in part to lack of money and in part to fixation upon his mother. Canby does believe, though, that actual sex reared itself in Whitman's life, largely on the basis of what he calls the "intense, morbidly self-critical lines" of the July 1870 notebook entry. "It is impossible to believe that the man who wrote these lines had not desired with all his being the reality of passion, and not been always unsuccessful." Canby's boldness, of course, is due largely to his conviction that "a woman is clearly involved" in Whitman's self-flagellation. The deciphering of "16" and "164" that would hoist Canby's theory would not explode for another twenty years. Canby thus rejects the first of the two conclusions he feels can be drawn from *Calamus*, that is, "that Walt Whitman, the 'I,' was actively homosexual, and that his poems are not merely a sublimation of what he calls manly love, but a blind and an excuse" (this last phrase opaque but homophobic). He, like so many others, professes to see "not a scrap of evidence of actual homo-sexuality in Whitman's life."

The alternative Canby accepts is that Whitman was "psychologically" what he terms "intermediate in sex." He was thus capable of "exalted, yet passionate, physical"—but not *sexual*—"love for a man" as well as "the same kind of love for a woman." Canby, though, does grant that male love was "in Whitman's case easier." "Such men are very common," says Canby, "especially among strong creative intellects, whose imaginative sympathies penetrate beyond sexual differences. They are very seldom homosexuals in the vulgar sense of the word." To escape completely from the vulgarity of full-frontal homosexuality, Canby retreats (as, we shall see, many have done since) into emphasis upon the narcissistic, phal-loskeptic Whitman: "He was in love with himself, in love with his own body. . . . This auto-eroticism in diffused form penetrates, invigorates, and sometimes debilitates many of the *Leaves*."

In Van Wyck Brooks's study, when the subject of sex is aroused, all the usual high-minded ploys are also marshaled. Attention is riveted on sex-as-procreation: "He instinctively identified the sexual impulse with biological procreation. . . . Whitman's lovers were primarily parents." His feminine (and therefore harmless) passivity is emphasized: "there was much of the woman in Whitman's composition." Brooks quotes Doyle's remark that Whitman "permitted no familiarities" in order to convince us of his profound sexual restraint. Then he performs this astonishing feat of long-distance psychosexual analysis: "There was something austere . . . in Whitman's sexuality, while personally he was rather under- than over-sexed, mildly bisexual and mostly unconscious of the homosexual impli-cations of *Calamus*." Besides, Brooks adds with fatuous complacency, "Homosexuality in the sense of perversion could scarcely have thrived in the climate of his time and place or in one who so liked 'manliness' and all that was bracing, hardy, and sane."

Brooks's efforts to elide the "sense of perversion" in Whitman are quite transparent, not to say blatant. His efforts, like those of many other high-minded critics, are inept, self-revealing, and, well, farcical. He is utterly hopeless of being permitted familiarity with Whitman, and just doesn't know it. His hope seems nil, too, of catching even a glimpse of the sexual "root of roots: the life below the life" in *Leaves of Grass*. This is because he is what Whitman called, with teeth clenched, a *civilian*. "To a Certain Civilian" attacks with cool vitriol those readers who would have from Whitman "peaceful and languishing rhymes"—flaccid rhymes, he might have said. More to his taste, he retorts, is the sexual and arousing "convulsive throb" of the military drum. The poet ridicules those readers who ask for "dulcet rhymes," just as one is inclined to ridicule those (like Trimble, Perry, Holloway, Brooks, even Symonds) who lull themselves with castrating interpretations of *Leaves of Grass*. Such readers deserve the brusque dismissal Whitman visits upon his impertinent civilian: "go lull yourself with what you can understand, and with piano tunes, / For I lull nobody, and you will never understand me." As I suggested in the Foreword, the whiff in this of Hamlet ridiculing Rosencrantz and Guildenstern is strong.

It should be observed at this point that the inclination to assume Whitman's naiveté about his own sexuality and the sexual politics of his poetry was by no means monopolized by heterosexual civilians. E. M. Forster, for example, wrote in a 1915 letter about the just-finished manuscript of his daringly gay novel *Maurice*: "Whitman nearly anticipated me but he doesn't really know what he was after, or only half knew—shirked, even to himself, the statement." Monumental crust, this condescension about shirking the bold statement coming from Forster, one might well think. Whitman, after all, waited only until his late thirties to publish his gay personality. Forster, on the other hand, kept the *Maurice* ms. in his desk until he died at the age of ninety-one. (To be sure, homosexuality was a punishable offense in England until 1967.) The author safely dead, the novel finally appeared in 1971, a perfectly timed literary aubade to greet the post-Stonewall era.

Now, it would be pleasant to say the voice of the civilian finally trailed off after Stonewall. But in fact coy evasion of the plunging seminal muscle by civilian sexologists has continued up to the present. Paul Zweig, for example, in what is otherwise one of the two most trenchant books on Whitman (Burroughs's *Whitman: A Study* of 1896 is the other), allows his courage to weaken when he poses the crucial questions: "A century later, Whitman's sexual life is still a mystery. Was he homosexual? Did he become openly homosexual in the 1850s, his new poetry a celebration of erotic freedom?" Instead of boldly answering these questions with the obvious "yes," Zweig refers at some length to the "dozens" of names of young workingmen that Whitman listed in his notebooks of the 1850s and simply wonders, "Were these men Whitman's lovers? Possibly, but so many?" Then he backs away with charming equivocation, saying that these lists "do not tell us that he was homosexual or, if he was, that he performed athletic feats of intercourse and kept a score sheet." These lists, Zweig lamely adds, only tell us of Whitman's "collector's mentality."

Zweig's nervous birds-and-bees session ends with this astonishing generalization about the great American celebrator of two-bodied—that is, *transitive*—sex: "Few poets have written as erotically as Whitman, while having so little to say about sex. For the most part, his erotic poetry is intransitive, self-delighting." For good measure, he adds this fillip of Van Wyck Brooksian speculation on Whitman's sex life: "In practice, I suspect, Whitman was fairly [!] chaste, the remote, edgy side of his character flaring up in intimacy, interposing an obstacle to love relationships of any sort." Zweig's finesse of shifting from sex to "love relationships" is too obvious. Besides, finding sex or getting involved in relationships is not beyond the reach of difficult, edgy, remote personalities; indeed, they are sometimes very adept at doing so. Stephen Sondheim celebrates the breed in his acid song "You Could Drive a Person Crazy."

Jerome Loving, discussing "Whitman's Idea of Women" in 1993, also performed a delicate, high-minded balancing act in the course of pursuing the poet's typically antic and obfuscatory remark, late in life, that *Leaves of Grass* was "essentially a woman's book." Though he grants that "Whitman's heterosexual encounters never reach closure" (the lit-crit euphemism for orgasm is telling), he is unwilling to suggest he was more than a "latent" homosexual and pronounces himself doubtful whether his "homosexual tendencies" were "ever fully acted upon."

Any hope that civilian pontificators on Whitman's sex life might finally become hoarse was banished by David Reynolds's ambitious *Walt Whitman's America: A Cultural Biography* in 1995, something of a case study in "civilian" rhetoric about sex and sexuality. Reynolds, too, boldly asks the question, "What kind of sex life did the poet of sex have?" But he quickly dismisses some "scattered gay readings in the 1870s" as not quite fitting "the facts" and revives "evidence Whitman had one or two affairs with women." Reynolds hastily assures us, however, that "he was certainly no womanizer, even though his poetry can make him sound like one." Whitman, a womanizer in his poems! No quotations, of course, support this preposterous view. We also learn, again without a single supporting citation, that Whitman "had an eye for female beauty." When Americans of Whitman's day talked about sex, says Reynolds with impressive assurance, "they were referring to sex between men and women." And so, Reynolds would have us believe, was Whitman. To make his point he finally quotes from the eminent septuagenarian's aria to Traubel about sex: "Sex is the root of all: sex—the coming together of men and women." Inevitably, Reynolds quotes the remark about *Leaves* being "a woman's book" and approves: "It was so, in the most far-ranging sense." But then, he also quotes with approval Whitman's description of the Real Woman as "strong and arrogant," "well-muscled," and capable of "brawny embraces"—not seeming to see in this the arrant "why can't a woman be more like a man" misogyny of Bernard Shaw's Henry Higgins. Whitman proved himself a perfect Higgins, in fact, talking one day about the much admired wife of his friend Joe Gilder: "Jeannette Gilder—Jennie—was here today, with some beautiful girls. She is large, splendid, frank, *manly*—yes, she should have been a man."

Reynolds's main theme, though, is that "strikingly ardent" and "passionate" *but nonsexual* relationships between "same-sex friends" were "unself-conscious and widespread" in mid-nineteenth-century America, and he makes much of "the cult of romantic friendship, the phrenological notion of adhesiveness, and the idea of passional social bonding" (whatever that might be) in the course of his elaborate evasion of the blunt reality of the plunging seminal muscle. Reynolds disengages same-sex love/affection/passion from sexual acts; he works hard to make America at midcentury safe from the latter. The Civil War, he observes, validated Whitman's "sense that same-sex affection was . . . a common part of public behavior in America." Indeed, in the War "same-sex affection came to be widely seen as pious and improving." Whitman's relations with men, Reynolds is thus able to assert, "can be best understood as especially intense manifestations of the kind of same-sex passion that was seen everywhere in antebellum America."*

These "manifestations," it is clear, do not involve the exchange of bodily fluids. The "*Calamus* Love," we learn, is "sanctioned by philosophy" and illustrates the "philosophical view of friendship." With his characteristically asexual diction, Reynolds says the *Calamus* poems give a "heightened" version of comradely affection. The "midnight orgies of young men" that Whitman boasts of sharing, it seems, are only the harmlessly "uninhibited gatherings that working-class comrades enjoyed." The American scene is painted by Reynolds in a fashion to make Pollyanna proud: "In the free, easy social atmosphere of pre–Civil War America, overt displays of affection between people of the same sex were common. Women hugged, kissed, slept with, and proclaimed love for other women. Men did the same with other men." Sexual intimacy did not occur; semen was never ejaculated, we are to suppose, and vaginal fluid never exuded. Like Brooks, Reynolds works hard to leach Whitman's poetry of perversion, saying with high-minder piety, for instance, that he "treated sex and the body in a physiological[?], artistic way as a contrast to what he saw as the cheapened, often perverse forms of sexual expression in popular culture."

Reynolds subsequently poses a version of the question about Whitman's sexual life I have been asking: "Did antebellum same-sex love involve sex?" The answer is stunning: "Certainly yes, if 'sex' is defined as hugging and kissing. Most historians [*who* are they?] agree that genital sex was rare among romantic friends [*how* do they know this?]." Reynolds gallantly concedes that "romantic friends could have genital contact without necessarily feeling guilty." This allows him to grant that Whitman "could kiss or spend the night with Doyle openly and without guilt in a culture that accepted intense same-sex passion." What Whitman had to "guard against," Reynolds suggests, were "homoerotic feelings that threatened to upset the equipoise and chasteness he prided himself on." He reads the famous 1870 notebook entry in which Whitman admonishes himself to avoid the "perturbations" of his affair with Doyle (see below, pages 140–142 and 192), in typical high-minder's fashion, as a vow of chastity and devotion to the "Whitman Myth" he was building. The possibility that the entry shows us a fifty-one-year-old man trying to talk some sense into himself over the folly, danger, and inevitable disappointment of becoming sexually involved with a twenty-three-year-old does not occur to Reynolds.

The ultimate effect of Reynolds's discourse is a radical neutralizing (neutering, rather) of Whitman's sexuality: the "I" of his poetry becomes, as he asserts, "at times heteroerotic, at times homoerotic, at times auto-erotic." Sex omni- and non-, everything and nothing. Sex effectively becomes undiscussable. The result is ideal for this quintessential civilian critic who, though asking bold questions about what Whitman called "the thought and fact of sexuality," produces the sort of pallid, lulling parlor "piano tunes" that Whitman detested. Whitman, as Traubel observed, "objected to the piano," most obviously because that instrument resided in "respectable" parlors, Whitman's least favorite venue. The piano, Whitman said, "seems to be so unequal to the big things." We saw in the preceding chapter that it was not the prude harmonies of parlor tunes but the throbbing quasi-sexual rhythms of the opera that best addressed the "big things" Whitman was after in his debut poetry. And he reacted with the same lukewarmness to the "parlor tune" criticism of civilians during his lifetime. One such critic was Stedman, who, we have seen, exasperated Whitman in spite of their friendship because he let erudition get in the way of insight. Stedman just didn't get it, Whitman made clear. Recent civilian critics, like Reynolds, are also reflected in Whitman's remarking, again about Stedman, a week later, "With all its scholarliness, its kindliness, its receptivity . . . it still lacks root—still misses a saving earthiness: what shall I call it?—a sort of brutal dash of elemental flame."

If sex has anything to do with Whitman's "elemental flame," then even

Harold Bloom comes up short in the Stedman fashion. Bloom achieved nearly the same result as Reynolds a decade ago, though without breaking Reynolds's critical sweat. Instead of leveling all sexuality in Whitman, he simply mystifies it, calling the poet's psychosexuality "labyrinthine in its perplexities." But he, too, is finally able to obviate the possibility of seminal exchange by finding, like Paul Zweig, that the poetry is "auto-erotic rather more than it is homo-erotic . . . his most authentic sexual passion is always for himself." And with a typically grand episcopal gesture he ventures: Zweig "surmises that Whitman might have experienced little actual homosexual intercourse. I suspect none."

Harold Bloom suspects none. This is rich—verges, indeed, on the quaint. I, on the other hand, suspect lots.

Which puts me in a difficult position. For, as Reynolds wisely says, "The search for details of Whitman's private sexual activities may be doomed to failure." He might have gone farther and said "*is* doomed." Reynolds cites from the very first Whitman biography, by Burroughs, the statement that between 1837 and 1848 Whitman "sounded all the experiences of life with all their passions, pleasures, and abandonments" and calls it "maddeningly vague." And so it most certainly is. Our search for details is doomed because, as Whitman himself scribbled on a scrap of paper just after Burroughs's book appeared in 1883, "How little posterity really knows about the facts [of] a far-back person or book in his or its own time!" The notion that the author of the first *Leaves of Grass* already, in 1883, seemed a "far-back person" to Whitman himself is poignant. It is also daunting, for that author is now a very much more "far-back person."

His sex life, especially, is lost in Prospero's "dark backward and abysm of time"—as our civilian critics of Whitman are pleased, perhaps too pleased, to remind us. Indeed, they have found a too cute way to make this point. In a suave and witty 1989 essay on how to address "the sex problem" in Whitman, his biographer Justin Kaplan observed, "we know that Emerson married twice and fathered four children. To reduce this to simple acts, we know for a certainty at least four more things about Emerson's sex life than we've ever been able to find out about Whitman's." Reynolds opened his sex talk with a curiously similar caveat. "His sister Mary had five children: although next to nothing is known about her, we know for certain five more things about her sex life than about Walt's." With a rueful paradox, Kaplan also calls all the recent critical curiosity about the role sex actually played in Whitman's life "unusually aggravated (although fully justified)" and, in view of the unknowability problem, suggests the time has come to call the whole thing off. "The cycle of discussion, as far as the sexuality issue is concerned, seems to have completed and maybe even exhausted itself: Whitman himself is most to blame for this. But perhaps it's time to move on to a broader focus." My difficult position, then, is in part that of having come too late to the critical orgy. Discussion is "exhausted." Everywhere, detumescence—and smoke curling from the postcoital cigarettes of enervated Whitman scholars.

The other difficulty of my position, of course, is that this is all a keyhole business. One has to peep and pry and be, well, prurient. There is constant danger of looking inept, comical, or merely gutter-minded as one goes about one's task. The English writer Edmund Gosse, in an essay written the year after Whitman died, in fact used the keyhole image to express the extraordinary difficulty confronting those who wish to get at the sexual "life behind the life" in Whitman. Gosse takes his simile from Bluebeard's fatal, forbidden chamber and conjures "the little room called 'Walt Whitman' " in the castle of literature. "We all know that discomfort and perplexity await us there, that nobody ever came back from it with an intelligible message, that it is piled with the bones of critics; yet such is the perversity of the analytic mind, that each one of us, sooner or later, finds himself peeping through the keyhole and fumbling at the lock."

Gosse's eloquent conceit and all the caveats of Kaplan, Reynolds, and many others are certainly intimidating, but "perversity" does make me reluctant to relinquish my preoccupation with that plunging seminal muscle. I am, I confess, of Symonds's harping tendency when it comes to sex, and so I am frankly suspicious of all these "civilian" critics who seem eager to pronounce the lubricious matter a dead end and discussion of it exhausted. (In a typical fit of civilian impatience, Reynolds not long ago declared that the topic of "Whitman and Contemporary Homosexuality" has been "done to death.") For these critics are precisely the ones most likely to "fumble at the lock" on the door of truth about Whitman's sex. Indeed, they seem doomed to fumble at it. "We have got so in our civilization," Whitman told Traubel in 1889, "that we are afraid to face the body and its issues. . . . we shrink from the realities of our bodily life." He was referring to "the business of having a baby," about which we have become much less squeamish in the age of Lamaze. But his point has lost none of its force, a hundred years later, when it comes to the realities of the "bodily life" of homosexuals—and the candid discussion of them.

We have heard, in other words, too much from civilian readers like Brooks and Bloom and Reynolds, who remain fixedly flaccid in the presence of Whitman's "grand assumptions" about the bodily life or simply refuse to acknowledge their existence. On this subject we have not heard enough from readers, so to speak, within the Whitman ranks—not enough, that is, from such witnesses as the "stranger" in *Calamus* #16 who reads Whitman with the intimacy of a lover. The poet gives us a more elaborate description of such a privileged reader/lover, and the critical acumen he can bring to bear, in *Calamus* #41 (1860 version):

> Among the men and women, the multitude, I perceive one
>   picking me out by secret and divine signs,
> Acknowledging none else—not parent, wife, husband, brother,
>   child, any nearer than I am;
> Some are baffled—But that one is not—that one knows me.
>
> Lover and perfect equal!
> I meant that you should discover me so, by my faint indirections,
> And I, when I meet you, mean to discover you by the like in you.

Here is the exact counterpart to Whitman's "Certain Civilian," who finds the first editions of *Leaves* "so hard to follow." Here is Whitman's ideal reader, alive to the "secret and divine" hints and indirections that reveal the "life behind the life," the sex life. A multitude of family members, casual friends, his numerous journalistic employers, Broadway bystanders, even the critics of posterity are baffled. Whitman's brother George, in fact, recalled that their father "never had an idea what Walt was up to, what he meant. To him, like to all the rest, Walt was a mystery." But there is no mystery or bafflement for the perceptive reader of "secret" signs fantasized by the poet in *Calamus* #41. He *knows* Walt.

Let me now express a thought that has often occurred to me while perusing all the civilian commentary on Whitman's sex life. This thought—temerarious but, I would like to think, also Whitmanesque—is that, in certain important circumstantial respects, I am a more nearly "perfect" and "equal" reader of Whitman (well, lover too) than these civilians. Like Whitman, I am a gay man. Like him, I also have been deliriously happy in love, later profoundly miserable for a time. Like Whitman, I have spent nearly two decades of my prime in New York, happily arriving in this exciting "city of eros" from more staid environs. I have become, like Whitman, part of the metropolitan gay "scene." Perhaps most important, I am not too many years older than Whitman was when he published his gayest—also, and not coincidentally, his greatest—edition of *Leaves of Grass* in 1860.* Much of this book was written, in fact, at a desk facing a panoramic view of what Whitman called "the beautiful masculine Hudson."

And so I have found myself reading the civilian commentary on Whitman's sex life with a mixture of emotions that range from bemusement and hilarious disbelief to anger and disgust. Whitman once said of a painting of him by one of his circle, "his picture is very benevolent, to be sure: but the Walt Whitman of that picture lacks guts." One feels similarly about the picture of the sexual Whitman civilians have given us, though a different part of his anatomy appears to be lacking. I fancy it is possible to do better by being more attuned to the "faint indirections" that Whitman emplaced throughout his poetry, prose, letters, and notebooks in order to allow posterity's "secret" lovers and perfect equals to discover him. That is, at least, what I hope to demonstrate in the following pages, which will offer a view of Whitman's sex life from 1841 when, as a twenty-two-year-old, he first resided in Manhattan until that grim evening in 1861 when the Secession War rang down the curtain on the time of his life.

That is, the time when, as he wrote in a dry run for "Crossing Brooklyn Ferry" in 1856, he was "drenched with joy,—had my friends, loved them, was loved by them . . . Had my hopes and dreams,—laughed, slept, had my amours." On his last birthday, 31 May 1891, Whitman, surrounded by friends, recalled this "preparatory and inauguratory" time of his life: "New York, Brooklyn, experimentation in strange ways, not such as usually go to make poetry and books and grand things, but the flash of active life—yes, in New York, Brooklyn (to me the greatest cities in the universe) . . ." "Strange" experimentation? The "flash" of active life? Surely Whitman is here alluding, with ginger diction of course, to the joy- and sex-drenched days of his amours. For these certainly helped him to create those "grand things," the early *Leaves of Grass* editions.

CITY OF ORGIES

"New York" does not appear once in Whitman's poetry. He always preferred "Manhattan" or the more aboriginal "Mannahatta." One of his nieces was even graced with this name, doubtless in his honor. It was a characteristic preference, rejecting a bourgeois, Old World name like New York in favor of a more earthy, primeval, native one. Likewise for Paumanok, a.k.a. Long Island. One afternoon in the summer of 1889, Whitman happened to ask Traubel if he knew what the word "Mannahatta" meant. He must have been thinking of the short poem "Mannahatta" he had published the year before in *Sands at Seventy*—

My city's fit and noble name resumed,
Choice aboriginal name, with marvellous beauty, meaning,
A *rocky founded island—shores where ever gayly dash*
   the coming, going, hurrying sea waves.

—when he offered Traubel this explanation: "The Indians use the word
to indicate a plot of ground, an island, about which the waters flow—
keep up a devil of a swirl, whirl, ebullition—have a hell of a time."

   Whitman himself had "a hell of a time" in his years living in Manhattan or just an East River ferry ride away, as his later reminiscences and
the early editions of *Leaves* make abundantly clear. Is there a better word
for these editions than "ebullition"? This perhaps explains why imagery
of swiftly roiling waters often occurred to him in describing the "mettle-
some, mad, extravagant city" of his own extravagant prime. "Turbulent"
was a favorite adjective: "this teeming and turbulent city"—the "turbulent musical chorus" of "Manhattan crowds"—"proud, friendly, turbulent
city." Of such a city he became a most famous son: "Walt Whitman, a
kosmos, of Manhattan the son, / Turbulent, fleshy, sensual . . ." And several times he deployed a version of the Native American definition of
Mannahatta to express the thrill of the fast pace of city life. The most
memorable instance is his promise, in "Proto-Leaf," the first poem of the
1860 edition, to include among his "programme of chants" the

Chants of the Mannahatta, the place of my dearest love,
   the place surrounded by hurried and sparkling currents,
Health chants—joy chants—robust chants of young men . . .

These lines are typical of the early, ebullient Whitman: exulting in the
joys of the present; deliriously, volubly, and robustly affiliated with young
men; and playing coyly with sexual ambiguity. Is his "dearest love" the
city? Or the young lover he has found there?

   But swift currents, however sparkling, can wear one down as one ages
and/or grows up. The pleasure of a joy ride can slowly, sometimes suddenly, turn into the disconcerting feeling of being swept away. The fast
life takes its inevitable toll, perhaps all the sooner for those who maintain
at the outset the highest velocity. With the perspective conferred by the
passing of time, the frenetic, promiscuous life begins to appear in a new
light. For Whitman, as we shall see, it was the racy bohemian company at
Pfaff's saloon, the "whorearchy" and "blab" of the Broadway pavement,
the piers of his "city of ships," the dark recesses of the upper tiers of theaters and opera houses, the all-male dinners and carouses, perhaps even

the all-male "bull-dances" he mentions. For robust young men today it is the bars, their "back rooms," the sex clubs, the mystic deliria of poppers and drugs, the disco palaces that hit their stride as the sun rises. In Whitman's day, as in ours, those who served in Manhattan's "galleys of pleasure" were eminently subject to exhaustion.

There are signs that even in the mid-1850s Whitman, as must (almost) every manic Manhattan party-lifer, was beginning to find his fuel running low. I have heard uttered in weary self-disgust, have heard — *myself* utter, Whitman's "O hotcheeked and blushing! O foolish hectic! / O for pity's sake, no one must see me now!"—a recrimination that introduces one of the sexiest yet most vulnerable, angst-ridden passages in the 1855 *Leaves*. Whitman's move down to the hospital wards of Washington in 1862 was, I think, an acknowledgment that this hectic, sometimes embarrassing, empty busyness could not go on forever, that there must be something more important in life than hanging out with roughs and poetizing. Circumstances, rather well timed for a forty-three-year-old man, forced him to relinquish the "joy chants" of an *ars vivendi* and begin to fashion, amid the staggering carnage of the Civil War, an *ars moriendi* or, at the very least, an *ars amatoria*. (The AIDS epidemic has performed a similar function for thousands and thousands of Manhattanites in the 1980s and 1990s.)

I know of no more poignant expression of this transformation of the reckless, hedonistic, carefree Early Whitman into the more earnest, sober, caregiving Late Whitman than a letter he wrote to a young soldier named Elijah Douglass Fox from his old Manhattan stomping grounds, which he was briefly revisiting in November 1863. The poet's former rambunctious life seems strangely distant to him now; he is discovering that he has changed and is not shy about telling young Fox that he is the reason for this change. Whitman says he feels he has

> had enough of going around New York—enough of amusements, suppers, drinking, & what is called *pleasure*. . . . I do not think one night has passed in New York or Brooklyn when I have been at the theatre or opera or afterward to some supper party or carouse made by the young fellows for me, but what amid the play of the singing, I would perhaps suddenly think of you—& the same at the gayest supper party, of men, where all was fun & noise & laughing & drinking, of a dozen young men, & I among them, I would see your face before me in my thought as I have seen it so often there in Ward G, & my amusement would be all turned to nothing. . . . you are so much closer to me than any of them that there is no

comparison—there has never passed so much between them & me as we have—besides there is something that takes down all artificial accomplishments, & that is a manly & loving soul.

We're not in Mannahatta anymore. Whitman's two "New York's" nicely suggest this, as does the fact that he began to remove some of the joyous all-male carousing and sexual exploits from his post–Civil War editions of *Leaves*. The "O foolish hectic!" lines and their erotic sequel disappeared, for instance. So did the three splendid lines about Mannahatta "joy chants" quoted above.

The sex-laden "joy chants" of 1860 apparently came to seem, with the passing years, mere boasts of "artificial accomplishments." Whitman's former style had been to revel promiscuously in the joys of the present moment. In the valedictory poem of the 1860 edition, in fact, he pronounced this supreme motto of Youth: "all I know at any time suffices for that time only—not subsequent time." But, chastened by the war and the approach of his fiftieth birthday, Whitman gradually lost his *carpe diem* vivacity and began to take more care for his future and posterity. And so, for the fourth *Leaves* edition, when the poet was forty-eight, the motto of Youth was suppressed forever. The poet became, at disastrous artistic cost, attentive to "subsequent time" rather than to that absolutely fabulous site for sex: the present.

Youth cannot be told any of this, of course. It must learn the hard way. Whitman, as most all of us do, had to learn some time after the fact that many of his "accomplishments" on Mannahatta—some pretty awful poetic juvenilia, countless mediocre newspaper stories, some promiscuous plunging of his seminal muscle, perhaps even *Leaves of Grass* itself—were "artificial." Our interest in this chapter, however, is in Whitman before this dour wisdom descended upon him. As New Yorkers today grow into middle age, they observe the sheer hedonistic stamina of the next generation of new arrivals from Bozeman, Fresno, Lebanon (Indiana), Hollidaysburg, Fort William (to name the native towns of some from my circle of friends and former flames), or my own hometown, Alhambra, California, with a mixture of astonishment, bemusement, and envy. Decade after decade has brought homosexuals in particular from oppressive small-town or big-town environments to the anonymity and freedom of the city. These naive, untutored, wide-eyed phalanxes have come as Whitman came: to pursue fame and fortune, no doubt, but also, as Whitman suggested to Fox, to pursue *"pleasure"* and enjoy with one's own kind the "fun & noise & laughing & drinking." And who but the most earnest prude would not add "sex" to that list?

Whitman could have been describing these waves of immigrants yearning for more sexual freedom—he was obviously describing himself—in this passage from *Franklin Evans*, a story he published in the *New World* newspaper when just twenty-three: "Yes, here I had come to seek my fortune! A mere boy, friendless, unprotected, innocent of the ways of the world—without wealth, favor, or wisdom—here I stood at the entrance to the mighty labyrinth, and with hardly any consciousness of the temptations, doubts, and dangers that awaited me there." Then the "robust youth of about twenty years" adds these very true words: "Thousands had gone before me, and thousands were coming still." In 1862, Whitman met a red-faced twenty-four-year-old and confided a bit condescendingly to his notebook that the fellow was "countryfied." But Whitman had been countryfied once, too.

By chance, on his very first day young Franklin becomes acquainted with a twenty-five-year-old named Colby. His face shows that "fun and frolic" are his elements, and he is on intimate terms with "the dissipation of city life." The two new pals arrange to meet again, and Colby suggests, "Let us go out and cruise a little." Colby takes Franklin to a bar, then on to a theater. . . . Well, it would be easy enough for you or me to take "the story so far" and complete it as a clichéd "cute young thing arrives in Gotham and is swept away" story. But Whitman had been hired by the *New World* to write a temperance homily, and so Franklin is eventually ruined not by descent into a sexual underground but by the "dull lethargy of *drunkenness.*"

One thing is certain, though: the lower Manhattan in which Whitman arrived to live in May of 1841 was an extraordinarily dissipated den of venereal iniquity. The Broadway he fell in love with and praised in several memorable poems was a far from pretty sight, according to more "proper" observers. In 1840, the stuffy patrician George Templeton Strong sighed to his diary, "It's a pity we've no street but Broadway that's fit to walk in of an evening. The street is always crowded, and whores and blackguards make up about two-thirds of the throng." Ten years later he was prepared to call New York a "whorearchy." George Ellington, in his 1869 book *The Women of New York: or, The Under-World of the Great City* (published, need one add, in *Iowa*), predicted that the city would "out-Sodom Sodom."

Timothy Gilfoyle, in his study of prostitution in New York, *City of Eros*, confirms the views of Strong and Ellington, summarizing that 1836 to 1871 were "the halcyon years of commercialized sex" in the city, as well as the years in which "the beginnings of a distinct homosexual subculture" could be seen. The emergence of a generally "libertine subculture," in fact, was occurring at precisely the time Whitman made himself a conspicuous denizen of the "million-footed" Broadway pageant. Prostitution, according to census figures for the very year *Leaves of Grass* first appeared, ranked just behind tailor shops atop the list of most prosperous "industries" of the day (the manufacture of silver wire, steam engines and boilers, and ships were a *distant* third, fourth, and fifth). From 1850 to 1870 about forty percent of the metropolitan area's houses of prostitution were near Broadway. Sanitary inspectors noted these houses in their reports, and in 1866 such establishments in the vicinity were numbered at 208. And very little was done about this, either out of mere toleration, or regard for wealthy landlords and hoteliers (hotels were very busy places of assignation), or the purchased blindness of police and prosecutors. Guidebooks to brothels, and there were many, listed nearly 150 establishments, but in Whitman's raunchiest decade, the 1850s, only seven of them were charged with disorderly conduct. Gilfoyle finds reason to think that this toleration extended to the homosexual activity that must have been a part of the brothel subculture.

Whitman used Broadway in the titles of two poems. It is very odd that the one from 1860, "A Broadway Pageant," should be such a bland, garrulous thing. Unless, of course, by cheerfully boosting "Young Libertad" and Broadway's façades "alive with people" and festooned with banners and pennants, he was hoping to spruce up his beloved thoroughfare's sleazy reputation on the occasion of a reception for the Japanese embassy which visited that June. But in one of those rare very late poems that throw a candid glance back to his heyday, titled simply "Broadway," we get a far more historically accurate evocation of the street's venereal character (and also another variation on Whitman's definition of Mannahatta):

> What passions, winnings, losses, ardors, swim thy waters!
> What whirls of evil, bliss and sorrow, stem thee!
> What curious questioning glances—glints of love!
> Leer, envy, scorn, contempt, hope, aspiration! . . .
> Thou visor'd, vast, unspeakable show and lesson!

These lines can still serve as a superb evocation of Manhattan's "flagstones, curbs, façades"—especially in the livelier venues of nighttown.

Naiveté is short-lived there. A notably jaded Whitman, after all, was able to portray it in Franklin Evans just a year after he crossed the hurried, sparkling currents of the East River to take up residence in Manhattan. "A thousand vicious temptations," Evans is warned by a middle-aged, exceedingly neatly dressed acquaintance named Demaine, will beset him "on every side, which the simple method of your country life has led you to know nothing." These temptations are particularly strong for the cash-starved new arrivals who must live on the streets or in atrocious hovels off them. Today this would be the tiny East Village fifth-floor walk-up or squatters' commune; in Whitman's time it would have been one of the hundreds of boardinghouses that served unattached men. The surely autobiographical description of Franklin's encounters with several "solemn" and "sour" proprietors and their (to him) filthy, cramped premises is a perfect analogue of the depressing search, *Village Voice* ads in hand, for bearable premises and roommates that faces today's newcomer.

Once ensconced in some forlorn dump, of course, the eager newcomer will embrace all means of escaping from it. "I have often thought that the cheerless method of their accommodations," says the older-and-wiser Franklin who narrates the story, "drives many a young man to the bar-room, or some other place of public resort." So it does, and always will, in this city. Franklin is quite happy to be in the "seductive scene" of the "musical drinking-house," where "most of the inmates were young men . . . no small number quite on the verge of boyhood. They played the same as the rest, and tossed off glasses of liquor, without apparently feeling any evil effects from it."* On that first theater jaunt, by the way, occurs a perfect example of the serendipitous, it's-a-small-world-of-one's-own-kind coincidence that so often unfolds even in this populous city. A friend of Colby's named Mitchell joins them and insists they all go on to a theater filled with "Beautiful women and elegant men—moustached dandies and lively youth." During an intermission Franklin is riveted by a young gentleman in the stage box who seems to him a "pattern of perfection in dress and manners." "A fine looking fellow," says Franklin, and Mitchell agrees. After the performance Mitchell slyly suggests going round to one of the "fashionable refectories" nearby for oysters. Once seated, he says to Franklin, "do you know I have a fancy always to be served by a particular individual in this refectory? Just notice the man's face, now, and tell me what you think of my taste." When he is beckoned, lo! the waiter is the very "fashionable gentleman" of the stage box. A dandy earlier in his hours off, now waiting table—an immemorial Manhattan scenario.

Whitman ends the scene abruptly ("I changed the subject, and we finished our oysters"), but not before allowing Franklin to draw a time-honored lesson from his adventures with Colby and Mitchell. He says he is left more willing to "question the reality of things" and to "reflect that, though to appearance they were showy, they might prove, upon trial, as coarse as the eating-house waiter." He also confesses to losing "some of that reverence, and that awkward sense of inferiority, which most country folk, when they take up their abode in this brick-and-pine Babel, so frequently show."

In "Song of Myself" Whitman writes of the sex-charged "touch" of another person "quivering me to a new identity." The touch of Manhattan had the same effect, and in the years following the publication of *Franklin Evans* Whitman made it clear that he thought the annealing of a new identity in this burning fiery furnace of a city was a liberating and therefore desirable process. For all the "georgic" aura of his poetry—the scented herbage, the dalliant eagles, the old feuillage, and so on—there is considerable reason to agree with Leslie Fiedler that Whitman was "at his best" as "a singer of urban life."

And it is fitting, certainly, that his most eloquent expression of this urban bias appeared at almost exactly the midpoint of his days as a "lover of populous pavements, / Dweller in Mannahatta." This comes in one of his "Letters from Paumanok," which he wrote as a traveling correspondent for the Sunday *Dispatch*, a progressive New York paper. His third letter, which was datelined Southold on the north folk of Long Island and which appeared in October 1849, begins with "Some Poetical Comparisons between Country and City." These few pages can still stand as a splendid explanation for the magnetic draw of New York to restless spirits who find themselves mired in Peoria and Dubuque and Peru (Indiana) . . . or even the more proximate Morristown and Manhasset.

While granting, as most New Yorkers do, that he loves to get away now and then to the "freshness and quiet of the country" and escape "the ligatures and ceremonies of a life in town," Whitman then asks, "But to be born and 'brought up' in an out of the way country place, and so continue there through all the stages of middle life . . . and at last die and be buried there—is that an enviable lot in life? No, it is not. The burying part may be well enough, but the living is much such living as a tree in a farmer's door-yard." He was perhaps thinking of his own salvation from this dismal fate at the age of four, when his family moved from rural Huntington to Brooklyn, when he notes that Long Islanders are especially "tenacious of the place." This "vegetating forever in one little spot of this wide and beautiful world . . . the getting *set* in the narrow notions of the locality where they live," Whitman says, "serve to dwarf and distort much of the goodly elements of their own nature." And so he offers the "Messrs. of the city" the following emphatic precept (he left his schoolmasterly pose slowly):

Let everyone mix for at least some part of his earlier life with the bustling world of the great towns. Such towns have, for many an age, borne the accusations of moralists, and been warned against by timid fathers and affectionate mothers. Yet were we a coarse and unhewn structure of humanity without them. Living in the country, in an insulated way, never wears off the husk of one's manners, never sharpens conversational powers, rarely develops the intellect or the morals to the perfection they are capable of—and generally leaves a man in that condition of unbakedness, appropriately called "raw."

After discussing the life of an old couple on Shelter Island, Whitman closes his letter with an acknowledgment that his view is "by no means popular" and this coda: "Does any one infer that I would advise country-boys to betake themselves to the city right off? God forgive me, if it should tend that way: no! Yet . . . I say that, no matter what moralists and metaphysicians may teach, *out of the cities the human race does not expand and improvise so well morally, intellectually, or physically.*"

And artistically. For *Leaves of Grass* was superb improvisation and also expanded with a jolt the realm of American poetry. But what of the "moral" and "physical" improvisation Whitman writes of?

Perhaps one answer lies in the breathtaking autobiographical irony of the Southold dateline of this "Letter." Nearly a decade before, it seems, one of Whitman's many brief teaching stints ended in this town amid scandal and mystery. The twenty-two-year-old schoolmaster was denounced from the pulpit by the town's Presbyterian minister, Reverend Ralph Smith (Reynolds suggests 3 January 1841 was the likely day). The accusations must have been sexual, though the church records seem to have been tampered with and no factual evidence survives. Rumors of Whitman's being tarred, feathered, and run out of town on a rail have come down through several generations, and his schoolhouse was referred to as "the Sodom School" well into this century. He almost certainly taught there at the time. A painting titled *Walt Whitman's School at Southold 1840* is extant, and Reynolds has brought to light a letter written on 28 November 1840 that suggests Whitman was under a cloud.* The author, a Giles Waldo, writes from Southold to a friend in Washington, "I am most sincerely sorry that Whitman tho't it expedient to 'run a muck' under the chariot wheels of 'old Tip'—but hope he may escape unscathed." Reynolds thinks "old Tip" refers to Whitman's campaigning against the Whig candidate for president, William Henry Harrison.

But it bears noting that Whitman's sole use of the word is erotic and comes in a passage of "Song of Myself" that could (if one were not high-minded) easily be considered a vivid description of a forbidden encounter between a perhaps provocative student and a teacher unable to restrain his lust:

> To touch my person to some one else's is about as much as I can
>   stand.
>
> Is this then a touch? . . . . quivering me to a new identity,
> Flames and ether making a rush for my veins,
> Treacherous tip of me reaching and crowding to help them,
> My flesh and blood playing out lightning, to strike what is
>   hardly different from myself,
> On all sides prurient provokers stiffening my limbs,
> Straining the udder of my heart for its withheld drip,
> Behaving licentious toward me, taking no denial,
> Depriving me of my best as for a purpose,
> Unbuttoning my clothes and holding me by the bare waist . . .

Given all the facts and rumors of the Southold affair, Waldo's rather flippant remark is more likely about sexual than political heresy. His reference to Walt's demise under "chariot wheels" is thus also more plausibly viewed as witty sarcasm—an allusion to Plato's famous parable of the charioteer who cannot control his lusty horse. Waldo's correspondent, incidentally, appears to have known Whitman personally and thus would more likely have been privy to his risky activities. Four months later, in May 1841, Waldo asked in a letter, "Have you heard from Whitman . . . since I wrote last?"

By fascinating coincidence, we have already noted, this was the month Whitman became a Manhattanite. If there is any truth in the Southold story, he would not have been the first or last emigrant to arrive fresh from a hairsbreadth brush with small-town law or ecclesiastical pulpit-thumping or homophobia and eager to improvise on his sexual identity and desires in the "bustling world" of the "great town." In the first of Whitman's two poems titled "Mannahatta," this one in the 1860 edition, he spoke of the name as being "liquid, sane, unruly, musical, self-sufficient." As so often, Whitman's adjectives are extremely carefully chosen. It is clear that his coming to the island was to attain a liquid—that is, improvisational, even seminal—and self-sufficient life after the "moral" and "physical" straitjacketing he had experienced in the further reaches of Paumanok.

His joy in deliverance from the "abominable" diet and "heavy labors" routinely thrust on Long Island youths was soon evidenced in the pages of the *Aurora*, for which he wrote in early 1842. He pronounced New York "a great place—a mighty world in itself" that, he did not mind saying, displayed "every hue" of morality and vice, breeding and brutality, elevation and degradation. On a quick tour he points out Coleman's the bookstore and warns against pickpockets, walks up to "the most villainous specimen of architecture you ever beheld" (the Park Theater), then past Tammany Hall (calling it with sarcasm "the Mecca of democracy"), and on to the "region of Jews, jewelry, and second hand clothing." The tour ends at the Bowery, "the most heterogeneous melange of any street in the city," which fifty years later Whitman would recall as the place of his "dearest amusements." Polite society in Boston and New York "taboo'd" the extravagant acting of Forrest and Booth because, he said, they were "too robustuous." But he adds, "no such scruples affected the Bowery." Nor did they affect the rough, robust Whitman.

The day in March 1842 after the twenty-two-year-old ascended to the editorship of the *Aurora*, he favored his readers with a fancy civic encomium that began, "Whoever does not know that 'our city' is the great place of the western continent, the heart, the brain, the focus, the main spring, the pinnacle, the extremity, the no more beyond, of the New World—whoever does not know this, we say, must have been brought up in a place where they 'didn't take the papers,' and where the *Aurora*, in particular, has never scattered its effulgent light." Regarding light, Whitman remarks that when the sun "mounts the horizon" Broadway "is changed, and the patricians of our great metropolis take possession in force." Whitman himself, of course, despised patricians and all manifestations of polite society. He preferred the nighttime, when his own loafing, recreational, promiscuous kind reestablished their domain . . . and when they could perform untrammeled their "visor'd, vast, unspeakable show." Always requiring a visor from the sunlight of respectability, Whitman expressed his preference for hijinks in a letter to Doyle in 1868: "I always enjoy seeing the City let loose and on the rampage as it was last night to the fullest extent."

As it happens, he was referring to demonstrations evoked by a Democratic Party convention. But it seems clear that in the 1840s and 1850s his rampages and looseness had less to do with political oratory than with carousing and sexual marauding. Street-scene and tavern-scene vignettes from this loafing, epicurean, sex-charged life are scattered through the early *Leaves* editions. Whitman's fine eye catches, amid the "blab of the pave," the "Arrests of criminals, slights, adulterous offers made, accep-

tances, rejections with convex lips." In *Calamus* #18, which later became
the aptly titled "City of Orgies," he professes indifference to its interminable rows of houses, bright shopwindows, learned persons, and
soirees; his sole joy is Manhattan's "frequent and swift flash of eyes
offering me love, / Offering response to my own—these repay me, /
Lovers, continual lovers, only repay me."

There is surely no better expression of how Manhattan quivered
Whitman to a proud new sexual identity (or at least one more boldly
active) than these lines from "Crossing Brooklyn Ferry" (1856):

> I too walked the streets of Manhattan Island, and bathed in the
>   waters around it,
> I too felt the curious abrupt questionings stir within me,
> In the day, among crowds of people, sometimes they came upon me,
> In my walks home late at night or, as I lay in my bed, they came
>   upon me.
>
> I too had been struck from the float forever held in solution,
> I too had received identity by my body,
> That I was, I knew was of my body—and what I should be, I knew
>   I should be of my body.

Walt Whitman, in other words, came out. Manhattan's receptiveness—
or, amid the bustle, mere indifference—to "every hue" of morality and
vice gave him the freedom to improvise his answers to the "curious
abrupt questionings" of his identity.

That these questionings were sexual the poet had made very clear the
previous year in an erotic passage in the poem he would later title "The
Sleepers." Just after he finds himself, in his dream-vision, abed with a
lover ("his flesh was sweaty and panting") and just before the boss-tooth
(his or the lover's?) advances in the darkness toward white teeth,
Whitman finds himself confused, abashed, and "curious to know where
my feet stand . . . . and what is this flooding me, childhood or manhood . . . . and the hunger that crosses the bridge between." As the 1840s
and 1850s wore on, Whitman evidently began to satisfy his curiosity and
hunger. He crossed the bridge between his Long Island–Brooklyn childhood and his Manhattan manhood, and his confusion transformed into
conviction, as many of his *Calamus* poems show. Indeed, Whitman became in later years a poet of certainties rather than doubts, and so the
lines about sexual confusion in "The Sleepers" vanished after the 1871
edition.

On the crowded flagstones of the city Whitman achieved a gay non-chalance in public not possible even today, except perhaps in the few predominantly queer neighborhoods of our "great towns":

Yet comes one, a Manhattanese [*nota bene* not a New Yorker],
   and ever at parting, kisses me lightly on the lips with robust love,
And I, in the public room, or on the crossing of the street, or on the
   ship's deck, kiss him in return;
We observe that salute of American comrades, land and sea,
We are those two natural and nonchalant persons.

These lines from *Calamus* #19 reflect touchingly on the wide-eyed, awk-ward, but "robust" hero of *Franklin Evans* and his introduction to the city's "public room" culture by Messrs. Colby, Demaine, and Mitchell. With the passing of nearly two decades, Franklin's creator became a natural and nonchalant denizen of public rooms so crowded or rowdy or simply so "mixed" in their clientele that he could, with a little discretion, cultivate a circle of friends of his own kind without fear. From this circle he might even cull a lover. Of this sociable life Whitman gives us a strik-ingly candid impression in *Calamus* #29:

One flitting glimpse, caught through an interstice,
Of a crowd of workmen and drivers in a bar-room, around the stove,
   late of a winter night—And I unremarked, seated in a corner;
Of a youth who loves me, and whom I love, silently approaching,
   and seating himself near, that he may hold me by the hand;
A long while, amid the noises of coming and going—
   of drinking and oath and smutty jest,
There we two, content, happy in being together, speaking little,
   perhaps not a word.

Certainly with the appearance of *Leaves of Grass* there was not much sitting unremarked in corners of Whitman. The celebrity loafer and liter-atus was seen more and more in the famous basement-level saloons of Broadway (shades of the poet Hoffmann carousing in the rowdy dive, Luther's, in Offenbach's *Tales of Hoffmann*). Among these thriving bohemian venues—Murger's *Scènes de la Vie de Bohème* had appeared in 1851 and was all the rage—were Taylor's Saloon, Platt's Saloon, and, most notably, Pfaff's, which from 1857 to 1862 was located on Broad-way between Houston and Bleecker. The keeper of the "drinking-house" visited by Franklin was "not an American"; nor was Charles Ignatius

Pfaff. His establishment—which seems to have served a motley and marginal band of artists, courtesans, actors, sexual free spirits, and political radicals—became a favorite hangout for Whitman. At least one letter to him begins, "To the Prince of Bohemians Walt Whitman."

In his old age, in fact, the place came to evoke some of his fondest memories of his pre–Civil War, chimes-at-midnight days. On an 1881 visit to the city he returned to the old stomping ground (now on Twenty-fourth Street) and recorded his reunion with Pfaff:

> Our host himself, an old friend of mine, quickly appear'd on the scene to welcome me and bring up the news, and, first opening a big fat bottle of the best wine in the cellar, talk about ante-bellum times, '59 and '60, and the jovial suppers at his then Broadway place, near Bleecker street. Ah, the friends and names and frequenters, those times, that place. Most are dead . . . all gone. And there Pfaff and I, sitting opposite each other at the little table, gave a remembrance to them in a style they would have themselves fully confirm'd, namely, big, brimming, fill'd-up champagne-glasses, drain'd in abstracted silence, very leisurely, to the last drop.*

Pfaff's was known for its talk and talkers, but Whitman told Traubel that he "was never a great discusser" and was happy just to look on. From a corner table? Holding a lover's hand under the table? Perhaps, for some suggest that Whitman met his working-class lover Fred Vaughan at Pfaff's; he may even be the lover referred to in *Calamus #29*.

And Pfaff's, too, must have been the kind of public resort in which his circle of gay friends was able to grow. Though some infamous women of the day were well known at Pfaff's (among them the actresses Ada Clare, Queen of Bohemia, and Adah Menken, famed for her Naked Lady stage role) and Whitman included the names of two in his 1881 reminiscence, Pfaff's seems to have been for him a "boy bar." In a twenty-line poetic fragment, perhaps written at one of its tables but never published, Whitman leaves a distinctly all-male impression: "Laugh on laughers! / Drink on drinkers! / Bandy the jest! / Toss the theme from one to another! / Beam up—brighten up, bright eyes of beautiful young men!" By 1875, his mind had obliterated all memories of Pfaff's, except for the boys: "I often recall the old times in New York, or on Broadway, or at Pfaff's—& the faces & voices of *the boys*." On a visit to the city five years earlier, Whitman waxed just as nostalgic. And since his reminiscences were contained in a personal letter to his boyfriend of the time, Peter Doyle, the talk is all about the boys: "I fall in with quite a good many of my acquaintances of years ago—the young fellows (now not so young)—that I knew intimately here before the war—some are dead—& some have got married [as "lost" to Whitman as the dead!]—& some have grown rich."

Now, one's Manhattan gay circle is bound to include, over the years, some who can't take the pace, the filth, the always present dangers of city life and others whose hopes for success as actors, artists, or stockbrokers are dashed. And so they leave. Some do modestly well and remain to lead an agreeable existence. Others thrive, sometimes spectacularly, and end up resident in penthouses with wrap-around terraces. In his letter to Doyle, Whitman goes on to describe his reunion with one of the last type. He seems clearly gay—Whitman carefully avoids naming him—and thrilled to show off his nouveau riche affluence: "one of the latter [rich friends] I was up with yesterday & last night—he has a big house on Fifth avenue—I was there to dinner (dinner at 8 p.m.!)—every thing in the loudest sort of style, with wines, silver, nigger waiters, &c. &c. &c." One might think this the sort of atmosphere guaranteed to make the despiser of fashionable society restless, but Whitman explains, "my friend is just one of the manliest, jovialist best sort of fellows—no airs—& just the one to suit you & me—no women in the house—he is single—he wants me to make my home there." Whitman quickly assures Doyle, "I shall not do that, but shall go there very frequently—the dinners & good wines are attractive—then there is a fine library."

Whitman declines his rich friend's offer to move into the 1870s equivalent of an East Side townhouse or a duplex in Trump Tower, of course, because he was happier amid calico shirts and pewter than amid "nigger" waiters and silverware. Today, Chelsea or the East Village would probably be more to his taste. That he would even consent to become a regular visitor on Fifth Avenue and betray his beloved and sleazy Broadway hints at what reaching the age of fifty can do to even the most vocal and athletic celebrators of the bohemian life.

But while this life lasted—that is, until 1860—his partisanship for the "moral" and "physical" Other became increasingly clear. In its 1856 and 1860 versions, Whitman ended "By Blue Ontario's Shore" with this stunning cast of his vote: "I have learned why the earth is gross, tantalizing, wicked—it is for my sake, / I take you to be mine, you beautiful, terrible, rude forms." There was no "earth" in America more gross, tantalizing, and wicked than mid-century Mannahatta, nor could any native earth present more eligible creatures with beautiful, terrible, rude forms for his keen inspection. And so he became a typical "Manhattanese," eager for the sun to set and the "rude" hunt to begin. Examples of the type, which he finely sketches in his 1860 poem "Native Moments," can still be found in abundance in the city. Indeed, "Native Moments" could be the theme of the hundreds who patronize the Roxy, the Pavilion on Fire Island, or whatever disco palace is currently in vogue:

> Give me now libidinous joys only!
> Give me the drench of my passions! Give me life coarse and rank!
> To-day, I go consort with nature's darlings—to-night too,
> I am for those who believe in loose delights—I share the
>   midnight orgies of young men,
> I dance with the dancers, and drink with the drinkers,
> The echoes ring with our indecent calls,
> I take for my love some prostitute—I pick out some low
>   person for my dearest friend,
> He shall be lawless, rude, illiterate—he shall be one
>   condemned by others for deeds done;
> I will play a part no longer—Why should I exile myself from my
>   companions?

CONCEALED BUT SUBSTANTIAL LIFE

In 1859 or so, the question was rhetorical. When Whitman composed these lines, he had evidently already cultivated the friendship of a large circle of nature's darlings and experienced many loose delights. Ironically, just a year after "Native Moments" appeared, he would exile himself from these companions to follow the Army of the Potomac and tend the bedside of wounded and dying soldiers.

A long letter from Washington in March 1863 to a couple of his intimates back in New York, however, suggests that Whitman missed being relaxed and not playing a part among them. The letter has all the feel of a gay report from the front. He remarks on finding "always the sick and dying soldiers begin to cling to me in a way that makes a fellow feel funny enough"—"funny," surely, because he had so recently been accustomed to the "cling" of a very different kind ("two boys together clinging"). Whitman boasts of striking up "a tremendous friendship with a young Mississippi captain (about 19) that we took prisoner badly wounded at Frederiksburgh." He has "eyes bright as a hawk, but face pale—our affection is an affair quite romantic—sometimes when I lean over to say I am going, he puts his arms around my neck, draws my face down, etc., quite a scene for the New Bowery." Only the Bowery's "heterogeneous melange," apparently, could handle such same-sex passion. The "etc." is coyly tantalizing, like his promise, "I have some curious yarns I promise you my darlings and gossips, by word of mouth whene'er we meet." Indeed, he calls his two friends "gossips" and "darlings" several more times. The 220-pounder jokes about retaining "my usual perfect shape—a regular model" and ends his "astoundingly magnificent letter—certainly the longest I ever wrote in my life" by saying his "heart panteth" for news of "everybody." He hopes his "darling, dearest boys" will send him news of six fellows in particular, including one "twinkling and temperate Towle."*

This affectionately cheeky letter raises an obvious question. How did Whitman, later in the 1840s and early in the 1850s, gather his circle of "darling, dearest boys" about him? Locating prostitutes was scarcely a problem in his day. He shows us how it is done in "To a Common Prostitute," though the poet lost his nerve and changed the gender-concealing "My love" in his manuscript to a civilian-pleasing "My girl." But detecting and attracting "nature's darlings"—not to mention that one "Lover divine and perfect Comrade" among them—requires considerable finesse. How did Whitman manage this?

The brief answer lies in the steps down to the basement vaults of Pfaff's, where Whitman said he could carouse,

> While on the walk immediately overhead pass the myriad feet of
>   Broadway
> As the dead in their graves are underfoot hidden
> And the living pass over them, recking not of them . . .

This is a fine image for the life of the Other—and also of the carouse that is possible in the vault of the Closet, hemmed though it may be with the horror of spiritual death. Whitman, in other words, went underground: into a nether world "recked not" by the oblivious straight citizenry of midcentury New York. From his table at Pfaff's, he could see them, but they could not see him.

The unfinished poem about Pfaff's is titled "The Two Vaults": "The lights beam in the first vault—but the other is entirely dark." Whitman, one might say, left the entirely dark and profound lonely personal vault, whose presence is alluded to countless times in his early poems:

> I cannot say to any person what I hear . . . . I cannot say it to
>   myself . . . . it is very wonderful.

> These yearnings why are they? these thoughts in the darkness why
>   are they?

I hear secret convulsive sobs from young men at anguish with
  themselves . . .

Sullen and suffering hours! (I am ashamed—but it is useless—I am
  what I am) . . .

He moved, as it were, not out onto the sunlit flagstones of the city where
his desires and behavior might frighten the horses and many a civilian,
but into the *other* vault, with its beaming lights, carousing—and comrades. This transition is superbly evoked in *Calamus #6.*

In some remarkably candid lines he wrote for an early version of the
first *Calamus* poem, Whitman explained this transit into the festively
vaulted Closet:

Long I was held by the life that exhibits itself,
By what is done in the houses or streets, or in company,
The usual adjustments and pleasures—the things which all
  conform to and which the writers celebrate;
But now I know a life which does not exhibit itself, yet
  contains all the rest,
And now, escaping, I celebrate that concealed but substantial life,
I celebrate the need of the love of comrades.

These lines apparently, on further thought, were deemed *too* candid. The
final version of *Calamus* #1, though more strenuously poetical, is not
nearly as pointed, and the excellent phrase "concealed but substantial life"
is lost. Affiliating himself with this love of comrades that does not exhibit
itself, Whitman had to become a skilled cryptographer of the sexual identities and Closets of others, an adept at "piercing through to the accepted
hells beneath." For then—as, to a lesser degree, now—the gay life was inevitably quasi-cryptographic. It functions through the subtle emanation
and attentive recognition of "secret and divine signs." The searcher who
desires to find others with his "own odor" (*Calamus* #25), others with
"blood like mine" circling in their veins (*Calamus* #42)—this searcher
must become an expert in breaking down the barriers of concealment and
frightened indirection that are necessitated by the closeted life.

This Whitman did. For all the boastful *blague* about self-revelation in
Leaves of Grass, much of the energy and fascination of the early poems is
focused on the cunning, ingratiating penetration of the sexual identity of
another . . . or of the reader. Whitman jotted down in one of his early
notebooks a description of someone (manifestly himself) who "can tear

off all the husks and pierce straight through every stratagem of concealment and [go] to the actual." This image became a passage in "Song of
the Open Road" (1856) in which the prying urge is focused with bold
explicitness on the closeted, adhesive reader:

> Only the kernel of every object nourishes;
> Where is he who tears off the husks for you and me?
> Where is he that undoes stratagems and envelopes for you and me?
>
> Here is adhesiveness, it is not previously fashion'd, it is apropos;
> Do you know what it is as you pass to be loved by strangers?
> Do you know the talk of those turning eye-balls?

Whitman lulls us with the notion of a mutual process, but the reality of
Leaves is that the poet is the busily husking party, the eager searcher for
the "kernel" that will nourish his queer desire, the loving stranger poised
for the possibility that a turning eyeball will meet his and respond.

Whitman liked to boast about being "a candid and unloosed summer-
poet," as he did in "So Long!" But it would be exceedingly naive and
unwise to accept this at face value. To a sympathetic Dutchman he later
confided more honestly that his poetry operated "sometime by directions,
but oftener by indirections." The night and the manly, robust underground were his real Manhattan elements, and many of his early poems,
as he says in "Spontaneous Me," are "poems of the privacy of the night,
and of men like me." The poet's desire to maintain this privacy while still
"publishing" his Personality generated the hundreds, if not thousands, of
indirections in *Leaves of Grass*. He wanted, in other words, to celebrate
the concealed but substantial queer life without blowing its cover—or
his. Thus, the image he offered to another sympathetic foreigner, this
time the Englishman Edward Carpenter, about the writing of *Leaves*
makes the point perfectly. "There is something in my nature *furtive* like
an old hen!" he told Carpenter during a visit in 1884. "You see a hen
wandering up and down a hedgerow, looking apparently quite uncon-
cerned, but presently she finds a concealed spot, and furtively lays an egg,
and comes away as though nothing had happened! That is how I felt in
writing *Leaves of Grass*."

Whitman did not mind (probably enjoyed with conspiratorial glee)
allowing his civilian readers to go away thinking that "nothing had happened" sexually or homosexually in his poetry . . . or in his life. But
Whitman was sociable even in his furtiveness; he wanted an audience of
cognoscenti to enjoy his skills. He wanted *someone* to spot his hen's eggs

of adhesiveness and comradery. He says so in *Calamus #41*: "Ah lover and perfect equal, / I meant that you should discover me so by faint indirections." The "you" here, however, is not every reader but only the reader who, like Whitman, knows the ways of furtive, closeted hens—his reader, that is to say, familiar with "la cage aux folles."

Whitman recorded in a notebook sometime in the 1850s that the "greatest poems may not immediately be fully understood by outsiders any more than astronomy or engineering can," and by that standard the early *Leaves* editions constitute a great poem. Whitman once explained that one of the three "leading sources and formative stamps to my own character" was a "subterranean tenacity," and there is likewise in the early editions a furtive but tenacious queer subtext that outsiders or civilians are very unlikely to detect, or fully appreciate if they do.

When a homosexual was detected in Whitman's day, he was abhorred and, as "Native Moments" implied, "condemned by others for deeds done." "Beasts in human shape," the novelist George Thompson called gays in his 1849 novel *City Crimes; or, Life in New York and Boston*. If detected by the police, they might have been (though extremely rarely were) prosecuted under sodomy laws then in force. Glancing allusions to these laws are scattered through *Leaves*: the lovers of *Calamus #26* fulfilling their foray and "statutes mocking" in the process; the "outlaw'd offenders" scanned "with kindred eyes" by the poet in "Starting from Paumanok"; the poet not bothered by his "crimes" in "Me Imperturbe"; or the anti–sodomy law plea in *Calamus #24* for the "institution of the dear love of comrades" without "edifices or rules or trustees." But to be found out by detective Whitman was a much gentler fate, for to him "detected persons are not, in any respect, worse than undetected persons—and are not in any respect worse than I am myself." He himself wanted to be detected, and so furtively diffused his "faint clews and indirections." In "When I Read the Book," he says these clues and indirections are "few," but in fact they were very numerous.

Leaves of Grass must be thought of as, among other things, a gay *poème à clef*. Whitman clearly invested much effort in appealing to, challenging, and satisfying the great majority of those readers who, he knew, did not hold the key. Some, like Rufus Griswold, would grasp the key and explode in righteous dudgeon. Others, responsive to his poetry and his overall agenda, might still draw the line at its sexual implications. One such was William Sloane Kennedy, who met the poet in 1880 and eventually wrote a book about him. In a manuscript scrap Whitman says of him, "Among my special young men *littérateur* friends are W S Kennedy. . . . A young college chap—Greek, Latin &c—Accepts L of G,—

yet bolts at the sexual part—*but I consider Kennedy as a real & ardent friend both of self & book.*"

Still another class of readers might be so firmly closeted that the key would go unused. One suspects that twenty-six-year-old William Alcott, a Camden fireman who died in 1874, might have been one of these. Whitman says in a touching little eulogy that "our love grew fast and close," and adds mournfully, "I think there were currents of emotion and intellect undevelop'd beneath, far deeper than his acquaintances ever suspected—or than he himself ever did. He was no talker. His troubles, when he had any, he kept to himself." Alcott obviously defeated Whitman's efforts to tear off his husk and reach the kernel. Such frustration must have occurred to him often, as it seems to have done with the young soldier Benton Wilson in 1867: "I wish things were situated so you could be with me, & we could be together for a while, where we could enjoy each others society & sweet friendship & you could talk freely. . . . but [I] will not at present say much to you on the subject, in writing." Sometimes, as here, distance made intimacy difficult, but on other occasions it must have become clear that the wished-for sexual responsiveness would not be forthcoming.

The final rapture of *Leaves of Grass*, however, is achieved when a reader comes who grasps its key *and* desires to turn the lock, the reader who gladly nominates himself a "detected person." As he admits in *Calamus #2*, Whitman knew that readers up to the olfactory challenge of phallus-shaped *Calamus aromaticus* would be rare: "I do not know whether many passing by will discover you or inhale your faint odor, but I believe a few will." One such reader was the young Charles Warren Stoddard, who read *Leaves* and made bold to write an effusive, idolizing letter about his same-sex adventures in Hawaii. Whitman replied supportively but with a word of warning about being too emotive: "As to you, I do not of course object to your emotional & adhesive nature, & the outlet thereof [!], but warmly approve them—but do you know (perhaps you do,) how the hard, pungent, gritty, worldly experiences & qualities in American practical life, also serve? how they prevent extravagant sentimentalism?" Whitman adds, in closing, "I am not a little comforted when I learn that young men dwell in thought upon me & my utterances."

Another "detected person" was Bram Stoker, who also read *Leaves* and was moved in 1872, at the age of twenty-four, to write the author. The gushing letter he first composed, however, lay in a drawer for four years before the odor of *Calamus aromaticus* finally overwhelmed him and he mailed it. In his cover letter of 1876, Stoker says, "I write this openly because I feel with you one must be open."* (When Horace Traubel reread the letter to Whitman in 1889, Whitman said this sentence had "hit me hard" and added, "That's it: that's me, as I hope I am: it's *Leaves of Grass* if *Leaves of Grass* is anything.")

The pleasure Whitman must have felt when he read Stoker's original letter can be easily imagined. Stoker hopes first that Whitman will enjoy a letter "from a younger man, a stranger, across the world—a man living in an atmosphere prejudiced to the truths you sing." He calls *Leaves* "the most candid words that ever fell from the lips of mortal man" and, acknowledging his husk torn away by reading them, he writes, "a man cannot in a moment break the habit of comparative reticence that has become second nature to him; but I know I would not be long ashamed to be natural before you," and "You have shaken off the shackles and your wings are free. I have the shackles on my shoulders still—but I have no wings." But because Whitman is "different from other men," Stoker, though "naturally secretive to the world," seeks to reveal himself with his idol's honesty, even if rather unappetizingly: "I am ugly but strong and determined. . . . I have a heavy jaw and a big mouth and thick lips—sensitive nostrils—a snub nose and straight hair." Before closing he adds a remark that is *Leaves of Grass* if *Leaves of Grass* is anything: "sometimes a word or a phrase of yours takes me away from the world around me and places me in an ideal land. . . ."

Whitman responded with a short, rather stately thank-you saying the letters were "most welcome to me—welcome to me as Person and as Author—I don't know which most—You did well to write me so unconventionally, so fresh, so manly, and so affectionately, too." And he adds, "Live here quite lonesome, but hearty, and good spirits." Though an ocean separated Stoker and Whitman, *Leaves* had done its work. It had brought two persons—secretive because, as Stoker says, of an atmosphere of prejudice—into natural and nonchalant intimacy. And it had revealed to Stoker that, though concealed, his life was indeed substantial . . . and shared with others. This, surely, is the point he makes in the last sentence of his letter to Whitman: "I thank you for all the love and sympathy you have given me in common with my kind."

O I CRUISE THE OLD CRUISE AGAIN!

Whitman the Person, dweller in Mannahatta, must have evoked the same variety of responses to his own sex life as he did, as Author, in the sex life of *Leaves of Grass*. The blissfully ignorant of course left him to his recreations. Gossip, embarrassing encounters, slipups in his furtive "stratagems," or misguided attempts to bark up a heterosexual tree must have subjected him on occasion to homophobic ridicule. *Leaves* is scattered with allusions to this: the "slights and degradations cast by arrogant persons," the "mocking taunt," the awareness of "how it stings to be slighted," and the defenses of "venerealees" and those "others are down upon."

But the supreme task for Whitman as he walked the flagstones, rode the horsecars and ferries, haunted the theaters, opera houses, saloons, or roamed the parks and piers was to spot, meet, and ingratiate himself to the Stoddards and Stokers in his own midst. Among his most earnest pastimes, it seems, was "Picking out here one that shall be my amie, / Choosing to go with him on brotherly terms." That the object of his cruise was a sexual encounter seems sweatily clear in the equine image that follows in "Song of Myself":

> A gigantic beauty of a stallion, fresh and responsive to my caresses,
> Head high in the forehead and wide between the ears,
> Limbs glossy and supple, tail dusting the ground,
> Eyes well apart and full of sparkling wickedness . . .
> His nostrils dilate . . . . my heels embrace him . . . . his well built limbs
>   tremble with pleasure . . .

To corral such a creature, Whitman became, quite obviously, an ardent, inveterate, and keen-eyed cruiser. To "cruise my old cruise again" he counts among the joys of his 1860 poem, "A Song of Joys." In the passage "One of the Human Kinks" in *Specimen Days* he observes, "one is never entirely without the instinct of looking around, (I never am, and others tell me the same of themselves, confidentially,) for somebody to appear, or start up out of the earth, or from behind some tree or rock." Spoken like a true, ever-expectant cruiser out at large in the *al fresco* environs of Long Island, as Whitman often was.

Allen Ginsberg's famous line about Walt as a "lonely old grubber, poking among the meats in the refrigerator and eyeing the grocery boys" is catty, perhaps, but expresses a potent truth about him. His life's work, itself an elaborate poetical cruising machine with all manner of furtive bells and whistles, is rich in vignettes of the cruising style that will be instantly recognizable to any practiced gay veteran of New York. The prey, of course, is "one goodshaped and wellhung man." Whitman's "wellhung" is drawn from carpentry, but he would have understood and delighted in our current idiom, too. Though Stoker calls him a "keen physiognomist," his close attention could be drawn elsewhere. A "well-made man" appears in "I Sing the Body Electric," and Whitman takes slow ocular pleasure in his wellmadeness. As especially entranced cruisers will do, he undresses the man in fantasy (I quote the 1855 version):

> . . . it is curiously in the joints of his hips and wrists,
> It is in his walk . . the carriage of his neck . . the flex of his waist
>   and knees . . . . dress does not hide him,
> The strong sweet supple quality he has strikes through the cotton
>   and flannel;
> To see him pass conveys as much as the best poem . . perhaps more.

The gorgeous creature passes on, and the cruiser casts a final admiring glance at the departing torso: "You linger to see his back and the back of his neck and shoulderside."*

The cruiser's pose, especially in such a ravishing presence, is often a curious mixture of apparently blasé indifference and electric sexual tension. Of this there are also many glimpses in *Leaves*. Among the joys of "manly self-hood" is the power to "look with calm gaze or with a flashing eye." In the midst of the "pulling and hauling" of daily life, we learn in "Song of Myself," stands the loafing Walt "amused, complacent, compassionating, idle, unitary." And he stands there looking "with side-curved head curious what will come next, / Both in and out of the game"—a perfect evocation of the gay man on cruise control: complacently or aloofly uninterested one moment, then suddenly and secretly "compassionating" when an object of particular desire appears.

The difficulty of New York, though, is that there are so many potential objects of desire. The "So many men, so little time!" catchphrase, very popular just after Stonewall, now and then echoes in Whitman. His lovers are many but they are loved from afar. "I love him though I do not know him," says Whitman in "Song of Myself" of a young fellow driving an express wagon. "Do I not often meet strangers in the street and love them?" he asked rhetorically in another 1855 poem. In "Crossing Brooklyn Ferry" of 1856 he speaks about "many I loved in the street or ferry-boat or public assembly, yet never told them a word." He has even kept silent as he "Felt their arms on my neck as I stood, or the negligent leaning of their flesh against me as I sat."

The eager but always seemingly frustrated love-fantasy is repeated again in 1860, with the admission in *Calamus* #16 that the poet is given to secretly loving strangers: "O tenderly, a long time, and never avow it." Countless cruising scenes are split-second affairs, though sometimes powerfully implanted in memory. Whitman finely phrases this as Manhattan's "frequent and swift flash of eyes." An example is caught in these lines (later deleted) in "A Song of Joys": "O the streets of cities! / The flitting faces—the expressions, eyes, feet, costumes! . . . The memory of only one look—the boy lingering and waiting." Occasionally, a cruiser will become more intensely "involved" with a stranger, usually when paths cross in the course of daily routine. A kind of stalking begins to occur, yet nothing happens. A *Calamus* poem perfectly captures such an occurrence:

> O YOU whom I often and silently come where you are that I may be
>   with you,
> As I walk by your side or sit near, or remain in the same room
>   with you,
> Little you know the subtle electric fire that for your sake is playing
>   within me.

Cruising, with all its mute "talk of those turning eye-balls," is predominantly about failed communication, missed connections, and the fantasies they generate. Many gay newspapers, in fact, have "Missed Connections" or "Parting Glances" advertising sections with personals like this: "We took the E train together uptown at 23rd St. We danced with our eyes but never said a word. Now all I can hope is that you find this and call." Or: "You: on bench, green sweatshirt, cap with bike. Me: Latino too shy to say 'Hi.' How about another chance?" Or—very like Whitman—on a bus: "you had on a black sweater and a beautiful smile. Me: blue/gray sweatshirt. Got off at Powell, regret not talking to you. Can I have a second chance?"

The finest of Whitman's "cruising" poems, "To a Stranger" from *Calamus*, describes such a missed connection in just ten vivid lines, while also conveying the impetus for the cruising habit. It begins,

> PASSING stranger! you do not know how longingly I look upon you,
> You must be he I was seeking, or she I was seeking, (it comes to me
>   as of a dream,)
> I have somewhere surely lived a life of joy with you . . .

Whitman often added an alternative heterosexual phrase (here "or she I was seeking") to conceal a sexual implication, but the context of the sequence makes the homosexual implications clear. In the middle of the poem time stops; the poet experiences a dream-fantasy of spiritual union with the stranger. This ends with a more physical image: "You give me the pleasure of your eyes, face, flesh, as we pass, you take of my beard, breast, hands." Then the clock begins ticking again; the stranger vanishes. And the solitary cruiser is left behind, hoping the cruiser's quenchless hope:

> I am not to speak to you, I am to think of you
>> when I sit alone or wake at night alone,
> I am to wait, I do not doubt I am to meet you again,
> I am to see to it that I do not lose you.

But enough of the frustrating experiences of the cruiser who finally chooses to stay "out of the game." Sometimes, when the mood and the time and the face are right, the cruiser will jump into the game and attempt to make contact. The crucial finesse for these moments is to allow the "subtle electric fire" of sexual interest to be recognized, but discreetly. Whitman explains this etiquette of cruising in "Poets to Come":

> I am a man who, sauntering along without fully stopping,
>> turns a casual look upon you and then averts his face,
> Leaving it to you to prove and define it,
> Expecting the main things from you.

Whitman seems to have become a master of this ability to draw out the "main things" from his casual acquaintances, notably in the course of his constant trolling on Manhattan's vehicles of public transport. He boasts about this skill in "Song of the Open Road" when he asks, "What is it I interchange so suddenly with strangers? / What with some driver as I ride on the seat by his side?" He would later meet at least one great love, the horsecar conductor Peter Doyle, in this fashion.

Once skillful eye contact achieves its purpose and conversation is initiated, the cruiser's abilities to ingratiate come into play. Over the course of the 1840s and 1850s Whitman must have developed a very smooth line. Part of his agenda in *Leaves of Grass* was to expand the vocabulary for the "friendly sentiments" between men and to find what he called the right "impetus-words" to pursue his desires. "Comradeship," he said, was one such word, and we might add some other obvious ones: *manly, robust, athletic, adhesive,* perhaps even *gay.* Impetus-words were very useful in gaining the confidence, then the intimacy, and perhaps even the sexual society of the young men he was constantly meeting in the city. They aided him as he made his moves. The garrulous schmoozer boasts, in 1860, of this skill at "young men my problems offering—no dallier I— I the muscle of their brains trying."

Our best evidence for this skill comes from Whitman's memoirs, the references in his letters to so many young men who figured among his "darlings" and "gossips," and the long lists of such acquaintances that he kept in his notebooks. On his trip in 1848 down to New Orleans, he couldn't help noticing the groups of "tall, strapping, comely young men" at various stops on the river, and this epitomizes his ideal of male beauty. In the fascinating notebook lists we find confirmation of his preference expressed, in "Song of Myself," for the "well-tann'd" and those with "scars and the beard and faces pitted with smallpox over all latherers" (i.e. the clean-shaven).

In a period of several months in 1857, for example, he ran the gamut of young men. First, the obvious loser: a twenty-six-year-old named Charley he met on Fifth Avenue struck him as "hurt, diseased, deprived." Others displayed good and bad points: a "young [good] married [bad] man" on the #18 line with "bad teeth good eyes," a fellow on Fourth Avenue with a "thin face superb sonorous voice," a "broad-shouldered, six-footer, with a hare-lip," or one Jack who "had the French pox" but was "tall slender." An Edward Payne was a "youthful" twenty-four but, alas, "hectic."

Other acquaintances were most definitely not Whitman's type: an effeminate Bob, for instance, who is described simply as "hermaphrodite." One Traverce Hedgeman, a Seventh Avenue conductor, was ideally "young" but, being also "slight fair feminine," perhaps not quite Walt's cup. More plausible, apparently, to this connoisseur was one Arthur: "big round sandy hair coarse, open." But an Irishman, John Kiernan, must have been even nearer the Whitman *beau idéal*: "loafer young saucy looking pretty goodlooking."

Though no notebook entries seem to refer to the endowment of his comrades, it is hard to imagine the phallic singer not paying attention sometimes to how his pals were "hung." He was certainly familiar with the concept behind that modern slang in his Manhattan days. In 1889 a new slang expression, "He's not built that way," came up, and Whitman recalled, "Years ago in New York there was an expression similar . . . but that was indelicate. The phrase was 'He does not hang that way.' You can see its import. Of course that could not find adoption, especially in litera-ture. It was vulgar, had its brief day, is gone." Social mores, apparently, deprived us of a more colorful *Leaves of Grass* than we have.

And the word "hustler"? Traubel reports that Walt laughingly asked him what it meant one day. " 'Hustler' is a new vulgarism for a busy man," he said, and Walt responded, "Thought that must have been its meaning, but I did not know." Though Whitman did not learn the modern gay meaning of the term, he doubtless encountered the busy phe-nomenon itself among what he called the "he-harlots" of the streets and barrooms of the city.

Whitman was still proving no dallier in the few months just before he left for Washington in 1862. Like most veteran cruisers, he could be cruel in his judgments of those who turned him off, though, as will sometimes happen, sheer horniness might urge him on. We learn, for instance, about a desirably "tallish, thinnish" fellow who unfortunately had an "oily, labial way of talking," of a "harsh-faced" boy named Talbot, and of a twenty-three-year-old who lived with his mother and was, well, just "plain homely."

This raises the question, what was "good soma" for Whitman? He seems to have leaned strongly toward the tall and slender. These epithets appear often, as, for example, in the entry for a David Burver: "American stock—tall and slender." In a manuscript from the mid-1850s, in fact, is a revealing synopsis Whitman made of the four temperaments as revealed in body type. He obviously saw himself as the Sanguine type: "well-defined form—moderate plumpness—firm flesh . . . great fondness for exercise and air—Brain active . . . has hilarity and hope, lights up the countenance, impels to motion and to animal gayety." Such indeed is the essential Whitman pose. Less desirable or sexually auspicious was the Lymphatic type: "round form, soft muscle . . . Brain languid—other organs [!] ditto." Twice Whitman uses the word in his lists: once for a James Myers ("fat, lymphatic & rosy") and once for a John Campbell ("round light complex lymphatic, good-look"). The famously heavyweight poet, apparently, could make exceptions. The other two temperaments doubtless evoked small interest from Whitman. These were the Bilious ("black hair, dark skin, moderate stoutness, firm flesh, harsh features") and the Nervous ("fine thin hair—small muscles—thin skin—pale countenance").

Whitman's preference was for "butch" muscularity rather than "femme" slimness and uncommanding vocalism. He was also dead set against the world of what would now be considered cologned, monogrammed, designer-labeled faggotry. No Barney's, no Bloomingdale's. Strictly The Gap or L. L. Bean. This bias was made amusingly clear when he reminisced one Saturday afternoon in 1888 about a fellow named Ned Wilkins, one of his few vigorous defenders around the tables at Pfaff's in the early days: "Ned was courageous: in an out-and-out way very friendly to Leaves of Grass: free-spoken—always willing to let it be known what he thought. . . . He was always plucky." And Whitman adds, "let me say this: I never heard Ned say a foolish thing: every remark had its place, its point." But, alas, this fellow with an ACT-UPer's salient spirit was physically the Walt anti-type. He was remembered as "slim, sickish, dressy, Frenchy—consumptive in look, in gait: weak-voiced: oh! I think he had the weakest voice I ever knew in a man." His toilette was far too much for the "rowdyish" and "unrefined" poet. He was "what we nowadays call a dude: kid-gloved, scrupulous—oh! squeamish!—about his linen, about his tie—all that. . . . Ned's dressiness was immense—almost painful: his perfume, washèdness, strangely excessive." The type has not vanished.

Whitman adds that much "comment and amusement" was had at the expense of poor "naturally weak, loose-jointed, thin in the girth" Wilkins. It is disagreeable to think Whitman might have taken part in this all-too-familiar harassment of an effeminate homosexual, but more heartening to record a kind of eulogy for Wilkins ("full of feeling," Traubel noticed) with which Whitman ended his reminiscence. He was referring to the oppression of *Leaves of Grass*, but his words apply eloquently to the baiting of poor Wilkins and, by extension, to homophobia in general:

> Then W. said sadly: "You know, he died within a couple of years." W. added: "Such a defender at that time was appreciated. I don't know if you have ever realized it—ever realized what it means to be a horror in the sight of the people about you: but there was a time when I felt it to the full—when the enemy—and nearly all were the enemy then—wanted for nothing better or more than simply, without remorse, to crush me, to brush me, without compunction or mercy, out of sight, out of hearing: to do anything, everything, to rid themselves of me.

Whitman developed the habit of including in his notebooks details about the young men he met that might encourage or discourage hope for a sexual encounter. An Englishman named Tom, "good looking, 24 yr's," charmed him, but he learned Tom had "married young, has three children living." Joseph Cornell is "smallish, married," while the appealingly "blondish sandy" Cornelius Van Winkle is "married, no children." Whitman was no doubt sorry when he had to record that a boy like George Nauck ("aged 23, blonde and boyish") "lives home." More hopeful was the information that a Joseph Le Charlier has "parents in N.J." or that "John Gueey, Gooeey, Gwoeey"—he didn't quite catch the name—"20 yrs of age—little fellow, very youthful . . . does not board home." Many who flit into the cruiser's field of vision, of course, prove to be very speedy birds of passage. Whitman had met an eighteen-year-old "in the bath" but informs his journal that he has now "gone to California."

Many are the pitfalls and pratfalls of the cruising game. Sometimes a cruiser will be enticed and yet finally decide something is wrong with the picture. Perhaps this happened with one Philip he was with on a Broadway streetcar on 8 November: "black-eyed brownish sharp-faced, with a suspicion of a squint in his eyes—reckless—." On other occasions, the blend of off-putting and on-putting features can prove disconcerting, as happened when Whitman met James Doyle on a Madison Avenue streetcar the night of 3 October: "plumpish young fellow, always smiling . . . (hardly any chin) coarse pleasing smiling round face." It sometimes happens, too, that a likely boy proves not to be of the cruiser's sexual persuasion. Peter Calhoun, a twenty-three-year-old canalhand, caught Whitman's fancy, but he could not have been very happy to be regaled on a long streetcar ride with Calhoun's story of "his affair with the woman in Brooklyn and N.Y."* Also occasionally, one will encounter a plausible sex partner temptingly impaired by alcohol. One wonders if this happened the night of 7 October, when Whitman came upon a "young man, drunk" and walked him "home" up Fulton and High Streets. His own home? The boy's? And what happened? Did Whitman, staggering down Fulton, conclude the boy was straight or too drunk to function and so become a Samaritan? Or did the liquor loosen the boy's inhibitions and lead to an encounter? We'll never know, but neither scenario can be ruled out.

Some of Whitman's meetings were more agreeable. The young abolitionist, for example, he had met at Pfaff's on 16 August—"black eyed (with a cast)—pale—makes a good impression on me"—or the "welltann'd" driver he met three days later on Broadway, or the conductor on the #4 line who caused him to ride two trips on Thanksgiving night. A "thinnish, rather tallish" twenty-one-year-old Joseph Perry pleased Walt because he was "always cheerful and laughing." A Henry Kelly, about twenty-four, had a "florid face" and a "fresh and direct" manner, but "I notice a few gray hairs." On another day he chatted with a "fresh and affectionate" nineteen-year-old from upstate named Aaron Cohn. The poet was obviously pleased when Cohn "spoke much of a young man named *Gilbert L. Bill* (of Lyme, Connecticut) who thought deeply about *Leaves of Grass*, and wished to see me." Intrigued, Walt did research and learned that Bill was in law school at Albany.

An essential part of successful cruising, of course, is knowing where one's own kind are most likely to be accessible. Most famously for Whitman, this was public transportation. He enthused all his life about "the flush days of the old Broadway stages" and the "immense qualities, largely animal" of their drivers, so many of whom gave him "comradeship, and sometimes affection." Though he thought it might make his critics laugh, he even said their "declamations and escapades undoubtedly enter'd into the gestation of *Leaves of Grass*." Likewise for the ferries and their crewmen. What Whitman obviously didn't care for were the "roof'd rooms" and fancy parlors of the bourgeoisie and the upper crust. "In any roof'd room I emerge not," he warned in *Calamus #3*. Much better the rustic corners of the city and Long Island: in the same poem he says he is more likely to "emerge" to a lover "in some wood" or "back of a rock in the open air," or "on a high hill, first watching lest any person for miles around approach unawares."

"Song of Myself," in so many ways a cruiser's apologia, reveals much about the sites of Mannahatta that Whitman favored. In section 33 the poet unlooses his "ties and ballasts" and goes out "afoot with my vision." Many of the haunts he mentions there must have been part of his own cruising life. The world of the all-male drinking houses, for example, is captured in the line about "he-festivals, with blackguard gibes, ironical license, bull-dances [nineteenth-century slang for a same-sex dance], drinking, laughter."

Also mentioned in Section 33 are two extremely agreeable sites for cruising: "the gymnasium" and plunges where "the splash of swimmers and divers cools the warm noon." Anyone who has belonged to a Manhattan Y or health club will be familiar with the denizen who exercises his eyes more than his biceps and deltoids. Whitman suggests his priorities were similar when, one day in 1842, to rest up from a "sentimental afternoon stroll," Whitman visited Hudson & Ottingnon's gymnasium on Broadway. He reported in the *Aurora*: "After an hour's lounge" watching gymnasts and several pairs of boxers cavort, "we bid the gentlemanly proprietors good bye, resolved to recommend the use of their excellent establishment to all dyspeptic and misanthropic young gentlemen."

Whitman was much more enthusiastic about swimming, though here, too, lounging was his style: "My forte was . . . in floating . . . I was a first-rate aquatic loafer," he told Traubel. While editing the *Eagle*, he regularly visited Gray's Salt Water Baths at the foot of Fulton Street in the company of his favorite printer's devil, William Sutton. "It is a fine noble sport, to dash in the cool waters, of a hot summer day! a sport specially grateful to the young," he editorialized in the *Eagle* on behalf of free public baths. But his reference in the editorial to the need for regulations to "preserve order and propriety" and protect children from "dangerous companionship" suggests that public baths may have had a dubious reputation. Many years later, in 1857, he expressed outrage in the *Daily Times* at recent arrests for the "frightful crime" of bathing along Brooklyn's shores. "For our own part we would encourage boys and men, for both physical and moral reasons, to habituate themselves to practise swimming and daily ablutions." He adds, caustically, "Is it not a most filthy modesty that objects and is so terrified at the neighborhood of a few people at their agreeable and wholesome sports in the water?"

Civic-minded concern for sanitation was surely not the only reason for Whitman's exultant "O to bathe in the swimming-bath" of "A Song of Joys." He had a "soul hungering gymnastic" but also a *body*. Some of his steamiest passages involve swimmers. "The swimmer swimming naked in the bath, or motionless on his back lying and floating," for instance, who leaves "love-flesh tremulous aching." Or the "beautiful gigantic swimmer swimming naked" through the eddies of erotic fantasy in "The Sleepers"—a figure worthy of comparison with Christopher Marlowe's homoerotic swimmer Leander. Or, most famously, the twenty-eight bathers of "Song of Myself," whose "white bellies bulge to the sun" and who do not know that someone, in fantasy, "seizes fast to them" with an "unseen hand" and pants over them "with pendant and bending arch." Whitman says the hand belongs to a woman, but it seems clear that a "pendant" phallus is somewhere in the picture. No aquatic loafing here.

The bath is reprised later in "Song of Myself," when all the "lovers" the poet's "old cruise" has won for him gather in surreal convention around him. In one of the poem's several orgasmic crescendos, the following lines rehearse most of Whitman's sexual haunts (mentioned elsewhere in the poem are the piers, the "curtain'd saloon," and the ship's deck). Here we have the secluded bushes in some ramble like the one in Central Park, the concealing rocks by a swimming hole, the public drinking fountain, a theater's dark upper tiers at intermission time (notorious at the time for sexual activity). Note the one phrase lamely defusing the richly homoerotic ambiance:

> My lovers suffocate me!
> Crowding my lips, and thick in the pores of my skin,
> Jostling me through streets and public halls . . . . coming naked
>   to me at night,
> Crying by day Ahoy from the rocks of the river . . . . swinging
>   and chirping over my head,
> Calling my name from flowerbeds or vines or tangled underbrush,
> Or while I swim in the bath . . . . or drink from the pump at the
>   corner . . . . or the curtain is down at the opera . . . . or I glimpse
>   at a woman's face in the railroad car;
> Lighting on every moment of my life,

Bussing my body with soft and balsamic busses,
Noiselessly passing handfuls out of their hearts and giving them
    to be mine.

This passage brilliantly captures the fantasy-full yet empty life of the promiscuous cruiser, so busily creating a thrilling catalogue of lovers, some never spoken to, some never caressed, some never touched by his thumb of love. Or perhaps even more apt as a description of the cruising urge—since our subject is the birds and the bees—is the "hairy wild-bee that murmurs and hankers up and down" in Whitman's sexiest poem, "Spontaneous Me."

And there were so many streets to hanker up and down, and so many lovers to hanker after, in Mannahatta. It was wearing, this life of constantly being either the person "silently selected by lovers" or one of those who "silently select lovers," this life of sometimes refusing "my love to those that gave me theirs," this "resistless yearning . . . for any and each the body correlative attracting!" Wearing because so open-ended, so merely potential: the side-curved head always poised for the next to appear from around a corner or out of the darkness of a drinking house or dance hall.

Indeed, the penultimate "scene" of "Song of Myself" leaves the poet and reader frustrated at an impending Missed Connection and hovering longingly. The night is old and the poet is getting impatient: "Here you . . . . what have you to confide to me? / Look in my face while I snuff the sidle of evening [that is, end the nocturnal cruise] . . . . I stay only a minute longer." And the scene ends, as usual for the cruiser, on a note of postponed expectation. What will the next night's cruise bring? The fleeting image of the "boy lingering and waiting" in "A Song of Joys" returns as the poem ends:

> Failing to fetch me at first keep encouraged,
> Missing me one place search another,
> I stop some where waiting for you

The up-in-the-air touch of having no final period at the end is superb, inspired. (On a miserably anal second thought, Whitman added the period to all post-1855 editions.)

THE BODY CORRELATIVE ATTRACTING

But what, then, of the lucky nights Whitman did not miss his connection? Paul Zweig, we have seen, contemplated the notebook lists of young men and wondered aloud whether they were lovers. "Possibly," he thought, presumably with mouth agape, "but so many?"

Of course not. Not *all* of them. With any luck, however, cruisers do now and then fall into the company of perfect strangers: that is, perfectly suitable strangers. They hit it off from the very first conversational openers. Whitman certainly did, now and then. In a manuscript dated 20 March 1854, for instance, we learn about a "Yankee boy" named George Fitch. He was obviously to Whitman's taste. "Fine nature, amiable, of sensitive feelings, a natural gentleman—of quite a reflective turn." Whitman must have sympathized with the fact that Fitch left home "because his father was perpetually 'down on him.' " Otherwise, he found Fitch a "Good looking, tall, curly haired, black-eyed fellow, age about 23 or 4—slender, face with a smile—trowsers tucked in his boots—cap with the front-piece turned behind"—a nice 1990s sartorial touch.

An even more spectacularly appealing "find" was a fellow named Peter, who is described in the same manuscript. All that we know about Whitman suggests that Peter must have seemed heaven-sent, almost a doppelgänger of the heroic speaker in the *Leaves of Grass* poems he was probably writing at the time:

> Peter—large, strong-boned youn[g] fellow, driver . . . weighs 180.—Free and candid to me the very first time he saw me.—Man of strong self-will, powerful coarse feelings and appetites—had a quarrel,—borrowed $300—left his father's, somewhere in the interior of the state—fell in with a couple of gamblers—hadn't been home or written there in seven years.—I liked his refreshing wickedness, as it would be called by the unorthodox.—He seemed to feel a perfect independence, dashed with a little resentment, toward the world in general.

And then Whitman adds a sentence that is as good a thumbnail sketch of the poetic persona of the first three editions of *Leaves* as one could wish: "I never met a man that seemed to me, as far as I could tell in 40 minutes, more open, coarse [often a Whitman term of approbation: "O you coarse and wilful! I love you!"], self-willed, strong, and free from the sickly desire to be on society's lines and points."

Some years later Whitman called a new acquaintance he obviously liked, one William Pine, "Walt Whitman sociable." So too was Peter: the kind of man the poet must have had in mind when he was "afoot with my vision" on Broadway's pavements. Whether the exhilarating forty minutes of conversation led to sexual intimacy with Peter we shall never know for certain. One would like to think so: here was a "perfect Comrade" if ever there was one. In any event, the "perfect" stranger is, for any number of reasons, often unavailable: already has a lover, is not interested in you, is not feeling horny, perhaps on closer inspection is found to be straight.

On the other hand, it is not always necessary that one be perfectly matched in cultural background, interests, or even somatic preferences in order to indulge in a sexual encounter. The lists Whitman kept contain several entries that suggest he in fact did score now and then with nondescript young men. On a bitterly cold 28 December 1861, he met a Mike Ellis wandering at the corner of Lexington and Thirty-fourth: "took him home to 150 37th street,—4th story back room." Why up to that fourth-floor back room, if not for sex? On 29 May he met a "somewhat feminine" and bedraggled Daniel Spencer, who explained that he "did not drink at all" but had been in a fight; some months later, on 3 September, Whitman recorded that Spencer "slept with me." In August he met a deserter on the grounds of Fort Greene, and he "came to the house with me." On 11 October he met nineteen-year-old David Wilson, a worker in a naval blacksmith shop, walking up Middagh Street in Brooklyn. Whitman records that Wilson slept with him and they enjoyed "walks together Sunday afternoon & night." Ten days later he met one Horace Ostrander from Otsego while visiting a friend in the hospital: "slept with him Dec 4th '62." Later, in Washington, a soldier named Jerry Taylor of New Jersey "slept with me last night weather soft, cool enough, warm enough, heavenly."

Zweig, we have seen, thinks such entries tells us nothing of Whitman's sex life, only about his "collector's mentality"; they are likened to his poems' notorious "catalogue" passages. And David Reynolds believes that homosocial, as opposed to homosexual, sleeping together was pandemic in nineteenth-century America. Putting this construction on such entries as those just quoted seems perversely high-minded. It is more plausible—given the details of each meeting and the well-defined attractions of age and physique that motivate most of the entries in the lists—to assume Whitman was recording successful and even (though rare) "heavenly" pickups. Is it so outrageous to plausibility to think these entries tell us his collector's mentality extended to the collection of actual sexual intimacies and pleasures?

Nor is the assumption really very plausible that *all* of Whitman's sexual experiences with correlative bodies involved beds and the privacy of a small "roof'd room" like that of the fourth-floor walk-up on Thirty-seventh Street. There were then, still are, many alternative sites for sexual encounters. In an erotic night-terror passage of "The Sleepers," the dreamer awakens naked, his clothes "stolen while I was abed":

Now I am thrust forth, where shall I run?

Pier that I saw dimly last night when I looked from the windows,
Pier out from the main, let me catch myself with you and stay . . . .
    I will not chafe you;
I feel ashamed to go naked about the world.

Is this not a marvelous evocation of the excitement, fear, and sense of vulnerability that attends sexual encounters in public places? Perhaps Mannahatta's piers at night beckoned Whitman on occasion: a few lines later boss-tooth is advancing in the darkness and milky "liquor is spilled on lips and bosoms." Many years later, to Traubel, Whitman recalled such places and bound them clearly to the presence of men: "My own favorite loafing places have always been the rivers, the wharves, the boats—I like sailors, stevedores. I have never lived away from a big river."

There appears to be another allusion to the sexual attractions of the nighttown streets of Mannahatta in the randy juxtaposition of images in the poem "Respondez!": "let the few seize on what they choose! Let the rest gawk, giggle, starve, obey! / Let shadows be furnished with genitals!" This provocative poem, which appeared in 1856 along with "The Sleepers," also boldly advises "the she-harlots and the he-harlots" of the city to "dance on." Characteristically, Whitman in this poem also associates "genteel persons" with the sexually inactive, in this case eunuchs and consumptives.

Or maybe Whitman enjoyed hasty sex in the dark recesses of an opera house or theater—either when "the curtain is down at the opera," as he said in "Song of Myself," or when other ears are filled by the "colossal volume" of orchestral sound. Whitman's pleasure in opera, we have seen, was profoundly quasi-sexual: the soprano's voice so "delicious" that it goes "through one like a knife" and being like the pain of the thruster in his "love grip." Or the "vast, pure Tenor" voice that filled him "to the uttermost" and solved, temporarily, "the problem of human cravingness." In 1844, the year before New York established its first police department, Alderman Caleb Woodhull recommended the elimination of the third tier in all city theaters as a way of excluding "frailty from places of public amusement." Was Whitman among those who solved the problem of sexual cravingness by buying a ticket to the third tier and casting their eyes about for appealing and likely faces when the gaslights were up, as Franklin Evans does?

One is very tempted to answer "yes" after hearing him reminisce, in old age, about the joys of the upper tier. Whitman was not the first gay aficionado to insist he went up to the gods' for the fabulous sound ("it was at the top I heard best . . . *ensemble* most impressive"), but our night-wandering bohemian clearly went there for extramusical reasons too. To Traubel, in 1890, he waxed movingly nostalgic:

> I always went in my early days to the 25-cent place in the theatre, and it was my breath of life, what I got there, however cheaply secured. What opportunities were tallied! What gates opened! . . . I, too, used to meet and make new friends in the galleries. Often we would go in parties. We heard the best plays, operas, in that way. My early life especially was full of it. I suppose the average man doesn't object to high prices because he only wants to go to the theatre about twice a year. I suppose that satisfied him, but for the wanderers, for the Bohemians we are—many, many times are not too many.

Whitman then described how, as a journalist with a press pass, he fell from comradely grace: "The time came when I was on the papers, when I had a pass, by which means I fell literally from my high estate—from gallery to parquet, and it *was* a fall—I felt it to be such. It was comfortable to have the seat reserved, I admit *that*, but something was lost—the greatest something." Poor Walt, alone on the aisle and exiled from the boys—a perfect image for the aging, post–Civil War Whitman.

And what of sex amid the shore-brush, under the stars, or, as in *Calamus* #3, "by stealth in some wood"? "Smile O voluptuous cool-breath'd earth!" Whitman exulted in "Song of Myself," and in "Kosmos" a few years later he praised "the coarseness and sexuality of the earth." There is also much coarseness and human sexuality *on* the ground in his poems. Highly erotic is the memory in "Song of Myself" of the "transparent summer morning" in June when the poet loafed in the concealing grass with his far-from-bodiless soul:

> How you settled your head athwart my hips and gently turn'd over
>   upon me,

And parted the shirt from my bosom-bone, and plunged your
     tongue to my bare-stript heart,
And reach'd till you felt my beard, and reach'd till you held my feet.

The "plunged" and "bare-stript" are typically, wonderfully suggestive, even more so the beard located between heart and feet. Many years later Whitman would demand in America poetry a "tonic and *al fresco* physiology." He had certainly shown the way in his early *Leaves of Grass*, whose "presiding spinal purpose" he later said was to evoke his experiences of "the open air, the sky, the sea."*

Our "gymnosophist" was happy to find himself "rapt and austere in the woods"—rapt in the sexual sense and austere, perhaps, in the sense of naked. For the poet did enjoy walking naked on the beach or in the woods, or sunbathing at a creekside; witness "A Sun-Bath—Nakedness" in *Specimen Days*. Being alone could sometimes by itself be agreeable, as we learn in *Calamus* #11. Here the poet says he found happiness when he wandered "alone over the beach, and undressing bathed, laughing with the cool waters." But having company on such *al fresco* excursions (and feeling no need for "stealth") was even better, as "when I thought how my dear friend my lover was on his way coming, O then I was happy." The lover arrives at the shore the next evening and the poet hears

. . . the hissing rustle of the liquid and sands as directed to me
     whispering to congratulate me,
For the one I love most lay sleeping by me under the same cover in
     the cool night,
In the stillness in the autumn moonbeams his face was inclined
     toward me,
And his arm lay lightly around my breast—and that night I was
     happy.

Comparable to this sea-girt intimacy is the explicit sexuality of "The souse upon me of my lover the sea, as I lie willing and naked" in "Spontaneous Me" and the erotics of another 1856 poem, "This Compost," in which the sea "is so amorous after me, / That it is safe to allow it to lick my naked body all over with its tongues."

Similarly idyllic, though not so sex-charged, is *Calamus* #10, where happy days spent "far away, through fields, in woods, on hills" are recalled, the poet and his lover "wandering hand in hand, they twain apart from other men." And nothing in Whitman has more tonic and *al fresco* sexuality than his great poem of spring, *Calamus* #13. By the "wild woods" and "pond-side" are discovered "Breast-sorrel," "pinks of love," and "Love-buds . . . to be unfolded on the old terms." "Gushes from the throats of birds hid in foliage" resound; we glimpse "fingers that wind around tighter than vines"; and gifts are "offered fresh to young persons wandering out in the fields." When the poem was first published, the phallus more obviously presided over this spree of sexual innuendo, for its first line then was simply "CALAMUS taste."

In a Whitman notebook—one of four recently found after a mysterious half-century disappearance and now returned to the custody of the Library of Congress—there is an extraordinary one-page entry that moves beyond mere "*al fresco* physiology" to evoke a religious experience made possible through resort to the privacy of nature. Gender-revealing pronouns are carefully avoided, but surely the dramatis personae for this tryst are of the same sex. Here a yea-saying, Whitmanesque God is willing to avert his eyes discreetly from the horrible sin *inter Christianos non nominandum*:

> Fatigued by their journey they sat down on Nature's divan whence they regarded the sky. Pressing one another's hands, shoulder to shoulder, neither knowing why, both became oppressed, their mouths opened; without uttering a word they kissed one another. Near them the hyacinth and the violet marrying their perfume, on raising their heads they both saw God who smiled at them from his azure balcony: Love one another[,] said he[,] it is for that I have clothed your path in velvet; kiss one another, I am not looking. Love one another, love one another and if you are happy, instead of a prayer to thank me kiss again.

In another, earlier notebook, Whitman had observed that "the soul prefers freedom in the prairie or in the untrodden woods," but this epiphany makes it clear that, in Whitman's day as in ours, the "oppressed" body too might have reason to prefer the freedom conferred by *al fresco* sites. It struck me as an ideal epigraph for this book.

A sexual undercurrent seems also present in a short 1877 essay in *Specimen Days* called "The Oaks and I." In it Whitman described a favorite *al fresco* exercise:

> to pull on that young hickory sapling out there—to sway and yield to its tough-limber upright stem—haply to get into my old sinews some of its elastic fibre and clear sap. . . . At other spots convenient I have selected . . . strong and limber boughs of beech or holly, in

easy-reaching distance, for my natural gymnasia. . . . I hold on
boughs or slender trees caressingly there in the sun and shade,
wrestle with their innocent stalwartness—and *know* the virtue
thereof passes from them into me. (Or may-be we interchange—
may-be the trees are more aware of it all than I ever thought.)

What is missing here, of course, is a lover.

In fact, there may be one. He is figured in that *tall* and *slender*—
favorite Whitman epithets—hickory sapling. Edwin Miller has argued
that a curious passage in an 1878 letter to Anne Gilchrist contains a
ciphered reference to Harry Stafford, Whitman's main young male
acquaintance at the time: "At least two hours forenoon, & two afternoon, down by the *creek*—Passed between *sauntering*—the *hickory
saplings*—& '*Honor* is the *subject* of my story'—(for explanation of the
last three lines, ask Herby [Anne Gilchrist's son]—)." The plays upon
Stafford's initials turn the *Specimen Days* passage into a deliciously ribald
and graphic *jeu d'esprit*. Some color is given to this speculation by a marvelous little description of Whitman's spending a Sunday with Stafford
several months after writing Gilchrist. This manuscript makes it easier to
assume "The Oaks and I" and the veiled boast of the Gilchrist letter are
the work of a man who not only talked about the thing but did it:

> A delightful day, warm but breezy. Had much comfort with H.S., we
> two all day together, lazily lounging around, shady recesses, banks
> by the brook where the slight but coolish west wind set in—having
> long talks, interchanges, cheery and loving confidences, with vacant
> intervals.
>
> Soothing, human, emotionally-nourishing, most precious hours,
> costing nothing simple and cheap and near as air. Why should they
> be such rare oases?*

Was this truly a "soothing" nonsexual jaunt? Or did Whitman discreetly leave out the more invigorating gymnastics alluded to in *Specimen
Days*? Did Whitman spend some of these hours "between" Stafford's
legs—pulling on the tough-limber stem of that "hickory sapling"—
fanning his sixty-year-old sexual embers with the vitality of a twenty-
year-old? Impossible to tell. One thing is certain, though: the more erotic
scenes *en plein air* in the early *Leaves* editions indicate that, when Whitman was twenty-five years younger, he was much less interested in
putting on airs of asexual benignity.

Consider, for example, one of the most graphic passages in the first

Leaves, a passage, incidentally, that a proud Whitman made much of in one of his anonymous self-reviews. Here in "Song of Myself" a sudden, serendipitous—perhaps even anonymous—joining of correlative bodies unfolds:

> You sea! I resign myself to you also—I guess what you mean,
> I behold from the beach your crooked inviting fingers,
> I believe you refuse to go back without feeling of me,
> We must have a turn together, I undress, hurry me out of sight of
>   the land,
> Cushion me soft, rock me in billowy drowse,
> Dash me with amorous wet, I can repay you.
>
> Sea of stretch'd ground-swells,
> Sea breathing broad and convulsive breaths . . .
> I am integral with you . . .

In other words, the speaker is invited by "secret and divine signs" of another into some concealed site, clothing is hastily removed, bodies comfortably positioned, a rhythmic motion produces an agreeable ecstasy, and then, at the end, amid pants and throbbing breath, the speaker hopes for a simultaneous "amorous wet."

With much justice, Whitman, a few lines later, pronounces himself "Extoller of amies and those that sleep in each others' arms." Even more provocative, though—and more suggestive of the promiscuous sex life Whitman led in those salad days when he was grass-green in judgment and had "greensleeves" for the time-honored reason—is the ending he worked so hard at for his third *Leaves* edition.

I refer to the last few stanzas of the volume's valedictory poem, "So Long!" Whitman, it will be recalled, in 1855 ended his monumental "Song of Myself" with an elaborate image of failed consummation, however devoutly wished. For the end of his 1860 edition, an older, wiser, and more sexually practiced poet daringly chose to stage-manage his departure from his dearly beloved reader as a kind of archetypal anonymous, nocturnal, brief encounter of the sexual kind.

In the first of the last four stanzas the scene is set: "Is it night? Are we here alone? . . . / It is I you hold, and who holds you, / I spring from the pages into your arms." In the next stanza, as so often elsewhere in the 1860 edition, Whitman celebrates the "deliciousness" of sex:

> O how your fingers drowse me! [recall the "billowy drowse" of
>   "Song"]

> Your breath falls around me like dew—your pulse lulls the
>   tympans of my ears,
> I feel immerged from head to foot,
> Delicious—enough.

The next stanza, in which the speaker extricates himself from this sudden, illicit sexual act, gave Whitman considerable trouble. His various manuscript revisions, which become progressively more discreet, brilliantly evoke the fleeting, busy, promiscuous life that I am inclined to think Whitman actually led in the 1840s and 1850s. First he tries "O brief! O minute of us two. O secret and sudden." Then he expands on the quickness of the sexual climax: "O us two only! secret and sudden—impromptu and secret!" A third try, with its sexually rhythmic ecphonesis, is even more elaborate and offers a wonderful précis of quick sex, the one-night or even the stealthy ten-minute stand:

> Enough O contact abrupt and secret
> Enough O winding and unwinded arms!
> Enough O fastened and loosened twain!
> Enough O impromptu and gliding present!

Whitman, alas, finally settled for a stanza that left out the physically specific second and third of these lines.

After the heat of sex and exclamation subsides, the poet-lover regains his composure and prepares, with a little tender dignity, to take his leave. One can easily imagine Whitman saying (or thinking) these words as he parted from a Mannahattese sex partner on a street corner, in a theater lobby, or at the south gate of Fort Greene, where he met a twenty-three-year-old "English lad" one Sunday evening in 1862:

> Dear friend, whoever you are, here, take this kiss,
> I give it especially to you—Do not forget me,
> I feel as one who has done his work—I progress on,
> The unknown sphere, more real than I dreamed, more direct,
>   darts awakening rays about me—*So long!*
> Remember my words—I love you . . .

Words truly spoken, one might say, by a promiscuous "progresser."

It is perhaps in this sexual context that we can begin to sense the candor of Whitman's numerous boasts about "the lovers I recklessly love," the "lovers, continual lovers" he entertained as he does the reader at the end of "So Long!"—and the phalanx of "lovers" who suffocate him, "Crowding my lips, thick in the pores of my skin." So many men, in other words, so little time. What harm is there, exactly, in assuming that while swimming in Mannahatta's "hurried and sparkling currents" he used his sexual prime well? And what harm in assuming that he was being honest when he boasted, in his "Crossing Brooklyn Ferry" manuscript, of having "laughed, slept, had my amours"?

TO WISHES FIX AN END

In December of 1874, when he was fifty-five years old and had suffered for nearly two years the effects of a paralytic stroke, Whitman reported to a friend about a bossy new doctor he had recently consulted. He "comes every day—rather a curious fellow—a great bully, vehement, loud words & plenty of them." However, Walt was not unhappy. The doctor, he thought, seemed to talk sense: "& yet I value what *he* says & does for me—He is inclined to think the seat of all my woe has been (what no one ever whispered before,) the *liver*, acted upon largely also, perhaps almost primarily, thro the emotional nature . . ."

The liver, of course, had for centuries been considered the organ of sexual desire and passion. Falstaff, Shakespeare's would-be adulterer in *The Merry Wives of Windsor*, loves Mistress Ford with "liver burning hot," and utterly well behaved Ferdinand promises Prospero in *The Tempest* that "The white cold virgin snow upon my heart / Abates the ardor of my liver." Perhaps there was a reluctance among Whitman's friends and medical advisers to "whisper" about the liver because it would have carried the implication of criticism for his earlier life as a "venerealee." The patient, however, cottoned to this liver diagnosis that had been pronounced so loudly. Obviously, I would like to think—given my attempt here to imagine his sex life—that this is because Whitman looked back on his Mannahatta days and found the diagnosis plausible. The "liver-vein," says Berowne in another Shakespeare play, *Love's Labor's Lost*, "makes flesh a deity," and Whitman was now willing to accept that he was reaping woe for giving his "emotional nature" rein in Mannahatta. No poet, certainly, has deified flesh more spectacularly than Whitman did in his first editions of *Leaves of Grass*.

Whitman stuck by the liver theory for the rest of his life. He definitively, and finally, repeated it the year before he died: "this late-years palsied old shorn and shell-fish condition of me is the indubitable outcome and growth . . . of too overzealous, over-continued bodily and emotional excitement and action through the times of 1862, '3, '4, and '5." The "through" is worth emphasizing: Whitman is referring to his life *up to and including* the Civil War, which he believed was what finally broke his health.

But to all things, especially to an active sexual life, an end must come. *Certum voto pete finem*, Horace advised in one of his epistles: "To wishes fix an end."* There are many fascinating suggestions predating the 1873 stroke that show Whitman was beginning to entertain an end to his "overzealous" pursuit of bodily and emotional excitement in Manhattan. The city can, after some years, begin to wear one down. "Hot wishes," whether one dares not speak them or chooses to act upon them, are enormously energy-consuming. One can't stay up as late, drink as much, disco until other people's brunch time, or achieve orgasm more than once a night. One begins to think of strategies or extrication from the sexual busyness, the most drastic being simply to emigrate to calmer environs.

Whitman removed to Washington, doubtless for a combination of reasons: concern for his wounded brother George, abolitionist and Unionist patriotism, and perhaps (as we will consider in the following chapter) even the traumatic breakup of a serious love affair. But I suspect that a desire to get away to the more sexually calm (though infinitely more anguishing) wards filled with severely wounded soldiers may also have played a part. This is suggested in a letter of 1865 to William O'Connor in which Walt compared his volume of war poems, *Drum-Taps*, with *Leaves of Grass*. In his "unprecedentedly sad" new book, he explains, the "comradely" theme will not be nearly so stentorian as it was in *Calamus* and other poems of 1860. Rather, there is "an undertone of sweetest comradeship & human love, threading its steady thread inside the chaos, & heard at every lull." He adds, anticipating the liver diagnosis, "*Drum-Taps* has none of the perturbations of *Leaves of Grass*." His final observation about *Leaves* is that there are "some things in it I should not put in if I were to write now, but yet I shall certainly let them stand, even if but for proofs of phases passed away."

Awareness of the "perturbations" of his Manhattan phase seems strong in a poem Walt wrote in the same year of his letter to O'Connor. Its title is superbly apt: "Ah Poverties, Wincings, and Sulky Retreats." Its lines would be the equivalent of the disgruntled mopings one occasionally hears from the person sick and tired of the gay bar scene and its innocuous chatter, gratuitous insults, ego-bruising rejections, and frustrated or frustrating couplings. The poet begins to see "foes" on all sides:

You degradations, you tussle with passions and appetites,
You smarts from dissatisfied friendships, (ah wounds the sharpest
    of all!)
You toil of painful and choked articulations, you meannesses,
You shallow tongue-talks at tables, (my tongue the shallowest
    of any;)
You broken resolutions, you racking angers, you smother'd ennuis!

Ah, the poverty of our degrading tussle with our appetites for sex . . . and for love. The obvious thing to do, of course (and how often do we hear our friends or ourselves sound like this?), is make a solemn vow to turn over a new leaf, take charge of one's passions, and become a new person. "My real self has yet to come forth," the poem ends. This new self "shall yet march forth o'ermastering" and achieve the "ultimate victory." Fine. But easier said than done.

Also in 1865, Whitman published an extraordinary poem that is, I think, crucial to any large imagining of his sexual life, "Give Me the Splendid Silent Sun." It also happens to offer a perfect description of all the Manhattanites who ever have found themselves teetering nervously between attraction and repulsion at the city's stresses—and prolific sexual opportunities. The forty-line poem is superbly schizophrenic. In its first part Whitman paints a fantasy familiar to virtually all Manhattanites: this is of an escape to a rustic, sunlit eden populated with "serene-moving animals teaching content." "Tired with ceaseless excitement," the exhausted urbanite begs for "a rural domestic life" away from "the noise of the world." He wants to be blessedly alone, to regain his sane and sanitary center: "Give me to warble spontaneous songs recluse by myself, for my own ears only, / Give me solitude, give me Nature, give me again O Nature your primal sanities!"

And yet: though his heart cries to be far from the madding crowd, "still I adhere to my city." "O city, . . . you hold me enchain'd a certain time refusing to give me up, / Yet giving to make me glutted, enrich'd of soul, you give me forever faces . . ." The poet finally cannot *quite yet* free himself from the enticing gaze of faces in his old city of orgies. "Keep your splendid silent sun," he says, and then evokes once again the nighttime thrills and cherished places of public resort in the early *Leaves* editions:

Give me interminable eyes—give me women—give me comrades
    and lovers by the thousand!
Let me see new ones every day—let me hold new ones by the
    hand every day! . . .

Give me the shores and wharves heavy-fringed with black ships!
O such for me! O an intense life, full to repletion and varied!
The life of the theatre, bar-room, huge hotel, for me! . . .
Manhattan crowds, with their turbulent musical chorus!
Manhattan faces and eyes forever for me.

One senses, though, a protesting-too-much in these lines. Indeed, the poem may have helped Whitman begin to exorcise the "phantoms incessant" who still visited him in 1865 and made him nostalgic for old haunts and jaunts. We do not relinquish our pleasures—or our illusions of pleasure—easily, which may explain why we have this last great Whitman encomium to Manhattan. Or is "eulogy" the more apt word?

In any event, it did not take long for the splendid silent sun to become Whitman's principal planet during visits to the city. He spent a three-month furlough there three years later, in 1868, and described a typical day in a letter to Doyle. "Every hour is occupied with something," but the day's main event is going out after noon to "loafe somewhere" or take a long ride on a Broadway stage: "You know it is a never-ending amusement & study & recreation for me to ride a couple of hours, of a pleasant afternoon. . . . You see everything as you pass, a sort of living, endless panorama . . . & the gayety & motion on every side—You will not wonder how much attraction all this is, on a fine day, to a great loafer like me, who enjoys so much seeing the busy world move by him . . . while he takes it easy & just looks on and observes." Except for supper with his mother, Whitman mentions no nocturnal activity. Hardly an "intense life, full to repletion." Whitman had become a bystander, an observer not "both in and out of the game" but rather largely out of it. There is something sexual in the "Manhattan streets with their powerful throbs" that he mentions in "Give Me the Splendid Silent Sun," but there is nothing in the least sexual about the streets he tells Doyle about in his letter three years later.

About a year and a half afterward, in 1870, Whitman's difficult transit away from the world of sexual "perturbation" was further evidenced in the most famous of all his notebook entries, the passage in which he came to painful terms with the folly of his attraction to Peter Doyle. In the first part of this entry he tells himself to give up the campy, trivial badinage of his intimate circle. He should assume instead a "Cool, gentle, (LESS DEMONSTRATIVE) more UNIFORM DEMEANOR . . . *give no confidences*—never attempt puns, or plays upon words, or utter sarcastic comments." Then, with elaborate emphasis (italics, marginal lines, little finger-pointing fists), he makes this solemn vow: "It is IMPERATIVE, that I

Two pages from an 1870 notebook in which Whitman, feeling sickish and "opprest" amid steamy July weather in Washington, lectures himself about hoping for reciprocation from Peter Doyle, with whom he had become deeply infatuated. On the first leaf he warns himself not to fancy "what does not really exist in another." More specifically, he must "pursue her no more." Roger Asselineau was the first to notice that Whitman had first written "him," but then erased it and prudently replaced it with "her." On the second leaf, remarkable for emphatic, emotional underlining in black, purple, and red ink, Whitman makes a formal, dated oath to "give up absolutely" his "feverish, fluctuating, useless undignified pursuit of 16.4"—another gender-concealing ruse: Peter Doyle's initials are the 16th and 4th letters of the alphabet. Library of Congress.

obviate & remove myself (& my orbit) *at all hazards* from this *incessant enormous* ... PERTURBATION." On 15 July 1870 Whitman reread and reapproved this vow, then added that, as regarded Peter Doyle ("16.4"), he must "GIVE UP ABSOLUTELY & *for good, from the present hour, this* FEVERISH, FLUCTUATING, *useless* UNDIGNIFIED PURSUIT *of 16.4—too long, (much too long)* persevered in,—so humiliating—*It must come at last &* had better come now—*(It cannot possibly be a success)* LET THERE FROM THIS HOUR BE NO FALTERING."*

Immediately following this passage in the notebook, unsurprisingly, is a description of the new leaf that seemed in order, the "superb calm character" he now wished to become. This is a person who feels "complete in himself irrespective (indifferent) of whether his love, friendship, &c [could this "&c" stand for sexual advances?] are returned, or not." After this appear these four remarkable lines:

> Depress the adhesive nature
> It is an excess—making life a torment
> All this diseased, feverish disproportionate *adhesiveness*
> Remember Fred Vaughan

This was *Certum voto pete finem* with a vengeance. (Who Fred Vaughan was will be discussed in the following chapter.)

The astonishing extent to which Whitman hewed to this "just say no" vow is demonstrated in his first important prose work, *Democratic Vistas,* which he published the very next year. Sexuality suffers a sea change here. It loses its odors, seminal glisten, and feverish "*al fresco* physiology." Not surprisingly for a man beginning to experience signs of physical deterioration, "health" becomes the preoccupation in his *al fresco* excursions: "A strong-fibred joyousness and faith, and the sense of health *al fresco,* may well enter into the preparation of future noble American authorship." It certainly did in his own authorship over the next twenty years.

And Whitman's discussion of "adhesive love" (tellingly, in a footnote) is leached of all two-bodied feverishness. This love now becomes high-mindedly homo*social,* an avenue for the expression of political rather than genital impulses. "Fervid comradeship" no longer leads to affectionate hand-holding or a "long-dwelling kiss" but to "the counterbalance and offset of our materialistic and vulgar American democracy" and "the spiritualization thereof." His talk of adhesive love being "unprecedentedly emotional, muscular, heroic" and "having the deepest relations to general politics" leaves one thinking not of semen-glued bellies but of those huge, utterly unerotic statues of hammer holders in the old

Soviet Union. This highly successful depressing of the adhesive nature in *Democratic Vistas* is, well, depressing. Not so prosaic but more depressing is this short, thoroughly characteristic late-Whitman poem, also published in 1871:

> FOR him I sing,
> I raise the present on the past,
> (As some perennial tree out of its roots, the present on the past,)
> With time and space I him dilate and fuse the immortal laws,
> To make himself by them the law unto himself.

Sad demise for that sex-charged "dilate" of old, frustrated amid such tedious abstractions. Poignant too this odorless, bodiless "him." The poet of twelve years before who tasted the *calamus* root so deeply would certainly have sung "him" differently. To sexual desires, at least those expressed in his poems, Whitman was fixing an end.

More personal and more sad was the aftermath of his stroke two years later, in 1873. This event gave Whitman something like the fantasy wishes for a calmer, more reclusive life he had expressed eight years earlier in "Give Me the Splendid Silent Sun." He even got some splendid sun through the window of the third-floor room he occupied in his brother's New Jersey house. "My brother had a large room, very handsome, on [the] second floor, with large bay window fronting west, built for me," he wrote to Doyle in October 1873, "but I moved up here instead, it is much more retired, and has the sun." But he was still having trouble learning "content" among the "serene-moving animals" of blue-collar Camden. The "intense life" of busy Manhattan streets is a distant thing as Whitman sighs to Doyle, "I am very comfortable here indeed, but my *heart* is blank & lonesome utterly." Then he tells of a new acquaintance, and a glimmer of his old "list" style returns: "I have just been talking with a young married RR. man, Thomas Osler, I fell in with . . . he stood by the open window 1st floor, and talked with me, while I sat in an armchair inside—he is a regular RR. man—you could tell by the cut of his jib, low collar, cap, clean shirt (for holiday) dark complexion, & hard dark hands, I took quite a fancy to him and, *of course*, I suppose he did to me."

FROM BAWDY HOUSE TO CATHEDRAL

H. L. Mencken once wrote to a friend, "I seldom go to the opera; it is to music what a bawdy house is to a cathedral." The early editions of

Leaves of Grass, we have seen, were written by a poet steeped in opera. They *are* opera, a string of over-the-top ariosos and arias, cavatinas and cabalettas. They also constitute one of the bawdiest poetic houses of the nineteenth or any preceding century.

Later in life, however, Whitman became a more respectable poet and devoted considerable effort to making *Leaves*, as he said, into a cathedral. He ceased to be the singer of the "bedfellow's song" and the celebrator of the cruiser's life. He became, instead, a diplomat, a poet/prophet, an America-boosting master of ceremonies for the national pageant: "I chant America the mistress, I chant a greater supremacy." His relationship with the reader was no longer figured as an intimate one-on-one nocturnal encounter. Rather, one thinks of the bully pulpit or the orator's platform. The Whitman poetic voice loses its ability to sing *pianissimo* ("Talk honestly, no one else hears you") and tends to become rather boorishly stentorian, a voice "in the midst of the crowd . . . orotund sweeping and final." His delivery becomes browbeating, unsubtle, barky, as often happens with a once-fine voice in decline. And his rivetingly single reader becomes ineffably plural, one of "the crowd." In the later editions of *Leaves of Grass*, indeed, the crowd becomes posterity itself: his readers are "projected through time . . . an audience interminable."

The myriad ways in which Whitman transformed his private, dark-cornered, illicitly thrilling, for-comrades-only bawdy house into a kind of shiningly hypocritical crystal cathedral are fascinating. They were well, if genteely, summed up by Emory Holloway in 1920 when, by way of ending his essay on the poet's love affairs, he concluded that Whitman the Man and Whitman the Missionary "waged a long war." And the Missionary finally won out as the decade of the 1860s unfolded: "Battered in body and bruised in his affections, poor and generally rejected of critics, Whitman henceforth has less to say in praise of untrammelled natural impulses, but more and more to sing of democracy, of immortality, and of the soul."* For "untrammelled natural impulses" we can perhaps now more boldly say homoerotic genital impulses, and a particularly disheartening aspect of familiarizing oneself with the various editions of *Leaves of Grass* is observing how, through revision, Whitman frequently softened, subtilized, or simply neutered the genital impulse in the earlier versions of his poems. The very phrase "genital impulse," in fact, disappeared from "By Blue Ontario's Shore" after the 1871 edition.

Expurgation. Whitman professed hatred for the word. On a Saturday evening in 1889, Traubel asked for his last thoughts on it: "It's a nasty word: I do not like it: I don't think I ever thought expurgation in my life: Rossetti wished to cut out or change a few words: only a few words: I said, yes, do it: that was long ago: if the question came up today I would say no, do not do it: I think as time has passed I got an increased horror of expurgation." Whitman builds a head of steam and adds that self-censorship is "all bad, all wrong, all corrupt: it reduces a fellow to a cipher: seems just like an apology, a confession: it's a sort of suicide." Then he recalls proudly how "the gentle Emerson," before the publication of his bawdiest *Leaves* in 1860, "so far forgot who I was . . . to suggest that I should expurgate, cut out, eliminate: which is as if I was able to hide some of myself away."

It sounds wonderful. But this is not the only instance of late-Whitman persiflage that leaves one thinking Othello's "O vain boast." In 1890, just a year later, when Symonds wrote his famously probing letter, did not Whitman hide some of himself away with stupefying aplomb in his boast of six "jolly" fatherings? No, in the matter of expurgation Whitman desired, as was his wont, to have things both ways. His far more compromising practice, in fact, is captured in the letter to O'Connor in which he said he would let certain no longer satisfactory passages stand as "proof of phases passed away." Just two paragraphs earlier, however, he told O'Connor "there are a few things I shall carefully eliminate in the next issue, & a few more I shall considerably change."

The sexual—and more specifically homosexual—content of *Leaves* Whitman clearly treated in *both* of these ways after the 1860 edition. Many vividly erotic and candidly homosexual passages he left virtually untouched through all editions. But on many other occasions, in ways both large-scale and minutely detailed, the poet did proceed to perform a lengthy and meticulous sexual suicide. Oscar Wilde once defined the artistic life as "a long and lovely suicide," and the phrase applies with melancholy aptness to Whitman's efforts, over his last decades, to "depress" the sexual and adhesive content of his poetry.

The extant manuscripts for poems in the 1860 edition, in fact, show that Whitman was already a well-practiced self-censorer. Here, from one of his daybooks, is an exuberantly coital practice-run for his opening "Proto-Leaf":

> O ~~my~~ lands!
> ~~The O~~ Copious the embracing the many-armed,
>   interhanded, the
>   knit together, the
>   passionate lovers, the
>   and clasped
>   fused ~~ones~~ . . .

This became, in print, the sadly denatured snippet, "Inextricable lands! clutched together! the passionate lovers!" (and "lovers" was demoted to "ones" in the fourth edition of 1867).

Another example is found in the manuscript version of *Calamus #34*, a poem in which Whitman anticipates, for homosexuals, Martin Luther King Jr.'s "I have a dream" speech. The italicized words were deleted before publication:

> I dreamed in a dream of a city *where all the men were like brothers,*
> O *I saw them tenderly love each other—I often saw them, in numbers,
>   walking hand in hand;*
> I dreamed that was the city *of robust friends—*
> Nothing was greater there than *manly love*—it led the rest . . .*

The process of "careful elimination" was also at work in these lines from "Starting from Paumanok" when it appeared in the 1867 edition:

> Not he with a daily kiss onward from childhood kissing me,
> Has winded and twisted around me that which holds me to him . . .

The innocuous "friends from childhood" notion, however, had replaced these lines from 1860:

> Not he, *adhesive, kissing me so long with his daily kiss,*
> Has winded and twisted around me that which holds me to him . . .

And even more suggestive of an actual two-male-bodied embrace is the manuscript version Whitman had first entertained:

> Not he *whom I love,* kissing me so long with his daily kiss, has
>   winded and twisted around me that which holds me to him
>   *forever* . . .

In the manuscript for *Calamus #4*, several deletions tamed its homo-erotic bonding (expunged phrases are in italics). The poet is visited by the "spirits of dear friends, *lovers, comrades* dead or alive"; it is "a thick cloud of spirits [*lovers*]"; he will give the calamus root "only to them that love [*those comrades who love*] as I myself am capable of loving." The object of all Whitman's frantic search is likewise hidden away by this deletion from the ms. for *Calamus #14*: "Does the tide hurry, seeking something, and never give up? O I the same, *to seek my life-long lover.*"

And then there is the famous instance, in "Once I Pass'd through a Populous City," of Whitman purging the gender of his lover. His extant manuscript shows that it read "But now of all that city I remember only the man who wandered with me, there, for love of me, / Day by day, night by night, we were together." This became, in the final published version, "Yet now of all that city I remember only a woman I casually met there who detain'd me for love of me" etc. Likewise, in "To a Common Prostitute," the ms. reads "My love, I appoint with you an appointment," but in the printed version "My love" emerges as "My girl" and the kiss he salutes him/her with becomes a mere "significant look."

The more general urgings of a homosexual agenda are also occasionally censored by Whitman in his process of revision. In one of his manuscripts for *Calamus* Whitman wrote bravely, "I celebrate *that concealed but substantial life*, / I celebrate the need of *the love of* comrades," but in print, as we have already seen, he chose to hide some of himself away and wrote, "To tell the secret of my nights and days, / To celebrate the need of comrades." And for "Paumanok" he toned down this line: "I will therefore let flame from me the burning fires [*of adhesiveness*] that were threatening to consume me."

Some manuscript alterations that served to obscure homosexual life-experience were on a larger scale. Several decades ago Fredson Bowers discovered from Whitman's manuscripts that twelve of his *Calamus* poems were originally conceived as a sequence, "Live Oak, with Moss," that told of an unhappy love affair with a man. Bowers thought Whitman fair-copied it into a small notebook sometime in the spring of 1859. However, this sequence—remarkably akin to Shakespeare's sonnets to his Young Man—Whitman finally decided to dismantle and scatter among many other poems, thus obscuring his embedded autobiographical narrative. Alan Helms, the first to write about the implications of "Live Oak, with Moss," wittily suggests that Whitman was behaving like that furtive old hen when he so carefully "hid" his poems of personal heart's-loss in various corners of *Calamus*. Helms also believes this concealing dispersal foretells Whitman's "retreat from his sexuality" and a subsequent "degeneration" of his style. Retreat from a homosexual agenda continued after the 1860 edition appeared. *Calamus* #5 was perhaps Whitman's boldest "gay lib" utterance and included this stanza, which prophesies the mundane scene in Chelsea or the Castro today:

It shall be customary in all directions, in the houses and streets,
    to see manly affection,
The departing brother or friend shall salute the remaining
    brother or friend with a kiss.

In his own copy of the 1860 *Leaves*, #5 is almost wholly slashed through and marked "out all this piece for the present." In fact, it was permanently banished from all succeeding editions. Banished likewise was the "sore and heavy-hearted" *Calamus* #9 that so wonderfully describes the devastating feeling of seeing a lover "content himself without me."

There is also a merciless decimation of "lovers" in the later editions. The obviously masculine "superb lovers of the nations" and these "superb lovers names" in "To a Foil'd European Revolutionaire" are banished in 1881 and replaced by "heroes and martyrs." "Mon cher!" becomes "Dear son" and "Proceed, comrade" becomes "Listen dear son" in "Starting from Paumanok" after 1860. In his copy of 1860, Whitman contemplated adding "O my lover" six times to make very clear the identity of "Whoever You Are Holding Me Now in Hand," but he finally backed off on all of them. The lover in this line from "Song of the Open Road"—"No husband, no wife, no friend, no lover, trusted to hear confession"—is present in 1856 and 1860, but vanishes mysteriously in 1867. The disappearance of a "lover" is especially striking in "I saw in Louisiana a Live-Oak Growing," since it was originally the linchpin poem of what became the *Calamus* sequence. The lone tree images forth Whitman's lonely desolation: "I wonder'd how it could utter joyous leaves standing alone there without its friend, *its lover*, near, for I knew I could not."

Blasphemous and illicit sex is muted, too. Whitman's 1855 line "As God comes a loving bedfellow and sleeps at my side all night" very quickly became "As the hugging and loving bed-fellow sleeps at my side." Among the libidinous joys of "Native Moments" is that of taking "for my love some prostitute." This line vanishes by 1881, as does the reference in "Song of Myself" to the "Voices of prostitutes, and of deformed persons" who speak through the poet's voice. Bethinking himself of his sainted mother, perhaps, Whitman also changed his 1860 self-description in "Starting from Paumanok" as "lusty-begotten" to the much more respectable "Well-begotten, and rais'd by a perfect mother" of 1867.

The poet also quite literally loses his sense of touch in his later editions. The trend is exemplified in the way these quintessential early-Whitman come-hither opening lines of "A Song for Occupations" in 1860—

> COME closer to me,
> Push closer, my lovers, and take the best I possess,
> Yield closer and closer, and give me the best you possess.

—are jettisoned by 1881 in favor of this awful chamber-of-commerce bombast:

A SONG for occupations!
In the labor of engines and trades and the labor of fields
   I find the developments,
And find the eternal meanings.

Everywhere one looks, changes—some deliciously tiny—vitiate the arousing sexual "contact of bodies and souls" (this phrase itself, from the same poem, vanishes). In *Calamus #25* "sweet and lusty flesh clear of taint" is left in, but not the phrase that refers to its "love-power." A squeamishness about phallic allusion perhaps led Whitman to change "To be conscious of my body, so *amorous*, so large?" first to "so happy, so large" and later to "so satisfied, so large" in his "Song at Sunset."

In view of these minor changes, the disappearance of bolder phallic lines from the three early editions of "Song of Myself" was inevitable. For example, "Thruster holding me tight, and that I hold tight! / We hurt each other as the bridegroom and the bride hurt each other." Likewise expurgated—there is no other word for it—from "A Song of Joys" and from the song of sexual joy that was the whole 1860 *Leaves of Grass* are the loins, phallus, testicles, and seminal discharge, as well as dozens of exclamation points conveying the ecstasy of copulation: "O love branches! love-root! love-apples! / O chaste and electric torrents! O mad-sweet drops!"

In one wonderfully perverse revision of "Song of Myself," in fact, Whitman quite literally removed the "joy" of gay sex. Just after his lover/soul plunges his tongue to the poet's "bare-stript" heart, and indeed licks his entire body, comes this line describing the poet's ecstatic, not to say orgasmic, reaction: "Swiftly arose and spread around me the peace *and joy* and knowledge that pass all the *art and* argument of the earth." Gone after 1860 is the "joy" and "art" in this line, as well as much of the joy and art of sex in *Leaves of Grass*.

It says much for Whitman's equanimity—or the rhinoceros hide he boasted of—that some in his cherished inner circle were not shy about expressing their views on the attenuation of *Leaves* over the years. One day in 1888 Traubel was handed an "historic document," the very first letter Walt had received from his extremely close friend and adviser, Dr. R. M. Bucke. In this letter, written in 1870, Bucke reported reading the first of the devolutionary editions, that of 1867, and ventured, "I have compared the Walt Whitman [i.e. "Song of Myself"] in that with the same poem in the 1855 edition, and I must say that I like the earlier edition best." Whitman spoke of the letter admiringly: "he comes in quite frankly, quite frankly, without flattering adjectives, yet also without impudence." The friend most unashamedly idolized by Whitman in his life was William O'Connor, and he too was disgruntled by the later poems. The poet took the view manfully. Of the poems in Sands at Seventy (1888), Whitman reported, "O'Connor kicks against them—is unfavorable—seems to regard the new poems as in some sense a contradiction of the old—alien to the earlier poems—as if I had gone back on myself in my old age." On this July day, Whitman's response to such criticism was "I do not feel that way about them."

Six weeks later, however, on 30 August, Whitman was more open, even eloquent, on the possibility of "decline." His rummaging that day had produced an 1877 letter from one J. T. Trowbridge of Massachusetts, who wrote, "I am astonished that these latter-day critics should have so little to say of the first Leaves of Grass, or venture to speak of them only apologetically. They still stand to me as the most powerful prophetic utterances in modern literature." Feeling mellow, Whitman seems almost to embrace the view, coming, as he says it did, from "one of the early comers and long stayers, always loved and welcomed." Whitman adds, "I think I know what Trowbridge means, too: I do not consider his position unreasonable: there was an immediateness in the 1855 edition, an incisive directness, that was perhaps not repeated in any section of poems afterwards added to the book: a hot, unqualifying temper, an insulting arrogance (to use a few strong words) that would not have been as natural to the periods that followed." Whitman then admits, with great justice, "We miss that ecstasy of statement in some of the after-work." But then he quickly backs off, saying we "get something different, something in some ways undoubtedly better" in late Whitman. Finally, he throws up his hands: "But what's the use arguing an unarguable question?"

Now the question does seem hardly worth arguing about. Most readers today would cast their vote with Trowbridge and the more self-candid Whitman. Some months later, he would speak of the first Leaves of Grass as "my boyish exuberance put into concrete manifestation." It would have been very odd indeed if, having chosen to revise his one masterwork time and again for the rest of his life, Whitman had not bowed to the cycles of aging and left boyish—and sexual—exuberance behind.

Two anecdotes from the last Mickle Street years capture vividly the denaturing of the superb "physiology" of the early Leaves editions. Page upon page in Traubel's volumes are devoted to scrupulous debate over the pros and cons of the various paintings and photographs (there were upwards of 150 of the latter) made of Whitman. One likeness was done, in fact, by Traubel's father, a German-born lithographer. Whitman, who could very bluntly express his dislike for images of him, liked it and told Horace so, adding a remark that applied with huge irony to himself: "I hope he has not touched it since I saw him—it seemed to me on the whole there was nothing more to be done. The devil in artists is to keep pegging away at a thing after it really is all done—pegging away at it *done,* till it is *undone.*" Traubel, who did not share the view of some Whitman disciples that the later *Leaves* were marred by "pegging away," let the remark pass without comment. But one day, when Walt referred, as he often did, to his weight as being two hundred pounds, Traubel did record in his notes that the poet did "not seem to think he has lost weight, as he undoubtedly has"—another way, perhaps, to think of the quality of Whitman's later verse.

POSTCOITAL TRISTESSE

Several passages in the later editions of *Leaves of Grass* (or passages that vanish from them) are particularly haunting. For they seem to capture especially well the sadness of an author so busy to renounce the libidinous joys that made him the most revolutionary of all American poets. Or, in the words of Symonds, "the noblest of all the amatory poets" and "the most mellifluous of erotic singers."

There is, for example, the oddly wistful line from "A Song of Joys" that was deleted after 1860, a line that says so much about the emotional engine that drove Whitman the Broadway cruiser: "O young man as I pass! O I am sick after the friendship of him who, I fear, is indifferent to me." At the end of the same poem comes another singularly joyless moment when, in its final version, Whitman expresses the desire to be

> A ship itself, (see indeed these sails I spread to the sun and air,)
> A swift and swelling ship full of rich words, full of joys.

In 1860, however, the poem ended differently—and far more humanly, joyously, and *athletically.* "Athletic" always had a quasi-sexual connotation for Whitman. "An athlete is enamour'd of me, and I of him," he wrote in *Calamus* #36. In *Calamus* #38, a kind of mystic male union is described as "athletic": "Ethereal, the last athletic reality, my consolation, / I ascend, I float in the regions of your love O man, / O sharer of my roving life." Who, then, can read the original ending of 1860 and not wish that the poet, who first boasted of himself in 1855 as a "teacher of athletes," had left his "Song of Joys" unchanged:

> O to have my life henceforth my poem of joys!
> To dance, clap hands, exult, shout, skip, leap, roll on, float on,
> An athlete—full of rich words—full of joys.

Two other deletions deserve notice because they express not only Whitman's retreat from sexuality and an "adhesive" or homosexualist agenda, but his retreat, or emigration, from the supreme site of his libidinous joys. These exuberant lines, already quoted, Whitman deleted from his "programme of chants" after their sole appearance in 1860:

> Chants of the Mannahatta, the place of my dearest love, the
>   place surrounded by hurried and sparkling currents,
> Health chants—joy chants—robust chants of young men,
> Chants inclusive—wide reverberating chants . . .

And, even more sadly, he elided his identity as an ecstatic if mysterious dweller in Mannahatta when he came to turn his *Chants Democratic #10* of 1860 into "To a Historian" for the 1867 edition. In the process he became, preposterously, a "habitan of the Alleghanies," and these lovely lines describing the early, brilliantly unorthodox and sexual Whitman were lost:

> (Let the future behold them all in me—Me, so puzzling and
>   contradictory— Me, a Manhattanese, the most loving and
>   arrogant of men;)
> I do not tell the usual facts, proved by records and documents,
> What I tell, (talking to every born American,) requires no further
>   proof than he or she who will hear me . . .

In his vivacious public letter to Emerson appended to the 1856 *Leaves of Grass*, Whitman said, "The courageous soul . . . may be proved by faith in sex, and by disdaining concessions." Sad to say, he did not succeed in his post-1860 editions of *Leaves of Grass* in sustaining the extraordinary early courage of his sexuality.

3

WALT & HIS BOYS:
"TO SEEK MY LIFE-LONG LOVER"

What do you seek so pensive and silent?
What do you need, comrade?
Mon cher! do you think it is love?
　　　　　　　　—"Proto-Leaf" (1860)

ONE DAY IN 1913 the poet Guillaume Apollinaire, perhaps having had one absinthe too many, took it in mind to write a letter to the *Mercure de France* describing Walt Whitman's funeral. On a large tract usually "occupied by traveling circuses" three pavilions were set up: one for the body, one for a barbecue ("a popular treat at which beef and mutton are roasted"), one for drinking. Three thousand five hundred people attended, among them, said Apollinaire, Whitman's "former mistresses and cameradoes (he used this word which he thought was Spanish to designate the young men he loved in his old age, and he did not conceal his taste for boy love)." Even the young man "Whitman loved above all others" was there—Peter Connelly, though Apollinaire got his name wrong. "Pederasts came in crowds" and "everybody drank enormously" from tubs of whiskey, beer, and lemonade. There were "sixty fights," which led the police to make fifty arrests. The day-long affair ended at dusk with a grand procession preceded by bands playing ragtime. Apollinaire's communication to the *Mercure* appeared, appropriately enough, on April Fools' Day.

Stuart Merrill, Whitman's expatriate devotee of long standing, hastened to write a letter debunking this wicked whimsy, in the course of which he reiterated Apollinaire's point about the poet's gay following: "all our excited homuncules of Berlin, London and Paris have claimed him as one of theirs." A week later the *Mercure* published a letter from a Harrison Reeves, who reported on his travels among Whitman's old Long Island haunts: "In the course of conversation some of the oldest of these farmers spoke of the frequency of Walt's 'singularities' toward boys and of his 'special' morality, though none of these excellent people . . . seemed to consider him abominable on this account." Apollinaire, by the way, eventually owned up to his little hoax. Ragtime in 1892? Impossible.

It is fitting that, though delayed some twenty years, malicious gossip would attend Whitman to his very tomb in Camden's Harleigh Cemetery, for he had borne much during his life. Surely most of it (and the worst) never got back to him, but many a whiff of the innuendos and mocking ridicule must have come his way. Whitman did not take it shyly, either. "I have always craved to hear the damndest that could be said of me," he told Horace Traubel, "and the damndest has been said, I do believe." It stiffened, among other things, his resolve. In fact, apropos his "special morality" out on Long Island, Whitman had also told Traubel, "I have the hide of the rhinoceros, morally and in other ways— can stand almost anything." One wonders if Whitman could have stood Apollinaire's damnedest, though, for the poet had invested much effort and an enormous sum of money in an elaborate, dignified funeral vault— seventy-two tons of granite and five of white marble laid out over three hundred square feet. Drunken fisticuffs and barbecue sauce would have lowered the tone. Traubel tells us, in fact, that the funeral-day throng was "sedate, serious." And Walt hated lemonade: "It is a damnable drink."

In any event, a significant truth about Whitman is reflected in the *Mercure* brouhaha—namely, that his emotional and poetic economy was, if not misogynistic, deeply, overwhelmingly masculinist and male-homosexual. Indeed, his is not even a man's world but a boy's. The "singularities" of his life and of his greatest poetry were, as the Long Island farmers noticed, evoked by boys and boy (and b'hoy) love. When Traubel asked him when he founded the *Long Islander* newspaper, Whitman responded with one of his more reverberant generalizations about his masterpiece: "About '39 or '40—long before *Leaves of Grass* . . . I was a mere boy, then—it was in fact my boyish exuberance put into concrete manifestation." Boyishness was, early and late, a precious commodity for Whitman. "Undying childhood," he said, is an "*illimitably* important" aspect of character.

Whitman's "special" morality was that of boys, roughs, and mechanics, be they "inarmed" in public bonhomie or "clinging" together in private embrace. This morality was so special, in fact, that it required considerable fraternal reserve, privacy, and concealment breachable only by carefully read "secret and divine signs." The life behind the life could only be revealed in male intimacy, as happened, Whitman said (in an intimate chat with Traubel), in his dealings with Emerson: "Emerson was not inclined to talk to strangers ... would not unbosom himself easily.... But with me he was always quite free, easy, liquid—his own free self."

Several weeks later Whitman, in a particularly liquid moment, unbosomed himself to the thirty-one-year-old Traubel about those who truly shared his emotional life:

"Do you know, Horace," he said as I got up and was about to leave, holding my hand in his own, "the public has no notion of me as a spiritualistic being. Apart from a few—a very few—of you fellows— my *entourage*, household—you, Doctor [Bucke], perhaps several others—no one understands that I have my connections—that they are deep-rooted—that they penetrate shows, phenomena."*

In the preceding chapter, we considered the sexual Whitman and those "connections" he may have sought in order to satisfy his "shuddering longing ache" for physical contact. In the present chapter, the concern will be for the "spiritualistic" Whitman, his entourage of comrades, and those from the intimate circle with whom he had memorable "connections." The Whitman, in other words, in search not merely of the man-root but of that more deep-rooted, phenomenal thing called love—the Whitman in search of a lifelong lover. The Whitman, in short, who wrote in one of his early notebooks of "the young man of Manna-hatta, the celebrated rough, / (Him I love well—let others sing whom they may—him I sing, for a thousand years!)"

No Women in the House

Over the years Whitman offered up many generalizations about the "essence" of *Leaves of Grass* or the impetus for its creation. Some of these, like the remarks about boyish exuberance or the influence of opera (taken so seriously in Chapter 1), strike one immediately as very plausible. Others are more dubious. Whitman once ventured, for instance, that *Leaves of Grass* "has no narrow tendencies," but then added, "at least ... I hope it has not." But the work is rich in narrowing, hermetic tendencies, exclusions, and exclusivities. Still other obiter dicta strike one as so implausible or self-delusive as to be amusing. Among these, surely, is Whitman's remark, uttered in 1889, that *Leaves of Grass* is "essentially a woman's book."

In the very forward-looking Seneca Falls sense of what Whitman called "the woman rightsers" his assertion may have been justified, but in many other ways, to borrow one of Whitman's own squelches, this view "ain't worth shucks."* *Leaves of Grass* is no such thing—is almost as copiously and elaborately male-centered as that *ne plus ultra* of masculinist poetry, the sonnet sequence of Shakespeare. Whitman found small basis for comradery with Shakespeare in general, but *Leaves* and the *Sonnets* certainly see eye to eye in their projection of the cult of masculine friendship. A poet capable of writing—but fortunately not printing—"see here the phallic choice of America, a full-sized man or woman" would be a perfect reader for, say, Shakespeare's Sonnet 20 to the Young Man, which so wittily blends fraternity-house male bonding and misogyny and which ends with a phallic joke. Since Mother Nature has "prick'd" the Young Man out for women's pleasure by giving him a penis, the speaker cheerfully grants, "Mine be thy love, and thy love's use their treasure."

Indeed, late in the 1850s Whitman wrote down some thoughts for a "Lect. (To Women)" that exactly paraphrase Sonnet 20's notion of "spiritual" male-male affection ("love") being more treasurable than heterosexual fornication ("love's use"): "the love and comradeship of a woman, of his wife, however welcome, however complete, does not and cannot satisfy the grandest requirements of a manly soul for love and comradeship.—The man he loves, he often loves with more passionate attachment than he ever bestows on any woman." He ends with these breathtaking rhetoricals: "Is it that the growth of love needs the free air—the seasons, perhaps more wildness, more rudeness? Why is the love of women so invalid? so transient?" Whitman apparently (and happily) decided not to develop these sentiments for public utterance.

Most of his life, but especially in his later decades, Whitman was able to conceal the homophilia deep in his "spiritualistic being" reasonably well, and he presented an invariably gallant, courteous mien to the opposite sex. Bronson Alcott visited him and reported, with a dash of cynical vinegar, "A bachelor, he professes great respect for women." And profess he most certainly did . . . perhaps too much to be taken quite seriously. Once he even uttered that time-honored assurance that always leaves one a little suspicious: "Why—some of my best—in fact, my very best friends have been women." Two and a half years later, he reiterated the point with a suspiciously macho figure of speech: "I have great friends in the women. My best friends have been women. Put that in your pipe and smoke it." And he exploded in a grand show of fury, more than once, on recalling slanderous gossip that he had once said, "Women? What are women, anyhow? Nothing but a set of old cows!" Some color of truth is perhaps given to this nasty gossip, however, by an anecdote recorded by

Traubel: "Catching him in the act of saying something petulant concerning women [his doctor] Baker cried: 'I supposed from your books that you entertained quite other feelings about women.' W. at once came down. 'So I do: the books are right—I am wrong.' "*

By way of obliterating any disparity between his private and published views, Whitman's usual habit was to heap upon women such praise as to remove them from all physical existence. "I think the best women are *always* the best of all: the flower—the justification of the race—the summit, the crown—aureoling the shadows which make up the rest," he could enthuse without much trouble. On the very same evening he gushed so, in fact, Whitman summoned up the name of Anne Gilchrist, who had, through correspondence from England, fallen in love with Whitman and had even moved to Philadelphia for a time to be near him. "I know no other woman living who so attracts me." The "attraction" was, of course, utterly unphysical. He had always been more comfortable when Mrs. Gilchrist was three thousand miles distant. (Her artist son Herbert became a close acquaintance, though.) Gilchrist, by the way, had been safely dead four years when he gave her this supreme place in his heart.

Not nearly so disingenuous, to be sure, are Whitman's many admirable pronouncements in his writing and conversations on the subject of equality of the sexes in modern American life. "History teems with accounts of big men ... of the he-critters," he complained to Traubel, "but the women go unmentioned. Yet how much they deserve!" As early as the 1855 preface he was trumpeting "the perfect equality of the female with the male," and in the open letter to Emerson in the 1856 edition he speaks witheringly of "this empty dish, gallantry" being filled with something when "Women in These States approach the day of ... organic equality with men." But these more agreeable sentiments concern their political rather than their amorous welfare or their identity as women.

Gilchrist appears to have been the sole woman in Whitman's life who tried seriously to "bother him up," in the phrase of Peter Doyle. In an interview three years after the poet died, Doyle allowed that "Towards women generally Walt had a good way," but his main conclusion suggests that this was entirely a function of good manners: "I never knew a case of Walt's being bothered up by a woman. In fact, he had nothing special to do with any woman except Mrs. O'Connor and Mrs. Burroughs [wives of two Whitman disciples]. His disposition was different. Woman in that sense never came into his head. Walt was too clean, he hated anything which was not clean." Whitman's brother George echoed this summary: "As for dissipation and women. I know well enough his skirts were clean.

Any charge that he led a miscellaneous life is without a bottom."*
George nails the point by adding that "the stage-drivers, too, would tes-
tify to the same effect. Walt was always correct. I could quote all sorts of
things from these men." Straight men can be so charmingly naive about
their gay siblings.

That these views accurately reflect Whitman's complete lack of "connection" with women other than family is made amusingly clear in some
of the extant letters Doyle received from Whitman beginning in 1868.
That year Whitman paid a visit to very prosperous Providence, Rhode
Island, where he was entertained by a "party of ladies & gentlemen—
mostly ladies." In a "precious screed" to his "Dear boy & comrade,"
Whitman bragged wryly, "I also made love to the women, & flatter
myself that I created at least one impression—wretch & gay deceiver that
I am. . . . I am here at present times mainly in the midst of female
women. . . . You would be astonished, my son, to see the brass & coolness, & the capacity of flirtation & carrying on with the girls—I would
never have believed it of myself. . . . [I am] sought for, seized upon & rav-
ingly devoured by these creatures." Knowing his sheep-in-wolf's-clothing
performance would amuse, Whitman then assures his boyfriend this is all
"clean" fun: "Of course, young man, you understand, it is all on the
square. My going in amounts to just talking & joking & having a devil of
a jolly time, carrying on—that's all."

A few years later, on an 1870 visit to his mother in Brooklyn,
Whitman joked in a similar vein: "Pete, dear boy . . . I am going over to
New York to visit the lady I went down to the ferry with—so you see I am
quite a lady's man again in my old days." His real purpose for writing,
though, was to express more serious feelings. Of their parting in Washington he recalls: "I never dreamed that you made so much of having me
with you, nor that you could feel so downcast at losing me." He reports a
"cool breeze & the moon shining. I think every time of you, & wish if we
could only be together these evenings." He closes, "Love to you, dear
Pete—& I wont be so long again writing to my darling boy. Walt." A few
months afterward, in another letter to Doyle quoted earlier, the existence
of an all-male entourage is again jocularly mentioned. Whitman tells of
the very rich, manly, and jovial friend who invited him to live in his
Fifth Avenue mansion: "no airs—& just the one to suit you & me—no
women in the house—he is single. . . ." Whitman found it no effort to be
sociable with everyone. "He had an easy, gentle way" with people, said
Doyle, "no matter who they were or what their sex." But to be "Walt
Whitman sociable"—as he identified one young man in his notebooks—
meant something much more applausive . . . and masculine.

Nothing shows more emphatically than the notebook lists how Whitman never strayed far from his masculine bias of nature. Women appear occasionally, but they are only the odd great-aunt, widow, or celebrity. Not once is a detail of feminine physiognomy or physique recorded, as he routinely, often elaborately, did for young men and boys. There are many prefigurings of this bias in Whitman works that predate the notebooks. There is, for example, the very aptly titled story "The Boy Lover," first published in 1845, with its glimmer of an all-male Whitman entourage. The narrator's playmates are two "spirited, clever young fellows" named Wheaton ("very passionate, too") and Brown ("slim, graceful, and handsome . . . fond of sentiment, and used to fall regularly in love once a month"). Especially resonant is a little three-page story called "My Boys and Girls," published in *The Rover* in April 1844 when Whitman was twenty-five. It begins democratically enough: "Though a bachelor, I have several girls and boys that I consider my own." A baby girl and a "very beautiful" fourteen-year-old girl are mentioned briefly, and the rest of the story is devoted to eight males. Four are given names of Whitman's siblings; the other four, who are only given initials, form a homosocial entourage that clearly engages the affections of the first-person narrator. There is H. ("my 'summer child.' An affectionate fellow . . ."), M. ("a volatile lively young gentleman . . . an acquaintance by no means unpleasant to have by my side"), J.H. ("sober, good-natured youth, whom I hope I shall always number among my friends"), and finally a more nearly pubertal H.H. is "too large, perhaps, and too near manhood, to be called one of my *children*. I know I shall love him well when we become better acquainted—as I hope we are destined to be."

But the most heated paragraph of the story is devoted to a boy who has died. Much of the emotional freight carried in the early *Leaves* editions is miniaturized here: "No weary bane of body or soul—no disappointed hope—no unrequited love—no feverish ambition . . . may ever trouble him more. He lies low in the grave-yard on the hill. Very beautiful was he . . . and sad was the gloom of his passing." The last line about this youth so promising of "an honorable manhood" shows Whitman already suffering in his search for the divine and perfect comrade: "O bitter day! I pray God there may come to me but few such!"

With the appearance of *Leaves of Grass*, Whitman donned the gloves of a particularly pugilistic masculinism. (That the volume is at the same time brilliantly and combatively antipatriarchal is not the least of its paradoxes.) The hints of gender bias are sometimes small but telling. A few pages into the 1855 preface we hear of "the beautiful masculine Hudson" and may be permitted to wonder whether the (narrow? fast?

treacherous?) East River is by extension "feminine." Indeed, much later in life he did speak of the Hudson as "Not sluttish"! In his anonymous reviews Whitman was very clear about his readership: *Leaves* was intended as "an illustration, for the present and future of American letters and American young men." He was clear, too, about himself and the circle where his "connections" lay, calling himself "a person singularly beloved and looked toward, especially by young men and the illiterate."

A year later, via the Emerson letter, Whitman again touted his all-male entourage: "Every day I go among the people of Manhattan Island, Brooklyn, and other cities, and among the young men, to discover the spirit of them, and to refresh myself." The poet who boasted of "rugged" physiology was clearly writing as if he truly believed what he had scribbled in his "lecture to women": no "invalid" or "transient" and necessarily sexless womanly love could suffice. *Leaves* was his call for "more wildness, more rudeness"—a call that could only be answered by the phallic "wild old Corybantian dance" of men or the rhythmic thrust of their "slow rude muscle."

In "Song of Myself" Whitman made his debut as "the poet of the woman the same as the man," and twelve years later he repeated the assertion in a poem he eventually gave pride of place in *Leaves of Grass*: "The Female equally with the Male I sing." But these brave notions, too, fall ignominiously into the "O vain boast" category. What equality can there be from a poet proud of "lusty lurking masculine poems" and eager to paint landscapes "masculine, full-sized and golden"? And what disinterest in gender can there be from a poet who would entertain this early version of "Starting from Paumanok": "I believe the main purport of America is to found a new ideal of manly friendship, more ardent, more general"? For 1860 he toned this down, but only slightly: "I believe These are to found their own ideal of manly love, indicating it in me."

The masculinist purport of *Leaves* is often strikingly clear in the subtleties of Whitman's phrasing (the italics are mine): "I do not doubt that the *passionately-wept* deaths of young men are provided for, and the deaths of young women and the deaths of little children are provided for," he writes in an 1856 poem. In "Give Me the Splendid Silent Sun" he asks for "interminable eyes—give me women—give me comrades *and lovers* by the thousand!" In "Spontaneous Me" he promises to "saturate what shall produce boys [but why not also girls?] to fill my place when I am through." In "The Sleepers" the dream-traveler observes "The *sisters* sleep lovingly side by side in their bed, / The *men* [but why not "brothers," the obvious parallel?] sleep lovingly side by side in theirs." He also sees "The actor and actress . . . The affectionate *boy* [but why not "and girl" too?], the husband and wife." "I Hear America Singing" ends on yet another note of bias with the poet listening to

> Each singing what belongs to him or her and to none else,
> The day what belongs to the day—at night the party of young
>   fellows, robust, friendly,
> Singing with open mouths their strong melodious songs.

In the 1860 version of "Starting from Paumanok" Whitman called his chants "inclusive," but in fact they were predominantly the "robust chants of *young men*." Whitman was the supreme poet of well-deployed "impetus-words," of diction designed to encourage ambulation or, as he might have put it, getting a move on. But the movement he envisioned, for instance in "Song of the Open Road," is specifically intended "To gather the *minds of men* out of their brains as you encounter them— to gather the love out of their hearts, / To take *your own lovers* on the road with you." Whitman was, too, the great celebrator of the same-sex kiss, "the comrade's long-dwelling kiss" in *Calamus* #3 or the "good-by kiss" planted upon the "dear son" in "Song of Myself." But this did not prevent him from writing an editorial in 1857 for the Brooklyn *Daily Times* under the leader "Kissing a Profanation," in which he expressed regret over the "alarming increase of late years, in the custom of kissing among ladies." "A kiss should not be deemed a mere unconsidered trifle," he opined, "to be rudely pitched."

David Reynolds has recently asserted that Whitman had an "eye for female beauty" and also that what "today would be called heterosexuality was an essential part of his poetic program." These views are incredible, and Reynolds offers no citations from *Leaves of Grass* to make them less so. Whitman had virtually *no* eye for or interest in the physical beauty of woman. Nowhere is this more clear than in "I Sing the Body Electric" (1855). We are here riveted by the "play of masculine muscle through clean–setting trowsers and waist–straps," by "the joints" of a man's hips and wrists, and by "the flex of his waist and knees." The poet casts his eye on the naked swimmer floating belly-up and then upon five "massive, clean, bearded, tan-faced, handsome" sons of a farmer who has black eyes filled with "immeasurable meaning." But when he introduces "Girls, mothers, house-keepers" into the poem, they are without physical attributes; they are bodiless mirages and are "seen" only "in all their exquisite offices." Whitman wrote much to earn D. H. Lawrence's derisive summary of his representation of women: "Muscles and wombs. They needn't have had faces at all."

Later in the poem Whitman—as so often, especially in later years—shifts into what one might call his "Goddess excellently bright" mode, to borrow a phrase from Ben Jonson's "Hymn to Cynthia." That is, he idealizes the woman out of all physical (and hence sexual) reality. He speaks of the "contact and odor" of both men and women in this poem, but here and in *Leaves* generally all of the smell and touch has to do with male bodies. The woman rarely succeeds to a physique, remains instead sexlessly "formal":

> This is the female form,
> A divine nimbus exhales from it from head to foot,
> It attracts with fierce undeniable attraction.
> I am drawn by its breath as if I were no more than a helpless
>   vapor . . .

And when, a few lines later, sex is had with this vaporized wraith, the details are decidedly masculine: "love-flesh swelling," the "limpid jets" of semen ("quivering jelly of love"). Postcoitally the next morning, it is not the woman but "the dawn" that is "prostrate," not the woman who is "sweetfleshed" but "the day." That the poet has had sex with a nimbus is reiterated in the lines that soon follow: "The female contains all qualities and tempers them . . . . she is in her place . . . . she moves with perfect balance, / She is all things duly veiled." As regards his treatment of the female body, Whitman never wrote more truly than in that last line. For the woman's body a veil, and, as in "Song of Myself," in the woman's part Whitman himself, drawing his lovers near: "Come nigh to me limber-hip'd man and give me your finger and thumb."

No, the subject of physical female beauty had a way of causing the notoriously garrulous and graphic poet to close his lips and avert his eyes. Whitman had an *eye* for it? Perhaps the best response to this odd notion is simply to quote in its entirety his poem "Beautiful Women," which appeared in the third edition of *Leaves*:

> WOMEN sit or move to and fro, some old, some young,
> The young are beautiful—but the old are more beautiful than the
>   young.

One would not accuse the author of this poem of being engaged with his subject. For beautiful men Whitman wrought canto upon effusive canto; for beautiful women, this haiku. Here is the place to note, too, that there is only one extant photograph of Whitman with an adult woman, and in it the woman's face has been scratched out.*

Instances of the elided female body in *Leaves* are often striking, none more so than the famously voyeuristic passage of "Song of Myself." The bathers are "real," but "she" who watches them, tellingly, is a chrono-metric abstraction:

> Twenty-eight young men bathe by the shore,
> Twenty-eight young men, and all so friendly,
> Twenty-eight *years of womanly life*, and all so lonesome.

And "she" is also duly veiled—merely "handsome and richly drest"—while the poet's eye for physical detail is devoted to glistening male beards, moist temples and ribs, white bellies that "swell to the sun," and the "pendant" phallus and "bending arch" of a thrusting torso. Virtually the same scene is recast a few years later in *Enfans d'Adam #2* (1860), with the woman again imprisoned in abstract "form":

> The welcome nearness—the sight of the perfect body,
> The swimmer swimming naked in the bath,
>   or motionless on his back lying and floating,
> The female form approaching—I, pensive, love-flesh tremulous,
>   aching . . .

In "Give Me the Splendid Silent Sun" (1865), too, the woman has no body, merely breath: "Give me for marriage a sweet-breath'd woman of whom I should never tire." In his later decades even the breath vanishes amid marmoreal verbiage about the "towering feminine" of America, the "federal mother," and "womanhood divine, mistress and source of all."

Whitman, it seems obvious, did not "welcome nearness" to the female body, and many of the heterosexual feints and pronouncements in *Leaves of Grass* consequently have about them an air of lip service. On several occasions one senses Whitman indulging in a heterosexual "reflex" in order to disguise or at least tame his genuine sexual interest and agenda. For example, in "From Pent-up Aching Rivers," after invoking a kind of same-sex mating of "Two hawks in the air" and "two fishes swimming in sea" and the "oath of the inseparableness of two together," Whitman gives ground back to Propriety with a phrase about "the woman that loves me and whom I love more than my life." The heterosexual reflex in a line from "Spontaneous Me"—"The body of my love, *the body of the woman I love*, the body of the man"—is particularly shameless, since the rest of the poem is so deliriously and exclusively about phallic arousal, masturbation, and "limpid liquid" semen—which, characteristically, will produce "*boys* to fill my place" and "*Adamic* and fresh daughters." Adamic daughters, no doubt, who are like the "fierce and athletic girls" his "seminal milk" produces in "A Woman Waits for Me."

The heterosexual reflex is in play in many other poems. A few examples:

> . . . put your lips upon mine I permit you,
> With the comrade's long-dwelling kiss *or the new husband's kiss* . . .

> PASSING stranger! you do not know how longingly I look upon you,
> You must be he I was seeking, *or she I was seeking* . . .

> These yearnings why are they? these thoughts in the darkness why
>   are they?
> Why are there men *and women* that while they are nigh me the
>   sunlight expands my blood?

Whitman occasionally seems to have sensed that a heterosexual touch was too arrant. In the following passage from his 1856 poem "Excelsior," he decided to remove the italicized lines for his most homophilic *Leaves* edition:

> And who has receiv'd the love of the most friends? for I know
>   what it is to receive the passionate love of many friends,
> *And to whom has been given the sweetest from women,*
>   *and paid them in kind?*
> *For I will take the like sweets, and pay them in kind;*
> And who possesses a perfect and enamour'd body?

On this occasion, at least, the poet was behaving in the spirit of "candor" that he so loudly praised in the 1855 preface: removing the heterosexuality made "Excelsior" a more honest poem. His enamour'd though far from perfect body had probably for several years received the "passionate love" of many friends, assuredly all of them male.

That Walt's eyes were exclusively riveted on manly forms is amusingly suggested by the notes he made for an article on Manhattan's "democratic lager element," namely, the rowdy beer halls of the Bowery. One of these establishments, Lindmuller's, had a large dance floor, and Whitman's jottings leave the impression that there was not a woman in sight when he visited: "the waltzing band strikes up—very good music— the young fellows select their partners—waltzing altogether. . . . The young fellows are good looking—and still they waltz waltz waltz[—]some till they are red in the face—a gay assembly—a dance hall, perfectly respectable, I should think." To make the scene more emphatically "respectable" and to avoid the suggestion that this was an all-male 1860s tea dance (or "ram-reel" as such would have been called then), Walt added this jolly heterosexual touch to the article he eventually published in the *Leader* of 17 May 1862: "One fleshy young lady shines conspicuously like a full moon among the stars." Or was she indeed but one full-bodied fag hag among so many handsome, manly "stars"?

Perhaps the most spectacular example of Whitman's deployment of the heterosexual reflex, and of his homophilic bias, is *Calamus* #38. The poem begins promisingly for womanhood, though the large abstraction of the first word is a danger sign:

> PRIMEVAL my love for the woman I love,
> O bride! O wife! more resistless, more enduring
>   than I can tell, the thought of you!
> Then separate, as disembodied, the purest born,
> The ethereal, the last athletic reality, my consolation,
> I ascend—I float in the regions of your love, O man,
> O sharer of my roving life.

But those exclamation points are pure melodrama; the poet's love for the woman proves eminently resistible. In the third line he wafts, like one of Marc Chagall's dreamily floating figures, into shared and loving life with a man. Amid the poem's abstractions Whitman, as so often, reserves the one obvious sexual allusion for the man. The "last athletic reality" was sex, as Whitman made clear in the first *Calamus* poem, where he announced his resolve to sing only songs "of manly attachment . . . Bequeathing hence types of athletic love."

Whitman's women, of course, had no such "athletic" reality for him. Those who loomed in his life either were related by blood or marriage or were mothers or spouses of close friends, like Nelly, the wife of William O'Connor, or Susan, the mother of Harry Stafford. With them Whitman was on his best behavior, always ready with a flow of harmless, flowery gallantry. The one woman who threatened to breach his circle of comrades, Anne Gilchrist, was nearly buried in the molasses of his praise. There is no small drollery, given her three-year siege upon him, in Whitman's remembering her as no "blind dreamer—a chaser of fancies: she was concrete—spiritually concrete." She was also "concrete" intellectually rather than physically, which was fine with Whitman—"the finest,

[a]cutest, most womanly woman I have ever known." This woman who was all mind, in fact, was "a great woman . . . a woman who, I am fond of saying, goes the whole distance of justifying woman."

On some occasions, though, Whitman privately expressed a very understandable puzzlement over the eager embrace of *Leaves of Grass* by women. Thinking of Harry Stafford's mother, he remarked: "I always say it is significant when a woman accepts me." He felt it significant not least because he was very well aware, as he asserted to Traubel one day, that the *"physiological" Leaves of Grass* was nursed in "the occupations, habits, habitats, of men." Small wonder he would say to Traubel on another day that "it is very curious that the girls have been my sturdiest defenders, upholders." Curious, of course, because the author of *Leaves of Grass* knew where the "physiology"—the genital impulses—of his work truly lay.

A few weeks before remarking on his curious female Whitmaniacs, Walt had received a charming letter from one Jessie Taylor, an Englishwoman at the Girls' Grammar School in Queensland, Australia: "I am only what I think in America you call a 'school marm' and of no 'eminence' but I expect it's the average intellect you most want to touch as they form the bulk of the living beings." Reading *Leaves* and *Specimen Days* had left Taylor feeling "what a beautiful sane thing human life is," but she had one humble question: "I wish, as I am a woman, you had told us more of your views about us. I wonder what your ideal of woman is." After Traubel read the letter aloud for Whitman there was, very unusually, no discussion at all of its contents—or the topic raised. Whether Whitman was bemused or rankled by this query at once naive and devastating, we'll never know. But Miss Taylor's may be the best précis we have on womanhood in *Leaves of Grass*.

One day in 1890 Traubel told Whitman of a discussion in town: "did Walt Whitman not think the *male* human body a superior development to the female?" To which Whitman laughed and said, "It is like asking one which he prefers—East or West." This equanimity rings hollow, though, because Whitman had on countless occasions expressed his alienation from the *"haut ton* coteries" of the parlor-bound East and his spiritual affinity with the West and the robust, rough, unlettered, manly men who ventured there. Just six months earlier, in fact, he had told Traubel, "I am a sort of Pacific, Oceanic, Californian critter, anyway." Perhaps, as he made this observation, he recalled the letter the young man named Charles Warren Stoddard had written him about his homosexual adventures out in Hawaii and Polynesia, far away from the corsets and pruderies of the Eastern seaboard.

In the summer of 1950 Thomas Mann, then in his late seventies, was struck by how his "enthusiasm" for young men continued to be emotionally "stormy" (a handsome young waiter in the Grand Hotel Dolder in Zurich had left him atwitter). He confided to his diary a most Whitmanesque credo: "It is my axiom that 'god-like young men' are more worthy of admiration than everything female and arouse a yearning desire like *nothing* in the world." On such an axiom were the early *Leaves of Grass* editions significantly founded.

BECOME ELEVE OF MINE

By January 1891, a little over a year before he died, Whitman had long been mired in the sixth of Shakespeare's ages of man, his muscular shanks shrinking and, as Jaques says, using Whitman's favorite adjective, "his big *manly* voice / Turning again toward childish treble." Poised on the verge of the seventh and last age—"mere oblivion, / Sans teeth, sans eyes, sans taste, sans every thing"—Whitman (notably sans hearing and legs) had given the subject of nurses some careful thought. He told Traubel, displaying once again his bias: "They seem impossible in our time—certainly to America—the true nurse must be a male: that is the upshot of my experience. A male, at least, for men. There are a few women, girls, who take it up *intellectually*: but how far does *that* take us? Certainly there are no males." Whitman then laid out his particulars in a nurse: "What I need is a man to control me—to suggest, to initiate, to save me the trouble even to mention his duties. A man to nurse me, not one I must nurse. Oh! that is very essential."*

These desiderata were sensible enough. And yet they show the profound changes that age and illness had wrought in the Whitman who, "Sighing like furnace" as a lover does in the third age of man, had produced the three sex-charged early editions of *Leaves of Grass* thirty years before. For these were the work of a poet with enormous, almost ineluctable desire to control, suggest, initiate: to act rather than be acted upon, to move rather than be moved.

Whitman was a first-moving poet in an age, as he put it, of "universal ennui." His most characteristic words were what he called impetus-words ("comradeship" and "adhesive" were such words), and he demanded in *Democratic Vistas* a "language fann'd by the breath of Nature, which leaps overhead [and] cares mostly for impetus." In his prime he was the supreme poet of locomotion, which gives a specially melancholy flavor to his many rueful comments on his "slippered and pantalooned" Camden dotage in the conversations with Traubel. "I am getting more and more satisfied with my bed and chair, which is suspicious," he told Horace one day, and on another: "I was a great deal more vehement years ago than I am now. . . . I take on the usual privilege of years—to go slow, to be less vehement, to trust more to quiet, to composure."

The early Whitman was also the poet of putting the moves on: of self-conscious, manipulative, come-hither charisma. He could not have become, as Symonds with some justice enthused, "the most mellifluous of erotic singers" without such a relentlessly attractive and attracting energy of personality. Perhaps Whitman cultivated this energy all the more vigorously because he was not a conventionally handsome man. In *Calamus* #19, he candidly owned up to a "swarthy and unrefined face," and by 1850 or so he had begun to go seriously gray. In fact, in a telling manuscript jotting of plans for the *Enfans d'Adam* sequence of 1860, Whitman boldly cast against type and made himself the central Adamic figure. This projected poem cluster, he wrote, would present "a vivid picture . . . of a fully-complete, well-developed man—eld, bearded, swart, fiery—as a more than rival of the youthful type-hero of novels and love poems." In another revealing manuscript of the same pre-1860 period that manages to boil Shakespeare's seven ages of man into three, Whitman cast himself as a bearded, and also *athletic*, lover. The first age is "Infantum Juvenatum . . . a young mans moods"; the last is "Old Age   Natural Happiness   Love, Friendship." But Whitman clearly sees himself in 1859 (when he was forty) as the ideal of "Middle-age" and of the middle-aged lover: "Strong, well-fibred, bearded, athletic, full of love, full of pride & joy."

Walt Whitman, in other words, seems to have "come out" as a distinctly middle-aged man. And he decided to make the most of it. Though he may have harbored, even acted upon, forbidden sexual desires as early as 1840 or so, he clearly took much longer, until the mid-1850s, to "publish" his personality flamboyantly. Several comments made about him as a young man by his brother George suggest a classic example of the gay man shedding a carapace of conventionality once free of family and native haunts. George says he dressed "stylish when young," that is, in the normal fashion, and he was far from the "swart, fiery" poet of "Song of Myself." "He was always cool, never flurried," said George. He was apparently even *shy*. "His association with neighbors and strangers was not at that period so marked as later. . . . he was scarcely so apt to chime in—establish an acquaintance."

How this introverted young man became "Walt Whitman sociable" in Manhattan and Brooklyn we have already noticed. Perhaps liquor helped to unloose his poetic and sexual cantabile, for George says Walt never "drank at all till he was thirty," and that is precisely the time George began to notice striking changes in his brother. "He started in with his new notions somewhere between 1850–55." In any event, his cultural insouciance came steadily to the fore, as George particularly underscored: "he never cared what anybody thought of him, bad or good. Mother would wonder, 'What will people think?' but he would say, 'Never mind what they think.' We saw that Walt had different ways about him." Whitman's father, like those of so many soon-to-be-gay sons, also hadn't a clue. "I don't think his father ever had an idea what Walt was up to, what he meant," said George. "To him, like to all the rest, Walt was a mystery." That Walter Sr. died just a week after *Leaves of Grass* first appeared suggests wisdom, or at least ironic humor, on the part of the Quakers' Heavenly Goodness.

Even as a child, apparently, among Whitman's "different ways" was a pronounced aptitude for dominance and control. This, as George suggests, set him apart from and above his siblings. Walt "seemed as if he had us in his charge. Now and again his guardianship seemed excessive." This pleasure at being *in loco parentis* is vividly reflected in a little story called "A Legend of Life and Love" that Whitman first published in 1842. It is about two orphaned brothers, both beautiful youths. They are separated for fifty years, and on their reunion the elder—obviously Whitman himself—vents his wisdom. The story's last line: "As Nathan ceased, his brother looked up in his face, like a man unto whom a simple truth had been for the first time revealed." Walt's charisma extended beyond the family, too: "His opinion was not only asked by the family, even when he was quite young, but by neighbors. We all deferred to his judgment—looked up to him. These strangers, these neighbors, saw there was something in him out of the ordinary."

Unsurprisingly, George never breathes a hint, in this reminiscence recorded the year after Walt's death, of just how out of the ordinary his brother was as a sexual being. Indeed, he gives the impression of being honestly in the dark, a pristine civilian. But we can read between the lines of his amusingly unprobing memories and discern the beginning of Whitman's lifelong pattern of desiring and achieving a Socratic and sexually charged control over younger males to whom he was attracted. In ancient Sparta, where men lived together in military barracks until the age of thirty, same-sex relationships often involved an older man, the Eispnêlos or "inspirer," and a younger Aïtes or "hearer." From a remarkably early age, Whitman preferred the role of inspirer. Perhaps gratified to be asked his opinion even as a boy, Whitman made the obvious career choice. "Long ago we lived on a farm," George recounted. "Walt would not do farm work. He had things he liked better—school-teaching, for instance, and writing." George, in fact, was himself a student of Walt's for a year and notes that "it was said at the time that Walt made a very good schoolmaster."

Shortly after leaving the schoolmaster's life (or being forcibly driven from it by angry foes of sodomy), Whitman turned to journalistic fiction, and several of his early stories reveal glimpses of the Eispnêlos cruising for a favored Aïtes. His apparent debut as a short story writer was, in fact, with a little tale titled "Death in the School-Room (A FACT)" that appeared in August 1841. This almost hilariously melodramatic story tells of a cruel village schoolmaster who accuses "a slight, fair-looking boy of about thirteen" of stealing fruit from a garden. Tim Barker fits the favored juvenile type of Whitman's notebooks: "his face had a laughing, good-humor'd expression," and he displays "good looks" and a "pleasant disposition" that "made him many friends in the village." But, alas, "the countenance of the boy . . . was too unearthly fair for health; it had, notwithstanding its fleshy, cheerful look, a singular cast as if some inward disease, and that a fearful one, were seated within" (shades of Aschenbach's thoughts about the frail-seeming Tadzio in *Death in Venice*). Of Lugare, the teacher, we learn: "Punishment he seemed to delight in. Knowing little of those sweet fountains which in children's breasts ever open quickly at the call of gentleness and kind words, he was fear'd by all for his sternness, and loved by none." The boy is given an hour to sit at his desk and confess. He falls motionless as the hour passes, and when Lugare begins to flog him he makes a horrible discovery: "Death was in the school-room, and Lugare had been flogging a CORPSE." The story was reprinted more often (seven times) than any other he ever wrote.

That Whitman himself knew well how to sound "the call of gentleness and kind words" in the classroom and gain the affection of the Tim Barkers under his charge is suggested by a longer tale, "The Half-Breed: A Tale of the Western Frontier" (1845). This story sounds a more idyllic pedagogical note, its opening phrase being "Loudly rang merry peals of laughter from a group of children." With the relationship between the cheerful, smiling teacher and favorite student of this story, Whitman was making clear strides toward becoming the "teacher of athletes" of the 1855 *Leaves of Grass*: "Master Caleb, the teacher, as usually happens in schools, had his favorites. . . . Of all the rest, Quincy Thorne, the tall gentle boy, was the one whom he loved most, and whose company he preferred. Any other choice would have created some envy and jealousy—but all the children themselves were attached to the teacher's favorite, and gladly yielded to his good fortune without demur." Caleb and Quincy, in fact, are alone together loafing by a "little and verdant grass-patch" on the river when the story's main melodramatic events, which concern a local Indian named Arrow-Tip, begin to unfold. Whitman concludes his story with a fantasy-vision of comradeship between "inspirer" and "hearer":

> Master Caleb has risen in his fortunes. As the extent and population of the town . . . increased, it was thought fit to have an incorporated academy. Master Caleb is at the head of it. Quincy Thorne, a popular and intelligent young man, whom they think of holding up as a candidate for a respectable legislative office, still keeps communion of friendship with his early and excellent teacher.

Four years earlier, and just a few months after "Death in the School-Room" appeared, Whitman published a haunting story with a darker, more boldly erotic Eispnêlos-Aïtes relationship: "The Child and the Profligate." In a "straggling village some fifty miles from New York city"—was the author thinking of Southold? or Huntington?—a twelve-year-old named Charley is deeply miserable at having to do farm work all day (the autobiography here is blatant). Like Quincy, he is "a lively fellow" and "the young men of the place . . . were very fond of him." After being consoled by his widowed mother, he returns to his employer. But on the way he hears hijinks in the village's one drinking house and peers in. His eye is caught by a stranger, perhaps twenty-one or -two, well-dressed in "linen delicate and spotless as snow." He seems, says the author, like those who "may be nightly seen in the dress circles of our most respectable theatres." Carousing sailors spot the boy, drag him in and try to force some brandy down him. In the nick of time, the elegantly dressed young man ("no stranger to the pugilistic art") saves the boy from a "one-eyed mariner." The stranger sits the boy down next to him and they hold "communion together" for an hour as the boy tells his sad story: "More and more interested, drawing the child close to his side, the young man listen'd to his plainly told history." Midnight comes and goes. Taking shrewd advantage of the situation, the man, named Lankton, promises to liberate Charley from his "servitude" the next day and invites him to share his bed at the local inn. (When Whitman reprinted the story, he arranged separate beds for the two and made Charley older.) Charley obliges and, as might be expected, "very pleasant thoughts filled the mind" of the young man as they retire.

Whitman, of course, could not play out this time-honored pickup scenario to its sexual climax. The "pleasant thoughts" are not of fellation or buggery but of resolutions more agreeable to propriety: thoughts "of walking in a steadier and wiser path than formerly." And yet, Whitman ventures daringly far with this profligate alter ego of his. "All his imaginings seemed to be interwoven with the youth who lay by his side; he folded his arms around him, and, while he slept, the boy's cheek rested on his bosom. Fair were those two creatures in their unconscious beauty."

With his two characters abed, Whitman rehearses the elder's dissipated past. It turns out to have much in common with the carousing low life he himself was probably beginning to sample in Manhattan as he wrote the story. A resident on the west side of New York and trained as a doctor, Lankton has spent most of his time with a brandy bottle, "mixing in all kinds of parties where the object was pleasure" and often being obliged to bribe journalists to escape notoriety. Like Whitman the Manhattanese, he does not stand on propriety in choosing his comrades: "Lankton hesitated not to make himself at home with any associate that suited his fancy." In fact, "New York police officers were not altogether strangers to his countenance."

Just as Whitman would do in the *Calamus* sequence as a whole, he now proceeds, by way of denouement, to stage a kind of benediction for male lovers. He has "a gentle angel" approach "those two who slumbered there in each others arms." This inevitably male visitor, a benign voyeur, instantly kisses the innocent boy but pauses, fearful of taint, over the young dandy. Finally, "a very pale bright ray of sunlight darted through the window and settled on the young man's features." The angelic spirit "from the Pure Country" accepts the sign, kisses him, and vanishes. (In all subsequent appearances of the story, this provocative *ménage à trois* was entirely deleted.)

In a few short paragraphs Whitman ends the story, yet again with a fantasy-ideal of same-sex companionship, this one necessitating a heterosexual reflex at the very end. The author says he will not "particularize the subsequent events of Lankton's and the boy's history . . . how the close knit love of the boy and him grew not slack with time; and how, when at length he became head of a family of his own, he would shudder when he thought of his early danger and escape."

Lankton turns over a new leaf, severs "the guilty ties that had so long gall'd him," and returns to his own hearth—and respectability. Lankton's creator, however, appears to have done no such thing himself. If he enjoyed beatific interludes with waifs that began through casual barroom acquaintance, as "The Child and the Profligate" may suggest, no angelic spirit from the Pure Country seems to have inspired him to adopt a more conventional life. Though there is no record of his becoming familiar to New York police officers, he became ever more boastful, in his poetry at least, of affinity with those who mock statutes, who are "outlaw'd offenders," and who are imperturbable in their dubious "occupation, poverty, notoriety, foibles, crimes." If anything, the entwined acts of teaching and loving, which may have ruined him in Southold, became more emphatic as Whitman made America his classroom with *Leaves of Grass*. Indeed, the sequence in these lines from 1855 describing all manner of beautiful, unclothed sleepers perfectly expresses the erotics of pedagogy in the volume: "The breath of the boy goes with the breath of the man . . . . friend is inarmed by friend, / The scholar kisses the teacher and the teacher kisses the scholar . . ." A few years later the amorist and scholar reiterated his joint profession, counting himself in *Chants Democratic* #17 among the "teachers of all, and lovers of all." This boast he eventually placed, with good reason, among the "Inscriptions" poems that usher the reader into *Leaves*.

Leaves, in short, is a schoolmasterly project, a kind of elaborate visual and spiritual aid. And its driving urge is simultaneously to teach and seduce, as Whitman made brazenly clear in a characteristic boast about his pedagogical charisma in "Song of Myself":

> I teach straying from me, yet who can stray from me?
> I follow you whoever you are from the present hour;
> My words itch at your ears till you understand them.

And, more specifically, *Leaves* is a volume potently—if often cryptically and with many a gentle and genteel feint to make the "average" student comfortable—addressed to the Tim Barkers, Quincy Thornes, and Charleys among his readers. It is a volume of stupendous favoritism, a favoritism that, not surprisingly, is most evident in the *Calamus* poems. *Calamus* #3 sounds like nothing so much as a forbidding professor guarding his class sign-up list with the mien of Cerberus—

> I give you fair warning, before you attempt me further,
> I am not what you supposed, but far different.
>
> Who is he that would become my follower?
> Who would sign himself a candidate for my affection?

—and warning that *his* course will be hell:

> Your novitiate would even then be long and exhausting,
> The whole past theory of your life, and all conformity to the
>   lives around you, would have to be abandoned;
> Therefore release me now, before troubling yourself any further . . .

Of course, the best—the ideal—students, Whitman recognized, would rise to the challenge.

Burroughs thought *Calamus* #3 "the single poem that throws most light upon [Whitman's] aims and methods," but I am inclined to think that a much briefer *Calamus* poem evokes even more forcefully the erotics of Whitman's pedagogical vocation. In 1855 he had gestured with a flourish, "Eleves I salute you, / I see the approach of your numberless gangs." But who among these eleves, these students, would become his favorites? He explains in *Calamus* #41 (its later title, "To a *Western* Boy," note well):

> To the young man, many things to absorb, to engraft, to develop,
>   I teach, to help him become élève of mine,
> But if blood like mine circle not in his veins,
> If he be not silently selected by lovers, and do not silently select
>   lovers,
> Of what use is it that he seek to become élève of mine?

A main purpose of *Leaves of Grass*, in other words, was to cultivate Whitman's "favorites"—those of his own kind, in whose veins comradely blood also circled—not to stray but rather to come closer. The book translates into elaborately poetic "secret and divine" signs the methods Whitman obviously indulged in real life to ingratiate and charm into friendship (and maybe more) the young men he found attractive.

Leaves is the work of someone expertly and intensively *gemütlich*, a word that caught Whitman's fancy and that he copied out in one of his notebooks. Typically, his definition has a masculine spin: "(ga-mute eu ga-mute-lisch)—full of soul heart manliness affection." And all the synonyms assembled by Cassell's dictionary for *gemütlich*, indeed, present the essential pose of the Whitman persona: good-natured, genial, jovial, jolly, cheerful, sociable, easy-going, cosy, snug, agreeable, comfortable. Even among Italian musicians at concerts he attended, where language failed him, the simpatico signore could take his pleasure. "The concerts were always a treat," he told Traubel, "I was always on hand: the players were most of them Italian: spoke miserable English—a mere show of it: but I got along very well with them. They were likeable fellows: I think they thought I was a likeable fellow."

But in the orchestra, as in the classroom of yore, Whitman kept his eye peeled for a favorite. Traubel says that Whitman paused in his remembrance of the Italian players, became "serious," and added "in a fraternal mood": "I can now see one of those Italian players: he played

E-flat cornet, I think they called it: very bright, animated: one of the best if not the best. I was always loafing about: had a quick if not a technical ear. This man would come to the crucial passages with immense gusto—would often play solo interludes, whatnot: then would come the lull—a chance for others to whack away—he being silent for a space. Then it was I would see his dark eyes glancing about—catch me—as if to say, how was that? do you approve? are we agreed?"

Many moments in *Leaves of Grass* perform the same function, asking the chosen eleve/reader in effect, "do you approve? are we agreed?" Asking, that is, whether the reader is a "candidate" for Whitman's affection and whether the would-be eleve can summon the courage to accept his sexual identity and to abandon, in the phrase of *Calamus #3*, the self-denying "conformity to the lives around you." The young Irishman Bram Stoker, we have seen, accepted the challenge, writing, "You are a true man, and I would like to be one myself, and so I would be towards you as a brother and as a pupil to his master. . . . You have shaken off the shackles and your wings are free. I have the shackles on my shoulders still—but I have no wings."

Several years before, the young Charles Warren Stoddard had written from the Pacific in exactly the same vein—"I want your personal magnetism to quicken mine"—and Whitman, after hearing Traubel read the letter out loud for him twenty years later, made a poignant observation that explains the impetus (and I use the word advisedly) behind the early editions of *Leaves of Grass*: "It's wonderful how true it is that a man can't go anywhere without taking himself along and without finding love meeting him more than half way. It gives you a new intimation of the providences to become the subject of such an ingratiating hospitality: it makes the big world littler—it knits all the fragments together: it makes the little world bigger—it expands the arc of comradery."

VOICES, LOVED AND IDEALIZED

Throughout his adult life Whitman, too, cultivated an "ingratiating hospitality." He did so in order to expand his own "arc of comradery." So vigorous and successful in this pursuit was he that, in time, the arc came to form a circle: a circle of boy- and man-friends in whose company, one strongly suspects, the real Walt Whitman (as opposed to the "real Me" persona in "Song of Myself") was likely to be glimpsed. Of course, this is not to say he was a bear or a boor when he ventured beyond his intimate all-male circle of friends. To all and sundry—neighbors, children, women,

shopkeepers, literati, family, bigwigs, fellow writers, casual acquaintances—
Whitman was invariably cordial, polite, and, in a word, most Quakerly. His
disciple William Sloane Kennedy, in fact, included among his Quaker
traits precisely the benevolence, friendliness, plainness, sincerity, placidity,
and "respect for every other human being" that made him such a benign
presence on the American scene for so long.

But this Quaker was not, as Whitman liked to say, the "real critter." In
one of his early anonymous reviews, he pronounced the author of *Leaves* a
man who "loves the free rasping talk of men," and it was amid such talk that
the real critter emerged: both the perfectly casual and the emotionally
earnest Whitman. That is, the "substantial" Whitman, which he sought
sometimes to reveal in his poems, sometimes to conceal through various
modes of diffidence, coyness, or calculated ambiguity. His manuscript of
Calamus #1 shows that he first contemplated announcing, "I celebrate that
concealed but substantial life, / I celebrate the need of the love of comrades." That only the much tamer "I celebrate the need of comrades" got
into the 1860 edition is a shame. For the jettisoned phrase provides a crucial
warning about how to read *Leaves of Grass*, namely, with a sharp eye for the
substantial life that is concealed in its pages. This is the life of the Closet
and the Closet's inevitable corollary: a social world, transparent to civilian
view, within the arc of comradery. When Whitman marked down a boy
in his little notebook as "Walt Whitman sociable," it is possible he was
referring to this world.

This world was defined by sexuality. In another 1860 poem, *Enfans
d'Adam* #8, Whitman made very clear that his "native moments" were
entirely masculine and far from harmless. His were "libidinous joys only
. . . coarse and rank." He consorts after dark with "nature's darlings"—
young men—dances and drinks with them, even shares their "midnight
orgies." Over this robust, raucous fraternity he says he will preside:

> . . . Why should I exile myself from my companions?
> O you shunned persons! I at least do not shun you,
> I come forthwith in your midst—I will be your poet,
> I will be more to you than to any of the rest.

Without doubt, he made good on that promise. The poem would have
been even more shocking, of course, if Whitman had placed it where it so
obviously belongs, in the *Calamus* sequence.

The most striking and self-revealing part of *Enfans d'Adam* #8, however, is the moment when, amid the echo of "indecent calls," the poet
says, "I take for my love some prostitute [these first seven words disap-

peared after the 1871 edition]—I pick out some low person for my dearest friend, / He shall be lawless, rude, illiterate—he shall be one condemned by others for deeds done." Here is the poet performing that most substantial and riveting task of almost all gay lives, the search among one's own kind for a single "dearest friend." The search, that is, for Mr. Right, whether "right" for one night only—a span of time for which prostitutes are eminently suitable—or "right" for the remainder of one's life. The poet referred to such moments as this in *Leaves* as "outcroppings" of autobiography, and outcroppings of this most intensely earnest, sometimes traumatic aspect of Whitman's life give us many memorable passages in his prose and poetry, correspondence, and personal notes. John Whitman, the poet's forebear, came to America in 1640 on a ship called *True Love*, and this, one might say, was a ship for which Walt was constantly on the lookout, not infrequently from the very docks and ferry slips of the East and Hudson Rivers.

Outcroppings of the search begin very early. In the Long Island *Democrat* of 19 May 1840, exactly when the ominous events at Southold may have been unfolding, appeared a seven-stanza poem by a twenty-one-year-old Whitman titled "The Love That Is Hereafter." The verse may be doggerel, but, considered as an exhalation of a young man whose love dare not speak its name, two of its stanzas take on remarkable and highly prophetic weight:

> O, mighty powers of Destiny!
> When from this coil of flesh I'm free—
> When through my second life I rove,
> Let me but find *one* heart to love,
>   As I would wish to love:
>
> Let me but meet a single breast,
> Where this tired soul its hope may rest,
> In never-dying faith: ah, then,
> That would be bliss all free from pain,
>   And sickness of the heart.

A dozen years later and Whitman would indeed abandon (in the phrase of *Calamus* #3) "all conformity to the lives around" him and embark on a "second life" brilliantly roving and nonconformist both in its metrics and in its sexuality. Gender here, in 1840, is carefully cloaked; by 1855 and 1860, the gender of the one heart he sought to love would be elaborately confirmed. Whitman would return eloquently to the image of being "born again" into an ideal "second life" in *Calamus* #27, which ends: "O to disengage myself from those corpses of me . . . To pass on, (O living! always living!) and leave the corpses behind!"

There is also a hint of Whitman's early search for one heart to love in a short story he published four years later in 1844, "The Little Sleighers." As before, frustration over unrequited love is the crucial note. The narrator watches some winter child's play at the Battery and is left philosophical. His sentiments anticipate the central facts of the author's emotional life over the next half century: "Who can help loving a wild, thoughtless, heedless, joyous boy? . . . A man may keep his heart fresh and his nature youthful by mixing much with that which is fresh and youthful." The story's observer imagines the children he sees suffering various sad fates, among them this surely autobiographical outcropping: "Some will love, and have those they love look coldly upon them; and then, in their sickness of heart curse their own birth-hour." Resident in the womb of time were several fine Whitman poems on precisely this theme, poems written, one must believe, from personal experience. Whitman ends his "mottled reveries" on a lighter note, saying "Why, what a somber moralist I have become!" However, another decade or so of frustration, both professional and sexual, would eventually evoke from Whitman some of his best, and most somber, poetry.

Very little is specifically known about Whitman in the decade preceding the appearance of *Leaves of Grass* in 1855, or indeed of the following five years. It seems fair to assume, though, that his life then was irregular, unfocused, mundane, full of false starts and serendipitous comings, goings, and acquaintances. Like many a comer to Manhattan who feels he is not "making progress" or is at the mercy of the whims of others, Whitman probably got seriously despondent on occasion. Crises of confidence when careers and affairs of the heart sail into the doldrums are a commonplace to many an ambitious but struggling young Manhattanite. Whitman, in fact, recorded one such slough in his notebook, giving it the heading "Depressions": "Every thing I have done seems to me blank and suspicious.—I doubt whether my greatest thoughts, as I had supposed them, are not shallow—and people will most likely laugh at me.—My pride is impotent, my love gets no response.—The complacency of nature is hateful—I am filled with restlessness.—I am incomplete.—" The feeling of vulnerability and the connection made here between writing and "love" are especially worth noting. Whitman casts himself exactly as the deeply depressed speaker of Shakespeare's Sonnet 29: he too is "in disgrace with fortune and men's eyes," deeply bewailing his "outcast state" and "almost despising" himself. In fact, *Calamus #9* ("Hours continuing long, sore and heavy-hearted"), a poem Whitman cut from all editions after 1860, is a virtually exact translation of the emotions of Shakespeare's "outcast" lover. Whitman's speaker is lonesome, discouraged, distracted, and paces city streets "stifling plaintive cries." His lovelorn earth, like Shakespeare's, is "sullen."

Shakespeare's speaker in Sonnet 29 famously rescues himself from the dumps by fantasizing about his Young Man and the love they share. "For thy sweet love rememb'red such wealth brings, / That then I scorn to change my state with kings" runs the glowing final couplet. Sustaining such an ideal is an exhausting, ego-battering, emotional roller-coastering process, as the following ninety-five sonnets to the Young Man show. Whitman, too, sought to create through his poetry a sustaining ideal of a perfect sharer of his roving life. There is not a little of Shakespeare's boast in Sonnet 55 about "this pow'rful rhyme" outliving the gilded monuments of princes in Whitman's boast, in one of his manuscripts, "The one I love well—let other sing whom they may—him I sing, for a thousand years!"

We have sampled a few of "those beginning notes of yearning and love there in the mist" of Whitman's early manhood—to borrow a line from his greatest lovelorn poem, "Out of the Cradle Endlessly Rocking." But it was not until decidedly in middle age (like Shakespeare when he wrote his sonnets) that the poet's tremendous, almost obsessive search for a man to love was triumphantly delineated, that is, with the publication of the third edition of *Leaves of Grass* in 1860. There is irony here—and also an explanation of the brimming homosexual pathos of 1860—because Whitman appears to have suffered a devastating amorous defeat sometime in the preceding year or two. He had once noted that it would be a "good innovation" to introduce into American speech the antithesis "lover—lovee thing loved," and some very highly charged moments in 1860 capture the pain of seeing a "lovee" become aloof and distant.

The emotional linchpin of the third edition is "Out of the Cradle," which Whitman had published on 24 December 1859 in the *Saturday Press* under the title "A Child's Reminiscence." Civilians prefer to talk about this poem as a nostalgic ululation for a Long Island childhood, as a poem about a child's exposure to death, or even as a reflection of Whitman's sense of artistic isolation. All are plausible approaches, but surely this lavishly operatic *Liebestod* of a poem is, in keeping with its Christmas Eve appearance, above all about the loss of a savior-lover, the loss of an ideal relationship of "two together":

> *Shine! shine! shine!*
> *Pour down your warmth, great sun!*
> *While we bask, we two together.*
>
> *Two together!*
> *Winds blow south, or winds blow north,*
> *Day come white, or night come black,*
> *Home, or rivers and mountains from home,*
> *Singing all time, minding no time,*
> *While we two keep together.*

Though the memoir is ostensibly about a "he-bird" caroling over his lost "she-bird," the real emotional nexus of the poem lies in the narrator's identification and bonding with the feathered "lone singer, wonderful, causing tears": "Yes my brother I know, / The rest might not, but I have treasur'd every note." The real "two together" of the poem, united in their tears, are the frustrated lovers, narrator and he-bird. The she-bird vanishes not only from the nest, but from the emotional heart of the poem.

Read in the context of the *Calamus* poems, as it must be, "Out of the Cradle" becomes a resounding answer "Yes" to every abandoned lover's distraught cry: can there be others who are suffering as I am now? "Out of the Cradle" is, in fact, the answer to precisely this question, as it is finely posed in *Calamus* #9:

> Hours of my torment—I wonder if other men ever have the like,
>   out of the like feelings?
> Is there even one other like me—distracted—his friend, his lover,
>   lost to him?
> Is he too as I am now? Does he still rise in the morning, dejected,
>   thinking who is lost to him? and at night, awaking, think who
>   is lost?
> Does he too harbor his friendship silent and endless?
>   harbor his anguish and passion?
> Does some stray reminder, or the casual mention of a name, bring
>   the fit back upon him, taciturn and deprest?

To any he-bird thus oppressed and doubtful, the author of "Cradle" stood ready to say, "Yes, my brother, I know. . . ." The emotional accuracy of these lines, as all who have felt the sting of rejection will agree, is superb.

This is, however, far too anguished a way to begin our look at Whitman's poetic evocations of his search for the "lover and perfect equal" and the life of two together. It is necessary, first, to imagine the excitement Whitman must have experienced when he began to "publish" his name and hang up his "picture as that of the tenderest lover"— and when he began to open his arms to the gay world of Manhattan and Brooklyn that became ever more visible to him by the 1850s. In an 1856 poem—later aptly titled "Salut au Monde!"—he boasted of his "divine rapport" with the "equals and lovers" he found "in all lands." An exhilarating optimism about going public with this "divine rapport" (not unlike that of the first post-Stonewall decade) is also part of the 1860 edition. *Calamus* #37, for instance, envisions "natural persons old and young" displaying their affection in public: "You twain! and all processions moving along the streets! / I wish to infuse myself among you till I see it common for you to walk hand in hand." And in *Calamus* #19, we have seen, Whitman hoped for an etiquette that would include the public kiss "on the lips with robust love."

Also often thrillingly invoked by Whitman in 1860 and before is the joy, as it were, of two he-birds riding out the oppressive "hoarse surge" of the homophobic storm. This joy is akin to that of the togetherness Lear proposes to Cordelia in *King Lear*'s last act: "Come, let's away to prison: / We two alone will sing like birds i' th' cage." The coincidence of the aviary image is happy, for it serves to emphasize the sense of oppression that makes the ideal of "two alone" so potent for Whitman. Lear's "Come, let's away" fantasy is reflected, for instance, in these lines, where two birds become two fishes and hawks:

> Hark close and still what I now whisper to you,
> I love you, O you entirely possess me,
> O that you and I escape from the rest and go utterly off,
>   free and lawless,
> Two hawks in the air, two fishes swimming in the sea
>   not more lawless than we . . .
> O you and I! what is it to us what the rest do or think?

That these lines are set apart by parentheses in "From Pent-up Aching Rivers" is emblematic of the privacy that surrounds many of the intimacies between men in *Leaves of Grass*.

Other instances of being alone together, laced with pleasurable fantasy, are more mundane but probably also closer to the reality of Whitman's New York days. Some offer familiar urban images of "escape" in the midst of an oblivious crowd. "To You," a short 1860 poem Whitman eventually removed from *Leaves*, for instance, could almost be the transcript of what he must have said to attractive young Manhattan men he desired to inveigle into conversation:

> LET us twain walk aside from the rest;
> Now we are together privately, do you discard ceremony,
> Come! vouchsafe to me what has yet been vouchsafed to none—
>   Tell me the whole story,
> Tell me what you would not tell your brother, wife, husband, or
>   physician.

The glowing image of the couple holding hands under their barroom table in *Calamus* #29 we have already sampled, but its last line bears repeating: "There we two, content, happy in being together, speaking little, perhaps not a word." Intimate pleasure was obviously found, too, far from society. The lover's "happiest days" in *Calamus* #10 have been spent "far away through fields, in woods, on hills, he and another wandering hand in hand, they twain apart from other men." Whitman was surely anticipating these moments of "private" homosexual parentheses *en plein air* when he warned, very earnestly, in "Song of Myself," "I swear I never will translate myself at all, only to him or her who privately stays with me in the open air." (If he was ever in private in the open air with a woman, the fact has gone quite unrecorded.) That privacy is necessary for a genuine "translation" of the poet's self is a notion fundamental to many poems in the first three *Leaves* editions.

One can see this instinct for privacy at work in Whitman's revisions of the *Calamus* poems. Bold as their published versions are, they could have been even more explicit about Whitman's search for a lover. The first poem in "Live Oak, with Moss," a twelve-poem narrative about a traumatic love affair among Whitman's manuscripts, became *Calamus* #14. It is worth drawing attention again to a crucial deletion Whitman made before publication: "Does the tide hurry, seeking something, and never give up? O I the same, *to seek my life-long lover* . . ." From a *Calamus* #2 ms. he deleted the phrases in italics: "O burning and throbbing, O *these hungering desires! . . .* you are not happiness . . . you are often too bitter! *Surely one day I will find the dear friend, the lover, who will . . .*"

Whitman wrote more often of the frustration of this private search, but on a few memorable occasions he put the thrill of victory into words. It is hard to imagine surpassing these last lines from *Calamus* #7, which describe the glowing sense of well-being the company of one's true lover can confer:

When he whom I love travels with me or sits a long while
    holding me by the hand,
When the subtle air, the impalpable, the sense that words and
    reason hold not, surround us and pervade us,
Then I am charged with untold and untellable wisdom, I am silent,
    I require nothing further,
I cannot answer the question of appearances or that of identity
    beyond the grave,
But I walk or sit indifferent, I am satisfied,
He ahold of my hand has completely satisfied me.

In the next *Calamus* poem in the 1860 edition, a sequel to this rapture, the poet happily performs the lavish gesture of renouncing all the world for love: "One who loves me is jealous of me, and withdraws me from all but love, / With the rest I dispense." The poem ends, "I will go with him I love, / It is to be enough for us that we are together—We never separate again." (Life on this peak of exhilaration is hard to sustain. Perhaps Whitman looked at *Calamus* #8 in the late 1860s with pain, rue, or determination to forget the lover the poem speaks of . . . and so chose not to include it in all subsequent editions of *Leaves*.)

Far more boisterous and operatic—indeed quasi-orgasmic, all those exclamatory, rhythmic O's—is the levitating close to the poem that Whitman gave pride of place in the 1860 edition, "Starting from Paumanok." Here is the "two together" Whitman in his mode of "high glee," and again hand-holding is the focal act:

O my comrade!
O you and me at last—and us two only;
O power, liberty, eternity at last!
O to be relieved of distinctions! to make as much of vices as
    virtues!
O to level occupations and the sexes! O to bring all to common
    ground! O adhesiveness!
O the pensive aching to be together . . .
O hand in hand—O wholesome pleasure—O one more desirer
    and lover,
O haste, firm holding—haste, haste on, with me.

O quick! (in other words) I am about to cum. It may be outrageous to Whitman's civilian devotees—but *not* to his adhesive spirit, I think—to suggest that the last line be read with the picture of two erect phalluses on the verge of simultaneous ejaculation firmly in mind. O wholesome pleasure! The next words the reader of the 1860 edition saw, on the facing page, were: "WALT WHITMAN. / I CELEBRATE myself . . ." The famed opening line is not an image of "one" alone but of "two together." Walt Whitman is with his comrade/reader as he speaks.

The passages just quoted vividly reiterate the desire for "*one* heart to love" that Whitman had expressed twenty years earlier in his medio-cre ballad. They are, one might venture, his climactic expressions of this theme. Afterward, the theme gradually detumesces. Whitman drops the code word "adhesive" from his vocabulary forever, and in the very next *Leaves* edition (1867) he transforms his flesh-and-blood "com-rade" of old from a sex partner into something more ethereal. When he adds the italicized line to "Song of Myself," amorous overtones give way to the orotund piety of a postsexual Whitman: "My rendezvous is ap-pointed, it is certain, / The Lord will be there and wait till I come on perfect terms, / *The great Camerado, the lover true for whom I pine will be there.*"

But while more mundane physical pleasures were still available to Whitman—before the capitalization and ascension of his camerado—did he himself experience the rapture of two together described in "Starting from Paumanok" and *Calamus #7*? Again, it is necessary to say that no known and explicit facts tell us that he did, or with whom. And yet, the wealth of circumstantial evidence seems to carry us far beyond a reason-able doubt that he did, that he may even have enjoyed a One Great Love, the haunting, wistfully nostalgic memory of which many gay men profess to carry with them the rest of their lives.

Two classic later examples of this are Thomas Mann and Gore Vidal. Mann, in his mid-twenties—before a fifty-year marriage and the father-ing of six children commenced—fell deeply in love with a man his age named Paul Ehrenberg. This drove him to compose such Whitmanesque passages as these in his notebooks:

> These are days of feeling alive!
> You have made my life rich. It is flowering—
> O listen, music!—it floats into my ear
> With a joyful shudder.
> I thank you, my savior! my joy! my star! . . .
>
> Here is my heart, and here is my hand
> I love you! My God . . . I love you!
> Is it this beautiful, this sweet, this charming to be a human?

In other words: "O my comrade! / O you and me at last—and us two only . . . O hand in hand." Thirty years afterward Mann confided in his diary that the "youthful intensity of feeling, the heaven-storming exultation and deep shock" of his affair with Ehrenberg was the "central affair of my heart," a phrase, we shall see, very similar to one Whitman used about one of his beloved. Was Mann's affair consummated? In 1947, just after completing *Dr. Faustus*, which contained a prominent homosexual episode memorializing his affair of more than forty years before, Mann wrote to a friend that Ehrenberg "was a charming fellow and one of my greatest love affairs [*Liebschäften*]—I can say it no other way." His recent biographer Anthony Heilbut is inclined to take Mann at his word (*Liebschaft* normally carrying a sexual connotation in German): "If Mann could say it 'no other way,' we should, paraphrasing Lawrence, trust both the tale and the teller."*

Gore Vidal, whose depiction of gay teenage sex in *The City and the Pillar* Mann found "glorious," leaves no doubt whatever about consummated sex. In his recent memoir, *Palimpsest*, he calculated that by the age of twenty-five he had managed more than a thousand sexual experiences, and yet all his life he has considered his Great Love to be a prep-school classmate who died on Iwo Jima. Decades later Vidal learned that the boy had written from Guam, shortly before a Japanese grenade killed him, to request from his mother a copy of *Leaves of Grass*. "This set off a tremor," Vidal writes. "He and I certainly lived out the *Calamus* idyll."*

The most obvious circumstantial evidence for Whitman's own full-fledged homosexual affairs is the large number of poems expressing the soul-shattering loss of a comrade's love he produced in the late 1850s. These poems are among the most moving he ever wrote and are often reminiscent of Shakespeare's most emotionally devastating sonnet, #120 ("That you were once unkind befriends me now"), with its affectingly plain-spoken grief: "O that our night of woe might have rememb'red / My deepest sense, how hard true sorrow hits." Whitman's descriptions of love's catastrophe also remind one often of C. P. Cavafy (1863–1933), the Greek homosexual who produced many fine poems on the subject of nostalgia for lost love. One such poem, a brief one titled "Voices," is particularly pertinent to Whitman, the great vocalist and lover of voices:

> Voices, loved and idealized,
> of those who have died, or of those
> lost for us like the dead.
>
> Sometimes they speak to us in dreams;
> sometimes deep in thought the mind hears them.
> And with their sound for a moment return

>   sounds from our life's first poetry—
>   like music at night, distant, fading away.*

When Whitman, in 1888, came to reminisce about his own life's first poetry and love, he chose to begin by setting precisely the mood of Cavafy's lines. "Perhaps the best of songs heard, or of any and all true love, or life's fairest episodes . . . is the résumé of them, or any of them, long afterwards, looking at the actualities away back past, with all their practical excitations gone. How the soul loves to float amid such reminiscences!" Whitman was here referring specifically to the poems he had written thirty years before, and these poems, he suggests, were born of emotional "actualities" and "practical excitations." His hint that these poems derive from autobiographical actualities deserves to be taken seriously.

Perhaps there is a hint of the Great Love, too, in an unusual parenthetical remark Whitman inserted in his memoir of a fine day in May 1876. Did one of Cavafy's "loved and idealized" voices waft through Whitman's mind as he luxuriated? "The last two days have been faultless in sun, breeze, temperature and everything; never two more perfect days, and I have enjoy'd them wonderfully. My health is somewhat better, and my spirit at peace. (Yet the anniversary of the saddest loss and sorrow of my life is close at hand.)" Whitman may have been alluding to the death of his mother on 23 May three years earlier, but one is tempted to think this rare departure from reticence might refer to the loss that occasioned the writing, in the fall of 1859, of "Out of the Cradle Endlessly Rocking." After all, it too recalls events that took place when the "Fifth-month grass" was growing, that is, in May, and the grass he refers to could be the marsh grass Calamus aromaticus, with its phallic associations.

It is certainly hard to read Whitman's poems about love's labors lost and then disagree with the many who have presumed that, in 1858 or 1859, he personally suffered such anguish. These poems bespeak much extraordinarily painful "excitation." In Calamus #20, which Whitman had originally intended as the second poem of an "adhesive" cluster, he describes the great moss-hung live-oak in Louisiana standing "alone there, without its friends, its lover near." The poet explains that the tree has become a "curious token" of what, having tasted true love, he can no longer be. The oak

>   . . . makes me think of manly love;
> For all that, and though the live-oak glistens there
>   in Louisiana, solitary, in a wide flat space,
> Uttering joyous leaves and its life, without a friend, a lover, near,
> I know very well I could not.*

It was one thing to fantasize the joy of finding "*one* heart to love" and feel the frustration of not finding that heart. It was quite another to experience the thrill, then have the pleasure torn from one's grasp: to learn the lesson of the live-oak, only to find oneself a solitary singer once again. About this misery the 1860 edition has much to say, as Whitman promises in its first poem. His "song of companionship" and of love, he says, will comprise both "sorrow and joy." The joys we have already tasted; Whitman's sense of how hard true sorrow hits is even more elaborately projected. It is thus not surprising that among the "sorrows of the world" catalogued by the poet in "I Sit and Look Out" (a new poem in 1860) is the "ranklings of jealousy and unrequited love, attempted to be hid."

The scene of the rupture in question is best set not in a poem published in 1860 but in the most famous and revealing of Whitman's manuscripts that produced the third edition. In *Enfans d'Adam* #9 (later "Once I Pass'd through a Populous City"), the poet recalls one single person, "a woman I casually met there who detain'd me for love of me." But a prior manuscript version analyzed by Fredson Bowers tells a different story:

> But now of all that city I remember only the man who wandered
>   with me, there, for love of me,
> Day by day, and night by night, we were together,
> All else has long been forgotten by me—I remember, I say, only
>   one rude and ignorant man who, when I departed, long and
>   long held me by the hand, with silent lip, sad and tremulous.—

Here the manuscript breaks off. But we get an idea of how Whitman might have continued (and also of why he gave up on such an explicitly homosexual revelation) in the remainder of the published version of *Enfans d'Adam* #9. For we read of "that woman who passionately clung to me" and of the poet dreaming, like Cavafy, of still having this idealized lover "close beside me with silent lips sad and tremulous."*

This revelation, if only to his notebook, of a long-term, passionate Manhattan affair with a "rude and ignorant" (as opposed to polished and parlor-bound) man reflects plausibly on several passages in the *Calamus* cluster expressive of doubt about the lover or misery at his withdrawal. The emotional responses in *Calamus* to these commonplace occurrences in the affairs of men still ring true. There is the agony of doubt about the requital of love in *Calamus* #10. The lover, separated from his beloved, lies "sleepless and dissatisfied at night," full of "the sick, sick dread lest the one he lov'd might secretly be indifferent to him."* Then there is the pain of seeing one's "lovee" happy to be elsewhere. The lover of *Calamus* #9 spends many "discouraged, distracted" hours because "the one I cannot content myself without, soon I saw him content himself without me." Time passes, yet thoughts of the beloved do not subside: "O weeks and months are passing, but I believe I am never to forget!"

Calamus #9, so obsessed with a "lost" lover, is succeeded in *Calamus* #17 by a superb dream-fantasy of the death and burial of the beloved . . . and the death of the lover's entire world.

> . . . I dreamed I wandered, searching among burial-places to find
>   him,
> And I found that every place was a burial-place,
> The houses full of life were equally full of death, (This house is now,)
> The streets, the shipping, the places of amusement, the Chicago,
>   Boston, Philadelphia, the Mannahatta, were as full of the dead
>   as of the living . . .

But especially Mannahatta, in those painful months after the breakup. *Calamus* #36, on the other hand, superbly expresses another commonplace fear in the mind of any lover conscious that an affair may be of unequal intensity: "For an athlete is enamour'd of me, and I of him, / But toward him there is something fierce and terrible in me eligible to burst forth." In other words, will one's own great passion frighten or intimidate the beloved?

Finally, toward the end of *Calamus*, comes a short poem in which, as all abandoned lovers must do, the poet tries to put his trauma into perspective and make some good use of it. *Calamus* #39, in its 1860 version, observed:

> SOMETIMES with one I love, I fill myself with rage,
>   for fear I effuse unreturned love;
> But now I think there is no unreturned love—
>   the pay is certain, one way or another,
> Doubtless I could not have perceived the universe, or written one of
>   my poems, if I had not freely given myself to comrades, to love.

Interestingly, this poem produced one of the very few occasions when Whitman made a poem *more* specific and personal upon revision. For the next edition in 1867, at a half dozen years' distance from the breakup, Whitman could speak more candidly of his pain. He dropped the long last line of the poem and added, in confidential parentheses, these two

lines: "(I loved a certain person ardently and my love was not return'd, /
Yet out of that I have written these songs.)"

Even so, as with all Great Loves lost, the melancholy mood can suddenly overwhelm one now and then, sometimes long after the immediate
crisis has passed. Several Whitman poems seem to reflect this Cavafy-
esque blend of forlornness, quenchless desire, and nostalgia, but one that
is very seldom quoted is particularly resonant, especially given the "adhesive" innuendo that so often accompanies the poet's references to the
West and to California. The poem is "Facing West from California's
Shores" and was new in the 1860 edition. It begins, "Facing west from
California's shores, / Inquiring, tireless, seeking what is yet unfound, / I, a
child, very old . . . look afar." In a half dozen lines the poet circles the
globe and returns "home again, very pleas'd and joyous." But then, in a
final two-line parenthesis like that of *Calamus* #39, the poet asks sadly,
"(But where is what I started for so long ago? / And why is it yet
unfound?)" Could Whitman, a child in spirit but at forty now feeling
"very old," have begun to doubt that he would ever find what he had
searched for so long—*one* heart to love?

Several poems in *Leaves of Grass*, then, urge us to take seriously
Whitman's assertion, which he could "not too often reiterate," that they
are genuinely revealing "outcroppings" of his "emotional and other personal nature." They seem to narrate the story of one momentous failure,
while numerous other lines and phrases in the early editions allude to the
countless minor rejections, mocks, insults, and derisive refusals that will
always attend the search for a lover in a metropolis. These poems also
help to establish, in Whitman's case, an inner conflict or psychomachia
that anyone who has lost a Great Love is bound to experience, namely,
the desire on the one hand to continue the great search and discover
another perfect, lifelong lover and, on the other, the desire to avoid the
pain of further defeat, retire from the arena, and ensconce oneself in self-
sufficing if solitary calm. Perhaps there is an element of this latter resolve
in his exclamation, in 1860, "O to be absolved from previous follies and
degradations . . . !" or in his wistful retreat from the frantic urban sexual
arena published five years earlier: "I think I could turn and live awhile
with the animals. . . . they are so placid and self-contained." When
Whitman was feeling blue, even the tedious life of a Long Island farm
began to appeal to him.

As early as the late 1850s, such lines suggest, Whitman began to feel
himself caught on the horns of this dilemma familiar to all—gay and
straight, male and female—who remain amorously and sexually eager
well into their middle age: to sally forth with one's banner and pennant

a-flapping and risk ego-battering defeat, or to become, in Whitman's case, a good gray poetic lion, couchant and regardant. By the late 1860s, as he arrived at his fiftieth birthday, this dilemma became a matter of considerable anxiety to Whitman. We know this for certain because one of his notebooks has survived, in a corner of which he collected his thoughts on the wisdom of retiring from the search for a lifelong lover. The editor of the notebooks for *The Collected Writings of Walt Whitman* calls these few pages, which we have already visited briefly in the preceding chapter, the "most important autobiographical document we have from WW." It would be hard to disagree.

Before looking into these notebook pages, it is necessary to pause and consider the word "adhesive," which occurs at a crucial point in them. In an entirely different notebook titled "The Primer of Words," which deals with vocabulary and usage, Whitman had occasion to observe that "the young men of these states" have "a wonderful tenacity of friendship, and passionate fondness for their friends, and always a manly readiness to make friends." He then adds, however, that the American vocabulary for this happy penchant was sorely undernourished. These young men "have remarkably few words, names for the friendly sentiments.—They seem to be words that do not thrive here among the muscular classes, where the real quality of friendship is always freely to be found. . . . the young men of these states rarely use, and have an aversion for [them];—they never give words to their most ardent friendships." "Adhesive," along with "comrade," were Whitman's famous contributions to combating this lexical deficiency.

He took the word "adhesive" from the then much bruited pseudo-science of phrenology, with which he became familiar very early. He first published on the subject in 1846 and frequented the shop of one of America's principal phrenologists, Orson Fowler, and also had his large, twenty-three-inch head "read" in 1849 by Fowler's brother, Lorenzo.* Fowler and his partner Samuel Wells, in fact, were the distributors of the first edition of *Leaves of Grass*. Adhesiveness, among phrenologists, referred in essence to any propensity for strong emotional friendship with another person of the same sex. Whitman's quite calculated purpose, however, was, as Michael Lynch has shown, to make adhesiveness "an exclusive reference to same-sex love. . . . Whitman's male-male Adhesive love was alone able to 'rival' male-female Amative love."* One can tell from Fowler's definition of Adhesiveness how perfectly it suited Whitman's agenda: "Friendship; sociability; fondness for society; susceptibility of forming attachments; inclination to love, and desire to be loved . . ." Adhesiveness was, in short, Whitman's word for homosexuality several decades before the neologism "homosexual" appeared.

Adhesiveness—Lorenzo gave Whitman 6 out of possible 7 in this category—could, like all faculties, be abused. The "abuses" of the Adhesive nature Fowler listed are, as we shall see, relevant to Whitman's notebook pages: "too great fondness for company, indiscriminately; grieving excessively at the loss of friends, etc." Fowler wrote often in his *American Phrenological Journal and Miscellany* about Adhesiveness, and in 1847 touched on how the adhesive nature can produce "improper associations." Fowler's male-male example unwittingly anticipates the angst of the *Calamus* poems: "The author once saw a young man who was rendered perfectly distracted by a sudden breach of friendship, or a supposed friend turning traitor. A break between him and his spouse could not have affected him more severely. In such cases the faculty requires restraint." Fowler's draconian advice to those experiencing such "excitations" is still taken by some who have parted from their once-perfect lovers: "Break up all association, all connection, all interchange of ideals and feelings with them. Exchange no letters, reciprocate no looks—no thoughts."

We turn now to the notebook pages and discover Whitman feeling as he once felt when writing his *Calamus* poems: deeply fearful that he was effusing unreturned love and angry with himself at how foolish and vulnerable his pursuit has made him. He is, in effect, lecturing to himself as the homophobic Fowler might have and trying to expel disturbing amorous "looks" and "thoughts." Whitman appears to have censored part of a notebook page (he had been too specific, perhaps), but Emory Holloway noted evidence of double underlining and an emphatic finger-pointing little fist on the remaining stub. Then the self-laceration begins in midsentence:

> . . . *Cheating, childish abandonment* of myself, fancying what does not really exist in another, but is all the time in myself alone— utterly deluded & cheated by *myself*, & my own weakness— REMEMBER WHERE I AM MOST WEAK, & most lacking. Yet always preserve a kind spirit & demeanor to 16. BUT PURSUE HER NO MORE.

Whitman first wrote "pursue him," then erased "im" and wrote in "er," obviously with the same concealing intent that led him to excise part of the page and to cipher with "16," Peter Doyle's first initial. Whitman, a decade earlier, had admitted in *Calamus* #19 that he filled himself with "rage" over unrequited love; now he was attempting to lecture himself into "A Cool, gentle, (LESS DEMONSTRATIVE) MORE UNIFORM DEMEANOR."

On a separate little square of paper, dated June 17th and garnished with underlining, marginal emphases, and little fists in red ink, he wrote in obvious agitation: "*It is* IMPERATIVE, that I obviate & remove myself (& my orbit) *at all hazards, from this incessant* enormous & abnormal PERTURBA-TION." Whitman appears to have reread and approved this resolution, writing next to it in red pencil, "Good! July 15." On a separate page just six inches by seven, dated the same day, Whitman records that he is writing in his Washington office and "not feeling very well—oprest with the heat." But it was clearly the feverish temperature of his love for Doyle that was really oppressing him. Feeling hurt, disgusted, foolish, and powerless, he recorded in his notebook the kind of solemn vow of renunciation that many an aging erstwhile lover of a much younger man has made:

> To GIVE UP ABSOLUTELY & *for good, from the present hour, this* FEVERISH, FLUCTUATING, *useless* UNDIGNIFIED PURSUIT of 16.4—*too long, (much too long)* persevered in,—so humiliating—*It must come at last &* had better come now—(*It cannot possibly be a success*) LET THERE FROM THIS HOUR BE NO FALTERING. . . . (NOT ONCE, UNDER *any circumstances*)—*avoid seeing her, or meeting her* [original "him" erased in both cases], *or any talk or explanations—or* ANY MEETING WHATEVER, FROM THIS HOUR FORTH, FOR LIFE   July 15 '70

The *Collected Writings* editor notes that the page is crammed with emphases in purple ink, red ink, and red pencil: "Only a color reproduction could do justice to the feeling conveyed by the ms. page."

On the final two notebook pages—the progression is very logical—Whitman, all passion spent after this near frenzy of anxiety and hopelessness, attempts to sketch the new leaf that his resolution implies. If one wished to epitomize the difference between the great, exciting, and profoundly perturbed poet of the first three editions of *Leaves of Grass* and the postwar, postsexual Whitman of the final seven editions, one could do no better than compare the seething emotion of mid-July 1870 with the grandiose admonitions on the last two pages:

> Outline sketch of a superb calm character
> his emotions &c are complete in himself, irrespective of whether
>   his love, friendship, &c are returned, or not
> He grows, blooms, like some perfect tree [shade of the live-oak!]
>   or flower, in Nature, whether viewed by admiring eyes, or in
>   some wild or wood, entirely unknown.

On the very last page, Whitman strikes the essential note of his last two decades with these melancholy jottings:

Depress the adhesive nature
It is in excess—making life a torment
Ah this diseased, feverish disproportionate adhesiveness
Remember Fred Vaughan
The case of Jenny Bullard
Sane Nature fit & full Rapport therewith
Merlin strong & wise & beautiful at 100 years old.*

In other words, that way madness lies, this search for the perfect comrade.

Though he failed by a long stretch to become a centenarian, Whitman did succeed in becoming something like a superbly calm character . . . and poet. He also succeeded in depressing his adhesive nature, at least, as we have seen, in his later poems and in his habits of revision. That he never succeeded in extinguishing his adhesive nature, however, will become clear as we consider some of the young men who came into his life and revived for him the ideal of comradery he had so exuberantly invented in the 1850s.

TOO HEARTFELT TO ALTER: FRED

Why did Whitman recall the "case of Jenny Bullard" in this context? Little is known of Sarah Jane Wollstonecraft Bullard (1828–1904), but this little may be enough: she never married, lived with two other women most of her life, and was described by Whitman's friend O'Connor as "strong, careless, laughing, large, regardless of dress or personal appearance." And she was also a devotee of *Leaves of Grass*. Perhaps Whitman wished to model himself after this freethinking woman in such apparently good rapport with her "Sane Nature."

Far more intriguing is "Remember Fred Vaughan." When Emory Holloway first examined the notebook pages and transcribed them for publication in 1921, he confessed in a footnote, "I have been unable to find any reference to Fred Vaughan which would indicate who he was or why he was to be remembered in this connection." Since then several letters from Vaughan to Whitman have come to light from the period 1860–62, as well as two highly revealing letters from 1874.* These give the distinct impression of a very close friendship, and several details in the letters suggest something more.

A younger man from Brooklyn and apparently a driver of some kind, Vaughan may even have been the lost lover celebrated in the *Calamus* sequence. For in a letter of 16 November 1874, Vaughan indicates that he had gotten to know Whitman's mother ("I used to tell your Mother you was lazy and she denied it") and had also domiciled with Whitman in Classon Avenue. He writes of now living "one door above Classon ave" on Atlantic Avenue and of visiting "our old home several times this summer." He also jokingly recalls first seeing the word "impecuniosity" in "a letter from R. W. Emerson to you while we were living in Classon Ave." (Whitman lived on this Brooklyn street for three years from 1 May 1856, precisely the period of the gestation of the *Calamus* poems.) But what is most telling in this charming, nostalgia-laden letter is the sense one gets of their former intimacy: "O Walt, what recollections will crowd upon us . . . To me the home so long long past . . . New York, the Stage box—Broadway.—Walt . . ." Perhaps the "rude and ignorant man" of the "Populous City" manuscript speaks in this letter's touching postscript: "Walt—please do not criticize my grammar, nor phraseology—it was written too heartfelt to alter. Fred."

The batch of earlier letters, mostly written to Whitman in Boston, certainly convey a feeling of *Calamus*-style intimacy. The picture of lovers holding hands under a barroom table in *Calamus* #29 is recalled to mind, for instance, in a letter of 19 March 1860 in which Fred says he visited Pfaff's two evenings in a row in the hope of seeing Walt, who had already departed to supervise printing of the third edition of *Leaves*. Fred is irresistibly fetching in a letter dated 27 March, in which he speaks of Bostonians as "a little too straight-laced for such free-thinkers as you and I are." He then responds to the news of Emerson's courteous meeting with Whitman, the one on Boston Common in which Emerson tried, unsuccessfully, to convince Whitman to tone down the sexual matter in *Leaves*: "You tell me Mr. Emmerson (one m to many I guess?) came to see you and was very kind." Fred reports that in the meantime he has heard Emerson lecture in New York on manners, not very successfully: "though very much pleased with the *matter*, I did not at all like his delivery. It appeared to me to be strained, and there was a certain hesitation in his speech and occasional repetition of words that did not affect the hearer very well." Still, when Fred recalled Emerson's kindness to Walt, he forgave his *"bad delivery"* and his "hea[r]t warmed towards him very much. I think he has *that* in him which makes men capable of strong friendships." Fred also reports that Emerson spoke on this occasion about great friendship, and Fred applied these sentiments to his relationship with Walt:

[He] said that a man whose heart was filled with warm, ever enduring *not to be shaken by anything* Friendship was one to be set on one side apart from other men, and almost to be worshipped as a saint.—There Walt, how do you like that? What do you think of them setting you & myself, and one or two others we know up in some public place, with an immense placard on our breast, reading SINCERE FREINDS!!!

Several of the more aggressively "out" and political of the *Calamus* poems—#19, #23, #24, #25, #26, #31, #35, #37—are shadowed in this exuberant passage.

There are charming touches in the other early letters, too, that suggest a very special intimacy. Knowing Whitman's penchant for workers on public transport, Vaughan advises: "If you want to form the acquaintance of any Boston Stage men, get on one of those stages running to Charlestown Bridge, or Chelsea Ferry, & enquire for Charley Hollis or Ed Morgan, mention my name, and introduce yourself as my friend." A few weeks later he chides, "How is this, Walt? I have written to you twice since I heard from you. Why don't you answer. . . . Come, Walt, remember I take a deep interest in all that concerns you and must naturally be anxious to hear from you." He also tells of an article about Whitman and their favorite meeting place in the *Morning Courier*: "It gives a good description of the Bohemian Club at Pfaffs in which you are set down as the grand master of ceremonies." In another letter he reports, "In accordance with not only your wishes, but my own I went to Brooklyn yesterday and saw your Mother. . . . She did not remember me at first but as soon as she did she was very much pleased." The letter ends, "If you come on here this [week] be sure and make it your business to call and see me. Do not neglect it please Walt, for I want to see you very much." The closing is "Ever yours, In a Hurry! Fred."

The next letter, of 7 May, begins, "What the devil is the matter? Nothing serious I hope.—It seems mighty queer that I cannot succeed in having one word from you.—I swear I would have thought you would be the last man in this world to neglect me.—But I am afraid.—" In the last extant letter from this period, written on the eve of Whitman's putting the third edition of *Leaves* to bed and returning from Boston, Vaughan almost pines, "Walt, I hope you will be home soon. I want to see you very much indeed. I have never thought more frequently about you than during the time you have been in Boston."

With Whitman's return to New York, correspondence of course ceased. The next letter that survives is dated 2 May 1862, exactly two years later. With what feelings must Whitman have read it?

Walt,

    I am to be marri'd tomorrow, Saturday at 3 o'cl at
      213 W. 43rd St.—near 8th Ave.
    I shall have no show! I have invited no company.—
    I want you to be there.—
    Do not fail please, as I am very axious you should come.—
    Truly yours, Fred

It is doubtful Whitman was present, for Fred much later refers to his wife as "one you could dearly love," as if they had never met. As must often have happened among the poet's young male circle, marriage became a bar to being "Walt Whitman sociable." The relationship appears to have waned for several years.

It did have, however, a striking coda. The two letters from 1874, a dozen years later, suggest that Fred's marriage was a classic case of a gay man marrying in order to achieve social respectability and profoundly suffering the consequences. On 11 August 1874 he wrote a letter that was intended to revive his connection with Walt. It begins pathetically: "I enclose you one of very many letters I write to you. I think I have written to you at least once a week for the past four years—sometimes I write long letters, sometimes short ones . . . and I often keep them months before I destroy them." He ends, "If you can Dear Walt write to me and acknowledge receipt of this.—If you cannot, I shall still keep writing in my own way. As Ever & always, Yours, Fred."

The undated letter Fred chose to enclose is indeed pure Walt. It records various scenes Fred has taken in among their old haunts: a bare-footed sailor in a blue shirt loosening a mainsail on a coal bark in the East River; "the ever plying ferryboats, the tugs, the Harlem Boats"; the "murmur of the sailors at dinner"; and the "laugh and wrangle of the boys in swimming." Then follows a most extraordinary confessional paragraph that suggests that Walt's "Remember Fred Vaughan" of 1870 was, a year or two later, reciprocated by the younger man:

With WmsBgh & Brooklyn—with the ferries and the vessels with the Lumber piles and the docks. From among all out of all. Connected with all and yet distinct from all arrises thee Dear Walt. Walt—my life has turned out a poor miserable failure. I am not a drunkard nor a teetotaler—I am neither honest or dishonest. I have my family in Brooklyn and am supporting them.—I never stole, robbed, cheated, nor defrauded any person out of anything, and yet

I feels that I have not been honest with myself—my family nor my friends.

As he watches a coal bark being loaded, Fred ends his travelogue-letter with one of the most haunting images of despair ever penned by a "rude and ignorant man." (Note that he adds in his address a reference to the street in which they had once lived.) "The old old Poem Walt. The cart backs up, the bucket comes up full and goes down empty—The men argue and swear. The wind blows the coal dust over man & beast and now it reaches me.—Fred Vaughan Atlantic Ave. 2nd door above Classon Ave. Brooklyn."

The 16 November letter of three months later, from which I have already quoted, includes an even more candid and pathetic confession in which Fred's entire life passes before him, the life of a married man and father whose attempts to "depress" his adhesive nature were not entirely successful. Among his "recollections" are those of

> ... the sea—the return—New York, the Stage box—Broadway.—
> Walt—the Press—the Railroad. Marriage. Express [office]—Babies—
> trouble. Rum, more trouble—more Rum—estrangement from you.
> More Rum.—Good intentions, sobriety. Misunderstanding and
> more Rum. Up and down, down and up. The innate manly nature
> of myself at times getting the best of it and at other times entirely
> submerged ... From causes too numerous and complex to explain
> except verbally, I found myself in June last in Brooklyn possesed of a
> wife and four boys—ages 12–9–4 years—and one of 8 months—no
> money, no credit—no friends of a/c [account?] and no furniture ...

From this abyss Fred reports pulling himself up somewhat. He now writes, he says, with his own pen and paper, in a hired room "lighted by my own oil" and with a "faithful-loving-honest" wife sleeping on a bed near him. And yet he also writes, movingly, "There is never a day passes but what I think of you. So much have you left to be remembered by." He recounts several typical moments with Walt ("a Fulton ferry boat, a bale of cotton on the dock ...") and summarizes: "All—all to me speak of thee Dear Walt.—Seeing them my friend the part thou occupiest in my spiritual nature—I feel assured you will forgive my remissness of me in writing— My love my Walt—is with you always."

If Fred and Walt corresponded thereafter, no letters survive. But the daybooks indicate that Fred visited Walt twice in 1876 and that they met on Chestnut Street in Philadelphia in 1878. Walt learned while on a visit to New York in 1879 that Fred was running an elevator in the New York Life Insurance Building; another entry from 1885 notes Fred's address as Harrisburg, Pennsylvania. The last known meeting—which must have been filled with emotion—took place in Camden on 10 May 1890, more than thirty years after they first saw each other, possibly at Pfaff's.

TERRIBLE, BEAUTIFUL DAYS: SOME SOGER BOYS

The *Calamus* poems suggest that the love trauma of 1859 or so left Whitman feeling alone and haunted, as Fred Vaughan was, by sounds and sights of the populous city reminiscent of happier days. Abandoned lovers often find it therapeutic to get away from the scene of defeat and amorous bereavement. If Vaughan was indeed the inspiration for *Calamus*, there may have been, in addition to a fraternal concern for his wounded brother George, an element of desire to start emotionally afresh in Whitman's leaving New York for Washington just a few months after Vaughan's marriage.

Though chastened, in any event, by whoever had ceased to effuse requited love, Whitman certainly did not relinquish his thirsting desire for a perfect comrade when he arrived amid the gory "many-threaded drama" of the "hospital part" of the Civil War. He famously wrote afterward in his memoirs that "the real war will never get in the books," but it is also true that Whitman's own amorous campaign for a perfect comrade during this time never got into *his* later poetry and prose—or into very many of the scores of books written about him in the last century.* But there are certainly hints enough in his hospital notebooks and his later correspondence that he made great efforts to extend the arc of comradery in the District of Columbia.

He certainly lost none of the eye for manly beauty displayed in his Manhattan notebooks. An Ohioan named Manvil Wintersteen, for instance, struck him as a "noble-sized young fellow." He cut some peaches for him and powdered them with sugar; "he relishes them much—he has suffered, but lies easy now—What a splendid neck, frame, & clean complexion." Another badly injured Ohio boy, one Oscar Cunningham, took Whitman's breath away: "he ought to have been taken by a sculptor to model for an emblematical figure of the west, he was such a handsome young giant, over 6 feet high, a great head of brown yellowy shining hair thick & longish & a manly noble manner & talk."

And some of Whitman's letters from this period suggest that he developed specially intimate circles of young male friends in which *Calamus*-style affection was discussable. In a letter of 21 April 1863 to a Tom Sawyer, he tells of being with a mutual friend, Lewis Brown: "Lew is so good, so affectionate—when I came away, he reached up his face, I put my arm around him, and we gave each other a long kiss, half a minute long." Whitman confesses to leading a "vagabond life," going "around some, nights, when the spirit moves me, sometimes to the gay places." And then he suggests that this "spirit" is the old search for a lifelong lover: "Tom, I wish you was here. Somehow I don't find the comrade that suits me to a dot—I won't have any other, not for good." Whitman then divulges to "my dear, darling comrade" his fondest wish: "if you should come safe out of this war, we should come together again in some place, where we could make our living, and be true comrades and never be separated while life lasts—and take Lew Brown too, and never separate from him." The letter ends: "if . . . we do not meet again, here on earth, it seems to me, (the way I feel now,) that my soul could never be entirely happy, even in the world to come, without you, dear comrade. (What I have written is pretty strong talk, I suppose, but I mean exactly what I say.)"*

Subsequent letters to Sawyer show Whitman trying, as he did in composing the *Calamus* poems just four years earlier, to accommodate himself to unrequited love: less than a week later, he closed, "I will bid you *so long,* & hope God will put it in your heart to bear me a little at least of the feeling I have for you. If it is only a quarter as much I shall be satisfied." A month later: "My dearest comrade, I cannot, though I attempt it, put in a letter the feelings of my heart—I suppose my letters sound strange & unusual to you as it is, but as I am only expressing the truth in them, I do not trouble myself on that account. As I intimated before, I do not expect you to return for me the same degree of love I have for you." Several further ardent letters to Sawyer and Brown were sent in the fall of 1863, but another infatuation also arose at this time. In a letter to Brown of 8–9 November, Whitman asks from Brooklyn about news of the gorgeous Cunningham and also wonders "whether Elijah Fox in ward G has gone home."

By coincidence, the next day Elijah Douglass Fox wrote a letter to Whitman at his Washington address that must have fluttered the poet's heart. Fox mentions that, his parents being dead, "Walt you will be a second Father to me. . . . I have never before met with a man that I could love as I do you[—]still there is nothing strange about it for 'to know you is to love you' and how any person could know you and not love you is a wonder to me." He also tells Whitman "what a vacancy there would be in my affections were I to be deprived of your love as well as your company" and addresses him as "Dear Comrade" and "Dear Comarade."

All of which may have been innocent affection and gratitude. But Whitman could not resist confiding to this possibly perfect comrade, in a letter the next week, that even amid the "gayest supper party" of young fellows in New York, he would think of Fox and wish to "leave all the fun & noise & the crowd & be with you." Then he adds, earnestly, "Douglass, I will tell you the truth, you are so much closer to me than any of them that there is no comparison—there has never passed so much between them & me as we have—besides there is something that takes down all artificial accomplishments, & that is a manly & loving soul." This would not be the last time he made such a flattering "You are the One" confession.

Poor Whitman! A letter from Fox, posted a few weeks later from Wyoming, Illinois, informed him, "I expect to go into business here with Brother but do not know certain." Fox then refers to what appears to have been the main story of Whitman's Washington search for true love: "Since coming here I have often thought of what you told me when I said to you I am certain I will come back to Washington. You said to me then that a gret many of the boys had said the same but none had returned. I am sorry it is so but after I had thought it over I concluded it would be better for me to go into some business that would be a periminent thing."

That Whitman's amorous quest in Washington for a "periminent" relationship of his own continued seamlessly from his Mannahatta socializing before the war is suggested in several letters he wrote then, either to soger boys or to his pals back home. His *Calamus* past, indeed, was but prologue to the search for emotional engagement amid the hospital cots and, when off duty, among the conductors and roughs of the capital's streets. Twenty-five years later, in 1888, he began divesting himself of drafts of these letters. One of them was the long letter he had written from New York to all his "dear comrades in the hospital" (the one describing his visit to the opera). Giving this letter up for good, Whitman explained to Traubel: "My relations with the boys there in Washington had fatherly, motherly, brotherly intimations—touched life on many sides: sympathetically, spiritually, dynamically: took me away from surfaces to roots."

Six weeks later, Whitman would define sex for Traubel as the "root of roots: the life below the life!" and "dynamically" is perhaps a finely chosen euphemism for the homoerotic life that pulsed beneath his kindly ministrations. Whitman certainly hinted at deeper emotions when he added, as he handed the hospital letter over, "I don't seem to be able to review that experience, that period, without extreme emotional stirrings—almost depressions. I'm glad you have the letters. . . . I don't want to wipe out the memory: it is dear, sacred, infinitely so, to me: but I would rather not have it recur too frequently or too vividly: I don't seem to be able to stand it in the present condition of my body." Two years later he found underfoot, "old, grimed," one of his tiny hospital memorandum books. He gave it up, too, alluding again to inexpressible bonds of engagement: "Every name, every date in it, recalls a thousand scenes, multifold memories—persons, events—army incidents—those fruitful years. The written record but a drop in the bucket—I may say a drop in the sea—to the whole story."

Whether in New York or Washington, Whitman's boys were "precious." As he explained to Traubel of these first Civil War years: "it was from the midst of things—to the midst of things: when I went to New York I would write to the hospitals: when I was in the hospitals I would write to New York: I could not forget the boys—they were too precious." Two days later, Christmas Day 1888, Whitman, in a deeply sentimental mood, gave up one of his 1863 draft letters to New York (addressed to Hugo Fritsch) and made the homoerotic *Calamus* connection explicit to Traubel: "I want you some day to write, to talk, about me: to tell what I mean by *Calamus*: to make no fuss but to speak out of your own knowledge: these letters will help you. . . . The world is so topsy-turvy, so afraid to love, so afraid to demonstrate, so good, so respectable, so aloof, that when it sees two people or more people who really, greatly, wholly care for each other and say so—when they see such people they wonder and are incredulous or suspicious or defamatory, just as if they had somehow been the victims of an outrage. . . . For instance, any demonstration between men—any: it is always misjudged . . . they meet, gossip, generate slander . . . confide in each other, tell the awful truth: the old women men, the old men women, the guessers, the false-witnesses—the whole caboodle of liars and fools." (Clearly, Walt was in the mood of my epigraph.) Traubel then read the Fritsch letter aloud, with considerable difficulty, since the draft was much criss-crossed and interlined.

The letter packs an emotional wallop. It is mostly devoted to describing an hour spent by a window on a "splendid soft moonlit night" reminiscing about one of their intimate circle, Charles Chauncey, who had just died:

. . . his looks, his handsome face, his hilarious fresh ways, his sunny smile, his voice, his blonde hair, his talk, his caprices—the way he and I first met—how we spoke together impromptu, no introduction—then our easy falling into intimacy—he with his affectionate heart thought so well of me, and I loved him then, and love him now—I thought over our meetings together, our drinks and groups so friendly, our suppers with Fred and Charley Russell &c. off by ourselves at some table, at Pfaff's off the other end [exactly the scene of *Calamus* #29, "A Glimpse"]. . . . Chauncey was frequently the life and the soul of these gatherings—was full of sparkle, and so good, really witty. . . . then I got to have occasionally quite a long walk with him, only us two, and then he would talk well and freely about himself, his experiences, feelings, quite confidential, &c. . . .

As so often, the "&c." at the tantalizing brink of revelation. Whitman then seeks to brighten his letter by expressing his desire to be back among "my dear boys' company and their gayety and electricity, their precious friendship, the talk and laughter, the drinks, me surrounded by you all (so I will for a moment fancy myself) tumbled upon you all, with all sorts of kindness, smothered with you all in your hasty thoughtless magnificent way. . . . Ah if one could float off to New York this afternoon." After asking for news of Chauncey's funeral, Whitman ends his letter. Traubel records, "I looked up as I finished reading. Walt's eyes were full of tears. He wiped the tears away with the sleeve of his coat. Put on a make-believe chuckle. 'It's very beautiful, Walt: right on the ground: where people are.' 'I hope so: that's where I belong: right on the ground.'"

Traubel personally supervised into print only the first three of the nine volumes of *With Walt Whitman in Camden*. Surely by intention and with poignant aptness, he chose to end the third volume with a conversation that took place less than a month later, on 20 January 1889. This session emphasized the centrality of Whitman's boys, comradery, and *Calamus* sequence to the achievement of the early *Leaves of Grass* editions. Again, a letter to Fritsch that Whitman is relinquishing generates powerful emotion—and eloquence. It was written on 8 October 1863 and before Chauncey's death, for Walt desires Hugo to say that "Fred & Charles Chauncey remain a group of itself in the portrait-gallery of my heart and mind yet & forever." Writing the letter, Whitman made clear, was an escape from the three to five hours he regularly spent at "the great government hospitals," where he witnessed "scenes of death, anguish, the fevers, amputations, friendlessness, hungering & thirsting young hearts, for some loving presence."

And yet, he could grant that he was finding something "fruitful" in these ghastly places: "I will confess to you, dear Hugo, that in some

respects I find myself in my element amid these scenes—shall I not say to
you that I find I supply often to some of these dear suffering boys in my
presence & magnetism that which nor doctors nor medicines nor skill . . .
can give?" That this magnetism and presence were in the same vein as his
carefree Manhattan comradery is underscored by the rest of the letter, in
which Walt jokes campily ("I have cut my beard short & hair ditto: all
my acquaintances are in anger & despair & go about wringing their
hands") and wishes he were back with his pals in the upper tier: "O Hugo
I wish I could hear with you the current opera—I saw [Donizetti's
Roberto] *Devereux* in the N.Y. papers of Monday announced for that
night, & I knew in all probability you would be there—tell me how it
goes, & about the principal singers." But the letter ends on a somber
note: "The suffering ones cling to me poor children very close. I think of
coming to New York quite soon to stay perhaps three weeks, then sure
return here."

No tears this time, though Traubel observed, "W. was quiet for a few
minutes after I stopped reading." He expressed relief when Traubel pocketed the letter: " 'That's right,' said W., 'now it's yours.' He was serious:
'The letters, my letters, sent to the boys, to others, in the days of the War,
stir up memories that are both painful and joyous.' " Whitman always
professed to admire the "letting-it-go kind" of man rather than the "judicial" sort, but in fact Traubel observed that in all his conversations
Whitman "rarely gives way externally to his extreme emotions." The
reading of the Hugo letter proved an exception, for Whitman in the next
few minutes became very heated on the themes that "there is nothing
beyond the comrade" and that in 1863–65 he was truly caught between
two "loves": "I was always between two loves at that time: I wanted to be
in New York, I had to be in Washington: I was never in the one place but
I was restless for the other: my heart was distracted." But his service
became, to use a hated word, his "religion": "A religion? Well—every
man has a religion: has something in heaven or earth which he will give
up everything else for—something that absorbs him, possesses itself of
him, makes him over into its image." And for this something, Whitman
believed all his later life, he gave up "the vitality of my physical self."

When Whitman answers the obvious next question—what did he get
in return?—we have one of the most pregnant moments in the millions
of words of the Traubel conversations: "What did I get? Well,—I got the
boys, for one thing: the boys: thousands of them: they were, they are,
they will be mine . . . I got the boys: then I got *Leaves of Grass*: but for
this I would never have had *Leaves of Grass*—the consummated book
(the last confirming word): I got that: the boys, the *Leaves*: I got them."

This ebullition, Traubel noticed, left Whitman "fired up . . . almost defiant." "All the wise ones said: 'Walt you should have saved yourself.' I did save myself . . . I saved myself in the only way salvation was possible to me. You look on me now with the ravages of that experience finally reducing me to powder. Still I say: I only gave myself: I got the boys, I got the *Leaves*."

The tremendous irony of these lines, of course, is that the soger boys' own great *Leaves of Grass* editions came *before* Walt had left the exuberant, carefree company of Hugo Fritsch and Charles Chauncey, *before* the Secession War had begun, and *after* the "dynamic" emotional logic of comradery had been definitively articulated in the *Calamus* poems of 1860. Whitman was wrong in his chronology ("my memory is such a devilish queer factor in my economy," he would later admit to Traubel), but right where it counted, namely, in his suggestion that the hospital days were indeed the "consummation" and "last confirming word" of the homoerotic impulse that is the "life below the life" of *Leaves of Grass*. And so the last paragraph of the last volume Traubel personally published constitutes a perfect last confirming word of its own: "I said to W.: '. . . you have no regrets.' 'No regrets: none: it had to be done.' I said: 'Walt, you gave up health great as health is for something even greater than health.' He said: 'Horace, that's what it means if it means anything.' "

Whitman's search among the rude and ignorant men in Washington for a "periminent" thing of his own continued after the war ended and he settled in as a clerk in the federal bureaucracy. Perhaps one Byron Sutherland auditioned for the role in 1865. Three years later Whitman wrote to Byron—now resident in New York—fondly recalling "the short time we were together, (but intimate,) in 1865." He reports life "dull" in the capital and says he is "still living in the same house, 472 M street, near 12th, where you staid with me a little while in 1865—and where you would be truly welcome to your old friend if you could come & stop with him again." He reports excellent health and jokes that he is "as fat and brown and bearded & *sassy* as ever." He closes, "Byron, I send you my love & friendship, dear soldier boy—and now that we have found each other again, let us try, as far as may be, to keep together." The sad old story: "together" but several hundred miles apart.

Was a boy named Alfred Pratt another such infatuation, this one from his nursing days? In July 1869 Whitman wrote with similar affection to him, ending, "Good bye, dear young man—I too have not forgotten those times when you lay sick in the hospital—& our love for each other—such things are not easily forgotten. . . . Good bye my loving boy." Two years later, and Whitman was devoting effusive attention to a young man named John Flood Jr. of Brooklyn. In a draft letter (which shows him softening his terms of affection several times and trying to cast their relationship as that of father and son), he writes, "Johnny, you say you should like to see me—Well, no more than I should to see you, my darling boy. I wish we were together this minute, & you had employment so we could remain with each other." In another draft letter a few weeks later, he says he is "at my desk, with a good lamp, all alone. So I thought of my dear boy." Flood was out of work, and Whitman suggested, "Dear son, if you feel to come on here on a visit, you come with me—you shall not be under any expense for board and lodging." What strings, one wonders, were attached to this invitation? Interestingly, these letters were written several months after the frantic attempt to "depress the adhesive nature" in July of 1870.

Whitman gave *Leaves of Grass* to another likely eleve of his, a Benton Wilson. Wilson reported back charmingly on 27 January 1868: "I will be candid with you, I think on the start I was more interested in it because it was your work, than for the good sentiments it contained, but as I got more acquainted with it I liked it for its own value, although I can not understand all of it, I can not find anything indecent about it." The author must have received his next letter from Wilson, whom he had met in a ward at the Armory Square Hospital, more wistfully: "My Wife wants me to send her love to you. . . . I remain as ever your Boy Friend with Love." The next year there was a shade of miserably married Fred Vaughan in another Benton letter: "I am a married man but I am not happy for my disposition is not right. I have got a good Woman and I love her dearly but I seem to lack patience or something. I think I had ought to live alone." The next year Benton reported more cheerfully, "My little baby Walt is well & Bright as a dollar."

Whitman carried his memories of moments of physical, if not sexual, intimacy with the boys of the hospital wards with him for the rest of his life. Traubel asked him one evening if he sometimes went back to Civil War days. " 'I do not need to. I have never left them. They are here, now, while we are talking together—real, terrible, beautiful days!' W. was in a very quiet mood. 'Kiss me good night!' he said." A week later, Whitman would recall one such loving wraith for Traubel, a "Kentucky youngster (a mere youngster), illiterate, extremely": "I found myself loving him like a son: he used to kiss me good night—kiss me. He got well, he passed out with the crowd, went home, the war was over. We never met again. Oh! I could tell you a hundred such tales."

DEAR LOVING COMRADE: PETE

A vast majority of the young men who were wounded or captured (or both) and brought to Washington soon returned, after the war's end, to far-flung homes or struck out, like Elijah Fox, to distant states in search of their livelihoods. One who decided to stay on in the capital was Peter Doyle, a Confederate soldier from Virginia who was wounded, captured, and interned in Washington. Doyle had emigrated from Ireland with his family (the father was a blacksmith) at the age of eight or so in the early 1850s.* He became, successively, a laborer, a conductor, and a brakeman on a Washington streetcar route, one that ran from Georgetown to the Navy Yard by way of the Capitol. In 1865 or 1866, Whitman met Doyle and commenced upon perhaps the most important adhesive relationship of the poet's life. Though it appears not to have generated any notably adhesive poems, the editor of the notebooks summarizes with good reason that the friendship amounted to "*Calamus* brought to life."

Not surprisingly, given Whitman's habitual streetcar comradery on Broadway, their first meeting took place in transit. In an interview with Horace Traubel and Richard Bucke three years after Whitman died, Doyle recalled the momentous occasion:

> You ask where I first met him? It is a curious story. We felt to each other at once. I was a conductor. The night was very stormy,—he had been over to see [John] Burroughs before he came down to take the car—the storm was awful. Walt had his blanket—it was thrown round his shoulders—he seemed like an old sea-captain. He was the only passenger, it was a lonely night, so I thought I would go in and talk with him. Something in me made me do it and something in him drew me that way. He used to say there was something in me had the same effect on him. Anyway, I went into the car. We were familiar at once—I put my hand on his knee—we understood. He did not get out at the end of the trip—in fact went all the way back with me. I think the year of this was 1866. From that time on we were the biggest sort of friends.

Whitman, for his part, remembered Doyle fondly too. "Pete was never a scholar: we had no scholar affinities," he told Traubel, "but he was a big rounded everyday working man full to the brim of the real substance of God." On another occasion Walt called Pete "a great big hearty full-blooded everyday divinely generous working man."

It is easy to imagine that an affair that began so suddenly and warmly was not merely homosocial, especially when one looks at Whitman's favorite picture of Doyle. The picture of the two comrades "looking at each other rather stagily, almost sheepishly" (as Traubel thought) is inscribed by the poet, "Washington, D.C. 1865—Walt Whitman & his rebel soldier friend Pete Doyle." (Doyle's memory about 1866 must have been faulty.) Several times in later years the photo came under somewhat embarrassed discussion. Whitman asked Tom Harned one day what he thought of it: "What do I look like there? Is it seriosity?" Harned replied with a witty edge, "Fondness, and Doyle should be a girl." The straitlaced O'Connor found the picture "silly—idiotic," but when Traubel noticed it on Whitman's floor in late 1890, the old man stood by it, alluding in a fleeting parenthesis, perhaps, to the nature of their relationship: " 'I know it is good of Pete—it is first rate: the best I have,' etc., and he exclaimed, 'Dear Pete! Many's the good day (night) we have known together!' " The two men, though apparently always maintaining separate residences, were constant companions for about eight years.

Whitman often warmed eloquently over cherished memories of the times he spent alone with Doyle. Thinking in particular of their wanderings in nearby Maryland "under the full or half-moon," Whitman paid Doyle the supreme compliment: "It was a great, a precious, a memorable, experience. To get the ensemble of Leaves of Grass you have got to include such things as these—the walks, Pete's friendship: yes, such things: they are absolutely necessary to the completion of the story." Whitman, of course, had largely completed the story of his Calamus love five years before Doyle made his entrance in the title role of rude and ignorant but perfect comrade.

Nothing is known for certain about the first three years of the Doyle-Whitman relationship. There is at least one very suggestive hint that it deepened, though not without eruptions of storm and stress like the one Doyle evoked in the summer of 1870. This is a four-line poem that exactly anticipates the notebook entry about "undignified pursuit of 16.4":

Not my enemies ever invade me—no harm to my pride from them
    I fear;
But the lovers I recklessly love—lo! how they master me!
Lo! me, ever open and helpless, bereft of my strength!
Utterly abject, grovelling on the ground before them.

"Not My Enemies" appeared in 1866, overshadowed by the debut of "When Lilacs Last in the Dooryard Bloom'd" in a small pamphlet called Sequel to Drum-Taps. Perhaps embarrassed later by its unseemly revelation,

Whitman and Peter Doyle in a photograph taken by M. P. Rice, Washington, D.C., *circa 1869. Whitman's dating of the photograph 1865 was probably incorrect. It was* *first published in 1905 in Eduard Bertz's German study of Whitman,* Walt Whitman: Ein Charakterbild, *one of the first to aggressively assert his* *homosexuality. Bayley Collection, Ohio Wesleyan University.*

Whitman decided this poem was *not* necessary to the completion of the *Leaves* story, indeed was subversive of the image of a good gray poet. (O'Connor published his "vindication" of Whitman, *The Good Gray Poet*, the same year, 1866.) And so it was banished from all later *Leaves* editions.

This omission is a shame because the poem finely expresses the agony of effusing unrequited love. The poem's suggestion that the emotional stakes were high for Whitman in this relationship is ratified by the first letters from him to Doyle that survive. They are from the fall of 1868, when Whitman visited New York for several weeks. The very first surviving letter, addressed "Dear Boy," begins an extensive correspondence on an affectionate note: "I think of you very often, dearest comrade, & with more calmness than when I was there—I find it first rate to think of you, Pete, & to know you are there, all right, & that I shall return, & we will be together again. I don't know what I should do if I hadn't you to think of & look forward to."* Shades of *Calamus* #11: "And when I thought how my dear friend, my lover, was on his way coming, O then I was happy." In subsequent letters Whitman conveys his pleasure at seeing Manhattan "let loose and on the rampage," tells of reunions with Broadway drivers who have been "much attached to me, for years & I to them," and jokes, as we have already seen, about his marauding "in the midst of female women" of Providence.

In 1869, a year later, also from New York, a fascinating letter bespoke considerable tension. Doyle had been depressed, apparently suicidal, about a skin ailment of some kind, possibly of a venereal nature, and their parting had been acrimonious. Whitman wrote at length to buck him up. "Dear Pete, you must forgive me for being so cold the last day & evening. I was unspeakably shocked and repelled from you by that talk & proposition of yours—you know what—there by the fountain. It seemed indeed to me, (for I will talk out plain to you, dearest comrade,) that the one I loved, and who had always been so manly & sensible, was gone, & a fool & intentional murderer stood in his place. I spoke so sternly & cutting." He then offers an idea: "My darling, if you are not well when I come back I will get a good room or two in some quiet place, (or out of Washington, perhaps in Baltimore,) and we will live together, & devote ourselves altogether to the job of curing you. . . . I have had this in my mind before, but never broached it to you." The letter closes with several effusive gestures: "Dear comrade, I think of you very often. My love for you is indestructible, & since that night & morning has returned more than before. . . . Dear Pete, dear son, my darling boy, my young & loving brother, don't let the devil put such thoughts in your mind again. . . .

Dear Pete, *remember*—Walt." Night and morning?—Had they spent this last night "lovingly side by side" in the same bed, like the men in "The Sleepers"? (Another hint of cohabitation may occur in Doyle's memory of being given the manuscript of *Drum-Taps* at some point after its appearance in 1865: "Walt made me a present of it. But somehow, when we moved, the manuscript disappeared—was either destroyed or stolen." Doyle also recalled in 1895 the "old days" when he "had always open doors to Walt—going, coming, staying, as I chose.")

A week later, calm seems to have descended on both parties. "I rec'd your letter of Aug. 24, & it was a great comfort to me. I have read it several times since—Dear Pete, I hope everything is going favorably with you. I think about you every day & every night." He ends more jauntily, "Now Pete, dear, loving boy, I don't want you to worry about me—I shall come along all right. As it is, I have a good square appetite most of the time yet, good nights' sleep—& look about the same as usual, (which is, of course, lovely & fascinating beyond description)." The closing salutation holds nothing back. "God bless you, dear Pete, dear loving comrade, & Farewell till next time, my darling boy. Walt."

Several months later, in February 1870, Whitman received a long letter from one of his Washington circle, Ned Stewart, then visiting Nova Scotia. Stewart gives the distinct impression he views Walt and Pete as a couple. He asks for their pictures ("if you have a double one of yourself & Peter I would like very much to have that"), uses the word "gay" several times with a curiously modern innuendo, and closes with what is probably some adhesive coyness about a coming date: "So Ile beg you to excuse this writing which is done in a very big hurry as I have made an Engagement to go out Driving in Sleigh with 'Her' & the time is drawing near a head So I'll close sending you & Pete much Love."

With the coming of spring, we have seen, something caused a crisis in the relationship, and Whitman made his heroic effort to disengage his deep emotions for Doyle. Part of his plan, perhaps, was his decision to get away and visit his now very frail mother in Brooklyn.

In the event, it seems that his effort was not entirely successful because his parting with Doyle turned out to be one of unexpectedly sweet sorrow. Whitman wrote in a letter of 30 July, "We parted there, you know, at the corner of 7th st. Tuesday night. Pete, there was something in that hour from 10 to 11 oclock (parting though it was) that has left me pleasure & comfort for good—I never dreamed that you made so much of having me with you, nor that you could feel so downcast at losing me. I foolishly thought it was all on the other side. But all I will say further on the subject is, I now see clearly, that was all wrong." A few days later, he fondly wrote (the 15 July resolution gone with the wind), "Good night, my darling son—here is a kiss for you, dear boy—on the paper here—a good long one—" He allowed this letter to lie around another day, and at the end of an addendum he added this loverly fillip so evocative of all the arms-around-neck imagery in *Leaves of Grass*: "*10 o'clock at night*—As this is lying here on my table to be sent off tomorrow, I will imagine you with your arm around my neck saying Good night, Walt—& me—Good night, Pete—"

Walt's next Sunday was spent idyllically, listening to a soprano next door practice hymns and old songs in her parlor. This put him in a dreamy mood: "Pete, I have just taken out your last letter, & read it over again—I went out on a kind of little excursion by myself last night—all alone—It was very pleasant, cool enough, & the moon shining—I think of you too, Pete, & a great deal of the time—" Doyle's letter was obviously a requiting one, and the fact that it does not survive encourages suspicion that Whitman later in life did destroy the young man's side of the correspondence with a view to secrecy. Pete reminisced that Walt was a "a long time after me to go to New York, while his mother was alive. I asked him: 'Will we stop there with your mother?' He was a little doubtful about that." The trip was made—when is not clear—and the couple stayed discreetly in Jersey City. They did dine with Mrs. Whitman ("a lovely woman") and rode the Broadway stages ("All the omnibus drivers knew him"), and Pete got himself taken to the opera "Polyato" (Donizetti's *Poliuto*).

The period of intimacy with Doyle came to an end around 1873, the year of the stroke that hobbled Whitman and caused his move to his brother George's house in Camden—and of his mother's death. There was much correspondence in the next few years, but the relationship seems to have fallen off sharply after 1876 . . . oddly, since this was about the time Doyle moved to nearby Philadelphia (he was for years baggage-master on Philadelphia–Boston trains). The stroke and the trailing off of the Doyle affair may explain why, in 1888, Whitman would speak of the years 1875–76 as "the most depressed year or two of my life."

Perhaps the physical part of the relationship simply subsided after the first five years, as Whitman's health began seriously to deteriorate and as the emerging literary lion found increasingly little in common with the nonliterate Doyle. He recalled, "Walt often spoke to me of his books. I would tell him 'I don't know what you are trying to get at.' "* Still, cordial if infrequent contact continued for many years, with Walt being very affectionate even as he alludes gingerly to the site of new emotional attachments at a place called Timber Creek. On 20 June 1877 he wrote,

"I have a fine secluded wood & creek & springs, where I pass my time alone, & yet not lonesome at all (often think of you, Pete, & put my arm around you & hug you up close, & give you a good buss—often)." In the late 1870s Doyle wrote every few months, and in 1880 he met Whitman at Niagara Falls, after the latter had visited Canada, and accompanied him back to Camden. Whitman's daybook entry for 7 December 1883 is "Pete Doyle with me this afternoon." The entry for 23 May 1885: "Pete Doyle—his mother is dying—$10—died May 24." On June fourth Doyle visited Whitman, as he had done the previous June fourth, possibly to commemorate his birthday, which was June third.

In November 1888, Traubel read aloud an old letter from the Englishman William Rossetti that mentioned Whitman's moonlight walks in Washington. Walt interrupted: "Oh! that's so fine—fine, fine, fine: he brings back my own walks to me: the walks alone: the walks with Pete: the blessed past undying days: they make me hungry, tied up as I am now and for good in a room: hungry . . . to get out of doors, into the woods, on the roads, to roll in the grass: to cry out: to play tom fool with yourself in the free fields."

Though Doyle did visit Walt on 15 June 1888 to give him some flowers, he was obviously becoming uncomfortable with the ménage in Mickle Street and having to "run the gauntlet of [the housekeeper] Mrs. Davis and a nurse and what not." Whitman's daybook says he "only staid two minutes." Yet his instinct was to return to Whitman's side. "I had a mad impulse to go over and nurse him. I was his proper nurse—he understood me—I understood him. We loved each other deeply. But there were things preventing that, too. I saw them. I should have gone to see him, at least, in spite of everything. I know it now, I did not know it then. . . ."

Glimpses of this continuing deep love occasionally surface in Traubel's volumes, as when Walt recalls that it was Pete who gave him his cane with a crook in it. "I like to think of it as having come from Pete—as being so useful to me in my lame aftermath." A few weeks later the cane leads him to think of Pete as "always a good stay and support." More moving, though, are these words recorded by Traubel during one of Whitman's delirious episodes after a series of small strokes: "Then he went astray again talking weird things about his friends, seeming to get them all jumbled together. Once he mentioned Pete Doyle. 'Where are you, Pete? Oh! I'm feeling rather kinky—not at all pert, Pete.' " A week later Doyle dropped by with his flowers.

A more amusing close shave with death occurred nearly two years later, on 20 April 1890. Traubel entered to find Whitman a bit shaken.

He had been reading the Philadelphia *Press* and said, "I was quite staggered here—it knocked the breath out of me—to read a headline—'The Death of Peter Doyle'—here in the paper: but it was not *our* Peter Doyle: it was some old man. . . . Oh! our good Pete—a rebel—not old—big—sturdy—a man, every inch of him! such a fellow—and health! . . . it was a shock!"

In 1895 Doyle ended his interview with Traubel and Bucke with a toast of beer. "You gentlemen take the glasses, there; I will drink right from the bottle. Now, here's to the dear old man and the dear old times. . . !" But the real heart-grabber had come earlier, when Doyle got up and announced, "I have Walt's raglan here [*goes to closet—puts it on*], I now and then put it on, lay down, think I am in the old times. Then he is with me again. It's the only thing I kept amongst many old things. When I get it on and [am] stretched out on the old sofa I am very well contented. It is like Aladdin's lamp. I do not ever for a minute lose the old man. He is always near by. When I am in trouble—in crisis—I ask myself, 'What would Walt have done under these circumstances?' and whatever I decide Walt would have done that I do."*

On Walt's side the final touches are melancholy ones of estrangement. When a visiting English "Whitmaniac," James Wallace, expressed in October 1891 a desire to meet Walt's most famous camerado, Doyle's whereabouts in Baltimore came as a surprise to the old poet and evoked this last recorded comment on him, a moving one: "I did not know of the change! The noble Pete! I hear but little from him. Yet that is not wonderful, either—I never did hear much. . . . He is a mechanic—an instance of the many mechanics I have known who don't write, won't write—are apt to get mad as the devil if you ask them to write. But of course I always humored Pete in that. It was enough for me to *know* him (I suppose for him to know *me*)."

Then there was the sad business of the wills. In the first one, occasioned by the stroke in 1873, Whitman left his gold watch—"a good time piece worth 130 to $150"—to his mother. In a new will of 1888, the gold watch went to Harry Stafford, a silver one to "my friend" Doyle. But in a final change made three months before his death, Walt left the gold watch to Traubel, the silver to Stafford. Doyle was to get nothing.

Doyle came to view Walt's body at Mickle Street in late March 1892 and, being unfamiliar to a policeman at the door, was almost turned away. He was also spotted on the periphery of the rites at Harleigh Cemetery, and Traubel recorded: "he was pointed out to me (by Burroughs) up the hill, twirling a switch in his hand, his tall figure and big soft hat impressively set against the white-blue sky." Later, as Doyle walked on the road back to town, Burroughs and Traubel spoke briefly with him: "Seemed immobile, not greatly moved by the occasion, yet was sincere and simple and expressed in his demeanor the powers by which he must have attracted Walt."

The ultimate fate of the gold watch, by the way, is melancholy too— and sadly suggestive of how long Whitman has remained, as he said, "*non grata* . . . not welcome in the world" to some folks. When Traubel's transcripts and other manuscripts came to reside permanently in the Library of Congress, the gold watch was found among them and thought inappropriate for housing with the collection. It was forwarded to a Traubel family descendant. Shortly thereafter the disgusted relative returned it—smashed.

CENTRAL FIGURE OF THEM ALL: HARRY

In June 1888 Whitman confided to his daybook, "Horace Traubel is invaluable to me." The nine volumes of Traubel's *With Walt Whitman in Camden* demonstrate overwhelmingly the truth of the assertion. Traubel's importance to the poet was not that of a boyfriend but of an amanuensis extraordinaire, factotum, conversational alter ego, vigorous disciple, and deeply devoted friend during the last four years of Whitman's life. That gold watch was richly deserved, as we shall see.

But what of the silver watch?

Harry Stafford, born like Traubel in 1858, was a different matter entirely. He was the last great "passional" attachment of the poet's life, the last to audition successfully for the part of perfect comrade. Though now approaching sixty, Whitman had, with Harry, dropped down a generation from Pete to maintain his habitual preference for the company of young men.

"Harry Stafford New Rep. printing office March '76 visit Kirkwood (White Horse) April 1, '76," runs a notebook entry. Whitman met the eighteen-year-old Stafford in March in the office of the Camden *New Republic* and apparently took an instant shine to the boy. By April first he had already visited Harry and his family at their farm in Kirkwood, which was about ten miles southwest of Camden via the White Horse Pike. On April fourth he wrote a secret letter to Harry's boss on his behalf: "I take an interest in the boy in the office, Harry Stafford . . . I am anxious Harry should *learn the printer's trade thoroughly* . . . want you to give him a chance (less of the mere errands &c)—There is a good deal really in the boy, if he has a chance. Don't say anything about this note to him—or in fact to any one—just tear it up, & *keep the matter to yourself private*."

This emotional engagement appears to have been reciprocated. In the next few years Walt and Harry spent much time together, which may explain the sudden fall-off in correspondence with Doyle after 1875. Harry sometimes stayed over in Camden for the weekend, and Whitman often sojourned at the farm, which was adjacent to Timber Creek. Whitman's excursions to the creek with Harry, we have already seen, became a highlight of his routine. Timber Creek, as Shively suggests, in fact "became Whitman's Walden and Tahiti combined"—a site for physical refurbishment and, it seems likely, secluded sexual encounters.* Within just six months the affair became so well established that Whitman made bold to give Harry a commemorative ring to wear. His daybook entry reads "talk with H S & gave him r Sept 26 '76—(took r back)." The parenthesis shows that the two quarreled and Walt demanded the ring back, but a month later peace was achieved, at least temporarily. The daybook entry for November first reads "Talk with H S in front room S street—gave him r again." At the end of the month Whitman records that he was "Down at White Horse— Memorable talk with H S— settles the matter." Well, apparently not quite. More than a year later, on 11 February 1878,

Two photographs of Harry Stafford from the late 1870s (above, Edward Carpenter Collection of the Sheffield Library, Great Britain; below, Library of Congress).

the scene was replayed: "Monday—Harry here—put r on his hand again." The ring, incidentally, appears to be on the little finger of Harry's right hand in a picture with Walt discovered ten years ago among the papers of Edward Carpenter.

By the end of the year the two appear to have been loafing in the same bed as well as on the pondside at Timber Creek. Walt took Harry to New York with him and inquired of a friend, "if you have plenty of room—My (adopted) son, a young man of 18, is with me now. . . . I feel somewhat at sea without him—Could I bring him with me, to share my room . . . ?" A few days later he writes, slightly altering the relationship, "My nephew & I when traveling always share the same room together & the same bed." To his more intimate friend Burroughs, some months later, he could afford to be a bit less coy. "Should like to fetch my boy Harry Stafford with me, as he is in my convoy like—We occupy the same room & bed." A typical daybook entry of this period records "Oct 17—Rec'd good letter from Harry—Wrote to H quite a long letter—/ Oct 19–20—Harry here—"

But the relationship had its storm and stress, too. When Whitman visited the farm in November 1877, he took the ring back to Camden with him, and Harry wrote immediately, "I wish you was down here with us; when you came back down Debbie [his eleven-year-old sister] said to me, it seems like home now Mr. Whitman is back. I wish you would put the ring on my finger again, it seems to me there is something that is wanting to compleete our friendship when I am with you. I have tried to studdy it out but cannot find out what it is. You know when you put it on there was but one thing to part it from me and that was death."

Shively suggests that one source of rancor might have been Walt's having a side affair with one Edward Cattell, a Timber Creek farmhand. A daybook entry for June 1876 reveals: "The hour (night, June 19, '76, Ed & I.) at the front gate by the road saw E.C. . . . Sept meetings Ed C by the pond at Kirkwood moonlight nights." A few months after these "meetings," Whitman, perhaps having difficulty juggling his two boys, wrote Cattell a letter warning him away from the Stafford farm: "do not call there at all any more—Don't ask me why—I will explain to you when we meet. . . . There is nothing in it that I think I do wrong, nor am ashamed of, but I wish it kept entirely between you and me—&—I shall feel very much hurt & displeased if you don't keep the whole thing & the present letter entirely to yourself. . . . as to Harry you know how I love him. Ed, you too have my unalterable love, & always shall have. I want you to come up here & see me."

If Whitman could petulantly demand back his ring, Harry was also subject to angry outbursts, for one of which he wrote to apologize on 1 May 1877. "Can you forgive me and take me back and love me the same. I will try by the grace of God to do better. I cannot give you up, and it makes me feel so bad to think how we have spent the last day or two, and all for my temper. I will have to *control* it or it will send me to the States Prison or some other bad place. Cant you take me back and love me the same. Your lovin, but bad-tempered, Harry." Three weeks later Harry is still pining. "You may say that I don't care for you, but I do. I think of you all the time. I want you to come up to-morrow night if you can. I have been to bed to night, but could not sleep fore thinking of you. . . . You are all the true friend I have and when I cannot have you I will go away some ware, I don't know where. . . . *Believe* me to be your true and loving friend, Harry Stafford."

A month later Whitman seems to have relented. "Dear son, how I wish you could come in now, even if but for an hour & take off your coat, & sit down on my lap."

Come mid-July and Harry was again feeling exiled. "I cannot get you off my mind somehow. I heard something that made me feel bad, and I saw that you did not want to bid me good bye when you went away yesterday. I will tell you what it was. I heard that you was going to Washington and stay and be gone for some time, is it so? I thought it was very strange in you, in not saying anything to me or about it. . . . I should like to come up to Camden next week, and stay all night with you if I could but I suppose I can not do it."

Again, Whitman returned Harry to his embraces, for on August sixth the boy wrote to thank Whitman for the "plesant time" and warn him, "I will be up to see you on Thursday to stay all night with you, don't want to go any wares then, want to stay in and talk with you. . . ." (Later that fall, Whitman got a similar letter out of the blue from Harry's young rival: ". . . it seems an age Since I last met With you down at the pond and a lovely time We had of it old man. i would like to Com up Som Saterday afternoon and Stay all night With you . . . I love you Walt and Know that my love is returned so i will Close, from your friend, Edward P. Cattell.")

A letter Harry wrote to Walt in early 1878 must have shivered the idyllic Timber Creek ethos of the relationship, for in it he reports, "I have found a girlfriend . . . a good and true friend to me." He hastens to add, though, "we have had many good times together, but none that hangs with me like those you and I have had." (By amusing coincidence, Harry's younger brother wrote Whitman on the very same day saying *he* "would like to come down & stay all night with you"!) In the next months Whitman seems to have reacted toward Harry with one of his "freezes." In July Harry wrote a pathetic letter in which he addressed "Mr. Whitman" and signed himself "Your loving son, H.L. Stafford." In the course of asking advice on his becoming "an educator," he mentions their tribulations: "we have had very many rough times to-gather but we have stuck too each other so far and we will until we die, I know."

In 1879 things proved quieter. Walt wrote his "Dear Son" from New York in May, striking as often a paternal pose (but with a sexual innuendo at the end?): "as to that spell you speak of, no doubt it was the devilish lemonade & cake—I always told you you was too heedless in the eating & drinking . . . (I tell you Harry, it is the *stomach, belly* & liver that make the principal foundation of all *feeling well—with one other thing*)."

With Harry reaching adulthood and slowly moving out of his social and emotional orbit, Walt seems to have been able to calm the perturbations that made their affair so full of fireworks. The tone of their relationship began to rise in 1881, most notably with Whitman's somewhat astonished pleasure at Harry's getting the hang of a copy of *Leaves of Grass* right away: "am a little surprised you take to L of G so quickly—I guess it is because the last five years had been *preparing & fixing the ground*, more & more & more—& now that the seed is dropt in it sprouts quickly." The irony of this is spectacularly droll: Harry, unbeknownst, had been playing a *Calamus* lover and living countless passages from *Leaves of Grass* all their years together. Whitman even seems to encourage Harry's signs of latent heterosexuality in his next letter, where he speaks glowingly of a neighboring nineteen-year-old ("handsomest woman & plesantest . . . I ever knew—full figure, blonde, good hair") and then adds, with richly smarmy hypocrisy, "O that I was young again."

A few weeks later Walt wrote an extraordinary letter to Harry that, in its way, is both the climax of the relationship and a benevolent kind of *frater ave atque vale* to the twenty-two-year-old poised to go out into the world. With poignant emphasis, Whitman tells Harry that all is forgiven:

Of the past I think only of the comforting soothing things of it all— I go back to the times at Timber Creek beginning most five years ago, & the banks & spring, & my hobbling down the old lane—& how I took a good turn there & commenced to get slowly but surely better, healthier, stronger—Dear Hank, I realize plainly that *if I had not known you . . . I should not be a living man to-day*—I think & remember deeply these things & they comfort me—*& you, my darling boy, are the central figure of them all*—

Of the occasional ridiculous little storms & squalls of the past I have quite discarded them from my memory—& I hope you will too—the other recollections overtop them altogether, & occupy the only permanent place in my heart—as a manly loving friendship for you does also, & will while life lasts.

In late 1883 Harry did light out to work for Whitman's disciple Dr. Richard Bucke at his asylum near Toronto, but the next year he returned to New Jersey. Whitman's daybook entry for 4 June 1884: "Harry Stafford is at Marlton, N.J.—is to be married soon." And for 25 June: "H S and Eva Westcott married."

Walt let Harry go his way. Now in his mid-sixties, he seems to have adjusted himself to the new dispensation, celebrating Thanksgiving of 1885 with Stafford and his wife and often receiving visits from Harry, the last one apparently being on 5 January 1891. In November 1888 Harry wrote a letter (now lost) that appears to have rattled Walt, who immediately replied that its contents were "quite a surprise to me, & a little *not understandable*—But you will tell me plainer when you come up & see me Saturday—Don't do any thing too hastily, & from great excitement." Perhaps, as Shively has speculated, Harry had informed him that he wanted to leave Eva and come live with the chanter of Adamic songs.

With the aging poet now apparently in earnest about avoiding "perturbation," Harry, like Pete, suffered a slow estrangement from the life at Mickle Street. In November 1891 Traubel noted, "Harry Stafford in to see W. the other day and rather puzzled and offended because W. seemed 'changed'—that is, reticent." Traubel also informs us that "after Stafford had been here the other day W. said to Mrs. Davis, 'Mary, why do you let everybody come upstairs? I don't know but I'll have to close all my friends out.'" The coldness of this, given Whitman's usual courtesy, is a little breathtaking, and Harry appears to have taken the inhospitable hint to heart. Though his wife and children would pay a happy visit to Walt a few weeks later, he seems never to have seen Whitman again. On Christmas Eve Walt sought to change his will and demote Harry from a gold to a silver watch. And Stafford was also conspicuously absent from the Mickle Street and Harleigh Cemetery obsequies.

A Dwindling Business

Several months after Harry's marriage, Whitman's daybook informs us that one "Charley Somer often visits me." A potential successor? But nothing more is heard of Somer, his audition having apparently failed. Then there was Will Duckett, a baby-faced teenager who, beginning on

1 May 1886, boarded for a few years in the Mickle Street house at (so he said) Walt's invitation. They had met the previous year, when Duckett and his widowed mother moved to Mickle Street a few doors away. His most notable function became driving the horse carriage that Walt's friends presented him with in September 1885. "Go out in wagon every afternoon—Wm Duckett drives," says the daybook in November.

The cheeky boy appears to have worn on Walt's aging nerves, however, and he eventually allowed Mrs. Davis to expel the boy for non-payment of board, while professing possibly theatrical outrage at the notion that he would have *invited* a boy to live with him: "think of it!—that I invited him here, that he was my guest!—the young scamp that he is! Why, that is downright perjury." In fact, Mrs. Davis successfully sued Duckett's trust from his dead father for $190 in arrears, just as she would later sue Whitman's own estate in 1894 for monies owed her; so successful was she in the latter effort that the poet's estate was effectively left bankrupt. Small wonder Doyle found intimidating the gauntlet of Mrs. Davis—whom Walt almost never mentions in the daybooks and who always insisted on calling him "Mr. Whitman."

In any event, Duckett had become "this young rascal" to Walt, as was amusingly apparent in November 1889 when Traubel brought in a Whitman personal that had appeared in *Current Literature*. It gossiped about "a young man of 12" who was the poet's driver and who "likes and will lecture on him after he is dead, having taken notes of all he has said." Walt was furious, calling it a "*lie* in big, big type" and adding with evident satisfaction, "Billy was here to see me the other day, but they [i.e., Mrs. Davis and his nurse Warrie Fritzinger] would not let him in." The last surviving connection between Walt and Billy was a letter from the latter pleading "pretty hard luck of late" and asking for "ten or Fifteen Dollars." Whitman's note on the envelope reads "sent back word I was quite sick & was hard up."

Well into the late 1870s and early 1880s, Whitman kept his gimlet eye out for the next lifelong lover who might appear suddenly from behind the steering-house of a Delaware River ferry or in the driver's seat of a streetcar. In January 1879 he noted in pencil in his daybook, "Harry Garrison RR man on ferry—blonde I meet." In March 1880 he jotted down a list of ten *"Drivers, Conductors, Ferrymen,"* among them "tall, young" John Williamson and "back eyed" John McLaughlin. He twice records "Wm Stillé, young man formerly at Coley's grocery," a nice anticipation of Ginsberg's line about eyeing grocery boys. Later that year he recorded meeting a Market Street driver, Robert McKelvey, who was "young, blackeyed, affectionate." And, as before, he sometimes notes significant family or domestic status: a Harry Cooper "boards—

Bill Duckett, briefly a part of Whitman's Mickle Street household, in two states: left, in a formal portrait, circa 1886 (Bayley Collection, Ohio Wesleyan University); below, in a photograph taken by Thomas Eakins in rooms of the Philadelphia Art Students League, circa 1886–92 (David Hunter McAlpin Fund, Metropolitan Museum of Art).

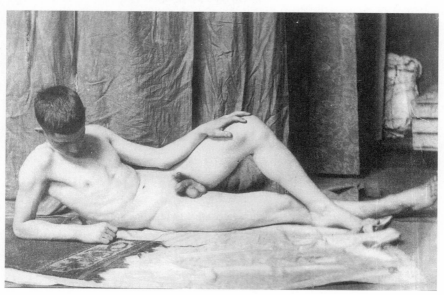

father dead," while another Market Street driver is a "widower, one boy 4 yr's old."

But as the 1880s progressed and Whitman fell under the more pressing distractions of a valetudinarian, the Whitman eye inevitably became cloudy and undiscerning—perhaps even uninterested in the male beauty that came his way. On 20 March 1888 Whitman pronounced himself "very ill" in his daybook and added that "these are dull even miserable days." An important reflection of this dull misery is the way all the defining epithets Whitman once deployed in memorializing the young men of his acquaintance— "sonorous voice," "broad-shouldered," "blondish," "saucy looking," and the like—slowly vanish from his daybooks. His young men lose their youth (he no longer makes a point of mentioning age) and all their fetching physical attributes. They become, like so much else in his later poetry, bodiless abstractions. Whitman told a correspondent in 1888, gamely but with rue, "I get out & have fun yet—but it is a dwindling business."

And yet . . . even amid the physical ruins there was the occasional effulgence of the ecstatic celebrator of male beauty who wrote *Calamus*. Three weeks after complaining of his dwindling life, he reported to Traubel that "some kind of labor agitator" had visited him earlier in the day. He was at first "sorry to see him come," admitting with a characteristic paradox that "I am somehow afraid of agitators, though I believe in agitation." Still, he allowed the youth in and reported with bittersweet gusto: "young, a rather beautiful boy—full of enthusiasms . . . I was sorry to see him come . . . but I was more sorry to see him go than come. Some people are so much sunlight to the square inch. I am still bathing in the cheer he radiated. O he was a beautiful boy! . . . Oh he was a beautiful boy—a daybeam: I shall probably never see his face again—yet he left something here with me that I can never quite lose."*

Less to his taste, but apparently appealing to look at, was a rather understated Harvard student who appeared on his doorstep a year later, having come south solely to visit Whitman, with two copies of *Leaves* ripe for autographing. Traubel amusingly notes that Whitman had to ask "questions that he cared nothing about to keep the ball rolling," and reports that Whitman confessed, "I always get Harvard and Yale mixed in my mind." Whitman was pleased to hear his visitor say that "there are many fellows up there who have the same feelings about you I do." After the boy—"young, with a New England accent. Slender, agile—complexion sallow"—left, Whitman remarked, "I rather like him—don't you? a modest, engaging fellow."

ᵂ   ᵂ   ᵂ

"The aging of my body and my beauty / is a wound from a merciless knife," wrote Cavafy, "I'm not resigned to it at all." Whitman, too, held up a hand mirror to himself and mercilessly found "No more a flashing eye, no more a sonorous voice or springy step," yet he resigned himself to old age with grace and amiability. Frequently, even, with humor: in his prefatory note to *Good-Bye my Fancy,* he likened himself to "some hard-cased dilapidated grim ancient shell-fish or time-bang'd conch (no legs, utterly non-locomotive) cast up high and dry on the shore-sands, helpless to move anywhere—nothing left but behave myself quiet." The stroke of 1873 had, of course, given him a long time to practice equanimity.

But like Cavafy, Whitman in his last decades sounded his retreat from love in part through poetry. "Bring your drugs, Art of Poetry," said Cavafy in the same poem, "they numb the wound at least for a little while." Unfortunately, "numb" must be an apt word for much of the later poetry to anyone who has read the early editions of *Leaves of Grass,* when the poet's search for a lifelong lover was still active and eager. Numbness, too, is perhaps the right word for what Walt's increasingly non-locomotive spirit made him say to an interviewer for the New York *Herald* in 1888, "I am an old bachelor who never had a love affair."

In private, however, Whitman was happy to flare about the *Herald* report, " 'Taint true! 'Taint true!" And a particularly droll cat-and-mouse game that took place between Whitman and Traubel for a couple years suggests, I think, that the poet's private view was the honest one. Whitman got into the habit of tantalizing Horace with a secret story from his past that he wanted to reveal, and Horace regularly broached the matter. On 1 October 1888, for example, he reminded Whitman that "that big story you were going to tell me: that's not coming very fast." Whitman "was grave at once. Took my hand in his: looked me straight in the eye: 'That couldn't come fast, Horace—that's too serious, yes— sacred: that must come in its own way, in its own time: but it will come.' W.'s good night more than usually tender. He kissed me."

Four weeks later, Whitman temporized again, but a bit more revealingly. "There are best reasons why I have not heretofore told you. . . . It's not so much that I desire to confide a secret to you as that I wish you on general principles to be made familiar with the one big factor, entanglement (I may almost say tragedy) of my life about which I have not so far talked freely with you." Traubel says he waited "for more but that was all he said—except that, seeing inquiry on my face, he concluded: 'Not to-night, Horace, dear boy.' " The next month, as usual, Traubel is mystified. "I don't know what to make of it. I wonder what it is? Sometimes I think it is just his playfulness. Then again I get the feeling that he really has something serious to say to me. But I can't push him." And so it went for many more months, the "big-pow-wow" (as Walt put it) never taking place.

The lavish tomb Whitman had ordered built in Harleigh Cemetery threatened, for a time, to be the pretext for his finally divulging the dark secret. He had confided to Dr. Bucke and Tom Harned that he had two dead children by two "highborn" women, and he wished to move their remains to the tomb (there were eight crypts within). This, Traubel assumed, was "the 'long story' which he then said he wished to tell me but to which he never had recurred." Several attempts in December 1891 to evoke a telling of the secret failed. Once Whitman brushed the subject off by saying, "I am not in good condition today. Let it go for another time. It is a nasty story anyway." A few weeks later, Traubel asked Bucke if he thought Walt would ever tell the tale. "No, I don't think he will. I don't believe he will ever be *able* to tell it." Which turned out to be true. Walt's last comment on the tomb was simply, "I have no particular wish, except that father and mother be put there, I between them." In the end, one might conclude that Whitman simply did not have the gumption to continue perpetrating so bald a genealogical fib. (It may also be that he had a reason other than sexual disguise for telling this tall tale: more occupants for the very expensive mortuary monument would bolster its *raison d'être*. He had promised his dying mother that he would care for his institutionalized brother Eddy, and his huge outlays for the tomb did compromise Eddy's welfare. Whitman knew, too, that most in his inner circle disapproved of it.)

Still, it is tempting to imagine that Whitman's *true* "great secret" had something to do with the "saddest loss and sorrow" of his life that is mentioned in *Specimen Days*. Tempting, too, to speculate that it was about a great male love. Whitman could not quite summon the courage, even with Traubel (who was, at least apparently, just beginning to settle into heterosexual domestic bliss), to reveal his secret. Dr. Bucke once advised Whitman, "Don't be reckless," to which Whitman replied: "There's no danger: the phrenologists mark my caution at six to seven—nearer to seven than six—which amounts to cowardice." In respect of his secret, caution evidently won out.

And yet . . . perhaps his caution was in the end not complete. Did the furtive old hen leave at least one faint clue to the bitter truth about his long, often tumultuous, and finally unsuccessful search for a true lover? Is it in this terrible sentence, apparently a paraphrase of a despairing remark made by Charles Dickens, that he jotted down sometime after 1880 and left behind in a notebook for Traubel to do with as he thought best: "Why is it that a sense comes always crushing on me, as of one happiness I have missed—life, and one friend & companion I have never made?"

4

WALT & HORACE:
"MIRACLES FOR MYSELF"

That's all there is in life for people—just to
grow near together.

—Walt Whitman

I N THE LAST few years of Whitman's life, his health was poor, sometimes highly precarious. A stroke in June 1888 caused particular
worry. There was a flurry of concern over his last will and testament,
the now virtually nonlocomotive poet acquired a "wheeling chair," and
closer attention was paid to providing a full-time nurse. Dr. Bucke even
urged that Whitman move permanently into the hospital facilities at
Johns Hopkins in Baltimore for optimal medical attention in the event of
emergencies that began to seem ever more likely.

All in all, he appears to have met his physical tribulations with stoic
equanimity, almost never resorting to crotchety rancor or unkindness,
even on his worst days. But he did not mince words. "It is wearisome,
almost sad," he said one day in the fall of 1888, "to be confined in this
way, imprisoned, for days, months, years. Yet I have made up my mind to
be cheerful."* The month before, Whitman, who always blamed the
stress of his Civil War nursing for the initial collapse of his health in
1873, poignantly described how he typically felt with a vivid abolitionist
simile: "I have seen the iron collars on the slaves in the South—bits on
the wrist here, a chain—back of the collar a spike: the effect of all not
pain, not anguish but a dull weight—making its wearer incapable of
effort—bearing him down. It is such a collar I wear day by day: a burden
impossible to shake off—vitiating all my attempts to get on my feet
again."

Both of these remarks were made to Horace Logo Traubel in the privacy of the Mickle Street house. Traubel, nearly forty years Whitman's

Horace Traubel at the time of his close association with Whitman. Library of Congress.

junior, was the last of the young men with whom the poet developed a strong emotional attachment. He was also without doubt the most indefatigable prop of the poet's last years, performing the roles of confidant, amanuensis, news- and gossip-bringer, agent to his printers, archivist, and, I think it is not too much to say, "perfect Comrade." Though sexual intimacy seems quite unlikely, the relationship between Walt and Horace was extraordinarily close, physical, and gratifying. Just a few months after the transcriptions began, Horace recorded: "W. kissed me good night. He said: 'We are growing near together. That's all there is in life for people—just to grow near together.'" Two months later the point was reiterated, also with a kiss: "W. said: 'Come kiss me for good night.' He was still lying down. I reached over him and we kissed. He took my hand—pressed it fervently. 'I am in luck. Are you? I guess God just sent us for each other.'" Kissing became, indeed, something of a ritual. A few months later this exchange occurred: "He called me. 'Won't you kiss me good night. . . . It will be a last kiss, a last good-night sometime.' I said: 'You seem a bit gloomy.' 'No: I only face conditions.'"

Just after Christmas 1888, the two waxed nostalgic about their first meeting fifteen years before. Whitman always recalled 1873 as one of his darkest years: the first stroke occurred in January, followed by bouts of dizziness; his mother died in May; and by June he was in Camden at his not particularly favorite brother George's house, disabled for work and feeling isolated from his manly circles in Washington and New York. Late in the year, as he was regathering his forces, Traubel—fifteen years old, Camden born and bred, son of a Jewish immigrant from Frankfurt— appeared in his life. Recalling the time, Whitman struck again the "heaven-sent" note and also sang Traubel's appealing body electric: "life was reviving: I was getting a little like my old self: certainly was spiritually realizing life once more—tasting the cup to the full. Horace, you were a mere boy then . . . I remember you so well: you were so slim, so upright, so sort of electrically buoyant. You were like medicine to me— better than medicine." Whitman spoke also of their conversations under the trees down toward the Delaware River and of how voracious a reader Traubel was. "Oh! you were reading then like a fiend: you were always telling me about your endless books."

Traubel, for his part, chose to remember the day three years later when Walt attended the burial of his eight-month-old nephew. "Walt, do you remember the day you buried little Walter? How we met—walked a bit: how we had quite a little chat: how you took the car at Fifth Street—at Stevens there: how we met again an hour or so later on the [ferry] boat? I look back and see it all: you said: 'Horace, it does me good—this air does me good: sort of makes me *whole* again after what I have gone through to-day.'" At this Whitman was very quiet. Traubel asked if his memory was jogged. " 'Yes! now I do remember it: not all the details you mention but the circumstances: and I remember what maybe you have forgotten: that on the boat you bought some wild flowers from an old nigger mammy who had been all day trying to sell them in the city and was going home dispirited: you bought her flowers and handed them to me. Do you remember that?' When he spoke of it, yes. W. was palpably moved."

In these early years, the two seem to have enjoyed each other's company regularly, although, as Walt said, "not so often . . . not so intimately" as in the late 1880s. Attention sometimes turned from books to baseball on the Camden common. "I can't forget the games we used to go to together," Walt recalled; "they are precious memories." (Walt's interest in baseball—and boys—continued long. On 11 June 1889, Traubel recorded that Whitman "had just returned from his [wheelchair] 'jaunt' with Ed [Wilkins]. 'It was baseball today.' He takes great interest in the boys out on the common. Sits watching them for long stretches.")

There were many bases for sympathy with Horace, aside from his appeal to Whitman's eye. In fact, Traubel's late teens and twenties unfolded very much like Whitman's. He ended his formal schooling early and steered marvelously clear of the shoals of a university education. Yet he was widely and well read. Like Whitman too, he seemed content with several fairly menial positions for his livelihood, at first in printing-house trades (his father was a lithographer). In May 1888, Whitman did his part for the thirty-year-old with a letter of introduction to the Philadelphia publisher of *Leaves of Grass*: "The bearer Horace Traubel is a valued young personal Camden friend of mine—American born, German stock—whom

I wish to introduce to you with the best recommendations—He is of liberal tendencies and familiar with printing office matters and the run of books." Toward the end of his Whitman years, Traubel was the paymaster in a factory, then a clerk at Philadelphia's Farmers and Mechanics Bank on Market Street near the river.

In any case, Traubel's daytime work was clearly of no consequence to him or, indeed, to Whitman, who asks about it precisely once in the nine volumes of conversations that have been published since 1906—and even then he doesn't let poor Horace get a word of answer in edgewise. Traubel's real profession was Walt Whitman. From the day in March 1888 when he began scrupulously recording his talks with the poet in what he called "condensed longhand," he visited with him virtually every day, usually between five and eight in the evening and usually for twenty minutes to an hour. Sunday visits could be earlier, and by 1889 he often paid a midmorning visit as well. After several months of this routine Traubel noted, "Eight o'clock is his good hour invariably if there is a good hour in the day. For that reason I have mostly made it the hour for consultation." Whitman in turn made a conscious effort to perk up for these meetings. He often napped just before Traubel's arrival, explaining one day, "I want to be ready for you: you are the oasis in my desert." Flattered, Traubel responded jokingly that he had feared it might be the other way around, at which Walt laughed, "That's witty but there's not a damn bit of truth in it."

As he had in 1873, Traubel was clearly still giving Whitman his best "medicine." The housekeeper, Mary Davis, told him one day, "You seem to have waked Mr. Whitman up. He was dull enough all day." The invalid seconded this notion on several occasions. Once Traubel expressed fear that he was a "bother," and Whitman protested, "You bother me? you couldn't: you never victimize me—you wake me up. I am far more alert this minute, am feeling better, than I have been at any time during the day." A few weeks later he reiterated, "The instant you came into the room and hung your hat on the bedpost I felt better." Small wonder he became thoroughly addicted to Horace's clockwork appearances on the doorstep. Once Horace missed a Sunday visit and recorded that Walt "greeted me as 'a stranger'—for having been absent yesterday altogether." Some time later *two* whole days were missed. When Traubel finally appeared, Walt "called out 'Horace' with great cordiality—took and held my hand—said, 'I wondered what had become of you: was going to send up to ask tomorrow.'"

Love is not too strong a word for the relationship that grew through these daily visits. Traubel was certainly not shy about using the word and recorded several moments of great emotion that can still grab the reader's heart. He very aptly chose, for instance, to end the second volume of *With Walt Whitman in Camden* with this beatific scene, which occurred after Walt uttered a spirited monologue in praise of Heine (the most Whitmanesque of European romantic poets): "I gazed at W. His face shone—he regarded me with great love. I kissed him good night and withdrew. 'Good-night!' he called after me: 'Good-night! Good-night!' " Genuine affection for the old man is often displayed by Traubel, as one can see from passing comments on several visits between 1888 and 1890:

W. lay on the bed as I left. The tangerines and a book beside him: he played with them. I was happy. He seemed so well.

He was serenely glowing to-night. He stirred me. He rarely lets himself loose in this personal fashion.

Was in a very hearty mood, inclined to be strangely demonstrative of his cordiality.

Happy, this night's 20 minutes with W!

6 p.m. Spent a half hour of significant joy with W. He sat in his room, writing, the crazy quilt tied about his neck.

LOVING KINDNESS & INDUSTRY

Traubel paid dearly, though happily, for such golden moments, notably performing a wide variety of tasks crucial to the design and publication of Whitman's last volumes of prose and poetry. Occasionally he was run quite ragged. In August 1888, for example, he found himself "running about all day for W.—first to Bonsall's house for the *Book Maker*—then across the river for conferences at different places with Ferguson [printer], McKay [publisher], Magarge & Green (paper merchants), Brown, Bilstein (plate printers). Struck a paper for seven cents, by which we can save one hundred and forty dollars on the lot required." Such errands, added to the task of writing out each evening's conversation in full, sometimes made for a long day. One day's entry reads "I am writing this very late at night. Very tired. Walt's copy to run over and get ready for delivery to Ferguson in the morning." On some evenings he might get added homework, for instance a handful of "loving messages" Whitman had received. "I took these letters home with me and spent two hours examining them. Wrote a dozen replies."

Other mundane errands produce amusing exchanges. "I threaten to give you another commission," Whitman said one Saturday. "I want some of Thaddeus David's black ink and don't seem able to get it here in Camden at all. When I send Ed out first he brings me Thaddeus David's pale blue. It's as bad as it used to be when I sent Mary out a-searching for my socks. She could get everything in the world that I did not want. . . . There must be enough old codgers like me, grounded in the past, to make it still worth while to make that ink." Traubel, of course, found the ink—and several months later was able to run down the big quill pens the old codger liked to flourish. "Got him a box of Mammoth Falcons and a holder today: about thirty-six pens. He took [them] with the pleasure of a child. . . . 'I was on my last man,' he remarked, 'and would have sent Warrie [Fritzinger, a new nurse] out to skirmish for them tomorrow. These are the best yet.' "

Some errands were a little racier. Whitman was not above the occasional tipple. "[Dr.] Bucke knows I drink," he admitted one day, "at least I used to whenever I got the chance—was in the mood." Champagne (though *not* "lunar champagne," his term for New Jersey moonshine) he especially favored. When a correspondent with a gift in mind asked whether Whitman drank the bubbly, he replied with a laugh, "Does a duck swim? . . . Yes—let him send a sip or two—it has a wonderful lift for a man!" Whiskey also had its place in Mickle Street, and one day Traubel was told, "I intended asking you to bring me more whiskey. I am quite out of whiskey and Tom [Harned]'s is the bestest ever was! Oh! it is the genuine stuff. I know nothing near so good anywhere else."

Alcohol, in fact, eased Whitman's last months considerably, sometimes with drollery attached. One day he referred to "a temperance man, so-called—that is, a bigot." He greeted a new bottle of "medicinal" brandy with "there's a whole world in that bottle," and on another occasion "the brandy! Oh! that is good—it freshens me if anything can!" And his liquor purveyor evoked memories of his glory days as king of Bohemia. "He reminds me of Pfaff. You knew about Pfaff? . . . he would go down in his cellar and bring out from the cobwebs a bottle of choice champagne—the best. . . . Pfaff never made a mistake—he instinctively apprehended liquors—having his talent, and that talent in curious prolixity, almost. Often I would wonder—*can* he ever go *wrong?*" Whitman's final death spiral began, in fact, on about the day Horace records, "For the present he asks no more for brandy."

Certain more important tasks Traubel performed behind Whitman's back, notably fundraising to pay for a full-time nurse. This now and then required artful concealment, as when Horace read aloud a letter he had received from a mutual friend. "I did not read W. the first part of Stedman's letter. He does not know how I am paying for the nurse." But by far the most significant of Traubel's self-appointed functions, aside from transcribing the conversations, were those associated with bringing into existence the poet's last volumes: *November Boughs and Complete Poems and Prose* of 1888, *Good-Bye my Fancy* and the "deathbed" edition of *Leaves of Grass* of 1891, and the *Complete Prose Works* of 1892.

On 22 December 1888, as a kind of holiday present, Whitman handed Traubel a package and told him to take it home. "At home I opened the package: found in it the inscription that follows. It is the first time he has let himself go to me." The inscription, in a copy of *November Boughs*, is a moving and justly grateful tribute:

> To *Horace Traubel*
> from his friend the author
> Walt Whitman
> & my deepest heartfelt thanks go with it to HT in getting this book out—it is *his* book in a sense—for I have been closely imprison'd & prostrated all the time (June to December 1888) by sickness & disability—& HT has managed it all for me with copy, proofs, printing, binding, &c. The Volume, & especially "November Boughs" & the portraits, could not now be existing formulated as here, except thro' his faithful & loving kindness & industry, daily, unintermitted, unremunerated— WW Dec: 1888

Traubel in fact became quite proprietary about his position as the good gray poet's factotum. Once Whitman allowed a third party to run a printing errand, and Traubel made certain this did not happen again. "W. had returned yesterday's proofs through Baker today. I kicked. I said I ought to do all those errands myself in order to keep a supervising eye on our affairs. . . . I said to him: 'If I am to work with you it must be on this condition.' He at once came down."

Vital though these tasks were to the largely house-bound poet, Traubel functioned even more valuably for posterity simply as a companion, as a conversational drawer-out and principal historian of Walt-behind-the-scenes. As I have often suggested, we would not be greatly the poorer if those last two editions of *Leaves of Grass* Horace slaved over had never appeared; they amounted, more or less, to rearranging deck chairs on a slowly sinking ship, a ship that was getting increasingly long in the beam and unwieldy. But the nearly three-year-long colloquy memorialized in *With Walt Whitman in Camden* offers many a priceless glimpse into the autobiography whose presence in *Leaves* Whitman often boasted of.

Inevitably, much in these pages is mundane, ephemeral, or repetitious. There is, of course, much talk of health and physical deterioration, but even the sometimes drastic swings in mood and medical status can produce real pathos . . . or gallows wit. On bad days Whitman might complain, "I am old, weak, toppling, full of defections," tell of being "two days way down in the valley," or report that he felt "miseble, as the darkies say." On good days he might announce himself "almost quarrelsomely well" or "rather pert" or (as he did at the end of his seventieth birthday dinner) "gloriously well and sassy!" Most every daily entry begins with Traubel sizing up his man: "looked ill, tired, worn, almost haggard"; "W. in might good feather his evening"; "W. in somewhat depressed mood"; "eye unwontedly calm . . . very wakeful but very soul-dwelling"; "W. in bad shape all day—sleepy, confused"; "W. in bright, cheery humor—color good," and so on. Horace noted how seldom he was obliged to record "W. was rather cranky to-night" or "W. seemed a little testy (unusual)." On such occasions, or when Walt seemed taciturn, his visitor beat a quick retreat—one April evening, for example: "I did not prolong my stay. W. not in good talking mood. In such cases I never linger." Happily, most days found Whitman "brisk for talk."

Not all of Whitman's talk is brisk for us now. Countless pages recording lengthy lucubrations over proofreading, book design, and marketing, as well as Whitman's frequent growling over the "small economies, meannesses" of the book industry and the "devilishly cute—lot [of] publishing wolves," will be of great interest mainly to bibliographical scholars. Many political discussions address issues long forgotten, and many literary topics broached are now of small moment. Largely because some of Walt's friends were fascinated by the theory that someone other than the man from Stratford wrote *Hamlet* and its brethren, this was often discussed in Mickle Street. The poet mainly sat on the fence, but characteristically let his feet dangle on the subversive side. "I have never been what you would call a Baconian: yet I acknowledge as far as anti-Shakespeare: there I take my stand." Another topic endlessly (and most revealingly) debated was the success or failure of the countless painterly and photographic images of Whitman, especially the latter. "I doubt if any one realizes the value and depth and grandeur of first-class photos," he opined at his last birthday dinner, and page upon page recorded by Traubel attests to his preoccupation with the song of his photographed self. "No man has been photographed more than I have or photographed worse," he truly told Horace one day. "I've run the whole gamut of photographic fol-de-rol."*

All these wide-ranging if not exactly riveting discussions, however, do serve to underscore what a superbly literate, cultured, and knowledgeable companion Traubel made for the poet. One day he asked if Whitman had read Matthew Arnold's essay on America in *The Critic*. "No, he had not read it. I described its chief features." On another occasion he spent ten minutes describing the performances of the great Italian actor Salvini he had just seen. After he attended Wagner's *Die Walküre* he also gave Whitman a full report. On another day Whitman asked Traubel to explain President Cleveland's message of retaliation on a fisheries dispute with Canada. And he did.

But amid the occasional doldrums of *With Walt Whitman* there is much of great price that serves to bring us closer (as Whitman himself put it) to the "pulse and throb of the critter himself." Take, for example, the question of Whitman's sense of humor. It was abroad in America— with some justice, be it said—that the author of *Leaves of Grass* did not have one. This aspersion was now and then discussed in Mickle Street, once when Traubel told of someone asking if Whitman "ever laughed himself—could appreciate a joke." At this Walt remarked, "That is very funny. My intimate friends would have their best fun with a man who brought them such a doubt!" Whitman also said once that he prided himself "on being a real humorist underneath everything else," and it was one of Traubel's happiest accomplishments to get "underneath" where the humor lay and reveal its existence.

Whitman had humor, but it was not the jokey or tall-tale humor of the Mark Twain variety. Twain and Whitman, in fact, never really got on. As Walt summed up: "I have always regarded him as friendly, but not warm: not exactly against me: not for me either." (Twain did join the subscription to get the old man a horse and buggy.) Whitman's humor was, as he suggested above, born more of intimacy; it blossomed ideally amid an inner circle. It was the kind of humor he found in one of his most admired intimates, Colonel Robert Ingersoll. Ingersoll, indeed, elicits a splendid definition of Whitman's own sense of humor: "The noble Bob! Oh! What would I not give to be able to show him how deep he has entered into my respect—my nature: taken hold of the last fibre. And *humor*: Bob has humor—that last quality—not fun, not jollity, which too much narrows its meaning—but humor, in the sense of lubrication—has it richly, superbly."

A more lubricious biographer might make something of the superbly chosen word "lubrication"—might make bold to suggest that, over his many decades, Whitman must have eased himself into many a manly friendship through such humorous lubrication. One is sometimes even tempted to call his humor "camp," as the late Karl Keller did several years ago in a *jeu d'esprit* titled "Walt Whitman Camping." (This essay's cheeky exit line: "Does it go too far to suggest that Walt Whitman is the Mae West of American literature?"*) Certainly many instances of the "flamboyant facetiousness" and "serious teasing" Keller professed to find in *Leaves of Grass* are on display in Traubel's pages as well. One can see it, I think, in Whitman's fun with the mild recreation of his dear Canadian friend Bucke: "Doctor takes to sleighing like some men take to rum: he gets drunk with it—he goes on sleighing orgies." Another day, when in a silly mood, Whitman had an idea for dealing with a slow bookbinder: "That book has been there about a month . . . what must we do to get it? Go there: don't hurt him: ram a needle in his ass—not too far: not far enough to hurt him—only far enough to wake him up." Traubel records that Whitman "was so funny about this I burst into a furious laugh. This broke him loose, too, and he haha'd till the tears flowed down his cheeks like rain."

There is also much artful self-deprecating humor in the conversations that *Leaves* would not exactly lead one to expect. One day he recalled how O'Connor felt about the poet's taste in photographs of himself: "he always said that whenever I had a particularly idiotic picture taken I went into raptures over it." Then he added, "There may be good reasons for that: how often I have been told I was a particularly idiotic person!" And, of course, Whitman used humor to lubricate the way to his quietus. With his seventieth birthday approaching, he announced, "I have about made up my mind to live another year: why not? Considering all the things I have to do I will need at least a year." He was on homely, idiomatic terms with death. "No one knows better than I do that I may go to pot any minute—vamoose, as they say out West." "Kicking the bucket," Traubel noted, was "a most frequent phrase," with him, and one day he sighed, "I am a lame though not yet quite dead duck."

Some of the choicest drollery in *With Walt Whitman*, though, is produced simply by the daily serendipity of the Mickle Street ménage. One thinks of the day a couple of deaf and dumb visitors came, and Walt told Traubel, "We got along pretty well together—though silently!" Then there was the violin playing of Whitman's nurse, droll serenade for a poet declining into the "second childishness and mere oblivion" of man's seventh age. Traubel tells us, "W.'s favorite piece in Ed's modest repertoire is Rock-a-bye Baby. Ed says quaintly: 'I make it long for him—put in the chorus two or three times.'" But one day, alone with Horace, Walt

confessed the truth: "I don't altogether like the screeching, but I do altogether like Ed, so I can stand one for the sake of the other." His patience
with pianism was much thinner. One day, when Traubel went on about
Paderewski's picture in *The Century Magazine*, Whitman asked what he
did for a living. On being informed he was a pianist, Whitman dropped
the subject, Traubel noting, "I find he has no enthusiasm over the best
piano playing." The dread instrument of the high-toned parlor! The stiff,
apparently humorless housekeeper, Mrs. Davis, also evokes a chuckle
when we read of Walt's reaction to her occasional attempts to rectify the
Augean clutter of his bedroom-study: "You get everything out of place
and call it order."

One day the mail brings a letter from abroad addressed, "Walt
Whitman, America," and the poet is pleased for once with post office
efficiency: "it gets here sharply." Another letter, from a manufacturer of
bee-keeping supplies in Friendship, New York, expresses concern over
news of Whitman's sickness and financial straits and invites him to live
with him: "You have always been my favorite poet, and I think it is a
shame that you should be left in need." No doubt pleasing to Whitman
was the letter "from a Western man" that arrived a month before he died,
"expressing the pressure of his spiritual debt to W.W. and his gladness
that 'the most modern and liberal of our poets' " still lived.

Then there was the dog, its name being the one salient fact about
Whitman that Traubel failed to record. To Horace's aggravation, it let
out "his usual dismal howl" every time he arrived. One day Walt got to
fuming over the mutt: "Well, if there's anyone in the world he ought to
know by this time—would know, if he had any sense at all, as he has
not—it is you. He is the nastiest, noisiest, silliest, stupidest, horriblest
dog that ever was born, a pest, a continual sore in my side! . . . any manly
[!] dog—gets to know his friends, betters—but this dog, never!" A week
later: "The dog made a terrific howl as I entered—never learns to know
me. I said to W. jokingly: 'I'll shoot him some night, he don't get over
that.' W. at once responding: 'And I'll not complain of the deed in the
least! He howls a hundred times a day, at all hours. In the night too, generally about one o'clock when the rest of the world wants to keep quiet.' "
Two years passed and the dog *still* howled at poor Horace, eliciting these
"compliments" from its master: "He's as dumb as the devil! Don't seem to
have any dog intuitions." A few days later the big setter again made a
racket: "He is the dumbest dog that ever set foot in America!" Its perfect
name, it turns out, was Watch. (A previous Whitman dog had been
named—after the "treacherous" phallus in "Song"?—Tip.)

Glimpses into the foibles and whims of the old man also give

Traubel's pages the feel of being, like Eakins's famous photographs and painting of him, very much "from the life." "W. has a peculiar way of sitting with his glasses stuck on the thumb of his left hand while he uses the right hand for playing with his paper knife, resting both elbows on the arms of his big chair as he does so and talking straight on in the best of humors." This he did all evening, Traubel tells us, adding, "in other moods, when not feeling well, when depressed, he never drops into this playful physical demonstration but is curiously impassive." One day four of Mrs. Davis's doughnuts were packed up for Horace's mother and Walt said, "Tell her they are not doughnuts—tell her they are love."

Especially droll was the day Whitman found a volume of Boswell's life of Johnson on the floor and remarked to Traubel that "a good many of the things told by Boswell are contradicted by the notes of annotators, who intimate that this could not possibly have happened, or that, or the other, simply because the man was absent at the time, or dead." A not so subtle hint to his own Boswell about taking good factual care?

There is much to charm, too, in the meandering variety of Whitman's table talk. It would have been regrettable to lose his thoughts on smoking, for instance. One day Horace—who never touched cigarettes or whiskey—asked if Walt regretted never having smoked. "I would as lief regret that I had not murdered my mother." And a few weeks later he recalled of his Mannahatta days that "we were a no-smoking crowd" and made one of his many highly unsuccessful prophecies: "it is so filthy a practice taken for all in all that I can't see but people must inevitably grow away from it." Paeans to baseball are a continuing aggravation of life, yet it has to be said Walt uttered one of the warmest there is on an early April day in 1889. When Horace happened to remark that baseball was "the hurrah game of the republic," Walt became "hilarious" and took off: "That's beautiful: the hurrah game! well—it's our game . . . America's game: has the snap, go, fling, of the American atmosphere—belongs as much to our institutions, fits into them as significantly, as our constitutions, laws: is just as important in the sum total of our historic life."

Horace also preserved Walt's wisdom about the nation's capital ("this is a stupid place compared to New York") and a wonderful aperçu about the kinds of people who rise to fame there: "The world goes daffy after phantom great men—the noisy epaulette sort." Indeed, it was precisely because General Grant's epaulettes were quiet that Whitman admired him so deeply. "Grant was the typical Western man: the plainest, the most efficient . . . most impressive in the severe simplicity of his flannel shirt and utter disregard for formal military etiquette." And his acerbic put-down of Benjamin Harrison could easily apply to a few later presidencies: "a little, snarling, pecking administration, with a big tuft of pretended dignity."

Important too are the countless comments on the "bottom-meanings" of *Leaves of Grass* and his various, often contradictory, sometimes faulty recollections about the writing and reception of its various editions. Some, as we have seen, must be taken with salt, as for instance his assertion that *Leaves* contains no "cocked and primed philosophy." Of course it does, as I hope the Annex will make clear—though the phrase, we have seen, should really be read as referring to sex play rather than gunplay. Nor, as I suggested in Chapter 2, is it possible to agree with Whitman's notion that there had been "no apologies, no dickers, no compromises" in the post-1860 editions of *Leaves*. One day he wisely remarked, "You can detach poems from the book and wonder why they were written. But if you see them in their place in the book you know why I wrote them." The irony, of course, was that often over the years Whitman himself had ripped poems from their obvious and life-giving contexts, leaving readers (surely, on occasion, intentionally) mystified about why he wrote them.

Other obiter dicta are tantalizingly ambiguous. When he expressed wonderment at "how much is put into *Leaves of Grass* that I never intended to be there," was he merely griping about the meretricious inventions of critics, or was he amazed that he had put *more of himself* in the poems than he had originally thought, thus driving the Symondses of the world to badger him so disconcertingly?

We also learn through Traubel that Whitman not only never gave formal readings of his poems but did not even recite them. WW: "You know I never read my own poems." HLT: "Or recite?" WW: "I don't recite because I don't know them. *Could* not recite." It is also revealed that Whitman held if not a philosophy of poetry then one of letters—and a highly characteristic one at that: "A letter is very subtle! Oh! The destiny of a letter should be well-marked from the first. . . . It may seem queer for me to have a philosophy of correspondence, but I have. And of course, *freedom* is the charm of a letter—it before all other qualities. And a letter without freedom certainly has nothing left to it." Clearly, the poet enjoyed the same freedom to say as he pleased in his conversations in his Mickle Street lair. And this freedom was not always agreeably enjoyed. Traubel records on 18 October 1891: "To W. the darkeys were 'a superstitious, ignorant, thievish race,' yet 'full of good nature, good heart,' too."

We must also be grateful to Traubel for knowledge of the many colorful remarks Whitman made about literary celebrities of his day. These remarks, both squelching and praiseful, are far more candid and illuminating than anything he would have ventured to publish. His put-downs of the more high-toned, traditional English authors are unsurprising yet often amusing. Convinced that Shakespeare (or whoever) "stood for the glory of feudalism," Whitman cast many an aspersion at the plays' "countless prolixities." "There is much in the plays that is offensive to me," he told Traubel one day, "forced, false phrasing: much of it. . . . I find myself often laughing over its sophistication." Decidedly not to his taste were Milton's blank verse ("turgid, heavy, over-stately") and Pope's rhymed couplets ("a machine—he wrote like a see-saw").

Thackeray, he said, "as a whole did not cast his sinker very deep." "I've tried Ruskin on every way but he don't fit," he confessed, and he struck out likewise with Arnold, "a man for whom I never seem to be able to get up any stir." On Dickens he was lukewarm; when a magazine reported the old poet's "greatest pleasure" to be rereading Dickens, Whitman chuckled, "That's news to me! I was a reader of Dickens from the first . . . but a dweller-upon, an enthuser, a make-mucher of, I never was—never—am not today. And you know, today I don't read him at all." Curiously, the European authors Whitman most regularly eulogized were Heine ("a genuinely great soul"), George Sand ("the brightest woman ever born" and her *Consuelo* "the greatest novel ever written"), Epictetus ("sacred, precious to me"), and Sir Walter Scott ("perennial . . . I can always go back to him and find him fresh").

Whitman's lifelong prejudices against the highly artificial or parlor-bound are also spicily evident in assessments of his American contemporaries. John Greenleaf Whittier, he thought, "has very few strings—very few—to his harp—only three or four—though, to be sure, these are pure and strong." Walt also pronounced him "a snivel" and a derivative one at that: "not a line he ever wrote or writes but is propped—leans up against something." Henry Wadsworth Longfellow was accurately summarized as one who "never broke new paths: in fact was a man who shrank from unusual things—from what was highly colored, dynamic, drastic."* Whitman told Traubel he was impressed "very favorably" by the presence of Poe when he met him ("dark, quiet, handsome . . . altogether ingratiating"), but he never cared for the way his "languid, tired out" demeanor was reflected in his fiction and verse.

Likewise, Hawthorne fared poorly—"I think he is monotonous, he wears me out: I do not read him with pleasure"—but not as poorly as the great American novelist and Closet Queen: "James is only feathers to me." As for lesser lights on the literary scene like William Dean Howells and Thomas Bailey Aldrich: "I have met and like them . . . but they are *thin*—no weight." Whitman adds the lovely phrase "they run a few temporary errands but they are not out for immortal service."

Immortal service was impossible for anyone who had been, as he put it, "stung by that respectability bee." Whitman felt that such service had been done in America mainly by Emerson and Thoreau. His public pose with them was always one of unmitigated praise, especially with the Sage of Concord. There are many encomiastic outbursts in Traubel's pages, Whitman calling Emerson's personality, for instance, "the most nearly perfect I ever came in contact with," or explaining one Christmas Eve that Thoreau remained close to him because of "his lawlessness—his dissent—his going his own absolute road let hell blaze all it chooses."

But fascinating and revealing indeed are the few occasions when Whitman, in private with Horace, hedged his praise. There is a splendid glimpse, for instance, of the tension created by Whitman's sexual radicalism of the 1850s when he reminisced about the two repressed New Englanders, "I did think that Thoreau and Emerson, both of them, years ago, in the Brooklyn days, were a little bookish in their expression of love." Whitman once described, quite wonderfully, the kinds of men he favored as "salient men—the men of elements—oxygenated men; the fellers who come and go like storms," and Thoreau and Emerson were decidedly not of this ilk. Several of Whitman's perceptive observations make this clear. "Emerson was always for poise," he said one day, "was almost poised to death sometimes." Though Walt hated to "allow anything that qualifies Emerson," he was still willing to tell Horace that he felt him "some ways rather of thin blood," that "his faculty was passive," and that he was "somewhat thin on the physiological side."

As between Emerson and Thoreau, Whitman said his "prejudices" were "all with Emerson," and perhaps the best explanation for this was something said in passing to Traubel in Mickle Street: "Thoreau's great fault was disdain—disdain for men (Tom, Dick and Harry): inability to appreciate the average life." As we have seen, a lifetime of pursuing the affections of average young men (Fred, Pete, and Harry, to be specific) lay behind this devastating remark.

WE *LOVE* YOU

Some of the most poignant moments preserved in *With Walt Whitman* are not specially pertinent to Whitman's "passional" life, yet irresistible. Had Horace not been so sharp-eyed, for instance, this wonderful vignette of Walt entering Morgan's Hall in Camden for his seventieth birthday dinner would have been lost: "How many saw the negro cook there in the hallway rush up to him to embrace and shake his hands? He had nursed her husband in the hospital at Washington." (Whitman told Traubel afterward that he had not shrunk from attending soldiers in black-only and venereal hospitals.) Nor would we know now of the black man who came to Mickle Street with remarkable praise. "A Negro came in the other day, an educated man: very simple: very black skin: he was a reader of *Leaves of Grass*: said: 'You will be of great use to our race.' " Somehow very moving, too, if one thinks back to the extremely "palpable" poetic voice of the early Whitman (and Alboni's palpable contralto), is Walt's explanation when Horace asked why he liked to hear old letters read aloud: "There are two reasons—1st, I like to hear your voice: 2nd, I like to hear these letters back in the voice of another . . . I like to read them in a palpable voice." And what reader can go unmoved by Traubel's report of the Sunday afternoon Whitman preferred not to hear an old letter palpably voiced, the day he chose to relinquish the last words from his mother sixteen years before:

> I took out the little sheet and read what was on it in trembling let-ters. I could not say anything. I put it back, holding it irresolutely in my hand: "Yes: I wished you to take it: it is safer in your hands than in mine." He was very grave. I still said nothing. "I was afraid you would ask me something about it," he said, chokingly. I kissed him good night and left. This was his mother's message: "farewell my beloved sons farewell I have lived beyond all comfort in this world dont mourn for me my beloved sons and daughters farewell my dear beloved Walter."

Many passages in *With Walt Whitman*—some as moving as this, others merely hilarious or charming—are, unlike the foregoing, very pertinent to Whitman's sexuality and to the affectional tastes, habits of mind, and experiences that have mainly concerned me here. Dozens of passages have already been cited in the preceding chapters, but a few others not mentioned hitherto deserve our notice here.

The mention of Whitman's dearly beloved mother, for example, calls to mind several illuminating comments Whitman made to Traubel about his family. He was a devoted (and very generous) son, brother, and uncle, but he clearly experienced most of his life a deep sense of spiritual isola-tion from his family. Amid so unprepossessing and down-to-earth a family as his, being not merely a poet but a homosexual must have encouraged this sense of apartness. Talk turned one day on the fact that

Whitman's father died too soon to read *Leaves of Grass*, for example, and Horace asked if "not one in the bunch" of his relatives was "in touch with what you have written." Walt replied, "Not one of them, from my dear mother down—not one of them: on the contrary, they are dead set against my book and what it stands for." On another occasion he said of his mother, "She stood before *Leaves of Grass* mystified, defeated," and he discouraged Horace from inviting his brother George to his 1889 testimonial dinner: "neither he nor any member of my family knows or cares anything about my literary work, fame."

When a mystifying early photograph of Whitman, from his New York days, turned up, Horace wondered if a family member could help to date it. The response, one cannot help feeling, could be spoken by many a homosexual who has chosen not to burden his family with knowledge of the realities of his private life: "My family know nothing at all: not one of them." Indeed, it is remarkable and probably telling that, among the 130 surviving photographs of the camera-adoring poet, there is not a single one taken of him and a parent or sibling. Traubel's narrative of Walt's burial day provides a perfect coda to the saga of his family's indifference to his achievement. "After the funeral, at 328 [Mickle Street], Bucke standing in the hall with George Whitman, called me. 'Listen, Horace, what do you think George is saying?' I found George incredulous as to the great applause greeting his brother today."

Revealingly contrasted with Whitman's coolness toward his Camden brother George, who is almost nonexistent in Traubel's pages, was his lavish affection for Horace himself. There are countless small hints of the sort of intimacy one associates with cohabiting lovers—lovers so familiar that they can anticipate, needle, joke with, and contradict each other quite freely. Whitman often teased Horace, for instance, about his hoarding instincts, and one day showed him an envelope with "from Ellen Terry" written on it. "He regarded me with a whimsical eye: 'You have a hungry look: I think you want the letter. Well—take it along. You seem to cultivate that hungry look: it is a species of pantalooned coquetry.'" Unfazed, Traubel pocketed the letter.

Horace had freedom of the house and sometimes entered the upstairs lair silently. Once Whitman joked when he saw him, "Well—you are my ghostly visitor! If I was in the theatrical business and needed a ghost, I would hire you." Horace asked, "Do I look like one?" "No indeed: it's all in the footstep!" On another occasion, Horace interrupted Whitman and Mrs. Davis, and the former said, "We were just telling each other about you." "Telling *what*?" Traubel asked, but Walt "only laughed—in a way to say, I guess I won't tell."

The two were also close enough to be candid or challenging with each other. Horace reminded Walt one day, "Once you said I was a damn fool—would never know how to write," and the old man charmingly got out of it: "Well, I was a damn fool to say it: I can't imagine what could have tantalized me into such an outburst. You're still a pretty green pippen but you'll ripen." (Perusal of *Optimos*, a volume of Traubel's poetry, reveals that Walt's initial view was accurate.) Horace could hold his own, too. One day he said, with justice, "I don't have any sycophantic regard for you. I don't worship the ground you tread on or kiss the hem of your garment or discover something oracular in everything you say." Some of their differences were amusingly minor, as when Walt growled about Dr. Bucke's handwriting ("It's all in up and down angles—sharp, like his voice") and Horace said he had no trouble with it at all. "W. smiled and replied: 'That's right—contradict me.' " But other incursions by Horace were more momentous and probing.

One day, for example, the first draft of "O Captain! My Captain!" from 1865 appeared amid the clutter and it was handed over. To Whitman's dismay the poem had become a verse chestnut, and he didn't half mind Traubel's low opinion of it. "You don't like the poem anyway," he challenged one day, and Traubel explained fearlessly, "I think it clumsy: you tried too hard to make it what you shouldn't have tried to make it at all—and what you didn't succeed in making it in the end." We are told "W. laughed and responded: 'You're more than half right.' " On another occasion Traubel seems to have tired of a theme Whitman often harped on and asked, "Walt, don't you sometimes put that American neglect [of Whitman] business a bit too strong?" They debated the point and Whitman was forced to admit, "That's a new point of view. . . . You're driving me hard along an unusual track."

A hilarious talk on a Friday evening in January 1889 found Walt getting "quizzy" and defensive when Horace needled him about his early unsigned reviews: "Walt, some people think you blew your own horn a lot—wrote puffs on yourself—sort of attitudinized and called attention to yourself quite a bit." The next month, feeling particularly feisty, Traubel ragged Whitman for exaggerating the sales of the 1855 *Leaves* in a letter to Emerson and calling him "master," a word Whitman later professed to hate. This lively and revealing colloquy ensued:

I laughed rather heartily. W. asked me why. I said: "I was wondering whether you were not bluffing Emerson." "You mean bragging? Well—maybe there was something of that sort in it." I said: "I can't forget either, that in that same letter you call Emerson 'master.'

Now you repudiate the word. What did you mean by it then?" He answered: "They were salad days: I had many undeveloped angles at that time: I don't imagine I was guiltless: someone had to speak for me: no one would: I spoke for myself." I said: "You didn't need to play Emerson: he was on your side without it." W. said in a fiery voice: "Who the hell talked about playing anybody?" I said: "You haven't made out a very good case for 'master' and 'readily sold.' I believe what you say because you say it but it hardly sounds plausible to me." "Do you mean to say I'm a liar?" "No: I only mean to say I'd like to know the real reason for 'readily sold' and 'master.' " He ended the quiz half petulantly, half jocularly . . .

Only very close friends—true lovers—could go at it like this and keep their affection intact.

In addition to such splendid evidence of Traubel's invigorating intellectual stimulation, the pages of *With Walt Whitman* offer many, though more fleeting, glimpses of Walt's relationships with his young male nurses. These show that the Whitman of Chapter 3 remained his old self to the very end. The nurse on hand when the conversations begin was a W. A. Musgrove. Horace noticed that he rubbed Walt "the wrong way" and was discouraged from physical contact—was not asked to "curry" or "pummel" (i.e. massage) Whitman. A comradely first name was never conferred on him, either. Then in November 1888 came the splendid Ed Wilkins down from Canada on Dr. Bucke's recommendation. Traubel, on meeting Wilkins for the first time, described him as "tall, young, ruddy, dynamic" and noticed how (no surprise here) "W. regarded him approvingly." Three days later we learn that Walt "takes to Ed. Calls him 'brawny—a powerful ally.' His first lament over Musgrove was his last."

Walt himself was downright effusive. "Ed is very stalwart—handled me well—helped me with the currying. . . . I am coming to see that he is just the man I needed: he is my kind: he is young, strong: I felt immediate wholesome invigorating reactions under the spur of his treatment: he gives me a sort of massage . . ." A week later Whitman refined upon this praise. "I like him. I wrote the Doctor so: he is just what he seems to be— straightforward, not inquisitive, hearty—best of all he is not intrusive: he does not push himself upon me, does not insist." Horace, for his part, observed that Whitman showed Ed "various little confidences and attentions." On Christmas Day, after Ed had been on hand for two months and Horace remarked that the new nurse suited him "to a T." Walt offered up this splendid homage: "Yes: he is vital, easy, nonchalant, self-sufficient (in the right sense): he throws out a sort of sane atmosphere: I always find myself at home, at peace with him." Dr. Bucke was delighted that his nomination had worked out so well. "I am real glad you seem pleased with Ed. W. I knew he would suit you . . . he is just what he looks—a good, simple minded, quiet, honest country boy—just the kind you like."

Soon, as Horace observed, Walt was allowing Ed to "help him more than usual nowadays," doubtless because our touching poet had found the perfectly sympathetic helper. "Ed is well fit in many ways," Walt said, but mainly because he had "one quality significant above all, essential—the quality of touch: has a touch which the patient likes." In addition to humoring Ed's musical pastimes (he took a violin lesson weekly), Walt showed him other kindnesses. In the summer he treated him to his first opera, with Horace as his escort. He had hoped Ed would catch one of his own old favorites, Balfe's *Bohemian Girl* or Auber's *Fra Diavolo*, but in the event they saw *The Chimes of Normandy*. A few months later Walt paid for a second trip, to see *Fra Diavolo*. Now and then he joked with Ed. When Horace noticed Ed's new haircut, Walt remarked in his hearing, "Yes, Eddy has been and had his picture taken—had to spruce up: the boy is a little like the women: they will fix up, whatever is said: if they have jewelry on it must go."

This amiable routine was to last not quite a year. On 19 September 1889, Wilkins said he would walk Horace down to the ferry dock. "On the way he told me of his resolve to go back to Canada Oct. 20. Had engaged with a veterinary surgeon to go with him on that date. This rather staggered me, as experience has shown how difficult it is to get a nurse for W. who combines qualities we desire." Three weeks later Ed screwed up the courage to tell Whitman. Traubel wrote on October ninth, "Ed has finally decided to go. Has spoken to W. about it. W. is 'adverse to change'— greatly likes Ed—but would not advise him to risk his future, if it was risked, as it seemed to be, by staying." There was some puzzlement in Mickle Street over why Ed would want to return to "a less than a quarter of a horse town" in Canada, but away he went . . . eventually to become a veterinarian himself with long years of practice near Indianapolis.

On 21 October Traubel recorded he had "today engaged Warren Fritzinger to take Ed's place" and that Whitman was "well pleased." Warrie, a neighborhood man in his mid-twenties whom Mrs. Davis had taken under her wing, had been an occasional and appealing presence in Mickle Street for some time. "I like him very much," Whitman had told Horace more than a year before; "he is such a lusty fellow—has been about the world so much—is a sailor." He enjoyed Warrie's sea tales, his affection (he always kissed the old man on departing), and sometimes just the sight of him. Walt had many months earlier asked Mrs. Davis to send him

Walt Whitman at the Camden, New Jersey, docks with his male nurse, Warren Fritzinger in 1890. Photograph by John Johnston, a visiting English admirer who published Diary Notes of a Visit to Walt Whitman and Some of His Friends *in 1898. The Library of Congress.*

upstairs, telling Horace before he appeared, "I like to look at him—he is health to look at: young, strong, lithe."

Just two days into Warrie's professional engagement Walt was ready to declare him an ideal replacement for Ed. "Warrie and I come to understand each other pretty well—*very* well. I like his touch and he is strong, a font of bodily power." He was especially enthusiastic about his "touch," explaining that Warrie "has that wonderful indescribable combination—rarely found, precious when found—which, with great manly strength, unites sweet delicacy, soft as a woman's." The next month Walt told an inquirer after his health that he felt better, in part because he had a good nurse. "I am under what they call a sort of massage treatment—Warrie rubs me every day—or twice a day—pummels me—and here I am!"

Finally, though, for my purposes the Traubel volumes are most valuable—indeed, often affecting—when they find Whitman alluding to his gay past or when they suggest something about the gay subculture of his day. "I like you to know just how our crowd got along in those old days of battle," he once told Horace, and that marginalized, embattled "crowd" of his was in part a homosexual one. Now and then, we have already seen, members of this "crowd" paid their respects at Mickle Street.

Consider, for instance, the mid-August morning in 1888 when an actor from his old Manhattan stomping grounds named Nestor Lennon sent up his card and was admitted. Was there then, as now, a large gay contingent among the American theatrical community? And was this why Whitman would acknowledge to Lennon a special affinity for male members of the profession? "I have a weakness for actors—they seem to have a weakness for me: that makes our meetings rather like family affairs." I would like to think so, for here is the suddenly moving scene that unfolded after ten minutes of casual chat and the dispensation of three autographs:

> When Lennon got up to go he cleared his throat, hitched his trousers, scratched his head, and blurted out to W. as if it was a hard job to get his message delivered right: "Mr. Whitman, do you need money? I've been delegated to ask you whether you need money. I know a hundred actors in places about and in New York who would like to get together and give you a benefit." W. was visibly touched. He frankly offered Lennon his hand and said with a voice that was shaken with emotion: "God bless you—God bless you all—for that! I have enough money, more than enough, for all my earthly wants, so I need not acquiesce in your beautiful plans: but you make me happy, nevertheless. I shall feed on your good will for many a day to

come. Tell all the boys what I have said to you about that—give them my love."

As the actor was leaving, Walt mentioned how much English theatrical people liked him, and Lennon, not to be outdone, replied, "Yes, I know, Mr. Whitman: they like you, no doubt—*like* you: but we—we *love* you." After Lennon disappeared, Walt said, "Did you notice how he set his American *love* up against the English *like*? It was very pretty, Horace . . . it took me unawares—almost bowled me over." It is very tempting to think he was bowled over because, though unspoken, he saw in the gesture an expression of solidarity from those of his real—his homosocial—family.

Many a passing and often rather vague remark caught by Traubel causes one to drift into similar tantalizing speculation. In the fall of 1889, for instance, Whitman fell into a retrospective mood and observed that "one's life is not always the thing it is supposed to be—has its periods and periods—dark, light, dark again—spots, errors, damned foolishnesses. Looking back over my own time—looking into the period starting with '61–'62—I have nothing to regret, nothing to wish reversed." In choosing those years, one is bound to wonder, was Whitman in effect confessing that his traumatic love affair(s) and promiscuity of the 1850s, and the superb poetry they evoked, now seemed to him "damned foolishnesses"? Or was he thinking of the great, tragic "loss" of that time, circa 1859–60, which was the last thing in his life he would "wish reversed"?

Sometimes a single word leaps out from the casual dialogue with special resonance: "I was bred in Brooklyn: initiated to all the mysteries of city life—populations, perturbations: knew the rough elements—what they stood for: what might be apprehended from them." That *perturbations* takes us vividly back to the perturbations he had desperately tried to exorcize in 1870, but the context also suggests that Whitman still associated his Brooklyn and Broadway years with the mystery of emotional and sexual perturbation that came with apprehending what the "rough elements" of the city stood for.

But no moment in *With Walt Whitman in Camden* captures better the homoerotic drive that lay underneath the poet's sometimes impassive, sometimes ebullient surface—or, indeed, explains better what made Traubel such a dedicated helpmate—than the day Whitman suddenly said, "You are doing much too much for me nowadays. What can I do for you?" Traubel replied, "I am not doing anything for you. I am doing everything for myself." At this, Traubel recorded, "W. looked at me fixedly for a moment. Then he reached forward and took my hand."

What he then said speaks volumes about all the "adhesive," emotional enrichment that his lifetime of associating with "rough elements" and dying Civil War soldiers had given him. It is also the perfect exit line from this excursion behind the arras in Mickle Street. "I see what you mean, Horace. That is the right way to look at it. People used to say to me: Walt, you are doing miracles for those fellows in the hospitals. I wasn't. I was, as you would say, doing miracles for myself."

The miracles Traubel performed in the last six months of Whitman's life have only recently come to light, with the publication—incredibly, over a century after the fact—of the ninth and last volume of the transcribed conversations. His dedication was so boundless, indeed, that various Whitman intimates, especially those in England, began to warn him regularly to husband his energies and not to compromise his own health in serving Walt. These warnings were largely ignored. On but two days did he fail to see Whitman during this time, and sometimes he paid as many as four visits in a day. In January of 1892, in addition to the daily late-night transcription, he began answering Whitman's mail in bulk. On 21 January he noted, "I suppose 15 or 20 letters in all today," and four days later, "Wrote 15 or 20 letters between times at the Bank." A month later: "My letter-writing is assuming enormous proportions, but I must stick to it."

Traubel was undoubtedly dominant among the triumvirate (Tom Harned and Dr. Bucke being his colleagues) that supervised Whitman's welfare. "Our affairs belong, after me, to you," Whitman told him two months before he died and just a month before he told him succinctly and accurately, "You are our next necessary self."

The millions of words of conversation, though, will finally be Traubel's great legacy. While Whitman must have been conscious that they were being produced (the furious jotting could not possibly have been surreptitious), Traubel did make some pretense of secrecy about the project. We know this from the occasion when Traubel's wife carelessly revealed his modus operandi to a visiting Englishman, James Wallace. Wallace had himself attempted to record some of Walt's table talk verbatim for a circle of Whitmanites in Lancashire. Traubel wrote later: "Curiously—at tea—Wallace said, 'I read some of my notes to Mrs. Traubel and she thinks they are quite like Walt, I believe. But she tells me also, that you are doing the same sort of work, and have been for a long time.' I instantly perceived that Anne had left the cat out, so owned up." He apparently then allowed Wallace a glimpse at his mountain of notes. It is hilarious to picture the scene, about which Horace remarked: "Wallace seemed rather aghast by the extent of my accumulations."

A LAST EMBRACE

That this most stupendous "oral history" project in all of American letters was born of genuine and profound love is revealed on countless occasions, but never more powerfully and dramatically than in what might be
called the "deathbed" volume of *With Walt Whitman in Camden*, which
allows us to be with the poet in what he called the "night-coming time of
my life." The moments of kissing and parting are particularly emotion-
laden. On the last Christmas: "I reached over and kissed him. I could feel
his responding lips." On January sixth: "I leaned over and kissed him—
and felt his lips reach for mine. 'God bless you, boy—God bless your
blessings!' And then I kissed his hand." The next night, Horace tiptoes
in and gazes for a while in the light of a faint fire.

> "Is that you, Horace?"—and I knew I was recognized. I went over to
> the bed—kissed him—sat down on bed. Our hands were clasped
> during the whole of the talk, and I knew it was with genuine love he
> pressed mine time and again. . . . His loving warmth almost astonished
> me . . . and once with almost a passion he cried, in a whisper, "Dear,
> dear, dear, dear boy—we all love you!"—in such a tone as drew all my
> life together into one sense of recognition and response.

If Horace had taken seriously Walt's remark several months earlier—"I
am not a demonstrable being, even to my intimate friends. . . . It is not a
part of me: demonstration"—one can understand his astonishment.

Just days before Whitman died, the intimate scene was replayed:

> "I have gone down and down—as if resistlessly, hopelessly, inexorably,
> pressed. Oh! Horace, it is the *feeling of death*." Uttered calmly and
> sweetly, with no tone of complaint. The voice very weak, however.
> When I felt my time was up, I left the one side of the bed and walked
> about to the other, taking his hand and leaning over and kissing
> him—kissing both lips and forehead. I whispered [to] him, "Dear
> Walt, you do not realize what you have been to us!" And he whispered
> me back, "Nor you what you have been to me!" My eyes filled with
> tears. I kissed his hands—his eyes opened an instant—looked [at] me
> [with] ineffable love. I hurried off—wiped the tears away—turned
> down the light—passed into the other room.

One week later Horace records: "Every word a struggle. And again I
kissed him, and heard him say, 'Bless—bless.' Coughed—choked—

breathed heavily. I turned as I reached the door. His eyes opened. He smiled. That smile! And after I had gone I had yet to go back. Again to see him, to have his smile."

Then, with Whitman's last breath at 6:43 on Saturday evening, 26 March 1892, a remarkable epiphany: "The heart was still! No contortion, no struggle, no physical regret—and the eyes closed of themselves and the body made none of the usual motions towards stiffening out—towards rigidity. By and by [Dr.] McAlister and I together laid him decently and reverently straight. I laid his hand quietly down—something in my heart seemed to snap and that moment commenced my new life—a luminous conviction lifting me with him into the eternal."

But Traubel being his always eminently practical self, this epiphany did not prevent him from then coolly seeing that news of the death was announced. "The bulletin at door effected. I escape reporters entirely. The end so uneventful—so simple, quiet—so without dressings and puerilities—a simple few words will tell all." He also called in the undertaker, supervised the making of plaster casts of the head and hand, and informed the pallbearers and funeral speakers (among them, to the dismay of many stung by the respectability bee, the fiery Colonel Ingersoll). He also succeeded in overriding George Whitman's objections to the autopsy Walt had expressly asked for. He did not even flinch from attending the gruesome four-hour affair, during which the brain was extracted. "To hear the claw and dip of their instruments—to see the skull broken and opened and the body given the ravening prey of the investigator had its horrors—then its compensations. I looked beyond and saw science, man, with benediction sweet." That last phrase is splendidly Whitmanesque.

Burroughs was with Traubel when, in Mickle Street on 30 March, the coffin was closed for the last time. "Burroughs wept—and I?—yes, I wept, too—for somehow even this dead form reached up to me, as if for a last embrace, and I held it in my arms long and long and pressed it with a passion of love. . . . And as we stood there together, I heard the lid drop, the door closed, the face forever shut out, the new life begun."

WALT & ME:
AN AFTERWORD

O adhesiveness! O pulse of my life!
—Calamus #6

Autobiography, said Horace Traubel, is the only real biography. And Walt agreed.*

This notion, however, has discomfited many who have tried to pull Whitman's beard and find the "real critter." One such was the English critic Edmund Gosse, who began to find disagreeable the constant invitation to see himself in all the flamboyance of *Leaves of Grass*. He expressed his frustration over this unpleasant self-referential sensation in an essay that appeared a year after Whitman died, employing an elaborate image drawn from microbiology. "There is no real Walt Whitman. . . . Whitman is mere *bathybius*; he is literature in the condition of protoplasm—an intellectual organism so simple that it takes the instant impression of whatever mood approaches it. Hence the critic who touches Whitman is immediately confronted with his own image stamped upon that viscid and tenacious surface. He finds not what Whitman has to give, but what he himself has brought." Whitman, being a joyous contrarian, might have taken this as praise, but Gosse certainly did not intend it that way. No wonder Gosse, a very discreet, English-style homosexual and thoroughgoing literary aristocrat (he was librarian to the House of Lords for a decade), found far more agreeable the novels and personal friendship of that closeted Anglophile Henry James, who was "only feathers" to Whitman.

Still, Gosse's warning is salutary: one must always try to be conscious of the distinction between what the biographical subject "has to give" and what the biographer "has brought," even if, in some of the most provocative life-writing, the distinction blurs. My interest in writing about Whitman, I recognize now that I have done so, has often been driven by what I have brought to his "tenacious" surface. (On "viscid" I beg to differ with Gosse: semen, that most Whitmanesque of bodily fluids, is not viscid.) And I am by no means unhappy, like Gosse, that this has happened. Rather, I am of the mind of Ann Douglas, who recently published *Terrible Honesty*, a study of culture in 1920s Mannahatta that touched on many matters of autobiographical consequence for her. She remarked later, in an interview about her work, "I can't see doing a book that isn't all tied up with who you are." Nor did she offer any excuse for being "drawn to people who will allow you, by telling their story as honestly and objectively as you can, to also be expressing yourself."

Whether my narrative "honestly" reflects the evidence I have marshaled in the preceding chapters, it is my reader's business to decide. As to "objectively," however, I am much less sanguine than Douglas. Indeed, I am nearly careless, for I believe about life-writing what Bernard Shaw believed about music criticism: "there is no more dishonest and insufferable affectation in criticism than the impersonal, abstract, judicially authoritative air." I now see clearly that I have written a biography, in Douglas's phrase, all tied up with who I am . . . or have been. And so I hope it will be worthwhile, here in this afterword, to describe some of the ways my *Walt Whitman* veers into autobiography—sometimes uncannily, sometimes amusingly, now and then (for me) very poignantly. Shaw, an unsinkable self-singer of Whitmanesque proportions, also asserted, "The critic who cannot interest the public in his real self has mistaken his trade." One might think biography the least likely genre for a writer concerned to interest the reader in his "real self," but there is, with Whitman, something irresistibly apropos in such a paradox. Under the cover of exploring the "real Me" of Walt Whitman, I have also been adumbrating the real me, and the following pages lay out some of the more striking instances in which I experienced Whitman's gay life as a premonition of my own.

           ❧   ❧   ❧

This book began very specifically, in fact, one afternoon when the real me was sauntering down Broadway in Manhattan, as was Whitman's happy wont. I was passing along the west side of his beloved thoroughfare between Seventy-second and Seventy-third Streets when—under the brooding brow of Giuseppe Verdi, whose statue stands across the street in Verdi Square—I happened upon some old books laid out on the pavement for sale. A battered paperback caught my eye: *Walt Whitman and Opera*. I was intrigued.

Opera was the great artistic love of my life. I had been writing about it for many years, with special emphasis on the relationships between music and literature. My *Literature as Opera* appeared in 1977, followed by *Shakespeare and Opera* in 1990, and for several years I had been a contributor and correspondent for *Opera News* magazine. I also wrote about and occasionally lectured on opera in many other places. For Whitman, on the other hand, I had until then shown no particular affection. I still have the paperback facsimile of the 1855 edition of *Leaves of Grass* I used to study for my doctoral qualifying examination in English, and my marginalia suggest minimal engagement with his poetry. As one might expect of a panicky graduate student with well over a hundred major titles on his reading list, my main worry was to out-Forster E. M. and "only connect." Thus I found one passage very "Blake," another very "Wordsworthian." The line "You splash in the water there, yet stay stock still in your room" from "Song of Myself" struck me in the early 1970s as "very Emily Dickinson." But then, I had not yet come out to myself or anyone else, and so I missed the fine homoerotic undertow of the aquatic "twenty-eight young men" passage in which this line appears. Shakespeare and English Renaissance literature were then my main interests, so when I came to Whitman's line "any thing is but a part" I naturally remarked (thinking of the "No man is an island" sermon) that this was "a very Donnian perception." *Leaves of Grass*, like *Beowulf*, *Middlemarch*, or *The Sound and the Fury*, was bound to seem but one more title to "do" and tick off my reading list. And my graduate studies were being done at Stanford University, where the influence of the recently retired Yvor Winters, a famed poet, curmudgeon, and Whitman basher, was still strong. So Whitman was far from *de rigueur*.*

Meanwhile, back on the million-footed Broadway pavement, my interest in Whitman was momentarily and serendipitously kindled. I dug out a dollar and took home with me Robert Faner's 1951 study of Whitman the opera buff. It went unread for several months until, also by pure happenstance, I noticed a little room on the first floor of Columbia University's Butler Library with the sign "Book Sale" next to the entrance. Here books declared "withdrawn from circulation" were on sale for a few dollars, and, as always when an array of used books heaves into view, I had to have a look around. The thick and informative 1949 Inner Sanctum edition of *The Poetry and Prose of Walt Whitman* published by Simon and Schuster was on offer and, remembering that Faner's book still called for my attention, I became for the first time the owner of a more or less complete volume of Whitman. Miraculously, the margins of the battered book were nearly free of student graffiti. They now awaited my own.

The synergy of the two Whitman books on my shelf soon spurred me to action. Faner's study proved to be an eye-opening and very extensive one, laying out with admirable comprehensiveness Whitman's immersion in opera. The table of 206 musical terms in the poetry—from "accompaniment" to "war-drum"—was impressive, as was his tallying of the 13 operas mentioned in *Leaves of Grass* and the 117 times "sing" and the 154 times "song" occur in its pages. But something, I slowly began to sense as I finished the book, seemed to be missing. For all the valuable (Walt would have called it "processional") information assembled by Faner, the heart of the matter, the "final lilt" of opera's effect on the poet, was not being captured.

And that started me thinking.

One problem, of course, was that Faner wrote his book just prior to the spectacular reawakening of interest in the Italian bel canto repertory, which was the kind of opera Whitman attended and loved almost exclusively. Of the superb European singers who appeared in America in Walt's operagoing heyday, Faner wrote: "For these voices, as great as the world has ever known, there were available perfect vehicles like *Norma*, which today only the greatest vocalists dare approach, and *La Cenerentola*, which singers of today can no longer encompass." Faner could not have been aware that, as he wrote these words, the conductor Vittorio Gui was leading a pivotal revival of *Cenerentola* (one of Marietta Alboni's greatest triumphs) at Glyndebourne, inaugurating an extensive revival over the next twenty years of the Rossini repertory and eventually the Donizetti, Bellini, and early Verdi repertory as well. *Cenerentola*, the opera Faner found lost for lack of executants in 1950, is now available in at least *nine* different compact disc versions recorded since then. Surely our current vivid familiarity with live and recorded performances of the repertory that thrilled Whitman gives us an enormous advantage over Faner as we attempt to reimagine the poet's experience of opera.

The other—and obviously to me more significant—problem with Faner's book was that, unsurprisingly, he did not raise the issue of the relationship between Whitman's devotion to opera and his sexuality. And here autobiography came remarkably into play. Faner, of course, frequently mentions the great Alboni, and it gradually began to dawn on me that the inception of my own opera-loving experience had centered upon a singer almost exactly like Alboni, the thrilling Pennsylvanian mezzo-soprano Marilyn Horne.

It has been ventured that the modern revival of the florid bel canto repertory began in Los Angeles on 29 January 1964, when Horne, in the company of Joan Sutherland, sang for the first time the role of Arsace in

Rossini's *Semiramide* (another triumphant Alboni role).* Over the next decades she became a supreme exponent of many famed Alboni roles that had vanished from the stage over the preceding century: roles like Rossini's Tancredi, Malcolm in *La Donna del Lago*, and Isabella in *L'Italiana in Algeri*; Meyerbeer's acrobatic Fidès (*Le Prophète*) and Urbain (*Les Huguenots*); and Donizetti's Leonora (*La Favorita*) and Orsini (*Lucrezia Borgia*). Horne, it happens, was just about the first singer to bowl me over. Her flabbergasting dexterity and rich, manly (pardon the Whitmanism) timbre in *Non più mesta* and *Eccomi alfine in Babilonia* were on her early *Presenting Marilyn Horne*, the first recital disk I ever owned.

Inevitably, Whitman's praise for Alboni began to take on a peculiarly affecting force for me. The two singers appear to have had much in common. The description of Horne in the *Metropolitan Opera Encyclopedia* (which I happen to have authored) exactly mirrors the acclaim Alboni received from her New York critics, which we sampled in Chapter 1: "Horne's singing is distinguished by ebullient temperament, sound musicianship, and her extraordinary command of a flexible, wide-ranging mezzo." Like Alboni too, Horne's spirited personality had to overcome a lack of conventional beauty. Théophile Gautier's amusing euphemism about Alboni's "athletic and triumphant body" also applied to the stout, foursquare Horne. No wonder they were both successful in the male drag of several pants roles. One laughs at the mere thought of Alboni singing Zerlina, though she did. And Horne sang Carmen, gorgeously, but a fiery sexual terminator she most certainly was not.

But conventional feminine beauty, of course, was beside the point for Whitman, as it was for me. Thus he was able to say of his Marietta, "some thought her fat—*we* always thought her beautiful." That "*we*" was spoken like a true gay camerado of the family circle or the standees' line. It is also very much in the vein of gay Horne devotees I have known, who commonly employed a highly un-PC phrase for expressing awe at her brawny low G's and A's. Surely, the tour-de-force "Turkish delight" divertissement in *Ghosts of Versailles*, an opera that premiered at the Met in 1991, was written for Horne by the gay composer John Corigliano and the gay librettist William Hoffman in homage to her, as she approached career's end, for long and deeply appreciated service to opera queendom. In it she certainly radiated precisely the amiable, nonchalant, one-of-the-boys stage presence that critics were always remarking upon in Alboni's performances.

Thus, in thinking about how Alboni might have affected Whitman's successful discovery of his voice in the crucial years before the debut of *Leaves of Grass*, I found myself also pondering the, to me, still mysterious ways my early vocal "courtship" of Horne—and certain other singers, most especially the phenomenal Montserrat Caballé (who towered over Wayne Koestenbaum's beloved Anna Moffo just as Mozart towered, Shaw said, over the "infinitesimal" Grieg)—was intertwined with and, eventually, eased my emergence into a cognizant, active, and fulfilling gay life.

One particular aspect of Whitman's operatic experience also resonated very strongly with my own. Several years before I happened on *Walt Whitman and Opera*, a change had begun to occur in me so imperceptible that I had not yet really thought about it, let alone verbalized it: my interest in opera was waning. Maybe even my love for it was waning. It is possible that having to report, on a regular basis for seven or eight years, on relentlessly routine performances at the Met was eroding my verve. I turned ashen whenever I noticed the huge price printed on my reviewer's tickets, considering what was being delivered and how I would feel if I had to *pay* such a sum for the paltry fare. Perhaps, I also began to speculate, this was like any passionate, transporting, salad-days affair—impossible to sustain, it was now burning inevitably down to embers. Or was it, more generally, merely a midlife crisis thing? Then I also began to fear, horribly and mortifyingly, that I was beginning to sound like the grumpy old men who used to exasperate me years ago with coloratura sighing about "the singers in *my* day . . . *they* were the real thing!"

Or just maybe, glorious though the music is, I had, after the twelfth or twentieth outing with *Butterfly*, *Trovatore*, or *Tosca*, finally plumbed the shallows of human and theatrical interest. Several familiar operas were now getting slapped on my "never, *ever* again" list: *Samson et Dalila*, *Faust*, *Fanciulla*, *Werther*; also the once sacrosanct *Parsifal* (I delighted in a friend's proposal for an ideal way to attend this endless work: one act a year for three years). And others are getting shockingly close to following them: *Die Zauberflöte*, *Cav* (though not *Pag*), *La Bohème*, *Fidelio*, *Billy Budd*, *Turandot*, even *Carmen*, for heaven's sake. In fact, the last time I attended a *Carmen* and a *Zauberflöte* my not entirely unlibidinous purpose was, in each case, to take a new boyfriend who was utterly innocent of opera. My vicarious (voyeuristic?) pleasure in the new experience of my companion considerably exceeded my interest in the tired old plots and so-so singing. Recently, I threw caution to the winds and took an Octavian of mine to see *Der Rosenkavalier*, the great opera about aging gracefully. Never have I so identified with the Marschallin's wistful, "Ja, ja" at the end of the opera about "the young people" going their way.

When I was rotated off duty as a reviewer, the timing could not have been better. I haven't darkened the Met's door for a regular performance in several years and feel not the slightest sense of deprivation. The last time I felt moved to record a Saturday afternoon broadcast from the Met (once a common event), it was out of nostalgia worthy of Walt's memories of Alboni: Marilyn Horne, sounding almost exactly as glorious as she had a quarter-century before, was singing Arsace again in a revival of *Semiramide*. I never tire of hearing all the "brava's" that rained down after her *Eccomi alfine in Babilonia* aria.

This strange sea change in my opera queenery was beginning to seriously disconcert me as Whitman turned into more than a passing interest. I was therefore fascinated to discover that opera loosened its love-grip on him as well in his later years. Once ensconced in Camden in 1873, the poet whose early work was so thrillingly impregnated with lyric vocalism rarely ventured back into the opera house. Though it was easily accessible across the Delaware River, he almost never attended opera in his last twenty years. He was often yoked with Wagner as an aesthetic visionary, to his obvious satisfaction, but so far as we know he never bothered actually to attend a Wagner opera to verify the compliment. Horace Traubel's reports on Wagner performances seemed to suffice.

Because it was my own experience, it was not a little moving to me to discover that Whitman became more and more satisfied to dine upon extraordinarily happy memories of long ago rather than crave the reality of live performances at Philadelphia's Academy of Music. As he was able to waft back nostalgically, when opera was mentioned, to Alboni's Norma, Bettini's Fernando, or Brignoli's Ernani, so I have found it increasingly tempting to forgo the present pleasure of live opera and simply recall some of my sublime "firsts": my first *Rosenkavalier* (Schwarzkopf, Ludwig, Grist, Edelmann), *Otello* (McCracken, Gobbi, Kabaivanska), *Norma* (Sutherland, Horne), *Peter Grimes* (Vickers), *Salome* (Rysanek) . . . indeed, my very first opera of all, at age fourteen, an eternal *Meistersinger* with Konya, in Los Angeles's cavernous Shrine Auditorium, that still somehow managed to capture my imagination.

Why did Whitman—why did Walt and I—come to find opera had lost its hold on our imagination? The most obvious explanation is that, in the phrase of the Noël Coward song, "Maybe it's something to do with Spring." Opera was the musical love of our vernal prime when "A sort of lilt in the air, / A lyrical loveliness, / Seems everywhere"—which, come to think of it, is not a bad way to describe the "final lilt" of the early *Leaves* editions. But pleasure that tends to be concentrated in gusts, whether evoked by masterly vocal heroics or skilled erotic foreplay, cannot last forever. Vocal stamina and sexual drives inevitably descend from the heights to something that seems pallid and forlorn. An overmastering love for opera, in Whitman's case, devolved into something like amiable affection.

He treated his old loves, Alboni and opera, gallantly, though, on the very few occasions he mentioned them in his later years.

Coward, incidentally, had a special knack for expressing the bitter-sweet task of amiably relinquishing lost love. Two of his finest valedictions to love have now and then hummed through my mind as I've pondered Whitman's waning affair with opera. One is in "Let's Say Good-Bye," from the early 1930s musical *Words and Music*: "All these sweet moments we've known / Mustn't be degraded. / When the thrill of them has faded / Let's say 'Good-bye' and leave it alone." The other, more famous, song certainly captures the way Whitman, imprisoned by age and illness in his little Camden house, looked back upon the most thrilling decade of his life, the 1850s, when his party and his devotion to opera were at their height:

> Dancing time
> May seem sublime
> But it is ended all too soon,
> The thrill is gone,
> To linger on
> Would spoil it anyhow,
> Let's creep away from the day
> For the Party's over now.

Will I grow in the coming years similarly distant from opera? I hope not. But I will certainly not be able to plead surprise if I do.

✸   ✸   ✸

For those ineffable Coward lines, I consulted a volume of his lyrics that once belonged to my uncle Art. He was Henry Arthur Davis Schmidgall but always went by the more private inner two names. Born and raised in Murphysboro, a tiny town in southern Illinois, he made a beeline for Chicago the instant it was possible, and several years later, in the late 1930s, got into a Pierce Arrow and set out over the Rockies. He was enchanted by the "flashing and golden pageant of California," as Whitman put it in "Song of the Redwood Tree," and decided to settle there permanently.

Eventually he alighted in rather louche and not yet tourist-befuddled Carmel-by-the-Sea, 125 miles south of San Francisco. The 1939 Federal Writers' Project volume on California says Carmel was founded by some artistic bohemians around 1900 and that "dilettantes, charlatans, and idlers flocked in after them." The atmosphere of such a village apparently appealed to Art. While there, he befriended a wealthy elderly woman, Abby Beecher Abbott, and helped nurse her during her final illness. In return for this kindness, Abbott left him a small cottage she owned across Carmelo Street, a half block north of Carmel's main drag, Ocean Avenue.

The cottage looked out on Carmel Bay, with its whiter-than-pearl sand dunes and majestic Monterey cypresses, and was just a solid drive from the ninth green of the Pebble Beach golf course. To this cottage I began to come as a child in the early 1950s, at first on vacation with my mother and younger twin brothers and later, in my early teens, by myself for week-long stays. My solo trips were on the train from Los Angeles, where my father, Art's youngest brother, had settled after war's end.

Occasionally, Art would come to Los Angeles, and it was on these trips that he took me to my first play, A Midsummer Night's Dream with Bert Lahr as Bottom, and my first ballet, the Ballets Russes in "Les Sylphides" and "Gaîté Parisienne"—perfect choices. Chance left it to the middle Schmidgall brother, my uncle Ray, who knew nothing about opera, to make the bizarre choice of Meistersinger for a teenager's first opera, but it was Art, in fact, who was eventually responsible for igniting my love for the art form. He loved opera deeply, had a fairly large collection of records, and of course was devoted to the Metropolitan Opera's Saturday afternoon radio broadcasts. My career as a writer began, I am keenly aware, with the letters I wrote to him describing my own theater-, music-, and operagoing, notably when I was a college sophomore studying in Germany and attending opera in a couple dozen cities from London to Vienna to Rome.

A man of extraordinarily eclectic tastes and the only one of my relatives with the slightest regard for the fine arts, literature, or music, Art introduced me virtually single-handed to the cultured life. He gave me the sublime monologist Ruth Draper (her records are within arm's reach as I write), the zany Bea Lillie, Saki's stories, the music of Scott Joplin (what I usually play when I sit down at the piano), the special brand of Bay Area jazz epitomized by Lu Watters and the trombonist Turk Murphy (after an opera at the War Memorial Opera House we would sometimes decamp to Murphy's joint, Earthquake McGoon's), the plays of Shaw and Coward (a wonderful Carmel little-theater Misalliance, my first Shavian encounter, and a glorious Hay Fever I will never forget). Mon oncle also gave me Jacques Tati's Mon Oncle and his other movies; also took me, a bit daringly, to Fellini's La Dolce Vita . . . and into la dolce vita of art generally.

He also introduced me to Oscar Wilde, in the splendid reincarnation

Vincent Price toured with so memorably, and of course there were the constant replayings of his especially beloved Coward records. Art made his one trip to Europe in 1973, to visit me while I was on a predoctoral fellowship; the highlights for us were attending the first English-language festival performances of Wagner's *Ring* under Reginald Goodall at the English National Opera, a Glyndebourne performance of Strauss's *Capriccio* with Söderström, and, just after Coward's death, seeing the hit review *Cowardy Custard* at the Mermaid Theater. About a dozen years later, just before deterioration in his strength and eyesight forced Art out of his rickety but cozy cottage and into a nursing home, he sent me the last of several cassettes on which he recorded highlights from the collection he was leaving behind. Toward the end of it—his humor could be deliciously sly—he included Coward singing "The Party's Over Now."

I thank my lucky stars for Uncle Art. But for him I would have been as unlucky as Whitman, who had not a single cultural mentor in his extended family. He had to scratch and claw on his own at the lending libraries for his culture and had to achieve his love of opera from scratch. When I paid my last visit to Art in 1989, he was nearly blind, infirm, and perfectly miserable in his very caring but distinctly uncultured and unprovocative digs. We decided to spring the "inmate," as he wryly liked to refer to himself, for a visit to Carmelo Street. It was a terrible struggle with Art's walker down the path to the cottage (he never gave in to a wheelchair, as Whitman did). How miserably over and done with the "marvelous party" of our relationship seemed, we both must have thought, though not a word was uttered. He returned to the care facility mortified and deeply depressed by the final recognition that he would never be able to return to the cottage to live. His parting words as I left to return to a teaching job in Manhattan were: "Thanks for all the excitement." I will always regret not having had the presence of mind to reply, "No, thank *you* for the last thirty-five years of excitement!" Three weeks later he was dead. I have just now learned from the Social Security Administration that he had lied about his age to the tune of six years: he was not born in 1906, as his death certificate says, but in February 1900. It is pleasant to think that he and Oscar Wilde shared the planet for a few months.

Uncle Art and I became each other's closest living relative, my own family aside, and my Whitman project has often evoked memories of him. This is because, as the reader will already have guessed, my uncle was gay. The Pierce Arrow—droll allusion to the gay patron saint, Sebastian—that brought him to California in the late 1930s belonged to his lover, Allard Crosten Bradford, and the cottage from Ms. Abbott was given jointly to

both of them. Art worked as a
subclerk in the local post office,
while Bradford was a government
stenographer at the nearby army
base, Fort Ord.

At about the time I was born,
Bradford disappeared from Art's
life, whereabouts unknown, a
fact that would later cause me, as
executor of Art's estate, considerable grief and inspire some
clever detective work to find him
or his heirs. And so for all the
time I knew Art he lived a single
life while working as a secretary/
receptionist in one of Carmel's
larger real estate offices. Many
years later, during one of his

The author and his uncle Art.

infrequent reminiscences, Art told me that, when just on the verge of an
important promotion, he had lost his post office job in 1951 when his
homosexuality was discovered.

My mother and father were aware of Art's sexual orientation. I shall
be forever grateful that they did not let this stand in the way, as many
parents would have, of what was obviously becoming a very enthusiastic
and significant relationship, one that now and then featured memorable
opera- and playgoing weekends in San Francisco. Usually we would
ensconce ourselves in a room at the Fairmont Hotel, where the "hunt
breakfast" (featuring pancakes Oscar) in the long-gone Camellia Room
was the great treat before a Sunday opera matinee. The subject of Art's
sexuality, in fact, was never raised by them with me, even well after I had
come out, which may say more about my family's spectacular gift for reticence than about its tolerance, which is also considerable.

Art, for his part, repaid my parents' trust with faultless propriety,
unlike uncles one sometimes encounters in porno films. Whenever I
stayed in the cottage, he gave me his bedroom and retired to a small
cubicle downstairs, off his well-tended garden. He never made a false
move, and as I think back on all his Carmel "bachelor" friends to whom I
was introduced, it is clear they had been sternly lectured about the
slightest dropping of hairpins . . . or anything else. I was a cute teenager,
though; in fact, I recall overhearing myself referred to as "queerbait" by
an Eastern preppy classmate in my freshman year and wondering what

this meant. I can now well imagine the camp ribaldry that must have been uttered at my expense, unbeknown to me, among Art's gay circle during and after my visits.

Art did not even permit his crest to fall when for several months I appeared to be settling into heterosexuality and was living with a college girlfriend. With her he was his usual charming self. But it was when, in my late twenties, I began to appear on his doorstep for weekends with a boyfriend in tow that we finally began to allow each other glimpses into our gay identities. My coming out, in the years just after Stonewall, was rather effortlessly and untraumatically achieved, and Art became, in effect, one of my main ties to the kind of "concealed but substantial life" that gay men had been leading, with probably not very significant variation, since the time *Leaves of Grass* first appeared. I notice that Art, in his book of Coward lyrics, specially marked as a favorite the wickedly "out" song "Green Carnation" from the 1929 musical *Bitter Sweet*. This song, for all its sleek sophistication, is perfectly Whitmanesque in its vaunting of the "haughty boys, naughty boys" who make up the gay fraternity. Whitman would have hated the neat rhymes and the taste for elegant *objets d'art* (a taste my uncle very much shared), but otherwise the song's opening lines capture the gay-liberation thrust that is often present between—sometimes in—the lines of *Leaves of Grass*:

> Blasé boys are we,
> Exquisitely free
> From the dreary and quite absurd
> Moral views of the common herd.
> We like porphyry bowls,
> Chandeliers and stoles,
> We're most spirited,
> Carefully filleted "souls."

Uncle Art seems to have had a substantial circle of gay friends in "the Village," as Carmelites refer to it, and around the Monterey Peninsula. It was a situation not vastly unlike the life Whitman led in the rather small town of Camden. Discretion was necessary and for good reason: when I read of Whitman's dismissal from the Interior Department by Secretary Harlan on account of *Leaves of Grass*, I was immediately reminded of Art losing his job in the post office. "Spirited" gay souls, such as Coward describes, counteract the humiliations of such self-concealment, though, by various exotic strategies. Sometimes, as in Coward's "Green Carnation" or many a passage in *Leaves of Grass*, they shout the truth so loudly that no one can hear them. Sometimes, and this too we have seen often at work in Whitman's poetry, sheer pleasure is to be had in privileged communication with one's secret sharers under the nose of the "common herd." Noël Annan has written recently of this pleasure as lying at the heart of the "cult of homosexuality" between 1850 and 1950: "The delight in belonging to a fraternity, at once secret and illicit, with its own jokes, its own language, courting danger of prosecution, engaging in a conspiracy against the rest of society—perhaps this was one reason why the cult became a fashionable cult."

We have seen much of this kind of delight in Whitman's poetry and also in his correspondence and conversations with Traubel. Though I was not aware of it at the time, I now see that the same subtle pleasures were to be had in Carmel-by-the-Sea. Indeed, it fell to some gay friends involved with the famed Carmel Bach Festival, founded more than a half century ago by two lesbians, to tell me a few years later of how men regularly courted arrest and prosecution by certain *al fresco* recreations that took place in the sand dunes visible from Art's living room. Annan's remark about a private gay language reminds me, too, of the venerable "friend of Dorothy" mode of revealing one's gaiety. I am always tickled to hear this increasingly rare relic uttered, because one of Art's very best female friends was actually named Dorothy.

Contemplating the likelihood that Whitman destroyed compromising documents and memorabilia before he died also made me think of my uncle. After he had moved out of the cottage, it fell to me to clean it out for rental. In the chaotic basement I came upon a fascinating cache of papers that, I am pretty certain, Art would have destroyed if he had remembered their existence or had still had the eyesight to locate them. Among his own old letters were those chronicling a very painful breakup with Bradford. Indeed, one letter that at first escaped my eye and that I have just now read for the first time is a long one from Art to Bradford illuminating, at long last, the miserable details of their separation.

Bradford, it seems, had ended up in Berlin after leaving California and was caught living and having sexual relations with a German national. During an interrogation he and a Sergeant Ford (part of a gay circle at Fort Ord, apparently) broke down and, quite unnecessarily, chose to reveal Art's homosexuality to military authorities. In a long, bitter letter describing his own subsequent interrogation and dismissal from the civil service, Art wrote, "It would have been so easy for both of you to have refrained from this betrayal." I now understood why Art in the early 1950s ignored a request by Bradford to resolve the matter of the joint ownership of their Carmel cottage. While Art was still alive, I was able to discover that Bradford had died of cancer in Seattle in 1969, his will giving everything to a subsequent lover (but not mentioning the cottage). My visit to Bradford's now aged surviving lover to discuss the property was a strange and interesting one, but I could never summon the courage to tell Art, then in very frail shape, what I had discovered.

Also among Art's papers was his frantic appeal from the dismissal. The second of its eleven paragraphs reads sadly now: "After careful and persistent thought, I have reasons to believe that I am not a homosexual in the final analysis of the term. . . . I have no characteristics that point to the condition of being one. Since my history closed approximately six years ago there has been no interest or desire to return to those acts. I have since that time led a normal life." The fifth paragraph: "I fervently ask that I not be discriminated against." Attached to this appeal is a letter, dated 19 November 1951 from the Old Mint Building in San Francisco, denying his appeal. Art's Secretary Harlan was someone named Harry Kranz, regional director of the civil service.

Another letter from the basement took my breath away. This was the carbon copy of a very emotional letter written three years before I was born, in which Art urged my father not to marry my mother. My guess at the pain this letter would cause Art just *barely* won out over curiosity to see how he would respond to the staggering irony of his plea, given our extraordinary relationship. In the end, I never mentioned it to him.

There was also something more elaborately and picturesquely reminiscent of Whitman hidden behind the gardening paraphernalia in the cottage basement: a trove of letters from gay men around the country that dated from the early 1940s. Bradford, it seems, devoted many an evening and probably some stenographic doldrums to corresponding with gay pen pals and exchanging pornographic prose, poetry, and photographs. Some of these last, showing Bradford in full tilt, were left over. I can tell they were taken in the cottage living room where, years later, Art and I would converse so elevatedly and listen so intently to Tiana Lemnitz, Michael MacLiammóir, or Feodor Chaliapin. Bradford made contact with his pen pals through their advertisements in Strength and Health magazine, and later through one he placed himself under the pseudonym Geoffrey Clark. Several writers were from big cities, but many were from small towns like Whitman's Huntington or Southold. They ranged from Brown City, Michigan, and Beeville, Texas, to Beloit, Wisconsin, and Barton, Vermont. Fortunately, Bradford made carbon copies of many of his letters, so the course of several exchanges over the months can easily be followed now.

There is considerable pathos in these letters. Some derives from elabo-

rate beating-around-the-bush and careful coding of desire, most often in
the expression of interest in the two subjects of "physique" photos and
psychology. Addition of an interest in music was, of course, the dead
giveaway. Sobering, naturally, are the cares taken to protect correspondents from discovery. Addresses and full names are often dispensed with
after initial contact, and one writer says he pores delightedly over his
sexiest communications but then "I burn them up right away." There is
drollery, too—the writer who makes satire of the usual gay gossip ("don't
you think Betty Davis was simpleh divine in *Now Voyager?*") or the one
who emphatically prefers "UNdraped pics of yourself showing that grand
8½″ thing." It is amusing to see what was considered "hot" pornography
then, and surprising how rare so-called "action" photos seem to have
been (Bradford said in one letter that he had only seen one). Another
writer asked if homosexuals ever marry, to which Bradford replied, "My
dear idiot, you should live in Carmel."

Looking through this material again, now that my Whitman project is
done, I find Walt brought often and vividly to mind. "All depends on
physique," after all, was one of his "Says" of 1860. The most charming
Whitman moment is perhaps the amateur photo sent by the Vermonter,
a part-time lifeguard and defense factory worker. Worthy of Eakins, it is
identified on the back as "The Ole Swimming Hole." There may not be
twenty-eight naked young bathers in the photo, as in "Song of Myself,"
but a good half dozen at least have been captured by this voyeur. It was
this same fellow, Lee D., by the way, who offered in one of his letters a
fine homespun paraphrase of Whitman's remark on the "immanence"
and ineluctability of sex: "I know sex is a touchy subject, and unless one
is completely normal he has a tendency to stray from the subject but you
notice NEVER from its diversion. It is always there and you can't drive it
away with a pitchfork or anything else." One could also say the fundamental point of the "Walt & Marietta" chapter is reflected in this remark
made by Kurt F., a young Chicagoan who said he was "very much in favor
of nudism" and of playing around with fellows in the Indian Dunes
(shades of Walt amid the marshes of Paumanok and on the banks of
Timber Creek): "my favorite music is symphonic [but] I have several
famous operatic arias . . . when I play these I'm adrift in another world
which I would like to be in." Which, we have seen, is exactly how Bram
Stoker felt when he read *Leaves of Grass*.

Not surprisingly, given the bodybuilding ethos of the correspondence,
there is a thoroughly Whitmanesque preference for butch as opposed to
femme deportment in these letters. Bradford himself hopes that one pal
"won't conjure up any visions of 'queers' or 'fairies' " in his mind. "I don't

A picture that circulated among gay pen pals in the early 1940s. The site is somewhere in Vermont. The photographer has penciled on the back the legend "The Ole Swimming Hole" and indicated it is part of a collection.

A painting, redolent of Whitman and Eakins, by Ludwig von Hofmann. Die Quelle *or* The Spring *hung near Thomas Mann's writing desk in various residences from 1914 until his death in 1955, providing, as a recent biographer says, "Ganymedean muses" for the novelist. Mann's favorite resort, Travemünde on the Baltic Coast, was the site of the world's first nudist colony and the setting for his provocative homoerotic story "The Fight Between Jappe and Do Escobar." By 1911, when Mann visited the Lido and had his* Death in Venice *experiences, sunbathing in sexually segregated groups had become a German fad. Courtesy of the Thomas Mann Archive, Zurich.*

swish, at any rate, nor mince, nor speak flutingly, nor try to emulate the manner and gestures of my favorite actresses."

Ed of Milwaukee amusingly seconds this view in describing a hospital encounter with an intern after a sledding accident. "While I lay there helpless (?) in bed, he diddled my dick and did me. He wrote me a note— wants a return engagement, and then some, but I'm cold to him . . . his features are so sissified and that I can't take." (Did nurse Whitman ever aid a soldier thus?) Then Ed thinks of his just-departed boyfriend ("the Army got him too"). "Now, Tom *was* cute—in fact, I often wondered what there was about me that attracted him—he reminded me of Ronald Reagan. Who, I think, is very nice looking."

All the vocabulary of derision for effeminacy—"pansy," "blowboy," "queer," "fairy"—is scattered through these letters, which gives the letters the style of Whitman's frequent praise of the "rough" and the "manly." Many of Bradford's pals, by the way, wrote from military installations, and their letters naturally remind one of Whitman's extensive "soger boy" correspondence.

Time and again, the yearning and sexually supercharged Whitman of Chapter 2 is reflected in the stories told by these pen pals. His motto "Give me libidinous joys only!" is most emphatically theirs as well. And also theirs is Walt's paramount desire to escape from the paltry public life that "exhibits itself / By what is done in the houses or streets, or in company" and into the "concealed but substantial life" where acknowledgment of one's true nature is possible. The impulse that caused young Charles Stoddard or young Bram Stoker to write so effusively to Whitman is much the same impulse that produced these letters to and from Bradford. It is the impulse, I dare say, that gave us many of the sex-drenched poems of *Leaves of Grass*. In so many of the anecdotes in these letters, too, one is reminded of Whitman's superb thumbnail sketch of sudden, thrilling, illicit sex: "O contact abrupt and secret . . . O fastened and loosened twain!"

Are they still alive, one finds oneself wondering hauntingly, these pals who sought to quiver themselves to a new identity, to touch their person to someone else's through the medium of writing, as Whitman sought to do with that Mammoth Falcon quill pen of his? Is the now seventy-five-year-old dancing master of Charleston, Jules, able to fondly recall the grand jets of his sexual prime? What of the beautiful, silk-pajamaed Harry of Memphis? He'd be seventy now. Did another Harry, this one of Newport News, soon move, I hope, away from his mother and ninety-five canaries and get a life? And does the Texan named Ed, now in his eighties, still chide himself for that time he refused to let the trucker on the road to Rockford pull over and suck him off? And did Joey of Marlton, New Jersey (where Walt's beloved Harry Stafford got himself married), continue to be "satisfied" with his "6¼-inch p——"? Is the erotic doggerel epic poem "Danny," which Bradford said he wrote and which he included in many of his letters, still extant in caches like my uncle's?* Would these letters, if their authors were to read them now, cause them to become teary-eyed with nostalgia for their "halcyon days," just as such letters made Walt Whitman weep?

❦   ❦   ❦

The search for sex played out in the "Walt & Boss-Tooth" chapter and in the letters amassed by my uncle's lover evoked many shocks of recognition. But they were shocks that I was able to enjoy, on the whole, in a comradely way, knowing that, with minor variations, the focus of desire and the end results would be recognizable to my gay readers, at least. In other words, we of the adhesive kind are all in this together. Writing in the next chapter, "Walt & His Boys," about that more earnest task of searching for a true lover, however, proved uneasily affecting, simply because I found myself more specifically mirrored in these pages. Here, the invitations to think of Walt as a forerunning alter ego of mine, I became aware, were more personal, more provoking.

The most obvious similarity between Walt and myself, which I shall mention in a moment, is perhaps connected to the relative lateness of our true coming out. Whitman, we have seen, may have sensed his "proclivities" as early as his late teens or early twenties. He may even have acted upon them, though we will never know for certain. Still, it is abundantly clear that he did not come boldly, heroically to terms with his sexual identity and peel away the protective covering from his adhesive nature until the early 1850s, when he was in his mid-thirties. Something—or someone—caused him suddenly to behave as gay men behaved after the Stonewall riots: to leave an old, repressed life and "exhibit" a new, more authentic one.

My own coming out was also belated—phenomenally so, I'm left thinking whenever someone tells me he knew he was gay almost from the cradle. I managed to graduate from high school a virgin, in both the manual and two-bodied sense of that term. And from the ignominy of being a virginal college graduate only a visiting high school friend, a woman, saved me. A year-long flirtation both with law school and heterosexuality ended fairly abruptly a short time later. But it was not until my late twenties that same-sex sex began to seem significant to me and worth my serious preoccupation. With almost no premeditation to speak of, and without much emotional storm and stress, my sexuality was suddenly and very agreeably activated.

Within not many months I was living in San Francisco with my first lover—a painter of very high-end cars who had dropped out, utterly disgusted, from graduate studies in English at Yale. We lived in a small apartment near Alamo Square, and there I worked on my dissertation and walked Luther, my lover's black labrador, in the park across from those six gussied-up Victorian houses one always sees in advertisements, commercials, and movies. There they were again recently, in the television version of *Tales of the City*. At that time, by the way, the famous polysexual newspaper soap-opera was just a gleam in the eye of Armistead Maupin, whom Uncle Art and I had come to like as a very witty official in the San Francisco Opera publicity office. (I was a fledgling opera reviewer by then.)

At this time, too, I would arise once a month from a Murphy bed with one labrador and one lover in it and drive to the nation's most beautiful fort, the Presidio, where I was a clerk in the U.S. Army Reserve's Fifth Judge Advocate General's Detachment. I had enlisted in the JAG corps during my fleeting year in law school, just two days ahead of a draft notice that would have sent me to Vietnam. Before setting out, though, I would carefully tuck my long blond hair under a short-haired wig with a shockingly unnatural pinkish-blond tint to it. My JAG buddies gallantly pretended not to notice this preposterous tonsorial ruse. My army memories eventually became, to my astonishment, rather fond ones. The service, after all, had with charming thoughtfulness sent me to Fort Ord for basic training, so I visited Art regularly for R&R in nearby Carmel. And later, on the occasion of Fifth JAG summer encampments, Uncle Sam was responsible for my introduction to the lively gay bars of New Orleans and the District of Columbia—the latter filled, to my amazement, with military haircuts. The liveliest joint there, I will always remember, was practically under the eaves of the new J. Edgar Hoover Building.

But I digress. My point in drawing attention to the lateness of Walt's and my coming out is to suggest that this (in tandem with my long training to be a teacher) may explain why for many years, like Whitman, I have been drawn into Socratic and sexual relationships with younger persons—relationships, that is, of the venerable Spartan kind that involve an "inspirer" and a "hearer," as discussed in Chapter 3. I had occasion there to call *Leaves of Grass* a "schoolmasterly project," and in my own life many of the most important "passional" relationships have involved a significant pedagogical aspect. With the exception of my first (and fleeting) male sex-partner and my Alamo Square lover, my longer-term boyfriends have been younger than myself, sometimes much younger.

Whitman's great *Calamus* poem about the erotics of the pedagogical vocation, which he later titled "To a Western Boy"—

> To the young man, many things to absorb, to engraft, to develop,
>   I teach, to help him become élève of mine,
> But if blood like mine circle not in his veins,
> If he be not silently selected by lovers, and do not silently select
>   lovers,
> Of what use is it that he seek to become élève of mine?

—recalled to mind several Western boys from my past, California élèves with gay blood like mine circling in their veins. I then, of course, thought of Michael, the student from a little town in central Pennsylvania who appeared one day in my Chaucer-to-Milton survey course. We silently selected each other as lovers, and in time it came to pass. We lived together for more than ten years, especially happily early on, though nothing, I found, could induce him to like the sound of Maria Callas's voice.

Three or four times, in the course of writing "Walt & His Boys," I also was impelled to recall the devastating night several years ago when Michael informed me, abruptly and (I could be very dense, it seems) to my shock, that the main love of my life was over. That harrowing period evoked the wrenching amorous defeat that Whitman appears to have suffered in 1859 or so, when he was—I quickly calculated—just a few years younger than I. The poems that he wrote in the wake of this "saddest loss and sorrow of my life" I readily identified with. Most wrenching, of course, were "Out of the Cradle Endlessly Rocking," *Calamus* #8 ("Long I thought that knowledge alone"), *Calamus* #9 ("Hours continuing long"), and *Calamus* #17 ("Of him I love day and night"). Specially moving, too, was *Calamus* #20, with its image of the solitary live-oak "without a friend a lover near," and the manuscript version of *Enfans d'Adam* #9, which told of the lover who helped him to pass through the "populous city."*

Whitman, I began to think, might even help me to understand what had gone wrong. Was his assertion in "Song of Myself" that "I teach straying from me" applicable to my lover, who matured beyond the need for anything I could have taught him? Nor could I resist thinking of myself when I came upon Whitman's remark to Horace Traubel "Young fellows seem rather bowled over by me. . . . I fool 'em for a time, when they're in their teens, but when they grow up they can no longer be deceived."

I thought of myself too, and of the effort one must make to put one's life back together in the aftermath of a breakup, as I read Whitman's *Calamus* #39, a superb effort at self-consolation. "Doubtless I could not have perceived the universe, or written one of my poems," he ventured, "if I had not freely given myself to comrades, to love." And I was also tempted, like Whitman, to avoid forever this pain of rejection and to retire from the fray and live with animals, as he put it, that are "placid and self-contained." A cat, say, like Shoki, the Himalayan sealpoint who shared most of the years Michael and I were together. This placid (except when being brushed) and brilliantly self-contained animal was one of the most deserving acknowledgees for my Wilde biography, and he still travels now and then, a hostage to joint custody, between our two Upper West Side apartments.

But, also like Whitman, I was still driven by the desire to find, as he put it in his early doggerel poem, "*one* heart to love." The Whitman image in "Starting from Paumanok" still beckoned: "O hand in hand—O wholesome pleasure—O one more desirer and lover." And thus I was forced to confront the dilemma that caused Whitman so much anxiety in his later years: whether to remain sexually eager and active as one arrives at late middle age and risk ego-battering defeat or to retire gracefully, elegantly, aloofly from the sexual arena. Sex partners continue to be younger than I, and I am ever more aware that, as I age, it will be increasingly difficult to engage them.

I am exquisitely aware that I am now *precisely* the age Whitman was in 1870 when he confided to his notebook the frantic self-admonition not to make a fool of himself by "this feverish, fluctuating, useless undignified pursuit" of Peter Doyle, a lover more than twenty-five years his junior. Like Whitman, I have regularly been tempted to lecture myself on the almost certain humiliation and the unlikelihood of success in becoming involved in the "enormous & abnormal PERTURBATION" of such vulnerable-making affairs of the heart. Whitman, we have seen, swore off such affairs, "from this hour forth, for life," but he subsequently allowed his heart to be taken . . . by Harry Stafford and perhaps by others whose names are now lost to us.

I wonder how I shall fare. I am still attracted to younger partners, and I am still attracting them, perhaps in part because my blond hair, unlike Walt's, has so far not turned gray. It has not even begun to fall out, though according to the Spanish proverb it will in a hundred years. Whether I will devolve into an old codger eyeing grocery boys in the aisles of a supermarket, as Ginsberg imagined a modern-day Whitman, or become satisfied to ogle young athletes from my wheelchair, as Walt did on the Camden town common, or merely gratify myself with the muscular presence and touch of a male nurse like Ed Wilkins, of course remains to be seen.

§   §   §

As in the "Walt & Boss-Tooth" chapter, the instances of autobiographical resonance in the Annex that follows struck me as more shared with the gay fraternity than personal. Being in large part about the assertion of gay personality and presence in a hostile world, my extended comparison of Whitman and Wilde caused me to think often of the life that I—and the gay and lesbian movement in general—have lately led, at least since the epoch-opening events of Stonewall.

Alfred Kazin observed recently in *Writing Was Everything* that Hart Crane "didn't know how to escape the isolation of his homosexuality" but that "Whitman glorified" his homosexuality "in the name of togetherness—my city, my people, my America." Though Whitman was, as Kazin also notes, expert at being "personal" and "loving" in his poetry, he was also quite capable of the boldly subversive political gesture. Many passages in his most uninhibited, "Stonewalling" poems, the *Calamus* sequence, are sometimes as superbly in-your-face as tactics of Queer Nation or ACT UP. It is a little astonishing to read now Whitman's initial statement of his sexual-political agenda, *Calamus* #5, for it so precisely evokes the simultaneous coming out and coming together of the homosexual rights movement in the early 1970s:

> There shall be innovations,
> There shall be countless linked hands. . . .
>
> The most dauntless and rude shall touch face to face lightly,
> The dependence of Liberty shall be lovers,
> The continuance of Equality shall be comrades.

In the same poem he predicts that it "shall be customary in all directions, in the houses and streets, to see manly affection," and friends will salute each other "with a kiss." And that took me back, of course, to the times I spent in the Castro, San Francisco's premier gay enclave, where such public display of gay affection and solidarity has long been "customary." Indeed, my very first pickup at a gay bar took place at the venerable Twin Peaks at Market and Castro. I had recognized my friend for the night as a cast member of the almost as venerable *Beach Blanket Babylon* revue, which I had seen a few weeks earlier—though it did not occur to me just then to think, *Eccomi alfine in Babilonia!*

Calamus #25, with its lines about "Those of the open atmosphere" who are "never constrained, never obedient," also made me think of the early coalescing of gay and lesbian political advocacy. The most exhilarating manifestations of this new force were the joyous gay pride parades of the 1970s, the mood of which was also eloquently anticipated by Whitman in *Calamus* #25: "Those that go their own gait, erect, stepping with freedom and command—leading, not following, / Those with a never-quell'd audacity—those with sweet and lusty flesh." *Calamus* #26, too, with its image of boys "together clinging" and its superb vision of gay solidarity, made me think of the spread of these gay parades to many of the nation's great urban roads:

> Up and down the roads going—North and South excursions
>   making,
> Power enjoying—elbows stretching—fingers clutching,
> Armed and fearless—eating, drinking, sleeping, loving,
> No law less than ourselves owning . . .

Finally, though, I have to say it is not a *Calamus* poem but an unpublished notebook entry, in which Whitman jotted some notes about ancient Greek rites, that best captures for me the buoyant "sextroversion" of those early parades: "Phallic festivals—Wild mirthful processions in honor of the god Dionysus (Bacchus) . . . unbounded licences—mocking jibes and irony."

There is, too, in certain of the *Calamus* poems some of the utopian glee and optimism we experienced in the 1970s, which it is now hard to look back on with other than bittersweet nostalgia. We were, to use Walt's word, more "exalté" then than now, more in the mood for such exuberance as *Calamus* #37 ("A Leaf for Hand in Hand"), yet another fine Whitman evocation of gay pride processions: "You twain! And all processions moving along the streets! / I wish to infuse myself among you till I see it common for you to walk hand in hand." Nearly a century and a half ago Whitman was our Martin Luther King Jr., and he had a dream. This dream he confided to America eloquently enough in the published version of *Calamus* #34 in 1860, but even more movingly in this preceding manuscript version:

> I dreamed in a dream of a city where all the men were like
>   brothers,
> O I saw them tenderly love each other—I often saw them, in
>   numbers, walking hand in hand;

I dreamed that was the city of robust friends—
Nothing was greater than manly love—it led the rest.

And then came the fall. For Whitman, just a few years later, it was the cannonade at Fort Sumter and Jeff Davis's rebellion. Walt's hand-holding men transformed from robust friends and lovers into "soger boys" cradling fallen comrades; the thumb of love became a trigger finger. The carnal sting gave way to pure carnage. The "exalté" singer of "Health chants—joy chants—robust chants of young men, / Chants inclusive— wide reverberating chants" in "Starting from Paumanok" was soon confronted with the horror of civil war. And thereafter, quite clearly, he lost the sally-forth spirit that produced the *Calamus* poems. "These carols, vibrating through the air . . . For comrades and lovers," he had called them in *Calamus* #33. So abashed was this spirit, in fact, that Whitman removed the two "Paumanok" lines about "Health chants" from his later *Leaves* editions. He no longer had, so to speak, the spiritual vocal cords and diaphragm for such robust, joyous, reverberant chants.

If we require a reason for this loss of vocal inspiration, perhaps it is best expressed in a brief "reminiscence" jotted on a scrap of paper that is now in the Huntington Library:

> I saw the wounded and the dead, and never forgot them
> Ever since have they been with me—
>   they have fused ever since in my poems;
> They are here forever in my poems

In his 1871 poem "To Thee Old Cause," in fact, Whitman would even more bluntly assert about *Leaves of Grass*, "my book and the war are one." For us, in the early 1980s, it was of course the war against a far more stealthy and devastating enemy than the "seceshes." It was the AIDS virus, which has cast such a mortifying pall over the gay parades of recent years. Here too, autobiography has come often into play as my acquaintance with Whitman has deepened. I have been left, indeed, with the eerie sensation that our own war on AIDS and Walt's writings are also "one."

Whitman, most wonderfully, presents us with the heroic challenge to *genuine* and useful compassion. In 1855, with uncanny anticipation of the years of nursing the wounded that lay in his future, he wrote:

> Agonies are one of my changes of garments;
> I do not ask the wounded person how he feels . . . . I myself

become the wounded person,
My hurt turns livid upon me as I lean on a cane and observe.

The notebooks Whitman kept of his hospital visits—he estimated that he made six hundred of them and ministered to more than eighty thousand soldiers—are filled with the mundane acts of kindness that occur time beyond number in AIDS wards and hospices around the world every day. It is easy to recall being in such places, visiting one's own, when Whitman records, "Once in a while some youngster holds on to me convulsively, and I do what I can for him; at any rate, stop with him and sit near him for hours, if he wishes it." Or when he refers to the "tragedies of soul and body" that occurred daily before his eyes. Or when, with prophetic vision, he remarked in a letter about the profoundly homoerotic wellsprings of his nature, "There is a strange influence here. I have found attachments here in hospital, that I shall keep to my dying day."

Here, in a letter, is yet another familiar scene from the AIDS-volunteer trenches: "Above all the poor boys welcome magnetic friendship, personality (some are so fervent, so hungering for this)—poor fellows, how young they are, lying there with their pale faces, & that mute look in the eyes. O how one gets to love them, often, particular cases, so suffering, so good, so manly & affectionate." And here, in a conversation decades later with Horace Traubel, is Walt on the sometimes salutary agony (and ecstasy) of lying to the dying:

Any Doctor will tell you how necessary it is—a species of mind cure. I could not count the times I did it—for its own sake—not because I would not have preferred to tell the truth. I did not seek to have to say anything—but said what I felt to say to fit the gravity of the cases. Oh! You've no idea how the poor fellows would cling to the last—crave hope, cheer, sunlight; and all I could free—all that could flow out of me—was theirs, theirs.

On 13 May 1863, now thoroughly habituated to the hospital scene, Whitman recorded, "I see such awful things. I expect one of these days, if I live, I shall have awful thoughts and dreams." He did live, for another thirty years, and the experience, as he predicted, proved indelible. In 1888 he mused about a dedication "To all cut off before their time," and two years later, in one of his last poems, "A Twilight Song," confessed to often "Musing on long-pass'd war-scenes." It is very easy to identify with Whitman in this sad retrospective mood as, in this second decade of the

AIDS pandemic, my own archive of "awful thoughts" and memories steadily grows. The last stanza of Whitman's finest Civil War poem, "Dirge for Two Veterans," rises to a kind of orgasm of grief:

> The moon gives you light,
> And the bugles and the drums give you music,
> And my heart, O my soldiers, my veterans,
> My heart gives you love.

This stanza leaves me thinking of former veterans of my heart and my bed, lost to AIDS. Two in particular from my California days come to mind now, David and Mark, the first of my sometime lovers—and close comrades thereafter—to fall to AIDS. David, a sweet, guileless, ever smiling North Carolinian, was a waiter in the Castro. Mark was a swimmer, Stanford geology student, and relentless bon vivant from a well-to-do Maryland family. His spirit moved him one afternoon, unforgettably, to perform fellatio on me as I drove down the Bayshore Freeway in my MGB, giving "stick shift" a splendid new meaning.

One Sunday morning in October 1990, about a half hour apart, I received two phone calls. The first informed me that David had shot himself, with the revolver he had inherited from his father, in his Haight Street apartment (I had been forewarned of this exit strategy). The next call was from Mark's sister: he had died peacefully at his family's home near Baltimore at almost exactly the same time. On Monday morning, I was on the doorstep of the Gay Men's Health Crisis, beginning three years of part-time volunteer work.

When I think of Mark, David, or one of the relatively few other casualties of AIDS from my life—I have been lucky: one often hears of those who have lost scores of friends and lovers—I sometimes daydream about what would be said (or done) if one or the other were suddenly to appear at my door. My last long talk with Mark was by phone; he was high on marijuana and our reminiscing got very sexy and arousing for both of us. It was a perfect farewell, though we did not know at the time that it was our "ultimo addio."

This communion with my dead, which recurs not infrequently during idle moments, sometimes makes me think of Whitman's *Calamus* #17. Many of his poems are astonishingly prophetic, but none more so than this one. Its opening lines constitute the best evocation of the devastation of AIDS I know of, the curious combination of franticness and dull despair the disease has cast over us. These lines are also about the *ars moriendi* that AIDS has forced us to learn:

Of him I love day and night I dream'd I heard he was dead,
And I dream'd I went where they had buried him I love,
　　but he was not in that place,
And I dream'd I wander'd searching among burial-places to
　　find him,
And I found that every place was a burial-place;
The houses full of life were equally full of death, (this house is now,)
The streets, the shipping, the places of amusement, the Chicago,
　　Boston, Philadelphia, the Mannahatta, were as full of the dead
　　as of the living,
And fuller, O vastly fuller of the dead than of the living . . .

When Whitman brought out his 1867 edition of *Leaves*, he made the poem less "gay" by removing it from the *Calamus* sequence. But by placing it under the rubric *Whispers of Heavenly Death*, he was, unwittingly, encouraging association with the AIDS plague to come.

❦　　❦　　❦

Writing the final short chapter "Walt & Horace," as it happens, also evoked memories of my cherished vanished boyfriends Mark and David— happily more cheerful memories. This chapter also caused me to identify, for a change, not with Walt but the very much younger Horace Traubel. And thereby hangs a tale.

During my graduate-student years at Stanford, Virgil Keeble Whitaker was its most distinguished Shakespearean. He had been a Stanford undergraduate in the 1920s and, but for a few years teaching in Washington state and running the Indian educational system in New Mexico during World War II, had been a highly visible professor, department chair, and dean at the university, as well as the engine behind the wonderful Stanford Summer Festival for several years. A very portly though vigorous man, and diabetic, he lived alone in an elegant, vaguely Japanese-style house he had designed himself and built around 1960. It stood behind the campus and offered superb views of oak-strewn hills and what is now called Silicon Valley. Virgil liked, for health reasons and for company, to have a student live on the downstairs floor and do occasional errands in exchange for room and board. While I was studying in London on a dissertation fellowship, the possibility of my assuming these duties was raised. Though I had never studied formally with Virgil, I was working on a Shakespeare dissertation, and I was also familiar with his household through a good friend who had been one of Virgil's previous live-in students.

The situation seemed ideal, but since I had come out before leaving for London, I thought it would be best to inform Virgil and hope this would not present a problem. A week later I received a reply that very discreetly said "the matter" I had raised was of no consequence and my moving in was settled. Being of Uncle Art's cautious generation, Virgil added a PS: "I have destroyed your letter."

Over the next four years Virgil and I became extremely close, and a ménage developed that was in many respects like that at Mickle Street in Whitman's last years. Virgil was the august old party, a vivid and witty conversationalist, and I was the appreciative neophyte listener, sometimes putting up, as Horace did, with my share of what Walt called the "parrot-like repetitions" of the aged. Walt would doubtless have had trouble cottoning to Virgil, who was as grandly poised a professor as they come, at least in his donnish on-campus persona. And Virgil would certainly have had no patience with Walt's views on Shakespeare. One of his journal articles begins, "Whenever I encounter a misguided soul who believes that Francis Bacon or the Earl of Oxford or Christopher Marlowe wrote Shakespeare's plays, I reflect: 'There, but for the grace of a good graduate school, go I.' "

And yet, time and again, as I marched through the volumes of *With Walt Whitman in Camden*, I was struck by how similar Walt and Virgil really were. The key similarity, I suspect, was their devotion to youth. Walt wrote in one of his very early stories, "Little Sleighers," that "a man may keep his heart fresh and his nature youthful, by mixing much with that which is fresh and youthful." This was certainly the pattern for both men in their last years (as it was for Wilde throughout his adulthood). Virgil spent as little time with his contemporaries or even his middle-aged colleagues as he could; indeed, he almost never ventured down to campus after his retirement.

And he even gave up, quite happily, his scholarly work. His last big project involved Sir Francis Bacon and would have touched on Bacon's relationship with his parents and his homosexuality. In the last paper I heard Virgil deliver, he quoted a letter from Lady Bacon to his brother Antony about the thirty-two-year-old Francis's shameful behavior: "surely though I pity your brother, yet so long as he pitieth not himself but keepeth that bloody Percy, as I told you, yea as a coach companion and bed companion,—a proud profane costly fellow, whose being about him I verily fear the Lord God doth mislike . . . he hath nourished most sinful proud villains willfully." I would like to think that, had Virgil lived to publish his research, a discreet scholarly coming out just might have occurred because of my presence in his life. But whenever the graduate student would merrily chide the professor about getting to work, he would always smile beatifically and change the subject. The huge Spedding edition of Bacon's works was arrayed on his desk . . . but almost never touched.

In fact, what began to amuse and fascinate me was that Virgil was positively delighted by the burgeoning gay circle that was coming to his house on Cedro Way: a few professors, several graduate and under-graduate students I had met at Stanford's newly established Gay Students Union, new "friends" encountered in local or San Francisco bars who would appear suddenly with me for breakfast of a morning. Sex was cer-tainly not Virgil's metier. He spoke often, though always very vaguely, of sexual dysfunction and swore, I always assumed with perfect candor, that he had reached old age a virgin. But his life was not without its homo-erotic titillations. He loved nothing better than to awaken a drowsing corpse early in the morning with a few harmless pats, and he showed a lively interest in conversation about the life and times of me and my gay cohorts.

Particularly memorable, in this vein, were the lively Sunday brunches that took place on his enormous sundeck. The guest list presided over by me, these became something of an institution during my tenure on Cedro Way. Just about my favorite memory of Virgil is of him sitting at the end of a long table in front of a griddle, rapidly producing blueberry pancakes he could not himself eat, to the tune of much laughter. Periodically the cork from a champagne bottle would sail off into the azalea bushes below.

And, oh, how he doted on my boyfriends! Michael was much ad-mired. One day he gave him the pick of the splendid Indian bowls he had carefully collected in the 1940s while in Santa Fe, among them a now fabulously valuable black-on-black specimen from the hands of Maria Martinez of San Ildefonso. But Michael was reluctant to spoil the collec-tion and, because Virgil never recorded this gift formally, the whole col-lection went to the Stanford University Museum when he died. But David and Mark were Virgil's real favorites. In his will, some of his furni-ture went to David. And when Virgil conveyed me and all my worldly belongings, including a big upright piano, in his old diesel Mercedes, from California to the East Coast for my first teaching job, it was Mark who offered to accompany him back home via a lengthy detour through Canada. Some time later, Virgil told me that Mark—bless him!—one night did something that I, being far too uptight, would never have had the courage to do: he allowed Virgil to experience what a hard-on feels like.

Virgil was like Walt in many ways, now that I think about it. His instinct was that of an all-embracer. His taste in people, especially young people, was far wider than mine, and some denizens who showed up on his doorstep were not entirely distinguishable from drifters. One, whom he had known from the boy's childhood, died under mysterious circumstances in the Tenderloin, and the mother asked Virgil to say a few words at the funeral. Rarely had I seen him so distraught. He had also, like Whitman, been for a long time extremely devoted to his mother (she lived with him for many years), though she died long before I knew him.

There was even a somewhat Falstaffian jollity to his presence that comes through, too, in Walt's conversations with Traubel. About his girth he was, like Whitman, capable of humor: during a television interview he was once asked his favorite line from Shakespeare and replied without missing a beat, "O that this too too solid flesh would melt." Virgil's humorous streak, in fact, was rather like the sly, puckish subversiveness that often surfaces in Traubel's volumes. He was a connoisseur of off-color limericks, one of his favorites being perhaps worth including:

> There once was a choirboy from Devon
> Who was had in the choirloft by seven
> Libidinous beasts,
> They were Anglican priests,
> For such is the Kingdom of Heaven.

Virgil was also, like Walt, a remarkably amiable valetudinarian. He had been a very active traveler all his life and had driven cross-country more than a dozen times, but as his various ailments ganged up on him, he settled with little fuss and less self-pity into life in the big yellow chair in his living room. "I am getting more and more satisfied with my bed and chair, which is suspicious," said Walt. Virgil didn't get suspicious at all. And, just as Horace was on a few occasions present for medical crises, so was I. Indeed, Virgil had one of his preliminary heart attacks as I was driving him home from dinner with one of my gay friends in San Francisco, an outstanding cook. Virgil's love of good food got the best of him, and, having ignored dietary restrictions, he calmly informed me on the way down Highway 280 that he was having a coronary. I drove very nervously to the Stanford Hospital. Twenty minutes after he vanished into the emergency room, a doctor emerged to say Virgil had insisted I was in pretty bad shape and might need attention myself.

Horace Traubel and I had just about equal time with our beloved old critters: around four years of almost daily intimacy. And I must say the main memory for me is of the same brand of easygoing good humor that leaps from almost every one of Traubel's pages—that humor "in the sense of lubrication" which Whitman said he so admired in Colonel Ingersoll. But my memory of Virgil was also jogged in other, sometimes droll ways. Virgil's housekeeper and occasional cook, an invariably dour Polish woman, seems to have been pretty much on the order of Walt's Mrs. Davis, and she, like Mrs. Davis, was perfectly happy to be out of conversational earshot—and definitely not privy to all the same-sex gossip. Virgil also had a brother and, like Walt with his local brother George, they had absolutely nothing in common. The brother's wife was a stiff, purse-lipped sort who clearly disapproved of most of Virgil's friends. How Virgil rejoiced when his doctor forbade their sojourning with him for fear of upsetting his health!

Finally, though, all the wacky serendipity of the chats in *With Walt Whitman* is what most consistently reminded me of my time with Virgil: the many happy, quite aimless hours spent around the dinner table or in front of his fireplace: his telling of some favorite story for the umpteenth time*; the gossip about mutual friends and academic fools; the sudden eruption of doggerel poetry or bad English translation of opera that he had memorized fifty years before and had not managed to expunge; or hearing one of his countless odd anecdotes about Stanford past—like the day he was shown the minutes of a Stanford trustees meeting at which his scholarship and a sum four times greater for the services of a prize bull were approved.

My first two books were written, in large part, in Virgil's house. The one on Shakespeare, which grew out of my dissertation, I dedicated to him, and I was very grateful indeed that it appeared before he died. (The earlier book, *Literature as Opera*, I had dedicated to Uncle Art.) In his will, Walt bequeathed to Horace his gold watch. Virgil never affected a gold watch, but I still fared very well. I was left the old Mercedes, which shortly thereafter definitively kicked the bucket, his seven-thousand-volume library, which included some choice old works like a 1586 set of Holinshed's *Chronicles* (the source Shakespeare ransacked for his history plays), and a remainderman's share in his estate.

Virgil Whitaker.

When Walt died, Horace Traubel, as always, was assiduous in seeing that the memorial service was recorded for posterity, and I was honored to be one of the four who were asked to speak at Virgil's memorial service in Stanford's Memorial Church. Among the words I composed for the occasion were these: "Virgil displayed the Shakespearean power of embracing all aspects of humanity. Though his decidedly old-fashioned notions of feminine decorum and lack of ease in the presence of some women left him open to a charge of misogyny, Virgil on the whole seemed to dote on the quirks and quiddities of the most various kinds of people. He spread a far wider net of acquaintances and friends than most of us should ever wish to do. . . . He was an infinitely patient, intrigued, and keen observer of human behavior. And he was no snob in his affections, either." It did not occur to me then, of course, but it certainly does now: I could have been speaking of the author of *Leaves of Grass*.

ANNEX

WALT & OSCAR:
VOICES OF LIBERATION

He is a fine large handsome youngster—had the good sense to take a great fancy to me!

—Letter to Harry Stafford

What we most need, must always demand, is a clear road to freedom.

—Conversation with Horace Traubel

WHEN, ON THE afternoon of 18 January 1882, Oscar Wilde ferried across the Delaware River to meet Walt Whitman for the first time, he was twenty-seven years old. Whitman was sixty-two and had been gray-bearded for a good thirty years. The *Press* of Philadelphia, reporting on the meeting the next day, emphasized the difference in age with the subheadline, "The Aesthetic Singer Visits the Good Gray Poet."

But mere chronology can be quite deceiving. The two amiable celebrities—who spent, as Whitman told the *Press* reporter, "a good part of the afternoon" upstairs in his den conversing and emptying a bottle of wine—were, in that far more significant respect of spirit, about the same youthful age. In their inimitably Irish/English and American ways, one might even say, they were the great babies of their day. They created worlds of their own and became singularly stubborn, careless, and happy inhabitants of these worlds, which is the essence of child's play. By some willful, ingenuous alchemy of the soul, each was able to retain, in spite of the passing years, that schoolboy's "shining morning face" that signifies, according to Shakespeare, the second of man's seven ages.

Wilde's essential childishness was often remarked during his adult life. A few months after he visited Camden, a reporter for the New Orleans *Times-Picayune* shrewdly observed that his "face has an air of youthful, almost infantile sweetness, which perhaps is the real secret of Mr. Wilde's power over the people who admire him." This quality surely explains why his company would so delight his two sons several years later. The younger one, Vyvyan, wrote in his memoirs, "Most parents in those days were far too pompous with their children, insisting on a vast amount of usually undeserved respect. My own father was quite different; he had so much of the child in his own nature that he delighted in playing our games." In Wilde's glory days in the 1890s, his friend Max Beerbohm thought him overweight yet said he was "fat not after the manner of ordinary men, but rather as some huge overgrown schoolboy." Even after his conviction and imprisonment, it was easy to strike the childish note in speaking of him. "I think his fate is rather like Humpty Dumpty's," wrote his wife Constance, "quite as tragic and quite as impossible to put right." His chief caretaker in the last few miserable years of wandering on the Continent, Robbie Ross, admitted that his old friend had become "a sort of adopted prodigal baby."

Whitman radiated the same juvenile air. A longtime friend remarked that, having gone gray by thirty, Whitman "had a look of age in his youth." But the friend adds that he managed somehow to retain "a look of youth in his age." When the young American poet Stuart Merrill met him in his late sixties, he was struck by how "the eyes, candid and blue like a little child's, sparkled with roguishness and kindness" and how Whitman's complexion "recalled precisely that of a young blond boy still a trifle animated from running." Whitman's Leaves of Grass, of course, rather insistently encouraged readers to marvel at the impression of the author's eternal youth. In an anonymous review of the first edition, he described himself as one who "drops disguise and ceremony, and walks forth with the confidence and gayety of a child." A few years later he added to the third edition a short poem that begins "What am I after all but a child, pleas'd with the sound of my own name?"

For both Whitman and Wilde, however, youth was not merely a pose but a political position. They clearly shared the truculent view of the elderly expressed by Thoreau in Walden: "I have lived some thirty years on this planet, and I have yet to hear the first syllable of valuable or even earnest advice from my seniors." To an admirer several years his junior, Wilde once wrote almost the same words: "I have never learned anything except from people younger than myself and you are infinitely young." On this theme Wilde spun several of his most mordant witticisms. "The old believe everything; the middle-aged suspect everything; the young know everything." In "The Decay of Lying," Vivian says that "frequenting the society of the aged and the well-informed" is "fatal" to the imagination. Mid-nineteenth-century America was quite as "aged" as late Victorian

England, and *Leaves of Grass* time and again strikes the note of a child announcing that he will not listen to his elders. Whitman chose to ignore, flamboyantly, the adult world inhabited by "the vast army of Philistia, the respectable . . . the timid, the pampered, the prurient, the conforming, the bourgeoisie" in spirit (in the phrase of the first great Whitman student, John Burroughs). "Young and strong" he came instead, as America's affectionate "cheer-bringing God, with . . . indulgent words as to children." These indulgent words said, in effect: Yes, go and play.

Though Whitman asserts in "Song of Myself" that he is "of old and young . . . a child as well as a man," his partisanship is clear. His very life's work is an answer to a child's question: "A child said *What is the grass?* fetching it to me with full hands." The most striking—and most profoundly autobiographical—of the several memorable answers Whitman proceeds to offer is "I guess the grass is itself a child." The passage of some thirty years did not change Whitman's allegiance to youth. "I like the boys who are glad to be boys—the men who remain boys," he told Horace Traubel. "Why should any man ever give up being a boy?" A few years later, in his most important political essay, Oscar Wilde would similarly hallow the child's place: "It will be a marvellous thing—the true personality of man . . . It will be as wonderful as the personality of a child." Can it be coincidental that not a single photograph survives of Whitman with someone his own age?

The vastly varied responses to Whitman in the last century can thus be explained, in part, as reflecting the different ways adults react toward children. Some, like Charley Shively, will find nothing but delight: "Part of the joy and center of Whitman's poetry will always be his eternal boyishness, his wonderful adolescence." Some, like Willa Cather, will condescend: "He was . . . a man without the finer discriminations, enjoying everything with the unreasoning enthusiasm of a boy." And others, like the appallingly dismissive Yvor Winters or the derisive Wyndham Lewis, will become purse-lipped and tetchy in a child's presence: "Walt showed all those enthusiastic habits we associate with the Baby. . . . He was a great big heavy old youngster of the perfect Freudian type, with the worst kind of enthusiasm in the Greek sense of the word." This dyspeptic squelch, however, curiously echoes Whitman's description of Wilde to the Philadelphia *Press* reporter, which he obviously intended as high praise: "I was glad to have him with me, for his youthful health, enthusiasm and buoyancy are refreshing. . . . He seemed to me like a great big, splendid boy." But then, we have seen, Whitman's enthusiasm was "Greek" in the very best sense of that word.

Bring Walt Whitman and Oscar Wilde together, as happened in real life in the winter of 1882, and many remarkable parallels and inter-sections in their lives and work like these begin to appear.

AT EASE IN ZION

We have the Philadelphia publisher J. M. Stoddart to thank for this titanic meeting of the two who would become the century's most famous gay comrades. On 11 January he wrote to Whitman, "Oscar Wilde has expressed his great desire to meet you socially. He will dine with me Saturday afternoon when I shall be most happy to have you join us. The bearer, Mr. Wanier, will explain at greater length any details which you may wish to know, and will be happy to bring me your acquiescence." Whitman, ever (like Wilde) the shrewd self-publicist, chose instead to sit for a Philadelphia photographer on that Saturday afternoon. Whitman noted this invitation "to drive with Mr Wilde in Phila" in his daybook, but he clearly wanted the meeting to occur on his own turf, where an intimate conversation might be more likely to take place. When Stod-dart tactfully withdrew for several hours, Whitman's strategy worked.*

Whitman laid it on pretty thick for the *Press* article, of course. He told of insisting on first names and of Wilde putting a hand on his knee to say, "I like that so much." (A dozen years later, asked at his trial if he was on a first-name basis with all his young sex partners, Wilde would answer, "Yes. I always call by their Christian names people whom I like. People I dislike I call something else.") Whitman also took special pains to disarm all the American journalistic satire aimed at Oscar's effete views and effeminate bearing. "We had a very happy time together. I think him genuine, honest and manly. . . . He is so frank and outspoken and manly. I don't see why such mocking things are written of him. He has the English society drawl, but his enunciation is better than I ever heard in a young Englishman or Irishman before."

Whitman would not have found Wilde's *Poems* (1881) to his taste at all; his silence about them is perhaps telling. And he would have been a very restless visitor at one of Wilde's lectures on interior decoration. But when the two came to talk about art and letters, Whitman went out of his way to be a sweetly avuncular host. He says he evaded "with a smile" several inquiries designed to draw out his views on the aesthetic school, and recalls only one shot across the bow of Art for Art's Sake: "Why, Oscar, it always seems to me that the fellow who makes a dead set at beauty by itself is in a bad way." He preferred, rather, to let the "splendid boy" simply go out and play. "You are young and ardent, and the field is wide, and if you want my advice, I say 'go ahead.'" He even cast a glance at Wilde's "big proportions" and expressed the hope that he would "shove the established idols aside"—a hope that was to be spectacularly fulfilled. As the two-hour chat came to an end, Whitman noticed that Wilde looked thirsty and made him a big glass of milk punch. "He tossed it off, and away he went."

Wilde, for his part, played the respectful, flattering neophyte perfectly. He told of his ebullient mother, Lady Wilde (who thought she was descended from Dante and preferred to be called Speranza), buying one of the earliest copies of *Leaves of Grass* sixteen years before and reciting from it to her son. It was, he said, also a companion on the rambles of his Oxford schoolmates. "I have come to you," Wilde said, "as one with whom I have been acquainted almost from the cradle." Knowing Whitman would see the reflection of his own younger self and certainly approve, Wilde also confided his "frank criticisms of British Philistinism," his view that the "poet

Oscar Wilde, in one of several photographs made in New York by Sarony, the fashionable celebrity photographer, during the lecture tour that brought the Irishman to Whitman's house in Camden in 1882. Sarony also photographed Whitman on two occasions, in 1879 and 1885. Library of Congress.

or artist in any department who goes beyond beaten ruts and lines is pretty sure of a bad time," and his desire to be among those who would "break up the stagnation" of Victorian England. He remarked on "the evident superiority of the masses of people in America" to those of Europe: a shameless bit of ingratiation with a poet known for spread-eagleism. Whitman complacently told the *Press* this view was "nothing new" but said it showed "the young man has his eyes open." Wilde also repeated some of the "gushing things" he had said in public about Whitman, notably that "we in England think there are only two—Walt Whitman and Emerson." And with Whitman's farewell, "Good-bye, Oscar, God bless you," he took his leave with two photographs in hand, one for himself and the other for Swinburne.

There was an afterglow. On the trip back to Philadelphia, Wilde was accompanied by Stoddart, who found him unusually silent and apparently deeply moved by "the grand old man." Whitman and Wilde were both keenly aware of the uses of photography in nurturing celebrity. Whitman even admitted late in life that he had "been photographed, photographed, photographed, until the cameras themselves are tired of me." Wilde was similarly assiduous, and two weeks after the visit an obviously impressed Whitman wrote to a friend, "Oscar Wilde sent me his picture yesterday, a photo a foot & a half long, nearly full length, very good." A month later, while staying at a Manhattan hotel on Whitman's beloved Broadway, Wilde wrote his single extant letter to "My dear dear Walt." In it he quotes at length from a letter just received from Swinburne with high praise for Whitman's "noblest works" and asks him to autograph for Swinburne a copy of a Whitman pamphlet on poetry. He concludes: "Before I leave America I must see you again—there is no one in this wide great world of America whom I love and honour so much."

Did a second visit actually take place? The editors of the *Collected Writings* think not: "He did not see Whitman again." But Richard Ellmann, in his Wilde biography, suggests that in early May it did, crediting Wilde's remark to his friend George Ives that Whitman "made no effort to conceal his homosexuality" on this occasion. It is tempting, indeed highly enjoyable, to imagine that a truly off-the-record meeting, undivulged to the *Press* or any other newspaper, took place at which the two spoke candidly about their predilections and hearts' desires, though we cannot forget that an eleven-year marriage and the fathering of two sons still lay in Wilde's future. Even so, one can still picture a meeting in the intimate style of "Song of Myself": "This hour I tell things in confidence, / I might not tell everybody, but I will tell you." In fact, the poet Richard Howard, in a richly atmospheric and carefully researched duologue called "Wildflowers," some years ago imagined Whitman and Wilde meeting in Camden as prophets "at ease in Zion, without age, without agitation."

It is not necessary, of course, to imagine a second, truth-telling visit. For Whitman's press account of the first meeting is highly suspect. Whitman was, as Leslie Fiedler has said, "the slyest of artificers"—and never more so than when performing for reporters or concocting "items" about himself to plant in newspapers. A celebrity capable of using a cardboard butterfly for his famous portrait (the tiny prop, MIA since World War II, was recently liberated and returned to the Library of Congress) was certainly up to making public only what he wanted the public to know about his visit with Wilde. He was always, in the phrase of Jorge

Luis Borges, "dramatizing himself," and there is an obvious hint of this fact in a thespian image he uses in the *Press* article itself. Wilde, he told the reporter, "was in his best mood, and I imagine that he laid aside any affectation he is said to have, and that I saw behind the scenes." Whether each of these two skilled actors and concealers did permit the other to see "behind the scenes" we shall never know. But it seems very doubtful that readers of the *Press* were vouchsafed such a view. Whitman's own self-protective affectation was obviously not laid aside in his narrative of the event. He mentioned, for instance, getting "inside glimpses" of the life and doings of the "London literati" from Wilde but did not choose to elaborate.

That Whitman carefully avoided revealing "inside glimpses" of racier topics of conversation to the reporter is suggested, I am inclined to think, by a tantalizing letter Whitman wrote to Harry Stafford one week after the visit. Stafford, twenty-three at the time, appears to have been depressed, and the purpose of this letter is to buck him up. "You say you wrote a *blue letter* but didn't send it to me—dear boy, the only way is to dash ahead and 'whistle dull cares away'—after all its mostly in one's self one gets blue & not from outside." Whitman then expresses the desire to have heart-to-heart talks more often:

> I wish it was so you could all your life come in & see me often for an hour or two—You see I think I understand you better than any one—(& like you more too)—(You may not fancy so, but it *is* so)—& I believe, Hank, there are many things, confidences, questions, candid *says* you would like to have with me, you have never yet broached—me the same—
>
> Have you read about Oscar Wilde? He has been to see me & spent an afternoon . . .

Here follows the sentence that serves as the first epigraph for this annex. The letter's last persuasive gambit is charming: "you say you know you are *a great fool*—don't you know every 'cute fellow secretly knows that about himself—I do." The farewell, as for Oscar, is a benediction: "God bless you, my darling boy—Keep a brave heart." It is appealing to speculate that Whitman's recent memory of a satisfying conversation with Wilde—full of "confidences, questions, candid *says*"—caused him naturally to think of Wilde after making his touching self-revelation. He wanted Hank, too, to "take a great fancy to *me!*"

One could scarcely expect Whitman to have been as relaxed and candid with Wilde as he was with Stafford, whom he had known for five years. The rather ceremonial meeting of the young lion and the old one was no occasion for genuine debate. The effect of the elderberry wine would have been spoiled.

However, remarks made several years later in conversation with Horace Traubel suggest that Whitman was not entirely disarmed by Wilde's charm. One day in August of 1888 he said, "I never completely make Wilde out—out for good or bad. He writes exquisitely—is as lucid as a star on a clear night—but there seems to be a little substance lacking at the root—something—what is it?" He tells Traubel, though, that in spite of Wilde's dubiousness he has "no sympathy with the crowd of the scorners who want to crowd him off the face of the earth." Later that fall Whitman recalled the year of Wilde's American lectures with a similar horticultural reservation: "Wilde . . . may have been some of him fraud at the time, but was not all fraud. . . . He has extraordinary brilliancy of genius with perhaps rather too little root in eternal soils." The foister of cardboard butterflies and author of poems in which, as Fiedler says, "trickery is essential, not accidental" has a fine nerve talking about Wildean "fraud," but there is considerable truth in the balance of this assessment. (Bernard Shaw attacked Wilde mercilessly as a fraud in his pose as an art connoisseur.) The next year, Whitman made a most remarkable evaluation that is understandable when one recalls that it came on the eve of Wilde's authorial *annus mirabilis* of 1890: "Wilde was very friendly to me—was and is, I think—both Oscar and his mother— Lady Wilde—and thanks be most to the mother, that greater, more important, individual. Oscar was here—came to see me—and he impressed me as a strong, able fellow."

Though Whitman entertained doubts about Wilde in private, he was clearly loath to utter them and give satisfaction to their common enemy, the army of Philistia. Nor did he want to be perceived as too effusively embracing Wilde with "tearbaggy manners": "We should leave slobbering to the idiots." Still, he was not shy about suggesting that the fault may have been in the eyes of the visitor's satirical beholders: "Everybody's been so in the habit of looking at Wilde cross-eyed, sort of, that they have charged the defect of their vision up against Wilde as a weakness in his character." Would he have sustained his public support for Wilde if he had lived another three years and witnessed the arrest and trial? Or would he have scrambled to distance himself from the cordial atmosphere of January 1882 and gone more public with his not unreasonable view that Wilde lacked "a little substance" at the root? Given the hysterical denial and outrageous boast of fathering six children when J. A. Symonds asked him in 1890 if the

Calamus poems could be read as homosexual, it could well have been the latter.

In any event, it is amazing that Whitman and Wilde got along as well as they did. In many respects, aside from their vast difference in age, they made an odd couple. Their physiques, of course, made a striking contrast. In one of his 1850s notebooks, as we have observed, Whitman sketched the four Temperaments, and his own, clearly, was the Sanguine: "well-defined form—moderate plumpness—firm flesh . . . fair complexion—great fondness for exercise and air—Brain active. . . . impels to motion and to animal gayety." Wilde's, on the other hand, seems perfectly reflected in the Lymphatic temperament as Whitman summarized it: "round form, soft muscle, fair hair, pale skin, sleepy eyes, inexpressive face. Brain languid—other organs ditto. The system—a great manufactory of fat."

In other respects they were just as disparate. Wilde could boast a recent and stunning Double First in his Oxford examinations and had also won the prestigious Newdigate Prize for poetry there. Whitman had completed his formal education at the age of eleven. Wilde seems to have had no practical interest in botany, aside from the exact correctness of the floral display in his buttonhole. Whitman was a practiced outdoorsman and connoisseur of plant life. The titles of his life's work and of its most resonantly autobiographical constituent, the *Calamus* poems of 1860, are taken from the green world. Wilde's interest in objets d'art was certainly not shared by Whitman. Wilde had made a splash at Oxford with a witty remark about finding it "harder and harder to live up to my blue china," while Whitman poked fun at such china in an essay on wildflowers. He singled out "a beautiful weed cover'd with blue flowers" that he was "continually stopping to admire." The blue of the dime-size buds, he said, was that "of the old Chinese teacups treasur'd by our grand-aunts."

Their views of journalism also might have clashed. Though Wilde would often, like Whitman, make cleverly exploitative use of journalists, his view of the profession grew increasingly hostile. The fourth estate, he said simply, was "very bad, and wrong, and demoralizing." By "giving us the opinions of the uneducated, it keeps us in touch with the ignorance of the community." Whitman, on the other hand, had commenced as a journalist at the impressionable age of twelve and by the age of twenty-eight had edited six different newspapers and written for another six. With him, as Burroughs observed, "the printer's ink had struck in," and he "loved the common, democratic character of the newspaper."

Whitman was a great perambulator, happiest when hiking the beaches of Long Island, the length of Broadway, or the environs of the capital: "I tramp a perpetual journey. . . . I have no chair." Traveling, Paul Zweig has in fact ventured, "is Whitman's principal activity in the 1855 *Leaves of Grass.*" Wilde, on the other hand, was decidedly more sedentary, a creature happiest indoors, pontificating at an exhibition, smoking lazily in his drawing room, or holding court at a London dinner party. When he was asked in court whether the site for one of his assignations was not ten minutes' walk from his house in Tite Street, he haughtily announced his entire reliance on hansom cabs: "I never walk." Wilde, by the way, was elaborately devoted to cigarettes (Nellie Melba once discovered six cigarette cases on his person). This could not have pleased Whitman, who, according to Peter Doyle, "seemed to have a positive dislike for tobacco."

A more profound difference lay in the strong streak of snobbery in Wilde's character. Shaw ridiculed him as a "prime specimen" of a Dublin snob—Shaw was a Dubliner too and knew whereof he spoke—and was especially aggravated by Wilde's insistence on polite decorum. "He objected to be addressed as Wilde, declaring that he was Oscar to his intimates and Mr. Wilde to others. . . . The vulgar hated him for snubbing them; and the valiant men damned his impudence and cut him." This, we have seen from his insistence on Oscaring a stranger, was not Whitman's style. His pose was that of a rough Jacksonian democrat who refuses to perch himself upon propriety. In one of his anonymous reviews of *Leaves of Grass*, he cheerfully grants that he "likes to be called by his given name, and nobody at all need Mr. him." He also boasts that he is "not prejudiced one mite against the Irish—talks readily with them—talks readily with niggers—does not make a stand on being a gentleman."

In one of his manuscript jottings for "Song of Myself," Whitman associated the etiquette of address with the larger world of fashionable social decorum, which he heartily despised all his life:

> Cleanly shaved and grammatical folks I call Mister, and lay the tips of my fingers inside their elbows after the orthodox fashion . . . and pass the time as comfortably as the law allows.—But for the others, my arm leans over their shoulders, and around their necks. . . . Their indefinable excellence gives out something as much beyond the special productions of colleges and pews and parlors as the morning air of the prairie or the sea-shore outsmells the costliest scents of the perfume shop.

Here we have virtually the anti-Wilde. Wilde was always cleanly shaved, and the young men with whom he consorted seem to have been too.

(Good grammar was not always required, though.) He harassed at least two friends—George Ives and André Gide—into shaving their mustaches, and wrote once of a "beautiful boy" he met in prison whose main blemish was "a slight, but still *real*, mustache." Whitman, of course, was the great singer of the hirsute. "Here are the roughs and beards . . . that the soul loves," he wrote in his preface to the first *Leaves of Grass*. Oliver Wendell Holmes's ill-meant jibe, "Whitman *goes at her* [poetry] like a great hirsute man," would have been taken by the poet as a compliment.

Wilde was also a brilliantly grammatical party, famed as an exquisitely polished talker. William Butler Yeats recalled his first meeting with him as an "astonishment," because he had "never before heard a man talking with perfect sentences." Wilde's writings were in large part but an extension of his extemporal conversational gifts, and many of his acquaintances remarked that nothing he wrote measured up to the quality of this talk. The Englishman Edward Carpenter visited Whitman in 1877, on the other hand, and recalled that Whitman "was no great talker, and would generally let the conversation ebb and flow at its own will." Nor could Whitman hope to challenge perhaps the champion English-language epigrammatist.* His most memorable utterances tend to be brief and bluffly declarative; they are too hirsute and brawny to achieve the agile twist that is necessary for an epigram. Even his most ardent admirers must grant, as did Burroughs long ago, that Whitman is "deficient in humor" of a literary kind and that "the brilliant epigrammatist will surely find [*Leaves of Grass*] an offence, and will battle against it." The poetry of Whitman, Burroughs adds with some justice, is "death to epigrams."

Oh yes, and "the costliest scents of the perfume shops" were not unknown to Wilde. Just before his release from prison he wrote to Ross, specifying the personal effects he hoped would be ready for him. Among his wants were Peau d'Espagne or Sac de Laitue soap, Canterbury Wood Violet cologne, and Eau de Lubin toilet water from Pritchard's shop in King Street.

Wilde, then, at the time he met Whitman, was a brilliant habitué of the world of the beflowered and china-festooned parlor, the elegant drawing room, the chic dinner-party table—from which felicity Whitman eagerly and noisily chose to absent himself. The notes for "Song of Myself" just quoted begin: "How gladly we leave the best of what is called learned and refined society." And in one of his self-reviews he says Walt Whitman "would leave a select soiree of elegant people any time to go with tumultuous men, roughs, receive their caresses and welcome, listen to their noise, oaths, smut, fluency, laughter, repartee." It is ironic to think that, a decade later, Wilde would become, as it were, socially ambidextrous: equally comfortable at a select soiree or enjoying the smutty repartee of young roughs and rentboys.

But then, it seems that Wilde was already honing these recklessly democratic social skills in January of 1882. For Whitman told the *Press* that his guest appeared "glad to get away from lecturing, and fashionable society, and spend time with an 'old rough.'" He was probably right. Wilde had, in fact, come from a formal breakfast given by a Professor S. H. Gross and would go back to Philadelphia for an elaborate society reception that evening. Whitman could have joined him. He wrote to young Hank, however, "I was invited to receptions in Phila. am'g the big bugs & a grand dinner to him by Mr & Mrs Childs—but did not go to any." He'd had his "candid *says*" with Oscar in blue-collar Camden and did not need to hear Oscar's "English society drawl" being suavely deployed among Philadelphia's upper crust.

In notes Whitman probably wrote before 1855, he observed that literature for such learned and refined people "is a parlor in which no person is to be welcomed unless he come attired in dress coat and observing the approved decorums with the fashionable." He shunned the literature and literati (and piano tunes) of the parlor, underlining the fact by including a portrait of himself vestless, open-collared, and coatless in the first edition of *Leaves of Grass*. In contrast, though Wilde also entertained highly subversive sartorial views, he was entirely comfortable in the literary "parlor" world. It is a tribute to the values and agendas they shared (both patent and hidden) that the Irishman's aristocratic snobbery and the American's democratic snobbery were not allowed to spoil their "jolly good time" together.

TWO BOYS TOGETHER CLINGING

Seven years after the Camden visit, Wilde, writing in the *Pall Mall Gazette*, made his most important public statement about Walt Whitman: "The chief value of his work is in its prophecy, not in its performance. He has begun a prelude to larger themes. He is the herald of a new era. As a man he is the precursor of a fresh type."

There is no evidence that these words came to Whitman's attention, but if they had he would certainly have been deeply gratified. Wilde's assessment unwittingly describes the task Whitman had set for himself more than three decades before, prior to publishing his most provocative edition of *Leaves of Grass* in 1860. On a scrap of paper Walt jotted what he was after at this time of his life: "A poem which more familiarly addresses those who will, in future ages understand me, (Because I write with reference to being far better understood then than I can possibly be now.)" This desire must have generated in his "Poets to Come" (1860) the line "I myself but write one or two indicative words for the future." It certainly suffuses his short poem "Beginners" (also new in 1860), a poignantly autobiographical meditation on how it feels to be the precursor of a fresh type:

> How they are provided for upon the earth, (appearing at intervals,)
> How dear and dreadful they are to the earth,
> How they inure to themselves as much as to any—
>   what a paradox appears their age,
> How people respond to them, yet know them not,
> How there is something relentless in their fate all times,
> How all times mischoose the objects of their adulation and reward,
> And how the same inexorable price must still be paid for the
>   same great purchase.

In respect of Wilde, there is immense irony in these lines. For he was himself a beginner, as Whitman perhaps sensed when he encouraged him to "shove the established idols aside." Wilde was, as the poem has it, also a celebrity both dear and dreadful to his late Victorian audience, an insistently paradoxical presence, a man who evoked enormously varied response but, until the trials of 1895, was not truly known, a man dogged by "something relentless" in his fate. How, Wilde wondered aloud on several occasions, could his countrymen so mischoose the objects of their adulation as to admire Dickens, Trollope, Tennyson, or Kipling and not him? And of course, finally, Wilde paid an "inexorable price" for the pleasures he purchased at the expense of Victorian morality.

There is also a fine irony of chronology in the poem. Like Whitman, Wilde was a skilled self-praiser, and there is an element of self-praise in the description of his old American idol. Indeed, there is an almost psychic premonition in it. For when Wilde wrote his *Pall Mall* piece in 1889 he was just ending the decade of his life devoted to dithering Aesthetic connoisseurship (1879–83) and rather quiescent marriage, housemaking, and fathering (1884–89). He was on the eve of demonstrating—with the appearance of *The Picture of Dorian Gray*, "The Critic as Artist," and "The Soul of Man Under Socialism" in 1890–91—that another beginner, another herald of a new era, had arrived. In "The Soul of Man," in fact, he explicitly joined Whitman as a writer preoccupied with the future: "It is with the future that we have to deal. For the past is what man should not have been. The present is what man ought not to be. The future is what artists are."

Other curious chronological parallels in their careers also draw attention. Both men commenced as journalist/poets most inauspiciously, Wilde with the mediocre volume of poems in 1881 and Whitman with doggerel stuff he placed in various New York newspapers. Both churned out much unexceptional, ephemeral, sometimes windy reportage and reviews in their late twenties and early thirties. Then, at almost exactly the same age, the spectacular butterflies emerged from their colorless, unpromising, hackwork chrysalises. (Both men, like that other W, Whistler, were famously associated with the colorful insect: Whitman was photographed with one, and Wilde told a friend *The Importance of Being Earnest* was "written by a butterfly for butterflies.") In 1855, when he was thirty-six, Whitman brought forth his epochal first edition of a mere 795 copies of *Leaves of Grass*. In 1890, Wilde likewise being thirty-six, his epochal *Dorian Gray* appeared in magazine form, then in 1891 as a volume, with a print run of only a thousand copies. Each work initiated a half decade of flourishing productivity for its authors. Whitman wrote more than two-thirds of his poetry and nearly all of his finest poems between 1855 and 1860; Wilde wrote nearly all the works for which he is now remembered between 1890 and 1895. That is, in their late thirties.

And then, at almost exactly the same age, each writer experienced a kind of artistic "death" that can be rather specifically dated. Whitman's demise dated from 13 April 1861, when he was forty-one and news of the bombardment of Fort Sumter reached New York. His steady decline, in post–Civil War editions of *Leaves of Grass*, into bombast, celebrityhood, and self-imitation, though, lasted over thirty years. Wilde was stunned into silence (except for *The Ballad of Reading Gaol*) by his arrest on 5 April 1895, when he was forty. By forty-six he was dead. The really spectacular beginners who "appear at intervals," it seems, cannot sustain their brilliance for long. They are in the nature of fireworks, like the Remarkable Rocket of which Wilde wrote in one of his most poignantly autobiographical children's tales.

Beginners, too, are bound to suffer abuse. Some works, Wilde once told Gide, wait a long time to be understood because they bring "answers to questions that have not been asked; for the question often comes a frightfully long time after the answer." *Leaves of Grass* perfectly exemplifies Wilde's point. We have perhaps not even now articulated fully and satisfactorily the questions to which it brings such radical answers. Anyone who attempts to supplant the old questions and the proprietors of all the old answers, as Whitman and Wilde did, is bound to pay the "inexorable price" of contumely.

Indeed, the sputtering outrage among reviewers at their shocking debutant fictions is perfectly interchangeable. An unsigned review in the New York *Criterion*, written by Poe's literary executor in 1855, called *Leaves* a "mass of stupid filth" that indulged in "the vilest imaginings and shamefullest license." *Leaves* was, for this reviewer, a "gathering of muck . . . entirely destitute of wit." The next year the *New York Times* fumed: "Who is this arrogant young man who proclaims himself the Poet of the time, and who roots like a pig among a rotten garbage of licentious thoughts?" *Dorian* received, almost verbatim, the same treatment. The reviewer for *Punch*, one Baron de Book-worms, felt that a "loathly 'leperous distillment' taints and spoils" the novel. The *Scots Observer* snidely said it was written for "outlawed noblemen [i.e. exiled titled homosexuals] and perverted telegraph boys" and wondered, "Why go grubbing in muck heaps?" And the *Christian Leader* thought it portrayed "the gilded paganism which has been staining these latter years of the Victorian epoch with horrors that carry us back to the worst incidents in the history of ancient Rome."

Even at the time of the Camden visit, Whitman and Wilde had been perceived as "two boys together clinging" (*Calamus* #26) and were clamped in the same pillory. The 1881 *Poems*, which seem so mild and neutered today next to *Leaves of Grass*, were pronounced "salacious" by the Springfield *Republican* and "obscene" by the San Jose *Daily Morning Times*, while the appearance of a new edition of *Leaves of Grass* the same year gave the New York *Tribune* its opening: "After the dilettante indelicacies of . . . Oscar Wilde, we are presented with the slop-bucket of Walt Whitman. . . . The chief question raised by this publication is whether anybody—even a poet—ought to take off his trousers in the marketplace." This yoking of the two cultural pariahs reached a climax in Max Nordau's *Entartung*, which appeared in English translation as *Degeneration* for the first time three years after Whitman died and a few months before Wilde's arrest. How Whitman would have delighted to be damned, as Nordau damns Wilde, for his "purely . . . egomaniacal recklessness." And how many reviews of his own work would Wilde have been reminded of in Nordau's rant about the "moral obtuseness and morbid sentimentality" of "the effusions of Walt Whitman, that crazy American."

The heaped abuse and vitriol both men experienced early in their careers caused them to indulge throughout their subsequent lives in certain protective strategies. The first was to present themselves to the world

in a pose of unflappable confidence. "Abuse seemed to make no differ-
ence to Walt," said his brother George; "he never counselled with any-
body."* This pose is captured in the perfectly titled 1860 poem "Me
Imperturbe," in which the poet snaps himself "standing at ease in
Nature" and displaying "aplomb in the midst of irrational things."
"Aplomb" might be the single best word to describe the public image
Wilde sought to achieve, whether offering a curtain speech at a premiere
with gold-tipped cigarette in hand, haughtily replying to reviews of
Dorian Gray, or defending the Love that dare not speak its name from the
witness box in the Old Bailey. His credo on criticism, published in 1891,
is pure Whitman: "On the whole, an artist in England gains something
by being attacked. His individuality is intensified. He becomes more
completely himself." Indeed, Whitman had years before presented himself in this grand pose of hauteur when he wrote, "All great rebels and
innovators, especially if their intellectual majesty bears itself out with
calmness amid popular odium or circumstances of cruelty and an inflic-
tion of suffering, exhibit the highest phases of the artistic spirit."

Another strategy was, in the privacy of their writing desks, to become
more careful, pull in their horns, and censor the blatancies of their first
drafts. The extant typescripts and two editions of *Dorian Gray* (no manuscripts survive) reveal dozens of retreats, both minor and significant, from
untrammeled utterance. They are often very similar to the retreats and
concealments achieved by revisions we have seen Whitman making in his
later *Leaves* editions. Both authors had good reason to despise public censorship. *Leaves of Grass* had been removed from the shelf of Wilde's own
Trinity College in Dublin, and Wilde's play *Salome* was not performed
publicly in England until many years after he died. But each was prag-
matic enough to draw the line between heroic and foolish risk-taking.

A third strategy they shared was that of composing their work for two
audiences at the same time. They would write in such a way that the
mainstream of readers (the ignoscenti) would be entertained and unof-
fended while a chosen elite (the cognoscenti) would read between the
lines and revel in the pleasures of deciphering the concealed exotica.
That famously raunchy mid-twentieth-century writer Henry Miller
sensed this about Whitman: "America has never really understood
Whitman, or accepted him. . . . Whitman did not address the masses."
Paul Zweig, more recently, writes forcefully of the almost hair-raising
nerve Whitman displayed in publishing the 1860 edition without expurgation, knowing that the vast army of Philistia would not "get
it": "Nothing, not even the poems of *Calamus*, could make Americans
confront that sealed subject [homosexuality] openly enough even to be

outraged. It is as if the *Calamus* poems were not read, as if they slipped through blanks in the minds of readers." Wilde, too, often depended upon the "blanks" in his Victorian readers' minds. "The Portrait of Mr. W. H.," about Shakespeare's love for a boy actor, is the most *Calamus*-like of Wilde's fictions in this respect, but racy encoded allusions are even scattered in some of the children's tales and, of course, in *The Picture of Dorian Gray.**

One consequence of this bifocal strategy—and a mark of its success—is the fan letters both received from young gay men who felt themselves ideally cognizant readers. For example, Charles Warren Stoddard, we have seen, wrote a marvelously confessional, idolatrous letter to the author of *Leaves of Grass* from Hawaii in 1869. In it he makes bold to describe his freedom from constraint "in these very interesting Islands," and says that for the "first time I act as my nature prompts me. It would not answer in America, as a general principle,—not even in California, where men are tolerably bold." He tells Whitman every Hawaiian man has a "matchless physique," and he describes at length sleeping most agreeably with one of them, eighteen or twenty years old: "In the morning he hates to have me go. I hate as much to leave him." Toward the end of the letter Stoddard says, "I read your Poems with a new spirit, to understand them as few may be able to." He begs for a few lines ("I want your personal magnetism to quicken mine") and a photograph ("the small lithograph I have of you is not wholly satisfactory"), and gives Whitman a San Francisco postal address.* Whitman's brief response, with which he included a photograph, is charming: "Those tender and primitive personal relations away off there in the Pacific islands (as described by you) touched me deeply. . . . Farewell, my dear friend. I sincerely thank you and hope some day to meet you." In one of his early, pre-*Leaves* notebooks, Whitman had observed that "A man only is interested in any thing when he identifies himself with it," and he gave readers like Stoddard much with which to identify.

That the writings of Whitman and Wilde attracted very similar "avowal" letters (as Whitman called them) from heartened young gay men is charmingly demonstrated by Lionel Johnson, an undergraduate at New College, Oxford. As an eighteen-year-old, he wrote to Whitman on 20 October 1885 to say that "in all constant thoughts and acts of my last few years, your words have been my guides and true oracles. . . . I should feel shame for myself, were I not to show the reality of my gratitude to you, even through the weakness of words—you, whom I thankfully acknowledge for my veritable master and dear brother." Johnson says that he received *Leaves of Grass* "from the hands of a most dear friend" and assures Whitman that "the help and exaltation I have won from it have been won by many another boy and young man." Whitman's response on hearing this letter reread by Traubel: "That sounds very ripe for a boy of eighteen—ripe enough already to shed fruit. . . . Keep a weather eye open for that boy: he will appear again." Johnson apparently did not do so, but five years later (and still at New College) he did appear on Wilde's horizon. On 18 February 1890 Johnson wrote to a friend: "On Saturday at mid-day . . . I was roused by a pathetic and unexpected note from Oscar: he plaintively besought me to get up and see him. Which I did. . . . He discoursed, with infinite flippancy, of everyone: lauded the *Dial:* laughed at Pater: and consumed all my cigarettes. I am in love with him." Johnson, it might be said, was to prove the unwitting sealer of Wilde's fate, for it was he who lent his copy of *The Picture of Dorian Gray* to Alfred Douglas. Douglas became "passionately absorbed" in it—read it nine times over, he said—and succeeded in getting Johnson to introduce him to Wilde. The rest was to be sad history.

The Frenchman Gabriel Sarrazin was another partisan shared by Wilde and Whitman. In 1885 Wilde wrote to thank the thirty-two-year-old for the gift of a book of essays and complimented his "exquisite critical insight." Four years later Wilde spoke of inviting him to dinner in Tite Street, and it was at just this time Whitman received a thank-you letter from Sarrazin for a copy of *Leaves of Grass:* "I shall peruse the new pages with the same admiration I bore to the ancient ones, with all my love for one . . . of the best and greatest men of the time." Sarrazin had published a comprehensive study of Whitman in the *Nouvelle Revue* in 1888.

Wilde received many such idolatrous letters as those Stoddard, Johnson, and Sarrazin wrote to Whitman. Almost none survive, though several gracious responses by Wilde suggest the flavor of them. One letter that did survive was from Clyde Fitch, a gay man who later became the first hugely successful American playwright. He appears already to have been to bed with Wilde when he wrote a similar adulatory letter after reading "The Portrait of Mr. W. H." "*I* believe in Willie Hughes," he says, calling the story "great—and *fine*," and the letter ends with this astonishing salutation: "Invent me a language of love. *You* could do it, Bewilderdly, All yours Clyde."* Over the decades, *Leaves of Grass* succeeded in evoking from those readers who sensed some kind of special affinity numerous letters and not a few personal visits to Camden. Many were doubtless lost in the clutter of Mickle Street, and Whitman may have destroyed the more extravagantly explicit ones (like Fitch's to Wilde), but some of them survived long enough to get into Traubel's

hands and be recorded. They give us a flavor of how successful that elaborate long-distance cruising apparatus called *Leaves of Grass* was.

These letters, indeed, came to be considered a separate category of
Whitman mail, along with the missives of "autographites" (Whitman
always retained any enclosed stamp, "destroying the rest at once"),
money-beggers ("they have heard I am a kindly old man!"), and parties
wanting literary advice. Then there were the nasty, often unsigned letters
filled with vituperation. One day in January 1889, Whitman told Traubel
he received two anonymous letters telling him something "bad." When
Traubel asked where they were, "He smiled. Pointed to the stove. 'Gone
up in smoke.' " All such letters Whitman called "worrisome." More to his
taste were the "avowals." A week before the two letters hit the stove,
Traubel reported, "W. gave me another one of the 'avowals.' He said: 'It
is a beautiful thing.' . . . I had to read the letter to him of course." This
letter, dated 1876, happened to be from a woman who identified herself
as a friend of Joaquin Miller (yet another devotee of both Whitman and
Wilde).*

But virtually all of the "avowals" were from men—usually young and
often, one can guess, homosexual. Young Bayard Taylor, for example,
wrote Walt in 1866 to praise *Leaves* for two things he could find nowhere
else in the literature of the day: awe for human life "as expressed in the
human body" and "that tender and noble love of man for man which
once certainly existed but now almost seems to have gone out of the
experience of the race." Taylor, unfortunately, got sucked into what
Whitman called the "*finesse*, finish, polish" of "the New York clique" and
eventually turned against his former idol. Whitman was also much
charmed by the first letter of another later-to-be-famous author, Hamlin
Garland. Garland was twenty-six in 1886 when he enthused, "I am,
everywhere in my talking and writing, making your claims felt and shall
continue to do so. . . . your poems thrilled me, reversed many of my ideas,
confirmed me in others, helped to make me what I am." He then adds,
little knowing how this would delight Whitman, "I am a border-man,—
born in Wisconsin and raised on the prairie frontier."

Ten years before, in 1876, Edward Carpenter—perhaps the premier
homosexual apologist of his generation and deep admirer of Whitman
(among his numerous books: *Days With Walt Whitman*)—wrote one of the
most moving avowals in the Traubel volumes. When Walt handed it over
to Horace he called it "one of Carpenter's early fine letters." Amid its
praise is this *Calamus*-spirited remark: "Dear friend, you have so infused
yourself that it is daily more and more possible for men to walk hand in
hand over the whole earth. . . . I think indeed the time has come for

people to learn to unwrap these bands, and that from this time there will be a world-wide growth in the direction you have pointed out."* Later, alluding clearly to the gay liberation agenda he perceived in *Leaves*, Carpenter adds, "So while I regret sometimes that there are things in your writings which make it difficult, sometimes impossible, to commend them to some who might otherwise profit by them, yet I feel it is best that they should be there. Their presence delays the understanding and acceptation of your message, but your message would not be complete without it."

Another Carpenter letter, dated May 1889, ends with this allusion to his own search for love: "All goes well with me. I am brown, & hardy—and tho' I live mostly alone I have more friends almost than a man ought to have. Some kind of promise keeps floating to us always, luring us on. With much love to you, dear Walt." Perhaps Whitman's own deep sense of that "luring" promise of love made him tell Traubel he thought this letter "one of the leading best missives I ever had—goes to my heart." John Addington Symonds wrote many letters in this vein as well, some of them, as Whitman observed, "more intimate, more personal, more throbbing" than others.

Many of the "avowals," of course, were from correspondents whose names are now lost in the mists. One was a William Hawley of Syracuse, who wrote in 1869, "I would I could grasp your hand, look in your eyes and have you look in mine. Then you would see how much you have done for me. Yours with a brother's love." Another was a John Swinton. When Whitman gave his letter to Traubel he said, "This letter is almost like a love letter—it has sugar in it." The aging poet did not seem to lose his appetite for these sugary letters, though he wasn't shy about carping when they went over the top. Allen Upward sent him a voluble extravaganza from Dublin in 1884 which began, "O Walt! Take this Calamus leaf at the hands of him thou hast sought for. Lo! I am he." Walt found in it, quite rightly, "the same crude boy confidence, the same mix-up of instincts, magnetisms, revolts," as in the letters Stoker had written him. Even in the very last years, the letters continued to arrive. In March 1890 an Irish-born clerk in Melbourne, Australia, wrote with "Enthusiasm abounding" (as Traubel put it), beginning: "Dear Walt, my beloved master, my friend, my bard, my prophet and apostle . . ."

Some of these superheated letters with apparently gay subtexts generated bemusement, or even embarrassment. In September 1889 Traubel recorded, "W. received what he calls 'one of my funny notes.' A young man in Richmond, 'a Southern boy'—writes a novel—says publishers refuse it because it shocks' etc. Asks W. to read it—it is only 109pp. legal cap! Of course W. never answered." A year before, in December 1888, Whitman "drifted into talk about the odd letters sent him." Then he took out "a very curious letter" he had just received "from a great distance . . . you would not think it: Algiers." Whitman explains that it is from someone "who wants to acknowledge indebtedness: it is warm—almost fervid. . . . A young fellow, an Englishman—it would seem, a 'nob': he has lost his girl: grieves, is restless: turns away from home—travels . . . gets to Algiers. Whether he took it with him, or found it there, or some one directs him to it—somehow he falls upon a copy of *Leaves of Grass*: reads it—says he is helped by it: that it braces him up to bear his sorrow: is enthusiastic—feels he must write." Given Wilde's homosexual recreations as a married man several years later in exotic Algiers, the scenario seems transparent enough: a young gay aristocrat has employed *Leaves* to help him lift the burden of guilt from his shoulders. Whitman told Traubel there was "something in the case which appealed to him" but did "not know what."

One guesses, though, that he did know what—just did not want to talk about it. Perhaps the same reluctance to get into sensitive territory caused him to respond negatively when Traubel, mentioning William O'Connor's excellent idea of collecting all the "comrade letters" in a book, added, "he says they exemplify your revolutionary sympathies." To this the ever cautious Whitman replied, "Ah! is that his idea? they seem so personal: it might be done but not by me: I would not be the best one for such a delicate task."

That *Leaves of Grass* was perceived and embraced by its gay readers as (among other things) a "coming out" work and a manifesto for sane self-acceptance is eloquently shown in practically the last, and surely one of the most moving, "avowal" letters Whitman ever received. Its author was no less than John Addington Symonds, himself ill and also soon to die. This letter, addressed to Traubel, was written "in the deep night" of 27 February 1892 from Davos, in Switzerland, where he was just finishing his biography of Michelangelo and no doubt planning his last opus, a book on Whitman. His words deserve quotation at length:

> You do not know, & can never tell any one, what Whitman has been to me. Brought up in the purple of aristocratic school and university, provided with more money than is good for a young man, early married to a woman of noble nature & illustrious connections, I might have been a mere English gentleman, had I not read *Leaves of Grass* in time.
>
> I am not sure whether I have not abused the privilege of reading that book. It revolutionized my previous conceptions, & made me another man. . . .

I only know that he made me a free man. . . . he also made me love my brethren & seek them out with more perhaps of passion than he would himself approve.

Working upon a nature so prepared as mine was, the strong agent of Whitman's spirit could hardly fail to produce fermentation. . . .

To clinch all, he has only done for me good; & the harm which may come to me, from intemperate use of his precepts, is the fault of my previous environment and my own feeble self. . . .

If I have seemed to be cold, here & there, about Whitman, it is not because I am not penetrated by his doctrine; but because I know by experience how powerfully that doctrine works, & how it may be misused & misunderstood.

Yours

J.A.S.

Though Traubel brought this and another Symonds letter to Mickle Street on a "very bad day" for Whitman ("a day of incuriosity, silence—without appetite, relish, strength"), the invalid was very eager to hear them read: "Read them now—now—now." Traubel did so, and, as can be well imagined, the effect of so perfect, if extremely delicately phrased, an expression of gratitude for the sexually liberating *Leaves of Grass* "doctrine" was shattering. Traubel records: " 'Loving Symonds! Dear Symonds!' and several times he had me re-read passages. 'Do you hear it all?' [Traubel asks]. 'Every word, every word—I am attentive to every word,' which was very evident—the tears gushing out of his eyes, and his whole body and brain evidently stirred by the words of the letters." Two weeks later, Whitman was dead.

In late February of 1894, just a year before his fall, Wilde received from a young artist named Philip Houghton an obviously confessional letter like the ones just sampled. Wilde responded that he was "deeply moved" and offered in return one of his most important confessions about his own life. "To the world I seem, by intention on my part, a dilettante and dandy merely—it is not wise to show one's heart." The letter ends on an importantly earnest note. "But write to me about yourself; tell me your life and loves, and all that keeps you wondering. Who are you? (what a difficult question for any one of us to answer!) I, at any rate, am your friend."

Whitman, late in life, had occasion to tell his young friend Traubel of precisely the same care he had taken to avoid showing his heart to the world. "I have suffered all my life from the misjudgments of people who looked with suspicion upon all I do." In order to come to "conclusions

satisfactory to my own soul," Whitman tells of employing "very methodical . . . ways [that] are mine and are necessary to me. I need to isolate
myself—to work along very undemonstrative lines: I can never rush."
Neither he nor Wilde could have afforded to rush, for the "methodical"
calculations are complex that allow one to reveal the heart to one's true
readers while seeming "undemonstrative" to the rest of the world. Every
now and then, however, Whitman allowed his pride at doing so to burst
demonstratively forth, as in "To a Certain Civilian" (1865):

> . . . leave my works,
> And go lull yourself with what you can understand, and with
> piano-tunes,
> For I lull nobody, and you will never understand me.

The poem's context is military, but it surely reflects the sentiment
Whitman secretly entertained toward the "civilian" world five years
before, when he presented it with his *Calamus* poems. Toward his double
audience he was, as he boasted, respectively "the most loving and arrogant of men."

To be sure, some clever but hostile civilians grasped the sophisticated,
subversive innuendos and were not amused. In a ferocious but perceptive
attack, the poet Sidney Lanier exploded the notion of Whitman as a
democrat and revealed him as purveyor of "dandyism—the dandyism of
the roustabout. . . . Upon the most earnest examination, I can find it
nothing but wholly undemocratic; not manful, but dandy; not free,
because the slave of nature [read: sexual desire]." Lanier concludes that
Whitman, "instead of being a true democrat, is simply the most incorri-
gible of aristocrats masquing in a peasant's costume." His work thus is "a
blasphemy against real manhood, is simply tiresome." This, of course, was
the gist of much of the criticism, especially in dozens of *Punch* magazine
skits and cartoons, directed at Wilde and his decadent cohorts as he pursued his dandiacal ways in London in the early 1890s. "Sexomaniacs" was
Punch's word for them.

Their countrymen's rabid response to the two buoyant beginners
underscores one final similarity in their careers worth noting, namely, the
fact that each of them enjoyed extraordinary initial popularity abroad.
Wilde was received in France relatively benignly, but in Germany he had
an enthusiastic following. An entire scene from *The Importance of Being
Earnest* cut by Wilde for the London premiere was preserved in a 1903
German edition titled *Ernst Sein!*, and his executor, Ross, was able to
announce in 1908 that Wilde's estate was no longer in debt, thanks

largely to royalties from Germany. In spite of what Burroughs called Whitman's "passion for country," he long perceived himself as better appreciated in Europe than America. In 1872 he wrote to a Dutch admirer that "neither my poetic *Leaves* or *Democratic Vistas* is cordially accepted in the United States—nor do the chief literary persons or organs of the country admit the poems as having any merit. . . . abroad, my book & myself have had a welcome quite dazzling." A few years later he wrote a short item, apparently for placement in an English periodical, in which he complained that, while "Emerson and Whittier are well off, and Longfellow and Bryant are rich," he "alone keeps up the tradition of narrow means and wide afflatus. While his fame is fast filling Europe, he is unrecognizable in his own country, works daily as a clerk at three hundred pounds a year . . . and has not yet, it is said, the first shilling of return from his poetic volumes." A decade later his royalties had improved only slightly, but his European fame continued strong. In 1885 Whitman's total income of $1,333 included $67 in American royalties and gifts totaling $686 from English admirers.

All of which gives some color to H. L. Mencken's observation about Whitman's "intellectual foreignness and loneliness" in America. This seems, at first blush, a very strange remark to make about that most energetically spread-eagle and ingratiatingly come-hither of all American writers. But there is truth in it. As with Wilde, insights into Whitman have a way of deriving from—or devolving into—paradox.

PRINCES OF PARADOX

"What a paradox appears their age" to beginners, wrote Whitman. The feeling is almost inevitably mutual: harbingers of new ideas and sensibilities will be perceived by their age as paradoxes themselves. Strindberg, a late-nineteenth-century theatrical innovator, was delighted to call himself a paradoxist in the Whitman sense: "I am proud that I am not alone in my paradoxes, as all new discoveries are called." Paradoxes, of course, may cause befuddlement, amusement, consternation, or downright anger. The richly paradoxical presences of Whitman and Wilde evoked all these responses and more at one time or another; indeed, an essentially paradoxical nature is the most extensively ramifying and revealing of all their shared characteristics.

Dorian calls Lord Henry Wotton, the character in *Dorian Gray* fashioned in Wilde's own image, Prince Paradox. Perhaps the best, though unwitting, self-description we have of the novel's author is a remark he made a year earlier in "The Decay of Lying": "In Falstaff there is some-thing of Hamlet, in Hamlet there is not a little of Falstaff." Wilde somehow managed to contain, if not multitudes, certainly the reckless gaiety of Sir John and the withering, sable intelligence of the Prince. That is why paradoxes and oxymorons seem to come easily in descriptions of him. Prince Paradox left even his good friends and acquaintances with mixed feelings. His best friend, Ross, said, "It was natural to Wilde to be artificial." Another acquaintance called him a "contented ogre." Richard Le Gallienne reminisced with baffling ambiguity, "Doubtless, he was weak as well as strong, and wrong as he was right." But the reaction of an Oxford tutor who spent a week with Wilde, his boyfriend Lord Alfred Douglas, and Wilde's two sons at a vacation house (Constance was traveling on the Continent) perhaps best captures the paradox Oscar presented to the Victorian age. "I think him perfectly delightful," said Campbell Dodgson, "with the firmest conviction that his morals are detestable." And critics have produced many ingenious paradoxes to describe him since his death: serious playboy, genuine counterfeiter, con-formist rebel, for example.

Nor was paradox merely something at the core of Wilde's nature. It was also a chief element of his style. After the premiere of his drawing room comedy *A Woman of No Importance*, the London *Times* marveled at Wilde's "passion for paradox, persiflage, and proverbial perversity" (he also loved to alliterate). Henry James grudgingly acknowledged his "cheeky paradoxical wit" and observed, "Everything Oscar does is a deliberate trap for the literalist." For the beginner Wilde, the paradox was a superb weapon for subverting all the old answers and asserting new ones. One dictionary definition of paradox is "a seemingly contradictory statement that may nonetheless be true." Wilde defined it more shrewdly as a "dan-gerous" weapon when deployed in a society mainly populated—as soci-eties always are—by literalists. In "The Decay of Lying," Cyril (playing the literalist) asks Vivian, "But you don't mean to say that you seriously believe that Life imitates art, that Life in fact is the mirror, and Art the reality?" To which Vivian (playing Oscar) replies, "Certainly I do. Para-dox though it may seem—and paradoxes are always dangerous things—it is none the less true." The next year, Wilde vividly elaborated his defini-tion when he had Lord Henry Wotton say, "The way of paradoxes is the way of truth. To test Reality we must see it on the tight-rope. When the Verities become acrobats we can judge them."

Wilde's brilliant paradoxing gave the stiff, unexercised verities of Vic-torian England an exhausting workout. Whitman's *Leaves of Grass* tested the flabby verities of mid-nineteenth-century America, too, and paradox

played a very important part in the process. But their two styles of paradoxing aerobics were distinctly different. The graceful, lithe finesse of
slim acrobats was not to Walt's taste; he preferred the butch, brawny, big-
boned physique. He said he wanted American verities and citizens to be
"muscular and self-possessed." Wilde's paradoxing was a riveting public
performance, like that of an acrobat on a high wire; it is there, for all to
see, in the verbal texture of virtually everything he wrote. Whitman's
paradoxing is far more subliminal, present in the recesses of his own personality and behind the lines of his poetry. It transpires within the "me"
behind the "real Me" who vocalizes for us in his poems. It is extremely
artfully screened, just like the woman in "Song of Myself" who hides
behind the window blinds of her fine house to spy on twenty-eight naked
young men bathing—and yet who is able to pass an "unseen hand" over
their bodies and "seizes fast to them." This is a quintessentially Whitmanesque moment, desire being—paradoxically—both concealed and
revealed. Many more such moments were to follow, notably in the *cri de
coeur* of his oeuvre, the *Calamus* poems: "Here I shade and hide my
thoughts, I myself do not expose them, / And yet they expose me more
than all my other poems."

Wilde, in his letter to Whitman, praises the poet for being "simple
and grand." By the 1880s he had certainly become grandly good and gray,
but simple he never was. Rather, he was a spectacular equivocator and, in
his swaggering debutant song of himself, very boastful of the fact, calling
himself "One of that centripetal and centrifugal gang" and a man "Both
in and out of the game." He can pose as one "Hurrying with the modern
crowd as eager and fickle as any" and then, two lines later, as a night
dreamer "Solitary at midnight in my back yard." Small wonder that
Paul Zweig would summarize "to see Whitman we need bifocals," that
Leslie Fiedler would say his poetry is "precisely a matter of cardboard butterflies on real fingers," or that the poet John Berryman would become
annoyed at all these "paradoxes that writers on Whitman too readily
indulge in."

Writers may have to be forgiven, though. For paradoxes are constantly
causing the meditator on Whitman's life or the reader of his poems
to stop, cock the head at an angle, and let the mind squint a moment.
We are often invited, in other words, to assume exactly the pose of
Whitman's amused and detached "Me myself" who is always "Looking
with side-curved head curious what will come next." Indeed, it is only
when Whitman turns thirty and paradoxical that he becomes truly interesting. Zweig writes, in fact, of the years 1848–49, "We must now begin
to think of him as a paradox: on the one hand, a writer of limited origi-

nality . . . on the other hand, a writer obsessed with originality who had decided to reinvent the idiom of literature." Zweig later phrases the Whitman paradox even more starkly: "Here is the baffling, often irritating fact of Whitman's temperament: that he was a hack and yet was also America's most original poet."* Poor Berryman!

Some of Whitman's paradoxes leave not only a side-curved head but also a smile: the dreadful temperance novel *Franklin Evans*, for instance, which he wrote early in life with, he said, the help of "gin cocktails"; or the Whitman who never voted himself but always advised "everybody else not to forget." Two of his favorite running jokes, several times repeated, consisted of paradoxical advice. The first: " 'Horace: listen to this: Take one more piece of advice and then stop.' 'What piece?' 'Never take advice!' W. laughed heartily." The second: "Be radical—be radical—be not too damned radical!" (This was varied on other occasions with "bold," "cocky," and "individualistic.")

Superbly paradoxical is the reputation for being a "good gray" eminence and Whitman's well-known (at least to his intimates) gift for brusqueness. Edward Carpenter was astonished at how the jovial face could "become as a precipice, instantly and utterly inaccessible." Yes! resonates throughout *Leaves of Grass*, yet when Pearsall Smith visited the author he was most impressed by the "magnificent No!" he was capable of sounding in company. Whitman's "Dear boy Pete" Doyle likewise admired his ability to squelch anyone who "stepped across what he thought his private border-line": "He could shut a man off in the best style, you know. He had a freezing way in him—yet was never harsh."

Whitman's political utterances create many a paradox, too. How could the great Civil War poet have approved of a new Oregon constitution prohibiting black freemen or slaves from entering the state? Or retain in *Leaves* after 1865 a poem "To The States" in which he advises them to "*Resist much, obey little*"? And how could the "typical inevitable democrat" (as Burroughs called him) nevertheless challenge his 1860 readers so anarchically: "Mind you the timid models of the rest, the majority? / Long I minded them, but hence I will not—for I have adopted models for myself." These lines, written in the contrarious heat of the *Calamus* poems, must have become embarrassing to the growing booster of "the word En-Masse," for he dropped them in all later editions.

Wilde himself figures in some of the more provocative Whitman paradoxes. In an 1890 conversation Walt recalled being struck by "a splendid thought" Wilde had expressed while in America, namely, "that no first-class fellow wishes to be flattered, aureoled, set upon a throne—but craves to be understood, to be appreciated for his immediate active present power." But Whitman, as he grew older, delighted in flattery, as Burroughs acknowledged: "The shadow of Whitman's self-reliance and heroic self-esteem—the sort of eddy or back-water—was undoubtedly a childlike fondness for praise and for seeing his name in print." He did not mind at all the aureole that surrounded him when Colonel Ingersoll lauded him at a Philadelphia lecture or when he attended the festive birthday dinners he was given in his later years.

Or consider the paradox of the admirer of blacksmiths with "massive arms" and ample-necked Negro horsemen with "polished and perfect limbs" and the proponent of an "athletic and defiant literature" being himself something of a lay-abed. He talked a good game in his 1855 preface to *Leaves* about a great poet knowing how to arouse a "heavy and slothful" time, but his brother George said that "he would lie abed late, and after getting up would write a few hours if he took the notion." When Bronson Alcott visited Whitman in 1856, he too recalled him posing in the languid fashion of Wilde's Algernon Moncrieff or Lord Henry Wotton: "When talking he will recline upon the couch at length, pillowing his head upon his bended arm, and informing you naively how lazy he is." Indolence, Whitman revealed, was one of the "dangerous faults" of his character, according to a phrenologist he had consulted in 1849, though his former employer at the *Daily Eagle* did not need to be told this: "Slow, indolent, heavy. . . . He was too indolent to kick a musketo." Not surprisingly, George said Whitman "cared little for sport." As with Wilde, "gunning" was something he had "nothing to do with," and the only physical exercise they both indulged in was swimming—if, in Whitman's case, it could be called exercise. "I was a first rate aquatic loafer," he told Traubel. "I possessed almost unlimited capacity for floating on my back."

There is also rich Wildean irony in Whitman's numerous announcements of his taste for roomy, unprepossessing, simple masculine dress. "An American bard at last!" he cries in one of his anonymous reviews of *Leaves*. "One of the roughs . . . his costume manly and free." In another he boasts that he is "never dressed in black, always dressed freely and clean in strong clothes—neck open, shirt-collar flat." He put his sartorial agenda into "Starting from Paumanok" in 1860 with this stirring line— "See the populace, millions and millions, handsome, tall, muscular, both sexes, clothed in easy and dignified clothes." Here was a clarion call for the Rational Dress movements that would in fact burgeon in the last half of the nineteenth century. One might think all this anti-dandiacal and unWildean. But in fact Whitman worked with a dandy's attention to detail to achieve his air of careless deshabille. He began as a dandy in calico.

The picture Bronson Alcott gives of him in 1856 is not much distant from the "manly and free" costumes (Whitman chose his words well) one is likely to see everywhere in Western-style gay bars today: "Red flannel undershirt, open-breasted, exposing his brawny neck; striped calico jacket over this, the collar Byroneal [i.e. open and flat], with coarse cloth overalls buttoned to it; cowhide boots; a heavy round-about, with huge outside pockets and buttons to match; and a slouched hat, for house and street alike."* Whitman was fastidious, too, with the boys he dressed. Accompanying a gift to his "Dear boy Pete" were these instructions: "The blue shirt . . . is to wear *over*, loose—it is made large for that purpose—I like the looks of them, the blue shirt collar turned down low with a nice black silk neck-handkerchief, tied loose—over a clean white shirt without necktie—I think they are very becoming to young workingmen." Nor did Whitman cease his careful attentions to dress later in life. "Never have I seen a man so fresh, so neat, so immacu-late," said Stuart Merrill when he met the sixty-eight-year-old in 1887. "He wore, that day, a jacket of black velvet, a large unstarched linen collar, and handsome lace ruffles. For he was very stylish in his own fashion."

Whitman's ability to appear casual and unaffected in his dress while paying close attention to it derives from his more general (and Wildean) skills as an actor. He was well aware that there was a public personality and one that existed, as he told the *Press* reporter, "behind the scenes." This he expressed memorably in one of his *Calamus* poems:

> That shadow my likeness that goes to and fro seeking
>   a livelihood, chattering, chaffering,
> How often I find myself standing and looking at it where it flits,
> How often I question and doubt whether that is really me;
> But among my lovers and caroling these songs,
> O I never doubt whether that is really me.

The last two lines complicate the paradox, for Whitman behaved quite differently among his lovers—up, as it were, in his den with Oscar, responding to the letters of boyish admirers, giving young friends nice blue shirts—than when caroling his songs. Even as he announces that the "shadow" is "really me," one is left to ponder whether the author of the line is not an unrevealed third party. The poem is a characteristic example of Whitman behaving like Hamlet (whose creator referred to actors as "shadows"), a master of "ambiguous giving out." Perhaps this is why he shared Hamlet's affinity for players. "These actor people always make themselves at home with me," he told Traubel; "I feel rather close to them—very close—almost like one of their kind."*

This made him one of Wilde's kind, too. Wilde's wife called him a "born actor," and role-playing was an essential part of his life and authorial style. Among his most famous (and paradoxical) credos is his view that "Man is least himself when he talks in his own person. Give him a mask, and he will tell you the truth." Whitman's "shadow" and his "real Me" were such masks. The roiling emotional reality behind these masks Whitman vividly expressed in this short poem titled "Visor'd" from 1860:

> A mask, a perpetual natural disguiser of herself,
> Concealing her face, concealing her form,
> Changes and transformations every hour, every moment,
> Falling upon her even when she sleeps.

Artfully masked in the feminine gender, he was writing of himself.

Indeed, the virtuoso "performance" that both men gave on the literary and cultural stage of their day was expressed by themselves in specifically thespian terms. "Anybody can act," Wilde told the readers of the *Daily Telegraph*; "most people in England do nothing else. To be conventional is to be a comedian." But then he adds that to "act a particular part" is "a very different thing, and a very difficult thing." Wilde did precisely this to spectacular effect. André Gide recognized this and, needless to say, the insight was expressed in the form of a paradox: "the character he played was his own; the role itself, which his everlasting demon kept prompting him, was a sincere one." Wilde thus avoided the fate of most human beings. "Most men and women are forced to perform parts for which they have no qualifications," Wilde sadly concluded. "The world is a stage, but the play is badly cast." Whitman likewise chose to perform a "sincere" role, not one prescribed by that comic genius Society. Whitman shows precisely this determination to avoid the common fate—indeed, shows the desire to rewrite the play on his own terms—in a few marvelous lines from his manuscripts for the 1860 *Leaves of Grass*:

> Come I am determined to unbare my breast—I have stifled
>   and choked too long
> I will escape from the costume, the play which was proposed to me
> I will sound myself and love—I will utter the cry of friends . . .

Whitman was driven to write his own heroically idiosyncratic role, in large part, by the urge to "sound" his love and "utter the cry of friends."

But the very fact that he did not permit these lines to be published points to another rich source of paradox in the life and work of both Whitman and Wilde: the constant tension and tug-of-war between self-confidence and doubt, between self-revelation and concealment, between the self-protective instinct to remain in the Closet and the self-assertive urge to leave it. Both men, in other words, experienced profoundly the dilemma Wilde succinctly expressed in *De Profundis*, the agonized apology he wrote while in prison: "To speak the truth is a painful thing. To be forced to tell lies is much worse."

The two great boys were drawn irresistibly to the lilac-blooming play-space of the dooryard just outside the Closet, a playground they both knew to be forbidden, closely monitored, and well fenced. But both had the nerve of trespassers. After prison, Wilde wrote to a friend of strolling in Switzerland: "There are lovely walks here by the Lake, through the grounds of others: but then I am a born trespasser." Whitman told his friend Traubel the same thing—"I was never made to live inside a fence"—and had made that pose clear in 1855: "I troop forth replenish'd with supreme power . . . and pass all boundary lines." As trespassers, Wilde and Whitman indulged in very complex maneuvers, camouflaging and disguising their candor—their seemingly unevadable urge to be frank—in various ways. Whitman's poetry of the "real Me" Harold Bloom justly calls "intricate and forlorn," for it was difficult, degrading, but necessary, this business of concealing one's soul. Much of Wilde's writing is similarly intricate and forlorn.*

Friedrich Nietzsche and André Gide, it happens, expressed some very pertinent views about artists who find themselves in this excruciating position. Nietzsche seems almost to be thinking of Whitman when he writes, in *The Gay Science*, "Every noble spirit and taste selects its audience when it wishes to communicate itself; and, while choosing it, it at the same time erects barriers against 'the others.' All the more subtle laws of any style have their origin at this point: these laws at the same time keep away, create a distance, forbid 'entrance,' understanding . . . while they open the ears of those whose ears are related to ours." The subtle (and paradoxical) laws of Whitman's style have an important point of origin in this analysis. We have, first, the poet who keeps his civilian readers at a distance by positively stentorian assertions of candid self-confidence. "I tell things in confidence" and "It is time to explain myself—let us stand up" are the memorable poses of "Song of Myself." He also states grandly in his 1855 preface: "The great poets are also to be known by the absence in them of tricks and by the justification of perfect personal candor. . . . How beautiful is candor! All faults may be forgiven of him who has perfect candor." In

1860 he reiterated the point: "I announce the justification of candor and the justification of pride." This pose hoodwinked many, including, amazingly, John Burroughs: "The candor and openness of the man's nature would not allow him to conceal or feign anything."

But then we have another poet—the one whose voice is directed to those with ears related to his—who often reveals a keen acquaintance with feigning and concealment. Whitman describes these readers (and himself) when he ventures: "I believe you are latent with unseen existences." The mingled pain and joy of the *Calamus* sequence is caught in these lines from #15 challenging latency: "From my breast, from within where I was conceal'd, press forth red drops, confession drops." Years of furtively cruising Broadway lie in this passage from another *Calamus* poem: "O Manhattan, your frequent and swift flash of eyes offering me love, / Offering response to my own." Deeply moving is the allusion to the Closet's space in "Assurances" (1856): "I do not doubt interiors have their interiors, and exteriors have their exteriors, and . . . the hearing another hearing, and the voice another voice." And there is not a better poetic evocation of the thick-plated inferno of the Closet than occurs in "Song of the Open Road," from the 1856 edition of *Leaves*:

> Out of the dark confinement! out from behind the screen!
> It is useless to protest, I know all and expose it. . . .
> Behold a secret silent loathing and despair. . . .
> Another self, a duplicate of every one, skulking and hiding it goes . . .
> Smartly attired, countenance smiling, form upright,
>   death under the breast-bones, hell under the skull-bones . . .
> Keeping fair with the customs, speaking not a syllable of itself,
> Speaking of any thing else but never of itself.

Some of the most exciting moments in Whitman's poetry, like this one, come when the poet is speaking of himself. As it happens, Wilde, also an inveterate but cryptographic autobiographer in his fictions, can explain why: "Autobiography is irresistible. . . . When people talk to us about others they are usually dull. When they talk to us about themselves they are nearly always interesting."

Gide, in an angry entry in his journal in 1927, brilliantly analyzed the way Wilde chose to talk about himself. The analysis parallels Nietzsche's aphorism and, it will be seen, applies perfectly to Whitman. Gide's fury was ignited by an essay by André Maurois on Wilde that did not address the question of sexuality ("very much a lecture before a ladies' club," Gide sneered). Maurois, Gide felt, failed to recognize that "always, and often even without the artist's knowing it, it is the secret of the depths of his flesh that prompts, inspires, and decides." Gide observes that Wilde's plays "reveal, beside the surface witticisms, sparkling like false jewels, many oddly revelatory sentences of great psychological interest. And it is for them that Wilde wrote the whole play—let there be no doubt about it." Gide allows that he himself "always preferred frankness," and then goes on to describe Wilde's contrasting "methodical" and "undemonstrative" style:

> But Wilde made up his mind to make falsehood a work of art. . . . That is what made him say: "Never use *I*." The *I* belongs to the very face, and Wilde's art had something of the mask about it, insisted on the mask. . . . Always he managed in such a way that the informed reader could raise the mask and glimpse under it the true visage (which Wilde had such good reason to hide). This artistic hypocrisy was imposed on him by respect, which was very keen in him, for the proprieties; and by the need for self-protection. Likewise, moreover, for Proust, that great master of dissimulation.*

And likewise for Whitman. Though he made a great noisy fuss about abrogating the proprieties, Whitman was very attentive to them, became a master of dissimulation in respect of them. "Be radical, be radical," he urged Traubel, but then added his usual retreat to carefulness, "be not too damn radical."

In consequence, there is a dizzying coexistence of boldness and caution in his poems. No wonder his phrenologist gave him a very high 6 for both Combativeness and Cautiousness. He can apostrophize the "potent, felt, interior command" to fare forth that Columbus felt, or he can lie back and praise the Closet in lines he finally suppressed: "And now, escaping, I celebrate that concealed but substantial life, / I celebrate the need of the love of comrades." In the first *Leaves* he could be both brilliantly vocal ("I chant a new chant of dilation or pride, / We have had ducking and deprecating about enough") or utterly dumbstruck ("I cannot say to any person what I hear"). In a poem for *Leaves* a year later, the Whitman persona is agonizingly mute—

> When I undertake to tell the best I find I cannot,
> My tongue is ineffectual on its pivots,
> My breath will not be obedient to its organs,
> I become a dumb man.

—yet erupts in the end with operatic exclamation: "Say on, sayers! sing on, singers! . . . pile the words of the earth!"

Similarly, in an 1860 poem, he could almost simultaneously boast of "aplomb" and yet cry, "O to be self-balanced for contingencies . . . ridicule . . . rebuffs." His epitaph could have been the same as on a grave marker in one of his Civil War poems: *"Bold, cautious, true, and my loving comrade."* Or, if that is not succinct enough, then "O daring joy, but safe!" from his 1871 "Passage to India." Such paradoxing continues through the very aptly titled "A Riddle Song" of 1880, in which we are vouchsafed another stage-managed glimpse "behind the scenes." Here is Whitman, as ever, "Open but still a secret, the real of the real, an illusion . . . Hiding yet lingering." Lingering, that is, autobiographically in his verse—as Gide said Wilde lingered in his fiction—to be "picked up" by the reader who is his true lover. Interestingly, Thomas Mann put Gide (and himself) firmly in this tradition of simultaneously bold and cautious—"out" and "closeted"—writing for a dual audience—when he agreed that Gide was "a cautious radical and a daring conservative" and added, "precisely this mixture makes me confess to brotherly feelings."*

Toward the end of his *Calamus* poems, the hectoring poet of candor rather boldly (one would think) confessed his devious, side-curved ways:

> Among the men and women, the multitude, I perceive
>   one picking me out by secret and divine signs,
> Acknowledging none else—not parent, wife, husband, brother,
>   child, any nearer than I am;
> Some are baffled—But that one is not—that one knows me.
>
> Lover and perfect equal!
> I meant that you should discover me so, by my faint indirections,
> And I, when I meet you, mean to discover you by the like in you.

This confession, of course, was not so bold. Whitman was cautiously assuming (rightly, as it turned out) that his readers En-Masse would be baffled and uncomprehending of the sexual thrust of the sequence. Toward these readers Whitman can become "precipitous" and truculent: "Do you see no further than this façade, this smooth and tolerant manner of me?" On the other hand, he knew that the *Calamus* poems would, in Nietzsche's phrase, open the ear of the reader who might be his true lover. This perfect reader, he knew, would hear and truly understand the "faint indirections" of *Calamus* and be able to decipher them, just as such a reader would have solved the "uniform hieroglyphic" of his earlier "Song of Myself."

Lord Goring, the Wilde character in his play *An Ideal Husband*, is described in a stage direction as "fond of being misunderstood" because it "gives him a post of vantage." Whitman, like all adroit paradoxists, shared this fondness. But of course neither author desired his paradoxes to be misunderstood by the *entire* world—just by the respectable, conventional, literal-minded, mammon-worshipping, heterosexual "multitude." Each had, as Wilde suggested to young Houghton, a heart to reveal, but only to "perfect equals." Without such readers, they could not fully relish the "post of vantage" achieved by their paradoxes. This post stood on a giddy height. It required an audience of initiates alive to the "secret and divine signs" and able to sense when Wilde and Whitman were performing their self-revealing high-wire feats, as it were, without a net.

BUTTERFLY PHILOSOPHY

Toward the end of *An Ideal Husband*, Wilde reveals "the philosopher that underlies the dandy" in Lord Goring's character. Beneath the dandy in flannel and the dandy in brown velvet (Wilde's attire for Camden) also lay energetic philosophers, philosophers bearing proposals for a radically subversive *ars vivendi* or, in Foucault's more recent phrase, aesthetics of existence. But most of their respective countrymen were so distracted or mesmerized by their dandiacal poses and props—cardboard butterfly and slouch hat, ebony cane and gold-tipped cigarette—that their devastating critiques of contemporary mores were either not fully grasped or not taken seriously.

A few of Wilde's sharper contemporaries, however, saw that Victorian society had a serious, modern-day Socrates on its hands. Ford Madox Ford recalled, "When Oscar Wilde wandered down Bond Street in a mediaeval costume, bearing in his hand a flower, he was doing something not merely ridiculous. It was militant." G. K. Chesterton found his "philosophy of ease, of acceptance, and luxurious illusion" to be vile, but he admired the "pugnacious and propagandist epigrams" in which he clothed it. "This armed insolence . . . was the noblest thing about him," Chesterton elaborated; "he challenged all comers." But perhaps Le Gallienne put best his friend's brilliance at exploding contemporary morals and hypocrisies when he wrote that Wilde "made dying Victorianism laugh at itself, and it may be said to have died of the laughter."

His philosophy was, as Chesterton said, one of ease and acceptance:

more specifically, of easy, nonchalant *self*-acceptance, along with all the corollary adjustments society must make to accommodate the self-accepting person. Wilde pursued this thoroughly Whitmanesque philosophy from his college days. In one of his Oxford commonplace books he inscribed, in French, Baudelaire's prayer "O Lord! give me the power and courage to contemplate my heart and my body without disgust!" but he might well have inscribed any one of dozens of passages from *Leaves of Grass* to the same effect. Wilde's writings, especially those of the late 1880s when he was beginning to taste his true sexual identity, constitute almost a theme-and-variations on what Whitman called the "ego-style."

The good gray poet would surely have applauded Vivian's assertion in "The Decay of Lying" that egotism is "necessary to a proper sense of human dignity"—though Wilde's view that such egotism was "entirely the result of indoor life" would have appalled him. The next year Wilde reviewed a translation of the writings of the Chinese sage Chuang-tzu and found his "perfect man" to be much like Whitman's: "He lets externals take care of themselves. . . . His mental equilibrium gives him the empire of the world." A few months later Wilde cast the perfect artist in similar terms that capture the pose of America's Chanter of Personality: "The longer one studies life and literature, the more strongly one feels that behind everything that is wonderful stands the individual, and that it is not the moment that makes the man, but the man who creates the age." Art, he concluded, "springs from personality" and demands an intensified assertion of "individualism."* This constitutes as succinct a summary of Whitman's first preface to *Leaves of Grass* as one could wish.

Then, in 1890, appeared *Dorian Gray*, which contains Wilde's most famous enunciations of the Whitman agenda. "The aim of life is self-development," Wotton tells Dorian. "To realize one's nature perfectly—that is what each of us is here for." Later, in perhaps the Wildean *locus classicus* on the ego-style, Wotton tells Dorian and Basil Hallward, "To be good is to be in harmony with one's self. . . . Discord is to be forced to be in harmony with others. One's own life—that is the important thing." Whitman, in fact, offers a charmingly rural paraphrase of this sentiment in a letter to young Harry Stafford about his intentions in *Leaves of Grass*: "My own feeling abt my book is that it makes (tries to make) every fellow *see himself*, & see that *he has got to work out his salvation himself*—has got to pull the oars, & hold the plow, or swing the axe *himself*—& that the blessings of life are not the fictions generally supposed, but are real, & are mostly within reach of all—you chew on this." This radical opposition between the "fictions" of society and the "reality" of the self is the centerpost of Wilde's philosophy as well. Whitman, in fact, anticipated in 1888, with this remark, the effect Wilde would have two years later when he emerged in his full subversive splendor: "Now and then a man steps out from that crowd—says: 'I will be myself'—does, because he is, something immense. The howl that goes up is tremendous." And the howls Oscar elicited from Victorian England with *Dorian Gray* were indeed tremendous.

Whitman appears to have read none of Wilde's provocative works that appeared in the few years before he died. If he had, he might well have quipped—as Wilde once did to a dim interlocutor—"I not only follow you, I precede you." Decades before, he had brought this same bold new answer to the central questions of life. In 1855 he briefly summed up Wilde's theme: "Every existence has its idiom." Whitman's own poetic idiom was, of course, far removed from Wilde's soigné drawing room. His images are more fleshly and homespun, but they urge the same point. In "Song of Myself" he boasts that he finds "no sweeter fat than sticks to my own bones" and warns that "not any one else can travel that road for you, / You must travel it for yourself." The next year he asks, "Will you rot your own fruit in yourself there? / Will you squat and stifle there?" In "By Blue Ontario's Shore" (1856) he employs the now clichéd term "self-esteem" and exactly anticipates Wilde's "Critic as Artist" when he swears "nothing is good to me now that ignores individuals."

The 1860 edition of *Leaves of Grass* is Whitman's *Dorian Gray*. Here the dual theme of self-acceptance and self-assertion is climactically expressed. Whitman summarized a few years before he died that "allowing a place for every man's personality, idiosyncrasy" was "the keystone of the arch of my teachings," and the third edition is the one that most emphatically launches this agenda. The opening poem announces the desire to "effuse egotism and show it underlying all." This "habitué of the Alleghanies" will "treat man as he is in the influences of Nature, in himself, in his own inalienable rights." In *Calamus* #25 he prefers the "close companionship" only of those who "go their own gait, stepping with freedom and command . . . Those with a never-quell'd audacity." And among the joys he celebrates in "A Song of Joys" is

> the joy of a manly self-hood!
> To be servile to none, to defer to none . . .
> To walk with erect carriage, a step springy and elastic . . .
> To confront with your personality all the other personalities
>   of the earth.

After the 1860 edition, Whitman became more and more the arch-defender of the "federal mother," of Democracy, and of the "word En-

Masse." The bard of individual personality receded in favor of the abstraction-bound prophet, whose step was not nearly so springy and elastic as before. In the following lines from 1860, the watershed is clear. Whitman reiterates his familiar theme of freeing the soul or self from constraint, but the military analogy strongly anticipates the changed emphases of his Civil War poems and the post–Civil War editions of *Leaves*:

> WHAT place is besieged, and vainly tries to raise the siege?
> Lo, I send to that place a commander, swift, brave, immortal,
> And with him horse and foot, and parks of artillery,
> And artillery-men, the deadliest that ever fired gun.

It is significant that these lines were originally part of a *Calamus* poem, where the context encouraged the reader to see the brave "commander" as a savior of male lovers rather than military comrades. In the next edition, in 1867, the lines were taken out of *Calamus* and made to stand alone and thus savor solely of Civil War heroics.

The two teachers of, in Whitman's phrase, "the unquenchable creed, namely, egotism" inevitably became radical nonconformists and persistent iconoclasts.* Wilde—whose "egoism was superb," said his friend Ross—took great joy in harassing "the seven deadly virtues," making fun of Puritans, prigs, good conduct prizes, and do-gooders (the good was too often peremptorily devised by the doer). When the notoriously wayward Oxonian surprised everyone with a Double First in his exams, he exulted, "The dons are 'astonied' beyond words, the Bad Boy doing so well in the end!" The Bad Boy of course found "our modern mania for morality" and all its attendant hypocrisies very galling, especially when leagued with philistinism. When people "describe a work of art as grossly immoral," Wilde said, "they mean that the artist has said or made a beautiful thing that is true." He despised journalists who encouraged the public to moralize upon the lives of others. They "invite the public," he said, "not merely to give their views, but to carry them into action, to dictate to a man upon all other points ... in fact to make themselves ridiculous, offensive, and harmful." Whitman must have felt this way often.

One of Wilde's choicest subversive paradoxes (it was thrown up at him at his trial) runs "Wickedness is a myth invented by good people to account for the curious attractiveness of others." Whitman also reveled, though not with such dextrous phrasing, in the wickedness perceived by "good" people. Wilde's epigram, in fact, is virtually paraphrased in "Song of Myself," when the poet says he will love only the boy who is wicked "rather than virtuous out of conformity or fear." We have already met one boy, named Peter, whose wickedness proved curiously attractive to Whitman. In one of his notebooks he wrote of Peter as being a "man of strong self-will, powerful coarse feelings and appetites. . . . I liked his refreshing wickedness, as it would be called by the unorthodox.—He seemed to feel a perfect independence, dashed with a little resentment, toward the world in general." This, of course, is precisely the persona Whitman himself cultivated in his early poems.

These aberrant tastes made Whitman extremely allergic to constraint. Constraint, he believed in Wildean fashion, was itself an evil. In his earliest extant notebook he wrote, "Wickedness is most likely the absence of freedom and health in the soul." His advice in the preface for 1855 was to "re-examine all you have been told at school or church or in any book, dismiss whatever insults your own soul." His ideal of a "great city" was one where "outside authority enters always after the precedence of inside authority." Even the very cogent arguments of his idol Emerson for revising *Leaves* into more respectable form left Whitman feeling "down in my soul the clear and unmistakable conviction to disobey all." Here, as so often, Wilde followed him years later with an elegant paraphrase: "Disobedience . . . is man's original virtue."

Even their orthography reflected their boundary-crashing natures. One Oxford classmate recalled that Wilde's hand was "huge and sprawling" and that he "took no notice of lines" in his examination books. Whitman, likewise, insisted that Traubel find him Mammoth Falcon quill pens, because only they could match the size of his thoughts. He also cheerfully admitted, "I use ruled paper, but I don't write on the lines!"

Whitman's penchant for disobedience (though not Oscar's) also extended to trespassing beyond the lexical boundaries of Webster's. He liked to stretch words in odd and amusing directions or invent new ones. If one could have an appointment, why not a "depointment"? He disliked prudery so much that he made a verb out of it, complaining about contemporary America, where "everything is toned down, veneered, hidden, lied about, *pruded away*—note *that* word!" He complimented Traubel on the "great likeacality" of his manner, was also pleased that his friend Bucke was impressed by the "autobiographicality" of *November Boughs*. He liked an early photograph of himself for its air of "calm don't-care-a-damnativeness," while chiding Bronson Alcott for his "queerities" and man in general for being "a scamp . . . a wickedee." He thought that Lincoln was "not basically serious—at least, not to the point of seriosity." He also found himself, in April 1890, having "considerable of dubiosity" whether he would be fit to attend his seventy-first birthday dinner.

Even in his last pain-ridden months, Whitman exhibited a charming liberation from the ordinary word hoard. He was greatly amused when a stiff Presbyterian minister, all set to interrogate him severely, was abashed into silence by "the debrisity, the confusion, the air of don't care" at Mickle Street. He groused about the "toploftical" ideas that "splurgey" military men tend to get, but praised his own *Leaves* as having offered "a new, superiorially new, travel-road heretofore not trod by man." He warned his caregivers against any "doctorial hidings and seekings," that is, mincing of medical realities. And a few weeks before death he complained of feeling "an utter giving-out-ness" and an "exquisite sorification" on his tender right side.

His penchant for verbal freedom extended, as well, to borrowings from foreign languages. Defending himself to Traubel one day, Walt expressed his particular pride in his famous gay code word—appropriately enough, because it was "musical": "If I have the trick of *music*—verbal music—at all, I owe it to the great singers, actors: they were my teachers—I sat under their influence. Have I adopted many [foreign words]? Am I accused of many? I don't think *many*. There is camerado, and my great word, Presidentiad. . . . Those two—they are our *pride*."

Whitman saw invitations to disobedience in many far less trivial places, and his contrariness is often expressed in withering observations that recall Wilde's deft epigrams. Whitman strikes a still-timely note, for example, when he envisions a great city in which "the populace rise at once against the never-ending audacity of elected persons." (He also editorialized for fewer and shorter legislative sessions!) Wilde's put-down of politicians carries the same gist, but is more classically phrased: "The Lords Temporal say nothing, the Lords Spiritual have nothing to say, and the House of Commons has nothing to say and says it." Wilde's remarks that "we live in an age when unnecessary things are our only necessities" and that ours is "a thoroughly selfish . . . a thoroughly grasping age" are finely reflected in Whitman's coruscating précis of America in the 1870s: "Never was there, perhaps, more hollowness at heart than at present. . . . We live in an atmosphere of hypocrisy throughout. . . . the one sole object is, by any means, pecuniary gain. . . . The best class we show, is but a mob of fashionably dress'd speculators and vulgarians." The soul of man under mid-nineteenth-century Americanism, as under Wilde's Victorianism, seemed to Whitman a sorry thing. "Our country seems to be threatened with a sort of ossification of the spirit," he wrote in a probably pre-1855 notebook entry. "The current that bears us is one broadly and deeply materialistic and infidel. . . . The public countenance lacks its bloom of love and its freshness of faith.—For want of these, it is cadaverous as a corpse." When Whitman fumed one day to Traubel about the moralists' harassment of Byron, he veered, not surprisingly, to the image of joyful, naked bathers. "The whole spirit of the persecution of Byron is the spirit of the town police—just as the spirit of the obscenity hunter anywhere . . . the spirit that will ignore all the gigantic evils [and] steal away down to the shore—lay low—pull in a lot of little naked boys, there to take a bath—snake 'em in! It well pictures for me what is too commonly called the greatness and majesty of the law."

Both Wilde and Whitman blamed philanthropists, moralists, and reformers in large part for this ossification of the spirit. Whitman's remark "when I see the harm that morals do I almost hate seeing people good" is pure Wilde. Antimoralism constitutes Wilde's most bracing life-long theme-and-variations. Mrs. Cheveley in *An Ideal Husband* observes, "Morality is simply the attitude we adopt towards people whom we personally dislike," while Gilbert in "The Critic as Artist" remarks that "the desire to do good to others produces a plentiful crop of prigs." Finally, in "The Soul of Man Under Socialism," Wilde pronounced in emphatic italics his ban on all attempts by society to forbid the harmless behavior of others: *"Selfishness is not living as one wishes to live, it is asking others to live as one wishes to live."* The very word "vice," Wilde said, is "tainted in its signification with moral censure." Whitman shared all of these views, ridiculing any "blurt . . . about virtue and about vice" and refusing to assume the "fault-finder's or rejecter's gait." When he remarked to Traubel, "What would we do without the sinners? Take them out of literature and it would be barren," he was anticipating several of Wilde's most famous encomia to sin, among them the remark that, without sin, "the world would stagnate, or grow old, or become colourless."

Given the hostility to *Leaves of Grass* of such as the Philadelphia Society for the Suppression of Vice and Immorality and Anthony Comstock's New York Society for the Suppression of Vice, Whitman had good reason to ridicule reformers who would use their "favorite (pint) measure" to "ladle out the ocean." "It is pitiful," he concluded. In fact, at exactly the time of Wilde's visit, Whitman's Boston publisher was abandoning the 1881–2 *Leaves of Grass* under the threat of that city's district attorney to prosecute if the book were not withdrawn from the mails or expurgated. Whitman was naturally an enemy of morality laws and wrote editorials on the subject. Though not italicized, these words from a "memorial" against Sunday restrictions convey the same view Wilde expressed in "The Soul of Man": "We do not want prohibitions. . . . The citizen must have room. He must learn to be so muscular and self-possessed; to rely more on the restriction of himself than any restrictions of statute books, or city ordinances, or police." A germ of Walt's rabid antimoralism can also be found in his earliest surviving notebook: "Great latitude must be allowed to others."

It is scarcely a wonder that both Whitman and Wilde expressed themselves as spiritually more at home in the western reaches of America, where societies for the suppression of vice were much less likely to flourish. "The further West one comes," Wilde told the San Francisco *Examiner*, "the more there is to like. . . . The Western people are much more genial than those of the East." Indeed, the mayor led Wilde on a tour of San Francisco that included the opium parlors and brothels of Chinatown. Several years later Wilde gave Lord Henry his famous remark alluding to San Francisco's risqué reputation as the Hoodlum City: "It is an odd thing, but everyone who disappears is said to be seen at San Francisco. It must be a delightful city, and possess all the attractions of the next world."

Though Whitman never fulfilled his promise in *Calamus* #30 to travel to California, he certainly enjoyed and approved of the more relaxed and "genial" morals of the state (those discovered, apparently, by gay young Stoddard). Whitman was often mistaken for a Californian, which must have gratified him. In his notes he described humanity as being "freer and grander" there: "The passions are also stronger, the soul more clarified and apparent, life seems more intense and determined—there is more individuality and character." And in the West, to Whitman's mind, one was more blessedly free to live as one wished to live. In his early story "The Half-Breed: A Tale of the Western Frontier" (1845), he used for the first time the word he would later make famous—"in the west all men are comrades"—and observed that since "every one is in some degree or other an adventurer, few wish to investigate the former history of their neighbours. Inquisitiveness does not prevail there, as in some other sections of our republic."*

California, the West, and the "open road" in general represented for Whitman escape from the constraints of Eastern proprieties and Eastern nosiness. Whitman sensed that he and "robust love" belonged "inland, and along the Western Sea." It is droll, now, to consider the sexual implications of Whitman's response to an introductory letter from the young Hamlin Garland, who described himself as "a child of the western prairies" (he was from Wisconsin): "I always expect the men and women of the West to take to me . . . take me in one gulp! Where the East might gag over me the West should swallow me with a free throat." Thus, it is to a "Western Boy" in *Calamus* that he issues the invitation to "become eleve of mine." Wilde appears to have enjoyed his tour of America in this same comradely spirit, enjoying himself (one suspects) far more when drinking gin cocktails with a rowdy group of Leadville, Colorado, silver miners than at formal receptions like the one given for him in Philadelphia after he visited Walt.

The rejection of propriety in favor of freedom extended not merely to their tourism but to their dress. Beneath the elaborate self-consciousness of their vastly different costumes lay, as usual, a pugnacious philosophy of freedom. Whitman's boast "never dressed in black, always dressed freely" was also virtually Wilde's sartorial Golden Rule. He wrote admiringly to the London *Daily Telegraph*, for instance, of an actor allowed to wear colorful evening dress in a new play, that "its charm resides in the fact that the choice of the colour of the coat is left to the taste and fancy and inclination of the wearer. Freedom in such selection of colour is a necessary condition of variety and individualism of costume." Wilde approved of the controversial divided skirt for women because it was based on the principles of "ease and liberty," favored the loose cloak for its "freedom and comfort," and insisted that "for the sake of freedom" hats and boots be made of soft material and not according to "any stiff, stereotypical design of hat or boot maker." And Wilde reacted, as Whitman did, with the same scorn for moralists of fashion as for moralists of more important matters. Of one such nuisance, he hissed: "I hope he consults his own comfort and wishes in everything which has to do with dress, and is allowed to enjoy that individualism in apparel which he so eloquently claims for himself, and so foolishly tries to deny to others."

Whitman's dress, too, was a most significant part of his self-asserting revolt from the norm. Clearly, he shared the view of Wilde's Lord Goring: "Fashion is what one wears oneself. What is unfashionable is what other people wear." Bronson Alcott caught the note of sartorial willfulness when he reported that Whitman "wears his man-Bloomer in defiance of everybody, having these as every thing else after his own fashion." And many years later, when Whitman was on his deathbed, the New York *Advertiser* recalled him as a self-pleasing dresser: "He was almost the first to make the now fashionable fad of the flannel shirt in Summer his all the year round convenience and comfort."

The escape from propriety required a decisive deshabille. This Whitman suggests in a characteristic passage in his notes about gladly leaving "learned and refined society" in order to join "a party of fresh and jovial boatmen, with no coats or suspenders, and their trowsers tucked in their boots." Like Wilde, he hated the stiffly stereotypical starched collar, preferring something flat, open, "Byroneal." The citizen, he said, must have room; so must a man's body. His sartorial rule was, in a word, looseness. Twice, we have seen, Whitman urged his boy Pete to wear his new shirt "loose." This mundane advice perfectly captures the radical philosophy of Whitman and Wilde. In much of what they wrote, as well as what they wore, they proclaimed, in Whitman's words, "I am for those who believe in loose delights."*

"Loose delight" also happens to be a good way to describe the erratic flight of a butterfly. "Before I first met Oscar," wrote his dear friend Ada Leverson, "I had been told he was like a giant with the wings of a Brazilian butterfly, and I was not disappointed." This was her way of saying how charmed she was by his colorful, splendidly wayward, and ever surprising personality. In much the same spirit, Whitman had many years earlier chosen the insouciant insect as his symbol when he published his personality. It was a provocative choice to make in an age dominated by an utterly earnest, thoroughly grasping bald eagle—and a marvelously revealing choice as well. For when Emerson called Whitman a "wayward, fanciful" man, when Cather called him an "optimistic vagabond," or when Borges called him a "happy, semi-divine vagabond" each was, in effect, alluding to his butterfly philosophy. Like Wilde's, this philosophy ignored, with astonishing waywardness, the established idols. This philosophy fluttered in Nietzschean style beyond good and evil. Indeed, Whitman promised it would do so in the first *Leaves of Grass*:

> The vulgar and the refined . . . . what you call sin and what you
>   call goodness . . to think how wide a difference;
> To think the difference will still continue to others,
>   yet we lie beyond the difference.

TWO FISHERMEN

Whitman and Wilde had good reason to be resentful of those who busy themselves calling this "sin" and that "goodness"—and to desire to live their lives "beyond the difference." Perhaps, over the elderberry wine, they may have sensed and even discussed this special basis for their camaraderie.* The admiring remarks about "the grand old man" made by Wilde to the publisher Stoddart on the ferry back from Camden certainly suggest that a tiff over Art for Art's Sake could not vitiate the fundamental principles they shared.

It is, in fact, a remarkable irony that Stoddart was Wilde's companion for the excursion to Camden. Several years later, he would be instrumental in the writing of two Wilde fictions that display, better than any others, the profound alikeness of the two butterfly philosophers. In 1889, while in London looking for new material for *Lippincott's Magazine*, Stoddart dined with Arthur Conan Doyle and Wilde and came away with promises from both to write for him. Doyle produced the second of his Holmes novels, *The Sign of Four,* and Wilde eventually responded with "The Fisherman and His Soul," by far the longest, most ambitious and fascinating of his children's tales. Stoddart, however, apparently found the tale inappropriate for his readers and rejected it. Wilde's second submission, several months later, turned out to be *The Picture of Dorian Gray.* It occupied the first hundred pages of the July 1890 issue of *Lippincott's* and a year later, much revised and lengthened, appeared in book form. A few months after that, "The Fisherman and His Soul" was finally published in Wilde's second volume of children's tales, *A House of Pomegranates.*

When Stuart Merrill met Whitman in 1887, he marveled at how in the "beautiful old man" the "harmony of the body equalled that of the soul." This is the same charismatic "harmony with one's self" that Lord Henry Wotton would praise a few years later in *Dorian Gray.* "The Fisherman and His Soul" addresses the same subject, though obliquely. This tale is fundamentally about the terrible suffering that occurs when the body and soul are not able to enjoy harmonious union. Certainly, none of Wilde's writings more succinctly or eloquently displays him as an articulator of "the espousing principle" that, Whitman said, permeates *Leaves of Grass* and on which "the work must stand or fall." This was simply, wrote Whitman, that "the human body and soul must remain as an entirety." In the same passage, he pronounced his life's work a "song of Sex and Amativeness, and even Animality." The "marvellous song" of the Mermaid in Wilde's tale, we shall see, carries a similar meaning.

The tale relates how a young Fisherman one day finds in his net a beautiful but frightened Mermaid, whom he releases on her promise to return and sing to him about the Sea-folk and charm the "tunny-fish" into his net. He falls in love but is rejected by the Mermaid because he has a human Soul: "If only thou wouldst send away thy Soul, then could I love thee." In the same spirit as Dorian, he decides to do so. But since the Mermaid cannot tell him how, he must consult a Priest.

(Here we should note that Wilde, as so often, is writing disguised autobiography. He is the Fisherman, and the Mermaid is, gender notwithstanding, the embodiment of all the young men who were beginning to crowd his life at the time he wrote the story. She is described as having hair like "a wet fleece of gold" and a body of "white ivory." Wilde disliked the looks of Swiss boys, saying they were "carved out of turnips," but he doted on "English lads" and said they were "chryselephantine," that is, made of gold and ivory.)

The Fisherman's love causes him to sit "idle in his boat" and lose all "care of his craft" as he is drawn into the world of the Sea-Folk—just as Wilde was then himself courting professional and family ruin in pursuit of his own pleasure. Nor is it far-fetched to see the Sea-folk as representative of the Amative and Animal comrades in Whitman's poems, for the Priest, when he hears of the Fisherman's intentions, erupts with exactly the kind of derision heaped upon *Leaves of Grass*: "Alack, alack, thou art mad . . . it is a sin that may not be forgiven. And as for the Sea-folk, they are lost, and they who would traffic with them are lost also. They are the beasts of the field that know not good from evil."

The Fisherman tearfully responds to these "bitter words" with the moral question implicit throughout *Leaves*: "what doth my Soul profit me, if it stand between me and the thing that I love?" The Priest's answer is pure anti-Whitman diatribe: "The love of the body is vile . . . and vile and evil are the pagan things God suffers to wander through His world. Accursed be the Fauns of the woodlands, and accursed be the singers of the sea . . . and their perilous joys." The Priest's final gesture is excommunicating: "thy leman is lost, and thou shalt be lost with her," he says, and drives the Fisherman from his door. Accursed be the singers—like Walt Whitman!

There are many wonderful glosses on this repellent Priest in Whitman. Among his early notes is a reminder to create the "character of a ranting religious exhorter—sincere, but a great fool" and a longer diatribe, apparently for a lecture he intended to give. "Really what has America to do with all this mummery of prayer and rituals and the rant of exhorters and priests? We are not all deceived by this great show that confronts us of churches, priests and rituals—for piercing beneath, we find there is no life, no faith, no reality of belief, but that all is essentially a pretence, a sham." The conversations with Traubel are often spiced with colorful anticlerical venom: "I see no use for the church: it lags superfluous on the stage." "The world is through with sermonizing . . . the distinctly preacherly ages are nearly gone. I am not sorry."

One day Whitman was visited by a preacher and reported, "I don't remember his name—a clever fellow but preachery all over, like a man in a lather. It did my eyes good to look away from him." "Damn the preachers!" he burst out one Saturday evening, "the smooth-faced, self-satisfied preachers." By their standards, he growled, "probably nine-tenths of the universe is depraved—probably nine-tenths denied a right in the scheme of things—which is ridiculous." Perhaps with the events in Southold still reverberating in the back of his mind, he professed the "profoundest contempt" for the church as an institution and all the "damnable psalming, praying, deaconizing of our day."*

In the months before his death, vehement and sometimes amusing anticlerical outbursts were still well within Whitman's power. He could express fury at "the damned Methodistic snifflers, who know *everything*" and at an "infernal cabbage-head" of a preacher who would dare to call George Eliot an adulteress. "What was George Eliot if not *clean*? And this man, *unclean*—yes, full of poison, venom, hate." Which is to say, just like Wilde's Priest. When Walt was told that some had wondered why he didn't call in the clergy when he had his December 1891 health scare, he merely uttered a disgusted "Oh hell!" And after his death there was a momentary but heart-stopping preacher scare among his inner circle. When his sister-in-law took it upon herself to ask a preacher, one Dr. McConnell, to officiate at the graveside, Dr. Bucke exploded. "My God! It was like to wreck us all! I wouldn't go to the funeral—no, I wouldn't: couldn't—dear old Walt would be outraged!" After an earnest meeting with the sister-in-law, the preacher was deleted from the funeral. Traubel commented: "A narrow escape from catastrophe."

Whitman's boast to Traubel that *Leaves of Grass* "takes the ground from under the churches as churches" was by no means idle. In the 1855 preface Whitman performed a kind of preemptive excommunication of all the self-satisfied preachers he knew would suffer paroxysms over his poems:

There will soon be no more priests. Their work is done. They may wait awhile .. perhaps a generation or two .. dropping off by degrees. A superior breed shall take their place .... the gangs of kosmos and prophets en masse shall take their place. A new order shall arise and they shall be the priests of man, and every man shall be his own priest.

One of the pastimes of Whitman's two boys together clinging in *Calamus* is "priests alarming." And some of the rare moments of virulence in the poems are reserved for priests: "Allons! from all formules! / From your formules, O bat-eyed and materialistic priests." Among his "Thoughts" of 1860 is one of "the mumbling and screaming priest" who is "soon deserted." The disgusted response Wilde desired for his Priest (who is soon deserted by the Fisherman) is perhaps best reflected, however, in this passage from "By Blue Ontario's Shore":

Already a nonchalant breed, silently emerging, appears on the
     streets,
People's lips salute only doers, lovers, satisfiers, positive knowers,
There will shortly be no more priests . . .*

The Fisherman proves to be of this nonchalant breed and ignores the Priest. He prefers to become a doer and a lover, a "positive knower" of the Mermaid. In order to lose his Soul, he consults a Witch and has a midnight encounter with a strange, enchanting man dressed in a suit of black velvet—an event related, surely, to the "midnight orgies of young men" in which Whitman says he shares. Finally, divested of his Soul, the Fisherman takes the amative plunge. "The Tritons blew their horns, and the little Mermaid rose up to meet him, and put her arms around his neck and kissed him on the mouth." The Soul persists, however, for several years in urging the Fisherman to renounce his forbidden love. "And ever did his Soul tempt him with evil, and whisper of terrible things. Yet did it not prevail against him, so great was the power of his love." The Soul says "nothing is better than Wisdom," but the Fisherman replies that love is and plunges back "into the deep."

This Soul, of course, is the Soul of the priests: an instrument of tyranny, an incarcerating myth, and an effective weapon for imposing conventional "wisdom" and morality upon the Fisherman. When he recognizes that the Soul is not his own but a fiction presented to him by the priests, his resistance to its "evil" is heroic. Satan-like, the Soul urges him, with the repetitiveness common to children's tales, not to return to the sea, into which the Mermaid has disappeared: "And ever did his Soul tempt him by the way, but he made it no answer, nor would do any of the wickedness that it sought to make him do, so great was the power of the love that was in him."

Finally, the Soul begs for entrance one last time. But the Fisherman's heart is "so compassed about with love" that the Soul can find no entrance. The Fisherman's final renunciation of the harrowing "formules" presented by his Soul is finely captured in Whitman's lines in "Song of the Open Road": "I ordain myself loos'd of limits and imaginary lines . . . Gently, but with undeniable will, divesting myself of the holds that would hold me." And so, as the tale reaches its denouement, the Fisherman performs one final—and fatal—act of undeniable will. Sounds of mourning Sea-folk are heard, and he runs to find the little Mermaid lying dead near the "black waves." Entwining her in his arms as the tide rushes in, the Fisherman refuses to hear the Soul's entreaties to save himself. Wilde creates here a touching *Liebestod* (not unlike the one that ends Mann's *Death in Venice*) in which, at the moment of death, the Fisherman "kissed with mad lips the cold lips of the Mermaid, and the heart that was within him broke. And as through the fullness of his love his heart did break, the Soul found an entrance and entered in, and was one with him even as before."

It is a wonderful Whitman touch, the Fisherman's attainment of harmony with his Soul at the moment of a mad-lipped kiss. D. H. Lawrence
called Whitman "the first to smash the old moral conception that the soul is
something 'superior' and 'above' the flesh," and Wilde's tale is premised on
the same iconoclasm and the same view of the undivided half-interests of
the body and soul. Whitman, indeed, almost seems to be speaking of the
Fisherman's fate in a poem of 1856 in which he urges, paradoxically, that
true prudence will take heroic risks. Such prudence, Whitman says, "favors
body and soul the same" and recognizes that "the young man who compos-
edly peril'd his life and lost it has done exceedingly well for himself without
doubt." Not surprisingly, it is in the *Leaves* edition containing the *Calamus*
poems that Whitman pushed to the limit his demand that the reader "com-
posedly" peril his life by self-assertion. The reader must "fear not, be candid,
promulge the body and the soul" and pursue the "vehement struggle so
fierce for unity in one's-self." Thus, the Fisherman's bold decision is precisely reflected in the poet's climactic announcement at the end of *Calamus*
#8, a poem banished from all post-1860 editions:

> One who loves me is jealous of me, and withdraws me
>   from all but love,
> With the rest I dispense—I sever from what I thought would
>   suffice me, for it does not—it is now empty and tasteless to me . . .

But perhaps nothing in all of Whitman better captures the "mystic
deliria" of the Fisherman's fatal apotheosis on the beach than his "One
Hour to Madness and Joy":

> To escape utterly from others' anchors and holds!
> To drive free! to love free! to dash reckless and dangerous! . . .
> To ascend, to leap to the heavens of the love indicated to me!
> To rise thither with my inebriate soul!
> To be lost if it must be so!

The twofold "moral" of the Fisherman's fate is not difficult to frame.
The world is unkind to those who are steeled against the world's conventional wisdom and inebriated by the taste of their own soul—and yet, as
Whitman never tired of reiterating, nothing is more important than
remaining thus hardened, thus tipsy, even if it means becoming "lost" to
the rest of the world. "One's-self must never give way," he warned, "that
is the final substance—that out of all is sure." The other part of the moral
is that tasting the soul is a bodily function. This, too, was an old Whitman

truism, expressed notably in 1860 in "Starting from Paumanok": "Behold, the body includes and is the meaning, the main concern, and includes and is the soul." In 1887 he wrote to one of his "special young men *littérateur* friends" to downplay the influence of Emerson and explained, "*L. of G.'s* word is *the body, including all*, including the intellect and soul; E.'s word is mind."* The very next year, he published this view in even more emphatic terms: "the trunk and centre whence the answer was to radiate . . . must be an identical body and soul."

Near the end of his life, the author of "The Fisherman and His Soul" would express for the last time the same lifelong credo: "Permanence of temperament, the indomitable assertion of the soul (and by soul I mean the unity of mind and body), such are the things of value in anyone." Such, then, is the obvious—the "candid"—moral of the tale, which Wilde could well have ended with this line: "And the sea covered the young Fisherman with its waves." But Wilde did not end the story there. Instead, there is one more page in which another moral, one might say a "masked" moral, is sustained.

Toward the end of "Starting from Paumanok," the first poem of the 1860 edition, Whitman jubilates: "O camerado close! O you and me at last, and us two only . . . O something ecstatic and undemonstrable! O music wild!" In the charming music of Wilde's ending, something ecstatic and undemonstrable is also, in fact, subtly demonstrated by the Fisherman and the Mermaid, alone together at last in death. This something has to do with close comrades.

The Priest discovers the Fisherman in shocking, albeit posthumous, embrace and behaves brutally:

> Clasped in his arms was the body of the little Mermaid. And he drew back frowning, and having made the sign of the cross, he cried aloud and said, "I will not bless the sea nor anything that is in it. Accursed be the Sea-folk, and accursed be all they who traffic with them. And as for him who for love's sake forsook God, and so lieth here with his leman slain by God's judgment . . . bury them in the corner of the Field of the Fullers, and set no mark above them. . . . For accursed were they in their lives, and accursed shall they be in their deaths also.

And so the "dead things" are laid to rest where "no sweet herbs grow." Three years pass, and the Priest is surprised one day, as he approaches the altar, to find it covered with "strange flowers that he had never seen before. Strange were they to look at, and of curious beauty, and their beauty troubled him, and their odour was sweet in his nostrils, and he felt glad." He attempts to preach on the wrath of God, but the flowers magically enforce his lips to utter words only of "the God whose name is Love." He is led from his pulpit in tears and soon learns that the flowers have grown on the unmarked grave in the Fullers' Field.

The events of the last two paragraphs of the tale epitomize, in the form of a fairy tale fantasy, the transformation Whitman hoped to achieve in America with *Leaves of Grass*. He wanted, as he said in *Calamus*, to disengage himself "from those corpses of me," just as he wanted America to disengage from the corpses of itself and "pass on, (O living! always living!) and leave the corpses behind." The only way to emerge from this ossification of the spirit was to become the accepter and yea-sayer. His urge was to offer the wide embrace, as Cather suggested when she wrote that "he takes everything in the universe from fly-specks to the fixed stars."

Such a gesture ends Wilde's story. The Priest prays overnight and is transformed. He banishes the "fault-finder's and rejecter's gait" that Whitman despised and strides forth with his monks and musicians to perform a Whitmanesque sacrament of acceptance. He "came to the shore of the sea and blessed the sea, and all the wild things that are in it. The Fauns [Wilde often referred to attractive young men as fauns] also he blessed, and the little things that dance in the woodland, and the bright-eyed things that peer through the leaves. All the things in God's world he blessed, and the people were filled with joy and wonder." What a shame it is that Wilde did not think to specify that the overwhelming fragrance of love came from *Calamus aromaticus*!

The Priest, here, is performing a ritual version of the welcoming gesture that occurs so often in Whitman: "come listen all!"—"Embracing all, soothing, supporting"—"I give you my hand"—"Welcome are all the earth's lands." The priest, indeed, changes his style to that of Whitman's very aptly titled "Salut au Monde!" whose speaker says, "I see ranks, colors, barbarisms, civilizations, I go among them, I mix indiscriminately, / And I salute all the inhabitants of the earth."* This is a note Whitman sounded from the start. In what appears to be one of his earliest *Leaves* notebooks, he ventured buoyantly that "none shall be an exception to the universal and affectionate Yes of the earth." And late in his life he summed up his wide embrace with "I never object to a man—any kind of a man—but I object to a priest—any kind of a priest. The instant a priest becomes a man I am on his side." Could there be a better gloss on the denouement of Wilde's tale?

"Amelioration is one of the earth's words," wrote Whitman in "A Song of the Rolling Earth." Wilde's finest tales—"The Happy Prince," "The

Selfish Giant," "The Star-Child"—all end with a finely prepared moment of amelioration. In "The Fisherman and His Soul," the moment comes when the Priest, with his indiscriminate acceptance, banishes the possibility of shame. Also in "Rolling Earth" Whitman observed: "In the best poems re-appears the body, man's or woman's, well-shaped, natural, gay, / Every part able, active, receptive, without shame or the need of shame." That, in a word, is the masked moral of Wilde's story. Amelioration in this tale, as often in Whitman and Wilde, means enabling every part of the body to be "active, receptive" according to the lover's own desires, even when the lover desires a Mermaid, a woodland Faun . . . or a comrade.

Whitman often insinuated the agony of repressing and concealing such desires in his poems. In his 1856 poem "To You, Whoever You Are" is a chilling evocation of the sordid existence of fishermen who conceal or deny their love for mermaids—and of the poet's desire to reach out to such oppressed persons:

> The mockeries are not you,
> Underneath them, and within them, I see you lurk,
> I pursue you where none else has pursued you,
> Silence, the desk, the flippant expression, the night,
>> the accustomed routine, if these conceal you from others,
>> or from yourself, they do not conceal you from me . . .
> I track through your windings and turnings . . .

A few years later, in *Calamus #2*, he says to himself (and to the reader), "Spring away from the conceal'd heart there! . . . Do not remain down there so ashamed . . . I have long enough stifled and choked." But surely the most harrowing evocation of the agony of concealing one's "adhesiveness" is *Calamus #6*, with its "ribb'd breast" heaving, "long-drawn, ill-supprest sighs," "husky panting through clinch'd teeth," and "many a hungry wish told to the skies only."

Wilde ends his tale with a lovely, melancholy allusion to this pain of those who, because of Priests of one stripe or another, cannot be candid and, as Whitman says, "promulge" the body and soul: "Yet never again in the corner of the Fullers' Field grew flowers of any kind, but the field remained barren even as before. Nor came the Sea-folk into the bay as they had been wont to do, for they went to another part of the sea." This is a potent image of the scar and the cost of repressing sexual identity and reminds us, once again, of Whitman, who brought such seminal gusto and fine-scented herbage to the barrens of mid-century America.

"The Fisherman and His Soul," like all the best children's tales, is for adult readers too. In a letter accompanying a gift of his first volume of tales, *The Happy Prince,* Wilde said that his tales were "an attempt to mirror modern life in a form remote from reality—to deal with modern problems in a mode that is ideal. . . . They are, of course, slight and fanciful, and written, not for children, but for childlike people from eighteen to eighty!"

"The Fisherman and His Soul," however, is anything but slight and fanciful. The tale delicately masks a devastating critique of an important "modern problem" of sexuality in the Victorian age, the same problem that Whitman—also very inaptly called "fanciful" by Emerson—had addressed several decades before in *Leaves of Grass.* Though having nothing of the nursery about it, one could say that *Leaves of Grass* was also written for childlike people from eighteen to eighty. It was written, that is, in the spirit of Wilde's remark that when we see "the true personality of man" it will be "a marvellous thing. . . . It will be as wonderful as the personality of a child." Whitman's volume made such an uproar, of course, because this true personality ("the real critter," as he loved to say) was presented, as Burroughs acidly observed of Americans, to "perhaps the least like children of any people in the world."

Several years later, in the witness box at the Old Bailey, Wilde would have occasion to defend more openly a love on which anathema like the Priest's had been pronounced. This defense is cast in exactly the terms he had used to ennoble the Fisherman's love for the Mermaid:

> It is that deep, spiritual affection that is as pure as it is perfect. It dictates and pervades great works of art like those of Shakespeare and Michelangelo. . . . It is in this century misunderstood, so much misunderstood that it may be described as the "Love that dare not speak its name," and on account of it I am placed where I am now. It is beautiful, it is fine, it is the noblest form of affection. There is nothing unnatural about it. It is intellectual, and it repeatedly exists between an elder and a younger man, when the elder has intellect, and the younger man has all the joy, hope, and glamour of life before him. That it should be so, the world does not understand. The world mocks at it and sometimes puts one in the pillory for it.

Even this spirited defense of adhesiveness and comradery—which evoked a tremendous burst of applause in the courtroom—can be found to have many eloquent premonitions in Whitman.

Perhaps most in the spirit of this speech is one of his announcements of "superb friendship, exalté, previously unknown" in *Calamus* #28:

> . . . when I hear of the brotherhood of lovers, how it was with
>   them,
> How together through life, through dangers, odium, unchanging,
>   long and long,
> Through youth and through middle and old age, how unfaltering,
>   how affectionate and faithful they were,
> Then I am pensive . . .

Not for nothing had Whitman, doubtless like Wilde, read Plato's
dialogues *Phaedrus* and *Lysis* with fascination and joy. Among the notes
he made while reading Plato are these tantalizing hints of many
Whitman poems to come (and of Wilde's Old Bailey speech):

> He [Plato] makes Socrates the defender & eulogist of the platonic
> love . . . advocates it, plainly, but carries it into higher & purer
> regions . . .

> His whole treatment assumes the illustration of Love, by the attach-
> ment a man has for another man, (a beautiful youth as aforemen-
> tioned, more especially)—(it is astounding to modern ideas)—

> . . . he makes an ingenious comparison—the gross & spiritual in a
> human being in love. . . . They "lie down together" "kiss & fondle
> each other &c . . ."

This last note, of course, foreshadows the beautiful and erotic fifth section of "Song of Myself" in which, on a "transparent summer morning,"
the bearded speaker lies down to make love with his soul.

Wilde's tale and Whitman's book of poems both propose platonically
ideal worlds—moral worlds, as Whitman said, "astounding to modern
ideas." And they were worlds friendly to decidedly unplatonic intercourse. Both men obviously hoped that in the future—where their eyes
and art were keenly focused—the old questions would be retired along
with the priests and the new answers they proposed would gain acceptance. Neither was so foolish as to think the transformation would be
easily or soon accomplished, especially within the movement to give the
Love that dare not speak its name a singer's trumpet voice. Wilde makes
his awareness of this—and his final optimism—clear in the sole prophecy
we have from him about the political movement in favor of gay liberation: "Yes: I have no doubt we shall win, but the road is long, and red
with monstrous martyrdoms. Nothing but the repeal of the Criminal Law

Amendment Act [under which he was convicted and imprisoned] would do any good. That is the essential thing. It is not so much public opinions as public officials that need educating."

Yet again, there is a fine passage in Whitman to steal Wilde's thunder. At the ecstatic end of "A Song of the Rolling Earth," the poet expresses Wilde's mingled sense of struggle and optimism in a prophecy of his own. It is less practical and more ringingly exuberant than Wilde's, but it is also optimistic about the final achievement of what he would probably have preferred to call not gay liberation but comradely libertad:

> Work on, age after age, nothing is to be lost,
> It may have to wait long, but it will certainly come in use,
> When the materials are all prepared and ready, the
>   architects shall appear.

> I swear to you the architects shall appear without fail,
> I swear to you they will understand you and justify you,
> The greatest among them shall be he who knows you, and
>   encloses all and is faithful to all,
> He and the rest shall not forget you, they shall perceive that
>   you are not an iota less than they,
> You shall be fully glorified in them.

A
WHITMAN CHRONOLOGY

1819   Born 31 May near Huntington, Long Island; Whitman's family will consist of father Walter (1789–1855), mother Louisa Van Velsor (1795–1873), and siblings Jesse (1818–70), Mary (1821–99), Hannah (1823–1908), Andrew Jackson (1827–63), George Washington (1829–1901), Thomas Jefferson (1833–90), and Edward (1835–92)

1823   Family moves to Brooklyn (returns to Long Island ten years later)

1825–30   Attends public schools in Brooklyn

1830   End of formal education; office boy for a lawyer, later for a doctor

1830–35   Apprentice work in the printing trade in various offices

1836–41   Teaches in several Long Island schools for brief periods of time (East Norwich, Hempstead, Babylon, Long Swamp, Smithtown, Woodbury, Dix Hills, Whitestone, and Southold); possibly dismissed from Southold for misconduct

1841–47   Functions in several journalistic capacities (compositor, reporter, fiction writer, editor) for a number of New York area papers, including the *New World, Aurora, Tattler, Long Island Star*; publishes temperance novella, *Franklin Evans*, in 1842

1846–48   From March 1846 to January 1848 edits Brooklyn *Daily Eagle*; quits or is discharged and travels in February with brother Jeff to New Orleans to edit new paper called the *Crescent*; resigns a few months later; back in Brooklyn by mid-June

1848–54   Continues newspaper work in Brooklyn and Manhattan; also pursues carpentering, house building, stationery selling, and freelance writing

1855   Early July, first edition of *Leaves of Grass* published; father dies on 11 July; Emerson writes to express famous "greetings" on 21 July

1856   Late summer, second edition of *Leaves of Grass* appears; visited by Thoreau and, a year later, by Emerson

1857–59   Edits Brooklyn *Times*; unemployed by summer of 1859; frequents Pfaff's restaurant/saloon; *Calamus* poems probably written between May 1857 and May 1859; probably meets Fred Vaughan at this time

1860   Third edition of *Leaves of Grass* published by Thayer & Eldridge of Boston

1861   13 April, learns of bombardment of Fort Sumter after attending a performance of Donizetti's *Linda di Chamounix* at the Academy of Music

1862   December, travels to Virginia to search for wounded brother George; stays in camp two weeks at Fredericksburg

1863–64   Remains in Washington as unofficial nurse in various hospitals; returns briefly in 1864 to mother's Brooklyn house in broken health

1865   24 January, appointed clerk in Indian Bureau of Department of Interior; discharged by Secretary James Harlan in June; employed next day in Attorney General's office; meets Peter Doyle while riding on a Washington streetcar around this time; 14 April, assassination of Lincoln

1866   *Drum-Taps* with annex including "When Lilacs Last in the Dooryard Bloom'd" appears; William O'Connor's pamphlet defending Whitman, *The Good Gray Poet*, published

1867   Burroughs publishes *Notes on Walt Whitman, as Poet and Person*; fourth edition of *Leaves of Grass*

1869   English widow Anne Gilchrist becomes enamored at long distance of Whitman, lives for three years (1876–79) in Philadelphia to be near him

1870   *Democratic Vistas* published; distress and depression during summer, perhaps in part over his relations with streetcar driver Peter Doyle

1871   Fifth edition of *Leaves of Grass*

1873   23 January, paralytic stroke causes dizzy spells for over a year; mother dies, 23 May; unable to work, moves from Washington to brother George's house in Camden, New Jersey

1875   Meets Harry Stafford in Camden newspaper office, beginning several years of intimacy; spends much time at Stafford home near Timber Creek, southeast of Camden

1876   Sixth ("Centennial") edition of *Leaves of Grass*

1879   In New York, gives first of thirteen annual lectures on Lincoln; travels to St. Louis to visit favorite brother Jeff, then makes furthest westward journey to Colorado; next year visits Dr. R. M. Bucke, a future biographer, in Canada

1881   Seventh edition of *Leaves of Grass* published by Boston firm, James R. Osgood & Company

1882   Oscar Wilde visits in January; Boston District Attorney, urged by Society for the Suppression of Vice, forces Osgood to cease publication of *Leaves*; subsequent edition, published in Philadelphia by David McKay, quickly sells out

1884   Buys house at 328 Mickle Street, Camden, his residence for the remainder of his life; Edward Carpenter visits in June

1885   Suffers sunstroke; friends present him with horse and buggy; next year friends donate eight hundred dollars for cottage retreat at Timber Creek, never built

1888   28 March, Horace Traubel begins taking copious notes of Whitman conversations; June, another stroke; *November Boughs* and *Complete Poems and Prose* published

1890   Last Lincoln lecture, in Philadelphia; 19 August, in a letter to John Addington Symonds, rejects homosexual interpretation of *Calamus* poems and tells of fathering six children

1891   Publishes *Good-Bye my Fancy* and last ("deathbed") edition of *Leaves of Grass*; prepares *Complete Prose Works*, published the next year

1892   26 March, dies; is buried in Harleigh Cemetery, Camden, four days later in a large granite "burial house" designed by himself

1860 AND 1892 TITLES OF THE CALAMUS POEMS

#1—"In Paths Untrodden"
#2—"Scented Herbage of My Breast"
#3—"Whoever You Are Holding Me Now in Hand"
#4—"These I Singing in Spring"
#5—*only in 1860 edition*
#6—"Not Heaving from My Ribb'd Breast Only"
#7—"Of the Terrible Doubt of Appearances"
#8—*only in 1860 edition*
#9—*only in 1860 edition*
#10—"Recorders Ages Hence"
#11—"When I Heard at the Close of the Day"
#12—"Are You the New Person Drawn toward Me?"
#13—"Roots and Leaves Themselves Alone"
#14—"Not Heat Flames up and Consumes"
#15—"Trickle Drops"
#16—*only in 1860 edition*
#17—"Of Him I Love Day and Night" (transferred to *Whispers of Heavenly Death* section)
#18—"City of Orgies"
#19—"Behold This Swarthy Face"
#20—"I Saw in Louisiana a Live-Oak Growing"
#21—"That Music Always Round Me" (to *Whispers of Heavenly Death*)
#22—"To a Stranger"
#23—"This Moment Yearning and Thoughtful"

#24—"I Hear It Was Charged against Me"

#25—"The Prairie-Grass Dividing"

#26—"We Two Boys Together Clinging"

#27—"O Living Always, Always Dying" (to *Whispers of Heavenly Death*)

#28—"When I Peruse the Conquer'd Fame"

#29—"A Glimpse"

#30—"A Promise to California"

#31—"What Ship Puzzled at Sea" and "What Place is Besieged?" (two stanzas divided, the first moved to *Whispers of Heavenly Death*, the second put among *Inscriptions*)

#32—"What Think You I Take My Pen in Hand?"

#33—"No Labor-Saving Machine"

#34—"I Dream'd in a Dream"

#35—"To the East and to the West"

#36—"Earth, My Likeness"

#37—"A Leaf for Hand in Hand"

#38—"Fast Anchor'd Eternal O Love!"

#39—"Sometimes With One I Love"

#40—"That Shadow My Likeness"

#41—"Among the Multitude"

#42—"To a Western Boy"

#43—"O You Whom I Often and Silently Come"

#44—"Here the Frailest Leaves of Me"

#45—"Full of Life Now"

NOTES

A NOTE ON THE NOTES

Each quotation is identified by its opening phrase in boldface. An initial asterisk (*) indicates that further elaboration or additional relevant material is contained in the note. All italics within quotations are original to the work cited, except where noted.

All unidentified page references are from the Library of America edition of the *Complete Poetry and Collected Prose* (1982), which includes two complete editions of *Leaves of Grass*: the first of 1855 (pp. 5–145) and the last of 1891–92 (pp. 147–655). The third edition of 1860 is quoted from *Walt Whitman's Blue Book* (1968), a facsimile edition of Whitman's personal copy; it is cited as *1860 Facsimile*. I generally refer to Whitman's forty-five *Calamus* poems by their original 1860 arabic numbers and often quote these versions when Whitman significantly revised them (see pages 343–344 for titles of the 1860 poems). The date in parentheses after any poem title refers to the year of the *Leaves of Grass* edition in which the poem first appeared.

Quotations from Fredson Bowers's parallel text edition, *Whitman's Manuscripts* Leaves of Grass *(1860)* (1955), are identified as Bowers, MS1860. Citations of the New York University edition of *The Collected Writings of Walt Whitman* (1961–1984) are abbreviated as follows:

LGC   *Comprehensive Reader's Edition of* Leaves of Grass
Var   Leaves of Grass: A *Textual Variorum of the Printed Poems*
EPF   *The Early Poems and the Fiction*
NUPM   *Notebooks and Unpublished Prose Manuscripts*
DBN   *Daybooks and Notebooks*
Corr   *The Correspondence*

WWC   Quotations from Horace Logo Traubel's nine volumes of tran-
         scriptions of conversations with Whitman in 1888–92, *With
Walt Whitman in Camden*, figure prominently in this study. Traubel, who
died in 1919 at the age of sixty-one, supervised the publication of the first
three volumes (1906, 1908, 1914); the next four volumes were published
by the Southern Illinois University Press in 1953, 1964, 1982, and 1992;
the final two volumes were published by William Bentley in 1996. Quotations from these volumes are in most cases accompanied by the date of
the conversation in parentheses.

Other frequently quoted sources are abbreviated as follows:

Bloom   Harold Bloom, ed., *Walt Whitman: Modern Critical
                Views* (1985)
Calamus Lovers Charley Shively, ed., *Calamus Lovers: Walt Whitman's
                Working Class Camerados* (1987)
Drum Beats   Charley Shively, ed., *Drum Beats: Walt Whitman's Civil
                War Boy Lovers* (1989)
Faner   Robert Faner, *Walt Whitman and Opera* (1951; rpt.
                1972)
Hindus   Milton Hindus, ed., *Walt Whitman: The Critical Heri-
                tage* (1971)
Measure   Jim Perlman, Ed Folsom, Dan Campion, eds., *Whit-
                man: The Measure of His Song* (1981)
Reynolds   David Reynolds, *Walt Whitman's America: A Cultural
                Biography* (1995)
UPP   Emory Holloway, *The Uncollected Poetry and Prose*
                (1921; rpt. 1972)
Zweig   Paul Zweig, *Walt Whitman: The Making of the Poet*
                (1982)

WALT & US: A FOREWORD

xi   **After a man disappears:** *WWC*, 7:139 (23 September 1890). Geoffrey O'Brien ratified Whitman's assertion perfectly in the first sentence of his recent review essay on the poet in the *New York Review of Books* (19 October 1995, p. 23): "Like Lincoln or Jesus (to both of whom he addressed poems), Walt Whitman has entered irrevocably the realm of myth."

rejoiced exceedingly: *WWC*, 5:297 (16 June 1889).

good, gray: This famous phrase for the poet in his later years was invented by his partisan William O'Connor for an 1866 pamphlet, *The Good Gray Poet: A Vindication*.

xii   **W. is so hard:** letter of 26 January 1892, *WWC*, 9:401.

own tendencies: *WWC*, 5:165 (10 May 1889).

average human critter: *WWC*, 5:423 (8 August 1889).

style is to have: *WWC*, 1:105 (5 May 1888).

*I should say: *WWC*, 6:475 (24 June 1890). Whitman reiterated this view with emphatic redundancy for the thirty friends at his seventy-first birthday dinner: "I have uttered the *Leaves* for the last thirty-five years as an illustration of, as an utterance of, as a radiation from, the personal critter—the fellow, man, individuality, person, American." The "four hundred leaves of grass," he added, are "held together by that iron band of . . . individuality, personality, identity." (*In Re Walt Whitman*, ed. Horace Traubel *et al.* (1893), p. 312.)

almost farcical to write: *WWC*, 7:266 (11 November 1890).

This hour I tell: p. 45.

Come, I will take: "Recorders Ages Hence," p. 275.

Both in and out and **One of that centripetal** and **Open but still:** "Song of Myself," pp. 30, 77; "A Riddle Song," p. 587.

xiii **Do you suppose:** *1860 Facsimile*, p. 358.

I do not tell: *1860 Facsimile*, p. 181; line deleted after this edition.

You will never: p. 455.

He hates to have: *WWC*, 4:141 (13 February 1889).

W. is a slow: *WWC*, 2:369 (23 September 1888).

I am always uneasy: *WWC*, 1:47 (18 April 1888).

God Almighty how: *WWC*, 4:19 (24 January 1889).

He is a questioner: *WWC*, 1:185 (20 May 1888).

Walt Whitman and I and **it is good he:** *WWC*, 6:221 (30 December 1889).

xiv **I don't want:** *WWC*, 2:115 (16 August 1888).

I expected hell: *WWC*, 3:515 (11 January 1889).

Thirty years ago: *WWC*, 1:385 (26 June 1888).

He is wisest: *LGC*, p. 605. "Debris" appeared only in the 1860 edition.

I think there are: Carpenter, *Days with Walt Whitman* (1906), p. 43.

xv ***I broke in:** *WWC*, 1:338–9 (15 June 1888). One guesses that Traubel himself now and then censored dubious material Whitman gave him. An example may be the letter from a Scotsman with "curious things" in it that Traubel took home with him to read. "It was curious," he records, but whether it was a homophobic "damn" or an avowal from a gay admirer we will never know. Traubel chose not to reveal its contents. (*WWC*, 3:447, 2 January 1889.)

As I was leaving: *WWC*, 2:57–8 (29 July 1888).

xvi **I reminded W.:** *WWC*, 2:129 (12 August 1888).

And that from a bachelor: *WWC*, 2:328 (15 September 1888).

I never doubted and **stifled, unable:** *A Different Person: A Memoir* (1993), pp. 141, 34.

xvii **From all I did:** *The Collected Poems*, trans. Edmund Kelley, Philip Sherrard (1992), p. 195.

It is one of my dreads: *WWC*, 9:3–4 (2 October 1891).

xviii **The time for me:** *Ecce Homo*, (1888; trans. 1967), p. 259.

something very snubbing: *WWC*, 6:249 (16 January 1890).

esteem themselves: *WWC*, 4:40 (20 January 1889).

Poor Jesus: *WWC*, 7:38 (5 August 1890).

*Stedman is cute: *WWC*, 1:56 (21 April 1888). Though Whitman called Stedman "miraculously deft" and "our best man in his speciality—criticism," he still had exquisitely mixed feelings about him. One remark about Stedman unwittingly captures something of the difficulty Whitman himself presents as a subject for biography. Traubel reports saying, "Your opinions about Stedman do not always agree," to which

Whitman replied, "That's because I don't always agree with myself about Stedman. If I could admire Stedman as much as I love him I wouldn't have much trouble making up my mind" (*WWC*, 1:222–3, 28 May 1888).

*I am persuaded: *WWC*, 5:225 (26 May 1889). Whitman added a similar view of all the photographs of that most "biographized" of all Americans, Lincoln: "I know of no satisfactory picture of Lincoln. All sorts of pictures exist—many of them good in themselves, good as pictures—yet all of them wanting in the last, the essential touch."

xix **In all imaginative work:** *WWC*, 2:562 (31 October 1888).

*I consider it the bane: *WWC*, 2:562 (31 October 1888). Another, more witty, Whitman view of professors appeared in a piece in *Life Illustrated*, 30 August 1856: "A circus performer is the other half of a college-professor. The perfect Man has more than the professor's brains and a good deal of the performer's legs" (*New York Dissected*, ed. Emory Holloway and Ralph Adimari (1936), p. 196).

formal-cut men . . . They like portions: *WWC*, 7:391 (1 January 1891).

His letter is friendly: *WWC*, 1:286 (8 June 1888).

*euphemisms and awkward genteelisms: "The Persistent Itchings of Whitman and Poe" (*The Southern Review*, Winter 1967), in *The Boy Scout Handbook and Other Observations* (1982), p. 14. Fussell also expressed salutary aggravation that the emphasis in the Blodgett/ Bradley commentary was not on the early and sexual Whitman but "on the tiresome old gas-bag of the all-too-familiar cosmic and 'mystical' pretensions . . . [who is] embraced by those who insist that poetry be at once vague, portentous, solemn, and puritan." The same "genteelism" has dogged another author whose works are steeped in homoerotic themes, Thomas Mann. In his *Thomas Mann: Eros and Literature* (1996), Anthony Heilbut takes to task the prominent Mann biographer Richard Winston for trying to "downplay Mann's homosexuality" (p. 129) and notes that, as recently as 1989, an unnamed "veteran scholar declared any emphasis on homosexuality 'superficial.' " That veteran scholar would be delighted to meet David Reynolds, author of the well-received *Walt Whitman's America: A Cultural History* (1995): see my discussion of this biography in chapter 2.

I do not value: *WWC*, 1:58 (22 April 1888).

xx **Do you suppose:** *WWC*, 1:135 (11 May 1888).

They are mainly: *WWC*, 1:55 (21 April 1888).

he was a university man: *WWC*, 1:189 (21 May 1888).

He's the fellow: *WWC*, 3:191 (27 November 1888).

here is a woman: *WWC*, 7:42 (8 August 1890).

For a long time: *WWC*, 3:467 (5 January 1889).

xxi ***Traubel's "lover":** Martin Murray, " 'Pete the Great': A Biography of Peter Doyle," *Walt Whitman Quarterly Review* 12 (1994), p. 40. Murray refers to explicit correspondence between Traubel and Wiksell to be found in the Library of Congress. There were some in Camden who felt Whitman responsible for corrupting Traubel's morals. In 1921, Elizabeth Keller, a nurse who looked after Whitman in his last months, published a memoir about the experience, *Walt Whitman in Mickle Street*. At its end is added a "letter" by one Guido Bruno that recounts some vicious town talk about how Whitman "lived very immorally" and wrote "pornographic" poems "dangerous to the morals." One William Kettler, a corner druggist nearby during the Traubel years, proved quite happy to speak ill of the twenty-five-years-dead poet (pp. 196–9): " 'But what is the worst,' Mr. Kettler continued, 'Whitman has spoiled the life of Horace Traubel. . . . He devoted his life to Whitman. He took Whitman's morals for his own standard.' And Mr. Kettler proceeded to tell about Traubel's private life. Some stories a policeman's wife, Traubel's next door neighbor, had told him." Homophobic gossip, then as now, can be quite irresistible.

My method all along: WWC, 2:70 (1 August 1888).

*Horace, you are: WWC, 2:200 (26 August 1888). Several months earlier and just a few weeks after Traubel began transcribing conversations, Whitman cheerfully acknowledged Traubel's skills as a conversational picklock: "I just get going and go and can't even stop myself, especially when you come round, damn you! You have an odd effect on me—you don't ask me questions, you have learned that I hate to be asked questions, yet I seem to be answering questions all the time whenever you happen in." Traubel said Whitman "laughed at this sally" (WWC, 1:56, 20 April 1888).

xxii   **He is very lonesome:** WWC, 2:109 (8 August 1888).

I went over: WWC, 1:207 (25 May 1888).

*Some day you: WWC, 1:398 (29 June 1888). Whitman reiterated the point six months later: "As I left W. said: 'I'm doing all I can from day to day to put you in possession of papers, data, which will fortify you for any biographical undertaking, if any, you may be drawn into concerning me, us, in the future.' " (WWC, 4:43–4, 28 January 1889).

I see more value: WWC, 7:44 (8 August 1890). Whitman had read Kennedy's work in manuscript; however, the book, *Reminiscences of Walt Whitman*, did not appear until 1896, four years after Whitman's death.

xxiii   **Happy this night** and **the public has no notion:** WWC, 7:358–60 (16 December 1890).

*Sex, sex: always immanent: WWC, 3:453 (January 1889). At his seventy-first birthday festivities, I think Whitman again alluded to the amorous/sexual energies coursing through *Leaves of Grass*, though again his diction is carefully abstract ("spiritualistic" is replaced by "emotional"). After acknowledging with a sip of champagne the reading of a short toast from Tennyson, Whitman observed that "after all is said, I turn everything over to the emotional, and out of that I myself, the actual personal identity for my own special time, have uttered what I have uttered. To me, as I have said, back of everything . . . is the simple individual critter, personality, if you please—his emotionality, supreme emotionality. Through that personality I have myself spoken, reiterated. That is behind *Leaves of Grass*" (*In Re Walt Whitman*, p. 300).

belonged to our circus: *WWC*, 2:302 (11 September 1888).

At one point in the dinner: *WWC*, 7:156 (28 September 1890).

xxiv **away back he was:** *WWC*, 2:502–3 (19 October 1888).

Clifford is quite: *WWC*, 6:60 (11 October 1889).

How gladly: *NUPM*, 1:169.

daring dance: Aphorism #278 ("Analogy of the dance"), *Human, All Too Human* (1878; Eng. trans. Marion Faber, 1984), p. 169.

xxv ***teach us to dance:** Aphorism #206 ("Books that teach us to dance"), *Human, All Too Human*, pp. 124–5. In Aphorism #259 ("A male culture"), Nietzsche boldly expressed his admiration for the "erotic relationship of men to youths" that was "the necessary, sole prerequisite of all male education" in ancient Greece. "The treatment of young people," he added, "has probably never again been so aware, so loving, so thoroughly geared to their excellence *(virtus)*, as it was in the sixth and fifth centuries" (p. 157). As the first brilliant display of the essential Nietzschean style, *Human, All Too Human* was the equivalent of the 1855 *Leaves of Grass*. This work throws considerable light on *Leaves of Grass*, particularly where Nietzsche describes the emergence of "free spirits" from within "bound" societies (pp. 6–7, 138–40). As analyses of the coming out process, these passages can hardly be surpassed.

The boy I love: p. 242.

essentially the most splendid: *In Re Walt Whitman*, p. 304.

not enough genuine culture: *WWC*, 9:434–5 (8 February 1892).

Eros as statesman: "Von Deutscher Republik," *Werke*, 11:848–51. For a fascinating discussion of this remarkable speech see Anthony Heilbut, *Thomas Mann: Eros and Literature* (1996), pp. 376–83.

Nietzsche's place: "Five Years of Democracy in Germany," *Current History*, quoted by Heilbut, p. 384.

xxvi **the Greeks still make:** *WWC*, 1:121 (8 May 1888).

verging upon the licentiousness: *WWC*, 6:342 (28 March 1890).

Sometimes, after an interval: *WWC*, 2:370–1 (23 September 1888).

xxvii **all the puritan criticism:** *WWC*, 2:560 (3 October 1888).

America means: *WWC*, 3:277 (10 December 1888).

Dick was a: *WWC*, 2:130 (12 August 1888).

condemn it without and **I have a deeper:** *WWC*, 2:142–3 (15 August 1888).

xxviii **You remember what I:** *WWC*, 6:128 (9 November 1889).

I meet new Walt Whitmans: *WWC*, 1:108 (6 May 1888).

most sensitive spot: *WWC*, 1:51 (20 April 1888).

how people reel: *WWC*, 3:321 (17 December 1888).

*Several who have written: Writing and publication on Whitman's homosexuality has burgeoned since Stonewall. Among the books and essays one might point to are: Joseph Cady, *"Drum-Taps* and 19th-Century Male Homosexual Literature," in *Walt Whitman Here and Now*, ed. Joann Krieg (1985); Byrne Fone, *Masculine Landscapes: Walt Whitman and the Homoerotic Text* (1992); Alan Helms, "Whitman's 'Live Oak with Moss,' " in *The Continuing Presence of Walt Whitman*, ed. Robert K. Martin (1992); Karl Keller, "Walt Whitman Camping," *Walt Whitman Review*, December 1980, and "Walt Whitman and the Queening of America," *American Poetry*, Fall 1983; M. Jimmie Killingsworth, *Whitman's Poetry of the Body* (1989); Michael Lynch, " 'Here is Adhesiveness': From Friendship to Homosexuality," *Victorian Studies* 29 (Autumn 1985); Robert K. Martin, *The Homosexual Tradition in American Poetry* (1979); Michael Moon, *Disseminating Whitman* (1991) and "Reading Whitman under Pressure of AIDS," in *The Continuing Presence of Walt Whitman*; Charley Shively, *Calamus Lovers: Walt Whitman's Working Class Camerados* (1987) and *Drum Beats: Walt Whitman's Civil War Boy Lovers* (1989).

Still, resistance to a homosexual Whitman continues to be encountered. One purpose of a most recent collection of essays was, in fact, to challenge "the exclusion of the homosexual dimension of Whitman's life and writings" (*Breaking Bounds: Whitman and American Cultural Studies*, ed. Betsy Erkkila and Jay Grossman (1996), p. 252).

xxix It does a man good: *WWC*, 3:327 (18 December 1888).

the degree and kind: *Beyond Good and Evil* (1886), aphorism #75, in *The Portable Nietzsche*, ed. Walter Kaufmann (1954), p. 444.

how these damned saints: *WWC*, 9:61 (20 October 1891).

do not reach the tapstone: *WWC*, 9:84 (26 October 1891).

to be *con amore*: *WWC*, 6:215 (27 December 1889).

xxx *autobiography is the only: *WWC*, 4:184 (19 February 1889). Bernard Shaw, in the "Apology" for an autobiographical collection, *Sixteen Self Sketches* (1949), made a similar point (p. 19): "The best autobiographies are confessions; but if a man is a deep writer all his works are confessions."

A man only: *NUPM*, 1:57. This notebook, the earliest extant, seems to date from 1847–54.

It is so great: *WWC*, 2:30 (23 July 1888).

That sounds very ripe: *WWC*, 2:181 (22 August 1888). The young Englishman was Lionel Johnson; he reappears in the Annex, p. 299.

*Mann's *Death in Venice:* Heilbut (p. 261) puts the last-named work in the same league as *Leaves* and *Dorian Gray* with unminced words: "*Death in Venice* comprised a revolutionary breakthrough in the expression of gay desire. . . . Indeed, [it] does more than evoke a pederastic episode; it constitutes a virtual Baedeker's guide to homosexual love."

xxxi **Charlotte Cushman's great acting:** WWC, 4:190 (20 February 1889).

The young fellows: WWC, 1:209 (25 May 1888).

I wouldn't know what: WWC, 2:154 (17 August 1988).

xxxii **Walt, you seem:** WWC, 4:321 (10 March 1889).

*The Real Queen's Throat: Debate on the subject has centered around Wayne Koestenbaum's *The Queen's Throat: Opera, Homosexuality, and the Mystery of Desire* (1993). See also the concluding chapter titled "In Praise of Brigitte Fassbänder" in Terry Castle's *The Apparitional Lesbian* (1993), and Paul Robinson's perceptive essay "The Opera Queen: A Voice from the Closet" in the November 1994 issue of the *Cambridge Opera Journal*. A theatrical epitome of the opera queen is Mendy, the Callas devotee in *The Lisbon Traviata* by Terrence McNally (he subsequently wrote a play devoted to Callas, *Master Class*).

xxxiii **as connecter, as chansonnier:** "The Centenarian's Story" (1865), p. 434.

xxxiv **it won't pass for money:** WWC, 2:157 (17 August 1888).

*In the best poems: "A Song of the Rolling Earth" (1856 title: "Poem of The Sayers of The Words of The Earth"), p. 363. In his short story "Skinned Alive," Edmund White offers similarly contrastive ways to read the word "gay": "He told me he thought of me as gay in the Nietzschean sense, not the West Hollywood sense" (*Skinned Alive* (1995), p. 86).

I do not know why: WWC, 2:107 (8 August 1888).

xxxv **Whitman long ago:** *New York Times* obituary, 6 April 1997.

1

WALT & MARIETTA: ENTER THE DIVO

1 **If you have the voice:** "Si vox est, canta," *Artis Amatoriae*, ed. J. H. Mozley (1929), Book 3, 1.595, p. 54.

She roused whirlwinds: WWC, 9:49 (18 October 1891).

names of all the celebrities: NUPM, 3:1268. About this ms. the editor observes, "The irregular writing suggests a late date." (Many following citations of NUPM will contain its editor's estimates of dating.)

2 **I heard Alboni:** "Plays and Operas Too," *Specimen Days* (1882), p. 704.

by night among the sudorous: Ms. in Library of Congress, quoted by Paul Zweig in *Walt Whitman: The Making of the Poet* (1984), p. 214.

What perfect cataracts: 11 July 1846, UPP, 1:120.

traveling through: UPP, 1:257.

many of our regular concert-goers: 24 June 1852.

*In the present state: The critic was Richard Grant White, writing in the

Courier and Enquirer, 19 June 1852; this quotation also appears on p. 267 of Vera Brodsky Lawrence's *Reverberations* (1995). My research on opera in 1850s New York City was enormously aided by the generous assistance of the late Vera Lawrence, the premier scholar of nineteenth-century musical life in New York City. Typescript pages from this second volume of her monumental *Strong on Music: The New York Music Scene in the Days of George Templeton Strong* introduced me to the New York musical press and the New York Historical Society's resources. *Reverberations* covers the period 1850–56, a crucial time for students of Walt Whitman, and is certainly the most informative and scholarly illumination of the subject we have. See especially pp. 265–344, which are devoted to the year Alboni was in America.

an impression of something: *Musical Times,* 26 June 1852, p. 86. Richard Storrs Willis, its editor, presumably authored this remark.

Here at Last in Babylon: The Early Years

3   **brick-and-pine Babel:** *Franklin Evans, EPF,* 158.

5   **O, lovely, happy children:** *EPF,* 33.

    For vainly though: *EPF,* 9.

    *Suddenly, out of its stale: *EPF,* 38; I have changed the obvious typographical error "state" of its first printing to "stale." In revised form, "Resurgemus" appeared untitled as the eighth poem in the 1855 edition. Thomas Brasher, the editor of *EPF,* writes (p. 39) of Whitman in this poem, "His unconcern for the syllabic formalism and metrical regularity of traditional verse, his dependence on the rhythm of the accented syllables in a loosely iambic-anapestic line, are clearly perceptible as the beginnings of a new 'free verse' for the first time."

6   **Hasty to decide:** *EPF,* 58–60. The story appeared in the *United States Magazine and Democratic Review* in August 1841.

    I was so hard up: *WWC,* 1:93 (2 May 1888).

7   **We are no friends:** New York *Aurora,* 20 April 1842; see p. 99 of *Walt Whitman of the New York* Aurora, ed. J. Rubin and C. Brown (1950), hereafter *Aurora.*

    There is not a fact: Brooklyn *Daily Eagle,* 23 December 1846; see 1:229 of *A Gathering of the Forces,* ed. C. Rodgers and J. Black (1920), hereafter *Gathering.*

    A door or two: 8 March 1842, *Aurora,* pp. 18–9.

    Few evils: 22 March 1842, *Aurora,* p. 91.

    In our sun-down perambulations: 23 July 1846, *UPP,* 2:207.

    As a matter of personal: *Eagle,* 10 June 1846, *UPP,* 2:203.

8   **Sparkling in quality:** *Eagle,* 30 September 1846, *UPP,* 2:299.

    Paucity of News: 6 June 1847, *UPP,* 2:225.

Carelessly knocking and **J.J. Astor has:** 21 August and 3 April 1846, *Gathering*, 1:231.

What do you think: 12 August 1846, *Gathering*, 1:231.

IMPORTANT ANNOUNCEMENT: 22 December 1846, *UPP*, 2:342.

If the *Boston Post*: 10 October 1846, *Gathering*, 2:277.

RECEIVED WITH THANKS: 17 June 1847, *Gathering*, p. 228.

9 **Have something:** *Eagle*, 24 April 1846, *UPP*, 2:274.

It is not upon you: p. 311 (1856 title: "Sun-Down Poem").

What troubled her much *etc.*: *EPF*, 327–30.

12 **The body permanent:** "Eidólons," (1876), p. 170.

 *****Virtually nothing is known:** For some informed speculation on Shakespeare's whereabouts just before his theatrical coming-of-age, see E. A. J. Honigmann, *Shakespeare: The 'Lost Years'* (1985); see also my review of this book in the *Huntington Library Quarterly* 48 (1985), pp. 385–90.

So, welcome death: "Each Has His Grief," *EPF*, 17.

I celebrate myself: p. 27.

13 *****"sing" and "song" occur:** For a full analysis of Whitman's musical diction, see Faner, pp. 115–25.

beautiful masculine Hudson: Preface, 1855 *Leaves of Grass*, p. 7. All dates accompanying poems are for the edition of *LG* in which they first appeared.

turbulent manly cities: "Song of the Broad-Axe" (1856), p. 341.

lusty lurking masculine poems: "Spontaneous Me" (1856), p. 260.

voices of young men: "Crossing Brooklyn Ferry" (1856), p. 312.

distinct purposes: Unsigned review in *U.S. Review* (1856), in Hindus, p. 39.

to prove and define: "Poets to Come," p. 175.

14 **To get the final lilt:** "To Get the Final Lilt of Songs" (1888), p. 624. Whitman was here speaking of the likes of Homer, Aeschylus, Dante, and Shakespeare, but he clearly included himself in this company.

O you singer: "Out of the Cradle Endlessly Rocking," p. 393.

 *****an isomorphism between:** "The Opera Queen: A Voice from the Closet," *Cambridge Opera Journal* 6 (1994), p. 288. The subject of operatic singing as a metaphor for sexual expression naturally causes Robinson to think of Whitman: "the actual sound of operatic singing . . . is itself a form of physical vibration. It is, if you will, the body shaking. In the words of America's greatest nineteenth-century opera queen, Walt Whitman, 'I sing the body electric.' That vocal electricity, I'm persuaded, is a sublimation or upward displacement (as Freudians like to say) of the bodily vibrations and tinglings of the sexual act." Robinson also pertinently quotes Wayne Koestenbaum's autobiography of an opera queen on the soul-invading "penetration" of the operatic voice: "a singer doesn't expose her own throat, she exposes the listener's inte-

rior. Her voice enters me, makes me a 'me,' an interior, by virtue of the
fact that I have been entered" (*The Queen's Throat*, p. 43).

lithely overleaps the stars: *NUPM*, 1:126. The date of this ms. is "before
1855."

Chanter of Personality: "To a Historian," p. 167.

15   ***doubtless greatly influenced:** *Whitman: A Study*, p. 76. See also Louise
Pound, "Walt Whitman and Italian Music," *American Mercury* 6 (1935),
pp. 58–63; F. O. Matthiessen, *American Renaissance* (1941), pp. 558–63;
Faner, generally; Gay Wilson Allen, *The Solitary Singer* (1967), pp. 112–5;
Thomas Brasher, *Walt Whitman as Editor of the Brooklyn Eagle* (1970),
pp. 204–8; Floyd Stovall, *The Foreground of Leaves of Grass* (1974),
pp. 79–100; Zweig, pp. 45–9, 328; Reynolds, pp. 176–93.

implication is inescapable: p. 230.

Opera's greatest contribution: *Opera in America*, p. 184.

WALTER GOES TO THE OPERA

15   **the agonized:** *Eagle*, 3 April 1846, quoted by Thomas Brasher in his brief
note, "Whitman's Conversion to Opera," *Walt Whitman Newsletter* 4
(1958), p. 109.

dancing school bows: 4 December 1846, *Gathering*, 2:348–9.

an Englishwoman: *Eagle*, 5 August 1847, *Gathering*, 2:351–2.

American opera ... three banjos: *NUPM*, 1:152. The notebook in
which this entry occurs appears to date from about 1855–60.

16   **enjoyment was:** *WWC*, 3:511 (11 January 1889).

If the piece: *NUPM*, 1:394.

my opera days: *WWC*, 5:419.

among men: *Library of Congress*, ms. quoted by Zweig, p. 214.

slang, wit: "The Old Bowery, A Reminiscence of New York Plays and
Acting Fifty Years Ago," p. 1190. This essay first appeared in the New
York *Tribune*, 16 August 1885.

The great Italian singers: "The Primer of Words," *DBN*, 3:737.

During the intervals: *Daily Eagle*, 16 December 1846, in *Gathering*, 2:356.

17   **bring the opera:** *Life Illustrated*, 10 November 1855, in *New York Dissected*, p. 18.

18   **For the information:** *NUPM*, 1:393.

19   **I could not help:** *Emerson in His Journals*, ed. Joel Porte (1982), p. 99.

clear, firm, wonderfully *et seq.:* "Letter from Paumanok," New York *Evening Post*, 14 August 1851, *UPP*, 1:257.

20   ***I have always:** *WWC*, 3:423 (20 December 1888). In an essay called "A
Christmas Garland," Whitman compared Sand very favorably to Victor
Hugo: "Hugo ... runs off into the craziest, and sometimes (in his
novels) most ridiculous and flatulent literary blotches and excesses. ...

I like Madame Dudevant much better. Her stories are like good air, good associations in real life, and healthy emotional stimuli." (*UPP*, 2:53.) The eleventh edition of the *Encyclopedia Britannica* (1910–11) speaks of Sand's "novels of revolt," identifies *Consuelo* and its sequel as "*fantaisies à la Chopin*," and observes, rather dismissively, that Sand's "unmethodical method produces in her longer and more ambitious novels, in *Consuelo* for instance and its continuation, a tangled wilderness, the clue to which is lost or forgotten."

21   **decidedly ugly:** *Consuelo*, p. 4. Likewise p. 39: "Consuelo's ugliness—this strange, unexpected, and invincible drawback . . ." All quotations are from the Da Capo reprint (1979) of the English translation.

The broad and sweeping: *NUPM*, 6:2244.

with so firm: *Consuelo*, pp. 92–3.

22   **It was the first:** *Consuelo*, pp. 709–10.

I knew nothing: *Memoirs of an American Prima Donna* (1913), p. 27.

The man who: *Memoirs*, p. 35.

that 'incubating period': *Memoirs*, p. 29.

23   **Imagine playing:** *Memoirs*, p. 41.

As Linda I: *Memoirs*, p. 63.

OPERA'S SUPERB SUGGESTIONS

23   **(So firm—:** p. 625.

24   **chant, psalm:** *NUPM*, 4:1319. "The date is probably before 1860."

I am your voice: *NUPM*, 1:175 "These lines combined with the small neat writing suggest a date before or early in 1855."

The one duty: *NUPM*, 1:124–7.

entire health and **I want that tenor:** *NUPM*, 1:126–7. "The date is before 1855."

25   ***climactic high B-flat:** Simon Dedalus sings this aria from Flotow's *Martha* in the Ormond Bar ("Sirens" chapter, pp. 271–6 of the 1961 edition). The ringing high note "soared, a bird, it held its flight, a swift pure cry, soar silver orb it leaped serene, speeding, sustained, to come, don't spin it out too long long breath he breath long life, soaring high, high resplendent, aflame, crowned, high in the effulgence symbolistic, high, of the ethereal bosom, high, of the high vast irradiation everywhere all soaring all around about the all, the endlessnessnessness . . ." Whitman himself appears to have been greatly taken with this aria when he first heard it. A friend, Ben Starr, recalled being with Whitman at the time (possibly at the American premiere of *Martha* in November 1852 at Niblo's Garden): "Brignoli sang an aria which carried you away: you listened to it with your neck craned forward, drinking it in, dead, buried, and resurrected, till the last: then you sank back in your seat

exclaiming: 'Lord! the voice of an angel and the manners of a codfish!' "
Thinking back on the night more than three decades past, Whitman
doubted he would have hurled such an insult. "I was a great lover of
Brignoli: knew him, too, personally: I always stood up for him. These
things, like that of the fish, were often said of him by others. I doubt if
a singer ever lived, a tenor, with a sweeter voice than Brignoli had
then. . . . I never thought of his manners when I heard him sing: they
were not present: they were easy to forget" (*WWC*, 4:249–50, 1 March
1889).

A tenorial high note and eros-filled operatic ecstasy also figure in
Mann's *The Magic Mountain*. The novel's hero and author surrogate is
Hans Castorp: Castorp's soul-shaking, life-haunting crush on a boy
named Pribislav Hippe is pure autobiography, based on Mann's infatuation with one Willri Timpe. In a passage that attempts to out-Joyce the
tenor-loving Joyce and superbly evokes the operatic voice penetrating the
"veiled" emotional life of the closeted, Mann writes that one day "many
years before . . . Hans Castorp had been privileged to hear a world-famous
singer, an Italian tenor, from whose throat the power of grace-filled art
had poured out over the hearts of men. He had held a high note—
beautiful from the very first. And then gradually, from moment to
moment, the passionate tone had opened up, swelled, unfolded, grown
ever brighter and more radiant. It was as if veils, visible to no one before,
were falling away one by one—and now the last, or so they thought,
revealing the purest, most intense light, and then one more, the ultimate,
and then, incredibly, the absolute last, releasing a glory shimmering with
tears and a brilliance so lavish that a hollow sound of rapture had gone up
from the audience . . . and even he, young Hans Castorp, had felt a sob
well up within him" (trans. John Woods (1995), p. 481).

I hear the chorus: p. 214.

poor, indigent, watery: From the twelfth "Ramble," published in collabo-
ration with William Swinton in 1859 (under Swinton's name only),
NUPM, 5:1660. For a discussion of Whitman's authorship, see *NUPM*,
5:1624–6.

26   **somewhat lacking:** "Opera in New York," *Century Illustrated Magazine*,
May 1882, p. 207.

I exultant: p. 182.

I fling: p. 44.

an alarum: Letter to Harrison Blake, 7 December 1856, *Writings* (1902),
6:296.

long study: "A Visit to the Opera," *NUPM*, 1:394–7.

The voice: *NUPM*, 1:397.

rigid pre-requisites: *NUPM*, 6:2233. "Dated during or after 1857."

Drinking brandy: "An American Primer" (circa 1855–60), in *The Poetry
and Prose of Walt Whitman*, ed. Louis Untermeyer (1949), p. 573.

28 **Are you full-lung'd:** p. 509.

That music: "That Music Always Round Me" (1860), pp. 563–4.

chief histrion: "Passage to India" (1871), p. 536.

29 **An animated *ego-style*:** NUPM, 6:2230. "Rather loose handwriting" suggests "a date near 1860."

Broad, free: NUPM, 6:2244. "The writing is in the flowing style of the 1860s."

Play the old role: "Crossing Brooklyn Ferry" (1856), p. 313.

When a grand: NUPM, 1:116. "The date is probably between late 1853 and 1855."

greatest poet: p. 10.

Solitary, singing: "Starting from Paumanok," p. 176.

a very great poet: "Whitman" (1923), in *Selected Literary Criticism* (1956), pp. 399–400.

30 **Restrain and curb gesture:** NUPM, 6:2231–2; among notes "dated during or after 1857."

My freedom: *Memoirs*, p. 34.

Both are mystics: NUPM, 4:1502–3; circa 1868.

31 **Boldness. Nonchalant:** Quoted by Zweig, p. 121.

Whitman's bag of tricks: p. 250–1.

Perhaps soon some day: "As the Time Draws Nigh" (1860 title: "To My Soul"), p. 597.

Nature . . . is: "Leaves of Grass #1," 1860 *Facsimile*, p. 197. This poem was later titled "As I Ebb'd with the Ocean of Life."

The song is: "A Song of the Rolling Earth" (1856 title: "Poem of The Sayers of The Words of The Earth"), p. 366.

singing what belongs: "I Hear America Singing" (1860), p. 174.

if there is: *Zweig*, p. 14.

orchestrate his presence: *Ibid.*, p. 251.

32 **A *rule in Elocution*:** NUPM, 6:2227. "The neat handwriting and subject suggest a date in the late 1850s."

Hasting, urging: NUPM, 6:1443; "1857 or after."

Fiercely and: NUPM, 1:148.

a good word: NUPM, 5:1702.

My own voice: "Song of Myself," p. 75.

Come my boys: "Song of Myself," p. 75.

The preparations: "To Think of Time" (1855), p. 104.

the trill: "Song of Myself," p. 44.

33 **Do you take it:** "Song of Myself," p. 45.

come listen all: "Song of Myself," p. 241.

Through me: "Song of Myself," p. 50.

I dilate: "Song of Myself," p. 73.

My voice: "Song of Myself," p. 52.

I have embraced: "Song of Myself," p. 73.

I hear the sound: p. 53.

After continued: "A Backward Glance o'er Travel'd Roads," p. 657–8.

34   The human voice: "The Perfect Human Voice," *Good-Bye my Fancy* (1881), p. 1269.

electric personal idiosyncrasy: "The Old Bowery," p. 1191.

magnetism . . . What a joy: *WWC*, 5:152 (8 May 1889).

the importance of: *WWC*, 5:174 (12 May 1889).

I never think: *WWC*, 6:303.

THE ELEPHANT WHO SWALLOWED A NIGHTINGALE

35   Not a single: Quoted by Arthur Pougin, *Marietta Alboni* (1912), p. 86. All quotations from Pougin, my translation.

La Alboni has: Quoted by Pougin, p. 123.

All that was known: "Opera in New York," pp. 36–7.

36   At my first entrance: Quoted by Pougin, pp. 66–7.

large, simple, and grand: "Opera in New York," p. 38.

Men dissolved: 3 July 1852, p. 98.

38   *Let women learn: "Res est blanda canor: discant cantare puellae: / Pro facie multis vox sua lena fuit" *Artis Amatoriae*, Book 3, 11.315–6, p. 140. Ugliness is relative. Alboni was perhaps fortunate in succeeding Benedetta Pisaroni of the previous generation, whom White (p. 36) called "the greatest contralto and the ugliest woman that ever trod the Italian stage." We learn in Pougin (p. 84) that "Pisaroni was unfortunately, as Castil-Blaze said, 'ugly enough to cause fear,' and this ugliness was not incapable of causing some stupefaction in an audience."

39   a young Falstaff: White, p. 39.

the blithe Bacchus: *Putnam's Monthly*, June 1853, p. 698.

Alboni is: "A Visit to the Opera," *NUPM*, 1:396.

40   The stage did not: White, p. 38.

Three or four times: New York *Courier and Enquirer*, 28 December 1852, p. 2.

42   one of the last glories: *Le Menestrel*, 1 July 1894, p. 205.

VENUS CONTRALTO

43   Italia's peerless and Awaking from: pp. 527–8.

44   Here, take this gift: *1860 Facsimile*, p. 401.

The best songstress: "A Visit to the Opera," *NUPM*, 1:396.

certain actors: "Plays and Operas Too," pp. 703–4.

the best dramatic: "The Old Bowery," pp. 1186–7.

Mme. Alboni celebrated: *DBN*, 2:574–5.

Seems to me: *Prose Works*, ed. Floyd Stovall (1964), 2:694.

45   a considerable something: WWC, 2:173.

*Her mellow: Quoted by Richard Bucke, *Walt Whitman* (1883), p. 157. Ritter also recalled: "But above all, he said, while he was yet brooding over poems still to come, he was touched and inspired by the glorious, golden, soul-smiting voice of the greatest of Italian contralto singers, Marietta Alboni." In the essay "Walt Whitman and Oratory" in *The Complete Writings of Walt Whitman* (1902), 8:248, Thomas Harned quotes, from a manuscript apparently not surviving, another of Whitman's associations of Alboni with splendid vocalism: "A perfect reader [in public] must convey the same pleasure to his or her hearers that the best vocalism of the Italian singers does, just as much as the voice of Alboni, Bosio, Bettini, or Brignoli does. There must be something in the very vibration of the sounds of the mouth, something in the movements of the lips and mouth, something *in the spirituality and personality that produces full effects*" (emphasis added). In *Frank Leslie's Popular Monthly* of June 1892 appeared a piece by Whitman titled "How *Leaves of Grass* Was Made," which included yet another reference to Alboni: "Returning to New York, I alternated with the attendances mentioned by Dr. Bucke, especially the singing of the contralto Alboni and the Italian opera generally. All this and these, saturating and imbuing everything before I touched pen to paper on my own account" (*Prose Works 1892*, 2:772).

For me: WWC, 4:286 (6 March 1889).

*the consciousness of: WWC, 5:454–5 (23 August 1889). At the end of 1890 Traubel made the mistake of saying how the male voice meant so much more to him than the female "for expression of power and breadth of beauty." Whitman interrupted: "You never heard Alboni: you would not say that if you had heard her." When Traubel responded that he had heard Adelina Patti and was not impressed, Whitman laughed and offered a very shrewd distinction between "virtuose-dom" and "heart-music": "I see what you mean—another Jenny Lind. . . . The perfection of a singer to the average in trills, flutes, pirouettings, intellect, perfect poise—utter, invariable. But no—no—no!—*that's* not it, I am sure: it's something subtler, deeper, not so perfect!" (*WWC*, 7:368–9).

She roused whirlwinds: WWC, 9:49–50 (18 October 1891).

46   particularly susceptible: WWC, 1:102 (5 May 1888).

La mia estenzione: Quoted by Pougin, p. 1.

son of the brawny: "Excelsior" (1856), p. 588.

We convince: "Song of the Open Road" (1856), p. 303.

47   In the opera house: Letter of 21 September 1871, in *Verdi's Aida*, ed. Hans Busch (1978), p. 223. Galway Kinnell made a similar point in his poem "The Choir" that appeared in *The New Yorker* in 1979: "Everybody who sings becomes beautiful! / Even sad music / requires an absolute happiness in the face."

He was quite gray: The anonymous information is quoted by Bucke, p. 25.

city of robust: Bowers, *MS1860*, p. 114.

electric force: "The Old Bowery," p. 1189.

48   **without comb:** New York *Mirror*, 14 June 1852.

one of the exigencies: Quoted by Pougin, p. 76.

why should I venerate: p. 206.

50   ***We ought not to be:** "The Opera Queen," pp. 289–90. Robinson adds, "There is, I'm saying, an elective affinity between the code of gender and the code of sexual orientation, such that the operatic soprano is able to give voice to the otherwise mute protest of the gay man." Robinson goes on to note a second form of vocal transgression that may be significant in drawing gay men to opera. This, the exploitation of the low register or "chest voice," is obviously pertinent to Alboni. He writes that "they very often sing like men, altering their method of vocal production for the lowest notes so as to boom out tones of unimpeachable masculine authority." Robinson singles out Maria Callas in this regard, noting particularly the "terrifyingly masculine" sound of her descents in the "Suicidio" aria of Ponchielli's *La Gioconda*, and concludes, "If I am right in my speculation, the distinct gender ambiguity of this kind of singing holds the key to its homoerotic charms."

I think a quiet affair: *WWC*, 9:38–9 (17 October 1891).

51   **What play of Shakespeare:** Unsigned review in *American Phrenological Journal* (1856), in Hindus, p. 42. "Too much attempt at ornament is the clur [?] upon nearly all literary styles" is among "Rules for Composition" Whitman set out for himself in the 1850s (*NUPM*, 1:101).

tangled and florid Shakespeare: *NUPM*, 5:1862.

52   **throat-virtuosos:** *Musical World and N.Y. Musical Times*, 26 March 1853, p. 193.

boudoir amours: *WWC*, 2:177 (21 August 1888).

The Swedish Swan: "Letter from Paumanok," *Evening Post*, 14 August 1851, *UPP*, 1:257.

Jenny Lind's: *Walt Whitman's Revision of the Analysis of* Leaves of Grass, ed. Stephen Railton (1974), p. 69.

singular coolness: Quoted by Bucke, *Walt Whitman*, p. 25.

53   ***find a new:** "One Hour to Madness and Joy," p. 263. Among the "copious and rich" contributions of the French language to American English, Whitman included the word "nonchalance," which he defined as "cool carelessness and indifference." (*NUPM*, 6:1658–9.) Whitman writes of the "nonchalance that the soul loves" in his preface to the 1855 *LG*, p. 5. He uses a related French loan-word to make a similar point in one of his notebooks: "No one will perfectly enjoy me who has not some of my own . . . hauteur" (*NUPM*, 1:380).

broad-chested feller: *WWC*, 2:173 (21 August 1888).

***Alboni sings:** Quoted by Pougin, p. 78. The same sentiment concludes

Théophile Gautier's impressive précis after he had heard Alboni in *Semiramide* and *Cenerentola*: "There is always, and more than ever, the silvery and fresh timbre, that suave force, that easy power, that vigorous delicacy . . . that unrivaled equality, that unheard-of perfection, those sonorous chains of pearls wondrously strung, all the song so audacious, so neat and so pure, so classic and so modern, so full of elegance and of vigor, yet in which one never senses either fatigue or effort." (Quoted by Pougin, pp. 88–9n.)

54   **two natural and nonchalant:** "Behold This Swarthy Face" (1860), p. 279.

    *I think the greatest: *WWC*, 3:553 (16 January 1889). The last entry in a notebook Whitman used in writing *LG* shows him teaching himself the word "insouciance" and digesting its concept: "Insouciance / een soo se awnz / or the mettlesome action of the blood horse / and the unimpeachableness of the sentiment of trees / & jealous and haughty instinct" (*NUPM*, 1:155).

The Great Ms. Norma

55   **singers do not:** *NUPM*, 1:312.

    Across the stage: p. 527.

    Brief, and as quiet: "Seeing Niagara to Advantage," *Specimen Days*, p. 877.

56   **this terrifying score:** Quoted in Lanfranco Rasponi, *The Last Prima Donnas* (1985), p. 192.

    Yes, this queen: White, p. 39

58   ***luckily thinking of the Brindisi:** The allusion to this famously rousing *ballata* carries its own Whitman touch. For if the text of any Italian bel canto aria captures the "final lilt" of the early *Leaves of Grass* editions, it is this one in which Maffeo divulges the "secret of being happy," namely, *Profittiamo degli'anni fiorenti* (While we're young let us live our lives fully).

    One of the roughs etc.: Unsigned review in *U.S. Review*, in Hindus, pp. 34–7.

59   **Strangle the singers:** p. 1328. The letter was included as an appendix to the 1856 *Leaves*.

The Divo Retires

    Walt Whitman's method: New York *Saturday Press*, 7 January 1880, in *A Child's Reminiscence*, ed. Thomas Mabbott and Rollo Silver (1930), p. 20.

    positively last night: *Tribune*, 12 April 1861, p. 1

    News of the attack: "Opening of the Secession War," *Specimen Days*, p. 706.

60   **The American people:** *Memoirs*, p. 55.

O superb! O Manhattan: "First O Songs for a Prelude" (1865), p. 416.

Such singing: Letter to Lewis Brown, 8 November 1863, in *WWC*, 1:101–4.

I have been: Letter of 15 March, *Corr*, 2:169.

*So many of my friends: *WWC*, 2:116 (10 August 1888). Several months later he reiterated his willingness to imagine a Wagnerian affinity: "It's one of my regrets that the Wagner operas have never come my way—that I for my own part have not found it possible to indulge in them. I am quite well aware that they are my operas—belong to *Leaves of Grass*, to me, as we belong to them" (*WWC*, 4:445, 28 March 1889).

The music of the present: "Poetry To-day in America—Shakspere—The Future" (1881), p. 1021.

61   **Is it our opera:** *WWC*, 1:106 (5 May 1888).

Alboni fills up: 28 December 1852.

Now I will: "Song of Myself," p. 214.

baffled, balk'd: p. 395.

So I pass: "So Long!" (1860), p. 611.

*Ljuba Welitsch: The *Grove Dictionary of Opera* on Welitsch: "Her rise to international fame was meteoric but, sadly, ill-health and insufficient care of her voice denied her continued success in her grandest roles." Zweig estimates that Whitman wrote "almost two-thirds of his life's work in less than three years" (*Walt Whitman*, p. 278).

62   **I sing the endless:** "Song at Sunset" (1860), p. 604.

O so loth: "After the Supper and Talk" (1887), p. 636.

*a reckless present tense: *Walt Whitman*, p. 254. Willa Cather captured the big vocalism of "Song of Myself" more amusingly: "If a joyous elephant should break forth into song, his lay would probably be very much like Whitman's famous 'Song of Myself' " (*Nebraska State Journal*, 19 January 1896, in *The World and the Parish*, ed. William Curtin (1970), 1:281).

It throbs me: "Song of Myself" (1855 version), p. 54.

She bowed: *Memoirs*, p. 175.

No more a flashing: p. 408.

You, old throat and **O old throat:** Bowers, *MS1860*, pp. 249, 246. Whitman finally settled for "Hasten throat and sound your last" (p. 610)

muffled sonorous sound: p. 626.

strange inertia: p. 614.

Dull, parrot-like and **caged bird:** p. 615.

63   **chant old age:** "On, On the Same, Ye Jocund Twain!" (1891), p. 640.

lusciously under: "That Music Always Round Me," p. 564. Zweig speaks of this change too (p. 328) in comparing Whitman's Civil War poems—which "register a stripping down, a setting aside of personality"—with his "great early poems" in which "his naked self had caroused, more like a gigantic opera singer than a simplified seer."

make poems: "Starting from Paumanok" (1860), p. 183.

No special strains: "Eidólons" (1876), p. 170.

The song is: "A Song of the Rolling Earth," p. 366.

Avoid . . . the whole: *NUPM*, 1:233.

beautiful quiet Sunday: *Corr*, 2:104–5.

64   a most surprising compound: *Familiar Studies of Men and Books* (1882), p. 121.

sobbing dirge and dirge, the voices: "As I Ebb'd with the Ocean of Life" (1860; originally Leaves of Grass #1), pp. 394–6.

I love well: "To a Certain Civilian," p. 455.

65   in Hospital: *NUPM*, 2:869. "The date is in the late 1860s."

reedy monotones: "Locusts and Katydids," *Specimen Days*, pp. 788–9.

66   Labial gossip and Whispers of heavenly: "Whispers of Heavenly Death" (1868), p. 558.

deep musical drone: "Bumble-Bees," *Specimen Days*, p. 784.

superior landscape: "Art Features," p. 859.

strange effects: "Sundown Lights," p. 815.

delicate color-effects: "Hours of the Soul," p. 827.

the flageolet-note: *Specimen Days*, p. 787.

sweet, artless: "Spring Songs," p. 840.

liquid-simple notes: "A Meadow Lark," p. 815.

The air was: "A Contralto Voice," p. 876.

FINALE OF THINGS

Fierce-throated beauty: p. 583.

pianner-player: *WWC*, 1:223 (28 May 1888).

67   Emblem of: p. 570.

I fear: *WWC*, 1:28 (12 April 1888).

I am no longer: *WWC*, 1:456 (12 July 1888).

fish-shape Paumanok . . . populous pavements: "Starting from Paumanok," p. 176.

68   Outdoors is the: *NUPM*, 1:169.

*Poem—illustrating: *NUPM*, 1:145; from a notebook "most, if not all . . . written prior to 1855." The poem "I Heard You Solemn-Sweet Pipes of the Organ" (1861) also shows opera and the outdoors to be compatible: ". . . as I walk'd the woods at dusk I heard your long-stretch'd sighs up above so mournful, / I heard the perfect Italian tenor singing at the opera, I heard the soprano in the midst of the quartet singing . . ." (p. 266).

2
WALT & BOSS-TOOTH: "SINGING THE PHALLUS"

69   **Yet still sex:** *WWC*, 3:453 (3 January 1889).
   He was compelled: *Whitman: A Study* (1896), p. 190.
   the shuddering longing ache: "Song of the Open Road," p. 302.
   love-grip: In a manuscript he writes of the soprano who "convulses me like the love-grip of her in whose arms I lay last night" (*NUPM*, 1:125), but of course the "her" was surely a "he."
   Thruster holding me: "Song of Myself" (1855 version), p. 47.
   Push close my lovers: "A Song for Occupations" (1855 version), p. 89. In the edition of 1881, when Whitman was no longer physically close to lovers, this line vanishes.
   I merely stir: p. 215. Note also "I Sing the Body Electric," p. 253: "There is something in staying close to men and women . . . in the contact and odor of them, that pleases the soul well."
70   **this is no book:** "So Long!", p. 611.
   Persuader always of people: *1860 Facsimile*, p. 141; title in this edition: *Chants Democratic #2*. This splendid eighteen-line snapshot of the poet at about forty was deleted entirely after the third edition.
71   **would have nothing:** "Notes from Conversations with George W. Whitman," *In Re Walt Whitman*, p. 39.
72   ***Power enjoying:*** p. 282. Another marvelous instance of "armed" used in the limb-twining rather than the National Rifle Association sense occurs in a *Leaves* notebook (*NUPM*, 1:72): "Every room of your house do I fill with armed men / Lovers of me, bafflers of hell." Whitman himself encouraged a military image when he changed "men" to "force" in the published version of this passage in "Song of Myself."
73   **body and soul** and **hang on its neck:** p. 23.
   The white teeth: p. 110.
74   **the passional relations:** *WWC*, 1:173 (27 April 1888).
   he harps on: *WWC*, 1:202–4 (24 May 1888).

THUMB OF LOVE—UPRIGHT, EMOTIONAL

75   **blurt:** "Song of Myself," p. 209.
   applied to the morbid: *Whitman: A Study*, p. 190.
   effuse egotism: "Starting from Paumanok," p. 183.
   you don't need: 8 January 1895, *Briefe an Otto Grautoff und Ida Boy-Ed* (1975), p. 30.
   from his broad breast etc.: *NUPM*, 5:1881–3. "The ms. dates from 1859 or a little later."

76   **sex, sex: always immanent:** *WWC*, 3:453 (3 January 1889).
77   **here is my neck:** p. 233.
       Broad-shouldered: *The Journals of Bronson Alcott* (1938), Hindus, p. 64.
       My verse strains: Letter to Rudolf Schmidt of 16 January 1872, *Corr*, 2:150.
       Something I cannot see: p. 212.
78   **most ecstatic passages:** From *At the End of the Open Road* (1962), included in *Measure*, p. 258.
       a close connection; *WWC*, 5:376 (18 July 1889).
       Phallic festivals: *DBN*, 3:772.
       Dancing yet through the streets: p. 236.
       see here the phallic: *NUPM*, 4:1305.
79   **singing the phallus:** p. 248; later title: "From Pent-up Aching Rivers."
       genital impulse of: *Chants Democratic #1, 1860 Facsimile*, p. 119; earlier title: "Poem of Many in One"; later title: "By Blue Ontario's Shore"
       equal hemispheres: p. 321; later title: "Our Old Feuillage."
       perfect Comrade: p. 408.
       Leaves of Grass!: Quoted by Milton Kessler in a note, *Walt Whitman Quarterly Review* 11 (1994), p. 140. In a letter Whitman offered a more benign explanation for his choice of botanical hallmark: "It is the very large & aromatic grass, or rush, growing about water-ponds in the valleys . . . often called 'sweet flag' . . . The recherché or ethereal sense of the terms, as used in my book, arises probably from the actual Calamus presenting the biggest and heartiest kind of spears of grass—and their fresh, acquatic, pungent bouquet" (*Corr*, 1:347).
80   **you must be careful:** *WWC*, 9:38 (17 October 1891).
       To speak!: *1860 Facsimile*, p. 177.
       his mind: "Allen Ginsberg on Walt Whitman: Composed on the Tongue" (1980), in *Measure*, p. 235.

READING WHITMAN'S SEX

       I write with: *NUPM*, 1:338.
81   **disgusting Priapism:** Reported in a letter from William O'Connor to Whitman, *WWC*, 1:313 (12 June 1888).
       was the thing: *WWC*, 3:453 (3 January 1889).
       I give you joy: Letter of 21 July 1855, quoted in Reynolds, p. 341.
       It is as if the beasts: Letter of 7 December 1856 to Harrison Blake, in Hindus, p. 67.
       that dirty old man: *My Mortal Enemy* (p. 96), quoted in *The World and the Parish*, 2:279n.
       a great chastity: "The Achievements of Walt Whitman," *Texas Quarterly* 5 (1962), p. 46.

I cannot too often: "A Backward Glance o'er Travel'd Roads" (1889), p. 671.

Whitman inserted: p. 30.

82   **physical excursions:** In *Rare Early Essays on Walt Whitman*, ed. Carmen
      Dello Buono (1980), pp. 44–45.

      Don't you feel: *WWC*, 1:381 (25 June 1888).

      mass of stupid filth: Unsigned review, New York *Criterion*, 10 November
      1855, in Hindus, p. 67.

83   **You speak of Mr. Whitman:** Letter of 25 April 1862, *Selected Letters*
      (1986), p. 173.

      so pure, that they: Letter of 7 December 1856 to Harrison Blake, in
      Hindus, p. 67.

      A man was here: *WWC*, 1:381 (25 June 1888).

      Who is now reading: *1860 Facsimile*, p. 361. This poem appeared only in
      the 1860 edition.

84   **many happy hours:** Letter of 18 February 1872, reproduced in *WWC*,
      4:180–5.

      the fashionable delusion: p. 1335.

      a distinctly sensuous side *et seq.*: *Walt Whitman* (1893), pp. 72–5.

85   **Members of the Legal:** Excerpted in *Hidden from History: Reclaiming the
      Gay and Lesbian Past*, ed. Martin Duberman *et al.* (1989), pp. 106–9.

      an unhealthy mood: *Whitman: An Interpretation in Narrative* (1926),
      p. 173. For an analysis of Holloway's wrestle with Whitman's sexuality,
      see Jerome Loving, "Emory Holloway and the Quest for Whitman's
      Manhood," *Walt Whitman Quarterly Review* 11 (1993), 1–17.

86   **abundantly unclear** and **goes far:** *The Dial* 69 (1920), pp. 482, 477.

      substantially true: *Whitman*, p. 66.

      That Whitman had known: *I Sit and Look Out*, ed. E. Holloway and
      V. Schwarz (1932), p. 208n.

      intense, morbidly self-critical *et seq.*: pp. 176–202.

87   **He instinctively:** p. 183.

88   **Whitman nearly:** Letter to Edward Dent, 6 March 1915, *Selected Letters*
      (1983), 1:222.

      A century later *et seq.*: pp. 188–90.

89   **essentially a woman's book:** *WWC*, 2:331 (16 September 1888).

      Whitman's heterosexual: *Lost in the Customhouse*, p. 117.

      What kind of sex life: p. 197. Subsequent quotations from Reynolds are
      from pp. 194–218, 391–403, 427–30, and 487.

90   **Jeannette Gilder:** *WWC*, 9:78 (24 October 1891).

      *can be best understood: Reynolds also seeks to downplay ardently pas-
      sionate same-sex relationships by noting (p. 398) that an "implied hetero-
      sexuality" was often involved in them. That this strategy is a principal
      one for the closeted homosexual is not addressed by Reynolds; indeed,
      the strategies of the Closet are entirely ignored by him. Equally puzzling
      is Reynolds's assertion that "Although [Whitman] frowned on promis-

cuity, he believed in marriage." As often, one is left wondering where in Whitman's verse, especially his early verse, these frowns are to be observed, and it was of course easy enough for Whitman to believe in marriage . . . for those other than himself, even for those attractive young friends of his who turned out, alas, to be heterosexual. Grandiose (and utterly unsubstantiatable) generalizations asserting Whitman's radical displacement from sexual function continue to be made. In 1995, Stephen Railton opined that Whitman "could never bring himself to acknowledge that this attraction to men was sexual" and that "the circumstances of his own temperament made it necessary for him to disguise his sexual preference *even to himself*." ("The Performance of Whitman's Poetry," *The Cambridge Companion to Walt Whitman*, ed. Ezra Greenspan (1995), p. 15, emphasis added.) How does the critic *know* these things so categorically? This is a question one is often urged to ponder after encountering pessimistic speculations about Whitman's sexual activities.

91 **the thought and fact of sexuality:** "A Backward Glance," *LGC*, p. 572.

objected to the piano and **seems to be so unequal:** *WWC*, 1:56, 70 (21, 26 April 1888).

92 **labyrinthine in its:** Introduction, *Walt Whitman: Modern Critical Views* (1985), p. 4. Bloom also calls "accurate" Zweig's remark about Whitman having "so little to say about sex" (p. 5).

How little posterity: *NUPM*, 3:1183.

we know that Emerson: "The Biographer's Problem," *Mickle Street Review* 11 (1989), p. 82.

His sister Mary: p. 197.

93 **the little room:** The essay is reproduced in *Measure*, p. 20.

Whitman and Contemporary: Letter, *The New Republic*, 17&24 July 1995, p. 5.

We have got: *WWC*, 3:452 (3 January 1889).

never had an idea: In *In Re Walt Whitman*, p. 34.

94 ***gayest . . . edition of Leaves:** Roy Harvey Pearce strongly argues the thesis that it is "Whitman, the poet of 1860" whom "we must recover" ("Whitman Justified: The Poet in 1860," in Bloom, pp. 65–86). R. W. B. Lewis is also convinced (Bloom, p. 100) that in the first three editions of *Leaves* "most (not all) of the real Whitman is to be found." Paul Zweig, of like mind, ends *Walt Whitman: The Making of the Poet* just a few pages after he reaches the publication of the 1860 edition; with *Drum-Taps* and the Lincoln ode of 1865, Zweig writes (p. 345), Whitman's "great work was done."

beautiful masculine Hudson: Preface to the 1855 edition, p. 7.

95 **his picture:** *WWC*, 1:154 (14 May 1888). The artist was Herbert Gilchrist, the (probably gay) son of Anne Gilchrist, the great female love-interest of Whitman's life—the interest being all on her part.

drenched with joy: *NUPM*, 1:231.

New York, Brooklyn, experimentation: *In Re Walt Whitman*, p. 311.

CITY OF ORGIES

96   My city's fit: p. 613. In 1860 Whitman published a longer poem with the
same title; see p. 585.

The Indians use: *WWC*, 5:470 (30 August 1889).

Chants of the Mannahatta: *1860 Facsimile*, p. 7.

97   O hotcheeked: p. 109.

had enough of going: Letter to Elijah Fox of 21 November 1863, *Corr*,
1:187. By this time Fox had returned home to Michigan; a letter from
him a year later indicates he had married.

98   all I know: "So Long!", *1860 Facsimile*, p. 451; this line appeared only in
the 1860 edition.

99   Yes, here I had etc.: This and all subsequent *Franklin Evans* quotations
(from its first five chapters) are from *EPF*, 128–58.

countryfied: *NUPM*, 2:490 (verified by the Library of Congress website
(http://lcweb2.loc.gov:8080/wwwhome.html), LC #94, p. 22).

It's a pity: *The Diary of George Templeton Strong*, ed. A. Nevins and
M. Thomas (1950), 1:150 (entry for 11 October 1840).

whorearchy: *Diary*, 2:57.

out-Sodom Sodom: p. 198.

halcyon years: *City of Eros: New York City, Prostitution, and the Commer-
cialization of Sex* (1992), p. 141. Other facts in this paragraph are drawn
from Gilfoyle's sixth chapter, "Shoulder-Hitters, Porno Kings, and
Politicians" (pp. 119–41).

100   Young Libertad: p. 386. The poem first appeared in the 1865 edition with
the title "Broadway Pageant. / (Reception Japanese Embassy, June 16,
1860)."

What passions: "Broadway" (1888), p. 624.

101   *musical drinking-house: Gilfoyle (p. 129) has an interesting discussion
of the advent of what he calls "concert saloons," which by the end of
the Civil War "replaced the theater as the major form of urban
entertainment."

102   quivering me to: p. 215.

at his best: "Images of Walt Whitman," in *The Collected Essays of Leslie
Fiedler* (1971), 1:165.

lover of populous: "Starting from Paumanok" (1860), p. 176.

*Some Poetical Comparisons: Quotations from this "Letter" are from
the appendix in *The Historic Walt Whitman* (1973), ed. J. Rubin,
pp. 318–23. The deathless story of transition from the stifling homophobic boondocks to the thrilling promiscuity of New York City is told

once again in a recent book by Alan Helms, *Young Man from the Provinces: A Gay Life Before Stonewall* (1995); Helms pertinently chose *Calamus* #16 as the epigraph for his memoir.

103 ***the Sodom School** and **A painting titled:** See Katherine Molinoff, *Walt Whitman at Southold* (1966). Reynolds discusses the Southold facts and rumors at length (pp. 70ff); he also reproduces the painting.

104 **To touch my person:** p. 55 (1855 version).

liquid, sane: p. 585.

105 **a great place:** Issue of 8 March 1842, in *Aurora*, pp. 17–18.

dearest amusements: "The Old Bowery," *November Boughs* (1888), p. 1187.

too robustuous: p. 1189.

Whoever does not know: Issue of 29 March 1942, in *Aurora*, p. 19.

visor'd, vast, unspeakable: "Broadway," p. 624.

I always enjoy: Draft letter of 6 October 1868, *Corr*, 2:55.

blab of the pave: "Song of Myself," p. 195.

106 **frequent and swift flash:** p. 279.

I too walked: *1860 Facsimile*, p. 383, quoted since its punctuation is more clear.

his flesh sweaty: pp. 109–10 (1855 version).

107 **Yet comes one:** Whitman toned down this poem, *Calamus* #19 (*1860 Facsimile*, p. 364), for later editions; compare the alterations in "Behold This Swarthy Face," p. 279.

One flitting glimpse: This version (*1860 Facsimile*, p. 371) later became "A Glimpse" (p. 283).

108 **To the Prince:** Letter of Will Wallace, 5 April 1863, in *Drum Beats*, p. 210.

*Our host himself: "Some Old Acquaintances—Memories," *Specimen Days*, p. 911. For more on Pfaff's see Christine Stansell's essay "Whitman at Pfaff's: Literary Life and New York Bohemia at Mid-Century," *Walt Whitman Quarterly Review* 10 (1993), 107–26. William Dean Howells describes his first meeting in Pfaff's in *Literary Friends and Acquaintances* (1900), pp. 74–75; the passage is reproduced in *Whitman in His Own Time*, ed. Joel Myerson (1991), pp. 167–8.

was never a great discusser: *WWC*, 1:417.

Laugh on: "The Two Vaults," *LGC*, p. 660.

I often recall: letter to Edward Einstein, 26 November 1875, *Corr* 2:344 (Whitman's italics).

I fall in with: letter of 2 September 1870, *Corr*, 2:109.

109 **I have learned:** *1860 Facsimile*, p. 125. In the final version of the poem (pp. 482–3), these lines are followed by a dismally anticlimactic two dozen more.

110 **Give me now libidinous:** 1860 version (*Facsimile*, pp. 310–11). The final version of "Native Moments" mostly involved punctuational changes; see p. 265.

CONCEALED BUT SUBSTANTIAL LIFE

*always the sick: Letter of 19 March 1863 to Nathaniel Bloom and John F. S. Gray ("Dearest Nat, and Fred Gray ..."), *Corr*, 1:81–85. Among Whitman's notebooks is this description of Bloom: "Clever fellow, and by no means bad looking.—(George Fitch has roomed with him a year, and tells me, there is no more honorable man breathing.)—Direct, plain-spoken, natural-hearted, gentle-tempered, but awful when roused" (quoted by Shiveley, *Calamus Lovers*, p. 56).

111   While on the walk: *LGC*, p. 660.

I cannot say: "Who Learns My Lesson Complete" (untitled in 1855), p. 140.

These yearnings: "Song of the Open Road" (1856), p. 301.

112   I hear secret: "I Sit and Look Out" (originally *Leaves of Grass* #7 in 1860), p. 411.

Sullen and suffering hours: "Hours Continuing Long," *1860 Facsimile*, p. 355; also in *LGC*, pp. 596–7. Whitman banished this deeply despondent poem from all post-1860 editions.

Long I was held: Bowers, *MS1860*, pp. 66–8.

piercing through: Thoughts #1, *1860 Facsimile*, p. 408. This poem was deleted after 1867.

can tear off: *NUPM*, 1:135.

113   Only the kernel: p. 301.

a candid and unloosed: *1860 Facsimile*, p. 451. The boast was later deleted.

sometime by directions: Letter of 16 January 1872 to Rudolf Schmidt, *Corr*, 2:150.

poems of privacy: p. 260.

There is something: *Days with Walt Whitman* (1906), p. 43. The visit took place on 30 June 1884.

114   greatest poems: *NUPM*, 1:371. "Small, neat handwriting suggests a date in the 1850s."

leading sources: "Sources of Character," *Specimen Days*, p. 705.

Beasts in human shape: Quoted by Gilfoyle, p. 136.

detected persons: Thoughts #1, *1860 Facsimile*, p. 408.

faint clews: "When I Read the Book" (1867), p. 171.

Among my special: *NUPM*, 3:1136.

115   our love grew fast: "Three Young Men's Deaths," *Specimen Days*, pp. 811–2.

I wish things were: Letter of 12 April 1867, *Corr*, 1:323.

As to you, I do not: Letter of 23 April 1870, *Corr*, 2:97. Of Stoddard, more in the Annex.

*I write this openly: The letter is reproduced in *WWC*, 4:181–6 (19 February 1889). Stoker visited Whitman while assisting Henry Irving and

Ellen Terry on an American theatrical tour and gave "every evidence of being staunchly on my side" (*WWC*, 1:325, 14 June 1888). Stoker arranged for an autographed *Leaves* for Terry, who wrote Whitman, "Since I am not personally known to you I conclude Mr. Stoker 'asked' for me—it was good of him—I know he loves you very much" (*WWC*, 1:5, 30 March 1888).

Thomas Mann had similar "professional" experiences. In 1927 (aged fifty-two) he met and fell in love with a seventeen-year-old named Klaus Heuser while on vacation. Later, he was thrilled by the experience of lecturing on a Kleist play with Heuser present as his muse. To his gay son Klaus and lesbian daughter Erika he wrote, "I read in the theater . . . from my analysis of *Amphitryon*, on which 'he,' if one may say so, was not without influence." Then he adds, exulting in the concealed but substantial life, "The secret and most silent adventures in life are the finest" (Heilbut, p. 457). Fifteen years later, Mann read for a long time in his old diaries "from the Klaus Heuser time when I was a happy lover. Most beautiful and touching, our farewell in Munich, when I made for the first time 'the leap into a dream world,' and his temple rested against mine. Well, I have lived and loved: black eyes that shed tears over me, beloved lips that I kissed—there it was, even I had it. I will be able to say that, when I die" (Entry of 20 February 1942, *Tagebücher 1940–1943* ed. Peter de Mendelssohn (1982), pp. 395–6; three years later Mann destroyed his diaries from the Heuser period). Mann's *Young Joseph* was inspired by Heuser; Heilbut ventures (p. 549) that this novel "deserves comparison with Proust's *Cities of the Plain* as a statement of the splendors and miseries of homosexual love."

O I CRUISE THE OLD CRUISE AGAIN!

117   **Picking out here:** "Song of Myself," p. 58.
       cruise my old cruise: p. 326.
       one is never entirely: p. 801.
       lonely old grubber: "A Supermarket in California" (from *Howl!*, 1955), *Collected Poems 1947–1980* (1984), p. 136.
       one goodshaped and wellhung man: Preface to 1855 edition, p. 26.
118   ***it is curiously** and **You linger:** p. 118. A great twentieth-century author for whom the ocular intimacy of cruising proved a constant and deeply pleasurable part of life was Thomas Mann. In his probing, often witty, and refreshingly unjudgmental recent biography, Anthony Heilbut has frequent occasion to remark on such habitual delight in the male body, calling Mann a "world-class voyeur" (p. 209) and an "arch-voyeur" (p. 345) and noting that "the surreptitious glance is so typical of Mann"

(p. 53) and that beholding male beauty was "the one constant pleasure of his life" (p. 13). Mann's penchant for cruising is borne out in his diaries, in which he happily notes moments of locking eyes with a young man during a concert or while signing autographs. One day in 1921, after working on an essay on Goethe and Tolstoy, Mann notices some gardeners, "one of whom, young, beardless, with brown arms and open shirt gave me quite a turn." This leaves him mulling thoughts on "the importance of enthusiasm, love, dedication." To which (p. 370) Heilbut adds, "The advantages of sublimation could not be clearer." A few years later, a similar event took place, and Mann's diary entry (quoted p. 452) was more analytical—and decidedly more Whitmanesque: "Passing the plant nursery I was pleasantly smitten by the sight of a young fellow working there, a brown-haired type with a small cap on his head, very handsome, and bare to the waist. The rapture I felt at the sight of such common, everyday and natural 'beauty,' the contours of his chest, the swell of his biceps, made me reflect afterward on the unreal, illusionary and aesthetic nature of such an inclination, the goal of which, it would appear, is realized in gazing and 'admiring.' Although erotic, it requires no fulfillment at all, neither intellectually nor physically." Nearing fifty, it is perhaps wise to begin thinking this way—though, as we shall see was Whitman's case, it can be painful.

Small wonder that Heilbut has occasion (p. 398) to make much of the influence of "the voyeur Whitman" on Mann after he read him in a German translation published in 1922 by a close friend, Hans Reisiger. Mann's diary entry for 31 May 1921: "On Sunday evening Reisiger was here at the house and read from his translations, which led to a discussion of Whitman's homosexuality" (*Diaries 1918–30* (1982), p. 116). Whitman's democracy, Heilbut cheekily remarks (p. 377), "ratifies the voyeur's cruise: the sole erotic pleasure Mann never denied himself." Whitman's influence is spectacularly present in Mann's 1922 lecture "On the German Republic," which Heilbut calls "the most revealing public statement" of Mann's career (see pp. 376–83 for a discussion of this daring homosexualist political credo and the drastic censorship of its English translation). Heilbut later summarizes impressively that "Whitman, not Freud" was Mann's mentor (p. 409) and also observes (p. 557) that "America had influenced Mann long before he arrived there. Whitman's poetry inspired his politics during the early 1920s." Other parallels between the sexual politics of Whitman and Mann (and Wilde as well) are noted in the "Walt & Oscar" annex.

look with calm gaze: "A Song of Joys" (1860), p. 328.
pulling and hauling: p. 191.
I love him: p. 39.
Do I not: p. 90 (later titled "A Song for Occupations").
many I loved: p. 311.

O tenderly: *1860 Facsimile*, p. 362; this poem appeared only in the third edition.

frequent and swift flash: "City of Orgies" (originally *Calamus #8*), p. 279.

O the streets of cities: *1860 Facsimile*, p. 261.

119   O YOU whom: p. 286; originally *Calamus #43*.

120   PASSING stranger: p. 280; originally *Calamus #22*.

I am a man: "Poets to Come" (1860), p. 175.

What is it I interchange: "Song of the Open Road" (1856), p. 301–2.

impetus-words: "A Backward Glance," p. 667.

young men my problems: "So Long!", p. 611.

121   tall, strapping: *UPP*, 1:188.

well-tann'd . . . scars and the beard: p. 243.

hurt, diseased, deprived *et seq.*: From the lists in *NUPM*, 1:199–200, 249–59; 2:492–7, 845.

Years ago in New York: *WWC*, 5:143 (6 May 1889).

the word "hustler": *WWC*, 5:507 (13 September 1889).

122   well-defined form: *NUPM*, 6:2246–7.

Ned was courageous: *WWC*, 3:117–8 (17 November 1888).

124   *his affair with the woman: And yet, Whitman maintained a long friend-ship with Calhoun. In a letter to Peter Doyle of 9 October 1868 (six years later), he wrote: "the Broadway drivers, nearly all of them are my personal friends. Some have been much attached to me, for years, & I to them. . . . Yesterday I rode the trip I describe with a friend, on a 5th Avenue stage, No. 26—a sort [of] namesake of yours, Pete Calhoun. I have known him 9 or 10 years" (*Corr*, 2:57).

the flush days: "Omnibus Jaunts and Drivers," *Specimen Days*, pp. 702–3.

In any roof'd room: "Whoever You Are Holding My Hand," pp. 270–1.

125   After an hour's lounge: Issue of 29 March 1842, in *Aurora*, pp. 34–5.

My forte: *WWC*, 2:21 (20 July 1888).

It is a fine noble: *Eagle* issue of 10 June 1846, *Gathering*, 2:204–6.

For our own part: Issue of 20 July 1857, in *I Sit and Look Out* (1932), ed. E. Holloway and V. Schwarz, pp. 103–4.

126   O to bathe: p. 328.

soul hungering gymnastic: "Rise O Days" (1865), p. 427.

The swimmer: "From Pent-up Aching Rivers," p. 249.

beautiful gigantic swimmer: p. 545.

My lovers: pp. 80–1 (1855 version). The line "Or while I . . ." was cut after 1860.

127   silently selected by: "To a Western Boy" (originally *Calamus #42*), p. 285.

my love to those: *NUPM*, 1:231. The line appears in ms. notes that pro-duced "Crossing Brooklyn Ferry."

resistless yearning: "From Pent-up Aching Rivers," p. 248.

Here you. . . . what and Failing to fetch: pp. 87–8.

boy lingering: *1860 Facsimile*, p. 261.

THE BODY CORRELATIVE ATTRACTING

128   **Fine nature** and **Peter—large:** *NUPM*, 1:199–200.

O you coarse: "Apostroph," *LGC*, p. 601. This poem appeared only in the 1860 edition.

129   **Walt Whitman sociable:** *DBN*, 1:171.

130   **Now I am thrust:** pp. 109–10.

My own favorite: *WWC*, 2:71 (1 August 1888).

the problem of human: *UPP*, 1:256.

131   **frailty from places:** Quoted by Gilfoyle, *City of Eros*, p. 138.

it was at the top and **I always went:** *WWC*, 7:24–5 (25 July 1890).

by stealth: "Whoever You Are Holding Me Now in Hand" (*Calamus #3*), p. 270.

Smile O voluptuous: p. 208. This is reminiscent of Cummings's great spring-poem "O sweet spontaneous."

the coarseness and: p. 516.

How you settled: p. 192.

132   **tonic** and *al fresco*: "Poetry To-day in America," p. 1023.

*presiding spinal purpose: *WWC*, 7:414 (14 January 1891). Whitman boasted he was "nearly always successful with the reader in the open air" (*WWC*, 2:175, 21 August 1888). He also favored James Fenimore Cooper over Hawthorne because Cooper's influence was "always an outdoor influence; he is perennial fresh air, pure seas" (*WWC*, 7:4–5, 10 July 1890).

gymnosophist . . . rapt: "Song of Myself," p. 236.

alone over the beach: "When I Heard at the Close of the Day," pp. 276–7.

The souse upon me: p. 262.

is so amorous: p. 496.

wild woods *etc.*: "Roots and Leaves Themselves Alone," pp. 277–8; for original version, see *1860 Facsimile*, p. 359.

133   **Fatigued by their:** LC #94; p. 86 (http://lcweb2.loc.gov:8080/ wwwhome. html). My transcription varies from that in *NUPM* (2:499) based on Holloway; *NUPM* also guessed incorrectly at its placement in the notebook.

the soul prefers: *NUPM*, 1:64.

to pull on that young hickory: pp. 808–9.

134   **Edwin Miller has argued:** Shively rehearses this material in *Calamus Lovers*, pp. 148–9.

*A delightful day: *NUPM*, 4:1014 (ms. dated 14 July 1878). Whitman retold the sapling story many years later to Traubel, and one dearly wonders if his rehearsal (notice the word "fellow") was also a self-pleasuring with sexual overtones that he expected Traubel not to notice. Traubel remarks on the anecdote about Montaigne being amused by his cat and then wondering whether he amused his pet, causing Whitman to say: "I remember that a long time ago, down at Timber Creek—I would go

along the stream, looking, singing, reciting, reading, rumination—
and one fellow there—a splendid sapling—I would take in my hands—
pull back—so-so: let it fly, as it did with a will, into position again—its
uprightness. One day I stopped in the exercise, the thought striking me:
this is great amusement to me: I wonder if not as great to the sapling?
It was a fruitful pause: I never forgot it: nor *answered* it. I suppose this
is a new strophe—Montaigne in other dress" (*WWC*, 6:367–8, 16
April 1890).

135   **You sea:** p. 208.
   Is it night *et seq.*: *1860 Facsimile*, pp. 455–6; quotations from the ms. versions are from Bowers, *MS1860*, p. 248.
137   **laughed, slept:** *NUPM*, 1:231.

To Wishes Fix an End

   comes every day: Letter of 2 December 1874 to Charles Eldridge, *Corr*,
   2:315–6.
   liver burning hot *et seq.*: *Merry Wives of Windsor*, 2.1.117; *The Tempest*,
   4.1.55–6; *Love's Labor's Lost*, 4.3.72.
   this late-years palsied: Preface to *Second Annex: Good-Bye my Fancy*, p. 638.
138   ***Certum voto:*** The full context of this advice is pertinent: *Sperne volup-
   tates; nocet empta dolore voluptas. / Semper avarus eget; certum voto pete
   finem* (Scorn pleasures; pleasure bought with pain is harmful. The cov-
   etous is ever in want; aim at a fixed limit for your desires), Second
   Epistle, Book I (11.55–56), *Satires, Epistles, and Ars Poetica*, trans.
   H. Fairclough (Loeb edition, 1932), pp. 266–7.
   unprecedently sad: Letter of 6 January 1865, *Corr*, 1:247.
139   **You degradations:** p. 589.
   serene-moving animals: pp. 446–7.
140   **Every hour is:** Letter of 9 October 1868, *Corr*, 2:57.
   cool, gentle *et seq.*: *NUPM*, 2:887–90; also *UPP*, 2:94–7. See the discussion of this ms., "probably the most important autobiographical document we have from WW," in *NUPM*, 2:885, 891–4; see also my
   discussion on pp. 191–2.
142   **A strong-fibred joyousness:** pp. 981–2.
143   **For him I sing:** p. 171.
   My brother had: Letter of 3 October 1873, *Corr*, 2:248.

From Bawdy House to Cathedral

   I seldom go: Letter of 6 May 1925 to Isaac Goldberg, in *H. L. Mencken on
   Music*, ed. Louis Cheslock (1961), p. 202.
144   **I chant America:** "A Broadway Pageant," p. 386.

in the midst of the crowd: "Song of Myself," p. 234.

projected through time: "Starting from Paumanok," p. 177.

*waged a long war: "Walt Whitman's Love Affairs," *The Dial* (1920), p. 483. In his essay "Whitman Justified: The Poet in 1860," Roy Pearce vigorously reiterates Holloway's view: "Whitman, for whatever reason, after 1860 moved away from the mode of archetypal biography toward that of prophecy. He worked hard to make, as he said, a cathedral out of *Leaves of Grass*. He broke up the beautifully wrought sequence of the 1860 volume; so that, even when he let poems stand unrevised, they appear in contexts which take from them their life-giving mixture of tentativeness and assurance, of aspiration, and render them dogmatic, tendentious, and overweening" (Bloom, p. 84). Another eloquent critical variation on this theme comes from R. W. B. Lewis, who offers this thesis: "It was during those years, from 1867 onward, that Whitman— initially a very self-exposed and self-absorbed poet—became willfully self-concealing, while at the same time he asserted in various ways an entity, a being, a persona radically other than the being that lay at the heart of his best poetry." After 1871, Lewis adds, "Oratory and rant were unhappily notable even in the most interesting of the new poems" (Bloom, pp. 99, 123). D. H. Lawrence, in 1921, was more brutally succinct: "The individuality had leaked out of him" (Bloom, p. 13). Even one of the earliest Whitman disciples, John Burroughs, ventured this view, though it was not shared by the more doting Traubel: "Did not agree with Burroughs that W.'s late work lacked in the poetic" (*WWC*, 7:393).

It's a nasty word: *WWC*, 4:29–30 (26 January 1889).

145   **there are a few things:** Letter of 6 January 1865, *Corr*, 1:247.

a long and lovely suicide: Letter to H. C. Marillier of January 1886, *Letters* (1962), p. 185.

O ~~my~~ lands: *DBN*, 3:795; *1860 Facsimile*, p. 18. "Proto-Leaf" was later titled "Starting from Paumanok."

146   ***I dreamed:** Bowers, *MS1860*, p. 114. Whitman also deleted from *Chants Democratic #2* ("Song of the Broad-Axe") a line about a city of men who can be seen "going every day in the streets, with their arms familiar to the shoulders of their friends" (*1860 Facsimile*, p. 132).

147   **retreat from his sexuality:** "Whitman's 'Live Oak, with Moss,' " in *The Continuing Presence of Walt Whitman*, pp. 185–205. See Hershel Parker's response, "The Real Live Oak, with Moss," *Nineteenth Century Literature* (1996), pp. 145–60.

It shall be customary: *1860 Facsimile*, p. 350.

sore and heavy-hearted: *1860 Facsimile*, p. 355.

149   **I have compared:** *WWC*, 2:6 (16 July 1888).

150   **O'Connor kicks against:** *WWC*, 2:9–10 (17 July 1888).

I am astonished: *WWC*, 2:224–5 (30 August 1888).

my boyish exuberance: *WWC*, 7:373 (23 December 1890).

151   **I hope he has not:** *WWC*, 6:232 (6 January 1890).
       not seem to think: *WWC*, 6:340 (26 March 1890).

POSTCOITAL TRISTESSE

       the noblest of all the amatory: *WWC*, 7:274 (14 November 1890).
       O young man: *1860 Facsimile*, p. 261.
       A ship itself: p. 330.
       An athlete is: "Earth, My Likeness," p. 284.
       Ethereal, the last: "Fast-Anchor'd Eternal O Lover," p. 286.
       teacher of athletes: p. 242.
152   **O to have my life:** *1860 Facsimile*, p. 268.
       Chants of the Mannahatta: *1860 Facsimile*, pp. 7–8.
       Let the future behold: *1860 Facsimile*, p. 181. The "puzzling" in this passage was an even more apt "turbulent" in Whitman's manuscript version; see Bowers, *MS1860*, p. 152.
       The courageous soul: p. 1335.

3
WALT & HIS BOYS: "TO SEEK MY LIFE-LONG LOVER"

153   **What do you:** *1860 Facsimile*, p. 12; later "Starting from Paumanok," p. 181.
       occupied by traveling: This, Merrill's, and Reeves's letters are reproduced in *A Whitman Controversy: Being Letters Published in Mercure de France 1913–1914*, ed. Henry Saunders (1921), pp. 1–9.
154   **I have always:** *WWC*, 7:113 (11 September 1890). On another occasion Whitman summed up the gamut of responses to *Leaves:* "Some adulation—(a little's enough): some cussing: now and then somebody goes for me—gives me hell. If I had made a collection of such documents I'd have had some queer stuff for you to preserve" (*WWC*, 4:6, 21 January 1889).
       I have the hide: *WWC*, 7:98 (3 September 1890).
       sedate, serious: *WWC*, 9:617 (30 March 1892).
       It is a damnable drink: *WWC*, 5:219 (25 May 1889).
       about '39 or '40: *WWC*, 7:373 (23 December 1890).
       Undying childhood: *WWC*, 7:391 (2 January 1891); original emphasis. Whitman was here praising Robert Ingersoll and William O'Connor, but as often his praise of others was also self-praise.
       Emerson was not: *WWC*, 7:107 (8 September 1890).
155   ***Do you know, Horace:** *WWC*, 7:360 (16 December 1890). Whitman often expressed this kind of fraternal "gay underground" sentiment in

conversations. He said of Symonds, for instance, that he "has got into our crowd in spite of his culture: I tell you we don't give away places in our crowd easy—a man has to sweat to get in" (*WWC*, 1:388, 27 June 1888).

the young man: *NUPM*, 3:1304. Whitman deleted the "Him" and replaced it with "The one" in the manuscript.

NO WOMEN IN THE HOUSE

essentially a woman's book: *WWC*, 2:331 (16 September 1888).

the woman rightsers: *WWC*, 9:53 (19 October 1891).

156   ***ain't worth shucks:** *WWC*, 7:93 (29 August 1890). That Whitman had something of a feminist battle cry in mind is clear from the remark's full context: "*Leaves of Grass* is essentially a woman's book: the women do not know it, but every now and then a woman shows that she knows it: it speaks out the necessities, its cry is the cry of the right and wrong of the woman sex . . . speaks out loud: warns, encourages, persuades, points the way." Sherry Ceniza pursues this theme of Whitman's grateful reception by early feminist figures—like Mary Chilton, Adah Menken, Abby Price, and Paulina Davis—at persuasive length in "Some Nineteenth-Century Women's Responses to the 1860 *Leaves of Grass*," in *The Cambridge Companion to Walt Whitman*, pp. 110–34. She particularly draws attention to Juliette Beach, who defended Whitman in print but also wrote in a letter to the editor Henry Clapp, Jr. that *Leaves of Grass* "delights me—that defiant ever recurring I is so irresistibly strong and good." Beach also wrote that she admired Whitman's "fierce wild freedom from anything conventional" (pp. 123–4), an admiration wholly understandable among freethinking American women just after midcentury.

see here the phallic choice: *NUPM*, 3:1305.

the love and comradeship: *NUPM*, 1:341. "The writing suggests WW wrote this in the late 1850s."

A bachelor, he: In Hindus, p. 65.

Why—some of my best: *WWC*, 5:196 (18 May 1889).

I have great friends: *WWC*, 9:46 (17 October 1891).

*Women? What are women: *WWC*, 7:180, 124 (5 October 1890, 17 September 1890). Misogynistic sniping in gay circles goes back a long way. The second-century poet Strato wrote, "every dumb animal copulates in one way only, but we, endowed with reason, have the advantage over animals in this—we invented anal intercourse. All who are held in sway by women are no better than dumb animals" (*The Greek Anthology*, Book XII, #245, trans. William Percy in *Pedagogy and Pederasty in Archaic Greece* (1996), p. 55).

157   ***Catching him in the act:** *WWC*, 1:322 (14 June 1888). Several other

comments Whitman made in male company might be perceived as male chauvinism. "I have been more than lucky in the women I have met," he said to Traubel, but added, "a woman is always heaven or hell to a man—mostly heaven: she don't spend much of her time on the border-lines" (WWC, 2:140, 14 August 1888). A few months later he had occasion to say one friend was "virile," the other "feminine," then hastily (but not entirely convincingly) added, "I don't mean any disrespect by that word—I don't mean what people mean when they say sissy" (WWC, 3:352, 21 December 1888).

I think the best: WWC, 7:338 (8 December 1890).

History teems: WWC, 7:440 (29 January 1891).

the perfect equality: p. 8.

this empty dish: pp. 1334–5.

Towards women generally: Calamus: A Series of Letters Written During the Years 1868–1880, ed. R. M. Bucke (1897), p. 21.

*As for dissipation: In Re Walt Whitman, p. 36. George suggests he was often asked about his brother's relations with women (why? surely, to confirm suspicions about his sexuality), and he remarks earlier in his reminiscence (p. 34), "I am confident I never knew Walt to fall in love with young girls or even show them marked attention. He did not seem to affect the girls."

158 **party of ladies:** Letter of 18 October 1868, Corr, 2:62.

Pete, dear boy: Letter of 30 July 1870, Corr, 2:101–2.

no airs—& just: Letter of 2 September 1820, Corr, 2:108.

159 **spirited, clever young fellows:** EPF, 303.

Though a bachelor: EPF, 248–9.

beautiful masculine Hudson: p. 7.

160 **Not sluttish:** "The Hudson is quite another critter [than the Mississippi]—the neatest, sweetest, most delicate, clearest, cleanest river in the world. Not sluttish—not a trace of it and I think I am pretty familiar with it . . . for the matter of 200 miles or so" (WWC, 5:402, 31 July 1889).

an illustration and **a person singularly:** Hindus, pp. 46–7.

Every day I go: p. 1327.

wild old Corybantian dance: "Proud Music of the Storm," p. 528.

slow rude muscle: "A Woman Waits for Me," p. 259.

the poet of the woman: p. 207.

The Female: "One's-Self I Sing," p. 165. The poem's last line is more accurate: "The Modern Man I sing."

lusty lurking masculine: "Spontaneous Me," p. 260.

masculine, full-sized: p. 216.

I believe the main: Bowers, MS1860, p. 12.

I do not doubt: "Assurances," p. 563.

interminable eyes: p. 447 (emphasis added).

saturate what shall: p. 262.

The *sisters*: p. 543.

161   Each singing: p. 174.

robust chants: *1860 Facsimile*, pp. 7–8.

To gather the *minds*: *1860 Facsimile*, pp. 325–6.

the comrade's long-dwelling kiss: "Whoever You Are Holding Me Now in Hand," p. 271.

good-by kiss: p. 242.

alarming increase: Issue of 15 September 1857, in *I Sit and Look Out*, p. 114.

an eye for female and today would be: *Walt Whitman's America*, p. 198.

play of masculine muscle: pp. 251–2.

Muscles and wombs: *Selected Literary Criticism*, ed. Anthony Beal (1956), p. 397.

162   Goddess excellently bright: *Oxford Authors: Ben Jonson*, ed. Ian Donaldson (1985), p. 482. The poem begins "Queen and huntress, chaste and fair," the last two epithets capturing the essence of most of Whitman's praise of womanhood.

Come nigh to me: p. 127.

WOMEN sit: p. 413 (1860).

*the woman's face has been scratched out: The picture, of playwright Francis Williams and Whitman arrayed with her three children, is reproduced by Ed Folsom in "Whitman's Calamus Photographs," in *Breaking Bounds*, p. 197. Folsom believes Whitman scratched out the face.

163   Twenty-eight young men: p. 36.

The welcome nearness: *1860 Facsimile*, p. 289; later title: "From Pent-up Aching Rivers."

Give me for marriage: p. 446.

Two hawks: p. 249.

The body of my love: p. 261.

164   put your lips: "Whoever You Are Holding Me Now in Hand," p. 271.

PASSING stranger: "To a Stranger," p. 280.

These yearnings: "Song of the Open Road," p. 301.

And who has receiv'd: *Var*, 1:243.

democratic lager: Article reproduced in Charles Glicksberg, *Walt Whitman and the Civil War* (1933), pp. 61–2.

the waltzing band: *NUPM*, 2:484 (LC #84, pp. 83–5).

165   PRIMEVAL my love: *1860 Facsimile*, p. 375.

of manly attachment: "In Paths Untrodden," p. 268.

blind dreamer: *WWC*, 2:268 (6 September 1888).

the finest, [a]cutest: *WWC*, 6:22 (27 September 1889).

166   a great woman: *WWC*, 5:12–3 (11 April 1889).

I always say: *WWC*, 2:20 (20 July 1888).

"physiological" Leaves of Grass: *WWC*, 6:133 (12 November 1889); original emphasis.

it is very curious: *WWC*, 3:117 (17 November 1888).

I am only what: *WWC*, 2:450–1 (8 October 1888).

did Walt Whitman not think: *WWC*, 7:8 (12 July 1890).

haut ton coteries: *Democratic Vistas*, p. 944.

I am a sort of: *WWC*, 6:187 (11 December 1889).

167   It is my axiom: Entry of August 28, *Notizbücher 1949–50* (1991), pp. 257–8;
Mann's emphasis.

BECOME ELEVE OF MINE

*They seem impossible: *WWC*, 7:400 (7 January 1891). Three years earlier, when the subject of a nurse was first raised to Whitman, he said:
"Be sure you get a large man—no slim, slight fellow" (*WWC*, 1:291,
9 June 1888). He clearly wanted a nurse whose sight would be therapeutic, as will be seen in "Walt & Horace" (pp. 243–6).

universal ennui: *Democratic Vistas*, p. 988.

language fann'd: p. 992.

I am getting more: *WWC*, 1:200 (24 May 1888).

168   I was a great deal: *WWC*, 5:405 (1 August 1889).

the most mellifluous: This praise came to Whitman's attention, having
been quoted in a clipping from the *Manchester Guardian* of 28 October
1890 that was sent to him (*WWC*, 7:274, 14 November 1890).

swarthy and unrefined face: *1860 Facsimile*, p. 364. By the fifth edition of
Leaves, Whitman eased up on himself and deleted "and unrefined."

a vivid picture: *NUPM*, 1:431.

Infantum Juvenatum: *NUPM*, 4:1360.

stylish when young *et seq.*: *In Re Walt Whitman*, pp. 34–9.

169   As Nathan ceased: *EPF*, 119. The story appeared in the *U.S. Magazine
and Democratic Review* of July 1842 and was reprinted in the Brooklyn
Daily Eagle in 1846.

170   a slight fair-looking boy *et seq.*: *EPF*, 55–60.

Loudly rang *et seq.*: *EPF* 273–63, 291.

171   straggling village *et seq.*: *EPF*, 68–79. The story first appeared in the *New
World* of 20 November 1841; all quotations are from this original version. The story was reprinted with many major and some bowdlerizing
changes in 1844, 1847, and in the *Collect* (1882); see *EPF* notes for its
publishing history.

172   outlaw'd offenders: "Starting from Paumanok," p. 182.

173   occupation, poverty: "Me Imperturbe" (originally *Chants Democratic* #18
in 1860), p. 173.

The breath of the boy: "The Sleepers" (1855 version), p. 116.

teachers of all: "On Journeys through the States," p. 172.

I teach straying: p. 83.

I give you fair warning: *1860 Facsimile*, pp. 344–5; later title: "Whoever You Are Holding Me Now in Hand."

174   **the single poem:** *Whitman: A Study* (1896), p. 81.

      Eleves I salute you: p. 71.

      To the young man: *1860 Facsimile*, p. 377. This was the climactic final poem of a twelve-poem sequence, "Live Oak, with Moss," that is extant in Whitman's manuscripts; it was later expanded to become the *Calamus* poems.

      (ga-mute eu . . .): *NUPM*, 2:728.

      I can now see one: *WWC*, 3:511 (11 January 1889).

      You are a true man: *WWC*, 4:182 (19 February 1889).

      It's wonderful: *WWC*, 4:269 (3 March 1889).

VOICES, LOVED AND IDEALIZED

176   **respect for every:** "Quaker Traits of Walt Whitman," *In Re Walt Whitman*, pp. 213–4.

      loves the free: In Hindus, p. 46.

      I celebrate: Bowers, *MS1860*, p. 68.

      Why should I exile: *1860 Facsimile*, p. 311; later title: "Native Moments."

177   **O, mighty powers:** *EPF*, 9.

178   **O to disengage:** *1860 Facsimile*, p. 370.

      Who can help loving: *EPF*, 255–6. The story first appeared in the *Columbia Magazine*, September 1844.

      Every thing I have: *NUPM*, 1:167.

179   **The one I love well:** *NUPM*, 4:130. This ms. "may be dated in 1855 at the earliest."

      those beginning notes: p. 388.

      lover—lovee: *DBN*, 3:675.

180   *Shine! shine!:* p. 389.

      Hours of my torment: *1860 Facsimile*, pp. 355–6.

181   **lover and perfect equal:** "Among the Multitudes" (originally *Calamus* #41), p. 286.

      picture as that: "Recorders Ages Hence" (originally *Calamus* #10), p. 276.

      divine rapport: p. 296.

      You twain!: "A Leaf for Hand in Hand," pp. 283–4.

      Come, let's away: *King Lear*, 5.3.8–9.

      Hark close and still: "From Pent-up Aching Rivers" (originally *Enfans d'Adam* #2), p. 249.

182   **Let us twain:** From the "Messenger Leaves" cluster, *1860 Facsimile*, p. 403.

      far away through fields: "Recorders Ages Hence," p. 276.

      I swear I never will: p. 84 (1855 version).

Does the tide hurry: Bowers, *MS1860*, p. 92.

O burning and throbbing: Bowers, *MS1860*, pp. 70–1.

183   **When he whom I:** "Of the Terrible Doubt of Appearances," p. 275.

One who loves me: *Calamus #8, 1860 Facsimile*, pp. 354–5.

O my comrade: *1860 Facsimile*, p. 22. The flamboyance of this passage was later severely compromised by revision; see later version in the Library of American edition, p. 188.

184   **My rendezvous:** p. 241.

These are days: *Notizbücher*, ed. Hans Wysling and Yvonne Schmidlin (1989), 2:44–6; my translation.

185   **youthful intensity of feeling:** Entry for 6 May 1934, *Tagebücher 1933–1934*, ed. Peter de Mendelssohn (1977), pp. 411–12; my translation.

was a charming fellow: Letter to Walter Opitz, 28 February 1947, quoted by Heilbut, p. 142.

*****If Mann could say:** p. 142. Heilbut asserts that Ehrenberg was the inspiration for Mann's two superb stories of 1903, "Hunger" and *Tonio Kröger*, as well as the model for Adrian Leverkühn's one adult affair with a man in *Doctor Faustus* several decades later. Leverkühn on an amorous cloud nine—Heilbut (p. 139) calls this "one of the great homosexual love arias"—is pure *Calamus*: "A man came into my life. . . . He released the human in me, taught me happiness. It may never be known or be put in any biography. But will that diminish its importance, or dim the glory which in private belongs to it?" Heilbut adduces a Mann letter written to his brother Heinrich during the affair (1 April 1901, quoted by 128) that also suggests Mann was experiencing a *Calamus*-like exhilaration. He feels "boundless gratitude" for Ehrenberg: "My sentimental need, my need for enthusiasm, devotional trust, a handclasp, loyalty, which has had to fast to the point of wasting away and atrophying, now is feasting." Next year he wrote of Paul to Paul's half sister, "I have made him a little more literary and he has made me a little more human. Both changes were necessary!" (14 March 1902, *Letters 1889–1955*, p. 27). Mann was deeply saddened to learn, after the war, that Ehrenberg had been a Nazi.

*****This set off a tremor:** *Palimpsest* (1995), p. 25. The chapter on the boy, Jimmie Trimble, is often pertinent to the subject of this chapter; see pp. 21–40. Vidal's early gay novel *The City and the Pillar* (1948) is based in part upon the affair and carries the dedication, "For the memory of J.T."

*****Voices, loved and:** *The Collected Poems*, rev. ed. George Savidis (1992), p. 20. The parallels between the poems of Cavafy and Whitman are remarkably numerous and resonant. By way of example one might point to how Cavafy evokes Whitman's haunting of Pfaff's bohemian saloon in "At the Café Door" (p. 55 of the *Collected*), or to "In the Evening" (p. 73), in which Cavafy revels in the "echo from my days of sensuality" in his own Mannahatta, the exotic Egyptian metropolis of Alexandria.

Cavafy's brief poem "To Sensual Pleasure" (p. 74) could serve perfectly as an epigraph for any of the first three editions of *Leaves of Grass*, just as his "Theatre of Sidon (A.D. 400)" (p. 126), with its disgust at "puritans who prattle about morals," echoes many a Whitman thrust at the prim and proper. A Whitmanesque nostalgia for halcyon days of sexual ecstasy is finely captured in Cavafy's "Following the Recipe of Ancient Greco-Syrian Magicians" (p. 174). "September, 1903" (p. 189) is a powerful expression of frustration over lost amorous bliss, and it was written at the age of forty—precisely the age Whitman was when he experienced his own catastrophic New York love affair. "Growing in Spirit" (p. 188), written at the age Walt was when composing his *Calamus* poems, begins with a quintessentially Whitmanesque call to disobedience: "He who hopes to grow in spirit / will have to transcend obedience and respect." The poem also offers the utterly characteristic *Leaves of Grass* notion that "Sensual pleasure will have much to teach" the person who hopes to "grow in spirit." Many other Whitman themes—the compulsive urge to sexual activity, the aesthetic pleasure of the young male adult body, the awareness of one's illicit desires, the etiquette of cruising—are all prominent in Cavafy's verse.

186   **Perhaps the best of songs:** "A Backward Glance o'er Travel'd Roads," p. 656.

The last two days: *Specimen Days,* pp. 784–5.

*makes me think: *1860 Facsimile,* p. 365. Another deeply homoerotic tree is here worth remarking upon. Hans Castorp, the author's alter ego in Mann's *The Magic Mountain*, has an upheaving first love affair with a fellow adolescent. Castorp's favorite tune, which he often whistles, is "Der Lindenbaum" by (the also apparently gay) Schubert. The lime tree in the song—*Baum* is fortunately masculine in German—beckons to a young lad who has often dreamed in its shadows to come to it in the dead of night: "Come here to me, lad, here you will find your peace!" The restless boy, however, refuses this embrace and flees. Still, many hours distant, he hears the siren call. You "would have found peace" with me, he hears the tree say in the song's last line. The same longing for two-bodied love, one is inclined to think, is expressed in Whitman's "solitary" live-oak "uttering joyous leaves."

187   **song of companionship:** "Starting from Paumanok," p. 179.

sorrows of the world: p. 411.

a woman I casually: p. 266.

But now of all that city: Bowers, *MS1860,* p. 64.

*that woman who: p. 266. Cavafy treats precisely the same lovers' parting in a poem titled "Gray." It ends with these lines:

. . . Those gray eyes will have lost their charm—if he's still alive;
that lovely face will have spoiled.

Memory, keep them the way they were.
And, memory, whatever you can bring back of that love,
whatever you can, bring back tonight.

*sleepless and dissatisfied: "Recorders Ages Hence," p. 276. A line that Whitman eventually cut from the 1860 version of "A Song of Joys" (*Facsimile*, p. 261) expressed a similar fear: "O I am sick after the friendship of him who, I fear, is indifferent to me."

188   **the one I cannot:** *1860 Facsimile*, p. 355.

   I dreamed I wandered: *1860 Facsimile*, p. 362. This poem, titled "Of Him I Love Day and Night," Whitman later removed from its homosexual context in *Calamus* and placed in the "Whispers of Heavenly Death" cluster.

   For an athlete: "Earth, My Likeness," p. 284.

   SOMETIMES with one: *1860 Facsimile*, pp. 375–6.

189   **(I loved a certain . . .):** "Sometimes with One I Love," p. 285.

   Facing west from: p. 267.

   could "not too often reiterate": "A Backward Glance," p. 671.

   O to be absolved: *Enfans d'Adam* #6, *1860 Facsimile*, p. 308.

   I think I could: "Song of Myself" (1855 version), p. 58.

190   **the young men of these states:** *DBN*, 3:740–1. Traubel says Whitman compiled his primer in the late 1850s.

   *head "read": Whitman included a full report of his reading, which obviously flattered his self-image, in a footnote to one of his unsigned reviews of *Leaves* (Hindus, p. 47). The scale ranged from "very small" (1) to "very large" (7). Among Whitman's highest scores were Cautiousness (6), Benevolence (6–7), Combativeness (6), Sublimity (6–7), Firmness (6–7), and Self-Esteem (6–7). His lowest scores were for Acquisitiveness (4), Secretiveness (3), Time (3), Tune (4), Marvellousness (3), and Veneration (4). Whitman referred several times to this reading in old age, being especially proud of his score for Cautiousness.

   *an exclusive reference: Michael Lynch, " 'Here is Adhesiveness': From Friendship to Homosexuality," *Victorian Studies* 29 (1985), pp. 90–91. Lynch cites other important articles on Whitman's discovery and deployment of phrenology (pp. 69, 89) and gives an excellent short history of phrenology.

191   **too great fondness** and **The author once saw:** *American Phrenological Journal*, quoted by Lynch, p. 87.

   Cheating, childish abandonment *et seq.*: *NUPM*, 2:885–90. See also the illuminating discussion of this ms. in the appendix immediately following (pp. 891–4).

193   ***Depress the adhesive:** Whitman's frantic resolutions about renouncing pursuit of Doyle are in fact bracketed at both ends in the notebook by entries that admonish calm. Preceding the excised third of a page are

two significant entries. The first is a "Description of a Wise Man" redacted from Epictetus, the Stoic philosopher. The qualities of this wise man are obviously commendable to the fearful and desperate gay lover: "If any one reproves (? or insults) him he looks with care that it do not irritate him . . . All his desires depend on things within his power. . . . His appetites are always moderate . . . *He is indifferent whether he be thought foolish or ignorant* . . ." Epictetus, it happens, was very important for Whitman, who first read him when sixteen, probably because the Greek (born circa A.D. 60) counseled calm in the face of worldly (and sexual) desire. In 1889 Walt told Horace Traubel that he always remembered "the advice of Epictetus: 'Do not let yourself be wrapt [Traubel's mistake, surely, for "rapt"] by phantasms'" (*WWC,* 4:371)—a nice paraphrase of what, in his notebook, he was trying to tell himself about the phantasmal love for Peter Doyle. On another occasion, Epictetus came up in conversation with Traubel in connection with the "secret" that Whitman regularly threatened to tell about his past life:

> W. said: "This book has become in a sense sacred, precious to me: I have had it about me so long—lived with it in terms of such familiarity." I nudged him a bit about the "secret." "You haven't said anything about it, Walt." He was serious at once: "But I have not forgotten: I want you to know it—know all about it: you." I can't make it out. He has something on his mind. (*WWC,* 3:253)

Is it possible that Whitman's sudden mood swing was caused by his thinking of how Epictetus helped him survive the trauma of a devastating amorous defeat many years before?

Following the précis of Epictetus in the notebook is a similarly stoic "Extract from [Heinrich] Heine's Diary (Paraphrased & varied)": "to live *a more Serene, Calm, Philosophic Life.—reticent, far more reticent—* yet cheerful, with pleased spirit and pleased manner—far less of the gusty, the capricious—the puerile—No more attempts at smart sayings, or scornful criticisms, or harsh comments on persons or actions." Here, apparently, Whitman was depressing his adhesive nature by renouncing the high style of the bitch queen. Whitman had an extremely high regard for both Epictetus and Heine. He often carried his "dear, strong, aromatic" compact edition of the *Encheiridion* around with him in his pocket, and he told Traubel, "I always stand up for Heine . . . am eager (more than willing) to recognize his high estate: to excuse (if excuses are needed, as they are not) his improprieties, his erraticism, his strayings off from conventional standpoints" (*WWC,* 2:553, 29 October 1888). Whitman, obviously, saw much of himself in Heine.

Not coincidentally, Heine was (along with Nietzsche and Whitman's much loved Goethe) a favorite writer of the young Thomas Mann. In a student essay on Heine written at eighteen in 1893, Mann contended, in *Leaves of Grass* fashion, that the "good" and "bad" of Philistines do not apply to artists, who indulge in the "practical egoism of living," and that art is beyond morality—a very Whitmanesque (also Wildean and Nietzschean) view (*Gesammelte Werke* (1960), 11:711). Mann's own overwhelming influence, the equivalent of Whitman's Epictetus, however, was the homosexual Romantic poet August von Platen (1796–1835). Platen's radically subversive eroticism would doubtless have been read with pleasure by Whitman if the poems had been available to him, and Mann's 1930 lecture on Platen at several points sounds oddly like a lecture on Whitman. Pure *Leaves of Grass* are Mann's remarks that Platen's "poetic immorality is in truth a radical anti-morality" and that his "erotic libertinage unites all that is free and generously 'useless' in an alliance against all that is anxious, ordinary, and parsimonious in life" (in *Adel des Geistes* (1955), p. 448; my translation). In this lecture Mann also made a point of complaining about the reluctance of critics to deal with Platen's sexuality (p. 443). "Literary history, out of lack of knowledge and with an old-fashioned propriety, has, through silly circumlocution, attempted to skirt the decisive fact of Platen's life: his exclusively homoerotic tendency." Would that Whitman and Mann were themselves no longer subject to silly propriety and circumlocution in respect of *their* sexual "tendencies." About the Platen lecture Heilbut summarizes (p. 503), "Platen, and Mann speaking through him, becomes an avatar of gay liberation, a phrase that might have sprung from Mann's critical vocabulary."

Too Heartfelt to Alter: Fred

193   **strong, careless:** Letter of 19 October 1865, quoted in *WWC*, 1:85. See also *NUPM*, 2:890n.

I have been unable: *UPP*, 2:97.

***letters from Vaughan to Whitman:** Shively gathers these letters together and discusses Vaughan in *Calamus Lovers*, pp. 36–50. There is no doubt in Shively's mind that "Fred inspired Whitman to write the *Calamus* poems" (p. 38). All extracts from Vaughan's letters are taken from Shively (pp. 41–50). Whitman's address book for circa 1856–64 includes the entry "Fred Vaughan 1393 Broadway" (*NUPM*, 2:490 / LC #84, p. 22).

TERRIBLE, BEAUTIFUL DAYS: SOME SOGER BOYS

198 **many-threaded drama** and **the real war:** *Specimen Days*, pp. 778–9.

*scores of books written: Shively devotes a chapter to Whitman's special "soger boys" in *Calamus Lovers*, pp. 62–88; far more elaborate is Shively's discussion and gathering of correspondence in *Drum Beats*. Shively's setting himself at odds with "university people" and his some-times over-the-top queering of his pitch has caused his two collections of Whitman material to be largely ignored by civilian Whitman scholars. Consider, for example, Shively's view (*Drum Beats*, p. 55) that "Whitman's doctrine quite simply was that cocksucking, butt-fucking and boy-loving were religious activities equal to what some Christians called 'god's love.' "

noble-sized young fellow: *Drum Beats*, p. 243.

he ought to have been: *Drum Beats*, p. 244.

199 ***Lew is so good** *et seq.*: *Corr*, 1:91. Four months later, in a letter of 1 August (*Corr*, 1:121), Whitman revived the concept of a domestic if not sexual *ménage à trois* in a letter to Lewis Brown: "I have thought if it could be so that you, & one other person & myself could be where we could work & live together, & have each other's society, we three, I should like it so much—but it is probably a dream."

I will bid you: *Corr*, 1:94.

My dearest comrade: Letter of 27 May 1863, *Corr*, 1:107.

Walt you will: *Calamus Lovers*, pp. 79–80.

Douglass, I will tell: Letter of 21 November 1863, *Corr*, 1:187.

200 **My relations with:** *WWC*, 3:110–1 (16 November 1888).

201 **Every name:** *WWC*, 6:227 (4 January 1890).

it was from the midst: *WWC*, 3:367 (23 December 1888).

I want you some day *et seq.*: *WWC*, 3:385–8.

202 **Fred & Charles Chauncey:** *Corr*, 1:159.

203 **letting-it-go kind:** *WWC*, 3:322 (12 December 1888).

rarely gives way: *WWC*, 2:261 (4 September 1888).

204 **my memory is:** *WWC*, 7:33 (30 July 1890).

I said to W: *WWC*, 3:583.

the short time we: Letter of 20 September 1868, *Corr*, 2:44.

Good bye, dear young man: Letter of 1 July 1869, *Corr*, 2:82.

205 **Johnny, you say:** Letter of 23 February 1871, *Corr*, 2:118.

at my desk: Letter of 8 March 1871, *Corr*, 2:118.

I will be candid *et seq.*: *SDB*, pp. 215–23.

I do no need to: *WWC*, 1:115 (6 May 1888).

Kentucky youngster: *WWC*, 1:146 (12 May 1888).

Dear Loving Comrade: Pete

206   **at the age of eight:** Evidence conflicts as to Doyle's exact age: a Whitman notebook (*NUPM*, 2:891) gives his birth as 3 June 1845 in Limerick; Doyle, in 1895, said he was born in 1847; his Philadelphia death certificate indicates 1848. In his detailed, lengthy biographical essay on Doyle, " 'Pete the Great': A Biography of Peter Doyle," *Walt Whitman Quarterly Review* 12 (1994), 1–51, Martin Murray asserts that 3 June 1845 is the correct birth date.

Calamus **brought to life:** *NUPM*, 2:891. An informative summary of the Doyle-Whitman relationship, to which I am here indebted, is to be found in an appendix in *NUPM* (2:891–4).

You ask where I: Doyle gave this highly revealing interview about Whitman to Traubel and Bucke in May 1895; this is presented along with their correspondence in *Calamus: A Series of Letters Written During the Years 1868–1880*, pp. 21–33. Quotations from Doyle's memoir are from these pages.

Pete was never: *WWC*, 3:75 (11 November 1888).

a great big hearty and **What do I look like:** *WWC*, 3:543 (16 January 1889).

207   **I know it is good . . .:** *WWC*, 7:265 (10 November 1890).

It was a great: *WWC*, 2:512 (21 October 1888).

Not my enemies: *Var*, 2:546.

208   ***I think of you:** Letter of 25 September, *Corr*, 2:45. Whitman saved very few of Doyle's letters (some suspect he destroyed them at some point), but Doyle saved most of those from Whitman and they were published by Bucke as cited above. The magisterially closeted Henry James reviewed the collection (*Literature*, 16 April 1898; in Hindus, p. 260), depositing a thick layer of condescension on it, yet concluding favorably: "In this little book is an audible New Jersey [not adhesive!] voice . . . and the reader will miss a chance who does not find in it many odd and pleasant human harmonies. . . . [Its] record remains, by a mysterious marvel, a thing positively delightful. If we ever find out why, it must be another time. The riddle meanwhile is a neat one for the sphinx of democracy to offer." Several of Doyle's letters are quoted by Shively in *Calamus Lovers*, pp. 104–14.

Dear Pete, you must: Letter of 21 August, *Corr*, 2:84–5.

210   **I rec'd your letter:** Letter of 3 September, *Corr*, 2:86–7.

if you have a double: Letter of 25 February 1870, reproduced in *Calamus Lovers*, pp. 110–12.

We parted there: *Corr*, 2:101.

211   **Good night, my darling:** Letter of 3 August, *Corr*, 2:104.

the most depressed year: *WWC*, 1:202–3 (24 May 1888).

*Walt often spoke to me: A poignant example of Doyle's occasional bewilderment at Whitman's learning comes with Doyle's recollection (p. 27) that "Walt knew all about the stars. He was eloquent when he talked of them." In a letter to Doyle from Brooklyn in August 1870 (*Corr*, 2:103–4), Whitman amusingly recalled one of these starry lectures: "Dear son, I can almost see you drowsing & nodding since last Sunday, going home late—especially as we wait there at 7th st. and I am telling you something deep about the heavenly bodies—& in the midst of it I look around & find you fast asleep, & your head on my shoulder like a chunk of wood—an awful compliment to my lecturing powers."

212   **I have a fine secluded:** *Corr*, 3:87.

Pete Doyle with me *et seq.*: *DBN*, 2:325, 335, 357, 358.

Oh! that's so fine: *WWC*, 3:131 (20 November 1888).

I like to think and **always a good stay** and **Then he went astray:** *WWC*, 1:349, 415, 298 (18 June, 3 July, 10 June 1888).

213   **I was quite staggered:** *WWC*, 6:371–2.

*****I have Walt's raglan:** *Calamus*, p. 29. Doyle continued his bachelor life in Philadelphia until he died of uremia in 1907. His grave is in the Congressional Cemetery in Washington at 18th and E Streets. *NUPM* quotes (2:894) from the obituary tribute to Doyle by a Whitman devotee from Boston, Percival Wiksell: "Pete was a cranky fellow, the boys said, but he held them close by his singular magnetic personality. Ale always tasted better when he was along. . . . You could hardly talk five minutes with him before he was quoting Walt for some fact or opinion, or was telling some story he got from Walt."

I should like: Quoted in *Calamus Lovers*, p. 103.

I did not know: *WWC*, 9:34 (16 October 1891).

a good time piece: *NUPM*, 2:919. The story of the watch's fate was related to me by Jeanne Chapman, editor of the just-published final Traubel volume.

he was pointed out: *WWC*, 9:619–20 (30 March 1892).

CENTRAL FIGURE OF THEM ALL: HARRY

214   **Horace Traubel is invaluable:** *DBN*, 2:64.

Harry Stafford New Rep.: Quoted in *Calamus Lovers*, p. 138.

I take an interest: Letter to Daniel Whittaker, *Corr*, 3:37.

215   *****became Whitman's Walden:** *Calamus Lovers*, p. 139. Shively's discussion of Stafford and extensive extracts from the Stafford-Whitman correspondence (pp. 137–71) deserve consultation. All quotations from Stafford's letters are from Shively.

talk with H S *et seq.*: *DBN*, 1:44, 48, 49, 85.

216   **if you have plenty** and **My nephew and I:** Letters of 13 and 19 December 1876 to John Johnston, *Corr*, 3:68.

Should like to fetch: Letter of 13 March 1877, *Corr*, 3:79.

I wish you was: Letter of 17 November 1877, *Calamus Lovers*, p. 160.

The hour (night, June 19 . . .): Quoted in *Calamus Lovers*, p. 144.

do not call there: Letter of 24 January 1877, *Corr*, 3:77. The charmingly unlettered Cattell also wrote, on 21 October 1877, saying he could not respond as soon as he would like to an invitation. "i would Com up To see you But i Cant get of a day now for we are so Bisse now husking Corn! . . . i Would like to Com up to town. i think of you old man think of the times down on the Creek . . ." (*Calamus Lovers*, p. 156.)

217   **Can you forgive** and **You may say:** *Calamus Lovers*, pp. 151–2.

Dear son, how I wish: Letter of 18 June 1877, *Corr*, 3:86.

I cannot get you off: *Calamus Lovers*, p. 153.

I will be up: *Calamus Lovers*, p. 154.

it seems an age: *Corr*, 3:77n.

I have found a girlfriend: Letter of 18 January, *Calamus Lovers*, p. 162.

218   **addressed "Mr. Whitman":** Letter of 27 July 1878, *Calamus Lovers*, p. 165.

as to that spell: Letter of 28 May 1879, *Corr*, 3:155.

am a little surprised: Letter of 11 February 1881, *Corr*, 3:211.

handsomest woman: Letter of 7 March 1881, *Corr*, 3:212.

Of the past I think: Letter of 28 February 1881, *Corr*, 3:215.

219   **Harry Stafford in:** *WWC*, 9:162–3 (19 November 1891).

quite a surprise to me: Letter of 21 November, *Corr*, 4:236. See *Calamus Lovers*, p. 147.

A DWINDLING BUSINESS

Charley Somer often: *DBN*, 2:351.

220   **think of it!:** *WWC*, 4:64 (1 February 1889).

a young man of 12: *WWC*, 6:167 (29 November 1889).

pretty hard luck: Letter of 20 December 1889, in *Calamus Lovers*, p. 184.

Harry Garrison RR man *et seq.*: *DBN*, 1:37, 43, 88, 89.

222   **very ill . . . these are dull:** *DBN*, 2:487.

I get out: Letter to William O'Connor, 25 April 1888, *Corr*, 4:161.

*****some kind of labor agitator:** *WWC*, 1:166–7 (16 May 1888). Thomas Mann uttered similarly effulgent remarks about fetching male youths in his old age. With one, a Zurich waiter named Franz Westermeier, he became particularly infatuated in 1950 (at seventy-five); he even told his wife Katia that he was losing sleep over the boy. He wrote achingly, "Worldly fame is empty enough to me, but how little weight it carries compared to a smile from him" (*Tagebücher 1949–50*, ed. Inge Jens (1991), p. 215 (my translation). On one occasion Mann's wife and lesbian daughter Erika—two sons, Klaus and Golo, were also gay— gallantly arranged a last meeting before the family left Switzerland. "It makes for a rich Mannian episode: the two women observing Mann as he extends his glance to a beloved youth," writes Heilbut (p. 433). Mann's eye was also ravished by the "Hermes-legs" of an Argentinean tennis player at his hotel. As with Whitman, an accounting of Mann's "passional" life produces a list consisting entirely of boys and young men: Armin Martens, Timpe, Ehrenberg, Klaus Heuser, Westermeier, and presumably others whose names—or fetching body parts—appeared in diaries that Mann destroyed.

questions that he cared: WWC, 4:501–2 (6 April 1889).

The aging of my body: "Melancholy of Jason Kleander, Poet in Kommagini, A.D. 595," Collected Poetry, p. 113.

223   **No more a flashing eye:** "A Hand-Mirror" (1860), p. 408.

some hard-cased dilapidated: p. 638.

I am an old bachelor: Quoted by Justin Kaplan in Walt Whitman: A Life (1980), p. 43.

'Taint true!: WWC, 2:425 (3 October 1888).

that big story: WWC, 2:415 (1 October 1888).

There are best reasons: WWC, 2:543 (27 October 1888).

I don't know what: WWC, 3:120 (17 November 1888).

224   **the "long story" which:** WWC, 9:146 (13 November 1891).

I am not: WWC, 9:199 (2 December 1891).

No, I don't: WWC, 9:263 (23 December 1891).

I have no particular: WWC, 9:313 (7 January 1892).

Don't be reckless: WWC, 2:100 (6 August 1888).

Why is it that: NUPM, 3:1099.

4

WALT & HORACE: "MIRACLES FOR MYSELF"

225   ***It is wearisome:** WWC, 3:92 (14 November 1888). All following citations are from WWC unless otherwise noted.

I have seen: 2:544 (27 October 1888).

226   **W. kissed me:** 1:171 (17 May 1888).

W. said: "Come kiss . . .": 2:82 (2 August 1888).

He called me: 1:169–70 (24 November 1888).

life was reviving: 3:407–8 (28 December 1888). The nephew, son of George Whitman, died on 12 July 1876.

227   **I can't forget:** 4:223 (23 February 1889).

had just returned: 5:282.

The bearer: 1:171 (18 May 1888).

228   **asks about it precisely once:** 5:433 (14 August 1889).

Eight o'clock is his: 3:194 (28 November 1888). On 24 December 1890,

Traubel visited at 8:55 P.M. and noted (7:374), "Very late to get to W.'s—latest, I believe for me, on record."

I want to be ready: 4:88 (5 February 1889).

You seem to have waked: 2:207 (27 August 1888).

You bother me: 2:244 (1 September 1888).

The instant you: 2:351 (20 September 1888).

greeted me as: 6:145 (18 November 1889).

called out "Horace": 7:389 (2 January 1891).

229   **I gazed at W:** 2:563 (31 October 1888).

W. lay on the bed: 3:370 (23 December 1888).

He was serenely glowing: 3:515 (11 January 1889).

Was in a very hearty mood: 7:122 (7 September 1890).

Happy, this night's: 7:358 (16 December 1890).

6 p.m. Spent a half hour: 7:454 (9 February 1890).

LOVING KINDNESS & INDUSTRY

running about all day: 2:193 (25 August 1888).

I am writing this: 1:264 (4 June 1888).

I took these letters: 1:326 (14 June 1888).

230   **I threaten to give:** 5:314 (22 June 1889).

Got him a box: 7:400 (7 January 1891).

Bucke knows I drink: 2:197 (25 August 1888).

Does a duck swim: 6:337 (24 March 1890).

I intended asking you: 6:304 (19 February 1890).

a temperance man *et seq.*: 9:55, 486, 520, 370–1.

231   **I did not read:** 2:141 (14 August 1888).

At home I opened: 3:363.

W. had returned: 1:362 (21 June 1888).

232   **I did not prolong:** 5:79–80 (24 April 1889).

I have never been: 4:499 (5 April 1889).

I doubt if any one: *In Re Walt Whitman*, p. 303.

*No man has been photographed: 2:45 (27 July 1888). Ed Folsom explores Whitman's scrupulous and calculating deployment of self-images in two recent articles: "Appearing in Print: Illustrations of the Self in *Leaves of Grass*," in *The Cambridge Companion to Walt Whitman*, pp. 135–65, and "Whitman's Calamus Photographs," in *Breaking Bounds*, ed. Betsy Erkkila and Jay Grossman, pp. 193–219.

233   **No, he had not:** 1:72 (25 April 1888).

ever laughed himself: 7:25 (25 July 1890).

on being a real humorist: 4:49 (30 January 1889).

I have always regarded: 4:391 (20 March 1889).

The noble Bob: 7:387–8 (30 December 1890).

234   *Does it go too far: "Walt Whitman Camping," *Walt Whitman Review* 26 (1980), p. 144. Likewise, Frederick Lubich finds a "sublime camp" in the "increasingly explicit and illicit sexuality" and "erotic irony" of Thomas Mann's later writings, though this camping is done scant justice by Lowe-Porter's translations. See "Thomas Mann's Sexual Politics—Lost in Translation," *Comparative Literature Studies* 31 (1994), pp. 119–21.

Doctor takes to sleighing: 4:89 (5 February 1889).

That book has been: 4:282–3 (5 March 1889).

O'Connor always said: 1:335–6 (15 June 1888).

I have about made up: 1:201 (24 May 1888).

No one knows: 1:248 (2 June 1888).

Kicking the bucket: 4:89 (5 February 1889).

I am a lame: 2:132 (12 August 1888).

We got along: 4:8 (22 January 1889).

W.'s favorite piece: 3:135 (19 November 1888).

235   I don't altogether like: 3:155 (22 November 1888).

I find he: 9:500 (2 March 1892).

You get everything: 1:280 (6 June 1888).

Walt Whitman, America *et seq.*: 9:10, 186, 494.

Well, if there's anyone and The dog made: 6:114, 137 (6, 14 November 1889).

He's as dumb and He is the dumbest: 9:166, 178 (20, 25 November 1891).

236   W. has a peculiar way: 4:32 (26 January 1889).

Tell her they are: 1:25 (10 April 1888).

a good many of the things: 1:272 (6 June 1888).

I would as lief regret: 3:345 (20 December 1888)

we were a no-smoking crowd: 4:45 (29 January 1889).

the hurrah game: 4:508 (7 April 1889).

this is a stupid place: 4:270 (3 March 1889)

The world goes daffy: 3:562 (18 January 1889).

Grant was the typical: 2:139 (14 August 1888).

237   a little, snarling: 9:385 (25 January 1892).

cocked and primed philosophy: 5:310 (21 June 1889).

no apologies, no dickers: 2:107 (8 August 1888).

You can detach: 1:105 (5 May 1888).

how much is put: 7:11 (14 July 1890).

You know I never: 9:124 (6 November 1891).

A letter is: 9:3 (2 October 1891).

To W. the darkeys: 9:48 (18 October 1891).

238   stood for the glory: 4:54 (30 January 1889).

There is much in the plays: 1:234 (30 May 1888).

turgid, heavy, over-stately: 3:185 (26 March 1888).

a machine: 1:126 (9 May 1888).

as a whole did not cast: 2:552 (29 October 1888).

I've tried Ruskin: 1:92 (2 May 1888).

a man for whom: 2:112 (9 August 1888).

That's news to me: 5:395 (27 July 1889).

a genuinely great soul: 2:560 (14 August 1888).

the brightest woman: 3:35 (6 November 1888).

the greatest novel: 9:206 (5 December 1891).

perennial . . . I can: 4:100 (6 February 1889).

has very few strings: 6:294 (13 February 1890)

*never broke new paths: 3:24 (4 November 1888). Walt would have been thoroughly irked by Longfellow's predictable comment about him, reported by Oliver Wendell Holmes: "I believe the man might have done something if he had only had a decent training and education." Holmes himself left in his notes for *The Poet at the Breakfast-Table* a tart one-word assessment: "Walt Whitman—mush-bag" (Eleanor Tilton, *Amiable Autocrat: A Biography of Dr. Oliver Wendell Holmes* (1947), p. 437).

dark, quiet, handsome: 4:23 (25 January 1889).

I think he is monotonous: 1:111 (6 May 1888).

James is only: 1:78 (28 April 1888).

I have met them: 1:111 (6 May 1888).

239 **stung by that:** 9:193–4 (1 December 1891).

the most nearly perfect: 4:167 (17 February 1889)

his lawlessness: 3:375.

I did think: 2:52 (28 July 1888).

salient men: 2:177 (21 August 1888). O'Connor, of whom Whitman also said "William will die with a hurrah on his lips," inspired this phrasing. Whitman also called O'Connor "a human avalanche" (3:352) and said once (4:70–1) he "would talk alive with a dagger in his heart. . . . I can't conceive of anything that would dethrone his buoyant cheer."

Emerson was always: 3:266 (8 December 1888). Horace begged to differ: "I jerked in—it's not true."

allow anything: 1:23 (9 April 1888).

his faculty was passive: 1:70 (26 April 1888).

somewhat thin: 1:461 (13 July 1888).

Thoreau's great fault: 1:212 (26 May 1888).

WE *Love* YOU

240 **How many saw:** 5:250 (31 May 1889).

A Negro came: 4:429 (26 March 1889).

There are two reasons: 3:375 (24 December 1888).

I took out: 4:514 (7 April 1889).

241 **not one in the bunch:** 4:473 (1 April 1889).

She stood before: 1:227 (28 May 1888).

neither he nor any member: 5:232 (27 May 1889).

My family know: 4:387 (20 March 1889).

After the funeral: 9:626 (30 March 1892).

He regarded me: 1:5 (30 March 1888).

Well—you are: 6:85 (23 October 1889).

We were just telling: 7:208 (15 October 1890).

242   Once you said: 3:558 (22 December 1888).

I don't have any: 4:142 (13 February 1889).

It's all in: 2:23 (21 July 1888).

You don't like the poem: 2:333 (16 September 1888).

Walt, don't you: 4:61 (31 January 1889).

Walt, some people think: 3:459 (4 January 1889).

I laughed rather heartily: 4:152 (14 February 1889).

243   the wrong way: 2:51 (28 July 1888).

tall, young, ruddy: 3:29 (5 November 1888).

takes to Ed and Ed is very stalwart: 3:52 (8 November 1888).

Yes: he is vital: 3:385. Earlier in December he also called Ed "a gem: just the right man" (3:293) and "so gentle, so strong" (3:348).

244   I am real glad: Letter of 9 November 1888, *The Letters of Dr. R. M. Bucke to Walt Whitman*, ed. Artem Lozynsky (1977), p. 81.

help him more: 3:407 (28 December 1888).

Ed is well fit: 3:451 (3 January 1889).

Yes, Eddy has: 3:363 (22 December 1888).

On the way he told: 6:8.

Ed has finally: 6:52.

today engaged Warren Fritzinger: 6:76.

I like him very much: 1:282 (8 June 1888).

246   I like to look: 1:391 (28 June 1888).

Warrie and I come: 6:82–3 (23 October 1889).

I am under: 6:136 (13 May 1889).

I like you to know: 2:82 (2 August 1888).

I have a weakness *et seq.*: 2:145 (15 August 1888).

247   one's life is not: 6:140 (15 November 1889).

I was bred: 3:205 (30 November 1888).

You are doing: 1:332–3 (15 June 1888).

248   I suppose *et seq.*: 9:372, 383, 476.

Our affairs: 9:309 (6 January 1892).

You are our next: 9:406 (13 February 1892).

Curiously—at tea: 9:36 (16 October 1891).

A LAST EMBRACE

249   **I reached over:** 9:270.
       I leaned over: 9:309.
       Is that you, Horace?: 9:312–3.
       I am not a demonstrable: 9:128 (8 November 1891).
       I have gone down: 9:518 (7 March 1892).
       Every word a struggle: 9:544 (15 March 1892).
250   **The heart was still:** 9:600.
       The bulletin: 9:602.
       To hear the claw: 9:605 (27 March 1892).
       Burroughs wept: 9:622.

WALT & ME: AN AFTERWORD

251   *****Autobiography . . . is the only:** WWC, 4:184 (19 February 1889). It is
       interesting to note that Thomas Mann, a fundamentally homosexual
       man who could *honestly* boast of having fathered six children (three of
       whom were homosexual), held a very similar view of literary criticism.
       Heilbut writes of Mann (p. 38) that he "turned criticism into, as Oscar
       Wilde says, the most civilized form of autobiography: indeed, without
       knowing Wilde's definition, he assumed that good criticism had to be
       grounded in autobiography. 'Criticism that is not confessional in char-
       acter,' he said, 'has no value.' " Near the end of his life, Mann took an
       apologetic tone about the Whitman-like incessancy of autobiography in
       his oeuvre. He told Hermann Hesse he could "never quite bring" him-
       self to put his own work in Hesse's league: "It always strikes me as too
       personal, too much of an ad hoc arrangement with art to allow being
       mentioned in the same breath with the 'real thing.' " (*The Hesse/Mann
       Letters*, ed. Anni Carlsson and Volker Michels, trans. Ralph Manheim
       (1976), p. 153.)
       There is no real Walt Whitman: Excerpt in *Measure*, p. 21.
252   **I can't see doing:** *New York Times*, 17 May 1995.
       there is no more insufferable: *Shaw's Music*, ed. Dan H. Laurence (1981),
       3:237.
       The critic who cannot: *Shaw's Music*, 3:238.
253   *****Whitman was far from *de rigueur*:** A classmate of mine, who knew
       nothing of poetry or Winters's fame, earned extra money gardening for
       him. One day he asked the famous man who his favorite poets were and
       reported to me, much puzzled, that he had heard several unfamiliar
       names, including one "Folk Gravel." Little did I know that a few years
       later I would be writing a term paper on a poem by Fulke Greville, Lord

Brooke (1554–1628), and studying under his major biographer, Ronald Rebholz, also in the Stanford English department.

254 **For these voices:** p. 33.

*It has been ventured: The assertion was made by a longtime member of the Stanford English department, Herbert Lindenberger, in *The Words-worth Circle* (1993). Lindenberger is the author of *Opera: The Extrava-gant Art* and a member, as I am, of the Stanford Opera School. This school of opera criticism was given its name by my friend the longtime Stanford history professor Paul Robinson (author of *Opera and Ideas*), who wittily observed that to belong to the School it is only necessary to have no connection with the Stanford music department.

255 **athletic and triumphant body:** Quoted by Pougin, p. 87.

some thought her fat: NUPM, 1:396.

258 **All these sweet** and **Dancing time:** *The Lyrics of Noël Coward* (1973), pp. 125, 148.

262 **Blasé boys are we:** *Lyrics*, pp. 82–3.

263 **The delight in belonging:** "The Cult of Homosexuality in England 1850–1950," *Biography* 13 (1990), p. 197.

268 ***epic poem "Danny":** A few particularly Whitman-tinged stanzas from this poem, whose explosive climax occurs (much later!), unsurprisingly, on the bank of a rural pond:

> But Danny'd no use for these generous [female] charmers,
> For his rolls in the hay he liked brawny young farmers,
>   The same as himself, with hard, hairy chests
>   And eggs and a turkey below in their nests.
>
> In the fields, at their work, stripped bare to the hips,
> He rejoiced in their sun-bronzed young torsos—the strips
>   Of crisp, curling hair at the tops of their jeans
>   That sprang from the roots of their fucking-machines.
>
> He admired their muscles, their powerful backs,
> Their tapering thighs, the suggestion of cracks
>   Where their hard, flexing ass-cheeks divided beneath
>   The snugness of jeans fitting close as a sheath.

270 **To the young man:** *1860 Facsimile*, p. 377.

*without a friend a lover: p. 280. My favorite melancholic loss-of-a-lover poem besides those of Whitman is Song IX ("Stop all the clocks") by W. H. Auden, part of Benjamin Britten's 1936 cycle *Twelve Songs*. The last two of its four stanzas:

> He was my North, my South, my East and West,
> My working week and my Sunday rest,

My moon, my midnight, my talk, my song;
I thought that love would last for ever: I was wrong.

The stars are not wanted now: put out every one;
Pack up the moon and dismantle the sun;
Pour away the ocean and sweep up the wood;
For nothing now can ever come to any good.

272   **didn't know how to escape:** *Writing Was Everything* (1995), p. 117.
There shall be innovations: *1860 Facsimile*, pp. 350–51.
273   **Phallic festivals:** *DBN*, 3:772.
I dreamed: Bowers, *MS1860*, p. 114.
274   **Health chants:** *1860 Facsimile*, pp. 7–8.
I saw the wounded: This ms. (HM 94) is titled "Reminiscences 64" (presumably 1864).
Agonies are one: "Song of Myself" (1855 version), p. 65.
275   **Once in a while:** "After First Fredericksburg," *Prose Works 1892* (1963), 1:33.
tragedies of soul: Letter to Louisa Whitman, 13 May 1863, *Corr*, 1:99.
There is a strange: Letter to N. Wyckhoff or D. Northrup, 14 May 1863, *Corr*, 1:102.
Above all the poor boys: Letter to Abby Price, 11 October 1863, *Corr*, 1:162.
Any Doctor will tell: *WWC*, 7:356 (14 December 1890).
I see such awful things: Quoted by Shively, *Drum Beats*, p. 69.
276   **The moon gives:** p. 448.
277   **Of him I love:** p. 561.
278   **a man may:** *EPF*, 255.
surely though I pity: The letter, dated 17 April 1593, appears in the Spedding edition of Bacon's works (8:244).
280   **I am getting more and more:** *WWC*, 1:200 (24 May 1888).
281   ***umpteenth time:** The one story that never failed to make me laugh was of a professor railing at faculty teatime about a recent visiting lecturer. "That lecture was terrible!" she fulminated, adding, "It wasn't even second-rate. Why, it was positively third-rate. *I* could have done better than that!" At which a meek faculty wife, who hardly ever uttered a word on such occasions, piped up, "That's right, dear, you always *were* second-rate."

ANNEX

WALT & OSCAR: VOICES OF LIBERATION

283   **He is a fine:** Letter of 25 January 1882, *Corr*, 3:264.
What we most need: *WWC*, 4:33 (26 January 1889).

The Aesthetic Singer: The story is reprinted by Rollo Silver as "Oscar Makes a Call" in *The Colophon* (1935), n.p.

face has an air: The story is reprinted in E. H. Mikhail, *Oscar Wilde: Interviews and Recollections* (1979), p. 90.

284   **Most parents:** Vyvyan Holland, *Son of Oscar Wilde* (1954), p. 41.

fat not after: *Anglo-American Times,* 25 March 1893, in *Letters of Reggie Turner* (1964), p. 286.

I think his fate: Letter of 26 March 1897, p. 515n of *The Letters of Oscar Wilde,* ed. R. Hart-Davis (1962), hereafter *Letters.*

a sort of adopted: Quoted by William Rothenstein, *Men and Memories* (1931), p. 362.

had a look: Quoted by Bucke, p. 25.

the eyes, candid: "Walt Whitman," in the Belgian review *Masque* (1912), trans. John Espey, *Walt Whitman Newsletter* (1957), p. 57. Merrill, disinherited by his father for supporting the Haymarket Riot defendants, later settled in Paris; he wrote a notable obituary on Wilde for *La Plume* in December 1900 (see Mikhail, p. 355).

drops disguise: *U.S. Review,* in Hindus, p. 37.

What am I: p. 516.

I have lived: *Walden,* ed. J. L. Shanley (1971), p. 9.

I have never: Letter to H. C. Marillier, 8 November 1885, *Letters,* p. 181.

The old believe: *Miscellanies, The First Collected Edition* (1908; rpt. 1969), p. 178.

frequenting the society: "The Decay of Lying," *The Complete Works* (1966; rpt. Harper Collins, 1989), p. 973. Unless otherwise noted, all subsequent quotations from Wilde are cited by page number in this edition.

285   **the vast army:** *Whitman: A Study,* p. 90.

Young and strong: "Chanting the Square Deific" (1865), p. 560.

A child said: p. 192.

I like the boys: *WWC,* 3:533–4 (14 January 1889).

It will be: "The Soul of Man Under Socialism" (1891), p. 1084.

Part of the joy: *Calamus Lovers,* p. 20.

He was . . . a man: *Nebraska State Journal,* 19 January 1896, in *The World and the Parish,* 1:280.

Walt showed: Lewis, quoted by Leslie Fiedler, *Collected Essays,* 1:167.

AT EASE IN ZION

286   **Oscar Wilde has** and **to drive with Mr Wilde:** *DBN,* 2:280.

*Stoddart tactfully withdrew: Whitman had many subsequent dealings with Stoddart. As late as April 1890 he wrote to Whitman requesting poetry from him (*WWC,* 6:382); just six months earlier Stoddart was in

London commissioning fiction from Wilde. Several months later Walt gratefully remembered Stoddart's tact in leaving him alone with Oscar. "There is no airisfines about him—no *hauteur*. Years back he came over with Oscar Wilde, when Wilde was here in America and the noise over him was at its height. They came in great style—with a flunky and all that. And what struck me then, instantly, in Stoddart, with his eminent tact. He said to me 'If you are willing—will excuse me—I will go off for an hour or so—come back again—leaving you together,' etc. I told him, 'We would be glad to have you stay—but do not feel to come back in an hour. Don't come for two or three'—and he did not—I think did not come till nightfall. And all I have had to do with him since is equally to his credit" (*WWC*, 7:366, 19 December 1890).

Yes. I always: H. M. Hyde, *The Trials of Oscar Wilde* (1948; rpt. 1962), p. 125.

288   **been photographed:** *WWC*, 1:367 (22 June 1888).

Oscar Wilde sent: Letter to Harry Stafford, 31 January 1882, *Corr*, 3:266. The portrait was probably one of several well-known shots Wilde had taken in Manhattan by the Richard Avedon of the day, Napoleon Sarony.

My dear dear Walt: Letter postmarked 1 March, Chicago, *Letters*, pp. 99–100.

He did not see: *DBN*, 2:282n.

made no effort: Journal entry for 6 January 1901, p. 4305 of ms. at the University of Texas, quoted by Richard Ellmann, *Oscar Wilde* (1987), p. 171. Ellmann assumes that the second visit was entirely private and also cites Ives's report that Wilde told him, "The kiss of Walt Whitman is still on my lips."

This hour I tell: p. 206.

at ease in Zion: *Two-Part Inventions* (1974), p. 16.

the slyest of artificers: "Images of Walt Whitman," *Collected Essays*, 1:172.

289   **dramatizing himself:** "The Achievements of Walt Whitman," *Texas Quarterly* (1962), p. 47.

You say you: Letter of 25 January 1882, *Corr*, 3:264.

290   **I never completely:** *WWC*, 2:192 (24 August 1888).

Wilde . . . may: *WWC*, 2:279 (7 September 1888).

Wilde was very: *WWC*, 5:284 (11 June 1889).

tearbaggy manners: *WWC*, 4:79 (3 February 1889).

Everybody's been: *WWC*, 2:289 (7 September 1888).

291   **well-defined form:** *NUPM*, 6:2246–7.

harder and harder: Quoted by Ellmann, p. 45.

a beautiful weed: *Specimen Days*, p. 830.

very bad, and wrong: "Soul," p. 1094.

giving us the opinions: "The Critic as Artist," p. 1048.

the printer's ink: *Whitman: A Study*, pp. 93–4.

292   **I tramp:** p. 241.

is Whitman's principal: *Walt Whitman*, p. 242.

I never walk: Hyde, *The Trials of Oscar Wilde*, p. 130.

seemed to have: *Calamus*, ed. Richard M. Bucke (1897), p. 24.

prime specimen: Frank Harris, *Oscar Wilde: His Life and Confessions* (1930; rpt. 1959), p. 335.

likes to be called and **not prejudiced:** Brooklyn *Daily Times* (1856), in Hindus, p. 46.

Cleanly shaved: *NUPM*, 1:169.

293   **beautiful boy:** Letter to Reginald Turner, 7 June 1897, *Letters*, p. 601.

Whitman goes at her: Quoted by Edward Carpenter in *Days with Walt Whitman*, p. 30.

never before heard: *Autobiography* (1958), p. 113.

was no great talker: *Days with Walt Whitman*, p. 19.

*champion English-language epigrammatist: Consider: in the Microsoft *Bookshelf* CD-ROM database of quotations (1994) there are 264 items by Shakespeare but an astonishing 384 by Wilde (Whitman has 71).

deficient in humor: *Whitman: A Study*, p. 181.

the brilliant epigrammatist: *Notes on Walt Whitman as Poet and Person* (1867), p. 45.

Peau d'Espagne: Letter of 6 May 1897, *Letters*, p. 535.

would leave a select: Brooklyn *Daily Times*, in Hindus, p. 46.

294   **I was invited:** Letter of 25 January 1882, *Corr*, 3:264.

is a parlor: *NUPM*, 1:144.

TWO BOYS TOGETHER CLINGING

The chief value: 25 January 1889, in *Reviews* volume of *The First Collected Edition* (1908; rpt. 1969), p. 401.

295   **A poem which:** *NUPM*, 1:338.

I myself: p. 175.

How they are provided: pp. 171–2.

It is with the future: p. 1100.

296   **written by a butterfly:** Letter to Arthur Humphreys, 12 February 1895, *Letters*, p. 382.

answers to questions: *Oscar Wilde: A Study* (1910), pp. 26–7.

297   **mass of stupid filth:** Rufus Griswold, in Hindus, pp. 32–3.

Who is this arrogant: Quoted in *The Poetry and Prose of Walt Whitman*, ed. Untermeyer, p. xxvii.

loathly 'leperous distillment': 19 July 1890 issue, p. 25.

outlawed noblemen: 9 July 1890, quoted in *Letters*, p. 265n.

the gilded paganism: 3 July 1890, in Stuart Mason, *Oscar Wilde: Art and Morality* (1912; rpt. 1971), pp. 137–8.

After the dilettante: Quoted by Untermeyer in *The Poetry and Prose*, p. 38.

purely ... egomaniacal and **moral obtuseness:** *Degeneration* (1895), pp. 230, 319–20.

298 ***Abuse made no:** In *Re Walt Whitman* (1893), p. 35. George's views about Walt's stubborn self-confidence were discussed by Whitman and Traubel many years later: "George once said to me: 'Walt, hasn't the world made it plain to you that it'd rather not have your book? Why, then, don't you call the game off?' I couldn't give George any reason why which he would have understood. . . . I said nothing: George was disappointed: he said: 'You are stubburner, Walt, than a load of bricks.'" Walt then added, to Traubel: "I admit that—but what can I do? I can't surrender: I won't defend myself: that made George, makes others, madder than if I told them to go to hell" (*WWC*, 4:267, 3 March 1889).

On the whole: "Soul of Man Under Socialism," p. 1093.

All great rebels: *UPP*, 1:246.

America has never: "Walt Whitman" (1954), in *Measure*, ed. Jim Perlman *et al.* (1981), p. 115.

Nothing, not even: Zweig, p. 141.

299 ***encoded allusions:** See my discussion of the tales in *The Stranger Wilde* (1994), pp. 145–68, and my introduction to the Signet Classic paperback edition of *The Picture of Dorian Gray and Other Stories* (1995), pp. xix–xxx.

*first time: *WWC*, 4:267–9. A letter from Stoddard the next year began, "In the name of CALAMUS listen to me!" (*Corr*, 2:97n).

A man only: *NUPM*, 1:57.

in all constant thoughts: *WWC*, 2:180–1 (22 August 1888).

300 **On Saturday at mid-day:** *Letters*, p. 254n.

exquisite critical insight: *More Letters of Oscar Wilde*, ed. R. Hart-Davis (1985), p. 60.

I shall peruse: *WWC*, 4:221–2 (25 February 1889).

*I believe in: Ms. letter in the Clark Library, UCLA. See my discussion of the very colorful Fitch in *The Stranger Wilde*, pp. 154–6, 178–81, 441–43. Whitman would probably also have agreed on "The Portrait of Mr. W. H.," for he suspected (*NUPM*, 5:1742) that "the ancient Greek friendship seems to have existed" between Shakespeare and "the beautiful young man so passionately treated" in his *Sonnets*.

301 **He smiled:** *WWC*, 4:26 (25 January 1889).

*W. gave me another: *WWC*, 3:555 (17 January 1889). Miller (1837–1913), a journalist and poet, defended Wilde in print when he was on his American tour, and Wilde wrote him a long letter of thanks (see *Letters*, pp. 97–9). Whitman had high regard for Miller, calling him "rugged, careless, happy-go-lucky, earthy" (*WWC*, 3:32, 5 November 1888).

as expressed in: *WWC*, 2:153 (17 August 1888).

finesse, finish, polish: *WWC*, 5:203 (20 May 1889).

I am, everywhere: *WWC*, 2:160–1 (18 August 1888).

*Dear friend, you have: *WWC*, 3:414–8 (29 December 1888). Carpenter evoked one of Whitman's most fiery expressions of solidarity with a gay apologist: "He is a man who shares the view of Jesus, of Bacon,—who says, don't let us talk of faith any longer—let us *do* something. Any man can jabber, tell a story—any fluent-tonguey man can do that. But the man who can live the virtues, needs no courier, no announcers—*is* the fact that other men only dream of—he is the man we want—the man to *absorb* morality—to *become* it! Carpenter has the keenest sense of all that" (*WWC*, 6:317, 4 March 1890).

302   All goes well with me: *WWC*, 5:256 (2 June 1889).

more intimate, more personal: *WWC*, 6:211 (25 December 1899).

I would I could: *WWC*, 4:365 (16 March 1889).

This letter is almost: *WWC*, 1:23 (10 April 1888).

O Walt! Take this: *WWC*, 4:212 (4 February 1889).

Dear Walt, my beloved: *WWC*, 6:369 (17 April 1890).

W. received what: *WWC*, 6:2 (17 September 1889).

drifted into talk: *WWC*, 3:334 (19 December 1888).

303   comrade letters . . . he says: *WWC*, 4:270 (3 March 1889).

You do not know *et seq.*: *WWC*, 9:535–6 (12 March 1892).

304   deeply moved: *Letters*, p. 353.

I have suffered: *WWC*, 2:558 (31 October 1888).

305   leave my works: p. 455.

the most loving: "To a Historian," 1860 *Facsimile*, p. 181. This line does not appear in later editions.

dandyism—is: *The English Novel and the Principle of Its Development* (1892), p. 61. Lanier's vigorously hostile reading of Whitman (pp. 52–61) derived from lectures Lanier gave at Johns Hopkins University in 1881.

Sexomaniacs: 6 April 1895 issue, p. 157.

306   passion for country: *Whitman: A Study*, p. 149.

neither my poetic *Leaves*: Letter to Rudolf Schmidt, 16 January 1872, *Corr*, 2:151–2.

Emerson and Whittier: *NUPM*, 3:961.

total income of $1,333: See table, *Corr*, 6:xvii.

intellectual foreignness: *Smart Set*, October 1919, in *Smart Set Criticism*, ed. William Nolte (1987), p. 184. Mencken adds, "His countrymen . . . regarded him generally as a loafer and a scoundrel, and it was only after foreign enthusiasts began to cry him up that he emerged from the constant threat of going to jail."

PRINCES OF PARADOX

I am proud: Preface to *Miss Julie, Selected Plays,* trans. Evert Sprinchorn (1986), p. 207.

307 **In Falstaff:** p. 975. The last chapter of my *The Stranger Wilde* is devoted to a discussion of the Falstaff and Hamlet sides of Wilde's character.

It was natural: Quoted in *Letters,* p. 565.

contented ogre: Gedeon Spilett, *Gil Blas,* 22 November 1897, in Mikhail, p. 354.

Doubtless, he: *The Romantic 90s* (1925), p. 257.

I think him: Letter to Lionel Johnson, 8 February 1893, in *Letters,* p. 868.

passion for paradox: 23 April 1893.

cheeky paradoxical wit: Letter to Mrs. Hugh Bell, 23 February 1892, *Letters,* ed. Leon Edel (1980), 3:373.

But you don't: p. 982.

The way of paradoxes: *Dorian Gray,* p. 43.

308 **muscular and self-possessed:** *UPP,* 1:262.

Here I shade: "Here the Frailest Leaves of Me" (*Calamus* #44), p. 283.

One of that centripetal: p. 237.

Both in and out: p. 191.

Hurrying with: p. 223.

to see Whitman: *Walt Whitman,* p. 116. R. W. B. Lewis makes the same point: "Walt Whitman is the most blurred, even contradictory figure in the classical or mid-nineteenth century period of American literature" (Bloom, p. 99).

precisely a matter: "Images of Walt Whitman," *Collected Essays,* 1:172.

paradoxes that: " 'Song of Myself': Intention and Substance," in *Measure,* p. 152.

Looking with side-curved: p. 191.

308–9 ***We must now begin** and **Here is the baffling:** *Walt Whitman,* pp. 84, 115. Anthony Heilbut remarks often on Thomas Mann's fundamentally paradoxical life and writings, calling him "an author perpetually saddled with the burden of paradox" (p. 108) and one with an "unerring instinct for paradox" (p. 334). In a remarkably candid and richly prescient letter to his future wife, Thomas Mann described the husband she would be getting (the sketch fits the "Chanter of Personality" to a T): "I am quite conscious of not being the sort of man to arouse plain and uncomplicated feelings. . . . To inspire mixed emotions, 'perplexity,' is, after all, if you will forgive me, a sign of personality. The man who never awakens doubts, never causes troubled surprise, never . . . excited a touch of *horror,* the man who is always simply loved, is a fool, a phantom, a ludicrous figure. I have no ambitions in that direction" (to Katia Pringsheim, mid-May 1904, *Letters 1889–1955,* p. 31; Mann's italics). When Wilde joked memorably about Shaw that "he has no enemies, and none of his friends like him," Shaw did not mind at all and responded with Mann's view: "Only a non-entity has friends who like him unconditionally" (see my *The Stranger Wilde*, p. 466).

309   **gin cocktails:** See editorial note to *Franklin Evans, or The Inebriate*, EPF, p. 125.

everybody else not to: *WWC*, 6:113–4 (5 November 1889).

Horace: listen to this: *WWC*, 1:174 (18 May 1889).

Be radical: *WWC*, 1:223 (28 May 1888); see also 2:136, 3:122, 4:469.

become as a precipice and **magnificent No!:** *Days with Walt Whitman*, pp. 19, 49.

stepped across what: *Calamus*, p. 22.

approved of a new: *I Sit and Look Out*, p. 90.

Resist much: p. 172.

typical inevitable democrat: *Whitman: A Study*, p. 95.

Mind you the timid: *Calamus #19, 1860 Facsimile*, p. 364.

the word En-Masse: p. 209.

a splendid thought: *WWC*, 7:160 (29 September 1890).

310   **The shadow of:** *Whitman: A Study*, pp. 92–3.

He would lie: *In Re Walt Whitman*, p. 35.

When talking he: Hindus, p. 65.

Slow, indolent: Isaac Van Anden (proprietor of the *Eagle*), in issue of 19 July 1849, in Herbert Bergman, "Walt Whitman as a Journalist, 1831–January, 1848," *Journalism Quarterly* (1971), p. 204.

I was a first rate: *WWC*, 2:21 (20 July 1888).

An American bard: Hindus, p. 34.

never dressed in black: Hindus, p. 47.

See the populace: *1860 Facsimile*, p. 21. (This line was cut in later editions.)

311   ***Red flannel undershirt:** Hindus, pp. 64–5. Whitman was wearing about the same get-up several years earlier while editing the Brooklyn *Daily Eagle* (1846–48), dressing "like a farmer or a workman, with homespun trousers tucked into cowhide boots reaching mainly to the knee, a pea jacket seldom buttoned, a flannel shirt open at the throat, a red kerchief knotted at his neck" (Arthur Howe, quoted by Bergman, p. 203).

Dear boy Pete: Letter of 12 December 1873, *Corr*, 2:260.

Never have I: *op. cit.*, p. 57.

That shadow: *Calamus #40*, p. 286.

***These actor people:** *WWC*, 1:5 (30 March 1888). Yet another striking parallel with Thomas Mann: Late in the Nobel laureate's life an American scholar said, "Herr Mann, you are nothing but an actor," and Mann chose not to deny it (Heilbut, p. 25). Mann, whether wittingly or not, had captured in his mid-twenties in his spectacularly successful first novel *Buddenbrooks* (1901) the actorly life of the closeted homosexual: "Thomas Buddenbrook's existence was no different from that of an actor—an actor whose life has become one long product, which, but for a few brief hours of relaxation, consumes him unceasingly. . . . All this made his life, his every word, his every motion, a constant, irritating pretense" (quoted by Heilbut, pp. 99–100). The diametrically opposite *ars vivendi* is to feel comfortable in one's own skin, and this is precisely what Mann wrote in homage to his two great idols, Goethe and Tolstoy, in the year he discovered Whitman: "one must go back to Goethe to find a human being so comfortable in his own skin" as Tolstoy. And Mann adds that both men manifested a "blessed, organic well-being" ("Goethe and Tolstoy," *Werke* (1990), 9:111). In a "Letter from Germany" that appeared in the September 1925 issue of *The Dial*, Mann specifically yoked Goethe and Whitman and the *Calamus* ethos: "These two fathers have much in common, above all sympathy with the organic, the sensual, the 'calamus.' "

312   **born actor:** Letter to Carlos Blacker, 20 March 1898, *Letters*, p. 718n.
  Man is least himself: "The Critic as Artist," p. 1045.
  A mask: p. 413.
  Anybody can act: Letter of 19 February 1892, *Letters*, p. 311.
  the character he played: *If It Die* (1920; Eng. trans. 1935), p. 296.
  Most men and women: "Lord Arthur Savile's Crime," p. 174.
  Come I am determined: Bowers, *MS1860*, p. 72.

313   **To speak the truth:** *Letters*, p. 502.
  There are lovely: Letter to More Adey, March 1899, *Letters*, p. 784.
  I was never made: *WWC*, 2:19 (20 July 1888).
  I troop forth: "Song of Myself," p. 231.
  *****intricate and forlorn:** "Introduction," *Walt Whitman: Modern Critical Views*, p. 9. These two epithets apply with peculiar aptness to the oeuvre of Thomas Mann, which in fact shares so much with that of Whitman and Wilde. Mann himself admitted that the intricacies and forlornness that attend communications from the Closet were at the core of his oeuvre in the essay "On Myself" which he wrote in 1940: "The howling triumph of the suppressed world of the instincts [is] the fundamental motif permeating and, as it were, holding together my whole work" (quoted by Frederick Lubich, "Thomas Mann's Sexual Politics"—Lost in Translation," *Comparative Literature Studies* 31 [1994], p. 122). Mann is clearly speaking here about what Whitman called the "life below the life" that is sex.
  Every noble spirit: Aphorism #381, *The Gay Science* (1882; aphorism added in 1887).
  The great poets: p. 19.

314   **I announce the justification:** "So Long!" p. 609.
  The candor and: *Whitman: A Study*, p. 93.
  I believe you: "Song of the Open Road," p. 298.
  From my breast: p. 278.
  O Manhattan: "City of Orgies" (originally *Calamus* #18), p. 279.

I do not doubt: p. 563.

Out of the dark confinement: p. 306.

Autiobiography is: "The Critic as Artist," p. 1010.

315   *very much a lecture and But Wilde made: *Journals 1889–1949*, pp. 405–6. In his early writings Gide behaved "furtively" very much in the Whitman and Wilde style. Here is a superb précis of Gide's delicately covert style made by an unfriendly contemporary critic, Henri Massis, in 1921, which could apply easily to the Wilde/Whitman literary method: "He doesn't want to be an open book: he needs an austere exterior. . . . His perversity is too conscious, too critical, not to have chosen an art that knows not to say everything, one where his troubling sincerities can find the right kind of shelter. . . . Gide does not permit one to find one's way immediately to his private quarters. He prefers us intelligent and attentive to his subterfuges—thus all those euphemisms, that reserve, all those obstacles that he carefully arranges, the better to extricate himself later" (quoted by Michael Lucey, *Gide's Bent: Sexuality, Politics, Writing* (1995), p. 13).

The profound nexus between Whitman and Gide is eloquently underscored by the closeness Thomas Mann felt to both of these authors. Heilbut observes (p. 471) that Mann "admired Gide's political engagement, his love of Goethe, Nietzsche, Whitman, and Dostoevsky, his devotion to reason, and—above all—his militant homosexuality."

Be radical: *WWC*, 1:223.

potent, felt, interior: "Prayer of Columbus" (1874), p. 541.

And now, escaping: Ms. version of *Calamus* #1, in Bowers, *MS1860*, p. 160.

I chant: "Song of Myself," p. 47.

I cannot say: "Who Learns My Lesson Complete?" p. 518.

When I undertake: "A Song of the Rolling Earth," p. 367.

316   O to be self-balanced: "Me Imperturbe," p. 173.

Bold, cautious, true: "As Toilsome I Wander'd," p. 441.

Open but still a secret: p. 587.

*a cautious radical: Quoted by Heilbut, p. 473. Several of Heilbut's remarks about Mann's ironic and convoluted playfulness in the vicinity of the Closet door are pertinent to Whitman's methods. For instance: "It's not unfair to call Mann the poet of the half-open closet" (p. 251) and "Mann's fiction is animated by the conviction that it takes one to know one; the spotting of a dissolute 'brother' is a perennial event" (p. 99).

Among the men: *1860 Facsimile*, p. 376.

Do you see no further: "Are You the New Person" (originally *Calamus* #12), p. 277.

317   fond of being misunderstood: p. 488.

BUTTERFLY PHILOSOPHY

the philosopher that: p. 548.

When Oscar Wilde wandered: *Memories and Impressions* (1911), p. 166.

philosophy of ease: *George Bernard Shaw* (1911), p. 28.

made dying Victorianism: *The Romantic 90s*, p. 270.

318   O Lord! give me: Quoted in Ellmann, p. 41.

ego-style: *NUPM*, 6:2230.

necessary to a proper: p. 970.

He lets externals: *The Speaker*, 8 February 1890, in *Reviews* volume, *The First Collected Edition* (1908; rpt. 1969), pp. 530–1.

*The longer one and springs from personality: "The Critic as Artist," pp. 1021, 1033–4. Naturally, the closeted Henry James hastened to draw the opposite conclusion in his hostile, unsigned 1865 review of Whitman's *Drum-Taps*: "art requires, above all things, a suppression of one's self, a subordination of one's self to an idea" (Hindus, p. 114).

The aim of life and To be good is: pp. 29, 69.

My own feeling: Letter of 11 February 1881, *Corr*, 3:211. Stafford was in his early twenties at the time.

319   Now and then a man: *WWC*, 1:433 (7 July 1888).

Every existence: "A young man came" (1855), later "Song of the Answerer," p. 315.

no sweeter fat: p. 206.

not any one else: p. 241.

Will you rot: "A Song of the Rolling Earth" (1856), p. 364.

self-esteem and nothing is good: pp. 479–80.

allowing a place for: *WWC*, 5:298 (16 June 1889).

effuse egotism: "Starting from Paumanok," p. 183.

treat man as he: "To a Historian" (1860 version), in *1860 Facsimile*, p. 181.

close companionship: "The Prairie-Grass Dividing," p. 281.

the joy of a manly: p. 328.

320   WHAT place is besieged: "What Place is Besieged?" (originally *Calamus* #31), p. 174.

*the unquenchable creed: *Chants Democratic* #2 (1856), in *1860 Facsimile*, p. 142. The line was among many cut from the poem when it later became "Song of the Broad-Axe." Zweig elaborates (p. 217) on the influences that helped to produce this creed: "Whitman spoke with the voice of his century which had placed the individual at the heart of social theory. Rousseau, Schiller, Blake, Kierkegaard, Carlyle, Emerson: such a dissonant chorus, yet all making the same potentially revolutionary judgment. Society succeeds in its great-souled individuals, fails wherever it constricts and mechanizes."

The Whitman creed also influenced two important twentieth-century gay apologists, one open, the other more closeted. The most important influence Wilde had upon the young André Gide was to teach Whitman's "unquenchable egotism." Wilde, Richard Ellmann concluded, saw that Gide was lacking in "flamboyant selfhood" and took it upon himself to "mischievously [prod] him to avoid the evil of self-suppression" (*Golden Codgers* (1973), pp. 89, 100).

Behind his sober suit and mien, Thomas Mann was also of Whitman's and Wilde's profoundly iconoclastic, antimoralizing bent. He could have been speaking of *Leaves of Grass* when he wrote in the essay "On Alcohol" (*Werke*, 11:718) that "almost all great works exist because of an act of defiance." In a 1911 essay, "Pornography and Eroticism," Mann mounted a thoroughly Whitman-like defense of sex-in-art that ridiculed the "foaming at the mouth" of Philistine zealots and contended that sexual passion was art's primeval source. Even more relevant to the homoerotics of Whitman and Wilde was a letter Mann wrote in 1920 to the publisher Paul Steegemann on the occasion of the publication of the "shockingly indecent" poems of Verlaine, which left Mann "shaken" and profoundly moved. In this letter Mann offered a paradox that both Whitman and Wilde would have applauded, "Great moralists have mostly been great sinners also," adding later that "the realm of morality is wide; it includes that of immorality." Mann's idols, like Platen, the homosexual lover of youth, "traverse the whole realm." Speaking of loving youths, it was at about the time of Mann's letter to Steegemann that he confided to his diary about his fourteen-year-old son: "Am enraptured with Eissi, terribly handsome in his swimming trunks. Find it quite natural that I should fall in love with my son." A few months later: "I heard some noise in the boys' room and came upon Eissi totally nude and up to some nonsense by Golo's bed. Deeply struck by his ravishing adolescent body; overwhelming" (entries of 25 July and 17 October 1920, *Diaries 1918–1939* (1982), pp. 101–3).

egoism was superb: Introduction for Ada Leverson, *Letters to the Sphinx* (1930), p. 16.

the seven deadly virtues: *Dorian Gray*, p. 147.

the dons are 'astonied': Letter to William Ward, 20 July 1878, *Letters*, p. 53.

our modern mania: *An Ideal Husband*, p. 495.

describe a work: "The Soul of Man Under Socialism," p. 1092.

invite the public: "Soul," p. 1095.

Wickedness is a myth: *Chameleon*, December 1894, p. 1205.

rather than virtuous: p. 242.

321   **man of strong:** Quoted by Shively, *Calamus Lovers*, p. 56.

Wickedness is: LC #80, p. 33 (http://lcweb2.loc.gov/ammem/080000.html).

re-examine all you: p. 11.

outside authority: "Song of the Broad-Axe" (1856), p. 335.

down in my soul: *Specimen Days*, p. 915.

Disobedience . . . is: "Soul," p. 1081.

huge and sprawling: G. T. Atkinson, *Cornhill Magazine* (May 1929), p. 560.

I use ruled paper: *WWC*, 5:164 (10 May 1889).

everything is toned down: *WWC*, 7:281 (19 November 1890); Traubel's italics.

322   the debrisity *et seq.*: *WWC*, 9:59, 78, 248, 420, 426.

If I have the trick: *WWC*, 9:88–9 (27 October 1891).

the populace rise: "Song of the Broad-Axe," p. 335.

The Lords Temporal: "Soul," p. 1094.

we live in: p. 79.

a thoroughly selfish: "The Critic as Artist," p. 1043.

Never was there: *Democratic Vistas* (1871), p. 937–8. He observes later in this work, "these savage, wolfish parties alarm me. Owning no law but their own will, more and more combative, less and less tolerant of the idea of *ensemble* and of equal brotherhood. . . ." (p. 966).

Our country seems: *NUPM*, 1:216.

323   The whole spirit: *WWC*, 5:473 (31 August 1889).

when I see the harm: *WWC*, 4:37; 27 January 1889. The full context of the remark: "It's a profound problem: teaching morals: they should be taught—yet also not taught: sometimes I say one shouldn't teach morals to anybody: when I see the harm" etc.

Morality is simply: p. 519.

the desire to do: p. 1042.

Selfishness is: p. 1101.

tainted in its signification: Letter probably to Arthur Clifton, 28 January 1891, in Ian Small, *Oscar Wilde Revalued* (1993), p. 47.

blurt . . . about vice and fault-finder's or: "Song of Myself," p. 209.

What would we do: *WWC*, 6:293 (11 February 1890).

the world would stagnate: "The Critic as Artist," p. 1023.

favorite (pint) measure: Brooklyn *Daily Times*, 19 April 1858, in *I Sit and Look Out*, p. 45.

We do not want: "Memorial in Behalf of a Freer Municipal Government, and Against Sunday Restrictions," Brooklyn *Evening Star*, 20 October 1854, *UPP*, 1:261.

324   Great latitude: *NUPM*, 1:56.

The further West: Lloyd Lewis and Justin Smith, *Oscar Wilde Discovers America* (1930), p. 243.

It is an odd thing: *Dorian Gray*, p. 159.

freer and grander: *NUPM*, 5:1949. Whitman appears to have learned this in 1857 from the reformer Eliza Farnham, who lived in California from 1849 to 1856. Whitman's geographical bias is especially noticeable in his view of Abraham Lincoln as being "quite thoroughly Western, original, essentially non-conventional" (*Democratic Vistas*, pp. 1197–8).

*in the west all men: *EPF,* pp. 257, 269. In the same story (p. 275) Whitman speaks of hunting in western forests because they afford "that strange, and exhilarating, and pervading sense of *freedom,* which strikes into all your sense and body, as it were, from the illimitable and untrammelled and boundless nature of every thing about you." One day in 1889 Whitman told Traubel, "I answered an autograph letter the other day—an unprecedented act: it was from the far west: from one of the territories, I think: there was something in it which moved me" (*WWC,* 4:338, 13 March). In a 1941 lecture at the University of California at Berkeley, Mann showed that he shared the Wilde and Whitman bias in favor of "Western" liberation by telling students that if Nietzsche were alive, he would be (like himself) an exile in California.

I always expect the men: *WWC,* 2:163 (18 August 1888).

325   **never dressed in black:** Unsigned review, Brooklyn *Daily Times* (1856), Hindus, p. 47.

its charm resides: Letter of 2 February 1891, *Letters,* p. 283.

ease and liberty *et seq.: Pall Mall Gazette,* 14 October 1884, *Miscellanies,* pp. 48–50.

I hope he consults: *Pall Mall Gazette,* 11 November 1884, *Miscellanies,* p. 52.

Fashion is what: *An Ideal Husband,* p. 522.

wears his man-Bloomer: Hindus, p. 64. The bloomer was a costume for women introduced about 1850, consisting of a short skirt and long loose trousers gathered closely about the ankles. Whitman also called himself a man of "costume free" in *Chants Democratic #2* (*1860 Facsimile,* p. 141).

He was almost: Letter of 10 January 1892, *WWC,* 9:414 (2 February 1892).

learned and refined society: *NUPM,* 1:169.

326   ***I am for those:** "Native Moments" (1860), p. 265. In his essay "The Dandy," Charles Baudelaire—who published his story "La Fanfarlo" ("The Dandy") in 1847—also emphasized the powerfully subversive effects of that "institution above laws" called dandyism. "For the true dandy," he wrote, an immoderate interest in personal appearance is "only a symbol of the aristocratic superiority of his personality. . . . It is a sort of cult of oneself." Whitman and Wilde are surely reflected in Baudelaire's observation that "Dandyism arises especially in periods of transition, when democracy is not yet all-powerful and aristocracy is only partially tottering or brought low. In the disturbances of such periods a certain number of men . . . rich in native energy may form a project of founding a new sort of aristocracy. . . . Dandyism is the last gleam of heroism in times of decadence" (*My Heart Laid Bare and Other Prose Writings,* ed. Peter Quennell (1951), pp. 54–7).

Before I first met Oscar: *Letters to the Sphinx* (1930), pp. 31–2.

wayward, fanciful: Quoted by Edward Carpenter, *Days With Walt Whitman,* p. 48.

The vulgar and: pp. 102–3. This poem was later titled "To Think of Time."

TWO FISHERMEN

*their camaraderie: Zweig (pp. 14–5) is of the same mind: "Whitman's counterpart is not the cocky Yankee peddler striding America's 'open road,' but Baudelaire's esthete and dandy, Samuel Cramer, in the short story 'La Fanfarlo'—or, more vividly, Oscar Wilde who, one likes to think, guessed Whitman's deepest nature when he made a pilgrimage to Camden to visit him."

327   beautiful old man: *Walt Whitman Newsletter* (1957), p. 57.

the espousing principle: Preface to *November Boughs* (1888), p. 669.

If only thou *et seq.*: pp. 248–72.

carved out of turnips: Letter to More Adey, March 1899, *Letters*, p. 784.

328   character of a: NUPM, 1:99.

Really what has America: NUPM, 6:2095. In one of his dry runs for "Song of Myself" (*NUPM*, 1:67) is the line "Let the physician and the priest timidly withdraw." In published versions (pp. 73, 232) this becomes "Let the physician and the priest go home."

I see no use: WWC, 1:110 (6 May 1888).

The world is through: WWC, 1:106 (5 May 1888).

I don't remember: WWC, 1:62 (23 April 1888).

Damn the preachers: WWC, 6:298 (15 February 1890).

*profoundest contempt and damnable psalming: WWC, 4:85, 5:17 (4 February and 13 April 1889). One day Whitman reported a letter from an extremely sensible preacher in Maine "who said if I wrote more like other people and less like myself other people would like me better. I have no doubt they would. But where would Walt Whitman come in on the deal?" (WWC, 1:150; 13 May 1888). A few months later he reminisced that he "went oftenest [to church] in my earlier life— gradually dropped off altogether: today a church is a sort of offense to me" (WWC, 2:51, 28 July 1888), and three years after Whitman's death Peter Doyle recalled that he "never went to church—didn't like form, ceremonies—didn't seem to favor preachers at all" (*Calamus*, p. 28).

329   the damned Methodistic snifflers *et seq.*: WWC, 9:24, 25, 438, 609.

takes the ground from under: WWC, 5:208 (21 May 1889).

There will soon be: pp. 24–5.

priests alarming: "We Two Boys Together Clinging" (originally *Calamus* #26), p. 282.

Allons! from all: "Song of the Open Road" (1856), p. 303.

the mumbling and screaming priest: p. 589.

*Already a nonchalant: p. 479. In his "To You" of 1856 (p. 376)

Whitman presents himself as a liberator from all outside authority: "I only am he who places over you no master, owner, better, God, beyond what waits intrinsically in yourself."

330   **I ordain myself:** p. 299.

331   **the first to smash:** "Whitman," *Studies in Classic American Literature* (1923), in *Selected Literary Criticism*, ed. Anthony Beal (1956), p. 401. Leslie Fiedler makes much the same point (*Collected Essays*, 1:159), saying that Whitman sponsored an image of himself "as the Defender of the Body against the overweening claims of the soul"—which could be seen as the fundamental thesis of "The Fisherman and His Soul."

favors body and soul: "Song of Prudence," p. 502.

fear not, be candid: "On Journeys through the States" (1860), p. 172.

vehement struggle: "Thoughts" (1860), p. 600.

One who loves me: *1860 Facsimile*, p. 354.

To escape utterly: p. 263.

One's-self must: "Quicksand Years" (1865), p. 563.

332   **Behold, the body:** "Starting from Paumanok," p. 184.

special young men: *NUPM*, 4:1136.

*****L. of G.**'s word is:** Letter to William Sloane Kennedy, 25 February 1887, *Corr*, 4:70. Among Whitman's notes (*NUPM*, 1:383) is the assertion "My two theses—animal and spiritual—became gradually fused in *Leaves of Grass*,—runs through all the poems and gives color to the whole." Also among his very early notes preparatory to writing the 1855 edition is a highly pertinent jotting about the "corporation" of the soul: "The effusion or corporation of the soul is always under the beautiful laws of physiology—I guess the soul itself can never be anything but great and pure and immortal; but it makes itself visible only through matter—a perfect head, and bowels and bones to match is the easy gate through which it comes from its embowered garden and pleasantly appears to the sight of the world" (*NUPM*, 1:58; this notebook is dated "between 1845 and 1854").

the trunk and centre: Preface to *November Boughs* (1888), p. 666.

Permanence of temperament: Letter to Frank Harris, 18 February 1899, *Letters*, p. 780.

O camerado close: p. 188.

333   **from those corpses:** "Oh Living Always, Always Dying" (originally *Calamus #27*), p. 565.

he takes everything: *The World and the Parish*, p. 280.

*****I see ranks:** p. 294. Several times Whitman emphasized to Traubel the wide embrace of *Leaves*: "*Leaves of Grass* has room for everybody: if it did not make room for all it would not make room for one" (*WWC*, 1:45, 18 April 1888); "That is what I wanted the book to be ... to include, combine, celebrate all: all: not the least jot missed: not the mouthpiece of classes, select cliques, parts ..." (*WWC*, 4:149,

15 February 1889); "in my philosophy—in the bottom-meanings of *Leaves of Grass*—there is plenty of room for all" (*WWC*, 5:227, 26 May 1889).

none shall be: *NUPM*, 1:64.

I never object: *WWC*, 1:144 (12 May 1888).

Amelioration is: p. 363.

334   **The mockeries:** "To You"; title and quotation from *1860 Facsimile*, pp. 392–3.

Spring away from: "Scented Herbage of My Breast," p. 269.

ribb'd breast: pp. 273–4.

an attempt: Letter to Amelie Chanler, January 1889, *Letters*, p. 237.

335   **the true personality:** "The Soul of Man Under Socialism," p. 1084.

perhaps the least: *Whitman A Study:* p. 91.

It is that deep: Hyde, *The Trials*, p. 201.

superb friendship: "To the East and the West" (originally *Calamus #35*), p. 285.

when I hear: "When I Peruse the Conquer'd Fame," p. 282.

336   **He [Plato] makes** *et seq.*: *NUPM*, 5:1882–3. In conversation with Traubel, Whitman also referred to the *Phaedo*, which describes the death of Socrates, as "a heart-book—a book one would have to love" (*WWC*, 6:66, 15 October 1889).

Yes: I have no: Letter to George Ives, 21 March 1898, *Letters*, p. 721.

337   **Work on, age:** p. 368.

INDEX